THE RESEARCH MANUAL

Design and Statistics for Applied Linguistics

1991

Evelyn Hatch and Anne Lazaraton

University of California, Los Angeles

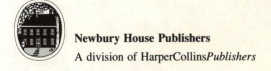

Newbury House Publishers

A division of HarperCollins*Publishers*

To our parents

Bodil and Alfred Marcussen
Mary and Ted Lazaraton

Director: Laurie E. Likoff
Production Coordinator: Cynthia Funkhouser
Cover Design: Caliber Design Planning
Printer and Binder: McNaughton & Gunn

NEWBURY HOUSE PUBLISHERS
A division of HarperCollins*Publishers*

Language Science
Language Teaching
Language Learning

The Research Manual: Design and Statistics for Applied Linguistics

Library of Congress Cataloging-in-Publication Data

Hatch, Evelyn Marcussen.
   Design and statistics for applied linguistics : the research
manual / Evelyn Hatch and Anne Lazaraton.
      p.   cm.
   Includes bibliographical references and index.
   ISBN 0-06-832678-8
   1. Applied linguistics—Research.   2. Applied linguistics—
Statistical methods.   I. Lazaraton, Anne.   II. Title.
P129.H39   1991
418′.0072—dc20   90-41922
                                                                        CIP

63-26789   94 93 92 91 9 8 7 6 5 4 3 2 1

Contents

iv   Contents

Contents   v

Acknowledgments

Books are never the product of their authors alone. We have many people to thank. First, four "critical friends" made substantive contributions to the manual. Lyle Bachman at the University of Illinois allowed us to trial an early version of the text with his students. His comments on the content for part I of the volume were very insightful. He also gave us valuable feedback on student reactions to the interactive nature of the workbook. This led to a major revision in the approach—from a highly interactive workbook to its current text plus practice format.

Fred Davidson helped us produce the original prospectus for the book. He made substantive suggestions about the content of the introduction and chapters 16 and 17. His enthusiasm for finding new and better ways to answer questions in applied linguistics and his love of measurement theory have been contagious to all his colleagues at UCLA.

Larry Bernstein of the University of Pittsburgh also gave us much needed input regarding loglinear procedures. An electronic-mail request for help was never set aside for another day. A question asked was answered in detail within minutes.

J. D. Brown of the University of Hawaii and Larry Bernstein read the entire text page by page. Their comments were offered in the true spirit of friendly, constructive criticism. Such criticism is so rare and so valuable that we felt both privileged and blessed to receive it.

In addition, Grant Henning at Educational Testing Service in Princeton, Brian Lynch at UCLA, and Thom Hudson in Guadalajara kept an interested eye on this project. Their help and enthusiasm cheered us up when our spirits lagged, eyes blurred, and typing fingers grew numb.

Our students have moaned and groaned as we asked them to fix yet another mistake in the many preliminary versions of the manual. But they have also been extremely encouraging, telling us what does and doesn't work for them. The result, we believe, is much more comprehensive because they were never shy about saying "but-but-but . . ." or "I don't get it." There were times when we didn't get it either. They showed us where the places were and they told us how to fix them too.

We thank the authors of the research cited in the text and activities sections. One of our major goals was that our readers learn to be wise and critical consumers of research. We also want our readers to understand the scope of "interesting questions" in the field of applied linguistics. Without all these examples, we would not have been able even to approach such goals.

The consulting staff at the Office of Academic Computing has been extremely generous of their time in helping us learn how to format the text of the manual (including all the beautiful math symbols). Dean H. Morris gave us access to UCLA's mainframe which allowed us to enter and compile the text. The computer has become semifriendly as a word processor and remains a super assistant in statistics. Our mainframe program, however, could not produce adequate copy for many of the figures included in this volume. We thank Sara Cushing and her marvelous Macintosh for coming to our rescue.

Finally, we thank the editorial personnel at Newbury House. Leslie Berriman was extremely helpful and encouraging as we planned the project. Laurie Likoff and Cindy Funkhouser have assisted us in getting the final manuscript in publishable form. Diane Hatch-Avis of Hatch and Hennessey assisted us in the preparation of the indices. We appreciate the time they have given us in their busy schedules.

All books contain errors. Those that remain in this text are ours alone.

Credits

We are grateful to the copyright holders of the following articles for permitting us to use material contained within them.

Altman, R. (1985). Subtle distinctions: *should* versus *had better*. *Studies in Second Language Acquisition*, *8*, 80–89. Reprinted with permission of Cambridge University Press.

Amastae, J. (1978). The acquisition of English vowels. *Papers in Linguistics, ff*, 423–458. Reprinted with permission of Boreal Scholarly Publishers.

Benson, M. & Benson, E. (1988). Trying out a new dictionary. *TESOL Quarterly*, *22*, 340–345. Copyright 1988 by Teachers of English to Speakers of Other Languages, Inc. Reprinted with permission.

Blum-Kulka, S. & Levenston, E. (1987). Lexical-grammatical pragmatic indicators. *Studies in Second Language Acquisition*, Special Issue 9, 155–170. Reprinted with permission of Cambridge University Press.

Brown, J. D. (1988). Components of engineering-English reading ability. *SYSTEM*, *16*, 193–200. Reprinted with permission of Pergamon Press, Inc.

Budd, R. (1988). Measuring proficiency in using English syntax. *SYSTEM*, *16*, 171–185. Reprinted with permission of Pergamon Press, Inc.

Call, M. E. (1985). Auditory short-term memory, listening comprehension, and the input hypothesis. *TESOL Quarterly*, *19*, 765–781. Copyright 1985 Teachers of English to Speakers of Other Languages, Inc. Reprinted with permission.

Crow, J. T. & Quigley, J. R. (1985). A semantic field approach to passive vocabulary acquisition for reading comprehension. *TESOL Quarterly*, *1*, 497–514. Copyright 1986 Teachers of English to Speakers of Other Languages, Inc. Reprinted with permission.

Daiute, C. (1986). Physical and cognitive factors in revising: insights from studies with computers. *Research in the Teaching of English*, *20*, 141–159. Copyright 1986 by the National Council of the Teachers of English. Reprinted with permission.

de Haan, P. (1987). Exploring the linguistic database: noun phrase complexity and language variation. In W. Meijs (Ed.), *Corpus Linguistics and Beyond*. Amsterdam: Rodopi. Reprinted with permission of Rodopi.

Geva, E. (1986). Reading comprehension in a second language: the role of conjunctions. *TESL Canada Journal*, Special Issue 1, 85–110. Reprinted with permission of *TESL Canada Journal*.

Ghadessy, M. (1988). Testing the perception of the paralinguistic features of spoken English. *IRAL*, *26*, 52–61. Reprinted with permission of Julius Groos Verlag.

Gibbs, R. W. & Mueller, R. A. G. (1988). Conversational sequences and preferences for indirect speech acts. *Discourse Processes*, *11*, 101–116. Reprinted with permission of Ablex Publishing Corporation.

Goldstein, L. (1987). Standard English: the only target for nonnative speakers of English? *TESOL Quarterly*, *21*, 417–436. Copyright 1987 Teachers of English to Speakers of Other Languages, Inc. Reprinted with permission.

Hudson, T. & Lynch, B. (1984). A criterion-referenced measurement approach to ESL achievement testing. *Language Testing, 1*, 171–201. Reprinted with permission of Edward Arnold.

Irujo, S. (1986). Don't put your leg in your mouth: transfer in the acquisition of idioms in a second language. *TESOL Quarterly, 20*, 287–304. Copyright 1986 Teachers of English to Speakers of Other Languages, Inc. Reprinted with permission.

Jafarpur, A. (1987). The short context technique. *Language Testing, 4*, 195–220. Reprinted with permission of Edward Arnold.

Jones, L. B. & Jones, L. K. (1985). Discourse functions of five English sentence types. *WORD, 36*, 1–22. Reprinted with permission of the International Linguistic Association.

Kirsner, R. (1989). Does sign-oriented linguistics have a future? In Y. Tobin (Ed.), *From Sign to Text: A Semiotic View of Communication*. Amsterdam: John Benjamins B.V., 161–178. Reprinted with permission of John Benjamins B.V.

Mann, V.A. (1986). Distinguishing universal and language-dependent levels of speech perception: evidence from Japanese listener's perception of English /l/ and /r/. *Cognition, 24*, 169–173. Reprinted with permission of *Cognition*.

Oller, J. (1983). Evidence for a general language proficiency factor: an expectancy grammar. In J. Oller (Ed.), *Issues in Language Testing Research*. New York: Newbury House. Copyright 1983 by Newbury House Publishers. Reprinted with permission of HarperCollins Publishers, Inc.

Porrcca, K. (1984). Sexism in current ESL textbooks. *TESOL Quarterly, 19*, 705–724. Copyright 1984 Teachers of English to Speakers of Other Languages, Inc. Reprinted with permission.

Reid, J. (1987). The learning styles preferences of ESL students. *TESOL Quarterly, 21*, 87–111. Copyright 1987 by Teachers of English to Speakers of Other Languages, Inc. Reprinted with permission.

Shimanoff, S. (1985). Expressing emotions in words: verbal patterns of interaction. *Journal of Communication, 35*, 16–31. Copyright 1985 Journal of Communication. Reprinted with permission.

Snow, M. A. & Brinton, D. (1988). Content-based instruction: investigating the effectiveness of the adjunct model. *TESOL Quarterly, 22*, 553–574. Copyright 1988 Teachers of English to Speakers of Other Languages, Inc. Reprinted with permission.

Tannen, D. (1982). Ethnic style in male-female conversation. In J. J. Gumperz (Ed.), *Language and Social Identity*. New York: Cambridge University Press, 217–231. Reprinted with permission of Cambridge University Press.

Tsang, W. K. (1987). Text modifications in ESL reading comprehension. *RELC Journal, 18*, 31–44. Reprinted with permission of SEAMEO-RELC.

Tunmer, W., Herriman, M., & Nesdale, A. (1988). Metalinguistic abilities and beginning reading. *Reading Research Quarterly, 23*, 134–158. Reprinted with permission of William Tunmer and the International Reading Association.

Introduction

Curiosity killed the cat.

We like to think that it is human nature to be curious. Every day of our lives, we ask ourselves questions. We wonder why a lesson that worked well last term doesn't work this time. We wonder what makes birds sing, why some people speak almost in a monotone, what signals people use to show that some things they want to say are new and important. We wonder about almost everything. It is curiosity that drives research.

If all of us are curious, does that make us all researchers? In one sense it does. We all wonder, we all ask questions, and we all search for answers to our questions. The ways we search for answers, however, will differ. The way we search differentiates simple curiosity from research. Research is the *organized, systematic search* for answers to the questions we ask.

Artist and scholar Elisabeth Mann Borgese was once asked how the world viewed her interest in teaching dogs and chimpanzees to type. Did the world of science appreciate her comments that the messages typed by her setter Arlecchino formed poems that rivaled, indeed surpassed, those of many modern poets? The world, responded the artist, has two answers to everything--either "I don't believe it" or "Oh, I knew *that* already." To these might be added a third response from the world of science--"Why should we care?" Let's tackle each of these comments in turn.

Research should be carefully designed to meet the first of these, the "I don't believe it" response. What is it that convinces us that answers are correct? This question requires that we think about what led us to particular answers and what evidence supports those particular answers. It requires us to consider the chance that we are deluding ourselves--that the lesson really worked just as well or better for most students but didn't work at all for a few. In research, what convinces us and what makes us doubt answers must be clearly articulated if we wish to overcome the first response of Borgese's world--"I don't believe it!"

Each of us as individuals has different criteria for believing or not believing the truth of claims. Different academic fields also have different criteria for accepting or rejecting the truth of proposed answers to questions. The first of these has to do with *where* we turn for answers. In many fields the first place to search for answers is to ask experts, colleagues, ourselves, and others. The "asking" may be quite informal or it may involve exceedingly complex questionnaire research. Such a research methodology is an excellent way to find answers to certain types of questions. And, of course, it is not a good way to search for answers to other kinds of questions.

In some fields another place to search for answers is to observe natural life situations using an ethnographic approach or an approach where the researcher is a participant-observer. The data collected may simply be a set of organized notes or it may involve elaborately coded videotaped records. The observations may cover only one instance or may run for months or even years. Another place to look for answers may be existing texts or transcripts. The observations may cover only a few records or pages or may include transcripts of thousands of lines. The questions and the data used will determine just how complex the analysis will be.

In some fields, more confidence is placed in answers where researchers have been able to manipulate or control the many factors that might influence or affect outcomes. When researchers have a good idea of the possible answers there might be to questions, they can manipulate variables in different ways to make certain that the variables truly act in the way they think they do. Experimental research allows researchers that option.

In library research all these methods may be combined. By surveying previous research, we can discover not only *where* but *how* experts have searched for answers to particular questions. But, to evaluate their answers, it is necessary to understand the methods each researcher used. This might include an understanding of questionnaire, experimental, ethnographic, participant-observer, and case study methods. In addition, we need to understand how the information given in these reports can be evaluated and combined as evidence in support (or nonsupport) of other candidate answers to questions.

Since we believe that research is primarily a way of convincing ourselves and others of answers to questions, it is important to know *where* to search for answers and *what* counts as evidence. It is also important to know just what standards any particular field may use as to what counts as valid evidence. In some fields, it is considered appropriate to ask ourselves questions, look within ourselves for answers, and, when asked why we believe our answers are correct, give examples as evidence in support of assertions. For example, in linguistics, it has been common practice to pose a question about acceptability of particular language forms and then answer it by "consulting native speaker intuition." If we think the sentence "He suggested me to take advanced statistics" is unacceptable, that is evidence enough. The use of example sentences (even those created by the researcher rather than actually used by someone) is also considered acceptable evidence in support of answers to research questions. Some fields consider "typical examples" as evidence whether or not "typical" is precisely defined.

In other fields, self-consultation and even typical examples fail to convince. The world that says "I don't believe it!" wants to know how many people think X (e.g., how many people consider "He suggested me to..." acceptable), how often X occurs (e.g., how often ESL learners produce such errors), or how much X was needed to influence someone to do Y or think Z (e.g., how many lessons would be needed to get students to use the structure correctly). Summary tables often appear in journals, giving this type of information in support of answers to questions. As with the use of examples, tables are very helpful in summarizing information. However, tables--like examples--must be carefully interpreted before we trust them as evidence.

Many fields expect that the researcher will not only give examples, frequency tables, or tables showing typical "averages," but that these will be annotated to show exactly how much *confidence* the reader can reasonably have that claims based on such findings are correct. Usually, such fields also place constraints on the acceptability of research designs, data-gathering procedures, and methods of analysis.

As individual researchers, none of us wants to make claims which are unwarranted. We want our findings to be both new and well substantiated so that we can face a world that already knows it all or doesn't believe us anyway. The way we search for answers to our questions will determine our own confidence in sharing our findings.

We also want to have confidence in answers given by others. We may be content with answers accepted by the field (we accept the answers and thus "know that already"). On the other hand, we may not be content without examining the evidence very carefully. Trust is a good thing to have but, when the cost of accepting or rejecting answers based on evidence is high, trust will not suffice. Careful examination of research reports requires not only common sense but also some degree of statistical literacy.

Research, then, is a means of balancing confidence and anxiety. The balance grows out of the need to answer a question and the fear of giving or accepting inaccurate answers. A well-designed research project will allow us to offer answers in which we can feel confidence. While it is important to keep in mind that different ways of presenting evidence and different types of evidence are used in different fields, the first thing is to convince ourselves--to establish confidence in answers for ourselves. After all, we posed the questions in the first place and so we are the first audience for our answers.

Let's turn to the second response of Elisabeth Mann Borgese's world. If the response is "I knew that already," the chances are that the world does not see the question as interesting, deserving of further research. What is it that makes a question interesting, worthy of research? This, too, varies from field to field. In a sense, the definition of what is an interesting question in any field defines the field at that point in time. In fact, it is often said that a field can be defined as a discipline in its own right to the extent that it has its own separate research agenda.

In disciplines that are engaged in the search for an overriding theory, questions are defined as worthy of research *only* if they contribute to theory formation. All other questions are held in abeyance (semi-interesting but not on track just now) or considered as irrelevant. For example, linguists wishing to construct a theory of *competence* have considered research on such *performance* factors as hesitation markers or such system components as turn-taking irrelevant and uninteresting. There is nothing more discouraging than to learn that the question most interesting to you is not interesting to the field. However, the direction in which the field is moving often makes it impossible for researchers to find an audience for their work unless it fits into the current mold, the current direction of work in the field.

In other fields where a central unifying theory is not a primary concern, research may branch in so many different directions that it is difficult to see how individual projects relate to one another. For example, studies on language mixing and switching, work on foreigner talk discourse, descriptions of the acquisition of temporality, studies of bilingual aphasia, and the English spelling systems of Chicano fourth graders may never be presented in a way that reveals the theoretical framework within which the studies were conducted.

You can imagine the problems that this creates across fields when researchers present their findings to one another. When theory formation is not discussed and, as is often the case, when outside researchers have limited access to the underlying assumptions of the field, it is almost impossible for them to understand why these particular questions have been posed in the first place--the "who cares" response. On the other hand, when theory formation *is* central, outsiders may consider the theory irrelevant to their own research world and wonder why such issues are important.

The "who cares" response (often voiced as "question is not interesting") is not uncommon in the research world. Unfortunately, such comments are too often taken at face value by researchers who, in turn, view these comments as coming from a group that is, at best, misguided and, at worst, arrogant and presumptuous.

We are fortunate in applied linguistics because the range of interesting questions is not limited to research where evidence could support or disconfirm some part of a central theory. Rather, our research questions are interesting to the extent that they can (a) apply to theory formation or theory testing, (b) apply to practice (e.g., curriculum design, materials development, development of language policy, test development), or (c) apply to both theory and practice.

While different fields determine what constitutes interesting questions and appropriate evidence, there are conventions in research that do cross fields of inquiry. Research plans have been designed and methods of analysis devised that give us confidence in findings. Such plans present "tried and true" ways of looking for answers. The tried and true are not the only ways and, with guidance, you will find that new methods can easily be designed. Your research approach can be as flexible as you wish. You may, in fact, want to take a multimethod approach in your search for answers. There is never a "one and only one" way to carry out a project. There is never a "one and only one" correct way to analyze the data. Some ways, however, are much better for some questions and other ways for other questions. By understanding how and why different researchers opt for different methods, you should be much better equipped to choose among methods yourself and to evaluate the research of others.

In terms of confidence, we are very fortunate to have access to computers to help us in our search for answers to questions. However accurate you may be in your computations, computers can be even more accurate. No matter how rapidly you can carry out computations, computers can do it faster. It is difficult, often, to get a computer to do what you want, and once done, the computer never knows if what it did is appropriate. Or, as is often said, "The data know not whence they came." Computers are even easier to fool than readers. They will believe you no matter what you tell them. They may issue you warning messages, but they will usually complain only if you use a language they cannot understand. They will never tell you whether you have compiled and analyzed your data in a sensible way. You (and your advisors) must determine that. The computer supplement that accompanies this manual will teach you how to carry out many of the analyses with a minimum of effort.

To decide whether the methods and procedures you use are appropriate, you will need to understand basic research design and statistics. We believe that the best way to do this is to work on your own research questions. However, for the novice researcher, this is not always possible. For the novice, it may be as efficient to begin by exploring the range of available possibilities.

Since this manual is written for the novice researcher, our approach will be to encourage you to form your own research questions while we present research questions and examples taken from the field of applied linguistics. We will look at ways to state research questions, to search for answers, to compile and analyze data, and to present findings. To do this, we have divided the book into three major parts. Part I includes chapters on defining the research question and planning a research project to search for answers. These plans form the research proposal (which later becomes the basis of the final report). That is, part I covers activities that allow the researcher to plan a well-organized research project. Part II shows how the evidence, the findings, can be described using simple descriptive statistics and visual displays. Parts III and IV present a variety of statistical tests that tell us how much confidence we can place in statements made as answers to research questions. We hope to show the choices that are open to researchers in all of these steps. In working through the choices we offer, we believe you will develop a stronger notion of the principles that underlie research procedures. We also expect that you will become comfortable with and confident of the help that computers can give you.

If you are not a novice researcher (and even if you are), you might want to turn to the pretest in appendix A now. If you know which procedures are appropriate for the data shown in the examples and if you feel comfortable using the terms listed in the pretest, then you already have the knowledge needed to meet the goals listed below. If you know some but not others, highlight the items you have yet to learn and focus on them during your study of this manual. If you are a novice, don't be discouraged! Just think how much you will accomplish by working through the manual. Our goals may seem overwhelming at the start, but you will be amazed at how much easier the pretest is once you have completed your work.

Our major goals are:

1. To promote basic understanding of fundamental concepts of research design and statistics, which includes the following.

   a. Statistical literacy: the ability to read and evaluate research articles that include statistically analyzed data

   b. Statistical production: the ability to select and execute an appropriate procedure (with flexible options)

2. To make research planning (both design and analysis) as easy as possible through the following.

   a. Simple practice exercises to be completed by hand

   b. Practice with interpretation of results

   c. Review of research reports that illustrate research design and statistical analysis

The book has been written as a combination text and workbook. At the end of each chapter you will find an activities section that relates published studies to the material covered in the chapter. These activities are meant to give additional practice in evaluating research articles and to stimulate your own research interests. In addition, you will find practice sections within each chapter. From past experience we know that students can read very rapidly through a discussion of a statistical procedure, feel that they understand and yet a moment later realize that they have not been able to "hold onto" the concepts presented. By including workbook features in the manual, we hope to slow down the reading process and allow practice to reinforce the concepts. Filling in blanks and working through examples as you read can be frustrating, especially if you are not sure that your answers are correct. For this reason an answer key has been provided for questions that have been marked with an arrowhead (▶) in the text. As you will see, other questions ask for your opinions, your research ideas, and your criticisms. For these there are no correct answers. We hope these will lead to useful discussion in your study group or classroom.

Once upon a time there may have been a cat that was killed by curiosity. More often, it is curiosity that is killed. We hope that the examples we have included in this book will stimulate, rather than kill, your curiosity about language learning and language use. We believe that the study of research design and statistical analysis will give you exciting, new ways to satisfy that curiosity.

Part I. Planning a Research Project

Chapter 1
Defining the Research Question

- *Sources of research questions*
- *Scope of research*
- *Feasibility of research*
- *Stating research questions and hypotheses*
- *Collecting research evidence*
- *Internal and external validity of studies*

Research has been defined as *a systematic approach to searching for answers to questions.* This definition is straightforward but deceptively simple. To truly understand it, we must understand how systematicity relates to defining questions, to defining search, and to defining answers.

(Basically operationalizing our definition)

Sources of Research Questions

Misconceptions reg. research

In a recent study where teachers were encouraged to become teacher-researchers, we asked teachers to talk about their research questions. As you might expect, the teachers initially discounted the notion that they had interests which might qualify for serious research. For them, research was something that people did at universities or labs. They described research as having great theoretical scope, with numbers and symbols that made it difficult to understand, and while important and valuable, of little use in terms of impact on their teaching.

After that meeting, we wrote down our thoughts in our research journals.

> *Do teachers have questions about teaching? Do they wonder aloud about teaching materials, about students, about techniques? Do they argue about curriculum design (e.g., whether a departmental arrangement where students have homeroom and then go to different teachers for math, English or ESL, science, history is "better" for fourth graders than a self-contained classroom)? Do they share their questions with students? with other teachers?*

> *Do teachers look for answers to their questions? If so, how do they go about doing this? If they find answers, do they share them with students and/or other teachers?*

What qualifies as an important question? If research findings aren't likely to have an impact on teaching, what makes them valuable and important?

Do teachers truly believe research is only conducted elsewhere by other people? If the research were not conducted at a university, would it be better? more relevant? less difficult to understand?

How do teachers define "theory"? What kinds of questions have theoretical importance? Is theory testing less relevant to classroom practice than research that does not test theory?

How can we go about changing teachers' notions about the nature of research?

An endless list could be generated from this experience, but our basic question was whether our expectations for teacher-generated classroom research were viable. Imagine you were a member of a university faculty and your president asked all faculty members to state their research interests. Think about how you would respond. We suspect that people *everywhere* react in similar ways to such top → down instructions regarding research interests. When asked to come up with a research question out of context and divorced from true curiosity, the results are probably predictable. We could compare such a situation to being asked to write a composition with an open-choice topic. Given lack of direction, it is difficult to think of anything and much time is spent complaining and/or worrying about how to please the person(s) who gave the directions. — Don't worry?

The first rule of research should be that the questions are our own, questions that we truly want to investigate. If we are going to invest the time, energy, and sometimes even funds in research, then the questions must be important to us. Of course, our questions are shaped by our experiences. Our teachers, colleagues, students, and the reading we do all guide us towards the important issues in our field. Advice is often given that urges us to follow up on a "hot" topic. This is good advice not just because the topic is current but because others will want to know about the results. Other teachers may benefit from the research or other researchers will want to build on the research. If the topic is "current," it will also be easier to get the research report accepted at the conferences of our field (TESOL--Teaching English to Speakers of Other Languages; SLRF--Second Language Research Forum; AILA--International Association of Applied Linguistics; AAAL--American Association of Applied Linguistics; MLA--Modern Language Association; AERA--American Educational Research Association; NABE--National Association of Bilingual Education). It will be easier to publish, and it may even help in getting a job. Nevertheless, unless the question is a question we care about, it is unlikely that we will have the motivation to sustain us in the research process.

Another source of research questions can be found in the journals of our field. If you scan these, you will again see how wide the range of "interesting" questions can be. The research does fall into major categories which, of course, change over time as new and old areas become the center of research efforts. The areas include classroom research, skills based research, learner characteristics, teacher characteristics, language analysis (for teacher reference or materials development), language use outside the classroom, interlanguage analysis, language policy/planning, testing and evaluation, and theory testing. Even if you only check the table of contents of a few of the journals listed in appendix D, you should soon understand how research in our field informs both theory and practice.

As you read the articles that interest you most, you may find the authors finish their reports with a list of "unanswered questions"--ideas for further research. Thus, journals show which questions are especially interesting at a particular time, the wide range of possibilities for research, and even offer us specific ideas for further research.

Many times, student research topics are defined by supervising faculty (research on noun complements, on reading comprehension, on reciprocity in argumentative prose are parceled out to participating student members for work). In such cases, personal pleasure and motivation can come from being a part of the research team, but unless the question captures our imagination, the process can seldom be as satisfying as we might like.

There is another reason why we pick particular research topics. While we often research what we like or what appeals to us, we also often research what we think we know already. We find ourselves pursuing a topic because, as we say, "Hey, I have some knowledge of that now, I think I can contribute something to that anyway."

There is a story about the writer William Faulkner that illustrates this point. It seems that when Faulkner was young he left his native north-central Mississippi and struck out for the booming town of New Orleans, Louisiana. There he hoped to make a name for himself as a writer. He did reach New Orleans, and did work about town, freelancing and writing whenever he could. He also produced his first two novels, considered by Faulkner scholars to be dismal failures.

Faulkner sensed that his writing was not improving. One day, someplace in New Orleans, he ran across an acquaintance (also to become a well-known author), Sherwood Anderson. Faulkner expressed to Anderson his desire to become a great writer. Anderson replied something to the effect: "Then what are you doing here? Go home! Go back to Mississippi! Write about something that you know!"

Faulkner took that advice and returned to Mississippi to begin his lifetime cycle of works about the area he knew best: Mississippi. His very next novel was *The Sound and the Fury*, considered by many to be a modern masterpiece and quite possibly the single work in his life most responsible for his Nobel Prize.

One of the best ways to begin to define what interests you and your thoughts about what you already know is with a research journal. Each time you think of a question for which there seems to be no ready answer, write the question down. Someone may write or talk about something that is fascinating, and you wonder if the same results would obtain with your students, or with bilingual children, or with a different genre of text. Write this in your journal. Perhaps you take notes as you read articles, observe classes, or listen to lectures. Place a star or other symbol at places where you have questions. These ideas will then be easy to find and transfer to the journal. Of course, not all of these ideas will evolve into research topics. Like a writer's notebook, these bits and pieces of research ideas will reformulate themselves almost like magic. Ways to redefine, elaborate or reorganize the questions will occur as you reread the entries.

If you are not part of a research team, a second good way to begin is to form a study group. Here you can find "critical friends"--people who will feel free to ask all the critical questions they can *and* lend you the support that you may need. "Critical friends" (or "friendly enemies") are invaluable to the researcher. They help you reformulate your research questions, point out your errors and possible threats to the validity and reliability of the research, suggest other ways of gathering data, question your selection of statistical procedures, and argue over the interpretation of your results. Advisors can and do serve this function, but critical help from a group of friends is even better.

◇◇◇◇◇◇◇◇◇◇◇◇◇◇◇◇◇◇◇◇◇◇◇◇◇◇◇◇◇◇◇◇◇◇◇◇◇◇◇

Practice 1.1

1. As a study group assignment, start a research journal. Enter your notes and questions in the journal for one week. In your study group, compare the research interests of the group members.
Report on range of interests:_____
_____
_____
_____
_____

2. Select two articles from recent journals related to the field of applied linguistics. Attempt to fit each article into one of these broad categories.
Classroom research _____
Skills based research_____
Learner characteristics _____
Teacher characteristics_____
Language analysis_____
Language use _____
Interlanguage analysis _____
Language policy/planning _____
Testing and evaluation_____
Program evaluation _____
Theory testing _____
Other _____

3. What potential losses/gains do you see in advisor-generated research? Compare your responses with those of members of your study group. Report the variability you see in the responses and how you might account for different reactions to this practice.

4. Your course instructor will decide how best to form study groups in your class. However, think for a moment about what special characteristics you would look for in selecting your own "critical friends." List these below.

Objective, well-read honest, able to criticize constructively
hard working motivated, reliable, interested in being critical friends

(As a research project, you might want to collect the responses to the above question and, at the end of the term, ask the same question. Are you curious about whether and how the group process changes perceptions about which characteristics of "critical friends" truly are the most important?)

Would you prefer to participate in a study group where interests are very similar or where there is a wide variety of interests? Why? _Similar - focus & depth_
on an issue of interest to me while I'm getting lots of breadth
in coursework etc. this semester/year.

◇◇◇

Scope of Research

Aside from personal interest, research questions need to have other characteristics. They should be able to generate new information or confirm old information in new ways. To be sure that this is the case, a review of the literature on the research topic must be done. Imagine that you are interested in second language proficiency but instead of looking at students' use of grammatical structures, you want to investigate how well they can perform basic "speech acts." Obviously this is not a topic that one would select without some acquaintance with speech act theory. You also would not select the topic if you thought that it had already been sufficiently addressed.

Still, the first thing to do is undertake a review of previous speech act research to learn exactly what has been done in this area with second language learners. If you went to your university library, you might be able to get a computer search for this topic. Such searches, like ordinary library searches, begin by looking at "key words" and "key authors." Key words and key authors for speech acts might include terms such as *directive, assertive, commissive* or such authors as *Austin, Searle, Gumperz.* Think for a moment about how broad a key word like "speech act" might be in such a search. While it is not as broad a key word as, say, *linguistics*, the number of articles and books generated by a search with this key word would be very large (and very broad).

A search using *bilingual* as a key word would also generate a huge number of items. Many of these would not be useful for, say, a language policy study of bilingualism in Peru. The question is how to narrow the scope of the search and at the same time find all the relevant entries.

Hopefully, this question illuminates one of the first problems regarding the definition of research questions--the questions are stated too broadly. To say we want to know more about how well second language learners carry out speech acts is a little like saying we want to know how well learners use language. Precisely *which* speech acts do we want to investigate? What types of second language learners--beginners, advanced--are we talking about? Are the learners adult Korean immigrants in Los Angeles or Japanese high school students in Kyoto? In what kinds of situations should the speech events be investigated? Is the research meant to support test development? materials development? theory development? Where above we called for narrowing via key words, now we can narrow further via key sentences.

Using these questions as a guide, we can redefine the research question by narrowing the scope. For example, the scope could be narrowed from:

> *Investigate how well second language learners perform speech acts.*

to:

> *Investigate Korean ESL students' ability to recognize complaint behavior appropriate in an academic university setting.*

Here "performance" has been narrowed from total performance to recognition (one portion of the total performance skill). "Second language learners" is narrowed to "Korean ESL students," and "speech acts" has been narrowed to one speech act subcategory "complaints." The events in which the subcategory might occur have been narrowed to those relevant to the university setting. There are, of course, many other ways in which the question might be narrowed.

In narrowing the scope of the research, we may lose interest in the topic because it no longer addresses the larger question. An appropriate balance needs to be struck between scope and interest. It is possible to maintain the original research interest by carrying out a number of studies with limited scope. Together these studies would address the broader, general area of interest.

A review of previous research will help us to define the scope of research in another way. We've already noted that the scope of the research must be realistic. But, even a fairly narrow question may need to be more carefully defined. Previous researchers may already have done this. For example, many teachers are concerned with student motivation. Motivation, like bilingualism, is a very broad concept. Previous researchers have, however, grappled with this problem and have subcategorized the concept into types of motivation--for example, *intrinsic* and *extrinsic* motivation or *instrumental* and *integrative* motivation. In narrowing or subcategorizing the concept, operational definitions must be given to show the scope of the subcategory.

operational definition

Sometimes well-established *operational definitions* exist for terms that are crucial to your research. Such a definition gives a "tried and true" definition and an accepted method for observing or assessing it. However, sometimes there are no such accepted definitions or no agreement as to what the terms mean. There are, for example, many abstract theoretical concepts that have been "constructed" in our field. These *constructs* are shown in abstract terms such as *acquisition, motivation, need achievement, monitoring, compound bilingualism.* We may share a basic understanding of such theoretical concepts, but even these *theoretical definitions* are difficult to formulate. For example, precisely *how* would you define *bilingual?* A commonly-shared definition of *bilingual* is "speaking two languages." We all know that the term may be applied to people who are at all points of fluency in the two languages (even to absolute beginners of a second language). To use such a term in research would be almost meaningless. A more precise definition is given, for example, *Arabic-English bilinguals who scored a 3+ or higher on the FSI inventory participated in this study* or *Children who had participated in the Arabic immersion program in Cleveland schools in grades K-3 constitute the bilingual group in this study.*

When broad terms for constructs are used in research questions, we cannot rely on a *theoretical definition* even if one is readily available. Terms must be "operationally" defined. An *operational definition* is a clear statement of how you judged or identified a term in your research. This is important for three reasons. First, you will need to be absolutely consistent throughout the research process in your definition. Second, it is important for consumers of your research so that they do not misinterpret your findings. Third, it is important to the research community that your study be replicable. Different results might be obtained by other researchers if they carry out a similar project and use a different definition of *bilingual.*

Good operational definitions can often be drawn from the existing literature. Sometimes, however, research is difficult to carry out because operational definitions cannot be found that will satisfy the researcher. Sometimes no operational definitions exist in the literature and the researcher must define terms. We know very little, for example, about how language is represented in the brain. Yet, many models of language acquisition talk about "acquisition devices," "filters," "parameters," "L1 → L2 transfer" as *internal* mechanisms. It is, of course, possible to create and define an operational definition for these terms for an individual project. A clear definition would be crucial to the research. (In some cases, we develop an operational definition for such concepts but then find ourselves questioning the "reality" of the concepts themselves. The attempt to establish concepts is an important area of research.)

◇◇◇◇◇◇◇◇◇◇◇◇◇◇◇◇◇◇◇◇◇◇◇◇◇◇◇◇◇◇◇◇◇◇◇◇◇◇◇

Practice 1.2

1. Write a research question that narrows the scope for the study of speech acts in a different way. _____

What key words would you use to search for relevant studies for this research question? _____

_____

Compare your question with those written by members of your study group. Which statements still appear to need further narrowing of scope? How could this be accomplished? _____

_____

_____

_____

Which of the questions generated in your study group are good candidates for contributing answers to the large general study of speech act performance?_____

_____

_____

_____

How much more research would need to be generated to begin to answer the broad general question? How large a research team do you think might be needed to work on an issue with this scope?

_____

_____

_____

_____

_____

maybe
in-class
do w/

2. In our example of speech act research, we talked about "performance," but we still must operationally define "perform" so that we will know precisely how it is measured. How might "performance" be defined and measured? Has the definition further narrowed the scope of the research?

But w/ term in class project

3. Imagine that your research question contained the key words *acquisition* and *L1 → L2 transfer*. First write a definition giving your general understanding of these concepts.
*Acquisition*_____

_____

Transfer _____

_____

Now write an operational definition for each term that shows precisely how you would measure or observe each.
Acquisition in my study means _____

_____

and will be measured or observed by _____

Transfer in my study means _____

_____

and will be measured or observed by _____
_____

How close do you think your operational definitions are to the theoretical definitions of these constructs?

_____
_____

How likely is it that the theoretical definitions of these concepts actually reflect reality (i.e., how metaphorical are they)? _____
_____

List other abstract constructs for which either operational definitions or the constructs themselves might be problematic.

_____
_____
_____

our class list

4. Select one research topic from ~~your research journal.~~ Identify key terms and give operational definitions ~~for each.~~ Ask members of your study group to critique these operational definitions and make recommendations of ways to narrow scope. Which of these recommendations can you use to improve the study?

good - if students had a res. journal at this point!

_____
_____
_____
_____

◇◇

Feasibility of Research

So far, we have suggested that research questions should

1. interest us

2. promise new information or confirm old information in new ways

3. have reasonable scope

4. have key terms that are clearly defined and operationalized

Before we turn to stating the questions in a more formal way, we need to consider whether or not the research is feasible.

Many factors affect feasibility of research. To decide whether a research project is feasible or not means that you must know how much time the project will take and whether or not you have that amount of time to spend. When the topic is very broad--as that of language learners' performance of speech acts--it might take a lifetime to investigate the topic. We have already talked about ways to narrow the scope of the research to make it more feasible. One of the major reasons we narrow scope is the amount of time we have available to carry out the research. If your research is for a course and the course is only 10 or 18 weeks in duration, the scope must be tightly constrained.

Assume that your sister and her husband have a first child. Your sister's husband speaks Spanish as a first language. They use Spanish at home rather than English. The other members of your extended family speak mainly English although, except for your mother who is monolingual English, they all use Spanish sometimes. You are very interested in investigating "bilingualism as a first language" since the baby, Luisa, will develop the language(s) simultaneously. It might take years, if not a lifetime, to complete such a project.

Longitudinal studies, which follow an individual or group over a period of time, can be very time-consuming. This is one of the reasons that many researchers prefer a *cross-sectional approach* rather than a longitudinal study. In this approach, data are gathered (usually only once) from different groups of learners of different ages or different levels of proficiency.

If we assume that the data of the longitudinal study were described in terms of actual age (in the following chart, the number before the colon stands for years and the number following it represents months), the cross-sectional equivalent might look like this:

years   months   Longitudinal Study of Luisa
0:9   1:0   1:3   1:6   1:9   2:0

Cross-Sectional Study of 30 Children
5 at 0:9   5 at 1:0   5 at 1:3   5 at 1:6   5 at 1:9   5 at 2:0

The assumption is that the data of the children at each of these age levels would be similar to that of Luisa at that age. The advantage is that all the data could be collected at one time rather than spread out over two years. This makes the study more feasible. The problem might be in finding children exactly these ages, all of whom were simultaneously acquiring English and Spanish.

For a research question where the *order* of acquisition (i.e., *when* forms *first* appear) is more important than *accuracy*, another possibility is to incorporate more acquisition data from other children into the design. For example, you might try the following:

Time Periods for Observational Data

0:9-1:0	1:1-1:3	1:4-1:6	1:7-1:9	1:10-1:3	1:4-1:6
Luisa	Luisa				
	Juan	Juan			
		Maria	Maria		
			Ernesto	Ernesto	
				Susan	Susan

This would allow you to collect observational data in six months rather than two years. The one-period overlap could help substantiate the similarity of developmental stages at these age levels. Again, it might be difficult to locate children of appropriate ages for the study. In addition, your research advisor might warn you that age is *not* a very satisfactory way to equate stages for such studies and suggest the use of a type of utterance length measure instead. That would mean collecting data from a fairly large group of children to find those who fit stages defined by this utterance length measure. MLU

Such quasi-longitudinal plans for data collection have the advantage of cutting the time span of the research, but the researcher must be able to locate appropriate learners and have time to collect the data from each of them.

Time, of course, is not the only thing to think about in determining how feasible a study might be. Imagine that you want to look at some aspect of language use by bilingual children in elementary school classrooms. If you are not already located at a school with a bilingual student enrollment, you may have great difficulty in gaining access to the classroom. For access to be granted, many schools and teachers require a statement that the research will not disrupt regular instruction. In some school districts (and for good reasons), there is a monumental amount of red tape involved with school-based research. It simply may not be feasible for you to gain access.   #2 access

Feasibility may be determined not only by time and access, but also quantity and quality of access. For example, assume the government was interested in finding out the extent of bilingualism in your state. One way they could do this is by including questions on the next United States census questionnaire. First, the quality of the sample is likely to be biased given the existence of undocumented aliens, who may or may not want to be part of the census count. Second, quantity--the number of questions that could be allocated to this issue on the questionnaire--would be severely constrained. Third, the cost, if bilingual census takers must be found to conduct census taking, might not make the project feasible. A phone survey (using every *n*th telephone number in a directory) is another possibility, but we would need to know whether all people are equally likely to have phones or to be accessible to the phone during calling periods.

The dollar cost of research may also determine the feasibility of the research. In   #3 cost
planning a project, prepare a reasonable budget. Do you need tape recorders and tapes? Do you have the computer software you need for the study? If videotaped data are required for your study, are videocamera and tapes available? Can you operate the videocamera and observe a class at the same time, or must you hire a camera operator? Will the school and/or the learners expect some remuneration for participating in your study? Will you have to hire someone to help you code your data (to ensure that your codes are well described and can be followed by anyone)? Do you need paper supplies, travel to and from a school, photocopies of 200 essays or computer entry of text data (perhaps via an optical character reader)? Try to make a complete list of everything you need. You don't want to near completion of the study and find that you don't have the last $5.95 you need for supplies. Think, then, about possible sources for funding for your project. Does your school have equipment you can borrow? Can you arrange a "help ex-

change" with other researchers rather than paying outsiders to help with ratings, coding, or data collection? Will the school district fund research such as yours? Could you apply for a grant through the National Science Foundation or the Office of Educational Research on Instruction? Are there nongovernmental groups that provide grants you could apply to? Does the school district or the university have an office that can assist you in preparing a grant proposal? If so, they may know good sources for funding.

Practice 1.3

no

1. Consider the study of Luisa. List other ways that the study might be made feasible. Discuss these in your study group and list any remaining feasibility problems for the study.

_____

_____

_____

_____

2. If you hope to do research in a classroom, list the procedures needed to gain access to the classroom. Will restrictions be placed on the data-gathering procedure by the school? If so, will these restrictions make the study less feasible?
_____ Human subjects process _____

_____

_____

_____

3. In what kinds of studies might a telephone survey be less desirable than a personal interview survey? Why?_____

_____

_____

_____

4. As a study group assignment, select one of the limited-scope research topics from your research journal. Prepare a budget statement in the space below. In the statement include an estimate of time (and pay scale) for the principal researcher along with travel, supplies, and equipment estimates. (Every grant application has its own budget format, so the actual budget form will vary from that given below.)

Research Budget

_____
_____
_____
_____
_____
_____
_____

Total Cost _____

List possible sources (and amounts) of funding or help for the research project:

_____
_____
_____
_____
_____

Assuming that you obtained the support you list above, would it be financially possible for you to carry out the research? If not, why? (For example, would you have to give up other jobs in order to carry out the research?)

_____
_____
_____
_____

Discuss your budgets in your study group. List items which were overlooked in the various budgets.
Group report: _____

_____
_____
_____
_____

◇◇◇

Stating Research Questions and Hypotheses

Now that we have talked about the scope and feasibility of research questions, it is time to consider how these questions can be clearly stated. Imagine that you still wanted to describe the bilingual language development of the child, Luisa. Your basic research question was "Can I describe the bilingual language development of Luisa?" You realize that this is not feasible, so you have narrowed the question to "Can I describe the first 50 Spanish and first 50 English words acquired by Luisa?"

Let's imagine what would happen if you, as a student researcher, brought this research question to your advisor. You soon might find yourself commiserating with Elisabeth Mann Borgese's grandmother. Your advisor might ask why this is an "interesting" question? Luisa's parents might find it fascinating (and, in fact, they could easily be persuaded to collect the first 50 words for you). You might find it fascinating too. Luisa's development, however, is of *interest* only insofar as it can be interpreted as an indication of bilingual development in general (or as an indication of how lexical development differs in simultaneous acquisition of languages vs. sequential acquisition, or how the process might differ from that shown by monolingual children). What do you expect that the 50 words might show you about the process? Do you expect to see a change in meanings over time? Do you expect to see parallel words in the two languages? Do you expect that the types of words used will relate to interactions with specific people? Do you expect to be able to identify Luisa's meanings for these words accurately enough that you can check to see if more nouns are produced than any other category? Do you expect to be able to see whether she uses her first words to label objects and people or whether she uses them to request actions? What do you expect to see in the data?

We often begin research with questions like "Can I describe *X*?" rather than "Why do I want to describe *X*?" The answer to the "why" question shows us that we expect the description to have some bearing on a question which is important to the field. "Can I describe" questions are often difficult, for we seldom know how we will go about this descriptive task until we begin to examine the data. However, it helps to think about possible outcomes ahead of time so that we are ready to look for particular relationships as we begin the study. That is, exploratory research is seldom completely open.

To illustrate this further, consider the work that is done in "needs-assessment" research. The basic question in such research is "Can I discover how *X* perceive their needs regarding instruction (or whatever)?" Imagine that, as all teachers, you realize that you cannot possibly instruct your students in language and also in all the content material that they need to learn. You want to involve parents in the instruction process. You wonder which instructional needs parents see as being important *and* which of these they would take responsibility for at home. The research is of obvious importance to curriculum planning. It has high practical interest, but it is of interest to the field only if findings can be taken as an indication of parental involvement in curriculum and instruction in a more general sense.

Again, if you ask yourself what you expect to find out, all sorts of new questions pop up. Do you expect all parents to respond in the same way? If not, what factors might help explain differences in their responses? Will you remember to tap these factors (e.g., will you collect information on education, age, work patterns, and so forth)? Do you imagine responses might be different if the students are already doing very well at school than if they are not? Do you have these data easily available so you can check this relationship? What about older siblings? Should they be included as part of this study? Once we start thinking about what might happen in the data, we begin to think about how to explain the findings. We develop hunches about outcomes, and rephrase our questions taking them into account.

◇◇

Practice 1.4

Indiv. or in groups? *our list? a list for list.* *they do for list.*

1. Select one question from your research journal. Explain why it is an "interesting" question for the field. _____

_____
_____
_____

Frame the general research question for the study. _____

_____ *(maybe)*
_____

Consider the possible outcomes of the study. What factors may enter into the
research that might influence the outcomes? _____

_____
_____
_____

◇◇

It is at this point in the planning process that we should take time to read, to
observe, and to think about the project very carefully. We don't want to plunge
into a project without taking time to let our minds sort through the many possibilities. If you have kept a research journal, you will already have revised your
research question many times and thought about many alternatives and the possible outcomes. It is important not to hurry the planning at this point. The reason it is important not to hurry is that our thought processes are not just analytic
but holistic as well. One thing that has come out of all the recent work on "expert
systems" in cognitive science is that the mental representation of problems involves qualitative reasoning. "Expert" researchers don't approach problem solving in a straightforward, analytic way. They give themselves time to "sleep on it,"
to think about the problem when they aren't thinking about it. If you read widely
and keep a research journal, you will soon find that you do this too. In the initial
stages, novice researchers are pressed for time and this can lead to an end product
in which the researcher finds little pleasure or pride.

Usually when we have questions or when we wonder about something, we really
do not know the answers for sure. That doesn't mean that we have no idea about
what those answers might be or where to look for them. Our hunches about answers may come from reviewing the literature on the topic, from talking with
colleagues, or from observing classrooms. These hunches about answers, when
written in a formal way, are called *hypotheses.* We carry out the research to see
if these hypotheses are supported or not.

One very popular notion is that research is a way to *prove* that an answer is right
or wrong. Given the exploratory nature of much research in our field, we would
like to disabuse you of this notion at once. It will seldom be possible to *prove* that

Chapter 1. Defining the Research Question   23

When? (If ever?)

your answer is *the* right one for the question. Instead, you should consider the research process as one in which you can collect evidence that will *support* or *not support* the relationship you want to establish or the hypotheses you have stated. Why this is so will be explained in much more depth in the following chapters.

In formal terms, a hypothesis is a statement of possible outcome of research. The hypothesis may be stated as a *null* hypothesis and as an *alternative* hypothesis. Imagine you wished to discover if an order exists in the acquisition of English spelling patterns. This is all you wish to do. You do not want to see whether the order is different according to the age of learners or whether the learner's L1 might influence the order. In the null form, your hypothesis might be:

> There is no order of acquisition of English spelling patterns.

While you might never write this null hypothesis out, it should be in the back of your mind as you collect and analyze your data since that is what the statistical test will test. The alternative hypothesis would be:

> There is an order of acquisition of English spelling patterns.

You hope that your data will allow you to discount the null hypothesis and give evidence in support of the alternative hypothesis.

(As you will see later, it *is* possible to test an alternative hypothesis when there are *strong* theoretical reasons to do so or when previous research has already allowed researchers to reject the null hypothesis. However, in our field, where replication studies are few and far between, it is more customary to test the null hypothesis.)

The null hypothesis is often annotated as H_o. The alternative hypothesis is annotated as H_1.

Let's assume that spelling patterns have been scaled for difficulty--that is, there is a known order of difficulty for major and minor spelling patterns in English. The literature gives an operational definition of the spelling patterns with examples of each *and* the established order of difficulty. This order, however, was established using spelling tests of native speakers of English. The question is whether the order is the same for second language learners. If it is, then ESL beginners should be able to show accurate performance only on the easiest patterns. They would place at the bottom of the spelling order continuum. The more advanced the learner, the higher he or she should place on the continuum of the known order scale of difficulty for spelling patterns.

Now assume that you have been hired to design a course book on English spelling patterns for university students who are in intermediate and advanced ESL classes. You would like to arrange the instruction to reflect the already established spelling continuum. Before you begin, though, you wonder if spelling errors of ESL students change as they become more proficient overall in the language. This time, unlike the previous example, you want to look at a re-

lationship between two things--L2 proficiency and where students place on the spelling continuum. You might state the hypothesis in the following ways:

> H_o There is no relationship between L2 proficiency and placement on the spelling continuum.

This is the *null* hypothesis and it says that the evidence you gather will show no relation between a student's proficiency and placement on the continuum. If the *null* hypothesis is correct, then the continuum is useless as a guide to sequencing spelling patterns. If the *null* hypothesis is incorrect, then the continuum may be helpful.

The *alternative* hypothesis would be:

> H_1 There is a relationship between L2 spelling proficiency and placement on the spelling continuum.

With both forms, you can test the null hypothesis, H_o , against the alternative hypothesis, H_1 .

In addition, you may state the alternative hypothesis in a *directional* form (positive or negative). That is, on the basis of previous research in the field, you may believe that a relationship does exist and that you can also specify the direction of the relationship. If other researchers have found that the scale "works" for L2 learners--i.e., that the more proficient the learner is in general language development, the higher the placement on the continuum--you can use a directional hypothesis. If previous research suggests a positive direction, the directional hypothesis is in the positive form.

> H_2 There is a positive relationship between L2 proficiency and placement on the spelling continuum.

This says that the more proficient the student, the higher the placement on the spelling continuum. If it is correct, then your data substantiate previous findings and give additional evidence for the use of the sequence in materials development.

> H_3 There is a negative relationship between L2 proficiency and placement on the spelling continuum.

This says that the more proficient the student, the lower the placement on the continuum. This seems an unlikely hypothesis and would not be used unless previous research had suggested that the continuum which was established for first language learners not only does not apply to second language learners (in which case the null hypothesis would be correct) but that the continuum works in the opposite direction (the negative direction alternative hypothesis is correct). The spelling patterns in the continuum are reversed so that what was difficult for the L1 learner is easy for the L2 learner and vice versa!

Practice 1.5

▶ 1. To practice stating and interpreting the meanings of these forms of hypotheses, assume that you wanted to look at the *relationship* of language proficiency and spelling test *scores*. How would you state and interpret the null and alternative directional hypotheses?

Null hypothesis: _____

_____

Interpretation: _____

_____

Alternative hypothesis: _____

_____

Interpretation: _____

_____

Directional, positive hypothesis: _____

_____

Interpretation: _____

_____

Directional, negative hypothesis: _____

_____

Interpretation: _____

_____

_____

◇◇

In most research reports, the null hypothesis (even though it may not be formally stated) is tested rather than a directional alternative hypothesis. This is because there is seldom a body of research which has already established a relationship among the variables included in our research. Strange as it may seem, it is easier to find evidence that supports a directional hypothesis than it is to reject a null hypothesis. We will explain the reasons for this later. Nevertheless, there are times when a directional hypothesis is appropriate (when previous research has shown evidence in this direction). Different statistics will be used based on this distinction of whether the hypothesis is directional.

Sometimes it is necessary to write more than one hypothesis to cover the research question. For example, in the task of preparing materials for a spelling textbook, you might also want to know whether students from different first language groups (as well as of differing proficiency levels) get the same scores on general tests of spelling. The null hypothesis for first language membership could be stated as:

> *There is no relationship between first language membership and spelling test scores.*

This means you expect to find no difference among the groups. However, there is still a possibility that there could be large differences among students from different groups when students are beginning learners and that this difference might disappear over time so that there would be no difference among advanced learners. In such a case, our results would show an *interaction* where the effect of language proficiency interacts with the effect of the first language. This requires a hypothesis about the possible *interaction* between first language membership and proficiency with spelling scores.

> *There is no interaction between first language and proficiency and spelling test scores.*

If the results are such that an interaction is found, then you cannot say that either first language or proficiency act alone. Rather, they interact so that differences in first language groups do show up at some levels of proficiency but not at others.

◇◇

Practice 1.6

► 1. Imagine that the researcher was also interested in the possibility that men and women might differ in spelling scores. State a separate null hypothesis for the *effect* of sex on spelling scores (i.e., ignore proficiency). Then state all the interaction hypotheses (i.e., adding in proficiency and L1 membership) in the null form.

H_o for sex: _____

H_o for sex and L1: _____

H_o for sex and language proficiency: _____

H_o for sex, L1, and language proficiency: _____

Three-way interactions are often difficult to interpret. If there were a three-way interaction here, it might show that females from certain L1 groups at certain levels of proficiency performed differently from everyone else. If the H_o for the three-way interaction could not be rejected, how would you interpret the finding?

_____
_____
_____

2. State the null hypothesis and alternative hypothesis for the research you defined on page 22.

H_o _____
_____

H_1 _____
_____

Check the hypotheses generated in your study group. List suggestions for further clarification of your study.

_____
_____
_____
_____

◇◇◇

As we think about our hypotheses, we need to consider what kinds of evidence we can use to reject the null hypothesis. Just as there are caveats about scope and feasibility of research questions, there are some things to think about in terms of data gathering. As with our statements about scope and feasibility, these comments on data gathering are to help you to avoid (rather than to create) problems so that the research is easier to do. They should help rather than hinder your pursuit of evidence for answers to questions.

Collecting Research Evidence

In planning a research project, it is important to consider what kind(s) of evidence are needed so that your findings will allow you to support or reject your tentative answers (hypotheses). The next step is to determine the best way to collect the data. The data collection method is determined, in part, by the research question. Given the wide range of possible research questions in our field, it is impossible to review them here. However, we can discuss the issue of how to gather the evidence most efficiently.

Unfortunately for our field, there is no central data bank to which we can turn for oral and written language data. However, almost every agency, university, or university professor _does_ have data files and these files may already be entered into the computer. Carnegie-Mellon has a data bank for child language data. Your university may have the Brown corpus (1979) or the Lund corpus (1980) on line for your use. Individual faculty members may have precisely the data you need to help answer your research question. In some cases, for example in government-sponsored research institutes or centers, data banks may be open to public use. In other cases, restrictions are put on the data.

Efficiency, of course, relates back to the amount of time you have available to carry out the project. If you have an unlimited amount of time, you might think of many different kinds of evidence and devise many different ways of gathering that evidence. The case presented would be exceedingly strong if you could use a multimethod approach. However, that luxury is not often available unless the project is undertaken as part of a research team effort. (This is one drawback of individual research. The balance between autonomy vs. efficiency in the research process is one faced by every researcher.)

Consider, for the moment, that you wanted to look at the types of spelling errors written by men and women from different first language groups. To obtain data, you decided to contact English teachers in universities around the world and ask them to send you sample compositions of their advanced English students. There are a whole series of questions to be answered. How might you operationally define "advanced" so that you are sure the samples will come from the appropriate groups? How many compositions will you need to obtain to have an appropriate sample? Will words representing all the spelling patterns actually occur in all compositions? How difficult will it be to find and categorize each spelling error? How long will it be before all the sample compositions actually arrive?

The strength of this method of data collection is that the errors will be those committed by students during actual writing tasks. There are, however, many weaknesses to this method that make it ill-advised. The data, if and when it arrived, would likely not contain examples of all the error types of interest. The examples might be extremely difficult to locate and categorize.

Assume you had 48 hours to gather the data! Via electronic mail, you contacted administrators at ESL departments at thirty American universities who immediately agreed to administer a spelling test. The test requires students to select the best spelling (from four choices) of a list of 60 words. The test is computerized so that students enter their responses directly on the computer. There are spaces where students identify their first language background and sex. The results (in this most impossible of worlds) are returned via electronic mail the next day.

The method would certainly be efficient but the data collection procedure has changed the analysis of actual errors to the analysis of the ability to recognize correct spelling patterns. Subjects might be either intrigued, anxious, or bored with the task depending on their acquaintance with computers and electronic mail. Depending on their reactions, the method might or might not be effective.

Efficiency isn't everything. If the method you use is dull or frightening or boring or takes too long, it's unlikely that your subjects (Ss) will be motivated to perform as well as they might. One efficient method to trace semantic networks is by galvanic skin response (GSR). Ss are conditioned with a very slight electric current to a word, say *chicken*. A measurement is taken from (painless) electrodes attached to the skin. Once the person is conditioned, other words are presented and no current is used. Nevertheless, there will be a skin response if the new words are linked to the word *chicken*. So, a reading would be obtained for *duck* and, perhaps, *farm* or *barn* and so forth. Would you agree to participate in research that used this method if we assure you that it *is* painless? A similar method is to flash a light and create an eye-blink or pupil restriction as a response to words. Again, once the conditioning is accomplished, the reaction will occur to words by networks. If you wanted to know whether bilingual Ss showed the same semantic network reactions in their two languages, you would more likely select this second option. It's just as efficient and not so frightening.

Imagine that you wanted native speakers of French to judge the seriousness of 12 types of gender errors in the speech of American students studying French. Each student in your class has presented a talk which you have recorded. Since there are 20 students in the class, this amounts to 10 hours of tape. You want the native speakers to listen to all 10 hours, scaling the seriousness of each error on a scale of 1 to 9. Would you agree to participate in this study as a judge (if you were a native speaker of French)? Probably not, since the time commitment would be great and the task fairly dull. The researcher would need to plan time blocks and ways of relieving boredom for the raters.

The data collection method should not only motivate Ss to participate, but should allow them to give their best possible performance. Methods that work well with adults may not work well with adolescents or young children. The context of data collection has to be one that allows everyone to give their best performance. If not, our findings may lead us to make erroneous claims. For example, Piagetians, using certain kinds of tasks, have shown that young children are not supposed to be able to take another person's visual point of view. Donaldson (1978) created a new data collection method using a model with toy children hiding from toy policemen. The model was arranged so that only by taking each policeman's visual point of view could the children decide where the toy children should hide. Four- and five-year-olds succeeded even when they had to coordinate the points of view of two policemen whose views of the scene were different from their own. In teaching, we look for the optimal way to make principles learnable. In research, we should also spend as much time as possible working out procedures that will allow us to get the best possible results.

Assume that your school district will look into the value of multilingual/multiethnic education. All kinds of performance measures have been collected, but you also wish to assess the attitudes of relevant personnel to such programs. The relevant personnel are children enrolled in the programs (kindergarten through grade 4), teachers, administrators, parents, school board administrators, and community leaders. Assume that you have worked out a needs-press analysis questionnaire that works well for the adults. (In needs-press analysis the researcher first asks respondents to list and rate the most important needs for a program or whatever. Then, after the respondents have taken part, or observed, the program, the researcher asks how well each of the needs were met. The comparison of perceived needs and need satisfaction make up the study.) Obviously, such a procedure will not reliably tap the attitudes of the children. One possibility would be to use the happy-face method where children are asked how they feel about *X* or how they feel when *X* happens. They are presented with an array of happy to unhappy faces to point to. Whatever data-gathering technique you use with young children, you will want to pilot the technique several times until you are certain that you are getting reliable results.

We often use questionnaires as a way of gathering data. Time requirements and task boredom can discourage people from responding. To insure a better response rate on return of questionnaires, it is important to consider exactly what information must be obtained from the respondent and what information can as easily be gathered from other sources. For example, there is no need to ask students to list their GPA, SAT, or GRE scores if this type of information can be more reliably obtained from other sources. The longer and more complicated the questionnaire, the less chance of return.

Of course, the best suggestion we can give is that you consider the data collection procedures used by researchers who have carried out studies similar to your own. The method that you use to collect data will undoubtedly be influenced by that used by previous researchers. If you wish to elicit monologue data, you might follow Chafe's (1980) model and have people view *The Pear Stories* film and tell the story back as you tape. Or you might use a silent film such as the montage of extracts from Charlie Chaplin's *Modern Times* prepared by project researchers working in Heidelberg on the European Science Foundation Project (a project studying second language acquisition of adult immigrants in Europe). Of course you would need to review each film story carefully in order to understand how it might shape the choice of structures used in the narrative monologue. Or you could copy Labov's (1972) "danger of death" technique to elicit narratives. For investigations of grammar, you might want to use grammaticality judgments, sentence repetition, or translation. For vocabulary, you could adopt a card sort method to test the outer limits of core vocabulary items (e.g., pictures of various boxes, bags, chests, baskets, etc., to see where *S*s move from *box* to some other lexical items or pictures of cars, vans, station wagons, jeeps, VW's, limousines, etc., to see where *S*s move *car* to another lexical item). You might use a spew test where *S*s "spew" out as many examples of a core vocabulary item (or words that rhyme or start with the same sound or whatever) as possible in a given time period. To study communication components described as "foreigner talk," you may tape teachers in beginner classes or set up dyads where one person has information (e.g., how items are arranged in a doll house or how geometric shapes are arranged on a grid) which must be conveyed to another person who cannot see the arrangement. To investigate the reading or the composing process, you may ask *S*s to "think aloud" as they work. To check comprehensibility of input, you may ask *S*s to listen to one of their taped interactions, and tell you as accurately as they can just what was happening--a "retrospection" method. To study speech events, you may set up role-play situations where *S*s return defective items to a store (a complaint situation), issue invitations to parties (inviting and accepting/rejecting invitations), give/accept advice, offer/receive compliments, and so forth. The range of possibilities is never-ending. The important thing is that the procedures work for you and give you data that can be used to answer your research question. To find lists of tests which purport to measure particular constructs, consult Buros (1975), *Assessment Instruments in Bilingual Education* (1978), or other test guides in the reference section of your library. Previous research that relates to your research questions will, however, give you the best ideas as to the most appropriate methods to use to gather data. Once you have completed the literature review for the study, you should be well versed in the variety of techniques previously employed, be able to select from among them, or be ready to offer even better alternatives.

◇◇

Practice 1.7

1. What data sources are already available at your university or institution? ___
_____
_____

2. The two methods (GSR and eye-blink) of examining semantic associations we mentioned are rather exotic. What other ways might the data be collected? Compare these suggestions in your study group. What advantages or disadvantages do you see for each?
_____
_____
_____
_____

3. List another way (other than "happy face") to gather data on the attitudes of young children toward an instructional technique. Compare the suggestions in your study group. What possible problems do you see with these techniques?
_____
_____
_____
_____

Would the methods you have listed above work to elicit data on attitudes of adult nonliterate ESL learners? Why/why not?
_____
_____
_____

4. Most language departments and ESL programs have placement exams. What personal information is requested at the beginning of the test? This is "questionnaire data." Why is the information requested? What interesting research questions can be answered on the basis of this information? _____
_____
_____
_____
_____
_____

5. Select one research topic from your research journal. First, be sure that you have limited the scope of the question, have stated hypotheses and written operational definitions for key terms. Give two methods you might use to gather evidence to support or reject your hypotheses.

a. _____

_____

_____

b. _____

_____

_____

Review these procedures in your study group. What suggestions were made to improve your data gathering techniques?

_____

_____

_____

_____

_____

◇◇◇◇◇◇◇◇◇◇◇◇◇◇◇◇◇◇◇◇◇◇◇◇◇◇◇◇◇◇◇◇◇◇◇◇◇◇

Internal and External Validity of Studies

Researchers talk about threats to both *internal* and *external* validity of their studies. To distinguish between these two, Campbell and Stanley (1963) note that internal validity has to do with interpreting findings of research within the study itself. External validity, on the other hand, has to do with interpreting findings and generalizing them beyond the study.

Internal Validity

Some common threats to internal validity include subject selection, maturation, history, instrumentation, task directions, adequate data base, and test effect.

We assume, when we collect data to answer questions, that we will be able to meet all threats to internal validity. Sometimes, that is not easy to do. Imagine that you wished to replicate the study conducted by Ben-Zeev (1976), which showed mixed results. In one part of the study she checked to see if bilingual and monolingual children had the same flexibility in recognizing that there *can* be other words for concrete objects such as book, table, cat. (Or, like Mark Twain's Eve, do they believe that the symbol *is* the thing?) In one sample she had 98 Hebrew-English bilingual and English monolingual children. In a second sample, she had 188 Spanish-English bilingual and English monolingual children. The bilinguals outperformed the monolinguals in the first sample but there was no difference between bilinguals and monolinguals in the second sample. You want to see what would happen with a new sample.

To start the study, you collect data at a school, carefully checking that school records show which children are bilingual and which are monolingual English speakers. When you were on the playground, though, you notice that some of the "monolingual" children actually speak some Spanish with each other. Your data are compromised by poor subject selection, a major threat to internal validity. Not all children in the monolingual sample were truly monolingual. Until each threat to internal validity is checked, you will not know how much confidence you can place in the results. Let's consider some of the most common threats to internal validity in more depth.

Subject Selection

It is important that you carefully identify the subject characteristics relevant to your study and that the subjects match that description. If your *S*s are monolingual and bilingual students, then the *S*s selected must match your operational definition of each category.

Selection bias can also occur if there are preexisting differences between groups of *S*s. You may wish to compare the effect of some particular teaching technique for two groups of *S*s, but it is impossible if the two groups are not really equivalent at the start. To escape this threat to internal validity, all relevant subject characteristics must be listed and checked for group bias in the selection process.

In planning subject selection, you should also think about the potential for attrition. This is especially important in longitudinal studies. Does the area or the school district you work in have a stable student population? Another type of attrition is especially important when you are comparing instructional programs. Say that your university wished to increase the number of underrepresented ethnic minority students admitted to the university. A sample admissions test was given to 10th grade students intending to apply for college admission. Letters were sent to those students whose English language skill scores were low, inviting them to attend a special summer program that would advise them on ways to improve their chances of college admission. Fifty-five such letters were sent and 23 students volunteered for the program. If all 55 of the students actually applied for college and you wanted to compare those who had and those who had not volunteered for this course, the comparison might not be "fair." There is always a chance that differential attrition might occur during this time period. Might the very best students from either of the groups decide not to apply after all? Or the very weakest students? Is it likely that more attrition might occur in one group or another? *Differential attrition* (also known as *mortality*) can have important consequences to the outcomes in the research.

It is important, then, to take care in selecting people (or, in text analysis, pieces of text; or, in one-person analysis, pieces of speech--i.e., utterances). This is often called the *subject selection factor.* "Subject" is a conventional way of talking about the people who participate in our research. Abbreviations you will see are *S* for subject, *S*s for subjects, and *S*'s and *S*s' for possessive forms.

Maturation

or excited

Another factor to consider is *maturation*. Maturation relates to time. In addition to getting older, it includes getting tired, getting bored, and so forth. Sometimes we hope to show a relation between special instruction and improvement in language skills. It is possible that exactly the same results would have been obtained simply because learners have matured.

History

In addition to maturation, many other things could be happening concurrent with the research. Though you may be unaware of many of them, there is always the possibility they could affect results. These are called *history* factors.

Imagine you teach Japanese at your university. The department wants to carry out an evaluation of a new set of materials (and subsequent change required in teaching methodology). Unknown to the department, you have instituted an informal Friday afternoon gathering for your students at a Japanese Sushi bar. You have also arranged for "conversation partners" by pairing students with Japanese families you know. The families invite the students to their homes for informal conversation, and some of your students go on shopping and cultural field trips with their "adopted families." If the department carries out the evaluation, and you do not mention these concurrent activities, the results of the research will not be valid.

Practice 1.8

1. In the study of "monolingual" children who also speak Spanish, would your study be compromised if it were only a matter of two of the children who knew Spanish? Would it matter if these two really knew only a few words of Spanish and that they used these only on the playground? How might you solve this problem? _yes yes Omit those students. Operationalize b) better._

2. Studies frequently mention subject attrition. For example, *data were collected from 1,067 junior high Spanish-English bilingual children on a reading test, a spelling test, and a vocabulary test. Twelve students were absent for the reading test, 17 for the spelling test, and 91 for the vocabulary test.* The report includes a comparison of the students' performance on the three tests. Compare this study with that of the 10th grade minority students mentioned in the discussion of attrition (page 34). In which case would attrition be a potentially more damaging factor? Why? _Hard to tell w/ this info. (not enough info for w/ grades— ½ differ. Volunteers elect choice)_

3. Imagine that in the evaluation of the Japanese teaching materials you began the partners arrangement prior to any pretest evaluation. The gain scores from pretest to posttest are to be used in the evaluation. Is it still important that you inform the evaluators about the arrangement? Why (not)? _Yes._

_____ _Gains would be result of partners, not new_

_____ _material_

_____

_____

4. Select one research idea from your journal. What is the best way to select *S*s or texts for the study?

_____

_____

_____

Is it possible that the findings for the study could be compromised by the subject selection? _____

_____

_____

What history factors might influence the results? _____

_____

_____

How might maturation influence the results? _____

_____

_____

◇◇

Instrumentation   _Teach "validity" first, before read this!_

It is important that the test instrument or observations used in research are both valid and consistent. The type of evidence that you collect to support or reject your hypotheses will depend, in part, on the validity of your operational definitions of the key terms in your research. Those definitions must be valid or it will be difficult to persuade others of their appropriateness.

For example, if you operationally defined the abstract construct *acquisition* as accurate performance (80% level or higher on a written test) of students on 10 grammar points, and then presented the findings to teachers of these students, they might question your findings. First, they might argue that language acquisition is something more than performance on 10 grammar points. Second, their course syllabus may place heavy emphasis on oral language and, again, they

valid

might question findings based on a written test of acquisition. Third, they may remember the 20% error performance of their students and wonder if the criterion level in your operational definition reflects acquisition. Your narrow operational definition may not match their broader definition of *acquisition*.

Since there is always variability in performance (even for native speakers), you might argue that 80% is a good level for defining what is or is not acquired. How do you feel about students who reach the 79% level--do you believe they have not acquired the structure? Do the people who group in 0%-79% behave in similar ways as non-acquirers and the 80%-100% in another way as acquirers? How much confidence would you have in the validity of any claims made about acquirer/non-acquirer groups? These are questions the researcher must consider and justify to give validity to operational definitions.

valid

To be valid, a measure must truly represent what it purports to represent. Teachers and learners often question the use of highly integrative tests, such as the cloze test (where students supply every fourth or fifth word in a text) or an error detection test (where students identify parts of sentences that contain errors), as a measure of the construct *proficiency*. Imagine you are a language teacher who believes in teaching discrete grammar points or that you work with materials which are built around a grammar syllabus. If research defines *proficiency* in terms of more global tests, it is unlikely that you would accept them as adequate measures of proficiency. Conversely, if you are a language teacher who believes in communication activities, it is unlikely that you would accept a multiple-choice grammar test as an adequate measure of proficiency.

Since constructs are abstract (constructs such as *proficiency, motivation, self-esteem,* or *academic success*), particular care is needed in evaluating operational definitions. Often, we forget our objections to such definitions as we read the discussion and application sections of reports. For example, if *need achievement* is measured by persistence in a ring-toss game, and you think this is a poor measure of *need achievement*, you would not accept the operational definition and yet, in reading the results, you might accept the findings anyway because the operational definition of "need achievement equals ring-toss" is forgotten. As consumers of research (and as researchers), we need to keep the operational definition in mind as we evaluate the results of research reports.

Suppose that you wished to test the claim that there is a language of academic success which is abstract and "decontextualized," and that children who do not have this "decontextualized" form of language in their L1 or L2 are doomed to academic failure. While "decontextualized" language has never been defined, there are a number of features which could be attributed to it. If you chose one of these features (e.g., the use of indefinite articles for "new" information) and examined the language of young children for this feature, you could only discuss the findings in terms of that one feature, not in terms of contextualized or decontextualized language. The discussion should, then, talk about this feature, explain that it is one part of the puzzle and list, perhaps, other facets that might be measured on the contextualized/decontextualized continuum.

Construct validity, then, has to do with whether or not the pieces of data collected to represent a particular construct really succeed in capturing the construct. Because so many constructs (e.g., *acculturation, field dependence, motivation*) are extremely difficult to define, construct validation is a field of statistical research in itself. The problem such research attempts to solve is whether or not a set of items can be established that define a construct.

There are many factors other than construct validity that influence internal research validity. In particular, we should examine the method we use to gather the data. Our procedure for gathering the data can affect the validity of the research.

Task Directions

If instructions are to be given to the people who participate in research, these instructions must be carefully planned and piloted. This is especially true in the case of directions given to language learners. Sometimes, after carrying out research, we discuss findings only to discover Ss could have done the task accurately if they had understood exactly what was expected. If the instructions are not clear, the results are not valid.

Length of instruction is also important. A recent questionnaire distributed by a university began with two single-spaced pages of instructions. The questions required a code number response and the definitions of the codes were embedded in these instructions (not near the questions). If the results of this report (purporting to measure faculty interest in instruction) are to be valid we would need to believe that faculty have both time and motivation to read such directions. Further, we would need to believe that such directions can be easily kept in memory or that Ss will flip back to consult the code numbers as they work through the questionnaire. Neither assumption appears warranted.

These same instructions assured the respondents that the research was "anonymous," yet questions about years of service, sex, age, salary, department, and college were included. If anonymity were important to respondents, we could rightfully question the validity of the data.

Instructions, however, need not be aimed at the subject. There are also instructions for the person(s) collecting the data. As you collect observations in the classroom or administer a particular test, you may think of new ways to make the procedure clearer to your Ss. While the changes may make the task clearer and more pleasurable for all, the result is that the data may also change and no longer be internally valid. When this happens, the best thing to do is to consider the data collection to that point as a pilot study. You now have a better data collection procedure and you can start again, maintaining consistency in the collection procedure.

When you have a large project, it is often necessary to have assistants help in the data collection process. You must periodically check and retrain assistants to make sure the test instrument itself and the collection procedures remain constant.

Adequate Data Base

Another problem regarding validity of measures has to do with the number of times a particular item is observed or tested. For example, one research project tested the relation between age and comprehension of the distinction between *X is easy to V* and *X is eager to V*. The test for this distinction was as follows. The child was presented with a blindfolded doll and asked, "Is the doll easy to see?" A "yes" response was counted correct. If the child responded "no," the next direction was "show me the doll is easy to see." It is unlikely that this single item could provide a valid measure of the structure. Of course, other researchers noted this and worked out alternative data collection methods where many examples of the structure were tested.

If you have multiple items to measure one thing, those items should be carefully arranged. Assume you decided that you needed 30 items to test the *easy/eager to V* construction. As respondents react to the first two or three items, they set up expectations as to how they are to perform on the rest of the items. This is called forming a set response. *elaborate*

Consider some of the ways you might test the relation of age and pronunciation of a second language. You've been teaching Spanish to students in a home for the elderly. To lessen the pressure of the research, you ask them just to push a red button when the words (minimal pairs) sound different and to do nothing if they are the same. However, with anxiety heightened, some of the students have trouble inhibiting the motor response once it is set up. One way to get around the set response is to give several filler items in between the test items. Since other responses are required, the response pattern can be broken.

To be valid, the data-gathering procedure should allow us to tap the true abilities of learners. If the tasks we give Ss are too difficult, people give up before they really get started. Placing easy tasks first will give Ss the initial success they may need to complete the procedure. On the other hand, if beginning items are very simple, respondents may become bored. If they do not finish the task, the results again will not be valid. In questionnaire research, we suggest that demographic information (personal information regarding the respondents) be placed at the end of the questionnaire. People are not usually bored giving information about themselves. When these questions come first, Ss often answer them and then quit. You're more likely to get full participation if other data are collected first and personal information second. And, of course, Ss are more likely to return a questionnaire that is finished than one that is not.

To be sure that the order of items does not influence results, you might want to order items randomly in several ways to obtain different forms of the same task. Alternatively, you might reverse the order to obtain two forms and then test to see if order was important. *how?*

Test Effect

Another factor that may influence the validity of research is *test effect*. If the research begins with a pretest, that test can affect performance during the treatment and on future tests. The test alerts students as to what teachers expect them to learn. The pretest, then, can influence the final outcome. Note that the actual *form* of items decays very rapidly in memory while the *content* of items remains. (So, if your research is on grammatical form rather than content, the pretest may not have a strong influence on a subsequent posttest.)

Test effect is especially important if tests are given within a few hours or even days after the pretest. For this reason, many researchers try to create parallel test forms so that the pretest and posttest are parallel but half the group receives form A as the pretest and form B as the posttest and the other half receives form B as the pretest and form A as the posttest. You must be VERY sure that the test forms are equivalent (or know where the differences are between the forms) before you try this! Otherwise, you may wipe out any gains that might have been there.

◇◇

Practice 1.9

1. Select one abstract concept (e.g., *self-esteem, field independence, proficiency, communicative competence*). Give an operational definition used for the concept in a published research report. Do you believe the definition reflects the total concept? What parts are or are not covered? Can you suggest a better measure?

_____
_____
_____
_____

2. Designers of profiency tests are concerned with giving test directions to *S*s who may not be proficient in the language. It is important that the directions not be part of the test! Review the directions given on tests used in your program. How might they be improved? If the test was validated on the basis of previous test administrations, would a change in directions mean these figures need to be reconsidered?

_____
_____
_____
_____

We expect that test items will show a range of difficulty. For the tests you examined, is there an attempt to place easier items toward the front of the test? If not, on what grounds would you recommend a change (or no change)? _____

_____
_____

3. Imagine you wanted to compare ESL *Ss'* ability to use old/new information as a factor in deciding on relative acceptability of separated and nonseparated forms of two-word verbs (e.g., *call up your friend, call your friend up* vs. *call him up, call up him*) in written text. How many items with old/new information would you suggest for such a study? How might you design the study to avoid a set response? _____

_____

_____

_____

4. Look at the ways you have decided to collect data for your own research. Check to see if the measures seem to meet the requirements of adequate operational definitions, good task directions, adequate amount of data, and task arrangement. Discuss the problems you see with your study group partners and list your suggestions for improvement. _____

_____

_____

_____

5. In your study group, select one research question. Write out the task directions and a few sample items. Select two appropriate *Ss* (with attributes that match the intended *Ss* of the study) and pilot the directions. Compare your perceptions as to the appropriateness of the task directions following this pilot. List below the suggestions to improve directions.

_____

_____

_____

_____

_____

◇◇◇

There are many other threats to internal validity that could be discussed. As you will discover in carrying out your own projects, they can be never-ending. If you have begun with strong operational definitions of terms that are involved in your research, you will have formed a basis for dealing with many of these threats before they occur. Consistency in data collection and valid subject selection come with a carefully designed study.

External Validity

Just as there are factors which influence internal validity of a study, there are factors which influence external validity. First, if a study does not have *internal* validity, then it cannot have *external* validity. We cannot generalize from the data. For *internal* validity, we worry about how well the data answer the research questions from a *descriptive* standpoint for this specified data set. When we want to *generalize* from the data set, we are concerned not only with internal validity but external as well--how representative the data are for the group(s) to which we hope to generalize. We need to overcome the threats to external validity so that we *can* generalize, can make *inferential* claims.

Sample Selection

We often hope to be able to generalize the results of our studies to other circumstances. To do this we must start with a detailed description of the population to which we hope to generalize. This is the population from which we draw our random sample. For example, we may test a group of university-level ESL students and hope that we can interpret our results as applicable to other ESL students. However, if the group has been selected by "convenience sampling" (they happened to be the group that was available), no such generalization is possible. Sample selection is central to our ability (or inability) to generalize the results to the population we have specified. We cannot *generalize* anything from the results unless we have appropriate subject selection. If we have specified the population as ESL university students everywhere, then our sample Ss must be selected to represent ESL university students everywhere.

One way to attempt to obtain a representative sample is via *random selection*. In random selection every candidate (whether a S, a piece of text, or an object) has an equal and independent chance of being chosen. This can be done by assigning every candidate a number and then drawing numbers from a hat (or by using a table of random numbers which you can find at the end of many statistics books and in some computer software programs). The problems with this method are many. For example, it may be the case that there are more immigrant students in ESL classes than there are foreign students. There may be more men than women in such classes. There may be more Spanish than Farsi speakers in such classes. There may be more students from the sciences than from the humanities. These differences are important if the sample is to be truly representative of the group to which you hope to generalize results. The way to solve this, once you have determined which factors are important, is to create a *stratified random* sample. You decide ahead of time what portion of the sample should be male/female, immigrant/foreign, and so forth. All possible candidates are tagged for these characteristics and are then randomly selected by category.

Imagine that you wanted to look at the use of agentless vs. regular passives in written text. But what is a representative sample of written text? There are many types of genres and within each genre (e.g., narrative) there are many possible sources of written text (e.g., news accounts of happenings, science fiction stories, folktales, and so forth). One possibility for obtaining a representative sample of written text would be to use the Brown corpus and take a stratified random selection of words (the number to be based on the proportion of the total word count in each category) from randomly selected samples of each of the categories identified in the corpus (e.g., novels, social science, science, and so forth).

As you might imagine, subject selection with random stratified selection procedures can be an art that is especially crucial to large survey research projects (whether the survey is of people or of texts). If you would like to see how extensive this procedure is, you might want to consult your sociology department. Political science, psychology, health, and social welfare departments also commonly engage in large-scale survey research. Your research group might like to invite faculty engaged in such research to speak about methods they use in selecting subjects.

Consider the following situations. (1) You have a list of elementary schools in school districts in your state. You need thirty such schools to participate in your research. You begin to select schools randomly, contacting them to secure permission for the research. When you have 30, you stop. Have you obtained a random sample of schools? No, you have not. You have begun to develop a pool of volunteer schools from which the final random selection can be made. (2) You want to use community adult school students as the data source for your research. You want to avoid using established classes because you cannot get random selection. So, you advertise in the school paper for volunteer *S*s. The early volunteers (the first 30 who call) become your *S*s. Do you think you have selected a random sample? Again, you have not. You have begun a pool of volunteer *S*s from which a random selection might be drawn. Notice, however, that in both these examples, the sample is made up of volunteers. Volunteers may not (or may) be representative of the total population. *Likely not representative*

Hopefully, these paragraphs point out the difference between a random sample, random selection, and a representative sample. You can achieve a random sample if everyone or everything has an equal and independent chance of being selected. When, as in the case of people, *S*s must agree to be part of the sample, it is important first to get a large random sample of people who do agree and then make a random selection from that group for the final sample. It is also important to determine whether people who agree to participate are representative of the population to which you hope to generalize results.

Let's briefly compare the importance of subject-selection for both internal and external validity. Imagine that you collected data from ESL students in your program. The *S*s are from three different proficiency levels (beginning, intermediate, and advanced.) If you want to compare the data to see if there are differences among these three groups in your program, it is important that all the *S*s represent the level to which they are assigned. If the *S*s in the study are not representative of these three levels, then claims about differences in levels cannot be made with confidence. That is, there is a threat to *internal* validity. However, if this threat to internal validity has been met, the results are valid for these particular three groups of *S*s. Statistical procedures, in this case *descriptive* statistical procedures, can be used to test differences in levels.

Then, imagine that you want to say something about ESL (beginning, intermediate, and advanced) students in general. Not only do you want to compare the data of your *S*s across these three levels, but you want to generalize from these *S*s to others. However, it is unlikely that you will be able to generalize from three intact classes to all beginning, intermediate, and advanced students. The students and the levels in your particular program may not be representative of such students in programs elsewhere. There are a number of ways to address this problem of *external* validity. One is to use random selection of *S*s within the study.

Descriptive vs. inferential stats

There are times, however, when you doubt that straight random selection of *Ss* will give you a representative sample--representative of the group to which you hope to generalize. Perhaps the subject pool at your university consists primarily of Chinese *Ss* from the PRC (People's Republic of China) while you know that nationwide, the proportion of Chinese *Ss* would be much less. The purpose of selecting a stratified random sample is to assure that all *Ss* in the population are proportionally represented in the sample. Though researchers sometimes *do* make comparisons of proficiency levels, L1 membership, sex, or other factors taken into account to obtain the stratified sample, the intent of stratified random sampling is to obtain a sample that represents the population to which we hope to generalize. If threats to external validity are met, this will be possible. To accomplish this generalization, the researcher will use *inferential statistical procedures.*

Descriptive and inferential statistical procedures are presented in this manual. It is not important at this point that you know which are which but rather that you understand that statistics can be used to *describe* a body of data. It is important that the data have met all the threats to internal validity so that the description be accurate. In addition, statistical procedures can be used to *infer* or generalize from the data. To do this, a detailed description of the population to which you will generalize must be given, *Ss* must be randomly selected using that description, and threats to internal and external validity must be met. Otherwise, no generalizations can be made.

◇◇◇◇◇◇◇◇◇◇◇◇◇◇◇◇◇◇◇◇◇◇◇◇◇◇◇◇◇◇◇◇◇◇◇◇◇◇

Practice 1.10

1. Assume that you wanted to generalize the results of a study to ESL university students everywhere. List the characteristics the sample would need to include to be representative of this group. Compare your list with those of your study group partners. Determine which characteristics would be crucial and which not.

_____

2. Review the example of a text search for agentless vs. regular passive. Imagine that you decided to limit the search to advice-giving contexts (e.g., recipes, Dear Abby, "how-to" books on gardening, enrollment instructions in college catalogues) because you believe that procedural discourse will contain large numbers of passive constructions. How would you select a representative sample for the study? Compare the tags suggested by all the members of your study group and prepare instructions for the selection of samples. _____

_____

3. Assume you need 30 *S*s and there are two classes which have more than 30 students and these classes are taught by friends of yours so there would be no problem of gaining access to the classes. You worry about such convenience sampling, though, and decide to advertise in the paper. You get exactly 30 responses to the ad from people willing to participate for a small fee. As a study group assignment, decide which method of obtaining *S*s would be best. How might your selection affect your research outcome? Will you be able to generalize from the sample selected? Why (not)?_____

_____

_____

_____

◇◇◇◇◇◇◇◇◇◇◇◇◇◇◇◇◇◇◇◇◇◇◇◇◇◇◇◇◇◇◇◇◇◇◇◇◇◇

Although this chapter is titled "Defining the Research Question," we have given a great deal of space to the discussion of research validity. Imagine that you defined a research question and then discovered that your study *does* have a threat to validity. Of course, that is undesirable. But exactly what happens? What is it that is so awful? Consider the results of your threatened study: the data are untrustworthy. They contain "error." You cannot generalize from the results because the threats to validity caused the data to be, somehow and to some degree, wrong. You may have a maturation effect, and the posttest score you thought was due to learning was in fact due to simple maturation of the subjects (which is "error" as far as you are concerned--you are not studying maturation). There may be other factors that you did not consider, and thus your posttest is affected by more than you intended (again, "error" as far as you are concerned). You may discover that your *S*s were unique and that you cannot reliably generalize to other situations, and so your posttest is not accurate (i.e., it contains "error").

Now imagine that your study is excellent; you have controlled for all possible threats to its design validity. However, imagine that you suffer from threats to *measurement* validity. For example, you may have inadvertently used a grammar posttest when you were really intending to measure reading; this is a measurement validity problem (and, you guessed it, a source of "error"). Or, you may be giving a posttest on the effects of instruction but you neglected to check the test carefully against the syllabus of the instruction; this is a measurement validity problem also (and it, too, adds "error" to that posttest). You could have a posttest that is simply bad--the developers of the test paid little attention to test construction; this is a threat to measurement validity (and, yep, more "error").

In fact, any realized threat to validity creates some "error" in the data description and analysis of the data. A good way to visualize this relationship is to consider the following two diagrams:

LITTLE threat to validity in the study:

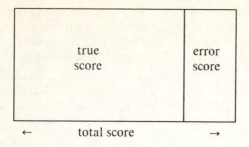

EXTENSIVE threat to validity in the study:

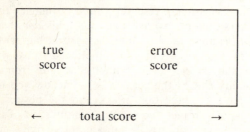

The concept is that any measurement you take ("total score") is composed of what you *want* to measure ("true score") and what you do *not* want to measure ("error score"). And, any threat to validity, be it to the design of the study or to the measurement instrument itself, *increases* error score.

Finally, have you ever wondered why test preparation courses are so popular? For example, in the United States, there are companies that do nothing but train people how to take law school exams, medical board tests, and so on. Those specialty schools do not teach the content of the exams; they do not teach the true score. Rather, they teach test-taking strategies and train for extensive familiarity with these major tests. In so doing, they reduce the examinees' error score. Now, if the examinees know the material already and if their true score would be high in the presence of little error, then you can see how these test-taking service companies make money: they help people reduce error score, display more of their true score (which is high since they know the material) and achieve a higher overall total score. What an elegant business concept!

Of course, if you go to a medical certificate training class and you do not already have medical training, no amount of "error score reduction training" is going to help you. And that is one of the first things such trainers will say, in the very first hour of the very first training class.

◇◇◇◇◇◇◇◇◇◇◇◇◇◇◇◇◇◇◇◇◇◇◇◇◇◇◇◇◇◇◇◇◇◇◇◇◇◇◇

Practice 1.11

w/ class proj. (later)

1. Think about one of your research questions. List two possible threats to the validity of the research project. Draw a "true/error" diagram to show how much you might improve your project by working out ways to eliminate these threats to validity or reliability.

a. _____

_____

b. _____

_____

Diagram:

2. If you have taught a course for students planning to take the TOEFL exam, how much time was spent on content? How much on types of exam questions? How much on general test-taking tips? For whom was the course most or least effective? Why?

_____
_____
_____
_____

◇◇◇◇◇◇◇◇◇◇◇◇◇◇◇◇◇◇◇◇◇◇◇◇◇◇◇◇◇◇◇◇◇◇◇◇◇

In this chapter, we have begun to think about the research process as a systematic search for answers to questions. We have begun to offer you some of the ways researchers have solved problems that confront every researcher--how to define the scope of research, ways to make research more efficient or feasible, and considerations of internal and external validity that make or break our research efforts. In the next chapter, we will consider a systematic approach to identifying and describing variables.

Activities

1. Below are brief summaries of five studies. On the basis of the summaries, write null hypotheses for each of the first 3

D. L. Shaul, R. Albert, C. Golston, & R. Satory (1987. The Hopi Coyote story as narrative: the problem of evaluation. *Journal of Pragmatics, 11,* 1, 3-25.)

tested the notion that, since stories have the same job to do the world over, narratives may be structured in the same way across languages. The authors show that the Hopi Coyote stories do not contain an evaluation section (a section which specifically points out why the story is told and thus validates the telling). The moral of the story is also usually unstated. The authors give examples and postulate reasons for this difference in narrative structure.

There's no rel. between narrative structure & L1.

yes

J. Becker & P. Smenner (1986. The spontaneous use of *thank you* by preschoolers as a function of sex, socioeconomic status, and listener status. *Language in Society, 15,* 537-546.) observed 250 3:6 to 4:6 year old children as they played a game with their teachers and then received a reward from either an unfamiliar peer or adult. Girls offered thanks more often than boys, and children from lower-income families thanked more often than those from middle-income families. Adults were thanked more frequently than peers.

no rel. between sex, ses, status & freq. of usage of thank you.

H. Warren (1986. Slips of the tongue in very young children. *Journal of Psycholinguistic Research, 15,* 4, 309-344.) Slips of the tongue (e.g., "with this wing I thee red") have long intrigued researchers. This study analyzed data of children in the 23 to 42 month age range. The number of slips made by the children was compared with the frequency of slips in the speech of adults (mother, teacher) with whom they interacted. Children made very few slips of the tongue. *No rel. btwn # slips tongue & age.*

no

M. Crawford & R. Chaffin (1987. Effects of gender and topic on speech style. *Journal of Psycholinguistic Research, 16,* 1, 83-89.) Men and women were asked to describe pictures that had previously been shown to interest men or women, or to be of neutral interest to both. The picture descriptions were coded for recognized features of "women's language" (WL). There was no difference between male and female *Ss'* use of these features in the descriptions. While male-interest pictures elicited more language than the other pictures, there were no differences otherwise. The authors speculate that the features of WL may actually be related to communication anxiety for both genders.

no

A. Pauwels (1986. Diglossia, immigrant dialects, and language maintenance in Australia: the case of Limburg and Swabian. *Journal of Multilingual and Multicultural Development, 7,* 1, 513-530.) studied language maintenance of German and Dutch immigrants to Australia. Some *Ss* spoke standard Dutch and German and others also spoke dialects (Swabian for German and Limburg for Dutch). There was no substantial difference in language maintenance of these groups although Limburg dialect speakers maintained only their dialect and not the standard variety. Second, language use patterns were examined to see how migration changed use of the first language.

2. Select ~~three~~ *one* of these studies. From the descriptions given here, identify the key terms which would require an operational definition to allow others to replicate the study. Write an operational definition for each key term.

3. Having completed 1 and 2 above, read one of the three articles you selected. Compare your hypotheses and operational definitions with those given in the article. Do you believe the author(s) did a good job in stating the research

questions and hypotheses and in offering operational definitions? Do you believe you have written clearer (or more adequate) hypotheses and definitions?

4. Authors usually present the broad research question in the introduction section of reports. The actual study may be much narrower in scope than the original general question. Select one of the above articles (or, even better, one related to your own research interests) and list, first, the broad research topic and, second, the actual question asked (or reported on) in the article. How completely does the actual report answer the broad research question? Does the author suggest other research that could be carried out to answer the broad research question more fully? If so, what suggestions were made? If not, what suggestions do you have?

5. In the study you selected to answer item 4, what threats do you see to internal and external validity? Was subject selection an important issue in the research? Could maturation have accounted for any of the findings? What history factors do you think might have been involved? Does the author generalize from the study? If so, how were the Ss selected? Are they truly representative of the group to which the author generalizes? If the setting for the study was tightly controlled (as in a laboratory), do you feel comfortable about generalizing to situations outside this setting?

6. For those studies you actually read, note the general layout of the reports. How similar/different are they? What evidence is presented in each case? What types of visuals (charts, graphs, pictures) are used to present the evidence? How effective do you think the report is in stating the question, in explaining how systematically the search for answers was carried out, and in presenting the evidence for answers?

References

Ben-Zeev, S. 1976. The influence of bilingualism on cognitive development and cognitive strategy. SCLR (Stanford Child Language Research) paper, Stanford University.

Buros, O. K. (Ed.). 1975. *Intelligence Tests and Reviews: A Monograph Consisting of the Intelligence Sections of the Seven Mental Measurement Yearbooks (1938-1972) and Test in Print II.* Lincoln, NB: The University of Nebraska Press.

Campbell, D. T. & Stanley, J. C. 1963. *Experimental and Quasi-experimental Designs for Research.* Washington, DC: AERA (American Education Research Association).

Center for Bilingual Education, Northwest Regional Laboratory, 1978. *Assessment Instruments in Bilingual Education: A Descriptive Catalog of 342 Oral and Written Tests.* Los Angeles, CA: California State University.

Chafe, W. (Ed.). 1980. *The Pear Stories.* Norwood, NJ: Ablex Publishing Company.

Donaldson, M. 1978. *Children's Minds.* New York, NY: Norton.

Francis, W. N. & Kucera, H. 1979 (revised and amplified). *Standard Sample of Present-Day American English* (the Brown corpus). Providence, RI: Brown University.

Labov, W. 1972. *Language in the Inner City.* Philadelphia, PA: University of Pennsylvania Press.

Svartik, J. and Quirk, R. (Eds.). 1980. *A Corpus of English Conversation* (the Lund corpus). Lund, Sweden: C.W.K. Gleerup.

Chapter 2
Describing Variables

- *Research variables*
  - *Variable vs. level*
- *Measurement of variables*
  - *Nominal scale variables*
  - *Interval scale variables*
  - *Frequency data vs. score data*
- *Function of variables*
  - *Dependent and independent variables*
  - *Moderator and control variables*
  - *Other intervening independent variables*

Research Variables

In chapter 1, we mentioned that we can expect variability in anything we observe. An ESL student's language skill may vary from week to week. You may be able to account for this variation in individual performance by considering amount of instruction. Skill does not remain constant. The ability of a group of American students learning Cantonese to recognize and reproduce the tone system may vary. You may be able to account for this variability by determining whether the students have learned other tone languages, whether they are young or old, male or female, or, perhaps, suffering from hearing loss. Different pieces of text may vary in frequency of "hedges." Academic science texts may include many more lexical hedges ("it appears," "it seems") to certainty of claims than other types of text materials. Variability and explanations of that variability are central to research.

A *variable* can be defined as an attribute of a person, a piece of text, or an object which "varies" from person to person, text to text, object to object, or from time to time.

One characteristic on which human performance varies is the ability to speak a variety of languages. Some people are monolingual, others are bilingual, and others multilingual. If we wanted to investigate multilingualism, we could code the number of languages spoken by each S. The number would vary from person to person. Notice here that the variable *multilingualism* is defined in terms of the number of languages spoken. Performance behavior in each of these languages also varies. If our research question asked about performance levels, then, with an operational definition of *performance*, we could investigate a variable, *L2 performance*, because this is a variable on which people vary.

Variables can be very broad or very narrow. For example, the discourse, semantic, syntactic, phonological elements of language are attributes of language. They are also something attributed to people in varying degrees of proficiency. A variable such as *phonological system* is broad, indeed, when assigned to *S*s. The variable *rising tone* is less so. The broader the variable, the more difficult it may be to define, locate, and measure accurately.

Variables can be assigned to groups of people as well as individuals. For example, the variable *bilingual* can be assigned to a society as well as to an individual. The variable is defined by its place in the research project.

In a study of written text, *text type* might be a variable. Pieces of text vary not only by type but in many other special characteristics. For example, different texts may vary in length, so *length* could also be a variable that one might examine in text analysis. Which characteristics are relevant will depend on the research questions.

Objects may be important in applied linguistic research and, of course, they too can vary in such attributes as color, size, shape, and weight. For example, in a test of reading, letter size or font style might be varied so that *size* or *font* would become variables. Color might be used in illustrations which are used to teach vocabulary. *Color* (vs. black and white) would be a variable on which the objects (illustrations) varied.

Practice 2.1

1. Imagine you wished to relate language proficiency and personal traits of learners. List two personal traits that vary across learners that might be included in the study. _____

How wide a range of variability is there within each of these variables? _____

_____

2. Assume you wished to relate language proficiency to traits of particular societies. List two variables attributed to societies that could be used in the research.

How wide a range of variability is there for these two variables? _____

_____

3. Imagine you wished to relate the use of *personal pronouns* (e.g., *we, you, I, they*) to text characteristics. List two variables of texts which might be investigated in the research. _____

_____

How wide a range is possible for each of these variables? _____

_____

4. Suppose that you were interested in descriptive compositions. You asked
students to write descriptions of various objects. List two variables attributed to
objects that could become part of the study of descriptive writing. _____

How wide is the range of variation on these two variables?

_____

5. Select one of your own research questions. List the variables for the research
question and the range of variability you might find for each.

_____
_____
_____
_____
_____

◇◇◇

Variable vs. Level

In a research project, we may wish to look at levels within a variable. For example, we might want to know how well ESL foreign students are able to do
some task. The variable is *ESL student*. That variable may be divided into *levels*
for the purposes of the study. If the study were designed to compare the performance of ESL students who are foreign students with those who are immigrant
students, the variable would have two levels. If the study concerned geographic
area, a student might be subclassified as South American, European, Middle
Eastern, or Asian so that comparisons among these levels of *ESL student* could
be made. The variable would consist of four levels. Or, for the purposes of the
study, we might want to divide the variable *ESL student* into proficiency levels
such as advanced, intermediate, and beginner. The variable would then have
three levels.

In our definition of variables, we can limit the range of levels or expand them.
For example, in object shape, we can say that a shape either is or is not a triangle.
The range is *yes/no* (+ or − triangle), two levels. We can enlarge the scope to
include various shapes of triangles, in which case *triangularity* is no longer *yes/no*
but *no* and all the individual triangle forms, several levels. Again, we can narrow
the variable to *right triangle* and the range, once more, is *yes/no*.

If we included *bilingual* as a variable in a research project, we might say that
people either are or are not bilingual (*yes/no* levels). The matter of proficiency in
each language would not be an issue in such a study. The research question,
however, might subclassify the bilingual *S*s on their proficiency in the second
language using school labels such as FEP (fluent English proficiency), LEP (limited English proficiency), and NEP (no English proficiency), three levels of the
variable *bilingual*. The selection of levels, as with the identification of variables,
depends on the research question.

◇◇◇

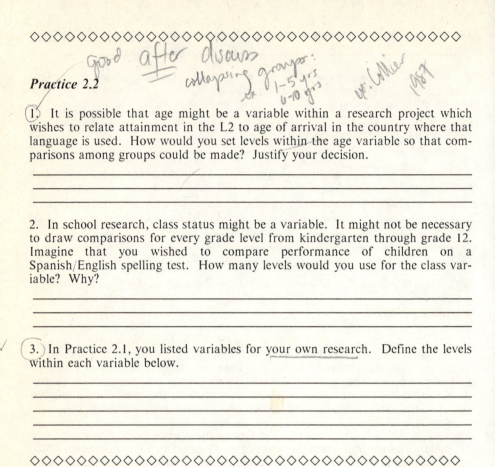

Practice 2.2

1. It is possible that age might be a variable within a research project which wishes to relate attainment in the L2 to age of arrival in the country where that language is used. How would you set levels within the age variable so that comparisons among groups could be made? Justify your decision.

_____

_____

_____

2. In school research, class status might be a variable. It might not be necessary to draw comparisons for every grade level from kindergarten through grade 12. Imagine that you wished to compare performance of children on a Spanish/English spelling test. How many levels would you use for the class variable? Why?

_____

_____

_____

3. In Practice 2.1, you listed variables for your own research. Define the levels within each variable below.

_____

_____

_____

_____

_____

◇◇

As mentioned in chapter 1, definitions of variables are very important in planning research. In addition to identifying levels of a variable that are to be contrasted, the operational definition needs to include the way the variable is measured and the function of the variable in the research project. The function and the measurement of variables are important because they determine exactly what kinds of statistical tests will be appropriate in analyzing the data.

Measurement of Variables

As we have just seen, the range along which an attribute varies can be small (e.g., a person either does or does not speak Arabic--*yes/no*) or very wide (e.g., the word length of pieces of text could vary from one to infinity). When variables are of the all-or-nothing, yes/no sort, we cannot measure *how much* of the variable to attribute to the person, text, or object. We can only say that it is or is not present. Variables will be quantified in different ways depending on whether we want to know *how often* an attribute is present or *how much* of the variable to attribute to the person, text, or object.

Nominal Scale Variables

A *nominal* variable, as the name implies, names an attribute or category and classifies the data according to presence or absence of the attribute. While you can use a yes/no notation in recording this information, it is customary (but not required) to assign an arbitrary number to each possibility instead. So, if the variable is *native speaker of French*, a 1 might represent *yes* and a 2, *no*. *The classification numbers have no arithmetic value;* they cannot be added or multiplied. If we tally all the 1s, we will have a frequency count of how many French speakers there are in the sample. If we tally all the 2s, we will have a frequency count of the number of non-French speakers there are in the sample. (We are not adding 1s or 2s but tallying the number of persons in each group.)

Nominal variables do not have to be dichotomies of *yes* or *no*. For example, the nominal variable *native language* in a study of English native speakers vs. non-native speakers might be 1 = NS and 2 = NNS, but it also could be 1 = English, 2 = Spanish, 3 = Cantonese, 4 = Mandarin, 5 = Arabic, 6 = Italian, and so forth. *Again, the numbers are codes to represent levels of the nominal variable and have no arithmetic value*.

It's easy to see that an attribute could be a yes/no variable in one research project and a level of the variable in another. For example, if the study includes student status as a research variable, this could be entered as 1 = yes (student), 2 = no. In another study, student status might be entered as 1 = elementary school, 2 = secondary school, 3 = undergraduate, 4 = graduate.

The numbers assigned to represent levels of a nominal variable have no arithmetic value. An average language of 3.5 (based on 1 = English, 2 = Spanish, 3 = Cantonese, 4 = Mandarin, 5 = Arabic, and 6 = Italian) makes no more sense than an average status of students of 2.25 (based on 1 = elementary, 2 = preparatory, and 3 = secondary). When we begin to tally the number of people who speak French and the number who do not, or the number of Canadian, Mexican, or European *S*s in a sample, these frequencies *do* have arithmetic value.

Frequency tallies are very useful in certain cases (e.g., when we want to know how many people participated in some study, how many were males or females, how many fell into the age categories of 19 and below, 20-29, 30-39, 40 and above, how many people enroll or do not enroll their children in bilingual education programs). In other cases, especially when we want to compare groups, open-ended tallies are a problem. For example, assume that you coded every clause in sample pieces of text so that all clauses are coded as 0 or 1 (yes/no) for relative clause, nominal clause, comparison clause, purpose clause, and so forth. The computer would tally these data so that you would know how many of each clause type appeared in the data. Imagine that you wanted to know whether samples drawn from different genres showed different numbers of certain types of clauses. However, the samples differ in the total number of clauses so a direct, meaningful comparison cannot be made. You might change the data into proportions so that you would show what percent of the total number of clauses in each genre were purpose clauses and so forth. In this case you have converted simple open-ended tallies of nominal variables into closed-group percentages. Comparisons can then be drawn across samples from different genres.

◇◇◇

Practice 2.3

1. A research project has been proposed to evaluate the English compositions of *S*s who have taken a composition course linked to a content course with those who took English composition separate from their content courses. What is the subject variable in this project? How many levels of the variable are there? Why is this classified as a nominal variable? _____

Type of courses student in	a) linked content/comp	presence/absence
	b) not linked	linkage

2. The foreign student office on campus wants to consider the distribution of majors in the foreign student enrollment. How many levels of the variable *major* would you suggest for such a project? How does the variable qualify as a nominal variable?_____
_____
_____

3. As a research project, you hope to show that student writing changes in quality depending on what type of writing task students are given. If you obtain writing samples from students on four different tasks, how many levels of task are there? Does *task* qualify as a nominal variable? _yo_____
_____
_____

4. Look at the variables you have defined for your own research. Which qualify as nominal variables?
_____
_____
_____

◇◇◇

Ordinal Scale Variables

Sometimes we have identified variables but have no easy way of developing a measurement to show *how much* of the variable to attribute to a person, text, or object. For example, if the variable is *happy* and this is not to be treated as a nominal variable in the study, we need some way of measuring degree of happiness. There is (to our knowledge) no reliable method of measuring precisely how much happiness one possesses at any moment. (Do those machines in fast-food restaurant lobbies measure happiness--you know, the ones where you insert your thumb and the little arrow moves over into the red zone?) However, we can say that a person is *very unhappy--unhappy--happy--very happy*. These can be assigned numbers from 1 to 4. In this case, the numbers *do* have arithmetic value. Someone with a 4 is happier than someone with a 1. The 4, however, does not say how much happiness to attribute to a person. Instead, it places the *S*s in a rank *order* with respect to each other. Persons rated 4 are ordered higher than those with a 3, and those with a 3 higher than those with a 2, and so forth. Ordinal measurement, then, describes a rank order measurement. The rank order can be of two sorts. First, one could take all *S*s and rank order them in relation to each other so that with 100 *S*s the rank order would be from 1 to 100. Another possibility is to rank order *S*s on a scale. Each *S* is placed on the scale and then all *S*s who rate 5 are higher than the group rated 4, and so forth. Each *S* can be ordered in relation to others, then, in two ways--first, an absolute rank; and, second, a ranking of persons who score at a similar point on a scale. In the first, each individual is ranked and in the second, groups are rank ordered.

While degree of happiness is seldom measured in applied linguistics studies, we do sometimes want to know students' attitudes towards particular lessons or sets of materials. In our happiness variable, we only gave four points to the scale. Most researchers who use scales prefer to use a 5-point, 7-point or 9-point scale. The wider range encourages respondents to show greater discrimination in their judgments (so responses don't cluster right above the middle point on the scale). You might like to use a Likert-type scale (after the researcher who first proposed such scales) to tap student attitudes. To do this you would set up a set of statements such as:

> *The lessons were boring*   1 2 3 4 5 6 7

and ask students to mark the strength of their agreement with each statement (7 being *strongly agree*, and 1 being *strongly disagree*).

While it is true that the scales in ordinal measurement have arithmetic value, the value is not precise. Rather, ordinal measurement orders responses in relation to each other to show strength or rank. That is, a person ranked 4 is not precisely twice as happy as one ranked 2. Nor is the increment from 1 to 2 necessarily equal to that from 2 to 3 or from 3 to 4. The points on the scales, and the numbers used to represent those points, are *not* equal intervals. This points out another reason researchers prefer to use a 5-point, 7-point, or 9-point scale. The hope is that wider scales encourage more precision in rating and thus approach equal intervals. For example, a *S* faced with a Likert 9-point scale is more likely to think of it as an equal interval statement of rating than a 4-point scale labeled *disagree, neutral, agree, strongly agree*.

Practice 2.4

1. Your research might require that you ask teachers to give judgments of overall student performance. What label would you assign this variable? How would you label the points on the scale?

_____

_____

_____

_____

2. In the absence of any precise measure, you might need to estimate the degree of acculturation of students. What labels would you use to define the points on the scale? _____

_____

_____

3. Examine the variables you have listed for your own research. How many of the variables could be measured using an ordinal scale? How would you label the points on the scale?

_____

_____

_____

Interval Scale Variables

Like ordinal scale measurement, interval scale data tell us *how much* of the variable to attribute to a person, text, or object. The difference is that the measurement is much more precise. The intervals of measurement can be described. Each interval unit has the same value so that units can be added or subtracted.

To demonstrate the difference between ordinal and interval scales, let's consider the measurement of pauses in conversations. It is extremely tedious to time every pause in conversation, so many researchers annotate pause length with +, + +, and + + +. These might be coded on an ordinal scale as 1, 2, and 3. However, if each pause is timed in seconds, then the seconds can be added to find total pause length. With such absolute interval scaling, you can give the average pause length in seconds while an ordinal "average" of 2.5 (ordinal + +.5) makes less sense.

In equal-interval measurement, we expect that each interval means an equal increment. This is true for absolute interval measurement, such as seconds, days, and so forth. For example, in measuring age, each year adds 365 days. However, in reality, you know that time does not equal aging, so that the difference of one year may actually be a very large interval and the difference of another year quite minor. In the same way, test scores are considered to be equal-interval yet (unless test items are appropriately weighted) this may not be the case. The difference in intervals between 1 and 10 in a test of 100 items might not be the same as the *(why?)* intervals between 90 and 100. In planning research, we need to think about just how equal the intervals of the measurement are.

By now it should be clear that the way you measure variables will depend in part on the variable itself and its role in the research, and in part on the options available for precision of measurement. In the operational definition of a variable, then, it is important that the researcher plan precisely how the variable is to be measured. There are often very good reasons for opting for one type of measurement over another. It is not always the case that more precise interval measurement is a better way of coding a variable. The measurement should be appropriate for the research question. For example, if we want to classify bilingualism according to the languages spoken, then nominal measurement is appropriate.

There are times when you may not feel confident that the interval data you have collected is truly equal-interval. Say that you had administered a test and then later felt little confidence in the test. You might, however, feel enough confidence that you would be able to rank students who took the test on the basis of the results. If you aren't sure that a person who scores a 90 on a test is 8 points "better" than a person who scores an 82, you might still be willing to rank the first student as higher than the second. Transforming the data from interval to rank order *give* measurement, however, means that some information about differences is lost. *ex.* You no longer know how many points separate a person ranked 30th from a person ranked 31st or 35th.

Whenever we convert data from one type of measurement to another, we should *☆* carefully consider the grounds for the decision. We will discuss these issues in much more detail later. For now, you might think about such decisions in relation to a balance between confidence in the accuracy of measurement vs. the potential for information loss or distortion in the conversion.

◇◇◇◇◇◇◇◇◇◇◇◇◇◇◇◇◇◇◇◇◇◇◇◇◇◇◇◇◇◇◇◇◇◇◇◇◇◇

Practice 2.5

1. Look at variables you have identified for your own research. Which of these are interval scale variables? How are they measured?_____

_____

_____

_____

▶ 2. In many studies in the field of applied linguistics *bilingualism* is a variable. Part of the operational definition of that variable will include the values that code the variable. *Bilingualism* may be coded as 1 = yes, 2 = no, or as 1 = French/English, 2 = German/French, 3 = French/Arabic, 4 = Cantonese/Mandarin, 5 = Spanish/Portuguese. In this case the variable has

the latter case?

been scaled as a(n) _____nominal_____ variable. Each number represents a _____level_____ (level/variable). *Bilingualism* might be coded as 1 = very limited, 2 = limited, 3 = good, 4 = fluent, 5 = very fluent. In this case, the variable has been measured as a(n) _____ordinal scale_____ variable. *Bilingualism* could be coded on the basis of a test instrument from 1 to 100. The variable has then been measured as a(n) _____interval scale_____ variable.

3. Assume that you gave a test and later decided that for the purposes of your research you would recode the data so that *S*s who scored 90 + are in one group, those who scored 80-89 in a second group, those who scored 70-79 in a third group, and those below 70 in a fourth group. What information would be lost in this transformation?

_____rank order w/i groups, intervals w/i groups_____

◇◇

Frequency Data vs. Score Data

Another way to think about difference in measurement is to consider whether the study measures *how much* on an interval or ordinal scale or whether it measures *how often* something occurs--the frequency of nominal measurement. For most novice researchers, it is easy to identify a nominal, ordinal, or interval measurement, but somehow the distinction becomes blurred in moving to studies where nominal measurement is now discussed in terms of frequency, and ordinal and interval measurement are grouped together as showing *how much* of a variable to attribute to a *S*. This distinction is important because it will determine the appropriate statistical analysis to use with the data.

Consider the following examples drawn from unpublished research projects of ESL teachers.

Lennon (1986) wanted to develop some ESL materials to help university students learn how to express uncertainty in seminar discussions. However, he could find no descriptions that said how native speakers carry out this specific speech function. In his research project, then, he tape-recorded seminars and abstracted all the uncertainty expressions uttered by teachers and students. He categorized these expressions into five major types plus one "other" category. First, the subject variable is *status* with two levels. The variable type is nominal. If he assigned numbers to the levels of a variable, these numbers would have no arithmetic value. Assume that a 1 was arbitrarily assigned to one level and a 2 to the other. If he added all the 1s for this variable, he would obtain the *frequency* for the number of students in the study. If he added the 2s, this would be the frequency for the number of teachers in the study.

The second variable in the research is *uncertainty expressions*. It, too, is a nominal variable. If Lennon found six hedge types in the data, he could assign numbers to identify each of the six hedge types. The numbers would represent the six levels. The total number of instances of each would be tallied from the data.

Practice 2.6

▶ 1. To be certain that the distinction between frequency counts and interval/ordinal scores is clear, work through each of the following examples. Compare your responses with those of your study group partners.

a. Brusasco (1984) wanted to compare how much information translators could give under two different conditions: when they could stop the tape they were translating by using the pause button and when they could not. There were a set number of information units in the taped text. What are the variables? If the number of information units are totaled under each condition, are these frequencies or scores (e.g., how often or how much)?

Group consensus: _Tape — stop or not (nominal)_
Info units — 0 — ? interval
freq.

b. Li (1986) wondered whether technical vocabulary proved to be a source of difficulty for Chinese students reading science texts in English. He asked 60 Chinese students to read a text on cybernetics and underline any word they weren't sure of. Each underlined word was then categorized as ±technical. Each S, then, had a percent of total problem words which were technical in nature. Among the 60 students, 20 were in engineering, 20 physics, and 20 geology. What are the variables? Are the data frequencies or interval/ordinal scores? If Li had compared the number (rather than the percentage) of ± technical words, would your answers change?

Need a control group to answer this Q
Variables: prob wrd: ± technical
Student major: eng, physics, geo.   # vs %

c. The Second Language Research Forum is a conference traditionally run by graduate students of applied linguistics. Papers for the conference are selected by the graduate students. The chair of the conference wondered if M.A. and Ph.D. students rated abstracts for the conference in the same way. Papers were rated on five different criteria using a 5-point scale (with 5 being high). Each paper, then, had the possibility of 0 to 25 points. What are the variables? Are the data frequencies or interval/ordinal scores?

criteria — 5 levels
Observations—papers, unknown #/   Variable — student status; M.A./Ph.D.
MA & PhD would have to rate each paper twice — by each group, to
be able to compare
Broken down or not?

d. Since her ESL advanced composition students seemed to use few types of cohesive ties, Wong (1986) wondered if they could recognize appropriate ties (other than those they already used). She constructed a passage with multiple-choice slots (a multiple-choice cloze test) for cohesive ties. The ties fell into four basic

Chapter 2. Describing Variables   61

types (conjunctive, lexical, substitution, ellipsis). Her students were from seven major L1 groups. What are the variables? Do the measures yield frequencies or scores? *Interval*

Tua - 4 levels / L1 - 7 levels

e. Hawkins (1986) taped the interactions of paired American and foreign students as they solved problems. She wanted to know how often Americans and foreign students showed they did not understand each other. What are the variables? Will they yield frequency or score data?

Variables: status Am/not
Indicate confusion ± FREQUENCY - how often

f. Since some of the problems were easier than others, Hawkins wanted to know if the number of communication breakdowns related to task difficulty. She classified five of the problems as easy and five as difficult. What are the variables? Do the measures yield frequency or score data?

Task diff: 1 easy 2 hard ordinal
#breakdowns: easy hard freq

◇◇◇◇◇◇◇◇◇◇◇◇◇◇◇◇◇◇◇◇◇◇◇◇◇◇◇◇◇◇◇◇◇◇◇

The difference between nominal variables that yield frequency data and ordinal and interval variables that yield score data is sometimes identified as *noncontinuous* vs. *continuous* measurement (or discrete vs. continuous measurement). *Continuous* data are data scored along either an ordinal or interval scale. *Noncontinuous* data are not scored but rather tallied to give frequencies. Nominal data, thus, may be referred to as noncontinuous. *Discrete* and *categorical* are other synonyms for *nominal* that you may encounter in research reports. To summarize:

> *Frequency data show **how often** a variable is present in the data. The data are **noncontinuous** and describe **nominal** (discrete, categorical) variables.*

> *Score data show **how much** of a variable is present in the data. The data are **continuous** but the intervals of the scale may be either **ordinal** or **interval** measurements of **how much**.*

◇◇◇◇◇◇◇◇◇◇◇◇◇◇◇◇◇◇◇◇◇◇◇◇◇◇◇◇◇◇◇◇◇◇◇

Practice 2.7

1. In your study group, discuss how each of the above teacher research projects is (or is not) "interesting" in terms of the research agenda of applied linguistics.

Can the results be applied to theory construction or theory validation? Can they be applied to practice (e.g., curriculum design, classroom methodology, materials development)? Can they be applied to both?

_____
_____
_____
_____
_____
_____

2. Select one of the questions you have defined for your own research. List the variables below. Identify variable type (nominal, ordinal, interval) and state how the data will be measured.

_____
_____
_____
_____
_____

◇◇◇

Functions of Variables

To understand how the variables in a study relate to one another, we need to be able to identify their functions. These functions grow out of the research question. That is, the functions depend on the connection we believe exists between the variables we have chosen to study. Sometimes we expect that two variables are connected or *related* to one another although we do not view one variable as *affecting* or causing a change in the other. (Correlation is an example of a statistical procedure that tests *relationships*.) In other cases, we describe one major variable and then observe how other variables *affect* it. (Analysis of variance is an example of a procedure that tests *effect*.) It is especially important to understand the function of variables in order to select the most appropriate way to analyze the data. A conventional way of classifying the function of variables is to label them as dependent or independent (and subtypes of independent variables such as moderating or control variables).

Dependent Variable

The dependent variable is the major variable that will be measured in the research. For example, if you wanted to study the construct *communicative competence* of a group of students, then the dependent variable is the construct and it might be operationalized as your students' scores or ratings on some measure of communicative competence. The measurement would be part of the operational definition of communicative competence for your study. This variable (*communicative competence*) is the dependent variable. We expect performance on the dependent variable will be influenced by other variables. That is, it is "dependent" in relation to other variables in the study. Let's consider two more examples.

Assume you wanted to know how well ESL students managed to give and accept compliments, one small part of communicative competence. Their videotaped performances during role-play were rated on a 10-point scale (10 being high) for giving compliments and a 10-point scale for receiving compliments and bridging to the new topic. The student's total score could range from 0 to 20. The rating, again, might be influenced by other variables in the research. The rating measures the dependent variable *compliment performance.* w/ 2 level - give
receive

In a text analysis, you hypothesized that use of English modals may be influenced by types of rhetorical organization found in texts. Each place a modal occurred in the text it was coded. Tallies were made of overall frequency of modals and also of each individual modal (e.g., *can, may, might, should*). The dependent variable would be *modal* and the levels within it might be the actual modal forms or, perhaps, the functions of modals (e.g., obligation, advisability, and so forth). The frequency of the dependent variable, *modal*, might be influenced by other variables included in the research

Independent Variable

An independent variable is a variable that the researcher suspects may relate to or influence the dependent variable. In a sense, the dependent variable "depends" on the independent variable. For example, if you wanted to know something about the communicative competence of your students, the dependent variable is the score for communicative competence. You might believe that male students and female students differ on this variable. You could, then, assign *sex* as the independent variable which affects the dependent variable in this study.

In the study of compliment offers/receipts, L1 membership might influence performance. *L1*, then, would be the independent variable which we believe will influence performance on the dependent variable in this research. There might be any number of levels in the independent variable, *L1*.

In text analysis, rhetorical structure may influence the use of modal auxiliaries. *Rhetorical structure* (which might have such levels as narrative, description, argumentation) would be the independent variable that affects the frequency of the dependent variable.

Practice 2.8

1. In the study of communicative competence, what attributes of Ss (other than sex) might serve as independent variables? Why would these be important to the study?

Degree of extraversion; degree of exposure to natural lng. for ex.
May affect comm. comp.

2. In the study of compliment offers/receipts, what other independent variables do you think might influence variations of performance on the dependent variable?

3. In text analysis, different genres of text might influence the frequency of use of modal auxiliaries. What different genres would you include as levels of this independent variable?

4. For your own research questions, list the variables and give the function (dependent, independent) for each.

◇◇

Moderator Variable

Sometimes researchers distinguish between major independent variables and moderating independent variables. For example, in the study of compliments, you might believe that sex is *the* most important variable to look at in explaining differences in student performance. However, you might decide that length of residence might moderate the effect of sex on compliment offers/receipts. That is, you might believe that women will be more successful than men in offering and receiving compliments in English. However, you might decide that, given more exposure to American culture, men would be as successful as women in the task. In this case, *length of residence* is an independent variable that functions as a moderator variable.

While some researchers make a distinction between independent and moderator variables, others call them both independent variables since they influence variability in the dependent variable. However, specifying variables as "independent" and "moderator" helps us study how moderating variables mediate or moderate the relationship between the independent and dependent variables.

Control Variable

A control variable is a variable that is not of central concern in a particular research project but which might affect the outcome. It is controlled by neutralizing its potential effect on the dependent variable. For example, it has been suggested that handedness can affect the ways that Ss respond in many tasks. In order not to worry about this variable, you could institute a control by including only right-handed Ss in your study. If you were doing an experiment involving Spanish, you might decide to control for language similarity and not include any speakers of non-Romance languages in your study. Whenever you control a variable in this way, you must remember that you are also limiting the generalizability of your study. For example, if you control for handedness, the results cannot be generalized to everyone. If you control for language similarity, you cannot generalize results to speakers of all languages.

If you think about this for a moment, you will see why different researchers obtain different answers to their questions depending on the control variables in the study. Comby (1987) gives a nice illustration of this. In her library research on hemispheric dominance for languages of bilinguals, she found researchers gave conflicting findings for the same research question. One could say that the research appeared inconclusive--some claimed left hemisphere dominance for both languages while others showed some right hemisphere involvement in either the first or second language. Two studies were particularly troublesome because they used the same task, examined adult, male, fluent bilinguals, and yet their answers differed. The first study showed left hemisphere dominance for each language for "late" bilinguals. The second showed the degree of lateralization depended on age of acquisition; early bilinguals demonstrated more right hemisphere involvement for L1 processing than late bilinguals, and late bilinguals demonstrated more right hemisphere involvement for L2 processing than early bilinguals.

The review is complicated but, to make a long story short, Comby reanalyzed the data in the second study instituting the control variables of the first study. Bilinguals now became only those of English plus Romance languages, handedness was now controlled for no family left-handed history; age was changed to one group--Ss between 20 and 35 years of age; and finally, a cutoff points for "early" vs. "late" bilingual were changed to agree with the first study. With all these changes, the findings now agreed.

It is important, then, to remember the control variables when we interpret the results of our research (not to generalize beyond the groups included in the study). The controls, in this case, allowed researchers to see patterns in the data. Without the controls, the patterns were not clear. At the same time, using controls means that we cannot generalize. Researchers who use controls often replicate their studies, gradually releasing the controls. This allows them to see which of the controls can be dropped to improve generalizability. It also allows them to discover which controls most influence performance.

In the above examples, we have controlled the effect of an independent variable by eliminating it (and thus limiting generalizability). The control variables in these examples are nominal (discrete, discontinuous). For scored, continuous variables, it is possible statistically to control for the effect of a moderating variable. That is, we can adjust for preexisting differences in a variable. (This procedure is called ANCOVA, and the variable that is "controlled" is called a *covariate*. ANCOVA is a fairly sophisticated procedure that we will consider again in chapter 13.) As an example, imagine we wished to investigate how well male and female students from different first-language groups performed on a series of computer-assisted tasks. The focus in the research is the evaluation of the CAI lessons and the possible effect of sex and L1 group membership on task performance. In collecting the data, we would undoubtedly notice that not all students read through the materials at the same speed. If we measure this preexisting difference in reading speed, we can adjust the task performance scores taking reading speed into account. Notice that this statistical adjustment "controls" for preexisting differences in a variable which is not the focus of the research. Unlike the previous examples, the variable is not deleted; i.e., slow readers (or rapid readers) are not deleted from the study. While reading speed may be an important variable, it is not the focus of the research so, instead, its effect is neutralized by statistical procedures.

Other Intervening Independent Variables

We often hope to draw a direct relation between independent and dependent variables in our research. For example, we might want to look at the relationship between income and education. We would expect that with additional education, income would increase. If you collected data, you might be surprised to find that the relationship is weak. Additional education might increase the income of some people and not help others. How can we explain the lack of a direct relationship between additional education → increased income? If you think about it for a moment, you can see that education is likely to increase the earning power of young people. They might earn the minimum wage at McDonald's while in high school and earn a much larger salary at IBM after college. So the increase in income is great. On the other hand, additional education is not likely to increase the income of older adults. Their salaries are already fairly high and the value of added classes may not be reflected in income. So for one age group the relation is that of additional education → higher income, but for the other group this is not the case. There is an intervening variable, *a variable that was not included in the study*, at work:

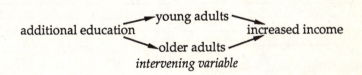

additional education   →young adults→   increased income
  →older adults→
intervening variable

As you can guess from this diagram, an intervening variable is the same thing as a moderating variable. The only difference is that the intervening variable has not been or cannot be identified in a precise way for inclusion in the research.

In planning research, we want to be able to identify all the important variables (or control for them). However, sometimes this is impossible. For example, intervening variables may be difficult to represent since they may reflect internal mental processes. For example, when we talk about L1 → L2 transfer or L1 → L2 interference, we are talking about an internal mental process that we may or may not be able to measure accurately. Intelligence and test-taking talents may not be directly measurable yet play some role in changing research outcomes. If you review page 46, you will see that intervening variables are a source of "error" in our research.

In all research, we can only account for some portion of the variability that we see in the major, dependent variable. We may look at the influence of many different independent variables to explain the variability in the dependent variable. However, there are many other factors which may or may not be important that we may fail to consider and that thus contribute to "error." However, whatever the findings, it is important to consider whether we have defined our variables well so that they reflect (as well as they possibly can) all the processes that we hope to tap.

Practice 2.9

▶ 1. To be sure that you have correctly grasped the definitions of variable functions, please review each of the research descriptions on page 60. For each study, identify the function of each variable (as dependent, type of independent, or intervening).

a. Lennon's study of uncertainty expressions.

_____
_____
_____
_____
_____

b. Brusasco's study of simultaneous interpreters.

_____
_____
_____
_____
_____

c. Li's study of technical vocabulary.

_____
_____
_____
_____
_____

d. Study of ratings of SLRF abstracts.

_____
_____
_____
_____
_____

e. Wong's study of cohesive ties.

_____
_____
_____
_____
_____

f. Hawkins' study of communication breakdowns.

_____
_____
_____
_____
_____

2. Identify the functions of the variables for your own research question. In your study group, check to be certain that all members agree on the identification of these functions.

Group consensus: _____

_____
_____
_____
_____
_____
_____
_____

◇◇◇◇◇◇◇◇◇◇◇◇◇◇◇◇◇◇◇◇◇◇◇◇◇◇◇◇◇◇◇◇◇◇◇◇◇◇

In the examples we have given in this chapter, the distinction between dependent and independent variables has been straightforward. In some research projects it is clear that we expect certain independent variables (such as proficiency level or major) to influence the dependent variable (such as performance on some test). There are, however, times when the assignment of one variable to dependent status and another to the function of independent variable is not so obvious. For example, we might expect that Ss' scores on a Spanish language placement exam might be similar to their scores on a Spanish language proficiency exam. One variable does not really influence the other; rather, we expect to see a relationship between the two sets of scores. Variable 1 relates to variable 2 and vice versa. The relationship is bidirectional. In such cases, the assignment of dependent and independent status is arbitrary.

In this chapter we have talked about variables and the functions of variables in research. Now that we have identified and categorized the variables in the research project, we will consider how these variables can be investigated within a research design.

Activities

1. Review the study summaries presented in the activities section of chapter 1. For three of these studies, list the variables involved in the study and label each for its function in the study and according to how it was measured.

2. P. McCandless & H. Winitz (1986. Test of pronunciation following one year of comprehension instruction in college German. *Modern Language Journal, 70*, 4, 355-362.) compared the pronunciation of American students learning German under two conditions. One group of 10 students received auditory input of German for 240 hours, 210 class hours, and 30 hours of listening comprehension tapes. Through the use of objects, pictures, and activities, students were taught to comprehend German. Grammar and reading were not taught. The second group of 10 students had a traditional program of equivalent time in which grammar, reading, and speaking were emphasized. Raters listened to each student read lists of sentences and gave each *S* an accent rating from excellent (*ausgezeichnet*) to poor (*mangelhaft*), on a 5-point scale. List the variables, their functions in the study, and variable measurement. If you were carrying out this research project, what alternative methods might you use?

3. V. A. Mann (1986. Distinguishing universal and language-dependent levels of speech perception: evidence from Japanese listener's perception of English /l/ and /r/. *Cognition, 24*, 169-193.) shows that although native speakers of Japanese may be unable to identify /l/ and /r/ correctly in spoken English, they respond like native speakers of English to the different acoustic patterns that convey /l/ and /r/ (as if they are sensitive to difference in the vocal tract movements that convey /l/ and /r/). The study contains the following table that describes the *S*s of the study.

Table 1. Oral English profile: <u>Japanese Ss participating in experiment</u>

| | College Testing | | Experience Prior to College* (0-5 pt. scale, 5 = extensive) | | | | |
	JACET max = 120	Koike max = 50	Before J.H.	Jr. High Sch.	Home	Sr. High Sch.	Home
Superior	97.5	48.4	1.95	3.63	3.32	2.74	1.42
Inferior	42.6	39.3	0.77	3.09	2.23	2.32	0.45

---

* Ratings computed by Ss' English professor on the basis of responses to a questionnaire.

Examine the table. *Superior* is "superior student" and *Inferior* is "inferior student." *JACET* and *Koike* stand for English language proficiency tests. Using the information in the table, write a description of the Ss' experience with English and their general proficiency in oral English.

4. J. Lee (1986. Background knowledge and L2 reading. *Modern Language Journal, 70*, 4, 350-354.) replicated Carrell's research project which showed that "unlike native speakers...nonnative readers show virtually no significant effects of background knowledge." Lee replicated the study design with three treatments: (1) $\pm$ a title page, picture page related to the topic, (2) $\pm$ a transparent lexical item which clearly revealed or obscured the content of the text, (3) $\pm$ familiarity with the topic of the text. In Carrell's study, Ss wrote what they recalled in the target language; in this study they wrote in the L1. Lee found a significant triple interaction of the treatment variables in contrast to Carrell's finding of no significant effects of background knowledge. List the variables (with functions and possible measurement). If this were your study, what alternative procedures might you use?

5. S. Shimanoff (1985. Expressing emotions in words: verbal patterns of interaction. *Journal of Communication, 35*, 3, 16-31.) investigated the speech act "expressive," one of the basic speech acts of communicative competence. College students were paid to tape their conversations for one day. All expressives (e.g., "I love it," "I felt fantastic," "I coulda shot him!") were pulled from these natural data. The expressives were categorized according to (a) expressive about self or other, (b) time, past or present, (c) source--person vs. object or event, and d) valence--pleasant or unpleasant. Each *S*, then, had data on use of pleasant/unpleasant, present/past, speaker/other, person/object or event. *S* gender did not influence the data so this variable was dropped from the study. List the variables (and functions and measurement). If this were your study, what alternative procedures might you use?

6. L. White (1985. The acquisition of parameterized grammars. *Second Language Research, 1*, 1, 1-17.) asked 73 adult ESL students (54 Spanish L1 and 19 French L1) to give grammaticality judgments on the acceptability of 31 sentences. Thirteen of the sentences represented grammatically correct or incorrect sentences that exemplify the subjacency principle (a principle in Universal Grammar that puts restrictions on the movement of certain kinds of features, for example WH-words). Subjacency in English, according to Universal Grammar, constrains the number of "bounding nodes" the WH-word can cross. Neither French nor Spanish have S (S = sentence, not Subject!) as a "bounding node" while English does. The research then looked to see whether Ss would transfer their L1 parameter to English or show sensitivity to the parameter setting of English in their grammaticality judgments. The author reports the results as inconclusive but believes the subject merits further research. What are the variables (functions and measurement)? If this were your study, what alternative procedures might you use?

References

Brusasco, D. 1984. Simultaneous interpretation and beyond: Japanese to English. Unpublished master's thesis, TESL, UCLA.

Comby, D. 1987. Hemispheric lateralization in bilinguals: a split issue. Unpublished master's thesis, Spanish & Portuguese, University of Texas, Austin.

Hawkins, B. 1986. Task difficulty and communication breakdowns. Unpublished English 283K paper, UCLA.

Lennon, D. 1986. Expressions of uncertainty. Unpublished English 283K paper, UCLA.

Li, X. 1986. Effects of contextual clues on identifying and remembering meanings of new words in discrete sentences. Unpublished master's thesis, TESL, UCLA.

Wong, J. 1986. Recognizing cohesive ties. Unpublished testing project, UCLA.

Chapter 3
Constructing Research Designs

- *Determining the design*
  Distinguishing the dependent and independent variables
  Confounded designs
  Repeated-measures vs. Between-groups (randomized) designs
  Mixed designs (split-plot designs)
- *Practice in drawing design boxes*
- *Classification of designs*
  Studies with intact groups
  One-shot design
  One-group pretest-posttest design
  Intact group--single control
  Time-series designs
  Experimental studies
  Random assignment posttest
  Control group pretest-posttest
  Ex post facto designs

Determining the Design

In chapter 2 all of the concepts have been presented that are needed for determining design. However, we will review them here as part of research design. In addition to determining the scope of the research question, stating the research question as clearly as possible, giving operational definitions to key terms, identifying variables, understanding the roles variables will play in the research and how those variables will be observed, we need to plan the overall design of the project. This is important for it will help us to determine how the data will be analyzed.

Distinguishing the Dependent and Independent Variables in Research

When novice researchers approach a consultant for help in analyzing the data, the first question the consultant asks is "Tell me about your research. What are you trying to find out?" If the research question is clearly stated, the consultant will probably say, "So X is your dependent variable and A, B, and C are your independent variables, right?" If the research question is not clearly stated, it may take time (which may or may not have to be paid for) to determine this first crucial piece of information: which variables in the research are which.

In chapter 2, we practiced identifying the function of variables. As a review, we will identify the dependent and independent variables in the following brief description of a research project.

> The university is concerned because, while many immigrant and foreign students enroll as science majors, few select a major in the humanities. As part of the admissions process, prospective students must score above 1200 on the SAT (Scholastic Aptitude Test). We believe that most immigrant and foreign students who meet this cut-off point do so by scoring very high on the math portion of the test (much higher than monolingual American students) but they probably score relatively low on the verbal portion of the test. We want to look at the math scores of American and immigrant/foreign students. We are also interested in comparing the math scores of students declaring an interest in the humanities with those planning to enroll in the sciences. (We may repeat this process for the SAT verbal scores or perhaps for the ratio of math to verbal scores of the *S*s in the two groups. Ultimately the information might be useful in the admissions process so that immigrant/foreign students interested in the humanities have a better chance of acceptance.)

Null hypothesis: There is no difference in the SAT math scores of native and nonnative speakers.
Null hypothesis: There is no difference in the SAT math scores of humanities and science students.
Null hypothesis: There is no interaction between student language (native/nonnative) and major area (humanities/science) on the math scores.

Dependent variable(s): SAT math scores

Independent variable(s):
(1) *S* type--two levels, native vs. nonnative speaker } How do these affect this?
(2) Major--2 levels, humanities vs. science

Try to visualize the data of this project as filling a box.

What fills the box? The data on math scores. Now visualize building compartments or cells in that box. The contents of the box in this project are subdivided first in two sections.

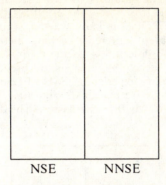

NSE   NNSE

The contents of the box have been subdivided so that the scores for native speakers are placed in one section and the scores of nonnative speakers in the other.

Now visualize the final division of the contents of the box:

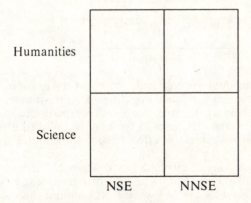

The data for the dependent variable have now been divided into four sections. That in the upper left corner are the data of the native speaker humanities students. In the upper right corner are the data of the nonnative speakers who are humanities majors. What data are in the lower left-hand corner? The scores of the science majors who are native speakers. In the lower right section are the scores of nonnative speakers who are science majors.

With the data partitioned, we can compare the two top sections with the two lower sections to find the differences between humanities and science majors. We can also look at native speakers vs. nonnative speakers by comparing the data in the left two sections with the right two. We can also compare all cells of the box individually to see which differ from the others.

Confounded Designs

Visualizing the design as placing data in boxes will help us avoid confounded designs. Confounded designs should be *avoided* if at all possible. These are designs where it is impossible to separate the effects of the independent variables. For example, suppose you wanted to know whether students in applied linguistics would learn the principles of different teaching methodologies depending on whether they not only read descriptions of the methods but also saw videotaped demonstrations of classes where the methods are used. Imagine you were also interested in knowing whether experienced ESL/EFL teachers would understand the principles better than novice teachers. You assign the treatments (read + video demo or read only) to two different classes. The design box would look like this:

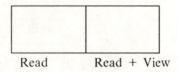

The teachers have been assigned to the classes on the basis of their experience. One class is for experienced teachers and one for novices.

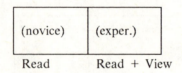

What happened? Once the data are collected, you could try to compare the two treatments. But any differences you found might be due to the teacher-experience variable. If you tried to compare the experienced and inexperienced teachers, any differences might be due to the difference in treatments. With this design, it is impossible to separate teacher-experience effect from treatment effect.

Hopefully, you see that you *cannot* attribute any difference that you find in the degree of understanding of the methodologies to *either* treatment *or* experience. These two independent variables are *confounded*. (Confound those confounded variables!) Sometimes, such a design is unavoidable but, in reporting the results, you would definitely have to ask for further studies to discover just how the two independent variables are related to differences in performance on the dependent variable.

Repeated-Measures vs. Between-Groups (Randomized) Designs

In the SAT example, you will notice that the math score of each *S* fell into *one and ONLY one cell of the box*. The data of a NSE who is a humanities major can only appear in the upper left section of the box. That of a nonnative humanities major can only appear in the upper right section. The comparisons will be drawn between independent groups in each of the four cells of the box. Therefore, this is called a between-groups (independent or randomized) design. This pattern is not always followed. Consider the following example:

> You have been given a Fulbright grant to teach American literature at the University of Helwan. Since you have never taught American literature to nonnative speakers of English, you are not sure just how appropriate your selection of short stories might be. Five different themes are presented in the stories. Since you will teach the course again in the second term and hope to offer the course during the summer at Alexandria University, you want to be sure of your choices. You ask each student to rate the stories on a number of factors. Each *S*'s ratings of the stories within a theme is totaled as that *S*'s score for the theme.

The ratings fill the box which is then divided into sections for ratings of the five themes:

T¹	T²	T³	T⁴	T⁵

The rating of each *S* no longer falls into *one and ONLY one* cell of the box. Each *S* gives a rating for the theme in each cell of the box. The themes will be compared using data collected from the same *S*s. Since repeated readings are taken from the same *S*s, this is called a *repeated-measures design*. This is not something to avoid. Rather, the distinction between independent groups and repeated-measures designs will determine in part the choice of an appropriate statistical procedure for analyzing the data.

◇◇◇◇◇◇◇◇◇◇◇◇◇◇◇◇◇◇◇◇◇◇◇◇◇◇◇◇◇◇◇◇◇◇◇

Practice 3.1

▶1. Decide whether the following studies involve a repeated-measures design or a between-groups design, or show a design which uses both.

a. Your university is considering removing credit from ESL courses for immigrant students though they will continue credit for foreign students. The claim is that the courses are remedial and give students credit for course work covered in high school. You survey faculty on whether or not they believe credit should be allowed both immigrant and foreign students. In your report you compare the responses of faculty who regularly have students from these groups in their classes with those who do not.

Repeated-measures, between-groups, or both? _____Between - looking at 2_____
Rationale: _____groups of faculty_____

b. In a cross-cultural analysis class, you ask students to watch a video and judge the appropriateness of small-talk behavior in each of five different episodes. The students are U.S., Canadian, Indian, and Vietnamese. — Do I use this info or not? not for this e.

Repeated-measures, between-groups, or both? _____ R & B _____
Rationale: _____
_____
_____

c. You believe that purpose clauses (e.g., "*To brown*, remove the foil, and continue baking for 5 minutes.") usually precede rather than follow main clauses. To test this claim, you search a random sample of oral data (from the Carterette & Jones corpus, 1974, or the *White House Transcripts*, 1974) and a random sample of written data (from the Brown corpus, 1979, or your own collection).

Repeated-measures, between-groups, or both? _____ oral _____ | prced | folw. |
Rationale: _____ written _____ | | |
_____
_____

d. You own an ESL school as a business. You have contacted local businesses, offering a course in "communication improvement" for their immigrant employees. You screen each student and prepare an individual profile on pronunciation, informal conversational skills, and oral presentation skills. ① At two-week intervals you reassess the students' abilities in each of these areas. At the end of the course, each student receives his/her record of improvement. ② Employers, who paid for the course, receive a report on course effectiveness for the students *as a group*. The report compares the scores of the groups at each point throughout the course.

week 1   week 5   etc.
Repeated-measures, between-groups, or both? ___ op ___
Rationale: ___ st. ___ | pron conver. oral pres | P c | |
R ___ st ___
___ st ___
st

e. Using a 30-item questionnaire, you ask native speakers of English and non-native students to decide whether a single verb or a two-word verb would be more appropriate in a given context. Each question contains a context and then a choice between a single verb (such as *telephoned*) and a two-word verb (such as *called up*). Fifteen items appear in a formal context and 15 in an informal context. Does context type influence verb type choice? No are (ns, nns) but implied

Repeated-measures, between-groups, or both? _____ B & R _____
Rationale: _____ used rf
_____
_____

◇◇◇◇◇◇◇◇◇◇◇◇◇◇◇◇◇◇◇◇◇◇◇◇◇◇◇◇◇◇◇◇◇◇◇◇◇◇◇

	single	2 word
formal 1		
2		
3		
15		
informal 30		

ns   nns

Mixed Designs (Split-Plot Designs)

We've noted that ==in between-groups comparisons, independent groups are compared==. For example, if we ask administrators of EFL programs, teachers in EFL programs, and students in EFL programs to complete a questionnaire reporting perceived value of courses as preparation for study in U.S., Canadian, or British universities, then the comparisons we draw are between different groups. On the other hand, if we survey all the students in modern languages regarding the value they placed on language vs. literature courses in their university training, then we have only one group of students and we are drawing comparisons for the courses by repeated measures of that one group.

What are the observations?

==Sometimes==, however, ==designs include *both* comparisons of independent groups and repeated-measures of the same group==. These are called *mixed designs* or *split-plot designs*. For example, imagine that you did carry out an attitude survey regarding the perceived value of a language skills program in preparation for university training in British, Canadian, or U.S. institutions. This will be one of several measures that you plan to use for the purposes of program evaluation.

> You are a "foreign expert" working at three different institutes in China. Prior to final selection for study overseas, Chinese students are given an opportunity to improve their language skills in one of these institutes. In each program, Chinese professors and Canadian, U.S., and British EFL teachers offer a variety of courses to the students. You administer the questionnaire to students at each institute at the start of the program. You want to compare the responses of these three separate groups. The questionnaire responses will show how valuable students in each group expect the program to be.

As a review, the H_o for this part of the study is that there is no difference in "expected value" ratings of the program across the three institutes. The dependent variable is the "expected value" rating. The independent variable is *institute* (with three levels). The design box for the study is:

What about teachers?

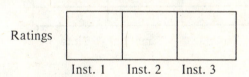

Ratings

Inst. 1   Inst. 2   Inst. 3

While the word *Ratings* is outside the box diagram, the ratings are, in fact, inside the three cells of the box. The ratings for institute 1 fill the first cell, the ratings for institute 2, the second cell, and the ratings for institute 3 are in the third cell. So far, the design is between independent groups.

> At the conclusion of the program, you administer the questionnaire again. You want to compare the responses on this questionnaire with that given before the start of the program to see whether Ss' value perceptions regarding the program have changed.

The questionnaire is completed by the *same* Ss. In addition to comparing the responses across the institutes (between independent groups), we also want to compare the responses of each *S* at time 1 with time 2 (a repeated-measures design).

The amended design looks like this:

	Time 1	Time 2
Inst. 1		
Inst. 2		
Inst. 3		
Ratings		

Again, the word *Ratings* outside the lower left-hand corner of the box tells us what is placed in each cell of the box. (That is, the top two cells of the box contain the ratings for institute 1 at time 1 and then at time 2, and so forth.)

> Six months after the same students have enrolled in university programs in Canada, U.S., or British universities, they were sent the third questionnaire form to fill out.

To compare the students' perceptions of value of the program, the questionnaire was administered three times. The comparison uses a repeated-measures design.

To compare students from the different institutes, the responses are put into three groups. The comparison, here, is between independent groups.

Here is the final design box for the study.

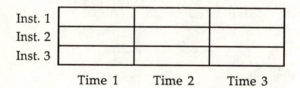

	Time 1	Time 2	Time 3
Inst. 1			
Inst. 2			
Inst. 3			

In this design, the same Ss participate in both a repeated-measures and an independent groups comparison. Fairly complex designs of this sort are common in applied linguistics research. The type of statistical analysis of the data will differ according to whether the comparisons are between-groups or repeated-measures. You can see why this is the case, if you think for a moment about how close your responses on two measures might be. If you are asked twice to give your perception of the value of grammar instruction, it is likely that your two responses will be more similar than would one of your responses and my response. Whenever you compare one person on different measures (or the same measure at different times), the performances are more likely to be similar than the performances between two people on different measures. (If by mistake you used a statistical test for between-groups with a repeated-measures design, the test *could* very well say that there was no difference between the groups when in fact a difference really exists. This gives rise to a *Type 1* error, a concept we will explain later.)

Practice in Drawing Design Boxes

One of the best ways to clarify a research design is to draw a box diagram (as we began to do in the previous discussion). The first thing to remember is that what goes *inside the box* is all the data on the dependent variable. (It is possible that you might have more than one dependent variable, but we will not cover such instances here.) The box will then be partitioned so that parts of the total data can be compared with other parts. When there is one dependent and one independent variable, by convention the levels of the dependent variable (what is being measured) will appear above each other on the left side of the box. The labels for the levels of the independent variable will appear across the cells at the bottom of the box.

D
E
P
E
N
D
E
N
T

I N D E P E N D E N T

In the purpose clause study above (see page 78), let's assume that the oral sample is from the tapes described and the written sample includes 200 words from an engineering lab manual, 200 words from *Always Coming Home* (a novel), 200 words from an economics textbook, 200 words from a geography book, and 200 words from a popular health science book.

The research question for this study in null hypothesis form is:

> There is no difference in distribution of purpose clauses (either before or following the main clause).

> There is no difference in the distribution of purpose clauses in written vs. oral language.

> There is no difference in the distribution of purpose clauses between the five samples of written text.

The dependent variable is position of the purpose clause (2 levels). The independent variable is language mode with two levels (oral vs. written).

Visualize the data as filling a box. The data inside the total box are all of the purpose clauses in the data. Now, look at the first null hypothesis. We make two divisions in the data, subdividing the purpose clauses into those in initial position and those in final position. We turn to the next null hypothesis and add two more divisions to the box. The data for initial position are divided in two and all the initial clauses from the spoken data are put in one cell and all those from written data in the other. Then the clauses in final position are divided and all final clauses from the spoken data go in one cell and those of written data in another. We have four cells. This leaves us with the final null hypothesis. How can we represent this subdivision? If you're not sure how to do this, read on.

If you look at the box diagram for this study, you will see that the division of the data has been quite regular up to the point where the written text was subdivided into sample types.

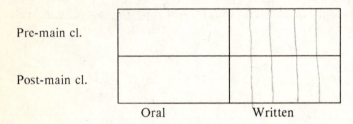

Pre-main cl.

Post-main cl.

Oral   Written

In the right two sections (the written data), we can draw vertical lines to subdivide each section into five parts for the five selections. These subdivisions represent the five levels of the written level. This obviously is not a neatly balanced study. However, again it is typical of much research in our field.

Let's try another example. Look at the following boxed diagram.

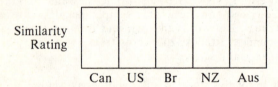

Similarity
Rating

Can   US   Br   NZ   Aus

Assume you have asked second language learners to listen to English speakers representing each of the above groups (Canadian, U.S., British, New Zealand, and Australian). They are asked to judge how similar they feel their own pronunciation is to each of these groups on, say, a 7-point scale. Think of the data as the total collection of responses of all Ss. Inside the complete box we find the similarity ratings. In the cell labeled *Can*, we find the ratings of similarity with Canadian English. If you wanted to look at how similar the students felt their own pronunciation approached that of the speakers representing New Zealand English, you would look at the cell labeled NZ.

Now, assume that the gender of students doing the judging might make a difference in their ratings. The box diagram would change to show this new division.

	Male	Female
Can		
US		
Br		
NZ		
Aus		

◇◇◇◇◇◇◇◇◇◇◇◇◇◇◇◇◇◇◇◇◇◇◇◇◇◇◇◇◇◇◇◇◇◇◇◇◇◇◇

Practice 3.2

▶ 1. Draw box diagrams for each of the studies on page 77, labeling the divisions.

a. Faculty survey re credit for ESL classes.

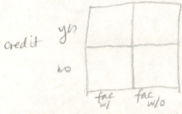

b. U.S., Canadian, Indian, and Vietnamese judgments of appropriateness of small-talk behavior.

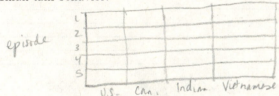

If you wanted to be sure that the judgments did not change across the episodes, how would you diagram the design?

w/i one student?
across students?

c. Purpose clause positioning.

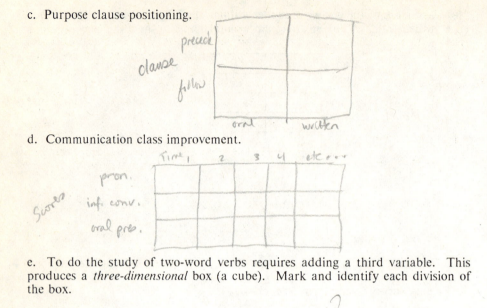

d. Communication class improvement.

e. To do the study of two-word verbs requires adding a third variable. This produces a *three-dimensional* box (a cube). Mark and identify each division of the box.

2. Compare your diagrams with those of others in your study group. Are they the same? If not, how do you account for the differences?

_____
_____
_____
_____
_____

◇◇

Classification of Designs

When you classify variables and their functions, you prepare the way for selecting appropriate statistical procedures for describing and interpreting your data. This classification of *variables* and their roles in your research is crucial. In addition, the classification of *designs* helps the novice researcher to consider threats to research validity.

Campbell and Stanley (1963) list 16 different design types and discuss the possible threats to reliability and validity inherent in each. There is no reason why you should know the names of all the different types of designs or the ways in which they are grouped together. The names, however, should be familiar so that when you read a report about an "ex post facto" design, you won't throw up your hands in despair at "technical jargon." You will know that it is a design classification and that you can always look it up in an index to refresh your memory if you decide that it is important to you. What *is* important is that you think about which type of design will work best for your particular research project.

In selecting an appropriate statistical procedure, one of the first things to decide will be whether or not there is random selection and assignment of *S*s (or of texts, or of objects) in the research. Designs, too, can be divided into those which do and those which do not show random selection and random assignment.

We have already said that research gives us support for our hypotheses rather than *proof* that we are right. However, we often do hope to establish *causal* links between variables. To make causal claims, the research must be carefully planned and closely controlled. For example, true experimental designs *require* random selection and, where treatments are compared, random assignment to groups. Sometimes, especially in classroom research, neither random selection nor random assignment is possible. The researcher must work with an established class of students, an *intact group*. Students are assigned to a class on the basis of scores on tests, on the basis of their compositions or oral interview skills, or by self-selection (the students decide which courses to take). Sometimes teachers select students in order to have a homogeneous class where they don't have to worry about extreme variations in student performance. Other teachers select students to have enough variation to allow them to use "cooperative learning techniques" (where all students become the experts in some piece of every task). When random selection is not possible, causal claims are also impossible.

Studies with Intact Groups

The majority of classroom research involves the use of classes where students have already been assigned on the basis of some principle. This is called an intact group. In this research it is impossible randomly to select students to begin with. Even where students could be placed in one of several sections of the same level, the assignment to those sections is seldom random. Students may self-select a section according to their timetables, and their timetables may reflect their majors. For instance, undergraduate engineering students may have a set number of required courses, courses which they must take, and so all ESL students from the engineering department might be in one section of a class. In intact group studies, we are unable randomly to select or randomly to assign students for research purposes. When random selection is required (i.e., when drawing inferences or generalizing to a population), the researcher should consider whether the design prohibits or allows for the use of inferential statistical procedures.

It is much easier to achieve random selection when dealing with text analysis. However, even here, random selection may not always be possible. Sometimes random selection is not desired and causal claims are not at issue. For example, if you are analyzing the use of special linguistic features in the poetry of a single author, you may need to use all of the data rather than a random selection of poems of the author. In carrying out an in-depth study of one fourth-grade class, the class behaviors of individual students may be followed and described in great depth. The descriptions are of this particular author or these particular students. Random selection is not desired and there is no intention of making causal claims or of generalizing the findings to all poets or fourth-grade students everywhere.

In classroom research where researchers wish to see the effects of a teaching/learning treatment, the design often uses the intact group. While such designs will not allow us to make *causal* (cause-effect) statements about the findings, they will allow us to *give evidence in support of* links between variables for these particular classes.

Intact designs are often the only practical way of carrying out research which will help find answers to questions. However, as you will see below, the researcher must think about how much confidence to place in the findings and interpret those findings with care. Replication will be necessary. As we will see in a moment, there are ways to improve designs to give us more confidence in findings that show a link between variables (although no causal claim will be made regarding the link).

One-Shot Design

In many teaching programs, teachers (and administrators) want to know whether students meet the objectives set for the course. At the end of the course (and whatever happened during the course is an example of "treatment" in research jargon), students take a test. The schematic representation for this design is:

$$T - X$$

where T stands for treatment and X for the test results.

This is a very simple design but the results must be interpreted with great care. While you may be tempted to say that the treatment "worked" and want to share the results with other teachers at the next TESOL conference, you should be wary of doing so. The results may not be valid and you cannot generalize from them with confidence. As we have said many times, the research process is meant to give you confidence in your description of results and (if you wish to go beyond description) the generalizability of your findings. The study has given you data that you can describe, but in interpreting the data you must caution listeners and readers to consider the possibility of threats to validity and reliability of the research. (You can quickly review these in chapter 1 if you don't remember them now.)

To try to take care of some of these problems, researchers sometimes use standardized tests with published norms. When possible, of course this is a good idea. However, Campbell and Stanley warn that we still can't say much about the results even if the T has been *carefully* described. That is, one might attribute any differences to many factors other than the treatment. (And, yes, that is "error" as far as you are concerned because you are not interested in these other factors.)

One-Group Pretest-Posttest Design

If you gave the learners in the above example a pretest on the first day of class and a posttest at the end of the course, you would have changed the design to the following schematic:

$$X_1 - T - X_2$$

By giving the pretest, you can assure yourself that students did not already know the material tested on the posttest. The administration of the pretest could be a threat to the validity of the research, especially if the time between pretest and posttests is short, the items very similar, or if the pretest gave Ss pointers on what to study.

The pretest and posttest do not have to be "tests". They can be observations. For example, you might observe the behavior of Ss using some observational checklist before and after some special instruction. Test is just a cover term for all kinds of observations.

Imagine that your school has a very poor record of parent involvement. Very few parents visit the school. You have a record of the number of visits by parents for the first three months of school. Some teachers believe that the parents are just not interested in their children's education. You don't agree. You think that the school does not appear to be a very "welcoming" place, particularly to parents of bilingual children. You have already been videotaping some of the classrooms and the tapes show children engaged in many different activities. You ask the children if they would like to have their parents see them on television on parents' night. They are all excited about this possibility. You and the students design special invitations to the parents. You ask the bilingual children to add a note in their first language to make the invitations even more special. The principal of the school agrees to collect and display some of the best compositions from various classes and put them on display. And, of course, some of these compositions are written in the home language of the children. Signs are posted not only in English but in the home language as well. Since none of the office staff speaks this language, several of the children are invited to come and serve as special interpreters to welcome the parents. Parents' night is a great success. Not only that, but some parents accept invitations to visit classes and do appear in the next two weeks.

The pretest measure is the number of visits by parents before parents' night. The posttest is the number after parents' night. It is difficult to say precisely what the treatment may have been. For the sake of the illustration, we will say it was parents' night (not all the preliminary activity). The pretest-posttest design for one group has many drawbacks that you can consider in your study group.

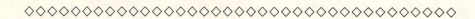

Practice 3.3

1. In the parents' night example above, do you believe that the pretest measure in any way influenced the posttest measure? *No*

_____

_____

2. If the treatment is activities during parents' night alone, are there activities between the pretest and the treatment that might affect the outcome? *Yes - taping, invitations etc. student involvement*

_____

If the treatment is parents' night alone, what *history* factors (rather than the treatment) might be related to improved parental involvement?

_____

_____

3. Having carried out the research, with whom would you want to share your findings?

_____

_____

If you shared the findings with teachers at a parallel school in your district, could you generalize your findings to their district? Why (not)?

_____

_____

4. You know that students at a nearby college can get stipends if they serve as interns in work programs. Some of these students are bilingual. How could you use the above information as evidence to secure an intern to work at the school to promote parent involvement? _____

_____

_____

Intact Group--Single Control

If you are working with a class and there are students in other sections of that same course, it is possible to establish a control group for the research. *S*s have not been randomly selected for the course nor randomly assigned to sections of the course. However, you could randomly assign the special treatment to the sections by the flip of a coin.

The representation for this design is as follows (*G₁* stands for the experimental group, a group which will receive your special treatment, and *G₂* stands for the control group.)

$$G_1 \text{ (intact)} - T - X$$

$$G_2 \text{ (intact)} - O - X$$

[handwritten margin note: O = means nothing happens out of ordinary. No treat.]

This design is an improvement over the previous design. The above schematic for this design suggests that only one treatment and one control is used in studies of this sort. It is quite possible that several treatments might be compared with single or multiple control groups. The distinguishing features of the design are that the groups compared are intact groups (*not* randomly sampled and randomly selected); there is a pretest and posttest measure; and there is a control group. *[handwritten: not true]* *[handwritten: Where?]*

Since this design is often used in our field for program or materials evaluation, let's review some of the other possible threats to validity and reliability of such a design. Imagine that you wished to evaluate the effectiveness of immersion programs. In these programs *S*s receive education in an L2 which is, typically, a minority language--for example, English-speaking children receive their early education in Spanish in Los Angeles, or in German in Milwaukee, or in Arabic in Cleveland. To show that such programs do not harm the children in terms of further first language development, the children might be compared with an appropriate control group on their scores on English language subject matter tests.

In this case, the treatment and control are definitely different We would, however, need to know precisely how they differ in terms of English use. That is, if activities in the treatment and control overlap, we need to know the extent of the overlap. If the overlap is great, then the outcomes would be different than if the overlap were slight. *[handwritten margin: COR]* *[handwritten margin: ?]*

It is also important to know that *S*s in these classes are (usually) volunteer students. They are, thus, not typical of all elementary school children. This could affect the results and generally limit generalizability. It would be important to check for differential dropout rates in the experimental and control groups. It is likely that *S*s who do not do well in the experimental program will de-select themselves and, perhaps, appear then in the control group. If they were generally the weaker students to begin with, and they shift groups, the results would be differentially affected. If some of the tests were observations conducted by trained observers, it would be important to know whether the observations were "blind" (i.e., the observer did not know what groups were observed--experimental or control--or the purpose of the observation.) The training of the observers could influence the outcome (the observations noted might be differentially affected). *[handwritten margins: cor, COR, COR]*

◇◇

Practice 3.4

1. Assume you wish to analyze the use of metaphor in the short stories of your favorite writer. Because you don't have access to an optical character reader, you have entered only one short story into the computer and coded all the metaphors. You want to report on the frequency and types of metaphor in the text. Identify the design classification and give the schematic representation.

On   shot   T→X

2. Your library research shows that, because this author was so successful, this use of metaphor became common in short stories between 1935 and 1940. Fortunately for you, you have been able to meet surviving members of the writer's family, and they tell you that the Huntington Library has a number of unfinished and unpublished manuscripts which were written while the author lived in Malaysia (1936-40). These manuscripts include several articles written on the birds of Malaysia. Once you read these articles and the unpublished stories, you believe the author's use of metaphor in short stories changed (you hope to establish a "bird period" as part of your dissertation research!) What is the best design for the research? Why? Identify the design and give the schematic representation.

Is Malaysia or some other event the treatment?

$$X_1 \quad \_ T \_ \quad X_2$$

3. Imagine that you wanted to evaluate the effectiveness of immersion programs as compared with foreign language programs. You have located schools where similar children receive instruction in Spanish, German, and Arabic. FLES (foreign language in elementary school) offers direct language instruction (rather than expecting children to acquire the language via instruction in content courses). In your study group, discuss the possible threats to the validity and reliability of such a comparison. How many and what types of control groups would you use in such an evaluation? In your discussions, consider the treatments being compared. Exactly in what ways do you imagine they differ? What factors (other than language immersion vs. language instruction) might influence differences between the groups?

Group report: _____

_____

_____

_____

_____

_____

_____

Time-Series Designs

Because of the problems involved with random assignment and the difficulties in finding control groups that match the experimental group in many ways, researchers often turn to time-series designs. While the Ss selected for such studies are not usually randomly selected (they can be to maximize generalizability), these designs solve the control group problem in interesting ways.

In a time-series design, the class is its own control group. The time series means that several pretests and posttests are administered. These don't have to be "tests," of course; they might be your observation records, student performance in the language lab, or answers to questionnaires. The schematic representation for the design might be:

$$X_1 - X_2 - X_3 - T - X_4 - X_5 - X_6$$

By collecting data prior to the treatment, you can establish the normal growth in performance over a period of time (say, three weeks), then institute the treatment and follow this with observations following the treatment (weeks 4, 5, and 6). There is no special number of observations required before giving the treatment. Once you feel you've established the growth curve, you can begin.

Let's use an example to see how this works. Imagine that your students are primarily from China and Southeast Asia. They use many topic/comment structures in their compositions as well as in their oral language. (Topic/comment structures are sentences such as *How to write acceptable English sentence, that is my first problem in picking up my pencil.*) During the first three weeks of class you note each student's use of topic/comment structures in written production. They produce large numbers of topic/comment structures. When you feel that you know the usage pattern, you institute a program to show and give practice in the ways that English manages to preserve word order and still fulfill the pragmatic need to highlight topic vs. comment. You continue, then, to look at the students' use of topic/comment structures to see whether they begin to diminish and whether the change is sustained without further instruction.

If you found results such as those shown below, you would be led to conclude that your instruction had no effect.

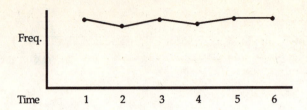

If you found that a rapid drop took place following instruction, you would assume it did have an effect. Students made fewer topic/comment errors in their writing.

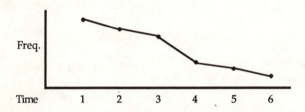

If you obtained a line similar to the following, you might believe that the instruction (1) was detrimental, or (2) totally confused some students but may have helped a few, or (3) that following a period of confusion the learning curve would be as dramatically reversed.

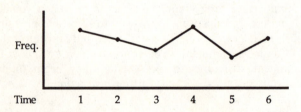

There are many possible variations in time-series designs. For example, if you wanted to know which of two techniques worked best, you could vary the design:

$$X_1 T_1 X_2 \rightarrow X_3 T_2 X_4 \rightarrow X_5 T_1 X_6 \rightarrow X_7 T_2 X_8, \; etc.$$

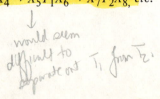

With this design you would alternate periods when you used one set of instructional materials (T_1) with times when you used the second set (T_2). Or, if you have two groups, you could alternate treatments so that, at time 1, group A received special materials and group B did not, and then reverse this at time 2 as in the following diagram.

	Time 1	2	3	4
Materials$_E$ Group	A	B	A	B
Materials$_C$ Group	B	A	B	A

If a time-series design does not seem possible for the particular research question you want to investigate, you could still find ways of letting your class serve as its own control. You could divide the class in two groups (using random assignment of students to the groups) and then randomly assign control and experimental status to the groups. This means that you'd have to prepare separate lesson plans for the groups and administer them in a way that neither group was aware of the treatment of the other. The problem, here, is that you are likely to end up with very few students in each group and--as you will learn later--the fewer the number of subjects in a group, the more difficult it will become to discover whether differences between the groups are "real."

Time-series designs are much more useful than a pretest given at the beginning of the year and a posttest at the end of the year for many applied linguistics projects. It is ideal for evaluation in materials development projects.

Some school districts and departments of education have professionals who engage in program evaluation. Evaluators of bilingual education programs often complain that one-year pretest to posttest evaluations on mandated tests cannot show the true gains made in such programs. They suggest that research be longitudinal, following children for a minimum of two years. A time-series design would be ideal for parts of such evaluations.

You will remember (that means you might not) that in chapter 1 we considered the possibility of making the study of Luisa more feasible by combining a longitudinal (time-series) design and cross-sectional design. The same sort of combination could be carried out for the evaluation of instruction. You might want to carry out a time-series design within your class at a series of points. In addition, you might conduct a cross-sectional study with other classes of students whom you expect to be at the same point of development.

Class A	X	T	X	T	X
Class B	X				
Class C			X		
Class D					X

There are definite advantages to the use of time-series designs. We know that even though we offer students instruction and they are able to perform well during the instruction period, they may not truly internalize the material unless it is recycled over a fairly long period of time. Since this is the case, longitudinal time-series studies are frequently used to discover how long it takes students to reach the goal and the amount of variability of performance along the way. There are disadvantages too. For example, if you conduct your research in schools and the families in your district are very mobile, the attrition and the new students constantly arriving will make it difficult to use such a design.

◇◇◇◇◇◇◇◇◇◇◇◇◇◇◇◇◇◇◇◇◇◇◇◇◇◇◇◇◇◇◇◇◇◇◇◇◇◇◇

Practice 3.5

1. Review the diagrams for the Chinese topic/comment study on page 91. How would you interpret the following two diagrams?

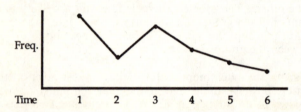

Explanation: _Initially effective at stopping X._
"" confused, so stopped X

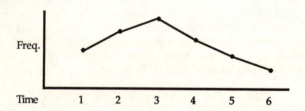

Explanation: _Initially effective at Time Y but_
long-term effects are minimal.

2. In working with these Chinese *Ss*, how might you incorporate control groups into the design to evaluate the effectiveness of an instructional program that addresses topic/comment in English?

_____

_____

_____

Would the design give you more confidence in your findings? Why (not)? _____

_____

_____

3. In your study group, consider how you might design a time-series project to evaluate a set of course materials. Assume that the new course materials *do* meet the same objectives as the previous course materials. (You might want to tackle the problem of how you might handle differences in the amount of time required in new materials versus old materials.)

Group report: _____

_____

_____

_____

_____

4. Summarize the advantages and disadvantages you see for time-series designs.

_____

_____

_____

5. Review the research questions you posed for your own research in chapter 2. Which could be carried out using a time-series design? _____
Give the design scheme below.

_____

_____

_____

◇◇◇

Experimental Studies

We have already mentioned that true experimental studies are relatively rare in applied linguistics. Yet, we strive to approach the "ideal" form of such studies.

True experimental studies do use control groups. They also assess and/or control for differences between groups prior to the start of the experiment. Most important, they require random selection of *Ss* and random assignment of *Ss* to control and experimental groups. Finally, the assignment of control and experimental status is also done randomly. This means that all *Ss* of an identified group have an equal chance of being selected to participate in the experiment. Once selected,

when treatments are compared (p. 85).

the Ss have an equal chance of being assigned to one group or another. The groups have an equal chance of being assigned to control and experimental status.

Random Assignment Posttest

The schematic for this design is:

$$G_1 (random) - T - X$$

$$G_2 (random) - O - X$$

Suppose a school has a very large enrollment of newly arrived students from other countries. In the past, these students were tested and placed at the appropriate level for ESL. However, the ESL program teachers believe that an orientation to school life and school responsibilities should also be available to these students. A program has been designed but, before the school commits money to the program and personnel, it would like to know that it promises to be effective.

All entering nonnative speakers designated as ESL students form the pool from which Ss are randomly selected for assignment to condition A or condition B. Obviously, the school does not want to do a straight random assignment for this study. It should be a stratified random selection. Following the stratified random selection and assignment to the groups, with a flip of the coin, group 1 is selected as the control group and group 2 is selected as the experimental group. The control group receives the regular ESL training. The experimental group receives ESL but for some part of the ESL program time, students also receive an orientation. At the end of the program, students are given a variety of measures to evaluate the effectiveness of the programs. The researchers expect to generalize the findings to all entering nonnative speakers (so long as they match the original group from which the samples were drawn).

◇◇

Practice 3.6

1. List the ways stratification might be done for the above study.

_____

_____

_____

In this study, were students randomly selected? No _____

Were they randomly assigned? Yes _____

Were the experimental and control groups equal to begin with? If yes, how was this insured? If no, why not? _____ *Who knows* _____

_____

_____

_____

2. How carefully should you describe the treatment? How might you go about making sure that the treatment really is as described? _____

_____

_____

_____

What history factors would you check out?

_____ *Previous Knowledge of school life/region.* _____

_____

_____

3. How might you assure that the posttests are kept anonymous (as to whether they are from the experimental or control group) during the coding or scoring process?

_____

_____

_____

_____

◇◇

Control Group Pretest-Posttest

The schematic representation for this experimental design is:

$$G_1 \text{ (random)} - X_1 - T - X_2$$

$$G_2 \text{ (random)} - X_1 - O - X_2$$

With the addition of a pretest, the design can be improved. (In the previous design you may have controlled for equivalence of the groups by specifying the skill level as one way of selecting a stratified random sample. Random selection also helps ensure equivalence of groups since every S has an equal opportunity of being selected and assigned to experimental and control groups.) With a pretest, you have a number of options. You can actually match individual students in the experimental and control groups on the basis of their pretest scores, and compare the performance of these matched groups. Another possibility is to subtract each S's pretest score from the posttest score and compare the *gains* (rather than the final test scores) of the Ss in each group. Finally, there are statistical procedures (e.g., ANCOVA) that will let you control for the student's pretest ability in analyzing the final test scores. All of these options increase the internal and external validity of the study. That is, you can feel more confident that any claims you make about differences in the two groups after the treatment are not due to pre-existing differences in the groups.

Let's illustrate this with another school project. Since U.S. schools across districts, and sometimes statewide, have certain units that are covered at each grade level, and because state ESL supervisors have decided to cover the ESL objectives using the content material for that grade level, new materials for ESL-math and ESL-social studies have been designed. One such ESL-social studies unit for the fourth grade covers the California Missions. Before the school year began all fourth-grade ESL classes (classes now act as though they were subjects in this study) in the school district were given an identifying number. Sixty numbers were then drawn at random to participate in the study. Thirty of these numbers were drawn and assigned to group A and 30 to group B. With a toss of a coin, group A was designated the experimental group and group B, the control. Schools were notified and teachers in both groups were given an in-service workshop on the California Missions. The teachers in the experimental group, however, were also shown how to use the unit to meet ESL objectives for the fourth grade. Pretests were sent to all participating schools and administered by school personnel other than the participating teachers. The course materials were taught and a posttest was given to control and experimental classes.

◇◇

Practice 3.7

1. Have the Ss (classes) in the Missions study been randomly selected? Have they been randomly assigned? Has status (treatment or control) been randomly assigned? If not, why not? _____

_____

_____

2. How would you feel if you knew that your class had been selected to trial the new ESL materials on the California Missions? _____.

_____

_____

Do you think it is important to notify teachers that their class will serve as a control group in a study? If not, why not? If so, how much information do you think they should be given?

_____

_____

_____

_____

3. What possible threats do you see to external or internal validity for the study?

Diff. teachers! Diff SES, Locations etc.

_____

_____

_____

4. Review the research topics you have posed for your own research. Which could be carried out using a true experimental design? Which design would you prefer? Why? How feasible is your choice?

_____

_____

_____

5. In some cases, you might not be sure whether it would be possible to use random selection, control for preexisting differences, or exactly how many control groups would be needed. Discuss these in your study group. Note the suggestions in the space provided.

_____

_____

_____

_____

_____

_____

_____

◇◇

Ex Post Facto Designs

Since it is not often the case that we can meet all threats to internal and external validity, and can arrange for random selection and random assignment, we are not able to make causal claims--claims of cause and effect of independent variable(s) → dependent variable(s). While we believe one should not make causal claims without satisfying the requirements of experimental design, we can still discuss the type and strength of the relationship of the independent and dependent variable in your particular study. When we cannot reach the ideal of true experimental design (random selection and assignment, control of preexisting differences among groups, and the use of control groups), what's a body to do?

One possibility is the use of ex post facto designs. In such designs you will look at the type of connection between independent and dependent variables or the strength of the connection without considering what went before. No treatment is involved. Good design requires, however, that you consider all the possible threats to the validity of the study and try to control for as many of them as possible.

As an example of an ex post facto design consider the following.

Your curriculum is set up for a total skills approach. You notice that there seems to be a great range within your class and also across all the course levels in terms of how quickly students are able to complete tasks. You wonder if this is due to slow reading speed. The first step, then, is to discover the average reading speed of students across the levels. Are students in the beginning sections reading more slowly than those in intermediate sections, and are students in the advanced sections reading most rapidly? Or, is it the case that there are such wide ranges in reading speed at each of these class levels that course levels are not really related to reading speed?

The dependent variable is reading speed. You want to discover whether class level (the independent variable) can account for differences in reading speed (the dependent variable). There are three class levels: beginning, intermediate, and advanced (the class level defined more precisely in the study). Class level is a nominal variable. Reading speed is an interval scale variable.

The design box is:

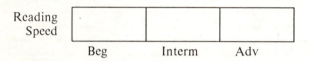

Beg	Interm	Adv

Reading Speed

In this project, is the research trying to show that performance has been improved on the basis of instruction? No, it is not. Are causal relations to be established? No. Are any of the variables being manipulated to cause a change? Again, no. So, the project is an ex post facto design.

This is the most common design type in applied linguistics for it allows us to discover "what is going on" rather than "what caused this." We may videotape our language class and then ask which students take the most turns--do boys or girls volunteer more often in the classroom? This will tell us "what is going on" and could lead to the design of a program to encourage more equal participation (though that is not part of the research). We might look at the amount of teacher talk vs. student talk. Again, this will tell us "what is going on" and could lead to the design of a teacher-training module on ways of encouraging more student participation. We might describe the types of feedback the teacher gives students or how students react to feedback from fellow students and from the teacher. The videotape data could be used to answer many "what is going on" kinds of questions. The design, in each case, is post hoc; it lets us describe some data and see how the values vary across groups of subjects, across tasks, and so forth.

We use post hoc designs for text analysis too. The research tells us what is going on, not the effect of some treatment. We can examine text features (e.g., use of modals) and see how they vary across genres (e.g., narrative vs. procedural text). The analysis will describe what is already there, not a change brought about by some instructional treatment.

Post hoc designs are common in reporting test results. We might want to compare the results of students from different first language groups, or those of immigrant vs. foreign students, or those of students who have gone through a series of courses in our program vs. those admitted at some higher level. Again, the research tells us about the relationship of variables in the data, not about the effectiveness of some instructional program or treatment. Ex post facto designs which incorporate random selection, of course, would allow for generalization of results to some degree. However, one reason these post hoc designs are so common is that many of our topics have nothing to do with a treatment. Rather, we want to discover the effect of some independent variable on a dependent variable (e.g., whether first language--not a treatment--influences the types of transfer errors of ESL students). Another reason, though, is that finding out "what is going on" is a first step in planning for instructional innovation. Once we have confidence in our descriptions of what is happening, we can plan for change. The evaluation of the treatment for bringing about change will, of course, require a different design.

Practice 3.8

1. A fellow teacher-researcher uses the Project Approach and wants to accumulate evidence that the approach "works." From a list of possible projects, Ss in this advanced ESL composition class decided to write an information brochure for deaf students who will spend six weeks on campus during the summer. The project requires that Ss interview leaders of community services, business, and government agencies regarding deaf awareness in the community, and recreation, transportation, cultural activities, work, worship, and business opportunities for the visitors. It also means compiling information on housing, meals, library, tutorial service, recreation, and so forth on campus. To keep track of plans and progress, the teacher and Ss will use computer electronic mail on linked terminals. The teacher envisions grouping Ss to be responsible for different sections of the brochure, peer critiques across groups, teacher critiques, assistance from the printing office on layout and formats, and final critique of the brochure from the Summer Sessions Office. In addition to interviews, Ss will give oral progress reports to the coordinator of the program, to Summer Sessions personnel, and to community leaders. They will give written reports to the campus and local newspapers. They might be interviewed or asked to write a paper on the composing process and how the brochure might be improved. The teacher is open to any suggestions concerning design and data collection.

In your study group, assign each member a design type. Use your assigned design type to design the study (or some portion of the study). List the strengths and weaknesses of the design type for this particular study. In the group, compare the results and determine which design, among those that are feasible, is best suited for this study. Report the results and justification for the choice below.

_____

_____

_____

_____

_____

2. Repeat this process for your own research topic. Design the study using each of the design types. Then select the best design type and justify your selection to your study group. Report the results below.

_____

_____

_____

_____

_____

◇◇◇

In this chapter, we have considered the construction of research designs. Such a consideration is important for several reasons. First, it will help you determine the best design for your particular study--ways of avoiding possible threats to internal and external validity. Second, it will clarify the research so that you can more easily determine which statistical procedures will be most appropriate for the analysis of the data you collect. Third, it is useful to think about possible threats to the validity and reliability of research in balance with the complexity of the final design. The simpler the design, the easier it will be to select an appropriate procedure and interpret results. Now, in the next chapter, let's turn to writing a project proposal using the information we've acquired so far.

Activities

1. L. Seright (1985. Age and aural comprehension achievement in Francophone adults learning English. *TESOL Quarterly, 19,* 3, 455-473.) The Ss in this study were military personnel enrolled in an intensive ESL course in Canada. Ss were classified as older (25-41) or younger (17-24) learners. Eighteen pairs of older/younger Ss were obtained by matching for (a) informal exposure to English, (b) the pretest, (c) nonverbal IQ, (d) education, and (e) previous ESL instruction. A pretest on aural comprehension was given prior to a 12-week course of instruction. Then a posttest was given. On the basis of this brief description, state the general research question. Which of the ways of matching Ss do you think are especially important to the research? Why? What other ways of matching do you think you might have used had this been your study? Give the schematic for the design.

2. J. T. Crow & J. R. Quigley (1985. A semantic field approach to passive vocabulary acquisition for reading comprehension. *TESOL Quarterly, 19,* 3, 497-514.) compared the effectiveness of an ordinary method of teaching vocabulary (with lists, derivations, matching exercises, multiple-choice, word substitutions in paragraphs, word puzzles) with a semantic-field approach. In this approach, a vocabulary word in context is identified with a key word and four other related words. For example, *rage* in a text would be given the key word

anger and four related words (*fury, ire, wrath, indignation*). Students had practice with activities such as picking out an unrelated word in a list of possible related words, substituting key words for target words, and so forth. Half of the words presented in the semantic-field condition were randomly selected and presented in the traditional method. In the study 42 *S*s were assigned to four sections of a class. Two of these sections became group 1, and two became group 2. A pretest was given to all *S*s at the beginning of the course. Group 2 classes were assigned to the experimental condition and group 1 classes to the traditional method. After instruction, the first posttest was given. Next the treatments were switched so that group 2 classes became the traditional group and group 1 classes the experimental group. Following instruction a second posttest was given. Two additional follow-up tests were given without intervening instruction using either method. From this brief description, state the general research question. Does this study qualify as a true experimental design? If not, how close does it approach the "ideal"? Draw a schematic representation of the design.

3. T. Robb, S. Ross & I. Shortreed (1986. Salience of feedback on error and its effect on EFL writing quality. *TESOL Quarterly, 20,* 1, 83-93.) One hundred thirty-four Japanese college freshmen were assigned alphabetically to four sections of English composition. A cloze test on the first day of class showed no differences among the four sections, but an initial in-class composition did show differences which were statistically controlled for in the final analysis. All sections received exactly the same in-class instruction. All *S*s were required to revise their weekly homework compositions on the basis of feedback they received from their instructors. There were four feedback techniques: (1) complete correction, (2) coded feedback (with a code sheet guide), (3) yellow highlighting of errors, and (4) listing the number of errors per line (*S*s had to find the errors). The compositions were graded on 19 different features which were then collapsed into 7 categories. Since no meaningful differences were found for the feedback treatments, the authors speculate that perhaps teachers spend too much time worrying about composition correction. From this brief description, sketch a schematic representation of the design. How would you classify the design type? Does the study have random assignment of *S*s? If this were your study, what other feedback techniques might you test?

4. B. Tomlinson (1986. Characters are coauthors. *Written Communication, 3,* 4, 421-448.) collected many examples of a prominent metaphorical story that novelists use to discuss the roles played by their characters in their composing processes. Authors talk about their characters coming alive, doing things the author didn't expect, suggesting what they want to say or do, wanting to take over the writing process, making evaluative comments, and so forth. The author gives many examples drawn from a review of over 2,000 published literary interviews and suggests that these are interesting metaphorical data that show how novelists *represent* their composing processes. If you had similar data and wanted to share the results with others, but your field did not accept examples alone as evidence for speculation, what might you do? Can you think of any way that you could redesign this study for another audience?

5. L. B. Jones & L. K. Jones (1985. Discourse functions of five English sentence types. *Word, 36,* 1, 1-22.) discuss the function of clefts, pseudo-clefts and rhet-

orical questions. They claim (on the basis of examples from written text) that all three serve the same basic function of highlighting the theme. Here are some examples:

Pseudo-clefts
What *X* liked
What *X* finally meant   (show theme)
What I am going to discuss
What I am going to do here

What was especially shocking was
What I like is   (show theme + emotive state
What is needed is   or right/wrong judgment)
What can/should be done is

Clefts
It is evidently a universal that   (show theme + discount
It is sheer conceit that   value judgment)

It is in the course of *X* that
It was *X* who   (show theme and assigned focus
It was a coincidence that   to crucial item related to theme)
It was not *X*, but *Y* that

Rhetorical Questions
How important is *X*?   (show theme for a few sentences)
The question is why/what/etc.

Assume that you wanted to validate this information. You have the Brown corpus so you can make a computer search. What is your research question? What is the research design?

In addition to making claims about the function of clefts, pseudo-clefts, and rhetorical questions, the authors also discuss extraposed sentences and sentential adverbs. The authors believe the function of these two structures is to mark author comments. They give examples to show that these structures appear in remarks, asides, and footnotes. Examples of these two forms are:

Extraposition
It should have been obvious that...but
It is clear that *X* is
It is unclear whether
It is conceivable that
It is astonishing to find that

Sentential Adverbs
Ironically, *X* is
Interestingly, *X* is
Incidentally, *X* is

How might you test this claim regarding the function and location of extraposition and sentential adverbs? Draw a design box for the study. Which of these two functions (author comments or theme identification) would you rather investigate? If you found the claims to be correct, which would be most useful in your language teaching?

References

Campbell, D. T. & Stanley, J. C. 1963. *Experimental and Quasi-experimental Designs for Research.* Washington, DC: AERA.

Carterette, E. C. and Jones, M. H. 1974. *Informal Speech.* Berkeley, CA: University of California Press.

Francis, W. N. and Kucera, H. 1979 (revised and amplified). *Standard Sample of Present-Day American English* (the Brown corpus). Providence, RI: Brown University.

New York Times. 1974. *The White House Transcripts.* New York, NY: Bantam Books.

Chapter 4

Writing the Research Proposal
and Report

- *Variation in formats*
- *Organizing the proposal/report*
  Introduction--related research, research question(s).
  Method--subjects, procedures, analysis
  Results and discussion
  Front and back matter--title page, abstract, references, appendices

Variation in Formats

Writing a plan for the research is the first chance we have to put all the pieces together. It can serve as a rough draft of the final research report. Therefore, you can save time and effort if you use the same format for the proposal as you will ultimately use in the final report.

The research proposal will answer the questions that any critic might ask when you first say that you have a question or questions that you want to address:

What is/are the research question(s)?
What has already been done to answer the question(s)?
What evidence do you expect to gather to answer the question(s)?
What are the variables in the study and how are they defined?
Where or from what *S*s (or texts or objects) do you expect to gather the evidence?
How do you expect to collect the data?
How will you analyze the data you collect?
What do you expect the results to be?
Exactly how will the results you obtain address the question?
What wider relevance (or restricted relevance) does the study have?
Are there any suggestions for further research?
Where can the related literature be found?
If new materials, tests, or instruments are proposed, what does a sample look like?
If funding is sought, what are your qualifications (your curriculum vitae)?
Timetable for the research
Budget for the research

This list looks formidable. Whether you will need to answer every question depends on the purpose for which you prepare the proposal. However, even if you don't write out an answer to each question, you should consider all questions carefully. For example, you may not apply for funding and the budget may not need to be specified. That does not mean you shouldn't think about it in preparing your plan.

If you prepare the proposal for anyone other than yourself, the first thing to do is to inquire whether there is a set format that you should follow. Grant agencies use forms that vary in detail. For example, a Guggenheim grant asks for no more than three double-spaced pages outlining the research plan. NSF (National Science Foundation) grants typically ask for a complete and detailed proposal. You can check with your university or library to find out where information on grants is available. Special grants (e.g., Woodrow Wilson grants, Fulbright research grants) may be available for graduate students.

Your department, if it is like ours, may give graduate students a detailed outline for thesis and dissertation proposals. You may be required to give not only an extensive description of the study but a list of relevant course work and a detailed timetable for completion of the project. Whether the format is open or extremely detailed, the same questions will need to be answered.

If your proposal is to be submitted in one of the more common formats such as the APA (American Psychological Association) format, the MLA (Modern Language Association) format, or the Chicago style sheet, computers can be very helpful. Nota Bene, and other personal computer software programs, offer you a choice of many of these formats. In addition, most universities have mainframe programs where a special software program formats the text in exactly the style required by the university. Once you become acquainted with such programs, they are invaluable--they make research more feasible by saving you time and money.

◇◇

Practice 4.1

1. Obtain instructions for writing a proposal from your department, university, or grant agency. Look at the instructions. How similar is the format to that given in this chapter? In what order do questions (those that must be answered in all research projects) need to be presented?

2. Check the range of computer software (and hardware) available for report writing and for data analysis. In your study group, evaluate the software avail-

able for your use. Which programs are best for your word processing needs?
Do these programs also offer possibilities for data analysis?

_____
_____
_____
_____
_____

◇◇

Organizing the Proposal/Report

Introduction

Typically, proposals and research reports begin with a short introduction. In
most research formats, the introduction is not labeled as such. Rather, the writer
begins with a brief statement that shows the question is timely and of importance.
Because novice researchers sometimes find it difficult to break the "writer's
block," it is worthwhile to pay attention to the almost formulaic phrasing of these
opening sentences. You may not want to use them yourself, but they are always
available to get you started.

> *Recent research has suggested xxx. Such (research, work, an interpreta-
> tion) has many strengths but...*

> *The issue of xxx is one which has puzzled researchers for many years. Re-
> cent work, however, has offered interesting ways in which we might ap-
> proach this issue.*

> *A number of proposals have been made in regard to xxx.*

> *Contemporary research into the nature of xxx emphasizes the role of xxx
> factors. A large part of this research has been based on the idea... However,
> in spite of the diversity/agreement of..., exactly how we might xxx is not well
> defined.*

> *The notion of xxx commands a central position in (theory, research, in-
> struction). While..., there is considerable controversy regarding...*

> *One of the most hotly debated topics in xxx has been the significance of...*

> *Researchers and teachers have been interested in X and Y throughout the
> twentieth century, but only recently have...*

Although xxx has always been recognized, scientific interest in this topic has developed slowly/rapidly over the past x years.

xxx and yyy are, for the (applied linguist, educational psychologist, language teacher), two of the most interesting facets of...

After the opening lines, the researcher provides a brief review of the most relevant research reports on the question. At the end of the review, it should not only be clear why the question is "interesting," but also why previous research has failed to answer the broad research question (e.g., not enough research to answer the broad research question; the research was somehow flawed; the research involved Ss that differ from those you wish to select; the procedures you wish to use will overcome previous threats to validity; and so forth).

Near the end of the introduction, the research questions are stated. Interestingly, some review committees (whether grant committees or department committees) as well as some journals prefer that the research question *not* be stated in the null form. The reason is, we believe, stylistic. Be sure to check with your advisor (or look at past issues of the journal) before deciding on the precise form of the research question. Operational definitions of terms may also be given here. And, at this point, the researcher may also place disclaimers to show limitations on the scope of the research.

If you are preparing a proposal for a thesis or dissertation, it is likely that the introductory section will be extensive. Typically, committees expect that you will review *all* the background studies in the research area as evidence that you are thoroughly prepared to undertake the study. This review may form a chapter of your final document. In rewriting the document as a journal article, only the research most directly relevant to the study would be used. Thesis proposals often give much more documentation to the importance of the study, the original contribution the study will make to the field, and its relevance to theory or practice. Again, this is evidence that the author is qualified to undertake the research. In preparing a journal article on this research, the author, with a few brief sentences, can make the connection between research and theory for readers.

Practice 4.2

1. Select one of the research articles you reviewed for the exercises in the previous chapters. Outline the introduction section for this study. Where are the research questions posed? How detailed is the introduction? How extensive is the literature review? Where are the research questions posed? Are formal hypotheses stated for the questions? Is there a "limitations to this study" section in the introduction? Are operational definitions given for the key terms in the research?

_____

_____

_____

_____
_____
_____

2. Compare the results in your study group across all the articles surveyed. How much variability is shown across the studies? How might you account for this variability?

_____
_____
_____
_____
_____
_____

◇◇◇

Method

The introduction tells us *what* the study is about. The method section tells us *how* the study will be carried out. The method section will, of course, vary according to the type of study. Typically, though, it begins with a section describing the data source--the "unit of observation" (the Ss and their characteristics, or the schools/classes and their characteristics, or the text classifications and characteristics, or the classes and characteristics of objects from which the data are drawn).

Subjects

The description of the data source should be as complete and precise as possible. In journal articles, we do not expect that every detail will be mentioned--journals do not have that kind of space nor do readers want to know every tiny detail. We do, however, expect that details will be given for variables that are important to the study. The major criteria in evaluating these descriptions are precision *and* replicability. When research is replicated, it is not unusual to consult the original author for further details. However, readers of articles also evaluate descriptions using these criteria. If the descriptions do not allow replication, then in some way they are not precise enough to allow the reader to interpret the results. As an example, consider each of the following fictitious descriptions. Is sufficient information given so that replication and/or interpretation of results would be possible?

> Subjects
> *Thirty native speakers and 30 nonnative speakers of Spanish will serve as subjects for this study. The nonnative speakers are enrolled in an advanced Spanish conversation class at Houston Community Adult School. The nonnatives have English as a first language. Three of these have studied other foreign languages in addition to Spanish.*

Comments on description of data source:

This description of *Ss* is complete in terms of information on number of subjects and their first language. While we know they are enrolled in an "advanced" Spanish class, we do not know much about how fluent they are in Spanish. We need an operational definition of "advanced" from the author. Other demographic data (e.g., age, sex, travel to Spanish-speaking countries) might be needed, depending on the research question.

Texts
The texts for this study are 30 200-word samples randomly selected from five short stories by American authors. The short stories appear in EFL: Vol 8, a reading textbook for advanced EFL students.

Comments on description of data source:
We do not know how the random selection was carried out. For a detailed description of random sampling procedures using a table of random numbers, you might consult Shavelson (1988, pages 10-11). We do not know how representative these stories are of American short stories. We do not know if the stories are original or were adapted (simplified). We do not know whether the sample size is sufficiently large to contain examples of the variables being studied. Whether these are important issues could only be determined by reading the remainder of the article.

Practice 4.3

1. Comment on the following descriptions.

Classes
The classes selected for this study include five fourth-grade bilingual classrooms located in a lower middle-class area where little residential mobility has been noted. The control classrooms are five fourth-grade bilingual classrooms located in a similar area where high residential mobility is the norm. Questionnaire interviews will be conducted with parents to obtain permission for the children to participate in the study. These interviews, conducted in the home language, will solicit further information on parents' education, employment, and length of residence as a check on school equivalence for the study. Other questions will tap data relevant to the research questions.

Comments on description of data source: _____
_____
_____
_____
_____

Speeches
Transcripts of presidential nomination speeches and nomination acceptance speeches given from 1920 to 1988 were obtained from published documents

(New York Times; Vital Speeches of the Day, 1971; and Los Angeles Times). These transcripts comprised the data base of the study.

Comments on description of data source:

_____
_____
_____
_____

◇◇◇◇◇◇◇◇◇◇◇◇◇◇◇◇◇◇◇◇◇◇◇◇◇◇◇◇◇◇◇◇◇◇◇◇

Whether the data sources are people, texts, classes, or whatever, permission must be obtained to use the data. The grant agency or your department or institution may have set forms to use as models in securing this permission. If for any reason you find no such formal requirements, you should still get written clearance to protect yourself as well as your *S*s.

No matter how willing your *S*s may be to have themselves identified by name in your research project, always assign pseudonyms, initials, or random identification numbers.

Sometimes it is crucial to a study that absolutely natural data be acquired. Many researchers feel the data will be compromised if prior permission is sought. Your department, grant agency, or institution may not allow you to collect data unless you secure permission to use the data before they have been collected. Some institutions will allow use of data when permission is sought after data collection. Be sure to check before collecting data.

◇◇◇◇◇◇◇◇◇◇◇◇◇◇◇◇◇◇◇◇◇◇◇◇◇◇◇◇◇◇◇◇◇◇◇◇

Practice 4.4

1. In your study group, collect examples of clearance forms. How similar are the forms? Discuss the ethics of prior vs. delayed permission requests with members of your study group. What consensus can your reach?

_____
_____
_____
_____

2. Critique the "Subjects" part of the article you chose to review on page 110. How precise is the description? Could you select equivalent *S*s (or texts or objects) based on the description?_____

_____
_____
_____

◇◇◇◇◇◇◇◇◇◇◇◇◇◇◇◇◇◇◇◇◇◇◇◇◇◇◇◇◇◇◇◇◇◇◇◇

Procedures

The next part of the method section typically contains a description of procedures. Some journals and research reports have separate sections to describe materials and procedures while others combine these into one section--procedures. If you combine them in one section, it is still customary to have headings for each within the section.

It is important that the materials (and, where relevant, any special equipment) and the procedures be described in enough detail that anyone could easily replicate the study. Consider the following description of materials:

> There are two versions of the test, A and B, each with two sections. The task-based section uses pictures and/or short instructions to elicit talk; the imitation section includes 10 sentences ranging from 2 to 12 words which students hear and repeat. Schematically, the forms are as follows:
>
> Form 1: Tasks A, Imitation A
> Form 2: Tasks B, Imitation B
> Form 3: Imitation A, Tasks A
> Form 4: Imitation B, Tasks B
>
> The order of presentation of the sections was varied to control for possible ordering effects; the two versions were created so that one could be used as a posttest.
>
> The task section includes a "warm-up" short-answer section plus five major tasks: description, narrative, process (giving directions), opinion, and comparison-contrast. Tasks were chosen on the basis of whether or not they fulfilled certain criteria: (a) their "authenticity" or naturalness--whether they were perceived as representing the kinds of speaking activities in which students engage in the university environment, as well as in everyday life; (b) their match with the rhetorical modes taught in our courses (even though the emphasis in these courses is on writing in these modes); and (c) their match with the kinds of speaking activities that take place in our courses, and thus their ability to serve as a basis for measurement of achievement. (Copies of the tests appear in appendix A.)

Comments on replicability:
Materials are replicable because tests are in the appendix. The order of administration of test sections is replicable. We do not know how the actual administration was carried out. This might not be important for interpretation but, if we wished to replicate the study, we would contact the author for precise procedure directions.

In proposal writing, complete copies of materials may be needed. In the final report, since journals do not always have space for a complete copy of the materials, you may only be able to give a few examples and either place the materials in the appendix or note where researchers can obtain a copy of the materials. Similarly, detailed instructions to Ss may be placed in the procedures section in a proposal and then, in the final report, simply summarized or placed in an appendix.

Practice 4.5

1. Evaluate the following fictitious example:

> *Participating Ss assembled in a quiet room and writing materials were given them. In session 1, participants in group A read instructions (see appendix A) to write an essay on the topic "The values of society are reflected in its popular music." A time limit of one hour was announced but no further instructions were given. Participants in group B read instructions to write an essay asking neighborhood residents to support a student project to convert a dilapidated house into a center for foreign students, and the time limit of one hour was announced. In session 2, participants assembled in the same room and were administered a concrete/abstract word-association test and the Simms role-taking task.*

Comments on replicability: _____

_____

_____

_____

_____

You may wonder about the emphasis on replicability. It is true that our field, perhaps, is unusual in that few replication studies are done. In other fields, the reverse is usually true. Once a finding is observed, the same researcher, and perhaps others, carries out replication studies to see whether the findings will be upheld. These studies may shift certain variables in the study or try a wider multimethod approach to the study. It is assumed that if a finding is important, then it is important to replicate the study to be sure of the stability of the finding. We have emphasized that we carry out research with the expectation of making an original contribution to the field. Replication studies, however, should be the meat of much of our work. Perhaps one reason for the present state of affairs is the mistaken assumption that findings can be generalized--usually an unwarranted assumption. Another may be the requirement that theses and dissertations make an "original contribution" to the field. Replication may not always fit an examiner's idea of originality. Nevertheless, replication studies should be an important part of our research agenda.

In cases where special equipment must be used, it may be important to include a description of the equipment or a note that the description can be obtained from the author.

If the data are to be coded, the procedures for coding are usually given in this section. For example,

> *Classroom activities will be coded using the attached check sheet (see appendix). Three observers (O_1, O_2, and O_3) will view the videotape records and at five-second intervals check the appropriate activity (e.g., teacher structuring move, teacher questioning move, teacher explication) on the sheet. Interrater reliability will be established as part of the development of the coding instrument. Observers will receive training prior to the study, and the training will be reviewed at two-week intervals throughout the study.*

Comments on coding description:
Coding procedures are clear, given that the check sheet appears in the appendix. We understand that training and review of the training are important to establish consistency in ratings but we do not know how interrater reliability will be measured and what constitutes "established" reliability. These are details that could be obtained from the author.

Practice 4.6

1. Comment on the following description. (The task is that undertaken by Flashner, 1987.)

> *All videotape records have been transcribed and entered in "idea units" form (see Chafe, W., & Danielewicz, J., 1985) in a computer data file. Each of the 5,431 units will be individually coded for mode (oral/written), genre (account, recount, event cast), clause type (the seven linguistic types described above), information (given/new), context (contextualized or decontextualized), data source (English monolingual, fluent bilingual, limited English speaker), lesson unit (four different units), and student I.D. This coding will be accomplished by creating "tables" using the RBASE (Microrim) computer program. Interrater reliability of code assignment will be established.*

Comments on coding description: _____
_____
_____
_____

It may seem obvious that the procedures should allow us to answer our research questions, but it is amazing how often something is forgotten. In preparing a proposal (and, of course, in reading proposals or reports of other researchers), look carefully at the procedure statements and check to see that they match the research questions. If you label each part of the procedure with the number for the question(s) it answers, you will know for certain that the procedures cover all of the questions.

◇◇

Practice 4.7

1. For the article you chose on page 110, critique the materials and procedures part of the method section. Are the descriptions precise enough to allow for replication of the study?

_____
_____
_____
_____
_____

2. Review the research questions posed and annotate the method section to show how each research question will be answered.

_____
_____
_____
_____
_____

◇◇

Analysis

Review boards often comment that the analysis section is the "weak link" of most proposals. This should not be the case if you have clearly stated research questions, have identified your variables appropriately, and have selected and classified the research design. The comparisons that are to be made will be clear; you know whether previous research suggests a directional hypothesis or not. You know the function of each variable in the research. You know whether the data for each variable is nominal, ordinal, or interval (or continuous or noncontinuous). You know whether comparisons are repeated-measures or for independent groups. These are precisely the criteria for selecting the appropriate method of data analysis.

The selection of the appropriate method of data analysis will be presented in the following chapters. At this point, however, you have already acquired the relevant information you will need for determining this selection.

In the final report, this analysis section will be embedded in the results section. That is, in the proposal, the analysis section lists the comparisons to be made and the appropriate statistics to do the comparison. In the final report, all the _wills_ are changed to past tense: that is, "An ANOVA will be used to determine ..." becomes "An ANOVA was used to determine..." However, because of the importance of the results, this section will form a new section of the final report. Rather than part of "Method," it is now "Results."

Results and Discussion

Again, it is possible that the results and discussion section may actually be two different sections. If the results section is especially long, it may be easier to present all the results of the analyses in one section and then explain and discuss the results in a separate section. However, if the research has not required comparisons of many different types (and all the accompanying tables), then the two can be compressed in one section. Some journals, because of lack of space, ask that the sections be shortened and combined.

When you are writing a proposal, these sections cannot be completed. It may be possible, on the basis of the proposed analysis, to speculate on possible outcomes and interpret what various findings would mean if they were obtained. This is good preparation for writing the final report. However, many grant agencies and university faculty committees believe that this should be left until results are in since speculation ahead of time may lead to bias in interpretation. That is, if you've already decided what the results (should they confirm or should they disconfirm your hypotheses) mean, you may not be able to interpret accurately the results that do obtain.

There are other differences between a proposal and the final report. In a final report, the researcher has had the opportunity to think about other ways the general research question might be addressed. Particularly in dissertations and theses, researchers discuss other possible research projects that might contribute to answering the general question. In fact, the discussion sections of dissertations are good places to look for research ideas.

Front and Back Matter

In addition to the body, the research reports must include material that publishers call front matter (usually, a title page and abstract) and back matter (references, appendices).

Title Page. Most proposals as well as final reports have a title page. The full title is given (a shorter title may be used as a running title at the top or bottom of the proposal itself). The researcher's name and affiliation is given on a separate line. If a date is relevant, this may also be given. Frequently, a statement appears on the title page to identify the institution or organization to which the proposal is being submitted.

The title should have three characteristics: it should be brief, it should be clear, and it should sell the project to the reader. Look at the following examples.

A description of the similarity of gender encoding errors of French and Spanish students for quantifiers, adjectives, and pronouns and the form and placement of object pronouns

Shorter version: *French and Spanish gender: similarities in errors of foreign language students.*

An investigatory analysis of several test approaches to discover which consistently measure language dominance in bilinguals

Shorter title: *Testing language dominance*

The title should be clear. The TESOL organization advises those who wish to submit papers to the conference to remember that the title will often be the only criterion a conference goer uses to decide which sessions to attend. Similarly, it may be the only criterion a reader will use to decide whether or not to read an article or a grant agency to decide whether or not to consider your proposal. On the other hand, the title does not necessarily have to be dull. It can interest the reader as well.

Each of the following titles are clear and short. Which would you rather read (or which would you select for a conference paper)?

The unitary language factor hypothesis in light of recent developments of IRT

A final nail in the unitary language factor coffin: recent developments in IRT

Some fields have had a period where clever titles (e.g., child sayings such as "Wait for Me, Roller Skate" for a study on directives, or puns such as "The Chicago Which Hunt" for a book containing papers on relative clause formation) were common. Can you imagine how difficult it would be to do a literature search with key words from such titles? If you are tempted to use a clever title, think first about how colleagues with similar interests will find your work. Second, if you are a graduate student, it might be wise to consult with your department to get their approval of titles prior to submitting your proposal.

Most dissertations and theses use the following general order for the rest of the front matter: dedication, table of contents, table of figures, table of tables, acknowledgment page, CV, and the abstract. Notice that this particular dissertation form places the CV in the front matter while most grant proposals require that it be placed in the back matter.

Abstract. Abstracts are exceedingly difficult to write. The first thing to do is to find out what restrictions there are on the number of words allowed for the abstract. Then, think about the most concise statement of your research question, how to identify the Ss and procedures as briefly as possible, how to summarize the findings, and also show the relevance of the study.

Much information, of course, will not appear in the abstract. The reader (if the abstract is interesting) will turn to the article to fir... .his information. If the article is organized in the usual format, the information will be easy to find. That's one of many reasons why journals adopt a research format and ask contributors to use it.

Consider the following abstract:

C. Haas & J. R. Hayes. 1986. What did I just say? Reading problems in writing with the machine. Research in the Teaching of English, 20, 1, 22-35. Sixteen computer-writers were informally interviewed about how they used the computer for writing tasks. While the writers felt that the computer was useful for their writing tasks, they also indicated that writing with the computer had disadvantages. They reported difficulty in locating information, detecting errors, and difficulty in reading the texts critically. Three experimental studies were conducted to compare the performance of college students reading texts displayed on a computer terminal screen and on a printed hard copy. Findings indicate that visual/spatial factors influence locational recall, information retrieval, and appropriate reordering of text. Copyright 1986 by the National Council of Teachers of English. Reprinted by permission.

Comments on information missing in the abstract--information that you would need to look for in reading the article: In what sections of the article would you expect to find each piece of missing information?

1. Operational definition of terms (end of Introduction)
2. Information on the 16 Ss. Are the Ss the same in the informal interview and in the three experimental studies? (Introduction and Method section, Subject heading)
3. Research design (Introduction and Method, Procedures heading)
4. Statistical procedures (Results section)
5. Software program used (Introduction and Method, Procedures heading)
6. Types of writing assignments (Introduction and Method, Procedures heading)

Comments on the title: Catchy title, informative.

Practice 4.8

1. Comment on the following abstract:

C. Daiute. 1986. Physical and cognitive factors in revising: insights from studies with computers. Research in the Teaching of English, 20, 141-159. This article argues that writing involves the complex interaction of parallel processes, in this case physical and cognitive processes. Phase one of this study indicates that the writing instru-

ment can affect the writing process. Junior high students using a computer word processor corrected more errors when they used the word processor than when they used pen. The computer word processor, however, was not used for more expanded revising activities. Phase two of the study contrasted the physical aids of the computer word processor with the direct cognitive aid of a <u>revision prompt program</u>. Ss who used the prompt program revised the drafts more closely and extensively than the students who used only the word processing program.

What information is missing in the abstract. Where would you expect to find the information in the article?

<u>#students ; name of program</u>

Comments on the title:

◇◇

Abstracts written for proposals differ from those written for journal articles. For one thing, they are usually longer. The abstract of a proposal will stress the possible outcomes of the project while an abstract for a journal will emphasize final findings.

Abstracts written for conference presentations may also differ from those of journals. Like a proposal abstract, they must "sell" the research to a review board. Writing such proposals is an art (or does it develop with practice?). It is always a good idea, when submitting an abstract for a conference or to a grant agency, to ask someone with experience to review your efforts and give you advice.

Journal abstracts are written for readers perhaps even more than they are for a review board. Most professionals have little time to read every article in journals relevant to their fields. Instead, they scan titles and from these select those that look promising. They read the abstract as a summary of the project. If the abstract promises important information relevant to their interests, then they will take the time to read the whole report. Well-written abstracts are extremely helpful to the profession.

References. At the end of the body of the document, you will find a list of references that the author has consulted. In a research proposal, and particularly for dissertations and theses, these reference lists may be extremely broad. They may even be annotated and grouped around topic areas. Such references demonstrate that the researcher is well prepared to carry out the research. In journal articles and most reports, the list will include *only* those references actually cited in the article. The actual format used for references should be consistent. Journals (and most university departments) specify the format to be used. It is extremely helpful if the references in the proposal and those in the final report can be prepared in exactly the same form.

Appendices. Appendices may be used to give information that, because of length, is difficult to incorporate into running text. Typically, these include descriptions of materials, measurement instruments, and special equipment when these are original and published descriptions are not available to the reader. They may also give additional information on procedures or information on the status of *S*s or schools used in the research. They almost always contain a sample release form used to get permission from *S*s, schools, parents, or authors to use the data source.

In addition to these general appendices, you may decide to place all the tables and/or all the figures in an appendix. Conventions such as "Insert Table 1 here" are used to mark the point at which the author intends the tables or figures to be read.

In some cases, you may find a data appendix. More likely the text will include a note that complete copies of the data can be obtained from the author, the agency, the school district, or the university. The appendix may, however, show sample data and the notation used in coding the data. Do not be surprised if an editor decides to cut many of your appendices for lack of space.

Indices are seldom required unless the report or dissertation is to be published in book form. This can be a horrendous or an easy task depending on whether or not you have access to a computer program that allows you to create automatic indices. Budgets, time tables, and researcher CVs are required for many proposals. If they are required, the best place to put them is in a special appendix. Appendices can also include details on availability, cost, and ordering of computer programs, particularly if a program is exotic or written especially for the study itself.

Practice 4.9

1. For the article you selected to review on page 110, check the reference section. What format was used for the references? Are the references complete and is the form consistent?

_____

_____

_____

_____

2. Critique the abstract of the article. Is it an informative summary of the article? If the author were allowed another 25 words, what additional information should be included?

_____
_____
_____
_____

◇◇

Conclusion for Part I

This concludes part I, the section of this book which was written to help you plan a research project. We have defined research questions, discussed procedures for gathering data in terms of design, and the possibile threats to internal and external validity associated with designs. Once you have completed the following practice, you will have completed the basics needed to write a project proposal. In part II, we will turn to initial ways of describing the data, the findings that are offered as evidence related to the research questions.

◇◇

Practice 4.10

1. Select one of your own research questions and carry out each of the following activities.

a. Select a title for one of your own research questions. Ask members of your study group to critique it. What suggestions did they make for improvement?

b. Write a few opening sentences for the research proposal (or report). If necessary, look at the samples given in this chapter on page 109.

c. Describe the data source (*Ss*, texts, or whatever) and the techniques used for data sampling.

d. Write a description of materials to be used in the study. Ask your study group members to critique the description for replicability.

e. Write out a procedures statement. Again, ask your study group members to critique the statement for you in terms of clarity and replicability.

f. Write an abstract for the research proposal. Ask members of your study group to critique it. What changes did they recommend? Did you agree? Why (not)?

g. Describe the requirements regarding back matter (e.g., appendices, budgets, CVs) and front matter (e.g., title, abstract, table of contents) for your institution.

h. Draw a box diagram for your study in the space provided. Then fill in as many items as possible in the following chart. (You are not yet prepared to fill in the entire chart.)

Research hypothesis?	_____
Significance level?	_____
1- or 2-tailed?	_____
Design	
Dependent Variable(s)?	_____
Measurement?	_____
Independent Variable(s)?	_____
Measurement?	_____
Independent or Repeated Measures?	_____
Other Features?	_____
Statistical Procedure?	_____

◇◇◇◇◇◇◇◇◇◇◇◇◇◇◇◇◇◇◇◇◇◇◇◇◇◇◇◇◇◇◇◇◇◇◇

Activities

1. S. Jacoby (1987. References to other researchers in literary research articles. *English Language Research Journal, 1*, University of Birmingham, Birmingham, England) investigated the ways in which researchers showed themselves to be the "humble receivers of tradition" and also "irreverent pioneers" who argue for the originality and rightness of their research. Being a receiver of tradition means that researchers build on the work of those who have gone before them. Researchers must show how their work relates to this tradition. Previous work is cited and traditional arguments credited. At the same time, as the irreverent pioneer, the writer must also argue against tradition, claiming new territory and new directions for research so as to establish the originality of his or her research. Jacoby's article considers how *literary* researchers accomplish this task. Outline a research project which would investigate this same issue using research articles from *applied linguistics* rather than literary research. (What other "English for special purposes" research topics can you propose that relate to how researchers accomplish report writing?)

2. J. K. Burgoon & J. L. Hale (1988. Nonverbal expectancy violations: elaboration and application to immediacy behaviors. *Communication Monographs, 55*, 58-79.) carried out a study to test the notion that the road to success lies in conformity to social norms. They found there are times when violation of norms has a favorable as opposed to a detrimental consequence. The introductory section of this article is actually longer than the method, results, and discussion. This often happens in research articles. Read the article and explain why this is so for this study.

3. M. Tarantino (1988. Italian in-field EST users self-assess their macro- and microlevel needs: a case study. *English for Special Purposes, 7*, 33-53.) gathered information on the linguistic problems of learners who use English in their profession (professors and researchers in different fields of physics, chemistry, and computer science, all of whom were collaborating in international projects). The questionnaire had three aims: (1) to classify the Ss on demographic variables, (2) to obtain information on experience which may have influenced language proficiency, and (3) to investigate their perceived competence in all skills in relation to their EST (English for science and technology) needs. Examine the questionnaire given in the appendix, grouping the items according to these goals. How might one set up a replication study for persons enrolling in an EST course (students who hope to become professors or researchers on such projects)? What other questions might you want to ask?

4. C. Kessler & M. E. Quinn (1987. Language minority children's linguistic and cognitive creativity. *Journal of Multilingual and Multicultural Development, 8*, 1 & 2, 173-186.) compared the performance of children in two intact classrooms: one group of monolingual and one group of bilingual sixth graders. The bilingual children outperformed the monolingual children in the quality of hypotheses they generated in problem-solving tasks. Their use of complex metaphoric language was also rated higher. Review the sections on Subjects, Procedures, and Measures. Given the descriptions, could you replicate the study with other groups of monolingual and bilingual children? If you carried out a replication, what part(s) of the study would you keep and which would you change? Why?

5. J. Lallerman (1987. A relation between acculturation and second-language acquisition in the classroom: a study of Turkish immigrant children born in the Netherlands. *Journal of Multilingual and Multicultural Development, 8*, 5, 409-431.) rank-ordered children on their acquisition of Dutch and also on acculturation in order to test the relationship hypothesized by Schumann. Since the rank order assignment of each child on acculturation and on acquisition of Dutch is based on several measures, the section on data collection is relatively long. Read through the descriptions of the measures and the method of combining several measures to achieve the rank order on each variable. Based on the descriptions, could you replicate this study with another immigrant group? What parts of the study would remain unchanged in the replication study and what parts would you elect to change? Why?

6. B. A. Lewin (1987. Attitudinal aspects of immigrants' choice of home language. *Journal of Multilingual and Multicultural Development, 8*, 4, 361-378.) measured the attitudes of English-speaking immigrants in Israel in relation to

their choice of L1 or L2 for communication with their Israeli-born children. Since this research was conducted with a 20-parent sample, the researcher is careful to mention this as a limitation of the study. Note the limitations the author points out and consider how you might replicate this study to overcome the limitations. Notice the placement of the limitations section in the report. Would you argue for placing it before the method section or in the conclusion? Why?

7. A. Doyle, J. Beaudet, & F. Aboud (1988. Developmental patterns in the flexibility of children's ethnic attitudes. *Journal of Cross-cultural Psychology, 19,* 1, 3-18.) were faced with the problem of finding measures appropriate for testing ethnic attitudes of young children (kindergarten to sixth grade). Read the descriptions of the procedures used with the Evaluative Attribution Task (which was created for this study based on the Preschool Racial Attitudes Measure II and the Sex Role Learning Inventory), the Crandall Social Desirability Scale, and Aboud's Ethnic Constancy Test. Would these be appropriate procedures if you replicated the study with another group of children? What parts of the study would you keep and which might you change in a replication study? Why?

8. The journal *English World-Wide* publishes summaries of theses on varieties of English in their fall issue each year. Read the abstracts provided in the 1987 issue (*8,* 2, 277-299). The abstracts are very brief. Select one abstract and list missing information and where you would expect to find it in the actual thesis,

9. *Dissertation Abstracts* has several headings related to applied linguistics. Check the most recent issue and review one abstract that relates to your own research interests. The abstracts, here, are longer and so give the reader more information. What information do you still need to find in the dissertation? Where in the dissertation do you expect to find the information?

References

Chafe, W. & Danielewicz, J. 1985. Properties of spoken and written language. In R. Horowitz and S. J. Samuels (Eds.). *Comprehending Oral and Written Language.* New York, NY: Academic Press.

Flashner, V. 1987. An exploration of linguistic dichotomies and genres in the classroom language of native and nonnative English-speaking children. Unpublished doctoral dissertation, Applied Linguistics, UCLA.

Shavelson, R. J. 1988. *Statistical Reasoning for the Behavioral Sciences,* 2nd edition. Needham Heights, MA: Allyn & Bacon.

Vital Speeches of the Day. 1971. New York, NY: The City News Publishing Company.

Part II.   Describing Data

Chapter 5
Coding and Displaying Frequency Data

- *Coding and counting values*
  Frequency--cumulative frequency
  Relative frequency--percent, proportion, cumulative percent
  Rates and ratios
  Coding numerical data
- *Data displays*
  Bar graphs and histograms
  Pie charts
  Frequency polygons and line drawings

Coding and Counting Values

In reading research reports, you will find many ways in which variables have been coded--as T-units, type/token ratios, MLU (an utterance length measurement), test scores, and so forth. Each of these is a simple way of giving numerical value to a variable. These values are seldom, if ever, displayed as a list of numbers. Rather, the values are condensed in some way to make them meaningful. If we want to know how many men and how many women took a particular test, we don't want to see a list of names with an M or an F after each. Rather, we want a total for the frequency of each. If we want to know about flexibility or variety of vocabulary choice in the writing of thirty students, we don't usually want to see a list of student names followed by numbers for total number of words and total number of unique words for each. Names and numbers can't give us information at a glance. We want the information presented in a way that allows us to understand it quickly. In this chapter, we will consider the various ways *frequency* data can be computed and displayed to give us the maximum amount of information in a descriptive display.

Frequency

You will remember that nominal variables tell us how often (how frequently) something occurs. The data are frequencies. In text analysis we are concerned with how often something occurs and with comparing the frequency of occurrence across genres, or in spoken vs. written text, or according to formality register. Imagine that you, like us, have an interest in the language used by children in elementary school classrooms. (Research that is similar to that described in the remainder of this chapter was part of our research agenda at CLEAR--Center for Language Education and Research, a center funded by the Office of Educational Research and Instruction. Many of the questions posed and some of the data samples come from this project. Preliminary findings from the project are presented in Flashner, 1987.) Video and audio recordings in the classroom have yielded a wealth of *oral* language data. The children's written work and journal entries comprise the *written* language data. All the language data--both oral and written--have been transcribed and entered into computer files.

Some of the students in the class are native speakers of English, some are fluent bilinguals (Spanish and English), and some are classified as limited in English proficiency (LEP). Descriptions of numbers of subjects are usually reported as n, where the n stands for the number of Ss. You may, however, sometimes find it shown with an f since that is the symbol for "frequency." The fictitious frequencies for each group are:

Classification	f
English Only	108
Fluent English Proficiency	94
Limited English Proficiency	81

Other frequencies might be used in describing these Ss as well, such as sex, native language, and so forth.

The first thing you might want to discover is just how *much* language--perhaps how many words or clauses or utterances--are produced by the children. The design box can be labeled to show how the frequencies for number of words would be divided for the variables of language classification (of the Ss) and language mode.

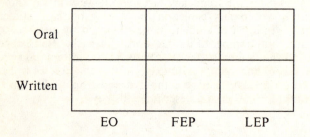

Oral

Written

EO   FEP   LEP

Do you think it might be important to separate the data of boys and girls? If so, we could amend the design to a three-dimensional box to allow for this comparison.

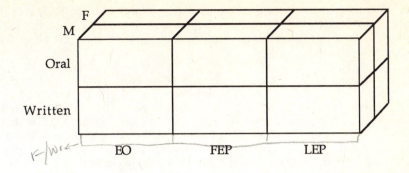

F

M

Oral

Written

r/wrc   EO   FEP   LEP

explain?

The easiest way to count the number of words is to have the computer do the counting. Once the data are entered into the computer, you can ask it to count the number of words by reading the spaces between words. If the data are entered in the computer so that the data source (the *S* and the *S*'s classification) and the mode (written or oral) are tagged, the computer can easily tally the word frequencies for the cells of the above design. The computer could give an automatic reading for the number of clauses if each clause were entered on a separate line and the program can count the number of lines. However, automatic reading is not always possible. When you work with natural language data, you may need to type in and, in addition, code the data before the computer can tally frequencies for you. For example, if you wanted to know how many turns each of the students took in various types of classroom tasks, you would need to code the turns and tasks so that the computer can find and count them. Or, if you wanted to know how many verbs or how many nouns or how many adjectives occurred in the talk of the limited English speakers, you would need to code the data so that the computer can find and count them.

If your research question has to do with the types of clauses children produce, there is no way that the computer can automatically find clause types in the data. For each clause, you would need to enter a clause-type tag and the computer would use the tag to count frequencies for each type. If punctuation marks are used at the ends of utterances, the computer, given program instructions, could give an automatic frequency count for number of utterances. If, however, you wanted a tally of the speech-act function of the sentences or utterances in the data, you would again need to add this information using a tag so that instructions can be given to the computer that will allow it to do the tally.

There are a number of computer programs available to analyze texts. Typically, they provide a word list in alphabetical order and a concordance. Each entry for a specified word is displayed, surrounded by the words of the context in which it occurred (along with information as to where in the text the word appeared). The programs also provide various statistics related to frequency of occurrence. If you

concordance —

use a computer concordance program such as WordCruncher (1988) or the Oxford Concordance Program (1980), much information can be found and tallied with little difficulty. Certain kinds of information, however, may not be so easily matched and retrieved.

If there is a way *not* to code, much time will be saved. If you wanted to count the number of turns and the transcript has been entered with the speaker's name at the beginning of each utterance, you will not need to code turns because the computer can count the number of times each person's name appears in the transcript. If you were doing a study of modals, it would be less time-consuming to ask the computer to find and tally the frequency of *can, may, might, will,* and so forth, rather than going through the data and marking each with a modal code and then using the code to pull up the examples.

Once the data are coded, the computer will tally and give you the total number of observations. This total is abbreviated as n. If the total is subdivided into categories, then N is used for the grand total and n is used to denote the number of observations in each category. Some researchers prefer to use the symbols for frequency, f and F, instead.

◇◇

Practice 5.1

1. Assume the computer gave you frequency information for numbers of words and frequency of each clause type for the monolinguals, the fluent bilinguals, and the LEP children in the study on page 130. Precisely what would be shown in each of the cells?

_____

_____

_____

What would this tell you? How useful is such information?

_____

What figures do you feel would be more important? Why? _____

_____

_____

_____

2. If you wanted to do a study of frequency adverbs in the speech and writing of these fourth-grade *S*s, how might you get the computer to do the counting without codes? _Id. the words, into count them_

_____

_____

3. If you had entered natural language data of *S*s and wanted a tally of number of turns for each speaker, how might you exclude names mentioned *during talk* from this count? _____

_____

_____

4. Look at the variables you have identified for your own research questions in previous chapters. Which of these will be coded with frequency counts?

_____

_____

Can the counts be automatically accomplished, or must the data first be coded so that you or the computer can find the instances to be counted?

_____

_____

It hardly makes sense to enter data into the computer if it takes as long or longer than it takes to tally the data by hand. How will you decide whether to do the counts by hand or with the computer?

_____

_____

_____

◇◇◇◇◇◇◇◇◇◇◇◇◇◇◇◇◇◇◇◇◇◇◇◇◇◇◇◇◇◇◇◇◇◇◇◇◇◇◇

Cumulative frequency

Cumulative frequency figures are presented when we wish to show a group of frequencies and the overall contribution of each to a total frequency. For example, imagine that the data base for one instructional unit in Flashner's work contained 1,293 clauses produced by the fourth-grade students. The data might be presented as follows:

Clause Type	Freq (f)	Cum Freq
transitive	587	1293
pred nominative	197	706
pred adjective	155	509
question	86	354
possessive	81	268
locative	74	187
intransitive	64	113
purpose	18	49
existential	13	31
passive	10	18
imperative	8	8

To obtain the cumulative frequency, the data are arranged in order of frequency (the most frequent at the top of the list). The least frequent clause type is imperative with an *f* of 8. The next clause type is passive with an *f* of 10. The cumulative frequency at this point is 18 (8 + 10 as shown in the arrows above). As each clause type is added, the cumulative frequency rises until the grand total *F* (1293) is reached. A formula for cumulative frequency, then, is:

$$cum\ f = \text{successive additions of frequency}$$

◇◇◇◇◇◇◇◇◇◇◇◇◇◇◇◇◇◇◇◇◇◇◇◇◇◇◇◇◇◇◇◇◇◇◇◇◇◇

Practice 5.2

▶1. Show the frequency and cumulative frequencies for clause connectors in a data set containing a total of 490 connectors. The frequencies of each are as follows: *after* 4, *and* 72, *as* 1, *because* 50, *but* 15, *how* 11, *if* 28, *like* 11, *okay* 12, *or* 12, introductory preposition 52, *so* 3, *that* 42, *to* 89, *well* 5, *what* 10, *when* 50, *where* 13, *who* 9, *why* 1.

Connector	f	cum f
to	89	490
and	72	
intr. prep	52	
when	50	
because	50	
that	42	
if	28	
but	15	
where	13	
okay	12	
or	12	
like	11	55
how	11	44
what	10	33
who	9	23
well	5	14
after	4	9
so	3	
as	1	
why	1	

◇◇◇◇◇◇◇◇◇◇◇◇◇◇◇◇◇◇◇◇◇◇◇◇◇◇◇◇◇◇◇◇◇◇◇◇◇◇

If you were interested in the differences in oral and written data, you would be less interested in the overall frequency of these clause connectors than in how the distribution compares in oral and written modes.

Another possibility for study of classroom discourse analysis would be to code the clauses according to what Heath (1986) calls classroom genres--kinds of language patterns shown in school-based behaviors. Flashner used Heath's genre categories for teacher-student interactions and Phillips' (1983) categories for student-student interactions. A brief definition of each is given below.

terrible names! (handwritten)

Term	Definition
label quest	student response to teacher's question for name or attribute (e.g., "What is this called?" "A rubber band.")
meaning quest *definition* (handwritten)	student response to teacher's question re meanings (e.g., "Does anybody know what an interview is?" **"Uhh, when you talk to somebody and ask questions."**)
account	student gives information unknown to hearer or reader (e.g., show-and-tell or a personal diary entry)
event cast	student talks about an act or event in progress or as it will happen
recount	student retells information already known to the listener
student question	student asks for information

Heath believes that label quests, meaning quests, and student questions are the three genres basic to classroom interaction. The other genres, in contrast, are those that require higher order manipulation and integration of information. Thus, it would be possible to group the clauses as having either higher or lower cognitive demand.

Phillips' genres for student-student interaction include the following (among others):

more lousy names! (handwritten)

Term	Definition
argument	student adopts alternative point of view
exposition	student acts like teacher in structuring a conversation (e.g., "Okay, yard slips, how many yard slips are there?")
hypothesis	student offers speculation or suggestion (e.g., "I think the best thing is to take out 'computer.'")
operation	student offers a running commentary on activity

◇◇◇◇◇◇◇◇◇◇◇◇◇◇◇◇◇◇◇◇◇◇◇◇◇◇◇◇◇◇◇◇◇◇◇◇◇

Practice 5.3

Imagine that the total for clauses in Flashner's data set was 1,153. Here are the frequencies for clauses in each of the above genres: *account* 476, *event cast* 348, *label quest* 112, *meaning quest* 11, *recount* 22, *student quest* 18, *argument* 12, *exposition* 17, *hypothesis* 16, *operation* 121.

▶ 1. Prepare a frequency and cumulative frequency table for the data:

Genre	f	cum f

12   23
11   11

2. Total the clauses that reflect Heath's basic interaction and those requiring higher order manipulation or integration of information. Does there seem to be much variability in the frequency of each clause type within each of the two categories? _____
_____
_____
_____

3. In which genre(s) do the children produce the fewest clauses? How would you account for this? _____
_____
_____

4. In which do they produce the most clauses? How do you account for this?
_____
_____

◇◇

Relative Frequency

Percent and Proportion

When you have only a small amount of data, it makes sense to present the raw frequency totals. It is easy to see how important each frequency is relative to the rest of the data. However, when numbers are large and/or when there are many categories, it is often more informative to show the relative frequency of each category as proportion or percent.

$$Proportion = \frac{\text{number of } X}{\text{total}}$$

Imagine that you have entered all the data from the fourth-grade class and tagged the types of clauses used by the children. You wonder how the kinds of clauses children use differ in oral and written modes. Ultimately, you want to know whether the language produced in these two modes shows the same kinds of differences in clause structure as found for adults in other studies. To make these comparisons with previous studies, you might count and display the distribution of the same clause types as those reported in the research on adults. The computer can tally these as raw frequencies, but it can also show you a percent for each clause type in all the written clauses counted. It can do the same thing for the oral language sample. For example, in coding the data for purpose clauses, adverbial clauses, and so forth, the raw frequencies look like this:

Clause Type	Oral	%	Written	%
Complex	44	6.5	151	32.2
Complex/Coordinate	2	.5	4	0.8
Coordinate	27	4.0	16	3.4
Fragment	194	28.0	7	1.5
Simple Finite	352	51.5	257	54.8
Simple Nonfinite	51	7.5	33	7.0
Nonmatrix Subordinate	14	2.0	1	0.3
Total	684	100%	469	100%

$\frac{44}{684} = .064 \times 100 = 6.4$

(Some of the percentages have been rounded to total 100%.) Note that we calculated the total number of oral clauses and then calculated the percent of that total for each clause type (and the same thing for written). You could also compute the percent of oral vs. written clauses for each clause type. The direction depends on the research question. If you want to know how many of the complex clauses in the data appear in written vs. oral data, the number of fragments that occur in written vs. oral data, and so forth, then the second method makes sense. If you want to know about the overall distribution of the clauses within oral data and then within written data, you would select the first method.

Another common use of percent or proportion in second language research is the use of "percent correct in obligatory instances." In such studies, a feature (say, the -s inflection of third person present tense) is to be evaluated for correctness in natural language data (oral or written). Rather than tally the number of -s inflections produced in a piece of text by the learner, the researcher first goes through the text and identifies all the places where the -s inflection would be used by a native speaker of the language. These are the "obligatory instances." Then the S is given a score for the correct uses of -s, expressed as a percent of the total number of obligatory instances in the text. Simple open-ended tallies of features can be changed to closed-group percentages in this way and comparisons can then be drawn across learners or groups of learners. That is, frequencies have been changed to percentages, moving measurement from nominal to continuous data.

Percents and proportions are exactly the same except that percents are presented as whole numbers (e.g., 68%) while proportions are presented as decimals (e.g., .68). It is important to give the reader a feeling for the frequencies as well as the percent or proportion. That is, a figure of 80% could represent 4 instances out of 5 or it could represent 80 out of 100. To overcome this difficulty, you might place the frequency data in the table and add the percent or proportion in parentheses next to each figure. Another, perhaps more common, solution is to present the percent or proportion and then note the n--the total number of observations on which the percent is based.

Cumulative Percent

Just as tables sometimes include a column showing cumulative frequencies, tables may include a column for *cumulative percent*. Cumulative percent is computed in precisely the same way as cumulative frequency.

$$cum\ f = \text{successive additions of frequency}$$

$$cum\ \% = \text{successive addition of percent}$$

We can arrange the data for clauses in the oral mode like this:

Oral Mode

Clause	%	Cum %
Simple Finite	51.5%	100.0%
Fragment	28.0%	48.5%
Simple Nonfinite	7.5%	20.5%
Complex	6.5%	13.0%
Coordinate	4.0%	6.5%
Nonmatrix Subord.	2.0%	2.5%
Complex/Coordinate	0.5%	0.5%

Interpreting Percent

One would think that the interpretation of percent would always be straightforward. Indeed, that is usually the case. However, there are a number of cautions to keep in mind. First, we need to know how large the n size is in addition to knowing the percent. If the data on clause types were subdivided for the three subject levels (EO--English only, FEP--fluent bilinguals, and LEP), the form of the table would change.

```
        oral                          written
       /  |  \                       /  |  \
   EO FEP LEP TOTAL              EO FEP LEP TOTAL
```

It would now be even more important to show raw frequencies as well as proportions if the data were presented in this way (rather than collapsed for all Ss) because the frequencies might be small. You will notice that the total number of clauses for this instruction unit was fairly large to begin with, but when it is divided into frequencies for each group, the n size drops. It is unlikely that equal numbers of clauses would be produced by the children in each of the three groups, but with the small n, the proportions might look very different while the actual raw frequencies might be quite close. For example, there are only 2 complex/coordinate clauses in the oral data. If both were produced by EO children, then the percentages would be 100%, 0%, and 0%. Somehow 100% and 0% seem to differ more than the raw numbers 2 and 0.

There is a second problem in interpreting percents. Notice there were only 14 nonmatrix subordinate clauses in the oral data. If 10 were produced by children in the LEP group, 4 by the EO group, and 0 by the FEP group, the percents would be 71%, 29%, and 0%. This might seem very informative until we remember that the number of EO, LEP, and FEP students is not equal to begin with. If the size of the groups was unequal to begin with, we should not expect equal numbers of clauses from each.

A third problem has to do with the amount of data available for interpretation. If it is the case that children in the LEP group contribute less data to the total data base, should this concern us? That is, if they produced *more* data, is it likely that the *proportion* of clause types in their data would change? This *is* a matter of real concern when we turn to interpretation.

It is also unlikely that the number of clauses produced in written and in oral modes would be exactly the same. Again, this should cause concern. That is, if the number of clauses in each mode were equal, would the proportion of clause types change for each mode? One way to solve this problem would be to select randomly 1,000 clauses from all of the oral data and 1,000 clauses from all of the written data and use these data for the calculations.

We do, of course, want to overcome as many threats to reliability and validity as possible. Equating the sample size and using random selection are usually good ways to do this. However, you can see that equating the number of clauses for each cell of the design might be problematic if we also want to search for infrequent structures. The possible threat to the study (because of unequal ns for Ss or for clauses in the written and oral categories) has to be weighed against the possibility of dealing with the threat means eliminating data you need. To deal with the threat, we are trying to change open-ended frequency data into closed continuous data (for example, the number of purpose clauses in a closed set of 1,000 randomly selected clauses). This conversion may not be warranted, particularly if it endangers the study by deleting the few clauses of certain interesting types that may appear somewhere in the data (but not in the 1,000 randomly selected clauses).

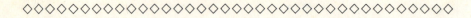

Practice 5.4

▶ 1. Using the percent figures given for the written data on page 137, calculate the cumulative percents and fill in the following table.

Written Mode

Clause	%	Cum %
	54.8	100.0
	32.2	45.2
	7.0	13.0
	3.4	6.0
	1.5	2.6
	0.8	1.1
	0.3	0.3

Rates and Ratios   *what are they? Explain*

Relative frequencies are most often presented as a proportion or percentage of a total. However, sometimes, the frequency is to be compared relative to some number other than the total number of observations. The most common of these comparisons are rates and ratios.

Rate is used to show how often something occurs in large data sets.

Rate = relative frequency per unit

It may not be that what you want to discover is "one in a million," but rather "one in ten" or "one in a hundred." The first thing to consider is the unit, the "per *X*" unit. For example, students whose first language is not English are usually given a language screening test on entering the school system. The students are then classified as English dominant (limited L1 skills), fluent bilingual (equal L1/L2 skills), limited English proficiency (limited L2 skills), or non-English-speaking (no L2 skills). These classifications are used to determine the best curriculum for individual children with differing L1 and L2 skills. The information from such a screening in a large school district might be reported as in the following fictitious data: *why this?*

L1 Group	N	Class	Rate/100 students
Spanish	4,750	EO	23
		Fluent L1/L2	38
		LEP	22
		NEP	17
Korean	2,688	EO	35
		Fluent L1/L2	50
		LEP	3
		NEP	12
Vietnamese	1,200	EO	5
		Fluent L1/L2	53
		LEP	8
		NEP	34

In a smaller school district, of course, a unit of per 100 would not make sense.

Rate might be useful in our fourth-grade study if we were interested in the frequency of clause types that are thought to reflect higher cognitive skills. Hypotheticals (e.g., *if/then, if not/then, unless/then*) and causals (e.g., *because*) are examples of such clause types. Assume the clauses have been tagged in the data so that the computer can tally how often these clauses occur. Do you imagine they might occur "once per 10 clauses?" If so, then 10 is a good unit to select. A unit of 100 or 1,000 clauses might not seem suitable.

While there is no standard unit, many text studies use "per 1,000 words." While "per 1,000 words" appears in most published articles on text analysis, this does not mean you must accept this as a standard for this study. You could use per 100 words, per 100 clauses, or per 1,000 clauses. The decision depends on the nature of the data. If you are investigating clause types, then the unit should be "per X clauses". However, if the data are not entered as clause units, you may be forced to use "per word."

Assume that we found that the rate for most of these "cognitively complex" clauses was 5 per 100 clauses. Also assume that few of these clauses were used by LEP children. Still, it is possible that it is not L2 proficiency but rather classroom task that influenced the frequency of such clauses in their data. That is, all the students may have the ability to produce these cognitively complex structures, but may not have had the opportunity to do so. To check to see if this is the case, we might work out an activity we think would encourage the use of such clauses. The activity selected is a board game similar to "Johnny, can I cross the ocean?" where permission is given or denied using such phrases as "yes, if *xxx*", "not unless *xxx*," or "no, because *xxx*." With this task, the number of such structures is dramatically increased for all *S*s. With such a mini-experiment introduced into a natural school setting, you can substantiate that all groups of *S*s are able to employ such structures appropriately but that they elect not to in certain classroom tasks.

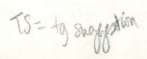

Imagine, too, that you are intrigued by the students' abilities to produce cognitively complex clauses in this mini-experiment. Such clauses are considered very difficult. In fact, they are believed to be typical of the language of "cognitive academic language proficiency" (Cummins' CALP, 1984)--the language needed for academic success. The mini-experiment took place in what would normally be thought of as "basic interpersonal communication" (Cummins' BICS) rather than in an academic task. In order to substantiate the notion that more of these clauses occur in academic tasks than in basic social interaction, you could do a survey of text structures in science, math, and social studies reading materials for the fourth grade. These counts could be compared with those of books used for nonacademic pleasure reading (such as comic books or children's novels). On the production side, you might compare counts of such clauses in children's diaries and letters as compared with their written reports in language arts, science, and social science. If you obtained the rate of cognitively complex clauses in each of these situations, you could compare rates in academic and personal communication tasks. The table on the findings might (or might not) look like the following fictitious data:

Frequency of Cognitively Complex Clauses

Acad Rdg	Rate	Non-Acad Rdg	Rate
432	4:100	210	2:100
Acad Writ	Rate	Non-Acad Writ	Rate
121	1:100	110	1:100

From this table (if the data were real), you could say that the frequency of cognitively complex clauses (as shown in the rates) for academic reading was twice that of nonacademic reading. For the novice writers--the children--you could state that the rates for frequency of cognitively complex clauses were the same in academic and nonacademic writing. The project breaks down when we try to compare the rates in the other direction. The notion that children produce fewer clauses of high cognitive complexity when compared to adults who are professional writers should not surprise anyone. If we try to talk about the cognitive demand of children's reading compared with children's writing, then the measure of cognitive demand (and our operational definition of cognitive demand) would be the production of such clauses. "Cognitive demand" would *not* include the cognitive demands of the composing process in writing vs. comprehension processes in reading--a very knotty area. Whatever we said about the comparison would have to be carefully limited so that readers would not interpret the statements of cognitively complex clauses as equivalent to cognitive demand in carrying out tasks.

While we usually think of rates with units of "per 100" or "per 1000," it is also possible to have a rate "per 1." One type of rate frequently used in applied linguistics research is the number of words or of S nodes (sentence nodes) per T-unit. These are measures of syntactic complexity. Roughly, a T-unit can be defined as an independent clause with any attached dependent clauses. Thus the utterance *Mari went to Chicago and then came to visit us* would contain 2 T-units (*Mari went to Chicago; (Mari) then came to visit us*). The utterance *Mari, who never loved flying to Chicago in winter, came to visit us* would contain only 1 T-unit. In this second utterance, the number of words per T-unit (13) is greater than the number of words per T-unit in the first (4, 5). In the first utterance, there is 1 S node for each T-unit (*Mari went to Chicago*--1 T-unit and 1 S node; *Mari came to visit us*--1 T-unit and 1 S node) and in the second, there are 2 S nodes (*Mari came to visit us; Mari never loved flying to Chicago in winter*) in 1 T-unit. When learners produce many words per T-unit or S nodes per T-unit, we can (if we accept "words per T-unit" as a good operational definition of complexity) infer that the syntax is complex.

Both rates and percents give us a way of comparing frequencies. Raw frequencies usually are not comparable because they are basically open-ended. By converting frequencies to rates or percents, we change them to closed-group frequencies which can be compared.

Ratios are also useful in displaying information about frequencies in relation to each other. There are a number of ratios we might want to display for the elementary school study mentioned earlier. For example, we might want to know the ratio of boys to girls in LEP classification in the total school district. If there were 80 girls and 360 boys, the ratio would be:

$$\text{ratio} = \frac{\# X}{\# Y}$$

$$\text{ratio} = \frac{80}{360}$$

$$\text{ratio} = .22$$

We could say the ratio of males to females is 1 male to .22 females. However, we don't usually talk about .22 of a person, so it is easier to multiply this by 100 and say the ratio is 100 to 22.

There are many other ratios we could display for the fourth-grade data. Since Goodlad's *A Place Called School* (1984) has shown that high school students have little opportunity to talk in school and since talk is important in language learning, we might want to know how the opportunities for talk vary across classroom tasks in the fourth-grade study. Some of the data collected are from teacher-centered activities. The teacher structures the interaction, calls on individual children for their responses, evaluates these responses, and poses more questions. She may also summarize the children's individual responses. In other tasks, the students are engaged in cooperative-learning activities. An example might be where children have to solve a problem and each child has some piece of information that others in the group do not possess. To solve the problem, each of these pieces of information must be presented and discussed. Kagan (1985) calls this the jigsaw technique. The teacher sets up the task but the students carry it out. We have the number of turns of talk for the teacher and for each of the individual students in teacher-centered and in cooperative-learning tasks. While we want to know how many turns children in each of the three language groups (EO, LEP, FEP) have in these two types of classroom activities, we are also interested in the number of turns in relation to the number of turns the teacher takes. Therefore, we could compute a ratio of teacher-to-student talk for each of the groups on each task.

Ratios are also used in the analysis of questionnaire and test information where the likelihood of falling into one group or another is compared. For example, the number of Ss who pass or do not pass the French proficiency test might be presented as an odds ratio. If 350 passed and 125 did not, the ratio is $350 \div 125 = 2.8$, almost three to one. If travel in France is included in the demographic data, then the odds ratio for pass vs. not pass can also be calculated. Perhaps the ratio for passing the test would be 4 to 1 for the +travel group and 1.5 to 1 for the −travel group.

Undoubtedly the most used ratio in applied linguistics research is the *type-token ratio*. This is a rough measure of vocabulary flexibility. While an overall word count can tell us about how much language a person can produce in some amount of time, the ratio of the number of unique words to the total number of words gives us a better notion of vocabulary use. The computer can easily count the total number of words and the number of unique words for each child. These ratios can then be compared across the three groups of children--EO, FEP, and LEP.

Practice 5.5

1. What prediction would you make for the ratios in the teacher-centered instruction? Do you think the ratios will be equal for all three groups of children?

_____
_____
_____

How similar do you imagine the ratios of teacher-to-student talk for the three groups would be in cooperative learning? _____

_____
_____

How similar do you predict the ratios would be between teacher-centered and cooperative-learning tasks?

_____
_____

2. What predictions would you make about the type-token ratios for the children for oral and for written data?

_____
_____

Coding Numerical Data

In discussing simple computations used to tally and compare frequency data, we have used examples drawn almost exclusively from natural language--data where these computations are difficult or at least time-consuming. With elicited data-- for example, data from experiments or from tests--the process is much easier. The researcher can enter information on each student or subject on a data sheet and enter numbers for most responses. The data do not have to be transcribed and the coding is much easier. *Why not?*

Suppose that teachers at the school where the fourth-grade research was being done attended an in-service workshop where the speaker talked about the diffi- culty many children experience in following consecutive directions. Given an applied linguistics perspective, you might suspect that it isn't just the number of steps in the directions but the order in which the steps are given that would effect comprehension. That is, you think a direction like:

> *Before you draw the triangle, turn the page.*

might be less comprehensible than a direction:

> *After you draw the triangle, turn the page.*

giving directions complexity

because the order of the clauses isn't the same as the order of required actions. You also think the connector itself may vary in difficulty. "Do X *and then* Y" (e.g., "Draw the triangle *and then* turn the page") might be easier than "Do X *before* Y" (e.g., "Draw the triangle *before* you turn the page"). Each child is tested individually on ability to follow directions where the order of mention is or is not the same as the order in which the actions are to be done, and where directions use connectors such as *and* or *and then* or *but first* compared with *be- fore* or *after*. (You might want to complicate the study by looking at conditionals in directions too!)

A data sheet could be prepared as follows. The data for each child would go on one row of the data sheet. At the top of each column place a label for the infor- mation that goes in that column. Columns 1-2 could hold the child's individual I.D. number (sometimes called a *case number*). The data will be easier to read if you leave an empty column between pieces of information (though this is not re- quired). Columns 4-5 might contain the child's age and column 7 might show the child's sex. You could use a 1 for female and a 2 for male. Column 9 might be used for classification. You could arbitrarily assign a 1 for EO, a 2 for FEP, a 3 for LEP and a 4 for NEP. *Why?*

If the test had had 10 items, you might use the following columns for that infor- mation. A 1 might indicate a correct response and a 0 an incorrect response.

ID	AGE	SEX	6. CLASS	I1	I2	I3	I4	I5	I6	I7	I8	I9	I10
1	8	1	3	1	1	1	1	0	0	1	1	1	1
2	9	2	1	1	1	0	1	0	1	0	1	0	1
3	10	2	4	1	0	0	1	0	1	1	1	0	1
4	10	2	2	1	1	0	0	0	0	0	1	0	1
5	9	1	2	1	1	1	1	1	1	1	1	0	1
6	10	2	3	1	1	0	1	1	1	0	0	0	1
7	9	1	1	1	1	1	1	0	1	1	1	0	1
8	11	1	4	1	1	1	0	0	0	0	1	0	1
9	10	2	4	1	1	1	0	1	0	1	1	0	1
10	10	1	2	1	1	0	1	0	1	0	1	1	0

Once the information is collected, it can be entered into the computer for tallying. With just a few instructions to the computer, you can learn how many boys and girls participated, the number of children in each classification, and the number of children who responded correctly or incorrectly to each item. Test items can be grouped and information on the number of total correct and incorrect responses for each group of items tallied. Of course, these tallies could easily be done by hand since the data are all right there on a single sheet of data paper. With large data sets, this is hard to do and of course the data are not easily accessible in natural language data bases. Once the data have been tallied, you will be able to give an informative display of the frequencies. The question that immediately springs to mind is whether or not the frequencies support your research hypotheses or not. This question (i.e., how big a difference do you need to be sure a difference is real?) will be discussed in the chapters of part III.

As you have undoubtedly realized, the coding and computations discussed in this chapter have been those used primarily for frequency data. In the next chapter we will discuss coding and displaying ranked (ordinal) and interval data. Before we do so, though, we will consider ways that the results of frequency computations might be displayed to make them more informative.

◇◇◇

Practice 5.6

1. Using the data table, compute the frequency for number of male *S*s. __5__
Compute the frequency for number of male *S*s who answered item 5 correctly.
__2__
What proportion of the *S*s answered item 9 correctly? _20%_ What is the ratio
of LEP *S*s to the other groups combined? _.20_   _.20_

2. Imagine for now that the hypotheses about the difficulty of clause types and
clause connectors (page 145) turned out to be supported by the data, what suggestions might you make at the next in-service workshop? (Don't forget our
warnings about research validity in previous chapters!)

_____
_____
_____
_____

◇◇◇

Data Displays

It has been said that a picture is worth a thousand words. Sometimes the picture
is used to represent numbers as well as words.

With sophisticated computer programs, data displays are becoming more and
more common. In the past it was expensive for journals to have draftsmen draw
figures and graphs with India ink to obtain 'camera ready' copy of high quality.
This problem is no longer an issue, so it is likely that data displays will more
frequently be used to describe data.

Dow Jones done like this

Bar Graphs and Histograms

Bar graphs are often used to show frequencies. The bars in the graph are not
attached to each other. In such graphs, there is no special reason for placing one
bar to the right of another. For example, males could be ordered first or second
in a display bar graph for sex of learners. Bar graphs showing frequencies for
L1 membership are also not ordered in any special way. The graphs can be ordered as you wish. By convention, many researchers place the largest number in
the center and build others out on either side, but this is not a rule by any means.

When the bars in a bar graph are arranged in some meaningful order, they are
often connected. These are sometimes called *histograms* rather than bar graphs.

Here are demographic data reported by Reid (1987) in her survey of learning styles. Among many other facts, Reid reports on the length of time her *S*s had studied English in the United States as follows:

Time Studying English in U.S.

Time	n
Less than 3 mos.	511
3-6 mos.	266
7-11 mos.	133
12-17 mos.	131
18 mos-2 yrs	48
Over 2 yrs	13
Over 3 yrs	53

The histogram could be arranged either from high frequencies to low, from low to high, or in order of length of time.

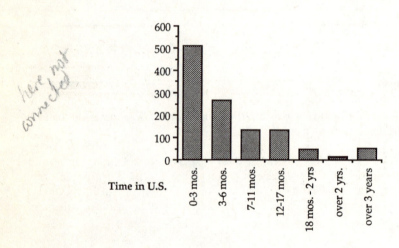

Data are also given on the educational status of the respondents. Class: Graduate, 424; Undergraduate, 851. The bar graph for this information might be displayed like this:

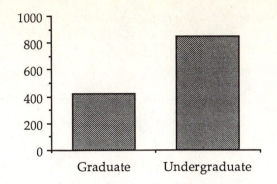

◇◇

Practice 5.7

▶ 1. Draw a bar graph for Reid's report on the sex of her respondents. Sex: Male, 849; Female, 481.

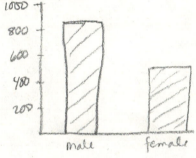

▶ 2. Draw a histogram for the data Reid gives on the age of her Ss.

Age	n
15-19	342
20-24	532
25-29	235
30-34	87
35-39	43
40-44	16
45-49	4
50-54	3
55+	1

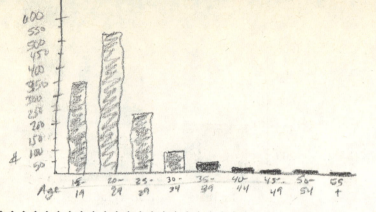

◇◇

Pie Charts

Some researchers feel that a pie chart is the best display for proportion or percent displays. Reid lists the major fields of study for her *Ss* as follows:

Major	*n*
Engineering	268
Business	277
Humanities	171
Computer science	130
Hard sciences	54
Medicine	43
Other	420

Here is a pie chart that illustrates this distribution.

Major

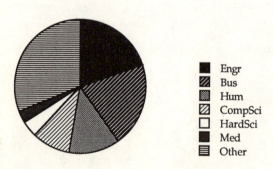

Engr
Bus
Hum
CompSci
HardSci
Med
Other

◇◇◇◇◇◇◇◇◇◇◇◇◇◇◇◇◇◇◇◇◇◇◇◇◇◇◇◇◇◇◇◇◇◇◇◇◇◇

Practice 5.8

▶ 1. Draw a pie chart that illustrates the proportion of male vs. female *S*s for the data in Reid's report.

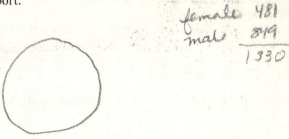

female 481
male 849
———
1330

2. Draw a pie chart that illustrates the breakdown for time studying English in the United States (data on page 148).

◇◇◇◇◇◇◇◇◇◇◇◇◇◇◇◇◇◇◇◇◇◇◇◇◇◇◇◇◇◇◇◇◇◇◇◇◇◇

Frequency Polygons and Line Drawings

With bar graphs and histograms, like items are stacked like bricks on top of each other to form a bar. When polygons are used, each item is not visually present in the stack. Instead, all like items are tallied and the frequency point is marked with some symbol. The symbol could be a small bullet, •, a small square, ■, or whatever symbols your computer program may use. These symbols are then connected either with a straight line or with a curve. Some researchers do use straight lines to connect the points, but most people prefer a curving line. The shape of the distribution shown by this curved connecting line is called a

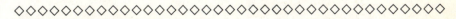

polygon. *Polygon* is an important term to remember. In future chapters we will use it to talk about the visual shape of the data. That is, we won't say "the shape of the bar graph or histogram" but rather "the polygon." It's important to make this connection now so that later you can process it with ease.

Polygons or line drawings are appropriate when frequencies are ordered in relation to each other. For example, if you want to display the ages of your *S*s, it makes sense to begin with the youngest age at the left and the oldest at the right. If you want to display the scores of a large number of students, it seems sensible to give the frequency for the lowest score at the left and then arrange the frequencies of all the following scores to the right.

Here is a frequency distribution of TOEFL scores as reported in Reid:

TOEFL	n
300-349	2
350-399	9
400-449	64
450-474	74
475-499	97
500-524	120
525-549	104
550-574	73
575+	63

Here is the polygon that presents this information in a visual form:

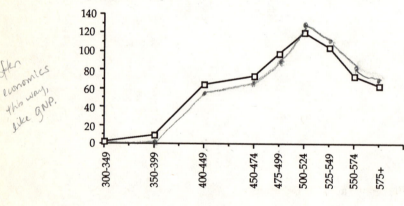

TOEFL Scores

It is possible to have overlapping polygon displays. For example, assume that you wanted to show these TOEFL scores but you wanted the display to show the number of males and females at each point on the distribution. With a bar graph you could make two bars for each interval. With a polygon, you can select one symbol to represent the frequency of females and another for males and draw two lines in overlay.

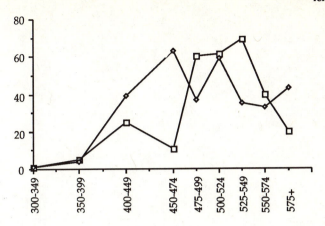

TOEFL Scores

◇◇◇

Practice 5.9

▶ 1. Let's imagine that Reid collected the TOEFL scores of these same students one year later and that the frequencies (fictitious) were as follows:

TOEFL	n
300-349	0
350-399	2
400-449	58
450-474	71
475-499	98
500-524	126
525-549	110
550-574	75
575 +	65

Draw a frequency polygon for this hypothetical data and place it in overlay on that given for the original data.

◇◇

Conclusion

In this chapter we have discussed ways in which the researcher can code, summarize and present information on frequency data. In the next chapter we will repeat this process using scaled and scored data.

Activities

1. G. Yan (1985. A contrastive textological analysis of restrictive relative clauses in Chinese and English written text. Unpublished master's thesis, TESL, UCLA.) compared the similarities and differences in the use and distribution of restrictive relative clauses in Chinese and English newspaper and journal articles, government agreements, and student compositions. Four major categories (and 20 subtypes) identified by Celce-Murcia and Larsen-Freeman (1983) were used for Chinese and English clauses and four additional types were added that occur in Chinese but not English. One table in this thesis shows the frequency of clause types in the English and the Chinese data sources:

English Type	f	%
OS	300	66.96
OO	69	15.40
SS	44	9.82
SO	5	1.11
S/Adv.	29	6.47
O/Adv.	1	.22

textological —

Chinese Type	f	%
OO	132	36.36
OS	127	34.99
SO	33	9.09
SS	29	7.99
TS	2	.55
TO	1	.28
O/Others	29	7.99
S/Others	10	2.75

Rearrange these tables to demonstrate cumulative frequency. While we have not identified all the relative clause types for you here, what can you say about the numerical distribution of restrictive relative clauses in the data based on this table? *not a lot until a comparable basis is set up.*

2. To compare the frequency of restrictive relative clauses in the different text types, a table is presented which gives relative clause frequencies in each text type and the total number of words in each corpus.

independent

	f Rel Cl *dep.*		Total No. Words	
Text Source	Eng	Ch	Eng	Ch
Comps	92	53	4,700	6,486
Newspapers	62	62	5,763	7,952
Journals	192	116	14,411	19,876
Agreements	102	132	6,299	8,741

Compute the occurrence of restrictive relative clauses per 100 words. Would some other unit seem more appropriate to you? *10000, so get whole #s*

Prepare a bar graph to show the distribution of clauses in these data sources.

3. B. Hayashi (1985. Language attrition: changes in the Japanese language over three generations. Unpublished master's thesis, TESL, UCLA.) investigated the Japanese used by first-, second-, and third-generation women in a family. Among several tables presented in the thesis is the following which looks at the degree of language mixing.

Use of Japanese in Main and Subordinate Clauses

	1st Gen.		2nd Gen.		3rd Gen.	
Clause Type	Main	Sub	Main	Sub	Main	Sub
Total	80	177	62	105	47	48
Japanese	78	176	51	81	17	28
%Japanese	98	99	82	77	36	58

Which woman uses the most English mixing? Would you expect that the third-generation woman would use more main clauses than subordinate clauses in general in speaking Japanese? Why (not)? Are you surprised at the frequency of mixing in her main clauses as compared with that in subordinate clauses? Why (not)?

4. K. Cruttenden (1986. A descriptive study of three ethnic Chinese schools. Unpublished master's thesis, TESL, UCLA.) gives demographic data on the families of students involved in three Chinese language programs.

Ethnicity	Total	School 1	School 2	School 3
Chinese	83	34	31	18
Non-Chinese	15	4	3	8

Compute the n for each school. What percent of the families is Chinese? Non-Chinese? What is the ratio of Chinese to Non-Chinese? What is the ratio of Chinese and Non-Chinese students enrolled in the programs at each of the three schools?

From questionnaires, the education statistics for the parents were:

Education	Total	School 1	School 2	School 3
BA/BS	30	10	13	7
MA/MS	32	24	4	4
Ph.D.	21	5	13	3
H.S.	20	5	1	14

Note that the N is not the same as that on ethnicity. How do you explain this? What proportion of the parents report having attained a college (not high school) degree? Do you think this is a representative sample of parents in the county? Why (not)?

The language or dialects of Chinese spoken by the parents include:

Language	Total	School 1	School 2	School 3
Mandarin	57	22	25	10
Cantonese	24	11	8	7
Taiwanese	23	9	11	3
Other dialect	14	4	4	6
None	13	5	2	11

Calculate the percentages for each school separately. Do the percentages appear very similar across the three schools? Compute the cumulative frequency and cumulative percentage figures for the totals for language groups.

Select any of the above statistics and prepare a pie chart to show the frequency distribution.

5. J. Graham (according to an article by J. Sanchez, "The art of dealmaking" in the *Los Angeles Times*, 2/15/88, Sec. 4, p. 3.) is a marketing professor at the University of Southern California who has studied the bargaining behaviors of businessmen from many different countries. Videotapes of bargaining sessions are reviewed for numerous characteristics of interpersonal communication. Here is a sample of some of the findings related to Japanese, Korean, Brazilian, German, British, and American businessmen. (a) The number of times "no" was used by each participant during 30 minutes of negotiation: Japanese 1.9, Korean

7.4, Brazilian 41.9, German 6.7, British 5.4, American 4.5. (b) The average number of minutes each participant looked at the partner's face per 10-minute period: Japanese 1.3, Korean 3.3, Brazilian 5.2, German 3.4, British 3.0, American 3.3. (c) The number of times "you" was used during 30 minutes: Japanese 31.5, Korean 34.2, Brazilian 90.4, German 39.7, British 54.8, American 54.1. (d) The number of overlaps (where both speak at once) in 30 minutes: Japanese 12.6, Korean 44.0, Brazilian 28.6, German 41.6, British 10.5, American 10.3. (e) The average number of silent periods (over 10 seconds in length) between turns in 30 minutes: Japanese 5.5, Korean 0, Brazilian 0, German 0, British 5.0, American 3.5. (f) The average number of times each participant touched partner (excluding handshakes) during 30 minutes: Japanese 0, Korean 0, Brazilian 4.7, German 0, British 0, American 0.

a. Prepare a graph to show all this information.
b. Draw an overlay figure and/or a line polygon showing the information from the six histograms.
c. Which display (graph or figure) do you feel is more informative and less misleading? Why?
d. What linguistic factor (rather than bargaining behavior) do you think might account for the high frequency for "no" in the Brazilian data?   Double neg. ?
e. If you were a consultant for a business firm, what other behaviors would you want to include in your research?

References

Celce-Murcia, M. & Larsen-Freeman, D. 1983. *The Grammar Book*. New York, NY: Newbury House.

Cummins, J. 1984. *Bilingualism and Special Education: Issues in Assessment and Pedagogy*. Clevedon: Multilingual Matters, Ltd..

Flashner, V. 1987. An exploration of linguistic dichotomies and genres in the classroom language of native and nonnative English speaking children. Unpublished doctoral dissertation, Applied Linguistics, UCLA.

Goodlad, J. I. 1984. *A Place Called School: Prospects for the Future*. New York, NY: McGraw-Hill.

Heath, S. B. 1986. Sociocultural contexts of language development. In *Beyond Language: Social and Cultural Factors in Schooling Language Minority Students*. Bilingual Education Office, California State Department of Education; Evaluation, Dissemination, and Assessment Center, California State University, Los Angeles, 143-186.

Hockey, S. & Marriott, I. 1984. *Oxford Concordance Program Version 1.0 User's Manual*. Oxford: Oxford University Computing Service.

Kagan, J. 1985. *Cooperative Learning and Sociocultural Factors in Schooling Language Minority Students*. Cooperating Faculty, School of Education, University of California, Riverside.

Phillips, S. 1983. *The Invisible Culture: Communication in Classroom and Community on the Warm Springs Indian Reservation*. New York, NY: Longman.

Reid, J. 1987. The learning style preferences of ESL students. *TESOL Quarterly*, *21*, 1, 87-111.

WordCruncher, Version 4.21. 1988. Electronic Text Corporation, 5600 N. University Ave., Provo, Utah.

Chapter 6

Describing Interval and
Ordinal Values

- *Measures of central tendency*
  - *Mode*
  - *Median*
  - *Mean*
  - *Central tendency and the normal distribution*
- *Measures of variability*
  - *Range*
  - *Variance*
  - *Standard deviation*
  - *Standard deviation and the normal distribution*
- *Ordinal measures*

In the previous chapter, we discussed some of the ways that frequency data can be displayed to give information at a glance. With ranking (ordinal) and interval measures, we are not concerned with "how many" or "how often" (as we are with frequency data). Rather, the data will tell us "how much," and the measure of how much is on an ordinal or interval scale. An example of ranked, or ordinal, data would be a teacher's rating of student performance on a five-point scale. A common example of interval data are scores obtained from a test. If 30 students in a class take an exam, the data consist of their individual scores. It doesn't make sense to add the scores and display them as a total. Instead, we want to know the most typical score obtained by students in the class. That most typical value is called a measure of central tendency.

Measures of Central Tendency

The term *central tendency* is used to talk about the central point in the distribution of values in the data. We will consider three ways of computing central tendency, the most typical score for a data set. The choice among these three methods can be made by considering particular reservations that go with each method. The choice of one measure of central tendency over another is especially important when we want to compare the performance of different groups of students (or the changing performance of the same students over time).

Mode

Mode is the measure of central tendency which reports the *most frequently obtained score* in the data.

Mode = most frequently obtained score

Imagine that you have designed a program that you believe will give newly arrived immigrant students the vocabulary they will need to deal with daily life in the community. The program includes an assessment vocabulary test. Here are the scores of 30 students on the test:

out of 50?
(p.162)

20	22	23	23	25
25	25	26	26	26
26	26	27	27	27
28	28	29	29	30
30	32	33	33	33
34	37	40	41	42

Drawing a frequency polygon will show the mode most easily. For these data, we would draw a horizontal line and divide the line into 1-point increments from 20 to 42, the high and low scores in the data set. Then, we would draw a vertical line at a right angle to the left side of this line and divide this line into 1-point increments from 0 to 6. The scores are shown on the horizontal line and the number of instances of each score is on the vertical axis. The lowest score is 20 and there is only one such score. If you check the intersect of 20 and 1, you will find a plot symbol (you can use a square, a dot, or a star--whatever you like) at that point. The rest of the data are plotted in a similar way.

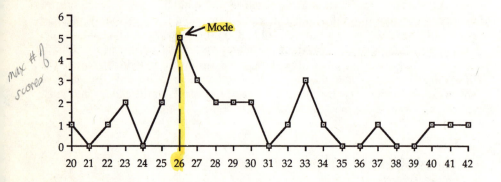

The curved line connecting the symbols is the frequency polygon.

If you drop a point from the peak of a frequency polygon to the baseline, the number on the baseline will be the mode. The mode, then, is really a *frequency* measure for *interval* data. It is a measure that shows us which score was the most typical for the most students (score 26 in this case).

or nominal, ordinal

There are several problems with using the mode as a measure of central tendency. First, it is possible that there will be no *one* most frequent term in a distribution or none that receives a frequency higher than 1. Obviously, when this happens, the mode cannot be used. Mode is also the measure of central tendency which is most seriously limited because it is so easily affected by chance scores. Look back at the set of scores on the vocabulary test. Imagine that the data had been misscored. One student scored as a 26 really missed another item and so should have been a 25. The people with 32 and 34 scores should have received scores of 33. The mode is now 33. This change in central tendency is quite a shift! As the number of scores increases, the chances of such large shifts in the mode become less and less likely.

Median

The *median* is the score which is at the *center of the distribution*. Half the scores are above the median and half are below it. If the number of scores is an odd number, then the median will be the middle score. If the number of scores is an even number, then the median is the midpoint between the two middle scores.

Median = center of the distribution

To find the median, then, the scores or observations are arranged from low to high and the middle score is obtained. This is the way the data were arranged for the vocabulary test. The median, the midpoint, for the values in the data set is 27.5.

The median is often used as a measure of central tendency when the number of scores is relatively small, when the data have been obtained by rank-order measurement, or when a mean score is not appropriate. As you will discover in later chapters of this workbook, the median is an important measure of central tendency for certain statistical procedures.

Mean

The *mean* is the *arithmetic average of all scores* in a data set. Thus, it takes all scores into account. And so, it is sensitive to each new score in the data. Imagine the scores distributed as weights along a horizontal line, the plank of a seesaw. The scores are the weights on the plank. To make the seesaw balance, you have to move the plank back and forth until you get the exact balance point. That exact point is the mean.

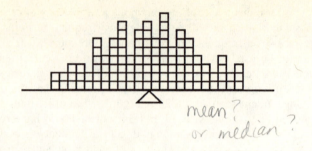

*mean?
or median?*

You already know how to compute the mean because it is the same thing as the "average" score: add all the scores and divide by the number of scores. If we add the scores in the first data sample for the vocabulary test and divide the sum by the number of scores, the answer is 29.1.

Now, let's begin to use some of the convenient symbols of statistics. $\sum$ is the symbol which means to sum, or add. X is the symbol for an individual score or observation. So $\sum X$ is the instruction to add all the scores.

The symbol for the mean is $\overline{X}$, pronounced "X-bar." (As you can imagine, this meaning of X-bar was around long before it was applied to linguistic description. X-bar in linguistics has nothing to do with $\overline{X}$!) The formula for the mean is "X-bar equals the sum of X divided by N":

$$\overline{X} = \frac{\sum X}{N} \qquad \text{MEAN}$$

Although the mean is the most frequently used measure of central tendency, it too has a limitation. It is seriously sensitive to *extreme* scores, scores that clearly do not belong to the group of scores. As an example, imagine that two additional students took the vocabulary test. Unfortunately, the test is not appropriate for students who do not read roman script. These two additional students were tested even though they could not read the script. Their scores were 0. If we add these two values to the data set for the vocabulary test, the mean for the group is now 27.3.

Extreme scores can change the mean so drastically that it will not be the best measure of central tendency. Extreme scores should be located and checked since there is always the possibility of error in data entry (or in test administration). When legitimate extreme scores are present, then the median may be a more appropriate measure of central tendency. If the number of Ss is small, it is also likely that the distribution will not be normal. For example, much of our research is conducted in classrooms where the number of students may be below 30. When there are few Ss and when they are in an intact group (that is, Ss are not randomly selected) the data may not be normally distributed. The median may be the more appropriate measure of central tendency.

Do w/ our project for this class

How do you know?

When there are no extreme scores and the distribution of scores appears to be normal, then the best measure of central tendency is the mean because it is the measure which takes the magnitude of each score into account.

◇◇

Practice 6.1

1. Identify each symbol in the formula for the mean.

N = ___*# of cases, etc.*___

Σ = ___*sum*___

X = ___*one case*___

$\bar{X}$ = ___*mean*___

2. In the vocabulary test example, imagine that the scores of two native speakers were placed in the data by mistake. Each received a perfect score of 50. How would these two scores affect the mode, the median, and the mean? _____
___*Doesn't affect*___ _↑ *will raise slightly*___
___*will raise more*___

▶ 3. The following table shows the distribution of reading speed scores for the 30 students who took the vocabulary test. One S's test was illegible so only 29 scores appear below. First scan the data for the mode on reading speed.

Reading Speed

Words/min.	f	
300	3	*900*
280	0	
260	0	*14.5 above/below*
240	2	*480*
220	1	*220*
200	3	*600*
180	4	*13 720*
160	8	⟶ *1280* } *but it's not ½*
140	4	*16 560* *above, ½ below*
120	3	*360*
100	0	
80	1	*80*
60	0	

When there are not a large number of values, it is easy to look at the distribution first for the mode. This gives a quick reading on the data. Mode = ___*160*___.

What is the median for the above data? ___*? 160.*___.

Now, compute the mean score. ___*179. 31*___. (Remember that you can't simply sum the wpm, but must multiply by f for each wpm score.)

Why are the mean, the mode, and the median different?

Higher w/ outliers (3 at 300 wpm)

4. If you visualize the scores as weights distributed on the plank of a seesaw, which measure gives you the best balance point for central tendency?

mode ?

Central Tendency and the Normal Distribution

If there are no very extreme scores and if you have 30 or more observations, you may have a *normal distribution*. A normal distribution means that most of the scores cluster around the midpoint of the distribution, and the number of scores gradually decrease on either side of the midpoint. The resulting polygon is a bell-shaped curve.

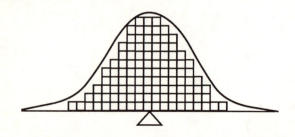

A normal distribution is a theoretical mathematical concept. The distribution of data is normal to the degree that it approaches this bell-shaped curve. Notice that the *tails*, the tail ends of the curve, show where the extreme values occur. These are the values that occur least often in the data. When the majority of scores fall at the central point and the others are distributed symmetrically on either side of the midpoint in gradually decreasing frequency, the distribution is normal, *and* all three measures of central tendency--mode, median, and mean--will be the same.

However, the distribution of data is not always normal: that is, the frequency polygon may not slope away from the central point in a symmetric way and the tails will not look the same. Let's consider what this means in terms of the measures of central tendency. Each of the polygons below differs from the normal distribution.

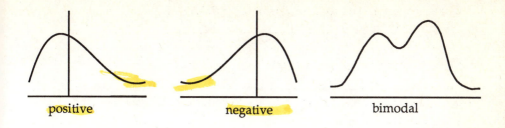

positive   negative   bimodal

Let's suppose that you gave the students in your class an examination. The scores were: 24, 25, 25, 25, 27, 27, 27, 27, 28, 28, 28, 29, 29, 29, 30, 30, 34, 36, 38, 39, 41, 45. Look at the three polygons. Which best illustrates these data? Polygon 1, right? Since some few scores are much higher (and there are no matching, much lower scores), the mean will be affected. It will be *higher* than it would be if the distribution were normal. Most of the scores cluster around a central point that is pulled higher than it normally would be. This is because a few extreme scores under the right tail of the distribution pull the mean to the right. This type of distribution is said to be *skewed*. Since the mean is moved to the right by the right-hand extreme scores, we say that it is *positively skewed*.

Now imagine that the scores on the exam were 16, 17, 18, 24, 25, 25, 25, 27, 27, 27, 28, 28, 28, 29, 29, 29, 30. The mean is *lower* than it would be in a normal distribution. Again, the distribution is skewed but this time in a negative direction (visually towards the left of the distribution) as shown in the second polygon. This is a *negatively skewed* distribution.

Skewed distributions are asymmetric. They show that extreme scores have pulled the point of central tendency in either a negative or positive direction. Look back at the skewed distributions. In the negatively skewed distribution, some students performed much worse than we might expect them to. Their data pulled the mean lower. In the positively skewed distribution, some students performed much better than we might have expected. Their data pulled the mean higher. (Because of the visual form of the polygon, people often reverse the meanings of positive and negative skew in discussing distribution.)

In either case, the data are not normally distributed and the mean may not be an accurate measure of central tendency. When this happens, it affects the kinds of statistical tests we can use. Many statistical tests, as you will see later, assume the data are normally distributed--that is, that $\bar{X}$ is the *best* measure of central tendency for the data.

The final polygon shows two peaks, two different modes. So, logically enough, it is called a *bimodal distribution*. There are two peaks in the distribution and the data spread out from each.

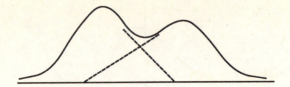

A bimodal distribution suggests that there are two very different groups of Ss taking this test--one group that scores rather low and one that scores higher. It might lead you to suspect that those that scored low had not yet taken the course. Another possibility is that they entered the course late. Another is that those with scores under the higher mode point are from languages which have many cognate words for the vocabulary tested. They may have had an advantage over other students. Or, possibly the students at the higher end of the distribution were those who had been living in the community for some time prior to enrolling in the course. As you may guess from this example, bimodal distributions are very important in research. They show us that some important independent variable with two levels may have been missed--an independent variable which has an effect on the dependent variable. For example, if you gave a Spanish test to a group of students and obtained a distribution like this, you might wonder if the data that cluster around the right mode might come from Ss who had an opportunity to speak Spanish outside class while the data clustered around the left mode might be from those Ss who had no such opportunities.

Looking at a distribution curve, it is also possible to see whether the data are "flat" or "peaked." Flatness or peakedness of the curve is called *kurtosis*. If the data spread out in a very flat curve (a platykurtic distribution) or in a very sharp peaked curve (a leptokurtic distribution), the distribution departs from the normal curve.

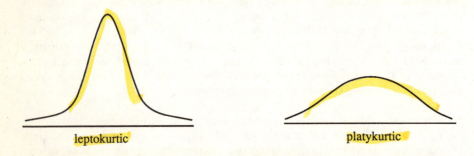

leptokurtic   platykurtic

Information on skew and the number and shape of the peaks in the curve help us to decide whether the distribution is normal. When the distribution is not normal, the three measures of the most typical score will vary. The decision as to which is the best measure of central tendency depends on this information, on the presence or absence of extreme scores, *and* on the purpose of the study. For example, imagine you wanted to offer a vocabulary class in your private language school. Only one class can be offered. If you had data from a vocabulary test for prospective students, the most useful measure of central tendency would be the mode. It would show you the level achieved by the *most* applicants. If many prospective students scored at the mode or close to it, you should have enough students to make the class financially viable for the school. You could also pitch the course (and your ads) at the appropriate level for the students. You can forget about the people who scored much lower or much higher than those at the mode.

Sometimes the median is the best measure of central tendency. If the distribution of responses in the data includes a number of scores that skew the distribution, then the median is the best option. As we have seen, the median is much less susceptible to extreme scores than the mean or the mode.

The mean is the measure of central tendency most frequently used when we want to compare performance or responses of different groups. When we talk about an entering class as having an average TOEFL score of 523 while last year's class had a 580, the numbers are assumed to be means of the two groups. Since we so frequently use the mean in comparing groups, it is important to know whether, in fact, the distribution of the scores was normal (i.e., whether or not the mean is, in fact, the best measure of central tendency). To do that, we need to consider variability in the data.

◇◇◇◇◇◇◇◇◇◇◇◇◇◇◇◇◇◇◇◇◇◇◇◇◇◇◇◇◇◇◇◇◇◇◇◇

Practice 6.2

▶1. Imagine that you received the following data on the vocabulary test mentioned earlier (see page 160):

20	22	23	23	23
23	23	23	24	25
28	29	30	30	30
30	30	30	31	32
32	33	33	34	35
35	36	36	37	37

Chart the data and draw the frequency polygon.

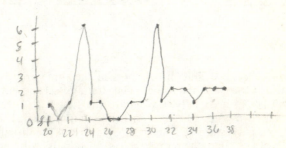

2. Compute the measure of central tendency which you believe to be best for the data. Justify your choice. Compare your choice with that of other members of your study group. What consensus did you reach?

Median because strongly positively skewed

_↘ 30_

3. Think of a test that you gave (or took) recently. If the distribution turned out to be bimodal, what hypotheses might you make about it? _____

◇◇◇◇◇◇◇◇◇◇◇◇◇◇◇◇◇◇◇◇◇◇◇◇◇◇◇◇◇◇◇◇◇◇◇◇◇◇

Measures of Variability

The measure of central tendency tells us the most typical score for a data set. This is important information. However, just as important is the variability of scores within the data set. Suppose that you gave the vocabulary test to three different groups of students. Each group achieved a mean score of 30. Does this mean that the performance of the groups was the same? No, of course it doesn't. The variability of the scores, how they spread out from the point of central tendency, could be quite different.

Compare the frequency polygons for these three different groups.

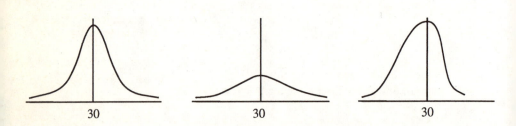

30   30   30

As you can see, the distribution of scores in the three groups is quite different while the mean for each is the same. The first and second curves are symmetric while the third is skewed. If we compare the first with the third, the third is negatively skewed by the scores under the left tail of the distribution. While the first and second curves are alike in being symmetric, the distribution of scores in the second is almost flat--the scores spread out almost equally across the range.

In the first curve, though, most of the scores in the distribution cluster around the mean.

In order to describe the distribution of interval data, the measure of central tendency will not suffice. This is particularly true, as we have just seen, when we wish to compare the performance of different groups. To describe the data more accurately, we have to measure the degree of variability of the data from the measure of central tendency.

Just as we have three ways of talking about the most typical value or score in the data, there are three ways to show how the data are spread out from that point. These are called *range, variance,* and *standard deviation.*

Range

The easiest way to talk about the spread of scores from the central point is range. For example, the average age of students in a particular adult school ESL class is 19. The youngest student is 17 and the oldest is 42. To compute the range subtract the lowest value from the highest.

$$Range = X_{highest} - X_{lowest}$$

$$Range = 42 - 17 = 25$$

The age range in this class is 25.

Imagine the distribution plank for this age data. Nineteen, the mean, is the balance point on the seesaw. The lowest "weight" on the seesaw is 17. The highest is 42. The balance point is much closer to 17 than 42, so we know many more Ss group at the lower end of the range. We can predict, then, that this is not a normal distribution but one that is positively skewed. The mean is higher than it would be if it were not for the extreme score of 42. Range is a useful, informal measure of variability. However, it changes drastically with the magnitude of extreme scores. If you had test score data where one person simply didn't do the test (scored zero), the range would dramatically change just because of that one score. Since it is an unstable measure, it is rarely used for statistical analyses. Yet, it is a useful, first measure of variability.

Because range is so unstable, some researchers prefer to stabilize it by using the *semi-interquartile range* instead. The semi-interquartile range (SIQR) gives the range for the middle 50% of the scores.

The formula for the SIQR is:

$$SIQR = \frac{Q_3 - Q_1}{2}$$

Q_3 is the score at the 75th percentile and Q_1 is the score at the 25th percentile.

For example, imagine that for the TOEFL test, the score at the 75th percentile is 560 and 470 is the score at the 25th percentile. The SIQR would be:

$$\frac{560 - 470}{2} = 45$$

One nice thing about the SIQR is that it is much less affected by extreme scores than the range is. Moreover, it can be used in skewed distributions where there are extremely high or low scores since the extreme scores are not considered in calculating the SIQR. In a skewed distribution, the median can be used as a measure of central tendency and the SIQR can be used as a measure of variability. Of course, the disadvantage of the SIQR is that percentile scores must be available or calculated.

◇◇◇◇◇◇◇◇◇◇◇◇◇◇◇◇◇◇◇◇◇◇◇◇◇◇◇◇◇◇◇◇◇◇◇◇◇◇◇

Practice 6.3

1. Look back at the first data set for the vocabulary test (page 160). The mean for the data was _29.1_. The range is _20_. Again imagine the distribution of the data with each score as a weight on a plank and the mean as the balance point. Does this picture appear to be a normal distribution? Why (not)?

_____No - pos. skewed_____

_____

2. Imagine that you are evaluating a special English reading program for a national Ministry of Education. On what grounds would you argue for and against using the median and the SIQR as the measure of variability (thus deleting data above the 75th percentile and below the 25th percentile)?_____

_____

_____

_____

◇◇◇◇◇◇◇◇◇◇◇◇◇◇◇◇◇◇◇◇◇◇◇◇◇◇◇◇◇◇◇◇◇◇◇◇◇◇◇

Variance

Suppose you were teaching an introductory linguistics class and when you returned a set of midterm exams, you announced that the mean score on the exam was 93.5. You can be sure that all students immediately check to see how close their scores are to the average for the test. If a student scores 89, the score is 4.5 points from the mean. This is the *deviation* of one score from the mean.

Students are interested in how much better (or worse) they perform than the average for the class. For research, however, we want to know more than just one individual's placement relative to the mean. We want a measure that takes the distribution of all scores into account. One such measure is *variance*.

To compute variance, we begin with the deviation of the individual scores from the mean. A lowercase, italicized x is used to symbolize the deviation of an individual score from the mean.

If we added all the individual variations of scores from the mean for the midterm exam, we would have the total for variability--$\sum x$. However, we know the total for variability is, in part, a reflection of the number of observations or Ss' scores in the data. So, we need to find an average variability for the distribution.

The following table shows the scores for the midterm exam. If you compute the $\overline{X}$, you will find that it is 93.5.

[handwritten: not italicized]

Midterm Exam

X	$x=(X-\overline{X})$	x^2	X	x	x^2
100	6.5	42.25	85	-8.5	72.25
88	-5.5	30.25	82	-11.5	132.25
83	-10.5	110.25	96	2.5	6.25
105	11.5	132.25	107	13.5	182.25
78	-15.5	240.25	102	8.5	72.25
98	4.5	20.25	113	19.5	380.25
126	32.5	1056.25	94	.5	.25
85	-8.5	72.25	119	25.5	650.25
67	-26.5	702.25	91	-2.5	6.25
88	-5.5	30.25	100	6.5	42.25
88	-5.5	30.25	72	-21.5	462.25
77	-16.5	272.25	88	-5.5	30.25
114	20.5	420.25	85	-8.5	72.25

[handwritten: sum of sq² total = total variability in data set]

In the second column are the individual difference values (x). Each value is the difference between the individual score and the mean ($X - \overline{X}$). This was the first step in the computation. If you sum these individual deviation scores, the result may surprise you. $\sum(X-\overline{X})=0$. Does the result surprise you? Remember that the mean is the balance point on the seesaw of the total distribution. If you add all the minus weights on one side of the seesaw and then all the plus weights on the other side, you should get zero because they balance each other out.

We have already said that we want an average of all the individual deviations from the mean. Obviously, adding them all and dividing them by the number of scores or observations won't work if the total is zero. To solve this dilemma, we *square* the deviation of each individual score from the mean (these are shown in the column labeled x^2) and add these. This total, sometimes called the *sum of squares*, shows the total variability in the data set.

Our next step is to find an average for this total variability figure, $\sum x^2$. That is, we don't want the measure of variability to increase just because there are lots of scores in the distribution. When we average a total, we usually divide by the number of cases (the N). It would be perfectly legitimate to do this, if we had a large N (over 100 scores).

However, with a small sample, mathematicians have determined that it is more accurate to divide the total by $N - 1$, since $N - 1$ produces an unbiased estimate of the variance. If we divide by $N - 1$, the result will be:

$$\frac{\sum x^2}{N - 1} = \frac{5268.5}{25} = 210.74$$

The formula for variance, then, is the following.

$$variance = \frac{\sum x^2}{N - 1}$$

Let's summarize the steps shown in this formula once again.

1. Compute the mean: $\overline{X}$.

2. Subtract the mean from each score to obtain the individual deviation scores: $x = X - \overline{X}$.

3. Square each individual deviation and add: $\sum x^2$.

4. Divide by $N - 1$: $\dfrac{\sum x^2}{N - 1}$.

◇◇◇◇◇◇◇◇◇◇◇◇◇◇◇◇◇◇◇◇◇◇◇◇◇◇◇◇◇◇◇◇◇◇◇◇◇◇◇

Practice 6.4

▶ 1. Prospective teachers can receive 20 points on an instrument developed to screen urban school teachers. Here are the scores of 10 prospective teachers.

S	Score	$X - \overline{X}$	x^2	
1	16	.6	.36	256
2	13	-2.4	5.76	169
3	13	-2.4	5.76	169
4	19	3.6	12.96	361
5	18	2.6	6.76	324
6	15	-.4	.16	225
7	20	4.6	21.16	400
8	11	-4.4	19.36	121
9	14	-1.4	1.96	196
10	15	-.4	.16	225

$\overline{X} = 15.4$ 2446

Fill in the values in the chart.

2. As a review of symbols, supply their values in terms of the example data.

$$(\Sigma X) = \underline{154}$$
$$\Sigma x = \underline{0}$$
$$\Sigma x^2 = \underline{74.4}$$
$$N = \underline{10}$$
$$\overline{X} = \underline{15.4}$$

▶ 3. What is the variance shown in the data for practice item 1 above?

$$variance = \frac{\sum x^2}{N-1} = \underline{8.26}$$

◇◇◇

Standard Deviation

If you understand the concept of variance, then you already understand standard deviation. The two measures are very similar. Variance is used in many statistical procedures, but standard deviation is more often reported in research articles and so the term may be more familiar to you. Both measures of variability attempt to do the same thing--give us a measure that shows us how much variability there is in scores.

While range simply looks at the scores at each end of a distribution, variance and standard deviation begin by calculating the distance of every individual score from the mean. Thus, they take every score into account. Because individual scores will be either below or above the mean and the mean is the balance point, the deviation of each score must be squared. Once squared, these deviations are totaled. To get an average for the deviations, the total is then divided by $N-1$. Up to this point the two measures are the same. Standard deviation goes one step further. Since we began by squaring the differences of each score from the mean, we now do the reverse. We change it by taking the square root of the variance.

You may see different directions, different ways of representing formulas. Can you see that the following directions say the same thing? (*s*, here, stands for standard deviation. You may also see it abbreviated as *s.d.* The symbol *s* is used in formulas but many researchers use *s.d.* as a label in tables and charts.)

$$s = \sqrt{\frac{\Sigma(X-\overline{X})^2}{N-1}}$$

or

$$s = \sqrt{\frac{\Sigma x^2}{N-1}}$$

If you have a problem with this, talk through it in your discussion group.

In order to clarify the concept of standard deviation, we have asked you to begin by subtracting the mean from each individual score. There is, however, a much easier way that uses raw scores instead. The formula is:

raw score formula

$$s = \sqrt{\frac{\sum X^2 - [(\sum X)^2 \div N]}{N - 1}}$$

Let's read through the formula. First it says to square each of the scores. Then the formula asks that we sum these. Let's do this with the midterm exam data:

Midterm Exam

X	X²	X	X²
100	10000	85	7225
88	7744	82	6724
83	6889	96	9216
105	11025	107	11449
78	6084	102	10404
98	9604	113	12769
126	15876	94	8836
85	7225	119	14161
67	4489	91	8281
88	7744	100	10000
88	7744	72	5184
77	5929	88	7744
114	12996	85	7225

The total for X, or $\sum X$, is 2431, and we must square this value according to the formula (5,909,761). Then, the $\sum X^2$ is 232,567. We can place these values in the formula. If you are confused, remember that $\sum X^2$ means to *first* square and *then* add. $(\sum X)^2$ means that you first sum and then square the total.

($\sum$x)² = add, then sq.
$\sum$x² = square, then add

$$s = \sqrt{\frac{\sum X^2 - [(\sum X)^2 \div N]}{N - 1}}$$

$$s = \sqrt{\frac{232567 - (5909761 \div 26)}{25}}$$

$$s = 14.52$$

If you work with a hand calculator, the formula that uses raw scores will save you time. If you have entered the data into the computer, the computer will, of course, do all this calculation for you.

What does the actual standard deviation figure tell us? We have said that it is a measure of variability of the data from the point of central tendency. While we will elaborate much more on the concept of standard deviation later, the important thing to realize now is that the larger the standard deviation figure, the wider the range of distribution away from the measure of central tendency. The data are more widely scattered. The smaller the standard deviation figure, the more similar the scores, and the more tightly clustered the data are around the mean.

[handwritten margin notes]: When overall range same, Thus s = 4.5 on test of 100 > means something. s = 1.2 on test of 100 vs on test of 20, who knows?

large s.d.   small s.d.

If you have been successful in visualizing a seesaw with data spread out on a plank and the mean as the balance point, the following visuals may be more helpful. Think of the standard deviation as a ruler that measures how scattered out on the plank the data actually are. When the data are widely scattered the standard deviation is large and the ruler is long. When the data are tightly clustered around the balance point of the seesaw, then the standard deviation "ruler" is short.

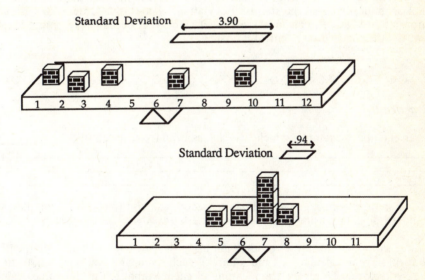

Standard Deviation   3.90

1 2 3 4 5 6 7 8 9 10 11 12

Standard Deviation   .94

1 2 3 4 5 6 7 8 9 10 11

How might this information on standard deviation help you? Imagine that you work in a language school where students are placed on the basis of an entrance exam. You will teach one advanced class and one low-intermediate class. There are three sections of each class; you can select your sections. (All three sections meet at the same time so convenience as far as time is concerned is not an issue!) You are given first choice. The director presents you with the following information:

Placement Exam Scores

Section	$\overline{X}$	s	
Advanced			
1	82.4	24.1	
2	81.0	4.5	homogeneous
3	80.9	8.2	
Low Intermediate			
1	30.1	1.1	
2	29.4	12.4	
3	25.8	8.7	

As you can see, the sections are arranged according to the mean score for the section. Look first at the difference in the mean scores for the three advanced classes. The means are very close together. Now look at the standard deviation values for the three advanced classes. The scores for section 2 are all close together. This class is the most homogeneous. Section 1, on the other hand, has much greater variability. If you are an advocate of cooperative learning, you might want a class where students are at different levels of ability. In that case, you'd probably select section 1. If you like to work with classes where everyone is at about the same level, you might decide between sections 2 and 3.

We can make more informed decisions if we consider not just the mean (or median or mode) but also the standard deviation. The standard deviation gives us information which the mean alone cannot give. It is perhaps even more important than the measure of central tendency.

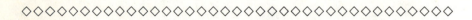

Practice 6.5

1. In the above example, which two classes would you select? Why?_____
_____
_____
_____

✓▶ 2. For the example given in the last practice exercise (page 172), compute the standard deviation using first the formula $s = \sqrt{variance}$. $s = $ _2.87_.

Now, recompute the standard deviation using the raw score formula. Remember you will have to calculate X^2, the square of each score, and $\sum X^2$, the sum of these squared scores. To review the meaning of each symbol, fill in the values below. Then place these in the formula for the standard deviation and show the results below.

$\sum X^2 =$ ~~2446~~
$(\sum X)^2 =$ _23716_
$N =$ _10_
$\sum X =$ _154_

$$s = \sqrt{\dfrac{\sum X^2 - [(\sum X)^2 \div N]}{N - 1}} = \sqrt{\dfrac{2446 - 2371.6}{9}} = \sqrt{\dfrac{74.4}{9}}$$

$$= \sqrt{8.27} = 2.875$$

◇◇

Standard Deviation and the Normal Distribution

Given that we already know that the larger the standard deviation, the wider the spread of scores away from the mean, what else can standard deviation tell us? If the distribution of the scores is normal, the standard deviation can give us a great deal of information. We already know that in a normal distribution, the mean, mode, and median are the same. The mean score then is equivalent to the median. When that is so, half the scores will be higher than the mean and half will be lower. Not only can we say that roughly 50% of the scores will fall above and 50% below the mean, but we can approximate the percent of scores that will fall between the mean and 1 standard deviation above or below the mean.

If the distribution is normal, 34% of the scores will fall between the mean and 1 standard deviation above the mean. Standard deviation works like a ruler measuring off the distance from the mean for 34% of the data in normal distributions. The same is true for 1 standard deviation below the mean. 68% of all the scores will occur between 1 standard deviation below and 1 standard deviation above the mean. Notice that we have not specified the numerical value of the mean in this statement. Nor have we specified the numerical value of the standard deviation. In a normal distribution, the most typical score is specified as the mean. Once we know the value of the standard deviation for the data, we have a "ruler" for determining the distance from the mean of any proportion of the total data. Look at the following bell-shaped distribution curve.

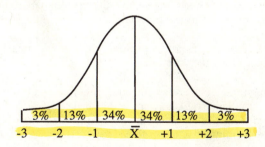

3%	13%	34%	34%	13%	3%
-3	-2	-1	$\overline{X}$	+1	+2	+3

50% (34 + 13 + 3) of the scores fall between the mean and 3 standard deviations above the mean. 50% fall between the mean and 3 standard deviations below the mean. 68% (34 + 34) of the scores fall between −1 standard deviation below and +1 standard deviation above the mean. 94% (34 + 34 + 13 + 13) of the scores are between ±2 standard deviations from the mean. That leaves 3% under each tail between 2 and 3 standard deviations above and below the mean.

In succeeding chapters, we will see how useful this information can be for research where we want to compare the performance of groups (or the changing performance of the same group over time). For now, you should realize that means of groups may be very similar and yet the groups, in fact, may be quite different because the distribution of scores away from the mean may be quite different. In some cases, the standard deviation may be very large because the data are spread out in the distribution. In other cases, the standard deviation may be quite small because the scores cluster around the mean. If we give a class a pretest, teach the content of the test and then give a posttest, we expect two things will happen. First, the $\bar{X}$ will be higher on the posttest, and second, the standard deviation will be much smaller. Sometimes, when the material to be learned is very difficult, large gains in the $\bar{X}$ may not occur but we would expect that instruction would have the effect of making students perform more similarly. The standard deviation should, therefore, be smaller.

Ordinal Measures

In chapter 5 we talked about ways frequency data might be summarized and displayed. In this chapter, we have presented the ways in which interval data are typically summarized. This leaves a gap regarding rank order, or ordinal, measurement. And it is precisely here that we believe (others may or may not agree) that it is important to be clear about just how variables are measured.

In many statistics books, the measurement of variables is treated as either discrete or continuous. *Discrete* refers to measurement of a nominal (categorical) variable which by its nature either is or is not present. There is no measure of "how much," for the choice is either 100% or zero. Such variables are tallied in frequency counts. Ordinal and interval data are then grouped together as *continuous* data as though they were the same thing. That is, ordinal measurement where variables are rated or ranked in relation to each other (and thus tell us "how much more") is seen as effectively the same as interval measurement where "how much" is measured on an equal-interval basis.

While it is true that in some instances ordinal and interval measurement may be very similar, in other cases they are not.

To begin to understand this issue, consider the following. Prospective ESL teachers in Egypt, studied by El-Naggar and Heasley (1987), were asked to respond to items regarding the value of microteaching (i.e., videotaped peer teaching where the performing teacher-trainee reviews the tape with peers and supervisor). The items were statements and each student responded according to how strongly they agreed with the statement. For example:

I prefer to receive feedback from my supervisor rather than from my peers.
1   2   3   4   5

The numbers show 1 = strongly disagree, 2 = disagree, 3 = neither agree nor disagree, 4 = agree, 5 = strongly agree.

→ Scale used for tax. evaluations at universities.

The question is whether the scale is equal-interval. How large an interval is there between *agree* and *strongly agree*? Between *neither agree nor disagree* and *agree*? Are these intervals the same? Can we use a mean score as a measure of central tendency for such data?

If we believe the intervals are equal, we should be able to compute a mean and standard deviation for the responses. If not, then it makes no sense to compute these measures.

Assume you were the teacher in this course and you gave the students the questionnaire before you assigned them their grades. How spread out do you imagine their ratings might be (i.e., what would you guess the range to be)? (If it is small, then we need to question whether this is truly a five-point scale at all.) If we think the scale is like interval data, then we would think responses to such questions can properly be summed to give a single numerical value that reflects each individual's attitude toward microteaching.

If you believe that the scale is really continuous or equal interval and that the distribution approaches the normal distribution, then it is quite proper to go ahead and use the mean and standard deviation in describing the data. If you do not believe this is the case, then you would more likely discuss each question separately, reporting on the number of teachers who selected a rating of 1 or 2 or 3 or 4 or 5, treating the data in terms of frequency. Thus, you could use the mode to show the most popular choice for the teachers on each item, or you could report the proportion of teachers who selected each point on the scale.

Let's consider another example. Interlanguage researchers (researchers interested in the the emerging language system of the second language learner) often use counts to show how frequently a particular grammar or phonological structure is used correctly by learners. They count the number of times the learner uses the structure correctly and the number of times it is incorrect (or omitted). This yields a "percent correct" figure for each structure. With such figures from many learners, researchers can make claims about difficulty of particular structures. Do you believe the scores have received interval measurement? Certainly percentage intervals are equally spaced. Many researchers would agree that such conversions do result in continuous interval data and that a "mean percent correct" is an appropriate description of central tendency for the data. We would argue that the data began as open-ended frequencies which, even though converted, still may not be continuous. The distribution of the data may not approach a normal distribution and so the mean and standard deviation are not appropriate statistics in such cases.

? explain

If you agree with us, would you, nevertheless, feel comfortable about rank-ordering the structures in relation to each other? That is, you might not want to say that a structure with a "score" of 88 was ten points higher than a structure with a "score" of 78, but you might feel justified in ranking one above the other *why?* without specifying the interval between them. The data would be ordinal, and the median would be used as the best measure of central tendency. Whichever choice you make, you should be prepared to justify your decision. This decision is important, for it affects the type of statistical procedure you will use in testing hypotheses.

Statisticians most often argue in favor of treating rank-order data as though it were interval data. They see ordinal scales as being continuous (with the mean as the appropriate measure of central tendency). Many argue that statistically it makes no real difference and that it is best to treat ordinal and interval as the same. In many cases we believe it is better to consider them as ordinal rather than as interval data, and especially so if the data are not normally distributed. We will argue--and this argument will continue in the succeeding chapters--that the researcher should make an informed decision, informed by the true nature of the data and that the decision should be justified in the research report. This decision is crucial because it has important consequences for selecting an appropriate statistical test for the data.

◇◇◇◇◇◇◇◇◇◇◇◇◇◇◇◇◇◇◇◇◇◇◇◇◇◇◇◇◇◇◇◇◇◇◇◇◇

Practice 6.6

1. Assume that you administered a 30-item questionnaire to teacher trainees as a replication of the El-Naggar and Heasley study. Would you feel comfortable summing each student's responses on the 30 items and treating this as an "attitude" score--similar to a test score? If not, why not? *No because Qs may not tap relevant attitudes and ...*

2. Our university, at the end of each term, requires students to evaluate courses and teachers. Questions such as "How would you rate the overall performance of your instructor?" are followed by a 9-point scale. Do you believe this 9-point scale does, in fact, represent a more continuous measure than shown in the previous example? If so, why? *More of a range for breakdown*

◇◇◇◇◇◇◇◇◇◇◇◇◇◇◇◇◇◇◇◇◇◇◇◇◇◇◇◇◇◇◇◇◇◇◇◇◇

Conclusion

In all research reports where rank-order or interval data have been collected, it is important to display a measure of central tendency (mode, median, or mean) _and_ a measure of variability (range, standard deviation, or variance). While we always want to know what the most typical score might be, the distribution of scores around that typical score is perhaps even more important. Why this is so will be illustrated in the next chapter. Before we turn to that issue, let's consider again why researchers select one or another measure of central tendency and when one might use one measure of variability rather than another.

If you review the section on measures of central tendency, you will remember that the mean score is very sensitive to extreme scores. If these extreme scores represent "outliers" that can clearly be shown to "not belong" to the data, it is possible (when there is strong justification) to remove them from the data and follow them as separate case studies. If such scores seriously skew the data, the distribution will not be normal. If the data do not approach a normal distribution, this will limit the types of statistical procedures that can be used in testing hypotheses.

Some researchers consider data removal a questionable procedure for there is no established methodology or set guidelines for deciding what constitutes an outlier or when outliers can safely be deleted. Of course when there is no clear explanation for outlier performance, they must remain in the data and the researcher would be wise to opt for the median as the best measure of central tendency. For example, if you work with census tract data (where data from census counts are displayed within mapped geographic areas) and find that some families report incomes that are extremely high or low compared to that of other respondents, there is no legitimate way of removing these families from the data sample. Therefore, the median is usually used for such data.

The mode or the median are often used in reports where data are drawn from beginning language learners, from preschool children, or from persons with language disorders. Performance in these cases may vary considerably. When this is so, the mode may be the most appropriate measure, but if there are only a few extreme scores, the median should be used.

If the data come from rank-order scales rather than true interval measurement, you should discuss the options available to you with an advisor or statistical consultant. If the rank scales are very interval-like and the distribution of the data appears to be normal, you should feel comfortable in reporting the data in terms of $\overline{X}$ and _s.d._ If they are not, you may present the information in terms of the proportion or number of persons who placed at each point on the scale. You might also give the mode, or the median, and the range (depending on the focus of the study). In the first instance, you would use the $\overline{X}$ and _s_ or _variance_ in testing the hypotheses. In the second, you might opt for the _median_. The decision is yours, but it is a decision which will have important consequences. These consequences will become clear in subsequent chapters of this volume.

Activities

1. Our university, worried about the legality of asking _immigrant_ students, like foreign students, to take an ESL English language proficiency test, thought they

might use a combination of SAT scores and length of residence to locate students in need of special ESL instruction. To check this, we found 69 students for whom we had ESL test scores, SAT scores, L1 background, and length of residence information. The following table is taken from the report.

VARIABLE	N	MEAN	STD DEV
ESL Test	69	109.043	20.217
SAT Verbal	69	307.101	76.660
SAT Math	69	540.970	105.923
Language	69	6.623	2.000
Months in US	69	61.723	39.118
SAT Tot	69	847.971	147.754

Interpret the table in the following terms. (1) Is it appropriate to display the means and standard deviations for each of these variables? If not, why? (2) If this were your study and you wished to display this information, would you arrange the information in the same way? (3) What sort of a visual display might you use for this information?

2. A. Spector-Leech (1986. Perceptions of functional and cultural difficulties by Japanese executives in Southern California. Unpublished master's thesis, TESL, UCLA.) administered a questionnaire to 411 Japanese business managers living in the United States. A table presents the following information on their ages:

	Age
$\overline{X}$	45.5 yrs
s	7.2 yrs
Youngest	26.0 years
Oldest	63.0 years

Do you imagine that this is a random sample of Southern California-based Japanese business managers? What is the age range? With an n of 411 can you assume normal distribution? If so, what is the mode? The median? Draw a normal distribution polygon. Using the value of the standard deviation, label the ages for 1, 2, 3 standard deviations above and below the mean. According to this curve, are some of the managers predicted to fall outside the age range actually listed? What proportion of the managers are predicted to be between 52.7 years and 38.3 years? How many people does this proportion represent?

3. D. McGirt (1984. The effect of morphological and syntactic errors on holistic scores of native and nonnative compositions. Unpublished master's thesis, TESL, UCLA.) noted that nonnative students and native students alike must receive undergraduate instruction in composition. Although they may elect to take ESL composition rather than English composition, students receive the same credit. Instruction in "parallel" courses is always an issue even though the students in these two classes may have very different instructional needs. One motivation behind this study was a desire to know whether students should cover the same material in the two courses (i.e., less emphasis on grammar and morphology in the ESL classes). American composition teachers were asked to give holistic ratings to compositions from these two groups. In one set, the ESL compositions

were typed in their original form and interspersed with those written by native speakers. In the second condition, the morphology errors in both ESL and native speakers' compositions were corrected before they were randomly ordered for ratings. The ratings were holistic (ranging from 1.5 to 15.5). Interpret the following chart:

Group	$\overline{X}$	s
Native speakers		
With errors	9.21	2.12
Without errors	10.10	2.13
Nonnative students		
With errors	5.80	2.21
Without errors	8.56	1.66

In which group of compositions was there the greatest agreement among ratings? In which was there least? Thirty native speakers and 30 nonnative students enrolled in ESL or English composition served as subjects in this study. Do you feel the Ss probably are representative of students normally enrolled in these classes? If not, why? The figure shows the scores given the compositions when errors were not corrected. Comment on the distribution of scores.

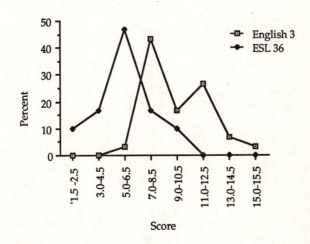

4. J. Phillips (1984. A comparison of the writing performance of immigrant and foreign ESL students at UCLA. Unpublished master's thesis, TESL, UCLA.) carried out an error analysis as one part of his thesis. The mean length of compositions for the two groups were as follows:

	Immigrant	Foreign
	$274.542 (\overline{X}_I)$	$240.143 (\overline{X}_F)$
	$76.713 (s_I)$	$80.123 (s_F)$

+1 sd 351.255   +sd = 320.266   +2sd = 400.389

+2sd 427.968

Those subscripts I and F look pretty spiffy, don't they! What do they represent? Which group appears to write longer compositions? In which group is there more variability? If you add 1 standard deviation to the mean of the immigrant group, what is the total? If you add 1 standard deviation to the mean of the foreign student group, what is the total? How different do the two groups appear at this point? At 2 standard deviations from the mean? Assume for the moment that the data are normally distributed and chart the two means and standard deviations onto an overlapping polygon. What does the distribution look like? *The F is wider, more spread out*

5. T. Mannon (1986. Teacher talk: a comparison of a teacher's speech to native and nonnative speakers. Unpublished master's thesis, TESL, UCLA.) counted the frequency of a number of structures a teacher used in her content lectures to native speaker students and in her lectures to ESL students. The talk data were entered as T-units (roughly equivalent to an independent clause). The forms (e.g., number of tag questions, imperatives, referential questions) were then counted per T-unit. The teacher, thus, would have a total number of T-units in a lecture. Some of these would, for example, include tag questions. A percentage figure for tag questions could thus be obtained. A series of charts, similar to the following, were presented for each structure.

	$\overline{X}$ tag Qs	s.d.
Teacher → NS	.65%	1.29%
Teacher → NNS	.91%	2.02%

Did the teacher use tag questions more or less often than once in 100 T-units? Using the mean and standard deviation figures, attempt to draw a distribution polygon for these data. What happened? Consult others in your study group to see what they think about the data. What conclusion can you reach?

6. R. Hinrichs (1985. WANDAH: A critical evaluation of objectives and uses among developers, teachers, and students. Unpublished master's thesis, TESL, UCLA.) asked 128 freshmen to rate a writing software package. The figure below displays means and standard deviations for their responses (a 9-point rating scale on effectiveness of the program for seven functions). The statements for the seven functions asked if the users found WANDAH saved them time in writing, helped them revise, help them organize their writing, made them better writers, was easy to read on the screen, whether the program was confusing, and whether they used the package for all their writing. Convert the display to a numerical table. If this were your study, which would you use for your final report? Why?

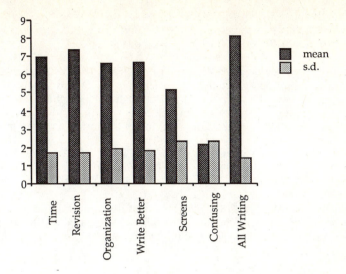

7. C. Holten (1984. The use of authentic language materials in low-intermediate ESL classes. Unpublished master's thesis, TESL, UCLA.) as one small part of her evaluation, asked observers to evaluate materials for three discourse units-- description, narration, and process. Here are tables for their ratings (1 to 5 with 5 being highest).

Description Unit	$\overline{X}$	s.d.
N = 6 observers		
Lesson Presentation	3.8	1.1
Materials Format	3.7	1.4
Teachability of Materials	4.4	.81
Student Participation	3.8	1.2
Student Reaction	3.7	1.0
Narration Unit		
N = 7 observers		
Lesson Presentation	3.7	1.3
Materials Format	3.3	1.4
Teachability of Materials	4.1	1.1
Student Participation	3.7	1.4
Student Reaction	3.5	1.4
Process Unit		
N = 5 observers		
Lesson Presentation	4.2	.87
Materials Format	4.3	1.0

Teachability of Materials	4.6	.68
Student Participation	3.9	1.1
Student Reaction	4.0	.77

In which ratings did the observers most closely agree? In which did their ratings vary the most? Consider for a moment the other options open for displaying these data. Would you have preferred to have a frequency chart for the ratings (1-5) with the number of observers who selected each (instead of the mean and *s.d.* for each)? Why or why not? Can you think of any other way you might want to display these data?

References

El-Naggar, Z. & Heasley, B. 1987. The effects of microteaching as an alternative to practice teaching: an experimental study. Paper presented at the 7th National Symposium on English Language Teaching, Cairo, Egypt, March 24-26.

Chapter 7

Locating Scores and Finding Scales in a Distribution

- •*Locating scores in a distribution*
    Percentiles, quartiles, and deciles
- •*Locating comparable scores in distributions*
    Standardized scores and the normal distribution
    z scores and T scores
- •*Distributions with nominal data*
    Implicational scaling (Guttman scalogram)
- •*Other applications of distribution measures*

When describing data (rather than testing our hypotheses) we often want to locate individual scores in a distribution. This location may be in terms of percentile ranks or by placement in levels such as quartiles or deciles. We frequently need to locate individuals in a distribution where information comes from several sources rather than just one. In addition, we sometimes want to look at a distribution to discover whether or not a single scale can be discovered within which individual Ss or observations can be ranked. All of these issues relate to distribution of data and the location of individual scores within that distribution.

Locating Scores in a Distribution

Percentiles, Quartiles, and Deciles

If you have ever taken an ETS test, the TOEFL, the Miller Analogies Test, or the Graduate Record Exam, you probably received a card in the mail with your score and the percentile level based on scores of Ss who took the test previously and established norms for students from your major (education, engineering, English, etc.). The report doesn't always say how well you did compared with students who took the test at the same time that you did, but rather how well you did in comparison with other people from your area of expertise who have taken the test. (You should always check the fine print to find out exactly how your percentile rank has been set.)

When we compute a percentile rank, we locate an individual score in a distribution. Basically, percentiles locate an individual score by showing what percent of the scores are below it. Actually, the measurement isn't just "below" the score, but rather below the score plus half of those that received the same mark. So, we usually say the percentile shows the number of scores "at or below" the individual score in the distribution. If you receive a card that reports you as being at the 92 percentile, this means that you did as well or better than 92% of people tested on the exam. For example, the TOEFL publishes the following information so that examinees can discover how well they compare with others taking the test:

TOEFL SCORE COMPARISON TABLE
(based on the score of 759,768 examinees
who took the test from July 1985 through June 1987)

SECTION SCORES

TOTAL Your Score	%ile lower	Sec 1 Your Score	%ile lower	Sec 2 Your Score	%ile lower	Sec 3 Your Score	%ile lower
660	99	66	98	66	97	66	98
640	97	64	95	64	94	64	96
620	93	62	90	62	90	62	92
600	89	60	85	60	85	60	87
580	83	58	78	58	77	58	80
560	74	56	71	56	69	56	71
540	64	54	62	54	59	54	61
520	52	52	52	52	50	52	50
500	41	50	41	50	40	50	39
480	29	48	30	48	31	48	29
460	20	46	20	46	22	46	22
440	13	44	12	44	15	44	15
420	8	42	7	42	10	42	10
400	4	40	4	40	7	40	6
380	2	38	2	38	4	38	4
360	1	36	1	36	2	36	2
340		34		34	1	34	1
320		32		32	1	32	1
300		30		30		30	

From the 1988-1989 *Bulletin of Information for TOEFL and TSE.* Reprinted with the permission of the Educational Testing Service, Princeton, NJ.

Practice 7.1

▶1. Use the TOEFL table to answer the following questions.

a. What is the percentile ranking for the following scores of one of your ESL students? Section 1: 54 ___62___ ; Section 2: 62 ___90___ ; Section 3: 42 __10__ .

b. If your student obtained a total score that placed her at the 52nd percentile, you could place her score as __520__ .

c. Since the percentiles are based on the scores of a set number of examinees, it is possible to turn these into actual frequencies. How many persons received a total score of 380 or less? __15,195__ .

d. If your school requires a TOEFL above 500 for student admission, how many of these examinees would not have met the admission requirement? __311505__ . How many would have met the requirement? __448263__ .

2. If your institution uses the TOEFL to screen applicants, what cutoff point do they use? _____ What percentile point does this cutoff represent? _____

◇◇

The student's percentile rank for the total test is usually the most important piece of information (since universities often use a set cutoff point for admitting or rejecting students). However, the percentiles for the sections also give us valuable information. For example, the overall percentile for a foreign student and an immigrant student might be the same but we would predict that immigrant students (who have had more opportunities to use the oral language) might outperform foreign students on some sections and perhaps do less well on other sections of the test. Students from different majors might also have the same percentile overall but differ in performance on the different sections. This information would be useful for placement purposes and for curriculum design.

To compute percentiles, we need to know what the distribution of scores looks like and the place of the individual score in the distribution. Assume you administered a test to 75 Ss entering your school's ESL program. The distribution of scores was as follows:

Score	Frequency (f)	Relative freq.	Cumulative freq. (F)	%ile
50	6	.08	75	96
→ 40	18	.24	69	80
30	27	.36	51	50
20	18	.24	24	20
10	6	.08	6	4

If you do not remember how the column labeled "Cumulative Frequency" (F) was computed, please review chapter 5, page 133.

The percentile requires that you locate the cumulative frequency at the point of the individual score. If the score was 40, 18 people received the score. The cumulative frequency for a score of 40 is 69. Divide this by the total N (which is 75 in this case). Then to make it a percent figure, multiply by 100. The result (92%) shows what percent of the Ss who took the test scored at or below 40. This figure is often reported as the "percentile." However, a more precise definition of percentile tells us how a particular S scored in terms of "as well as or better than" other *Ss* in the distribution. Percentile locates the score relative to the proportion of scores *at or below* it in the distribution. The *F* used, then, includes all the *Ss* who scored below and *half* the *Ss* whose scores place them at this particular point. Thus, the formula for percentile is:

$$Percentile = (100)\frac{\text{no. below} + 1/2 \text{ same}}{N}$$

$$= (100)\frac{51 + 1/2(18)}{75}$$

$$= 80$$

This formula will work to help you locate any score in a distribution. It locates the score by placing it relative to the proportion of all scores at or below it. Of course, you can easily locate the score relative to the number at or above it simply by subtracting from 100. If you took a test, scored 84 and that placed you at the 87th percentile, then 13% of the scores were at or higher than 84.

In school research, you may find reports of *quartiles* and *deciles* as well as percentiles. Quartiles and deciles are another way of locating individual scores within a distribution. The first quartile is the value where 25 percent (one-quarter) fall below the score. Seventy-five percent of the scores fall above the first quartile. However, if you say that a student's score is in the lowest quarter of the scores, you locate it anywhere in the first quartile. To say that a student scored *at* the 25th percentile is not the same as saying the student scored *in* the first quartile.

Deciles locate individual scores according to tenths of the cumulative rank. A score at the first decile is located so that 10% fall below and 90% above the score. The second decile is at the point where 20% fall below and 80% above the score. Again, to say an individual places *at* the eighth decile is not the same thing as *in* the eighth decile. The eighth decile locates a score so that 80% fall below and 20% above. At least 79% of all scores fall below those at the eighth decile. A score *in* the eighth decile would be within the range between the eighth and ninth decile.

Percentiles, quartiles, and deciles are similar in that they all locate an individual score relative to the number of scores below it. Scores of individuals are usually located in terms of percentiles. Deciles and quartiles are more commonly used to locate schools in a distribution. For example, schools may be required to give a statewide exam. For a specific grade level, the school achieves an average exam score based on the performance of its students. These averages are then used to place the school in decile or quartile divisions for all schools in the state.

Percentiles, quartiles, and deciles leave some unanswered questions in regard to locating scores in a distribution. For example, assume you want to compare two applicants for admission to your school. Each was the most outstanding person in her school. The percentile ranks of each at their respective schools might be the same--the 99th percentile. Yet, we don't know if one person dwarfed everyone else at her school while the superiority of the other might have been slight at the second school. Percentile information on the two students leaves us in the dark. We need another way of locating a score or value in a distribution that is sensitive to such differences. This second method is to use *standardized scores*.

Practice 7.2

▶ 1. Fill in the figures and compute the percentile rank for a student who scored 20 on the exam on page 189.

$$Percentile = (100)\frac{\text{no. below} + 1/2 \text{ same}}{N}$$

$$Percentile = (100)\underline{\qquad}$$

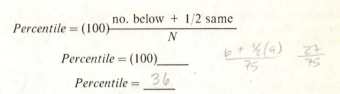

$$Percentile = \underline{36}$$

▶ 2. In what quartile of the distribution would the student's score be placed? _2nd_ . In what decile? _3rd_ .

3. Which method of placement--percentile, quartile, or decile--gives the most information? Why? _____ more detailed _____

_____

_____

4. On the basis of a statewide reading test, your school was placed in the second quartile of schools statewide. The local paper headlines this as among the poorest in the state. If the school serves mainly newly arrived immigrant students, what information might you ask for from the state department of education that would give you a more precise and appropriate placement for your school?_____

_____ w/i same group type _____

_____

_____

Locating Comparable Scores in Distributions

Standardized Scores

In the previous chapter, we discussed ways in which we can report a typical value or score for data. We also talked about three ways in which we could show how clustered or dispersed other values or scores might be in the data. We noted that one method, standard deviation, provides us with a "ruler" that will help us measure the dispersal of scores from the mean. That ruler can also help us locate individual scores in relation to the total distribution.

When the distribution of scores is normal, the standard deviation can give us extremely useful information. One use not mentioned in the last chapter is that of allowing us to compare scores of individuals where different tests have been used to measure performance. In the last chapter we asked you to select two classes to teach, given information on scores and standard deviations. Imagine, however, that this information came from two different tests--say, the department's ESL screening exam was used in two classes and a national test of English proficiency for the others. Scores that come from two different tests (although they purport to measure the same thing) do not allow us to make the needed comparison.

If the scores form a normal distribution and if you have the mean and standard deviation for each, there is an easy way to make such comparisons. This involves *standardized scores.*

Standardized Scores and the Normal Distribution

Before continuing, let's review the concept of normal distribution, for it is basic to the notion of standardized scores (and to many other procedures).

All of us like to think that we are unique, different from everyone else in what we can do. At the same time, we think of ourselves as being like all other humans in our capacities. In fact, the outcome of any sound measurement of human activity or behavior approximates a normal distribution. No matter what kind of behavior is measured or the type of measurement employed, the distribution of data in large samples tends to be normal. True, there will always be some people who score very high and some people who score very low on whatever we measure, but most of the data will fall around the point of central tendency and the dispersion of the data away from that point will be symmetrical.

How long do you think it would take you to learn 50 new vocabulary items in a language you do not now know? How different do you think your time to reach this criterion would be from that of your friends? Think of the best language learner you know. How much faster do you think this person might be at this task? Think of the worst language learner you know. How much longer do you think this person might take? Given this information, you could roughly estimate what a normal performance distribution would look like.

If you actually timed learning of these 50 items, you could begin tabulating the time period for each person. As you tested more and more people, you would find a curve emerging with most people around the middle point of the distribution (the central value). There would be a smaller number of people who *would* do better than the majority of people, as well as a smaller number who would *not* do as well. If you began the data collection with students enrolled in a private foreign language school, the times might be quite rapid and the data might cluster very tightly around the mean. If you then collected data from young children, you might find they clustered around a much slower point on the time scale, producing a bimodal distribution (one normal distribution for adults and one for children forming a bimodal curve).

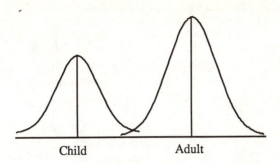

Child   Adult

As you tested more and more learners of all ages, these differences in the distribution would gradually become incorporated into a new overall curve and, again, most of the scores would cluster around one central value.

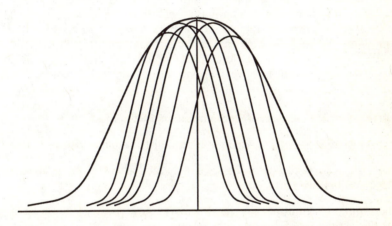

No matter what kind of behavior is measured, when large amounts of data are gathered, performance will approach this normal distribution. If a large number of students already enrolled in a graduate program are required to "pass" the ETS test in some foreign language (say French) for a Ph.D., you might imagine (given their sophistication in test-taking after this many years in school and their motivation) their scores would be high. This is true. Nevertheless, given the large number of Ss in this group who would take the test, their scores would approach a normal distribution. The scores would spread out symmetrically on either side of the mean. We would expect that the standard deviation would be small. That is, there would not likely be a wide dispersion of scores away from the mean. Rather, we would expect them to cluster fairly tightly around the high mean score.

Now imagine what the distribution on the ETS French test might be if were administered to all sorts of people from fifth grade on to students studying French in retirement communities. With a large number of scores, once again the distribution would approach the normal curve. The dispersion of scores would be wide (the standard deviation large) as the scores spread symmetrically away from the mean.

In each case, assuming a fairly large data sample has been collected, the distribution will tend to be normal. However, the distribution represents what is normal for the group from which that sample is drawn.

Given the fact that all of us share human abilities, it seems logical that human performance should approach a normal distribution. We do, of course, differ in how well or how fast we can do various tasks, but our behavior will fit in the normal range of behaviors. All of this seems logical enough. Yet, in fact, the normal distribution does not actually exist. We never get a completely normal data distribution. Normal distribution is an idealized concept. Still, the more data we collect, the closer we get to the normal distribution. So, we need a great deal of data if we hope to say much about general human language learning abilities. That is, we can't rely on the data from students enrolled in a private foreign language school to give us a normal distribution for *all* learners. The *S*s are not randomly selected as representative of all learners. In addition, the sample is not large enough. We can't rely on the distribution of 100 Ph.D. candidates on the ETS test of French to reflect that of all learners of French. The scores will be very close to a normal distribution, but obviously the distribution won't be representative of all learners.

The normal distribution has three important characteristics:

1. The mean, median, and mode in a normal distribution are all the same.

2. The first property results in the second characteristic--the distribution is bell-shaped and symmetric.

3. The normal distribution has no zero score; the tails never meet the straight line but stretch to infinity in both directions.

You know that half the scores fall above and half below the median. And since the mean and the median are the same in a normal distribution, the same can be said regarding the mean. Between the mean ($\overline{X}$) plus or minus one standard deviation ($\pm 1s$), we can expect to find 68% (more precisely, 68.26%) of the observations. Between $\overline{X}$ and $\pm 2s$, 95% (more precisely, 95.44%) of the observations are accounted for. And between $\overline{X}$ and $\pm 3s$, 99% (more precisely, 99.72%) of the data are entered. This leaves only 1% of the data to fall in the space shown under the outer stretch of the tails.

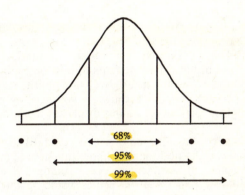

These proportions show the normal distribution of data for any behavior. This does not mean that all normal distributions look exactly like that shown in the above curve. Each of the following curves show a normal distribution. We can assume that in each case the mean, median, and mode are the same. None has a zero value and the tails never meet the straight line. The distribution is bell-shaped as the distribution of the scores from the mean spreads out symmetrically on either side of the mean. They differ in how widely the scores are dispersed from the the mean. In some cases, the scores cluster around the mean. The standard deviation is small. In other cases, the scores spread out from the mean so that the distribution is rather flat. The standard deviation is large.

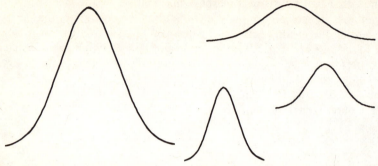

If we have a normal distribution, we can locate scores in relation to each other when we know the mean and standard deviation. For example, if we know that the mean for our ESL placement exam is 500 and the standard deviation is 50, we can locate the scores of individual students in relation to that distribution. If a student scored 550 (1 *s* above the mean), we know that the score is higher than 84% of the scores. To see that this is the case, you need only look back at the bell-shaped curve and the percentage figures displayed there.

If another student scored 400, the score is two standard deviations below the mean. From the normal distribution, we know that less than 3% of all scores will fall below this point. If a student scored 3 standard deviations above the mean, a score of 650, less than 1% of the scores would be above that point, and 99% would be below.

We have already shown, in talking about the normal distribution, that information on the the mean and standard deviation--coupled with the information on characteristics of normal distribution--allow us to locate individual scores in a distribution. *When the distribution is normal,* the characteristics of normal distribution also allow us to compute percentile ranks for all the observations in the data. However, to show what happens when the distribution is *not* normal, we will need to turn to the notion of *z* and *T* scores. First, though, review normal distribution by completing this practice.

◇◇◇

Practice 7.3

1. To conceptualize the normal distribution, consider how long you would be able to retain the meanings and forms of the 50 new words mentioned on page 192. In terms of retention, for how long a period do you think other people might be able to remember all fifty items?_____

_____

What do you imagine the mean length of time might be?

_____

How wide a range of time would be shown?

_____

Do you think the distribution would be normal? Why (not)?_____

_____

Would the distribution curve be flat (large standard deviation) or peaked (small standard deviation)?_____

_____

2. Imagine that you had the task of determining the cutoff point for fulfilling the language requirement for your Ph.D. program. ETS has sent you the scores of all your students on the exam and the mean and standard deviation for 3,000 humanities graduate students who took the test. How would you decide on the cutoff point? (Would you set it, say, 2 s.d. below the mean, assuming the scores are all incredibly high to begin with so that anyone attaining such a score could reasonably be expected to meet the requirement? Would you set it at 1 s.d. above the mean, assuming that your Ph.D. students should be somewhere "above average"?) Justify your choice. _____

_____
_____
_____
_____

3. Since we know that 68% of all scores in a normal distribution should fall within 1 s above and below the mean, 95% within 2 s above and below the mean, and 99% within 3 s above and below the mean, you can estimate where 1 s, 2 s, and 3 s occur in each distribution on page 195. Mark these estimates on the four polygons. In which is the standard deviation largest? _____ In which is it smallest? _____ Do means and standard deviations have fixed values in all distributions? Why (not)? _____

_____
_____
_____

If you're not sure, discuss this question in your study group and report your consensus below.

_____
_____
_____
_____

◇◇

z Scores

One of the most common ways of locating an individual score in relation to the distribution is to use a z score. To find it, we use standard deviation. Think, once again, of standard deviation as a ruler. Instead of being 12 inches long, it is 1 standard deviation in length. The z score just tells us how many standard deviations above or below the mean any score or observation might be. So, first we look to see how far the score is from the mean $(X - \overline{X})$. Then we divide this individual deviation by the standard deviation. This allows us to see how many ruler lengths--how many standard deviations--the score is from the mean. This is the z score.

$$z = \frac{X - \overline{X}}{s}$$

By finding the z score, we know where the score actually falls in the total distribution. For example, if a student scored 600 on the ESL placement test ($\overline{X}$ = 500, s = 50), then the z score would be +2.

$$z = \frac{X - \overline{X}}{s} = \frac{600 - 500}{50} = 2$$

The percentile for this score, assuming a normal distribution, is 98 (actually 97.72). If the z score were −2, the percentile score would be 2 (actually 2.27).

Of course, scores are not always exactly 1, 2, or 3 standard deviations away from the mean. Look at the following diagram. We gave a test to six people. Their scores are shown on the diagram below.

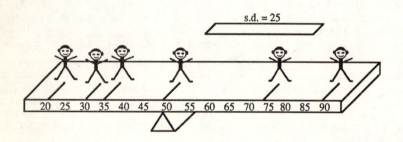

The mean, where the balance point is, was 50. The standard deviation turned out to be 25. The little ruler represents one standard deviation (1 z score in length, right?). Congratulations! You are the person who scored 90 on this test. Your z score is 1.6. One of the authors of this book is the person who scored 20. Her z score is −1.2.

To see how percentiles and z scores are linked in a normal distribution, examine the following chart which gives a more precise breakdown of the proportions of data in each segment of the curve in a normal distribution.

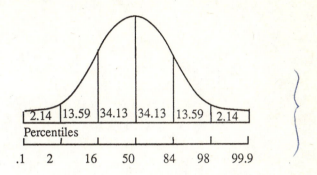

From this display, you might think that the percentile information is more important than z scores, or that the two are really the same thing. Neither is really true.

It is true that nobody would ever want to know that their individual z score was +2.1 or, worse yet, −1.4. Percentiles give information that makes more sense to most test-takers. However, z scores are useful in many ways. Imagine that you conducted an in-service course for ESL teachers. To receive university credit for the course, the teachers must take examinations--in this case, a midterm and a final. The midterm was a multiple-choice test of 50 items and the final exam presented teachers with 10 problem situations to solve. Sue, like most teachers, was a whiz at taking multiple-choice exams, but bombed out on the problem-solving final exam. She received a 48 on the midterm and a 1 on the final. Becky didn't do so well on the midterm. She kept thinking of exceptions to answers on the multiple-choice exam. Her score was 39. However, she really did shine on the final, scoring a 10. Since you expect students to do well on both exams, you reason that Becky has done a creditable job on each and Sue has not. Becky gets the higher grade. Yet, if you add the points together, Sue has 49 and Becky has 49. The question is whether the points are really equal.

Should Sue also do this bit of arithmetic, she might come to your office to complain of the injustice of it all. How will you show her that the value of each point on the two tests is different? It's z score information to the rescue! By converting the scores to z scores, it is possible to obtain equal units of measurement for the two tests even though the original units were quite different. That is, Sue picked up points on an easy multiple-choice test while Becky earned points when the earning was hard. As a general rule, then, when you want to compare performance over two tests which have different units of measurement, it's important to convert the scores to z scores.

Given z scores, it is easy to convert them back again to raw scores. For example, if the mean on the midterm was 40 and the standard deviation was 5 and a student's z score was -1, then

$$z = \frac{X - \overline{X}}{s}$$

$$X - \overline{X} = (s)(z)$$

$$X = (s)(z) + \overline{X}$$

$$X = (5)(-1) + 40$$

$$X = 35$$

z scores are useful in locating individual scores in a distribution. They are also useful when decisions must be made and data come from tests with different units of measurement. Percentiles and z scores both locate scores in a distribution but they do it in slightly different ways.

z scores, thus, are as useful as percentiles in locating individual scores in a distribution. Let's be sure we have dispelled the second notion as well--the notion that percentiles and z scores are basically the same thing. The chart on page 199 may be misleading, for it appears as though percentiles and z scores have an inherent equivalence. This is not the case. It is possible that identical z scores in two different distributions could have very different percentile ranks. You can see this is the case if you think of a distribution which is not normal. Imagine that five people took a test and they scored 2, 3, 6, 8, and 11. The mean is 6. Two people scored below the mean. They have negative z scores. Two scored above the mean. These z scores are positive. One person scored right on the balance point, 6. Here are the computed z scores and percentile ranks:

Score	z score	%ile
2	-1.09	10
3	-0.82	30
6	0.00	50
8	0.54	70
11	$+1.36$	90

If we locate each score (draw a small "brick" as a weight) on a distribution plank, it looks like this:

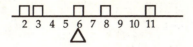

Now imagine that the scores of the five people were 0, 1, 2, 3, 14. The mean is 4. Four scores are below the mean. In the previous chart, the mean score was 6 and half the scores were at or below the mean. This is no longer the case, as you can see in the illustration.

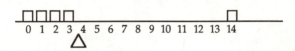

Here are the computed z scores and percentile ranks for these five scores.

Score	z score	%ile
0	−0.70	10
1	−0.53	30
2	−0.35	50
3	−0.17	70
14	1.75	90

Let's try to summarize this (without confusing you more). There is no inherent equivalence of z scores and percentiles. Each locates a score in the distribution in a different way. The percentile tells what percent of the scores in the distribution are at or below it. Does it say anything about its relationship to the mean? No, it doesn't. If one person receives a percentile rank of 98 and another a percentile rank of 99, does this necessarily mean that their scores are close to each other? No, it doesn't. A percentile just locates each score in proportion to the number of scores below it. The z score locates an individual score in relation to the mean but, unless the distribution is normal, it does not locate it in terms of the percentage of scores that fall above or below it. While both measures locate a score in a distribution, they do so in different ways.

T Scores

Another method of locating an individual score in a distribution is the standard *T score*. As you have no doubt noticed, z scores may be either positive or negative numbers. (If you add all the z scores in a distribution, the answer will be zero.) In addition, they often contain decimal points (a z score might be 1.8 standard deviations from the mean rather than just 1 or 2). This makes for error in reporting (it's easy to make a typo on decimals and + and − symbols). *T*

T scores

scores seem easier to interpret since they are always positive numbers and contain no fractions.

First, to get rid of all the fractions, the z score is multiplied by 10. So, a z score of 1.4 would be 14 at this point. A z score of .3 would be 3. To be sure we get rid of minus values, the mean (which was 0 for z scores) is changed to 50.

The mean of the *T* distribution is set at 50 instead of at 0 and the standard deviation of *T* scores is 10. To calculate any *T* score, simply find the z score and convert it to a *T* score:

$$T \text{ score} = 10(z) + 50$$

Since the mean is set at 50, we are sure to end up with a positive value. And by multiplying the z score by a set standard deviation of 10 and rounding off, we also come up with whole numbers instead of fractions. If the actual z score were 3.2 on a test, we could multiply by 10 to get the whole number 32. Then, adding the mean of 50, we get a *T* score of 82.

This conversion from z to *T* scores may not seem very important, but when you are reporting hundreds of scores, it's easier to convert them than to type in all the decimals and plus and minus values.

Whenever we compare or combine scores which have different units of measurement, we first convert them to standard scores. The choice of z or *T* scores is up to the researcher. If your interest is in language testing, there are other standardized scores, such as stanines and CEEBs (College Entrance Examination Boards), which you may encounter. We refer you to Henning (1987) for information on these types of standardized scores.

Practice 7.4

▶ 1. The $\overline{X}$ for a reading test was 38 and the standard deviation 6. Find the z score for each of the five following raw scores:

$$z = \frac{X - \overline{X}}{s}$$

Score	z score	
38	0	
39	.16	
30	−1.3	(Be careful to subtract!)
50	2	
25	−2.16	

Find the T score for the above scores: $T = 10(z) + 50$

Score	z score
38	50
39	51.5
30	37
50	70
25	28.3

2. If you converted all your data to T scores, why would you *not* ask the computer to calculate the $\bar{X}$ and standard deviation? What would the answer be if you did? _____

◇◇◇◇◇◇◇◇◇◇◇◇◇◇◇◇◇◇◇◇◇◇◇◇◇◇◇◇◇◇◇◇◇◇◇◇◇◇

Distributions with Nominal Data

So far in this chapter we have noted that school researchers may locate the performance of individual students (or of individual schools) in a distribution by using percentile, quartile, or decile ranks. When comparisons need to be made and information is drawn from tests where different units of measurement have been used, researchers locate scores in each distribution in terms of standard scores such as z or T scores. It doesn't make sense, however, to think of percentiles or z scores for nominal data. That is, if you look at sex as a variable you can obtain a frequency count of the number of boys and girls in a sample but you can't locate anyone at the 99th percentile or give anyone a 2.1 z score.

However, there are times when we want to see if a distribution exists within a whole series of nominal data frequency counts and whether observations (i.e., Ss, pieces of text, test items) can be reliably rank-ordered in the distribution. Again, this relates to normal performance on a set of variables. Think, for instance, of questionnaires you get in the junk mail or that you read in the Sunday paper. The questionnaires purport to measure how sensitive you are to extrasensory experiences, how well adjusted you are, or even how multilingual you are. The questions (each answered and thus measured as a yes/no category) might be:

1. Can you say *Merry Christmas* in another language?

2. Can you say *Good morning* in three languages?

3. Can you order a cup of coffee in four different languages?

4. Can you bargain for vegetables in five languages?

5. Can you write a letter to six friends each of whom speaks a different language?

6. Can you translate the Bill of Rights into six languages?

It is likely that almost everyone can say *Merry Christmas* in another language. If this were a nominal variable in a research project, most people would score a 1 (=yes) rather than a 0 (=no). Many people would also score a 1 on the next dichotomy; they would be able to say *Good morning* in three languages. The further we go through the list of questions--each a nominal yes/no variable--fewer and fewer people would answer yes and more and more 0s would be entered onto the data sheet. That is, the questions are arranged in a scaled order so that fewer and fewer people can claim to possess these attributes. When items are arranged in this way, most of the 1s will appear as a peak at the bottom of the scale and there will be a gradual decrease in frequency as the attributes are less and less possible in human performance. In a sense, the distribution curve looks a bit like half of a normal distribution polygon. There will always be a few people who do better than others and they are the ones who will win the Sunday paper's contest to find the "most multilingual person alive today."

This method of finding a scale in a set of dichotomous (yes/no) items is the basis of the Guttman procedure, often called *Implicational scaling* in applied linguistics research. The procedure has proved an extremely useful one for research on language learning.

Implicational Scaling

Much research in applied linguistics is aimed at trying to discover the orderliness (or lack thereof) in the language learning process. Of course the learning process of interest is not that reflected in the Sunday paper questionnaire. Rather, interlanguage research has as one of its goals documenting the gradual acquisition of the grammatical, lexical, and phonological features of language by learners over time. (Discourse features in interlanguage are also amenable to Implicational scaling. Although we know of no studies doing this, we don't see in theory why it couldn't be done.) One of several motivations for documenting the acquisition of these features relates to language teaching. In syllabus design and materials development, writers assume they know which structures, vocabulary, and phonology will be easiest to learn and they begin with lessons to teach this material first. They gradually increase the complexity of the material they present to learners. But much of this sequencing of teaching materials is based on intuition of what is easy or difficult. Interlanguage research seeks to document a learning sequence for learners by examining the language they produce.

Much of this research is observational; often studies report on only two or three Ss (and sometimes only one). The data from these observational studies are compiled and then compared. If similarities are observed, some sort of universals in terms of stages in acquiring various structures can be proposed. Many of the studies done in the 1970s on morpheme acquisition fit into this research pattern, so let's begin with an example of how the analysis might be done with Implicational scaling.

Scaling

Suppose that you were interested in the order in which English morphemes are acquired. The data you have might come from observational studies where you have charted the presence or absence of the morphemes in the speech of learners over several weeks or months.

Imagine that you were interested in the sequence of appearance of five different morphemes. For each S you prepared a chart and noted the presence or absence of each morpheme each week (1 = yes and 0 = no).

Morphemes

Difficult → Easy

Week	M1	M2	M3	M4	M5
5	1	1	1	1	1
4	0	1	1	1	1
3	0	0	1	1	1
2	0	0	0	1	1
1	0	0	0	0	1

The matrix shows that at the first data-collection session, week 1, the S produced one of the morphemes (M5) but none of the others. In session two, the same morpheme was present and another appeared (M4). Magically, week by week the learner acquired one more morpheme (and continued to use the ones learned in the previous weeks). In real life, of course, the process is never this neat and tidy.

Since the morphemes in the data appeared one after the other, it is possible to hypothesize a scale of difficulty from easy (for those acquired first) to difficult (for those acquired late). Prior to collecting the data the researcher may have little reason to suspect which might be easy and which difficult. As data from more and more learners are gathered, and if they fit the pattern found for the first learner, the researcher can claim that the variables form a unidimensional scale, and ultimately even decide to pose a *natural-order* hypothesis.

The claim that variables can be arranged in a scale order of difficulty can also be discovered using cross-sectional data. Realizing you haven't sufficient time to devote to observational research, you may have devised a game--or used the SLOPE (1975) or Bilingual Syntax Measure (1973)--to elicit language data from many learners at one point in time. Again, you would chart the presence or absence of the morphemes in the speech of these learners. The learners will not all behave in exactly the same way. Some will know and produce all of the morphemes; others none. Once charted, the data might look like this:

Morphemes

	M1	M2	M3	M4	M5
S^1	1	1	1	1	1
S^2	0	1	1	1	1
S^3	0	0	1	1	1
S^4	0	0	0	1	1
S^5	0	0	0	0	1

From this chart you should be able to see that Implicational scaling works in two ways. (1) It lets us arrange dichotomous items (yes/no attributes) to show their difficulty. That is, the more Ss that can perform with a "yes" on the variable, the easier the behavior must be. (2) It lets us arrange Ss in a performance order. That is, the more times an individual S can perform with a "yes" on the set of variables, the higher the S ranks on performance with respect to other Ss. Thus, implicational scales locate Ss in a distribution *and* establish a scale for the items as well.

When a data matrix is neat and tidy as ours have been, it is not difficult to see how items and learners should be arranged. The arrangement allows us to make predictions about the performance of other learners. We expect that a new S who produces morpheme 1 will also be able to produce morphemes 5, 4, 3, and 2. Given that knowledge, we would know where the learner should be placed on the matrix--i.e., at the top of the table.

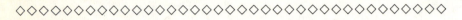

Practice 7.5

1. In the second morpheme chart (page 205), which learner produced the fewest morphemes? __S₅__. Which produced the most? __S¹__. Which morpheme appeared to be the easiest? __M₅__. The most difficult? __M₁__.

2. If a S produced morpheme 3 correctly, what predictions could we make?
   ___That M₄ & M₅ are also correct._____

   _____

Unfortunately, data are never this neat and tidy. Every piece of data does not fit or match such scaling. For example, if we gave the Bilingual Syntax Measure to absolute beginners, none of them would probably be able to produce any of the morphemes. Zeros would fill the matrix, and no order of difficulty and no order of Ss could be found. Similarly, if we gave the measure to advanced students, the matrix would be filled with 1s and nothing could be said about the distribution. Nor could we locate the performance of these individuals relative to each other since all perform in precisely the same way.

This points out a reservation regarding Implicational scaling that should be obvious. If all the items are roughly the same difficulty, no scale will be found. Conversely, if all the Ss are roughly at the same level, no scale in terms of their position in relation to each other will be discovered.

However, if we do have Ss at differing levels of proficiency (or the same Ss at longitudinally different points on their learning continuum), we should be able to scale items for difficulty. However, as we chart the data, it is unlikely that it will fall into a pattern precisely like those shown above.

Turn back to the Sunday paper's questionnaire on multilingualism. If we collected answers from six learners for these six questions, it is unlikely that the data would allow us to form a perfect idealized matrix. As with all performance, there will be error. Measuring the error is crucial in Implicational scaling. Since we are trying to discover a scale, the degree to which the data fit the idealized model depends on the degree of error. Error, here, refers to the number of entries in the matrix that violate the ideal model. If there were no error, the scaling would be perfect. Not only could we scale the items for difficulty but we could also absolutely predict that an individual S will know certain items but not others simply by his or her position in the matrix.

When the learner knows something we didn't predict she would know or when she doesn't know something we predict she will know, it's an error. The following matrix shows two deviations from the ideal model.

| | Difficult | | | | Easy | |
	Q6	Q5	Q4	Q3	Q2	Q1
S6	①	1	⓪	1	1	1
S5	0	1	1	1	1	1
S4	0	0	1	1	1	1
S3	0	0	0	1	1	1
S2	0	0	0	0	1	1
S1	0	0	0	0	0	1

Questions

Notice that $S6$ answered yes for five questions, including questions 5 and 6, which are the most difficult. For some reason, however, the S answered no to question 4. This shouldn't happen. We expect, from the performance of other Ss lower on the scale, that $S6$ should have a yes.

Now let's see how the "line" is drawn on the table because it is this line that shows us where "errors" occur (that is where Ss missed items they were expected to get correct or where they got items right but were expected to miss them). Start at the bottom of the chart. $S1$ got one question correct, so we draw a vertical line between the last two rows (between Q1 and Q2). $S2$ got two questions correct, so we draw a vertical line between columns 4 and 5 (between Q2 and Q3). $S3$ had three correct questions and so the vertical line moves over one more column (between Q3 and Q4). $S4$ had four correct, so the line moves over another column (between Q4 and Q5). $S5$ had five, so the line is now between Q5 and Q6. $S6$ also had five and so the line *stays between Q5 and Q6*. Thus, to locate the line, count the number of correct responses and place the line to the left of that number of columns.

Now to find the errors, look to the right of the line. Everything to the right of the line should be 1s. The 0 for Q4, which is not a 1, is an "error." Next look to the left of the line. Everything to the left of the line should be a 0. The 1 on Q6 is the second error. Thus, there are two errors in the data set. Not only did S6 miss an item that should not have been missed (given the pattern in the data), but S6 also answered an item correctly where the S's total score predicts the item would be missed.

Some research studies actually display a matrix as evidence to support their claims that particular structures can be ordered or scaled for difficulty on the basis of the performance of learners. Since a real data matrix won't match those given so far, the dividing line between the 0s and 1s in responses won't be as evident. For further practice, let's try this with a real data set. The following data were collected by Lazaraton (1988). This is a pilot replication of a study in which Scarcella (1983) suggested there might be a performance order for how well learners are able to do Goffman's (1976) universals of communication (such as conversational openings, closings, turn-taking and so forth). Ss took part in an oral interview where they were expected to give an opening greeting, perform a closing, respond to two preclosing moves, give a self-introduction, and respond to the interviewer's self-introduction. The data were entered for each S on a data sheet. Notice that the Ss and the "questions" are not yet ordered in any meaningful way. (That's the hard part!)

			Question			
ID	1	2	3	4	5	6
1	1	1	1	1	1	1
2	1	1	0	1	1	1
3	1	0	0	1	1	1
4	1	0	1	0	1	1
5	1	0	0	1	1	1
6	1	0	0	1	1	1
7	1	0	0	0	1	1
8	1	1	1	1	1	1
9	1	1	1	1	1	1
10	1	0	1	0	0	1
11	0	0	0	1	1	1
12	1	0	1	0	0	1
13	1	0	0	1	0	1
14	1	0	0	0	0	1
15	1	0	0	1	1	1
16	1	0	0	1	0	0
17	1	0	1	0	1	1
18	1	0	0	1	1	1
19	1	1	0	1	1	0

Now the hard part--constructing the actual matrix. The Ss must be rank-ordered so that the S with the lowest number of correct responses is at the bottom of the list and the S with the most correct responses is at the top of the list. Simultaneously, the communicative moves must be rank-ordered for difficulty on the chart (with the most difficult item first and the easiest last). The data are displayed in the following chart.

ID	SIntro Q2	RIntro Q3	PreC1 Q4	PreC2 Q5	Close Q6	Grtg Q1
1	1	1	1	1	1	1
8	1	1	1	1	1	1
9	1	1	1	1	1	1
2	1	0	1	1	1	1
3	0	0	1	1	1	1
4	0	1	0	1	1	1
6	0	0	1	1	1	1
15	0	0	1	1	1	1
18	0	0	1	1	1	1
17	0	1	0	1	1	1
5	0	0	1	1	1	1
19	1	0	1	1	0	1
7	0	0	0	1	1	1
10	0	1	0	0	1	1
11	0	0	1	1	1	0
12	0	1	0	0	1	1
13	0	0	1	0	1	1
14	0	0	0	0	1	1
16	0	0	1	0	0	1
Tot	14 5	12 7	6 13	5 14	2 17	1 18

0s 1s   *Marginals*

a fluke that this # of errors?

Notice the row of totals at the bottom of each column. For some reason, these totals are called *marginals*. The first number is the total number of 0s and the second is the total for 1s. Since the tables for the Guttman procedure are tedious to set up, it is easier to let the computer do the analysis for you. It will set up the table and print this out as a *scalogram*. The scalogram will show you precisely where the "errors" are located. However, to do this by hand, we must repeat the procedure of drawing in the lines on the chart. The directions are the same as before.

◇◇◇

Practice 7.6

▶ 1. To draw the dividing line on the chart, it is easiest to start at the bottom of the chart. How many people score 2--that is, got two items correct? __2__. So we draw a vertical line 2 columns from the right (between PreC2 and Close) for those *S*s. How many people have three correct items (remember it doesn't matter at this point *which* items they got correct, just *how many* items are correct for each *S*)? __5__. Continue the vertical line between columns 3 and 4 for these *S*s. How many have four correct items? __8__. Draw a vertical line four columns from the right (between RIntro and PreC1) for these *S*s. How many got 5 correct? __1__. Move the line over an additional column for this *S*. How many got all six items correct? __3__. The vertical line is now six columns from the right for these *S*s.

▶ 2. Now look to the right of the lines. Circle everything that is *not* a 1. These are "errors." *S*s got items wrong which they were expected to know. Look to the left of the lines. Circle every error (those that are *not* 0s.) How many errors are there in the data? ___18___. This time, what does an "error" mean? _____

In applied linguistics, some researchers set up an implicational table (including the lines) and stop there. For them a visual pattern is evidence enough that a scale exists. If you do this, don't be surprised if Grandmother Borgese stands up to say "I don't believe it!" So let's use a statistical procedure to give extra weight to the evidence.

When you run the Guttman procedure on the computer, it will produce several statistics for you. These include the *coefficient of reproducibility*, the *minimum marginal reproducibility*, and the *percent improvement*. These are steps towards determining the *coefficient of scalability*, the figure you want. Let's explain each of these steps in order to determine the final scalability coefficient. We'll do this first with the data in the chart on page 207 and then you can repeat the process using the pilot study data in the practice section.

Step 1: Coefficient of Reproducibility

The coefficient of reproducibility tells us how easily we can predict a *S*'s performance from that person's position or rank in the matrix. The formula, should you wish to compute this yourself, is:

over .90

$$C_{rep} = 1 - \frac{\text{number of errors}}{(\text{number of } Ss)(\text{number of items})}$$

In the morpheme example (page 207), we want to know whether we can claim that the items form a true scale. There are 6 *S*s doing 6 items with a total of 2 errors.

$$C_{rep} = 1 - \frac{2}{(6)(6)}$$

$$C_{rep} = .945$$

This means that almost 95% of the time we could accurately predict which questions a person answered "yes" or correctly by his or her rank in the matrix. By convention, mathematicians have determined that the value of the coefficient of reproducibility should be over .90 before the scale can be considered "valid."

Step 2: Minimum Marginal Reproducibility

The minimum marginal reproducibility figure tells us how well we could predict if we did not consider the errors (the places where people behave in ways not predicted by the model). The formula for this is:

$$MM_{rep} = \frac{\text{maximum marginals}}{(\text{number of Ss})(\text{number of items})}$$

less than C_{rep}

While the previous formula took into account all the errors, this one doesn't. Our ability to predict Ss' performance accurately will be greater when we pay attention to error than when we don't. This formula doesn't pay attention to error.

The only part of the formula you might not be able to decipher is the "maximum marginals." This refers to the totals at the bottom of each column. For *each* column select the *larger value*, whether it is the total for 0s or for 1s. Add these to obtain the value for "maximum marginals." In the example, we sum the number of 0s and 1s for each question as shown. For each column, we take the larger number and sum these.

$$\text{max } marg = 5 + 4 + 4 + 4 + 5 + 6$$

$$\text{max } marg = 28$$

We can now insert this into our formula for minimum marginal reproducibility:

$$MM_{rep} = \frac{28}{(6)(6)}$$

$$MM_{rep} = .7778$$

Our answer for these data should be less than .945 (the value of the coefficient of reproducibility for these data). That is, if we don't consider the errors, we won't be able to reproduce as well a *S*'s performance based on the *S*'s position in the matrix.

Step 3: Percent Improvement in Reproducibility

Percent improvement in reproducibility just shows how much improvement there is between the coefficient of reproducibility and the minimum marginal reproducibility.

$$\% \text{ improvement} = C_{rep} - MM_{rep}$$

$$\% \text{ improvement} = .945 - .7778 = .1672$$

The coefficient of scalability is the figure that indicates whether a given set of features are truly scalable (and unidimensional). It is this figure that is usually reported in studies that use Implicational scaling. It is equal to the percent improvement divided by 1 minus the minimum marginal reproducibility.

$$C_{scal} = \frac{\% \text{ improvement in reproducibility}}{1 - MM_{rep}}$$

For our example, the coefficient of scalability is:

$$C_{scal} = \frac{.1672}{1 - .7778}$$

$$C_{scal} = .753$$

If we reported the findings, we could now claim that *these* data are scalable. While the scalogram does not show us a perfectly scaled data set, a strong pattern of scalability is shown. Our coefficient of scalability is high, indicating a true scale in the data. Statisticians have determined that the coefficient of scalability must be above .60 before we claim scalability.

While it is not crucial that you understand the formulas given above for determining scalability, it is important that you understand that the Guttman procedure is testing the distribution of 1s and 0s for a series of variables to see if they can be ordered for difficulty. By preparing a matrix, you can locate individual Ss who may have achievement patterns that differ from other students. For example, it will locate Ss who have not acquired forms that their general level of achievement would suggest they had attained. It will also locate Ss who have acquired forms that, from their general level of achievement, you would not predict. This is useful information in language testing as well as in interlanguage analysis. And the coefficient of scalability figure should help convince you and your audience that the claims you make regarding the scalability of your data are correct. The procedure is *descriptive*; that is, the scale belongs to the particular data set from which it was drawn. Before we can generalize from these findings, further replication studies would be needed.

Practice 7.7

▶ 1. Let's repeat the procedure now using the pilot data collected to replicate Scarcella's study.

a. There are 19 Ss and 6 items with 18 errors in data set. Calculate the coefficient of reproducibility.

$$C_{rep} = \frac{1 - \text{number of errors}}{(\text{number of Ss})(\text{number of items})} \qquad \frac{17}{359}$$

moved (handwritten note above "1 −")

$$C_{rep} = \underline{\qquad}$$

At this point, does it appear that the data are scalable? How much better than a fifty-fifty chance have you of predicting a person's performance given his or her place in the matrix?

_____

b. Calculate the minimum marginal reproducibility.

$$MM_{rep} = \frac{\text{maximum marginals}}{(\text{number of Ss})(\text{number of items})}$$

$$MM_{rep} = \underline{\qquad}$$

The value for MM_{rep} should be smaller than that for C_{rep}. If it is not, check the answer key.

c. The percent improvement in reproducibility is found by subtracting MM_{rep} from C_{rep}. The percent improvement for this example is _____.

d. Now, the final step is to apply the coefficient of scalability formula:

$$C_{scal} = \frac{\% \text{ improvement in reproducibility}}{1 - MM_{rep}}$$

$$C_{scal} = \underline{\qquad}$$

2. The data do not show a clear scale. The C_{scal} is not large enough that we can feel confident in saying that a scale exists. Since the results do not support Scarcella's hypothesis, what explanations can you offer as to why this might be the case?_____

_____

_____

_____

3. If the data had shown a scale, could you claim that there is a natural order for second language learner performance on these communication factors? Why (not)? _____

_____

_____

_____

◇◇◇

Implicational scaling is easily done using the Guttman procedure in many computer software packages. It is tedious to carry the procedure out by hand. The calculations are simple, but arranging the data in a matrix can be confusing. To review, the procedure for preparing the matrix is:

1. Compute the number of 1s for each item.

2. Rank-order the items from difficult to easy across the top of the matrix on this basis.

3. Compute the number of 1s obtained by each S.

4. Rank-order the Ss in the matrix with the best student at the top and lowest at the bottom.

Once the data are placed in the matrix, the line marking the division between the 0s and 1s is drawn in. To do this, group the Ss who have the same number correct (even though the items correct may differ).

1. Find the number of Ss who have only one 1 response. Draw a line one column in from the right edge for these Ss.

2. Extend the line vertically until you find the first S with *two* 1 responses. Move the line in another column at this point (two columns in from the right edge for all Ss with two correct responses).

3. Extend the line vertically until you find the first S with *three* 1 responses. Move the line in another column.

4. Continue this process until the line is complete. If at any point there is no S with the number correct, go to the next number. For example, if there were Ss who had 3 correct, Ss who had 5 correct, but none with 4 correct, the line moves from 3 columns to 5 columns. That is, the number of items correct always equals the number of columns from the right for location of the line.

The next step is to locate the errors.

1. Look to the right of the line and find any 0s. Circle these as errors where the S missed an item he or she was expected to get correct.

2. Look to the left of the line and find any 1s. Circle these as errors where the S got an item we predict he or she would miss.

3. Total the number of errors.

In this final step, we need to determine the "marginals" for the data. This is the total for 0s and 1s at the bottom of each column. Add the *larger* number (whether 0 or 1) at the bottom of each column to find the maximum marginal value for the formula.

The Guttman procedure can be done by hand, but unless the number of items in the study is very small *and* the number of Ss is also small, it takes a great deal of time to sort all the data. It is much simpler to let the computer do the work.

There are, however, several cautions to keep in mind before you let the computer help you. The computer can't make a number of important decisions for you.

Problems with Implicational Scaling

Implicational scaling is a useful technique for the study of language acquisition. It is also a valued technique in dialect studies. For example, sociolinguists have used the technique to scale phonological features of certain American dialects. With the scale, it is possible to show that if a speaker uses the less frequent (higher on the scale) features of the dialect, he or she will also use those lower on the scale. Implicational scaling has, thus, been used to show orderliness in acquisition and orderliness in language variation data.

The major problem in dealing with variable data, though, is deciding when a form is acquired (thus, a 1) and when it is not (a 0). From your teaching and/or your own research, you know that learners use some forms correctly all the time, use others incorrectly all the time, but use a very large number of forms with varying degrees of consistency. For example, if you had collected free speech data from a learner, you might want to know whether or not the person uses the three forms of -s agreement for the third person singular present tense (e.g., "He laughs, dances, and plays the guitar"). You could go through the data and mark each place where the form is required (a.k.a. an *obligatory instance*). Then you could tally the proportion of times the -s was used (a.k.a. *percent supplied in obligatory instances*). Once this is done, you must decide on a cutoff point. If your criterion for acquisition is 80%, you check the percentage and, finding it is 84%, you enter a 1.

Happy about this, you decide to look at data from another student. This time, when you tally the percent correct, it turns out to be 79%, and you must enter a 0. This must give you pause for thought. Is a learner who supplies the ending in 84% of the cases really that much better than someone who supplies the ending in 79%? Is everyone over 80% an acquirer and everyone under 80% a non-acquirer? Obviously, the researcher *must* justify decisions made in this regard.

A second problem has to do with the question of what to do with missing data. When gathering observational data in natural settings, learners may simply not use the forms you wish to scale. Perhaps they use only a few of the forms. How many instances must occur in the data? What if the person talked about past experiences and there were only three places where an -s for present tense would have been appropriate? If the -s was supplied twice, the S obtains a 66% (a 0). With another topic, more -s forms might have been required and more supplied. The researcher must decide how many potential uses are needed. While convention requires five instances and an 80% cutoff point, there is no well-documented rationale for either of these conventions. If fewer than five instances occur, then a "missing data" symbol is placed in the matrix. (Imagine that a learner used only four instances of a particular morpheme but got all four of them. This might, indeed, change the scalability of the morphemes.) Again, the researcher must give the reader information on what grounds decisions were made to code missing data.

Finally, it is possible that reversals might occur in the acquisition of certain morphemes. For example, it's possible that beginning learners might obtain high scores for irregular past tense forms (e.g., "he sang," "I ran"). Later, at the intermediate stage, the same learners might get low scores using the more regular rule for past tense ("he singed," "I runned"). This is sometimes called a *U-shaped learning curve.* Such a learning pattern would definitely influence the scalability of the acquisition data.

In spite of these problems, the Guttman procedure is useful when we want to know whether there is a scale--an order of difficulty for items in a particular data set. If you do the procedure by hand, you will find it very tedious and, when a procedure is tedious, mistakes just seem to happen on their own. This is one of several procedures for which we urge you to let the computer do the work. Check the printout for the statistics you need. Since the computer usually excludes missing data from the analysis, check to see how many missing values there were. Consider all the other warnings we have given you regarding the Guttman procedure. That is, don't let the computer think or interpret for you, but do let it do the donkey work.

Other Applications of Distribution Measures

In this chapter we have looked at ways in which we can locate individual scores in a distribution, compare locations of scores in data where the units of measurement differ, and how we can determine whether or not we can predict student performance on a series of features (that is, whether the features will scale for difficulty so that we can predict student performance on the basis of place in a matrix).

The examples we have given in most cases have been taken from general applied linguistics research rather than from language testing. Yet, we can see that each of these issues is important in language testing and program administration. Administrators of language programs must understand these ways of locating scores in distributions in order to make decisions about who should or should not be admitted to their programs. They need to understand them in order to assign students to the courses that will benefit them most. When test scores come from different testing instruments, it is crucial that they understand standardized scores. Without this knowledge, decisions may be made that do a disservice to students.

Test designers, as well as researchers of interlanguage use the Guttman procedure to determine the difficulty order of items. Students who have high achievement scores should not make errors on items that were designed for beginning students. Nor should beginning students do well on items thought to be among the most difficult. Scalability of test items is important here too. In addition, test developers are often curious to know whether there is one underlying dimension to a total test or whether different parts of tests are tapping other language components. If there is one underlying dimension to a test, the Guttman procedure should show this unidimension with a high coefficient of scalability. (However, lack of a high coefficient of scalability can be due to "error," so this is not a good argument for multidimensionality in tests!)

Practice 7.8

1. Review the questions in your research journal. For which would Implicational scaling be an appropriate statistical procedure? Explain how you would overcome the problems that might be related to using the procedure or interpreting the output of the procedure for your project(s).

_____

_____

_____

_____

In this chapter we have looked, then, at issues related to locating values within a data distribution. We have recycled the notion of normal distributions. These and other issues will reappear in different guises in the following chapters.

Activities

1. M. A. Snow (1985. A descriptive comparison of three Spanish immersion programs. Unpublished doctoral dissertation, Applied Linguistics, UCLA.) includes the following table (among many others) in her study. *Site* refers to the locations of the three different programs.

MLA-Coop. Spanish Test Scores - Grade 6 Mean and Percentile Scores

Site	n	Listening score	sd	%ile	Reading score	sd	%ile	Writing score	sd	%ile
1	17	31.71	8.8	81.4	27.6	7.2	68.6	50.4	20.1	59.1
2	28	38.90	4.4	94.7	36.4	7.3	87.2	66.4	18.0	76.6
3	14	32.20	7.4	84.1	28.1	6.8	77.0	44.9	13.9	52.1

At which site does it appear the Grade 6 children score highest? At which site do the Ss appear to be the most homogeneous in performance? At which site do the Ss vary the most in performance? Look at the percentile figures. These percentiles are based on norms listed by the test publisher. Since the test is widely used, you can be sure that these represent a normal distribution. Note that the percentiles here are not for individual scores but rather for the group mean score. Select one school site and think about the variability of the distribution for each skill tested. What would you estimate (yes, guess) that the range of individual percentiles might look like for children in this class on each skill?

2. K. Hyltenstam (1977. Implicational patterns in Interlanguage syntax variation. *Language Learning, 27,* 383-411.) looked at the order in which *S*s from differing first languages acquired elements of the Swedish auxiliary system. Review the implicational tables given in the study. If this were your study, what changes would you make (and why)?

3. R. Andersen (1978. An implicational model for second language research. *Language Learning, 28,* 2, 221-282.) criticizes morpheme acquisition studies, regrouping the morphemes studied, and showing how the cutoff point affects the results. The data are from compositions written in English by Spanish speakers. What advantages might compositions have over oral language data when we wish to discover order in the acquisition process? What disadvantages do you see?

4. A number of researchers have listed the most frequent types of morphology errors of second language learners. These studies are usually based on proficiency examinations. What are the difficulties that you see in using proficiency exam errors to construct an implicational scale for ESL learners? What advantages might the Bilingual Syntax Measure or the SLOPE test have over a general proficiency exam for this purpose?

5. Data for such a study are given in the following table. Conversational language data were gathered from 33 *S*s in natural settings. The data were tape-recorded and transcribed. Each *S* received a 0 or 1 to show whether each of these individual morphemes were acquired.

Morpheme Matrix

S	PaR	Hv	3rd	Vn	PaI	AUX	ING	COP*
25	1	1	1	1	1	1	1	1
27	0	1	1	1	1	1	1	1
28	0	0	0	1	1	1	1	1
20	0	-	0	1	1	1	1	1
21	1	-	0	0	1	1	1	1
26	0	0	0	0	1	1	1	1
29	0	-	0	-	1	1	1	1
30	0	-	0	0	1	1	1	1
14	0	0	1	0	0	1	1	1
6	0	1	0	1	0	1	0	1
22	0	0	0	0	0	1	1	1
32	0	-	0	-	0	1	1	1
24	0	-	0	-	0	1	1	1
14	0	0	0	0	0	1	1	1
15	0	-	0	-	1	0	1	1
1	0	-	0	-	0	1	0	1
7	0	0	0	0	0	0	1	1
23	0	0	0	0	1	-	0	1
3	0	0	0	1	0	0	1	0
11	0	0	0	1	0	0	1	0
12	0	0	-	0	0	0	1	1
10	0	-	0	-	0	1	1	0
19	0	0	0	0	0	0	0	1
31	0	0	0	0	0	0	0	1
33	-	-	0	-	0	0	0	1
18	0	0	0	0	0	-	-	1
5	0	-	0	-	0	-	1	0
8	0	-	0	-	0	-	1	0
16	0	0	0	0	-	0	0	1
2	0	0	0	0	0	0	0	0
9	0	0	0	0	0	0	0	0
19	0	0	0	0	0	0	0	0
17	0	0	0	0	0	0	0	0

*COP = copula (*be*), ING = continuous, AUX = *be* as an auxiliary, PaI = irregular past tense, Vn = past participle, 3rd = third person singular present tense, Hv = present participle, PaR = regular past tense.

Draw in the line and determine the total number of "errors." Do a Guttman analysis of the data. What questions do you have regarding the results? If this were your study, how might you redesign it to answer the questions you have raised?

The cutoff point for the assignment of 1 vs. 0 in this table was 60% accuracy. Since we had access to a computer program, we reran the analysis using a cutoff point of 80%. While the morphemes appeared to be nicely scaled for difficulty when 60% was the cutoff point, that scaling was not so convincing at the 80% cutoff point. In fact, the order of difficulty for the morphemes at the 80% cutoff point is *different* from that obtained at the 60% cutoff point. If the claim of scalability can be made only in terms of the criterion level, what problems do you see for claims of a "natural order of difficulty" for these morphemes? How might the researcher determine which cutoff point is appropriate?

6. R. Scarcella (1983. Developmental trends in the acquisition of conversational competence by adult second language learners. In N. Wolfson and E. Judd, [Eds.]. *Sociolinguistics and Language Acquisition.* New York, NY: Newbury House.) hypothesized, on the basis of her analysis of conversational interviews, that there may be an "order of acquisition" for conversational competence. For example, she found that openings and closings were better performed than pre-closing moves. She also found that "requests for clarification" were less well managed than "repairs." This is the study for which we presented pilot replication data in this chapter. Imagine that you had the list of universals of communication proposed by Goffman (which contains communication signals beyond those tested by Scarcella) and wish to test the notion of a natural order of acquisition of these universals by second language learners. How might you design the project and how would you carry out the Guttman analysis (cutoff points, etc.).

7. J. Amastae (1978. The acquisition of English vowels. *Papers in Linguistics, 11*, 3-4, 423-458.) investigated the order of acquisition of English vowels by nine fluent Spanish-English bilinguals. In the following chart, a 2 represents standard form and a 1 represents fluctuation between standard and other forms. Notice that the table is not set up in the same way as our examples. Items with the most correct responses are on the right and the student with the most items correct is at the bottom of this chart. You will need to reverse directions in locating the line.

Implicational Scale for Vowels

S	/I/	/E/	/U/	/ae/	/o/
9	1	1	1	1	1
8	2	1	1	2	2
7	1	1	1	2	2
6	1	1	2	2	2
5	1	2	2	2	2
4	1	2	2	2	2
3	1	2	2	2	2
2	1	2	2	2	1
1	1	2	2	2	2

First, draw the line. Then, circle the responses that are "errors" (i.e., where Ss either use variable performance when they should have used standard or used standard when variable performance would be expected). Do a Guttman analysis of the data. What questions do you have regarding the procedure and the results? If this were your study, how might you redesign it and answer the questions you have raised?

8. P. Hopper & S. Thompson (1980. Transitivity in grammar and discourse, *Language, 56*, 2, 251-299.) listed 10 features they believe determine the degree of

transitivity of clauses in discourse. That is, a clause such as "I was drinking some of the punch" would have weak transitivity and a clause such as "I drank up the punch" would have strong transitivity. Strength of transitivity is determined by these 10 factors. The question is whether each factor weighs the same or whether we can determine a scale for the 10 factors. Can we predict which factors high transitive clauses will exhibit and which factors even low transitive clauses have? Do the factors exhibit a scale?

The clauses in the following data come from a casual telephone conversation between a brother and sister. In the chart, each clause has been coded as + or − on each of the 10 factors. The utterances are arranged so that the example with the largest number of factors is at the top and the utterances with the fewest factors is at the bottom. The features themselves are arranged from high transitivity to low transitivity across the top.

	Features*									
Utterances	1	2	3	4	5	6	7	8	9	10
10 I called him	+	+	+	+	+	+	+	+	+	+
17 I defended you	+	+	-	+	+	+	+	+	+	+
8 I washed some sheets	+	+	+	+	+	+	-	+	+	+
9 I'm also washing some sheets	-	-	+	+	+	+	+	+	+	+
15 I've gotta call her	-	-	+	+	-	+	+	+	+	+
16 We can call her	-	-	+	+	-	+	+	+	+	+
1 I was preparing for you tomorrow	-	-	-	+	+	+	+	+	+	+
12 He finally got one	-	+	+	-	+	+	-	+	+	+
2 I was thinking about it	-	-	-	-	+	+	+	+	+	+
14 Can you imagine Mother and Dad giving a Halloween party?	-	-	-	-	+	+	+	+	+	+
18 I'm gonna leave the door open	-	-	-	-	-	+	+	+	+	+
21 See you this evening	-	-	-	-	-	+	+	+	+	+
4 You have your car	-	-	-	-	+	-	+	+	+	+
6 You want me to tell Scott you're coming?	-	-	-	-	+	-	+	+	+	+
13 They're gonna give a Hallowe'en	-	-	-	-	-	+	-	+	+	+
3 Which will give me the week to	-	-	-	-	-	-	+	+	+	+
11 He's got an answering machine too	-	-	-	-	+	-	-	+	+	+
19 I can't believe it	-	-	-	-	+	+	-	-	+	+
20 You don't know me very well	-	-	-	-	+	-	+	-	+	+
5 That will make it quite easy	-	-	-	-	-	-	-	+	+	+
7 If you don't want me to come	-	-	-	-	-	-	+	-	+	+

*The features are:

1. Affectedness of object--how completely object is affected ("I drank up the milk" vs. "I drank some of the milk")

2. Aspect--action is completed ("I ate it" vs. "I am eating it")

3. Punctuality--verb has no "phase" between onset and completion ("kick" vs. "carry")

4. Kinesis--action verb vs. state verbs ("hug" vs. "like")

5. Mode--realis vs. irrealis

6. Volitionality--agent acting purposefully ("I wrote" vs. "I forgot your name")

7. Individuation of object--human, animate, definite, individuated ("Fritz drank the beer" vs. "Fritz drank some of the beer")

8. Affirmation--positive vs. negative clause

9. Participants--number of arguments of verbs (Note: matrix only contains two-participant clauses in the conversation as defined for this particular study)

10. Agency--degree of willing/ableness of agent ("George startled me" vs. "The table startled me")

Draw in the line and determine the total number of "errors." Do a Guttman analysis of the data. Are the data scalable? The data come from a section of one conversation. If you wished to establish scalability for Thompson & Hopper's factors in oral language, what other kinds of data might you want to include? Justify your choice. How might you be sure that the coding (the assignment of + or −) is correct in the data prior to doing the Guttman procedure?

References

Burt, M., Dulay, H., & Hernandez, E. 1973. *Bilingual Syntax Measure.* New York, NY: Harcourt Brace Jovanovich.

Fathman, A. 1975. The relationship between age and second language production ability. *Language Learning 25,* 2, 245-254.

Goffman, E. 1976. Replies and responses. *Language in Society, 5,* 3, 254-313.

Henning, G. 1987. *A Guide to Language Testing.* New York, NY: Newbury House.

Lazaraton, A. 1988. Interview format and function: implications for assessing oral communication. Unpublished manuscript, UCLA.

Scarcella, R. 1983. Developmental trends in the acquisition of conversational competence by adult second language learners. In N. Wolfson and E. Judd (Eds.). *Sociolinguistics and Second Language Acquisition.* New York, NY: Newbury House.

Chapter 8

Probability and Hypothesis Testing Procedures

In previous chapters, we have shown ways of describing data so that information on outcomes can be seen at a glance. In most research, however, we want to do more than describe. We want to know whether the data we have described can be used as evidence in support of our hypotheses.

If, in describing data, we see differences in frequencies or in scores, we want to know how confident we can be about any claims we want to make. Are the differences large enough? Might apparent differences just be normal variation in human performance? Are the differences real? Statistical tests have been created precisely to answer these questions. A statistical test checks the *probability* of any outcome and thus tells us whether we can have confidence in our claims. In some cases these claims are descriptive; the statistical test gives us confidence that the descriptions of the data are correct. The statistical test is used for *descriptive* purposes. In other cases, we hope to generalize, to make inferences from our data to other learners or other cases. This involves *inferential statistics*. Statistical tests give us confidence that our descriptions and/or inferences are correct.

The purpose of statistical tests, then, is to give us (as researchers or as readers of research) confidence in claims about the data. They do this by estimating the probability that the claims are wrong. When researchers report the *statistical significance* of their results, it means that they have applied a statistical test to the data and that this test has, via probability, told them how much confidence to place in their claims.

Probability

Probability is not an easy concept to define, but we all have a notion of what is probable and what is not. The weather reporter on the local TV channel tells us the probability of rain, our Lotto tickets tell us the probability of winning "The Big Spin"--about the same probability as being struck by lightning on the expressway. We are all surprised, and often delighted, when something improbable happens (not being struck by lightning, of course). We don't expect to win a million dollars, a trip for two to Tahiti, or even the local raffle of a chocolate cake. But there is always a chance.

In research, when we offer a hypothesis, we are making an educated guess about what is or is not probable. Similarly, the weatherman who says that the probability of rain is high isn't making a wild prediction. The prediction is based on previous information about rain at this time of the year given prevailing conditions, information gathered over many years. The prediction is often reported in terms of "chance"--e.g., that there is an 80% chance of showers occurring in the morning hours. This means that there are 20 chances in 100 that the weather forecaster may be wrong in claiming rain will occur. These odds relate to probability.

When we look at the frequencies, ratings, or scores that we have obtained in our research, we want to be sure that they truly support our hypothesis before we predict rain! And, we want there to be fewer than 20 chances in 100 that we are wrong. If we have stated our hypothesis in the null form, then we want to feel confident in rejecting it.

When we reject the null hypothesis, we want the probability to be very low that we are wrong. If, on the other hand, we must accept the null hypothesis, we still want the probability to be very low that we are wrong in doing so.

In many statistics books, writers talk about "Type 1" and "Type 2" errors. A Type 1 error is made when the researcher rejected the null hypothesis when it should not have been rejected. For example, the person said his group of Ss were better than a control group, when in fact, they probably weren't. A Type 2 error, on the other hand, occurs when the null hypothesis is accepted when it should have been rejected. That is, the person said his group wasn't any better when, in fact, it was. That's a Type 2 error. Statistical tests help us to avoid these errors. They give us confidence in our claims by telling us the probability that these particular results would obtain based not on simple odds but on statistical probability.

In research, we test our hypotheses by finding the probability of our results. Probability is the proportion of times that any particular outcome would happen if the research were repeated an infinite number of times. The way we are able to do this relates to our earlier discussions of the normal distribution. For any human activity, if we continue to collect data from more and more subjects or events, we will approach a normal distribution. It is possible then to locate the data of one S or event in the distribution and talk about how typical (how probable) it is in the total normal distribution. In addition, we will be able to locate data of groups in distributions and find how typical or probable it is in a similar way.

Probability of Individual Scores in a Distribution

In order to understand probability better, let's review what we already know about locating individual scores in a distribution. If we have the $\bar{X}$ and the *s.d.* of a distribution, we can locate any individual score in the distribution by using z scores. And we can find the *probability* of obtaining that particular z score in the distribution.

Imagine that you administered a general language proficiency examination to a group of 100 students at your school. The test publishers have told you that the $\bar{X}$ for the test is 75 and the standard deviation is 10. You have corrected the exams of your students. What is the probability that the very first paper you pick up will have a score above 75? The answer, if you remember the characteristics of the normal distribution, is easy. Remember that in the normal distribution, the mode, the median, and the mean are the same. The mean is the balance point on the seesaw. Half of the scores fall below the mean and half above it. The probability that the first paper will be above 75 is .50. The probability that it will be below 75 is .50.

Remember that the characteristics of the normal distribution tell us that 34% of the scores will fall between the mean and 1 standard deviation.

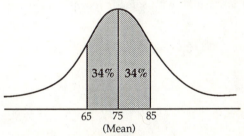

In this case, the probability that the ~~next~~ *same* paper you pick up will have a score below 85 is .84. Half (50%) of the scores are below the mean and 34% (more precisely, 34.13%) of the scores are between the mean and +1 standard deviation.

by taking out a paper, you change the odds. Leave that paper in...

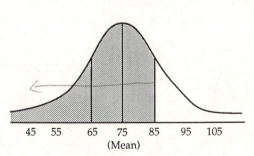

The probability that the next paper will have a score lower than 95 is 50% from below the mean + 34% (actually 34.13%) between the mean and 1 *s.d.* + 13% (more precisely, 13.59%) between 1 *s.d.* and 2 *s.d.* = 97.78% or 98%. The probability that it will be higher than a score of 95 is .02 (2.28% or 2 chances in 100).

For those *S*s who didn't do so well, the probability that the first paper you choose will have a score lower than 55 is .02 (again, the chances are very low--2 chances in 100).

When the probability level is .05, this means that there are 5 chances in 100 of obtaining this score given a normal distribution. There is only 1 chance in 1,000 that a *S* would obtain a score of 105 on this test. When the score is extremely high or extremely low, the probability level of such a score is *low*. There are very few chances of that score occurring.

When individuals obtain scores that have very low probability (either much higher than expected or much lower than expected), those scores fall under the tails of the distribution. Scores in these areas are scores that, because they are so improbable, need to be thought about carefully. Perhaps they are people who have certain characteristics, study especially hard, have received training of a special type, and so forth. Somehow these extreme scores "don't belong" in this distribution even though they are part of the distribution. The reason such scores "don't belong" may have to do with some independent variable we want to test.

Practice 8.1

▶ 1. Assume that you gave a listening test to 60 *S*s. The mean for the group was 25 and the standard deviation was 5.

a. What is the probability of scoring below the mean? __50%__. What is the probability of scoring below 20? __16%__. What is the probability of scoring above 30? __16%__.

b. Assume 15 is the "passing" cutoff point. What is the probability of not passing the test (getting a score below 15)? __2-3%__.

2. Assume 35 is the lower boundary for an "A" on the test. Draw a frequency polygon for this distribution. Label the mean and standard deviation points. Shadow the area for scores below the "A" point. What proportion of scores fall in this area? What is the probability of getting an "A" on the test? __2-3%__.

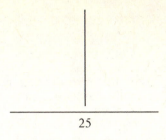

25

◇◇

The Normal Distribution (z Score) Table

Obviously, all scores in a distribution do not fall precisely at the $\overline{X}$, 1 *s.d.*, 2 *s.d.*, and so forth. Mathematicians, working with the concept of normal distribution, have given us tables that tell us precisely how probable any individual z score is for any test. You will find the table for the z score distribution in appendix C (table 1). If you know your score on a test (and the mean and *s.d.* so that you can figure out your z score), you can discover the probability of your score by consulting this table.

The first column of the table gives the z score obtained in the calculation. The second column is the proportion of scores we can expect to find between the z score and the $\overline{X}$. The third column is the proportion of scores in the curve on the *other* side of the z score (i.e., the *probability* of that particular z score). To keep the page looking balanced, the z scores continue from the bottom of the first three columns to the next group of three, and then the next group of three.

Notice the very last z score on the first page of the table. The z score is 1.64. The area beyond the z score of 1.64 is .05. This is the z score needed for an .05 probability level. That is, there are only 5 chances in 100 of obtaining a z score this high in this distribution. The probability of a score between a z score of 1.64 and the mean is .45 (from the second column in the table). There are 45 chances in 100 of getting a score between this z score and the $\overline{X}$ and 50 chances in 100 of getting a score below the $\overline{X}$. So, there are 95 chances in 100--a .95 probability of getting a *lower* score, but only 5 in 100 of obtaining a score this *high*.

Continue consulting the z score values until you find an "area beyond z" that equals .01. A z score of 2.33 shows us that the likelihood of such a score is 1 in 100. The z score needed to give us a probability of 1 in 1,000 (i.e., a probability of .001) is 3.08.

Thus, we can discover the probability of any score in a normal distribution if we compute the z score and consult the z score table.

Practice 8.2

▶ 1. Find the probability associated with the area between the mean and a *z* score of .34. _.1331_ . A *z* score of 2 has what area of the distribution beyond it? _.0228_ .

▶ 2. Find the probability associated with *z* scores of
1.28 _____
0.82 _____   → means area *z* (conflicts w/ definition on 224)
3.00 _____   beyond *z*

▶ 3. Find the proportion of scores ~~lower than one~~ with a *z* score of (remember the 50% below the mean!)
0.84 _____
1.99 _____
1.48 _____

▶ 4. Find the *z* score associated with a probability of
0.50 _0_
0.03 _1.88_
0.025 _1.96_

Probability of Group Scores or Frequencies in a Distribution

Now let's transfer what you know about the probability of individual scores in a distribution to the probability of group scores or frequencies in a distribution.

Just as we expect that individuals will display behavior which is within the range of normal human performance, we expect that groups of individuals will display behavior which is within the range of normal performance for groups. The same principle applies. We expect that if we find the mean score for our group it will fall somewhere in the normal distribution of means for all groups.

That is, if we give a test to many groups of students over and over again, we expect that the distribution of the means will approach a normal distribution. So, we can ask how probable it is that the data from our sample group of *S*s fit into that normal distribution. If we have given our *S*s some special new instructional program, we hope that our group score will be at the far right tail of the distribution polygon. The probability of that happening is not large if the null hypothesis is correct. If the probability of our group mean in the distribution of group means is .01, we should be delighted. The likelihood of our sample group of students scoring that high is 1 in 100. We have good cause to reject the null hypothesis.

Probability, then, is related to hypothesis testing. When the probability level is very low, we can feel confident that our sample group of Ss differs from other groups who may have taken the test in the past or who might take it in the future--that is the *population*. Our group of Ss forms a *sample* and we test whether the data from that sample "fit" with that of the population--all the other groups in the distribution.

You'll remember from earlier chapters that we state our hypotheses in the null form. Our aim is to reject the null hypothesis. The null hypothesis says there is no difference between the mean of our sample group and the mean of the population from which it was drawn. (This always seems strange since we hope that there *is* a difference.) We want to reject the null hypothesis and we use the probability of the location of our data in the normal distribution for this purpose. (Yes, in case you wondered, mathematicians have worked out special normal distributions for group means as well as for individual scores. They also have established probabilities for other special distribution curves where the median was selected as the measure of central tendency.)

The next issue is just how improbable a finding must be before we feel confident about rejecting the null hypothesis. Usually we want the probability to be very low indeed. The practice in most applied linguistics research is not to reject the null hypothesis unless there are fewer than 5 chances in 100 (.05 probability level) of obtaining these results. (So *that's* what the $p < .05$ means in all those tables in articles in our journals!) The .05 probability tells us there are fewer than 5 chances in 100 that we are wrong in rejecting the H_o. If the probability level is set at $p < .01$, there is only 1 chance in 100 of error in rejecting the H_o. If the probability level is set at $p < .001$, there is 1 chance in 1,000. We can have confidence in rejecting the null hypothesis.

Just to be absolutely sure the concepts we have been discussing are clear, look at the following visuals. If the score for our sample group falls in the shaded area, we will not reject the null hypothesis. The score is typical of that of all groups in the population.

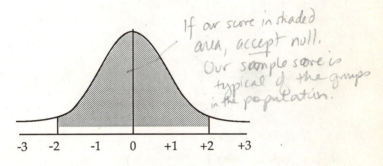

If, however, the score falls in one of the shaded areas in the following drawing, we will reject the null hypothesis. Our score is not highly probable in this distribution. (There are 5 chances in 100 of being wrong when we reject the H_o.)

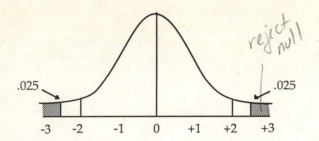

reject null

.025   .025

You will notice that although we set .05 as our probability level (level of signif-icance), we have had to divide the .05 in two, giving an .025 area to each tail of the distribution. Since we specified no direction for the null hypothesis (i.e., whether our score will be higher or lower than more typical scores), we must consider both tails of the distribution. This is called a *two-tailed hypothesis*. When we reject the null hypothesis using a two-tailed test, we have evidence in support of the alternative hypothesis of difference (though the direction of the difference was not specified ahead of time).

If, however, we have good reason to believe that we will find a difference (for example, previous studies or research findings suggest this is so), then we will use a *one-tailed hypothesis*. One-tailed tests specify the direction of the predicted difference. We use previous findings to tell us which direction to select.

In a positive directional hypothesis we expect our group to perform *better* than normal for the population. For a positive directional (one-tailed) hypothesis we can reject the null hypothesis at the .05 level if the scores fall in the shaded area:

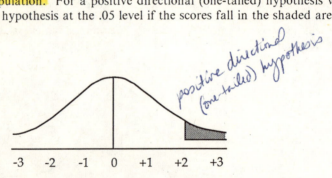

positive directional (one-tailed) hypothesis

With a negative directional (one-tailed) hypothesis, we expect our group to per-form worse than the population. For a negative directional hypothesis we can reject the null hypothesis at the .05 level of significance if the scores fall in the shaded area:

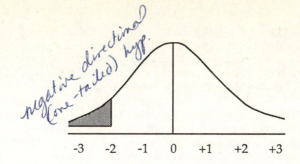

negative directional (one-tailed) hyp.

| -3 | -2 | -1 | 0 | +1 | +2 | +3 |

Let's see what this means, now, in reading the z score table in appendix C. In discussing the placement of individual scores in the distribution, we noted that a z score of 1.64 leaves an area of .05 beyond it under the tail to the right of the distribution. A −1.64 z score leaves an area of .05 beyond it under the tail to the left of the distribution. These are the values needed for testing a one-tailed directional hypothesis.

However, given the paucity of replication studies in our field, we seldom use a one-tailed directional test. Rather, we state a nondirectional null hypothesis. We can reject the null hypothesis if the z value falls under either the right or the left tail. If we set an .05 level for rejecting the null hypothesis, that .05 level must be divided between the right and left tail.

Turn to the z score table and scan the z score values until you find the place where the area beyond z is .025 (half of the .05 level). That value is 1.96, the z value needed to reject a null hypothesis at the .05 level. Now find the z score where the area beyond z is .005 (half of the .01 level). That value is 2.57, the z value needed to reject a null hypothesis at the .01 level of probability.

You might want to mark these values directly on the table. With practice, you will soon remember the values and not need the table at all. The values to remember are:

z Values Needed in Hypothesis Testing

	.05	.01
1-tailed (directional)	1.64	2.33
2-tailed (nondirectional)	1.96	2.57

As you can see, it is easier to reject a directional hypothesis that is one-tailed than a two-tailed nondirectional null hypothesis. When previous research has already shown that a null hypothesis can be rejected, there is less chance of making an error--either a Type 1 error or a Type 2 error in a replication study. Thus, it makes sense to use a one-tailed directional hypothesis.

We have said that the researcher decides on the level of significance--the probability level--at which he or she will feel confident in rejecting the null hypothesis. This p level--sometimes called the *alpha level* and noted as α--tells us how likely we are to be right or wrong in rejecting the null hypothesis. We also said that convention suggests this level be set at .05 where there are 5 chances in 100 of being wrong and 95 chances in 100 of being right. However, this is convention, not a hard-and-fast rule. It's true we want the probability of being wrong to be very low, but we don't want to overlook promising trends. For example, if you evaluated the effectiveness of a new computer-assisted program designed to teach technical English vocabulary and the probability of your outcome was .10, the outcome is worthy of notice. There are 10 chances in 100 that you would be wrong in rejecting the null hypothesis. That may be too many chances of error to give us great confidence. You would accept the null hypothesis in such a case, but it is still legitimate to report a *trend* in favor of the program. Otherwise, you and your audience might decide that the program was "worthless." Recognition of trends does *not* mean that one probability level is "more" or "less" significant than another. We set .05 as our cutoff point and on that basis we either can reject or cannot reject the H_o. We can talk about "trends" when p narrowly misses the established α (usually .05) cutoff point. Having set the cutoff point, we determine whether we can or cannot reject the H_o. We can discuss trends; however, we *never* look at values that do not make the cutoff point (say, a .12 and a .34) and say that one is more or less probable than the other. They are all simply typical values in the normal distribution.

In hypothesis testing the basic question is: *How sure are we that we are right?* There is, however, a second question: *What do we lose if we are wrong?* Statistical tests give us the answer to the first question--how likely we are to be right. This is a test of *statistical significance.* When we consider the implications of the results in practical terms, we apply common sense and a consideration of alternatives to answer the second question. This is a matter of *practical significance. Significance* is, therefore, a technical term and a practical term. Both questions are important, for both need to be answered when we make decisions based on research. In some fields, lives may depend on being right, so stringent levels must be set. In our field, we can usually afford to be more lenient. If the outcome of the research evaluating a computer-assisted program for teaching vocabulary showed a .10 or .15 level of significance, and you had set .05 as the level for rejecting the null hypothesis, you do *not* have statistically significant findings. However, you could still argue for continuing the program until you found something better based on the trend and on practical significance. That is, decision making is based on many factors where both questions--how sure are we of being right and what do we lose if we are wrong--are considered.

Decision making should not, of course, impinge on the research process. The two are separate. Researchers, however, usually undertake their work with the hope of influencing decision making, making recommendations. We want to feel confident that the recommendations we make are justified.

Practice 8.3

Think about decision making in the following examples. What weight do the statistical levels of significance have on practical decision making in each?

1. Your private language school is just three years old and is beginning to show a profit. A new set of very expensive and very innovative multimedia and computer-assisted teaching materials is now on the market. They report incredible student gains as a result of using this program (an .01 level of significance). Your students are also very impressed by technological toys.

What do you stand to lose if you do or do not purchase them?

_____
_____
_____
_____

2. The school district wants to apply for a state grant to revise and evaluate a special teacher-designed program in intensive oral language for ESL children. The teachers who developed the program want to add materials to transfer oral language skills to reading. In the grant request, they note that the oral language scores of children showed gains on certain grammar structures (.01 level for 5 structures, .05 level for 2, and .10 for 4). Without the special program to teach transfer, reading scores improved but not significantly.

The state has few grants to distribute. Does this look like a promising candidate for funding? Why (not)?

_____
_____
_____
_____

3. As a member of a research and development team, you have found that seven clause types are very difficult for young ESL learners. The statistical test you performed showed these seven to contrast in difficulty with twenty other clause types at the .001 level of significance. In your research report to the development team you suggest that such clauses not be used in the initial reading materials developed for young ESL children. The development team also receives a report from the art department which does the visuals and layout of the reading books. If these clauses are deleted and others substituted, it may mean that new illustrations and new layouts will have to be done. As a practical matter, what decisions would you make regarding revisions? Your justification?

_____
_____
_____
_____

◇◇

Steps in Hypothesis Testing

Let's summarize our discussion regarding probability and hypothesis testing with a list of steps:

1. State the null hypothesis.

2. Decide whether to test it as a one- or two-tailed hypothesis. If there is no research evidence on the issue, select a two-tailed hypothesis. This will allow you to reject the null hypothesis in favor of an alternative hypothesis. If there is research evidence on the issue, select a one-tailed hypothesis. This will allow you to reject the null hypothesis in favor of a directional hypothesis.

3. Set the probability level (α level). Justify your choice.

4. Select the appropriate statistical test(s) for the data.

5. Collect the data and apply the statistical test(s).

6. Report the test results and interpret them correctly.

We have discussed the first three steps on this list in some detail. We are ready now to consider just how we decide on a statistical test for research data.

Distribution and Choice of Statistical Procedures

We have said that when we collect sufficient data, the distribution of those data will approach the normal distribution. We often assume that *if* we carefully identify the population from which we want to draw our subjects (say, the population of language learners in general) and *if* we randomly select subjects from that population, the data from this randomly selected sample of Ss will be representative of that population. The scores from this sample will form a normal distribution which will fit into the normal distribution of the population from which the sample was drawn. Thus, we will be able to *draw inferences* about the population on the basis of our sample data.

When we want to generalize from our sample to the population it was drawn from, we must be certain that the sample is truly representative. We have talked about this issue in previous chapters. Random selection is an important issue here. However, another issue is how large a sample we need to be sure the distribution of the data will be normal and representative as well. One basic rule of thumb is that the sample must include 30 or more cases, but this is not a set rule.

Imagine that your research involved the ability of eighth-grade students to find errors in a written text. However, you wonder whether boys and girls might, in fact, perform differently. If you had only 30 cases (15 boys and 15 girls), you would not have met even this minimum requirement. You would need 60 Ss, 30 boys and 30 girls, to meet the minimum requirement.

The nature of the population you have identified for your study will also determine the number of cases needed. For example, if the population of concern is eighth-grade Korean girls who arrived in San Francisco and entered school this year, the population is limited. A sample of 30 cases might be drawn that could reasonably be expected to represent this population. If the population of concern is Korean students studying English in eighth-grade classes in the United States, a sample of 30 cases drawn at random would probably not match the population. If you wanted to generalize your findings to all Korean students studying English (rather than just eighth-grade students), the population becomes even larger. No matter how carefully you stratify this random sample, it is unlikely that you will get a true match on the distribution of the data drawn from this sample and that drawn from the total population of Korean students studying English.

Representativeness of the cases in any sample is important. A second factor of importance is the distribution of the data obtained from the sample. We have said that if the sample is large enough, the distribution of the data will approach a normal distribution. Again, 30 is the magic number at which we assume the distribution to be close enough to normal. However, it is important to check to be sure this is the case (not just to assume it is okay). Since we know the distribution will never be exactly that of a normal distribution, the question is: How close must it be?

Think for a moment of the diagrams we drew of skewed distributions. We suggested that skewed distributions occur when some scores (or observations) are so extreme that the mean is not an accurate measure of central tendency. This occurs because some of the Ss or observations are not typical of the group.

You can see that if care is not taken in selecting the sample, we cannot expect a normal distribution, and that if we do not obtain a normal distribution, we must conclude that the sample includes people who are not representative of the population we wanted to study.

Sometimes we cannot randomly select a sample but must work with an intact group, our very own class of students. We want to describe their behavior, not generalize to all such classes. Their performance (assuming it's a class of 30) may approach a normal distribution. However, the class may have a few individuals in it who give extreme data (either outperform or underperform all others). The distribution may not be normal, so the median, rather than the mean, should be used as the measure of central tendency. What are we to do? The answer to this question is solved by deciding just how to analyze and interpret data.

Practice 8.4

1. If you could draw only 30 Ss to represent the population of eighth-grade Korean ESL students in the United States, how would you stratify the sample to make it as representative as possible? _____

_____

_____

2. If you wanted to generalize to all ESL eighth-grade students, would a sample of 30 Ss suffice to represent this population? Why (not)?_____

_____

_____

3. If we have already randomly selected Ss and some of these skew our data, this is a warning that we must be cautious about generalizing. If we look at the special characteristics of those Ss who have skewed the distribution, we may find they have characteristics that suggest another subgroup within the population. If so, should we find a random sample of 30 such Ss, add these to our study, and test for differences among the subgroups? Or should we add more Ss to our study to get a more representative sample so that we obtain a more normal distribution?

Discuss this issue in your study group. If you had unlimited resources, how would you resolve these research problems? _____

_____

_____

_____

_____

Choices in Data Analysis

When we gather data and obtain results, we test the results to determine whether they support our hypotheses or not. If we claim that they do, we want to be certain we are correct. The use of statistical procedures, via probability, tell us whether we can have confidence in our claims.

The choice of an appropriate statistical procedure that establishes this confidence is extremely important. You can know all about various statistical procedures (just as you can know all about addition, multiplication, subtraction, and division), but if you don't know which procedure to use, this knowledge won't help much.

To select an appropriate statistical test for your data--the procedure that will tell you how much confidence you can have in the claims you make--means making decisions about a number of factors. We have mentioned many of these in earlier chapters.

The first deciding factor has to do with identifying the number of independent and dependent variables and the number of levels of each variable in your study. The number of variables and the number of levels of each variable determine, in part, the type of statistical procedure you will use.

A second factor that influences the choice of a statistical procedure is type of comparisons to be made in the study. Are you comparing the performance of individuals with themselves on different tasks or on the same task at different times? Are your comparisons among different people all doing the same task(s)? Are your comparisons among groups of people where each group receives a slightly different treatment?

The third has to do with how you measured your variable(s). Are the data frequency counts of nominal data--counts that say "how many" or "how often" rather than "how much"? Are they scaled, ordinal data where responses are ranked with respect to each other along a continuum? Or have you measured equal-interval data? Your answer to this question also determines, in part, the kind of statistical test you will use.

The fourth decision relates to continuous data. Do the data form a normal distribution? What is the better measure of central tendency--the mean or the median?

The fifth factor has to do with the shape of the distribution in the population from which the samples have been drawn and, finally, whether you hope to generalize to the population. In this case, does the sample adequately represent the population to which you hope to generalize?

All five of these factors are important. The last three issues, however, have much to do with whether the statistical procedure will be parametric or nonparametric.

Parametric vs. Nonparametric Procedures

A nonparametric procedure is one which does not make strong assumptions about the shape of the distribution of the data. Parametric procedures, on the other hand, make strong assumptions about the distribution of the data. First, strictly speaking, parametric tests assume that dependent variables are interval scored or strongly continuous. That is, a parametric test assumes that the data are *not* frequencies or ordinal scales but interval data where the $\overline{X}$ and *s.d.* are appropriate measures of central tendency and dispersion. Nonparametric tests work with frequencies and rank-ordered scales. They assume that the variable being studied has some underlying continuity and normality of distribution, but the assumption is weak compared with that for parametric tests.

While most nonparametric tests apply to data that are nominal or rank-ordered, they can be used with interval data as well. There are times when you may not feel all that confident about the "equal-intervalness" of the measurement and the use of $\overline{X}$ and *s.d.* to represent the distribution of data. You may be fairly sure that someone who scored a 60 is really better than someone who scored 30, but you aren't too sure about the difference between a 50 and a 60. In that case, you do think there is some underlying linearity to the data but you don't feel that the points on the line are really equally spaced. If a statistical test requires interval data where $\overline{X}$ and *s.d.* can be used, that is what is required. "Sort of" is not enough. If you're not happy with the intervalness of your measurement, use a nonparametric test.

Second (and following from the first), parametric tests assume that the data are normally distributed. You remember that the larger the sample size, the more likely you are to obtain a normal distribution. For many studies in our field, we have only a small number of Ss or a small number of observations. We cannot always be confident that these will be normally distributed so that the $\overline{X}$ and *s.d.* are appropriate statistics to describe the distribution. If interpretation of the test requires that the data be normally distributed and yours are not, you should turn to a nonparametric procedure. (If you have an excellent statistical package, your computer may be able to tell you if the distribution is or is not normal and just how far afield you are when you use a parametric procedure with such data.)

A third assumption of parametric tests is that we can estimate the distribution in the population from which the respective samples have been drawn. In parametric tests, the distribution of the data in samples is used to estimate the distribution in the population represented by the samples. This is possible only because so much is known about the nature of human performance and the normal distribution of that performance in very large groups (i.e., the population). With small size samples and sample distributions that do not appear normal, you might feel some hesitation in applying such tests. Again, nonparametric procedures may be more appropriate since they do not rest on such estimates.

A fourth assumption underlying most parametric tests is that the observations are independent. The score assigned to one case must not bias the score given to any other case. So, for example, if you score compositions, the score you give the first composition should not influence the value you give to the second composition. You know how difficult this is if you have ever taught composition. There is another type of independence required by many statistical procedures. This is that the data in one cell of the design should not influence the data in another cell. In repeated-measures designs, the data are not independent. That is, if we collect oral data and written data from the same Ss, the data are not independent. Some of the variability (or lack of variability) in the two things measured may have nothing to do with the variables but rather with the fact that the same person produced the data. Another example of nonindependence of data is frequency counts of particular grammatical features. When straight frequencies are used (rather than a rate of n per some number of words), high frequencies from one piece of text may contribute a great deal to the frequency of the structure overall. To be independent, each piece of text would have to be tallied as showing presence/absence of the structure (rather than contributing to some overall total of the structure for that text type). Independence of data is discussed in different ways depending on the statistical procedure. We will, of course, give you a warning about this for each procedure. In some cases, it will mean selecting a nonparametric procedure. In other cases, it will mean selecting a repeated-measures parametric procedure.

If, as we mentioned, nonparametric tests can be selected for nominal, ordinal, and even interval data, why would we not just opt for them all the time? The reason is that we want the most *powerful* test that we can find to test our hypotheses.

Power is a technical term in statistics, concerning the probability of a false null hypothesis. In selecting a statistical test we want one that gives us very little chance of making a claim when we shouldn't have done so. It is also one which gives us little chance of not making a claim when we should have. That is, the most powerful test allows us to be sure that when we reject the null hypothesis we are correct or that when we accept the null hypothesis we are correct. The most powerful test--and in a sense, the best test--is the one where there is the least chance of making an error in rejecting or accepting the null hypothesis. Parametric tests utilize the most information (i.e., the X and $s.d.$ use all the information in the data) and so they are more powerful when assumptions underlying the procedures are met. Also, tests which require normal distribution are more powerful because characteristics of the normal distribution are well-known. Parametric tests, because of this power, allow us to make our claims with confidence. If good design has overcome threats to internal and external validity, and if the requirements of parametric tests have been met, we can generalize with confidence as well. That is, we can make inferences from our findings to the population from which the sample data were drawn.

Parametric tests are, as a general rule, more powerful than nonparametric tests when assumptions underlying the procedures are met. (The power of nonparametric tests does increase rapidly as you increase the number of Ss.) In part this is because they are tests which utilize the most information. Also, tests which require normal distribution are more powerful because characteristics of the normal distribution are known. Therefore, parametric tests should be our first choice *if* the assumptions of the particular procedure are met and *if* we feel confident about the measurement of the variables and *if* we have overcome the many threats to the validity of the study so that we can generalize our findings. As you will see, some of the parametric tests are claimed to be "robust" to violations of their assumptions. Some computer programs will, in fact, show you how severe a Type 1 or Type 2 error you might commit if you use them in violation of the assumptions. However, we cannot know what happens if we violate more than one, or some combination of assumptions that underlie a procedure. It is important, therefore, that we check all the assumptions of any statistical test before applying it to data.

◇◇◇

Practice 8.5

1. Think back to the example in chapter 6 (page 178) regarding attitudes of teacher trainees toward microteaching. Would you say that the assumption of linearity (i.e., equal-interval linearity) for the scale is weak or strong? _____. Our university uses a set of 9-point ratings of teacher performance. Would you judge the linearity of the scale as weak or strong? _____. Is the $\bar{X}$ and *s.d.* an appropriate description of the distribution? Why (not)? _____

_____

_____

2. Assume that you wanted to give someone a score based on an oral interview. The measure shows the number of words per minute during a three-minute segment of the interview. Then, you also want to give the person a general fluency rating. Can this be done so that the two scores are independent? Why (not)?

_____

▶ 3. Think about each of the following examples. In your study group, decide whether a parametric or a nonparametric procedure seems best for data analysis.

Example A
As part of an evaluation project, you asked high school students whether or not they enjoyed studying languages prior to their enrollment in language classes. At the end of the year, you again asked them if they liked studying languages. There are 25 students in all. After you collected their responses, you looked to see how many people who didn't like languages to begin with changed their minds and liked studying them at the end; how many who said "no" still said "no"; and how many who said "yes" now said "no"; and how many said "yes" and still said "yes" after the course.

Measurement (nominal frequencies/rank-order scales/interval scores): nominal freq

Type of comparison (between independent groups/repeated-measures/combined design): _____

Representativeness of sample: _no_____

Normal distribution of data expected? _no_____

Can we generalize to all high school students? _no_____

Independence of measures? _no (repeated measures)_____

Choice (parametric/nonparametric) and rationale _Data are nominal, not interval; normal dist. questionable_

_____

Example B

Trainees in your TEFL program have designed a set of ESL lessons based on authentic language materials (materials prepared for native speakers of the language). These lessons are for beginning students. Using "convenience sampling," you find an "intact class" (an ordinary, everyday class to which Ss were assigned prior to the study) of beginners. Eleven students in this class of beginners use the materials for one of the units of the course (a unit on description). Ten students use the materials normally selected to teach this unit. A panel of judges who were unaware of the treatment read and ranked all the Ss on their descriptive compositions. The best S was rated 1, second best 2, and so forth.

Measurement (nominal frequencies/rank-order scales/interval scores): _rank_

Type of comparison (between independent groups/repeated-measures/combined design): _____

Representativeness of sample: _no_

Normal distribution of data expected? _no_

Can we generalize to all ESL/EFL students using such materials? _no_

Independence of measures? _no?_

Choice (parametric/nonparametric) and rationale _Not interval; questionable / a normal dist. can be expected._

Example C

Hensley & Hatch (1986) evaluated the effectiveness of a language lab listening comprehension program for Vietnamese students in a refugee camp on Bataan, the Philippines. Approximately half of the 400 students enrolled in ESL had participated in a listening comprehension program in the lab while the others had taken regular ESL classes. The duration of the program was 10 weeks. While the lab was a *listening* program, the hope was that listening skills would transfer to better *speaking* skills. The question was whether the lab group performed as well or better than the regular ESL group. Students were given scores for such things as pronunciation, syntax, confidence, and communicative ability based on their informal conversations with a native speaker.

Measurement (nominal frequencies/rank-order scales/interval scores): _quasi interval_

Type of comparison (between independent groups/repeated-measures/combined design): _____ _?_

Representativeness of sample: _ok — all members of population._

Normal distribution of data expected? _____ yes _____

Can we generalize to all ESL/EFL students using such materials? no _____

Independence of measures? _____ not if scores given at sometime/by ____
_____ stme score

Choice (parametric/nonparametric) and rationale _____
_____ or this cos' scales not equal-interval _____

Example D

Having studied conversational analysis, you would like to apply what you have learned to ESL teaching. You wonder whether you can effectively teach conversational openings, closings, and turn-taking conventions in phone conversations. In the first week of class you ask students in your class to phone you to talk about their goals for the class. In reviewing each call, you assign a score for each person's phone skills (reflecting openings, closings, and turn-taking) on a 10-point scale. During the term, you teach the unit on phone conversations that you prepared. At the end of the course, you asked the students to call once again and again ranked them on the scale. The research question was whether any improvement occurred. While there is no control group in this study, you want to share the results of this pilot research with teachers at your next ESL in-service.

Measurement (nominal frequencies/rank-order scales/interval scores): rank _____

Type of comparison (between independent groups/repeated-measures/combined design): _____

Representativeness of sample: __ no _____

Normal distribution of data expected? _ no _____

Can we generalize to all ESL/EFL students using such materials? _ No _____

Independence of measures? ___ no _____

Choice (parametric/nonparametric) and rationale __ non : rank, small n _
_____ non representative group _____

Example E

In the study mentioned earlier that evaluated the effectiveness of the language lab used by Vietnamese refugee students, we wondered whether lab students would improve on general oral language skills. This time, 30 pairs of students were matched on the basis of age, sex, and scores on a placement test battery. The oral skills test was a general oral language test given to all students at the end of the total 12-week course. Two teachers scored each test and an average score for each S was computed. Teachers did not know which students were lab students.

Measurement (nominal frequencies/rank-order scales/interval scores): __interval__

Type of comparison (between independent groups/repeated-measures/combined design): _____

Representativeness of sample: _How chosen? Since matched, probably most_

Normal distribution of data expected? _maybe_

Can we generalize to all ESL/EFL students using such materials? _no_

Independence of measures? _yes_

Choice (parametric/nonparametric) and rationale _____
_____
_____

Would your choice change if one person was ill on the final day and so only 29 matched pairs of students took part in the study? Why (not)? _30 @ minimum_
_____
_____

◇◇

Conclusion for Part II

In the first section of this volume, we presented some of the basic principles of research design. Data description has been the focus of part II. In this final chapter we have introduced the notion of using statistical tests to give us confidence that our descriptions are correct and/or that we can make inferences from the data.

We have discussed some of the issues that guide the researcher in determining the most appropriate statistical test for the data. The first two have to do with design, the third with measurement, and the last has to do with selection between parametric and nonparametric options:

1. Number of dependent and independent variables (and the number of levels within each variable)?

2. Comparison between groups or repeated-measures?

3. Level of measurement (frequencies, rank-order scales, interval scores)?

4. Assumptions of parametric tests

a. Truly continuous data?

b. Normal distribution?

c. Equal variances?

d. Independent observations?

Parametric procedures should always be our choice when (a) all the assumptions of parametric procedures have been met and (b) we wish to draw inferences about the population from which our sample data were drawn. This does not mean that parametric procedures cannot be used for descriptive purposes. They can (and should) be *if* (and that is an important "if") the assumption behind such procedures have been met. However, when parametric procedures are used for inferential purposes (when we want to generalize), then not only must the assumptions of parametric tests be met but the design must also allow for generalization. That is, threats to internal and external validity of the design must have been met.

Part III of this volume will cover statistical tests that allow us to draw comparisons between and/or among groups. Options will be given to allow you to select the most appropriate procedure, parametric or nonparametric, for such comparisons.

Activities

1. V. Nell (1988. The psychology of reading for pleasure: needs and gratification. *Reading Research Quarterly, 23*, 1, 6-50.) studied people who are sometimes called ludic readers--bookworms who read at least a book a week. Among many findings, such readers preferred to read materials which they themselves had judged to be devoid of merit. The null hypothesis for this part of the study might have been "There will be no difference in preference for books which have or have not been judged to have literary merit." The null hypothesis was rejected at the .001 level. How much confidence can you have in this finding (i.e., how many chances are there that the author may have made a mistake in rejecting the null hypothesis)? not much! 1/615

2. D. Ilyin, S. Spurling, & S. Seymour (1987. Do learner variables affect cloze correlations? *SYSTEM, 15*, 2, 149-160.) studied the correlation of cloze test scores with scores in other skill areas. (Correlation is a statistical measure of relationship between variables. If you want to know more now, flip ahead to chapter 14.) By grouping the learners, they were able to compare the correlations obtained for different types of learners. One of their findings was that cloze test score and listening test score correlations were higher for young learners than for older learners. Fisher's z indicated the difference was significant ($p < .05$). How much confidence can you have in this finding (i.e., how many chances are there that the authors might have been wrong in rejecting the null hypothesis of no difference in correlations for older and younger learners)? 5 in a 100.

3. J. M. Fayer & E. Krasinski (1987. Native and nonnative judgments of intelligibility and irritation. *Language Learning, 37*, 3, 313-326.) asked native and nonnative (Spanish) speakers of English to judge the speech of (Spanish) ESL students. In addition to these judgments, they asked whether errors distracted them or annoyed them. The study shows that nonnative judges reported more annoyance with ESL errors than native speaker judges did (p < .05). The null hypothesis could not be rejected for "distraction." That is, there was no significant difference in number of reports of distraction in response to the tapes on the part of native and nonnative speaker judges. State the null hypothesis for "annoyance." How much confidence can you place in the finding that native speaker judges reported less annoyance than nonnative judges?

4. M. Eisenstein, S. Shuller, & J. Bodman (1987. Learning English with an invisible teacher: an experimental video approach. *SYSTEM, 15*, 2, 209-216.) evaluated an experimental treatment described in the article. They also looked at learner variables to see if they might have affected the outcome on the final test score (Ilyin Oral Interview, 1972). Look at each of the following questions and convert them to null hypotheses. Then interpret the probability figures. Which would allow you to reject the null hypothesis? How many chances of being wrong would you have if you rejected the null hypothesis in each case?

Do females and males score differently? *p* < .646

Do Ss from different socioeconomic groups score differently? *p* < .05

Do Ss who plan to stay in the United States score differently than those who do not? *p* < .258

Some Ss prefer that the teacher correct them while other Ss prefer teacher and peer correction. Do these two groups score differently on the test? *p* < .284

References

Hensley, A. & Hatch, E. 1986. Innovation in language labs: an evaluation report. Report for Philippine Refugee Processing Center, ICNC, Bataan, Philippines.

Ilyin, D. 1972. *The Ilyin Oral Interview.* New York, NY: Newbury House.

Part III.   Comparing Groups

Qs leading to appropriate stats. test
  ① # of variables & their fns.
  ② type of measurement used
  ③ Data   a) between groups
            b) repeated measures

Chapter 9

Comparing Two Groups: Between-Groups Designs

In the previous section we discussed the major questions that lead to the selection of an appropriate statistical test. The first question has to do with the number of variables and their function in the research. A second question has to do with the type of measurement used. A third question is whether the data come from two different groups (a between-groups design) or are two or more measures taken from the same group (a repeated-measures design). In this chapter we will discuss tests involving one independent variable with two levels and one dependent variable. That is, we will compare the performance of two groups on some dependent variable. The measurement of the dependent variable will be continuous (i.e., interval scores or ordinal scales). The comparison will be of two different groups (a comparison of independent groups, a between-groups design). Repeated-measures designs are discussed in chapter 10.

There are several options available to us for comparing two groups. The choice has to do with the type of measurement and the best estimate of central tendency for the data. We will begin with the *t*-test, a procedure that tests the difference between two groups for normally distributed interval data (where $\overline{X}$ and *s.d.* are appropriate measures of central tendency and variability of the scores). Then we will turn to procedures used when the *median* is the best measure of central tendency or where certain assumptions of the *t*-test cannot be met.

Parametric Comparison of Two Groups: t-test

We have discussed at length how individual scores fall into the normal distribution. In research, we are seldom interested in the score of an individual student; rather, we are interested in the performance of a group. When we have collected data from a group, found the $\bar{X}$ and s.d. (and determined that these are accurate descriptions of the data), we still want to know whether that $\bar{X}$ is exceptional in any way. To make this judgment, we need to compare the mean with that of some other group.

In Case 1 studies, we compare the group mean with that of the population from which it was drawn. We want to know whether the group $\bar{X}$ is different from that of the population at large. In Case 2 studies we have means from two groups (perhaps an experimental group and a control group). We want to know whether the means of these two groups truly differ.

Let's imagine that you have been able to obtain a special computer-assisted videodisc program for teaching German. It's an expensive program, and your department chair asks for evidence that the program has been effective. You do have the results of a comprehensive vocabulary and structure test given at the end of the term. You can show the chair the $\bar{X}$ and s for the class on this test. You can say that the $\bar{X}$ of 80 looks much higher than the published mean of 65 for the test. You know he will just say, "Fifteen points? How much better is that?" Since there are other sections of German I, any of which could serve as a control group, you immediately ask a fellow teacher if he has the scores for his class. Unfortunately, he hasn't had time to score them and the chair needs the information by this afternoon. What can you do? Well, it is possible that you might do a Case 1 t-test. Some background is needed for us to understand how this works.

Sampling Distribution of Means

Assume there are 36 Ss represented in the $\bar{X}$ for your class. We need to compare this mean with that of many, many $\bar{X}$s from other groups of 36 Ss. Imagine that we could draw samples of 36 Ss from many, many other German I classes and that we gave them the test. Once we got all these sample $\bar{X}$s, we could turn them into a distribution.

The normal distribution is made up of individual scores. This distribution would differ in that, instead of being made up of individual scores, it is composed of class means. As we gathered more and more data, we would expect a curve to evolve that would be symmetric. This symmetric curve is, however, not called a normal distribution but rather a *sampling distribution of means*.

If we were able to build this sampling distribution of means, we could then see where the $\bar{X}$ for our German class fit in that distribution. We hope it would place at the right of the distribution, showing that our class scored higher than other classes. If the sample $\bar{X}$ fell right in the center of the sampling distribution of means, we would know that it is typical of all such classes, no better and no worse. If the sample $\overline{X}$ fell at the far left tail of the distribution, we would interpret this finding to mean that our class scored much lower than other classes.

If you had the $\overline{X}$s for the test from many, many schools and you plotted out the sampling distribution of means, you might be surprised at the results--especially if you compared the spread of scores within the sample from your class and the spread of $\overline{X}$s in the distribution of means. If you actually plotted the means from all the groups, you would immediately notice how much more similar they are to each other--much closer to each other--than the individual scores in your class are to the group mean.

Stop to think about it for a moment, though, and it will make sense. When we compute a mean ($\overline{X}$), the individual differences are averaged out. The high and low scores disappear and we are left with a central measure. The $\overline{X}$ is *the* most central score for the group. So, since our new distribution is made of $\overline{X}$s, it will naturally be much more compact than scores in a single distribution. Therefore, the standard deviation will be smaller in the distribution of $\overline{X}$s.

The size of the groups will also influence the sampling distribution of means. The larger the N for each group, the more the $\overline{X}$s will resemble each other. This is because the more scores there are in each group, the greater the chance of a normal distribution. And, with a normal distribution, the $\overline{X}$ becomes quite precise as a measure of central tendency. The $\overline{X}$s of large classes, therefore, should be very similar to each other (if they are all from the same population).

The following figures may clarify this difference in distributions. The first distribution is typical of a normal distribution of individual scores in a class of 30 Ss. The second is typical of a sampling distribution of means for groups of 30 Ss each. The final figure is typical of a sampling distribution of means for groups of 100 Ss each.

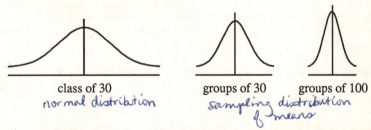

class of 30
normal distribution

groups of 30   groups of 100
sampling distribution
of means

When we take the average of a group of scores, we call that central balance point the *mean* and we use the symbol $\overline{X}$ for the mean. When we take the average of a group of means, we call that central balance point the *population mean* (not the "mean of means"!). And the symbol for the population mean is μ (the Greek letter *mu*).

The reason the mean for the groups is called the population mean is that it is drawn from a large enough number of sample groups (selected at random from

population mean = μ

the population) that it forms a normal distribution. Its central point should be equal to that of the population.

The sampling distribution of means has three basic characteristics.

1. For 30 or more samples (with 30 or more Ss per sample), it is normally distributed.

2. Its mean is equal to the mean of the population.

3. Its standard deviation, called *standard error of means*, is equal to the standard deviation of the population divided by the square root of the sample size.

The third characteristic may not be crystal clear. Why isn't the standard error of the means equal to the standard deviation of the population? Think back a moment to the two figures you just chose to represent the distribution of the means based on groups of 30 Ss each and that of groups of 100 Ss each. The sampling distribution of means depends on the *size* of the sample groups. The two figures (for groups of 30 vs. groups of 100) differed in the amount of spread from the central point, with the distribution representing groups of 100 being much more compact. Therefore, to make the standard error of means sensitive to the N size of the samples from which the means were drawn, we divide it by the square root of the sample size.

Now, the hard part. While you already have the published population mean for the German test from the publishers, you do not know the standard error of means for the test. You don't have time to find 30 other classes with 36 Ss each. There is a much easier way. We will estimate it, and that estimate will be quite precise.

When we carry out research, we gather data on a *sample*. The information that we present is called a *statistic*. We use the sample statistic to estimate the same information in the population. While a *statistic* is used to talk about the sample, you may see the term *parameter* used to talk about the population. (Again, *parameter* is a lexical shift when applied to linguistics. The two have little to do with each other.)

Perhaps the following diagram will make the picture clear:

Sample		Population
↓		↑
Statistic →	Estimates →	Parameter

Let's see how this works for estimating the standard error of means, the parameter $\sigma_{\bar{X}}$ (the Greek symbol is a small *sigma*):

$$\sigma_{\bar{X}} = \frac{\sigma_X}{\sqrt{N}}$$

$\sigma_{\bar{X}}$ = standard error of means

Since we will use our sample data to estimate the parameter, we use our sample statistics for the formula:

— sd of samples...

$$s_{\overline{X}} = \frac{s_X}{\sqrt{N}}$$

The formula says that we can find the standard deviation of the means of all the groups (called now the *standard error of means*) by dividing the standard deviation of our sample group by the square root of the sample size. Sample statistics are the best available information for estimating the population parameters. The correspondence between population parameter symbols and sample statistic symbols is:

$$\sigma = s$$

$$\sigma_{\overline{X}} = s_{\overline{X}}$$

$$\mu = \overline{X}$$

The standard error of means becomes a ruler for measuring the distance of our sample mean from the population mean in the same way that standard deviation was a ruler for measuring the distance of one score from the mean. The standard error ruler will, however, always be very short in comparison to the standard deviation ruler. This is because the sampling distribution of means is more tightly clustered and thus shows less spread from the $\overline{X}$. If this does not make sense, think back to the three distribution diagrams on page 251 and then discuss the matter in your study group.

Now let's apply all this information to a Case 1 *t*-test procedure.

Case 1 Comparisons

A Case 1 study compares a sample mean with an established population mean. The H_o for a Case 1 *t*-test would be: There is no *effect* of group on the dependent variable. That is, the test scores result in no difference between the sample mean and the mean of the population.

To discover whether the null hypothesis is, in fact, true, we follow a familiar procedure. First we ask how far our sample $\overline{X}$ is from μ. Then we check to see how many "ruler lengths" that difference is from the mean. The ruler, this time, is the standard deviation of the means rather than the standard deviation, right? The formula for our observed *t* value is:

$$t_{obs} = \frac{\overline{X} - \mu}{s_{\overline{X}}}$$

If the $\overline{X}$ for our class was 80 and the published μ for the test was 65, you can fill in the values for the top part of the formula:

$$\frac{80 - 65}{s_{\overline{X}}}$$

To find the value for $s_{\overline{X}}$, refer back to our formula for the standard error of means. The standard deviation for the scores of your German students was 30. The class size was 36. So,

$$s_{\overline{X}} = \frac{30}{\sqrt{36}} \qquad \frac{s_x}{\sqrt{N}}$$

Then,

$$t_{obs} = \frac{\overline{X} - \mu}{s_{\overline{X}}}$$

$$t_{obs} = \frac{80 - 65}{30 \div \sqrt{36}}$$

$$t_{obs} = 3.0$$

That's the end of our calculations, but what does this t value tell us (or the chair of your German department)? Visualize yourself as one of many, many teachers who have given the German vocabulary test to groups of exactly 36 students. All of the means from these groups have been gathered and they form a sampling distribution of means. The task was to find exactly how well the $\overline{X}$ of your class fits in this distribution. Can you say that they are really spectacularly better--i.e., your class $\overline{X}$ falls so far out under the right tail of the distribution that they "don't belong," "are not typical"? Can you reject the null hypothesis?

Before we can answer, there is one more concept we need to present--the concept of *degrees of freedom (df)*. You already know that the t value is influenced by the sample size. Sample size relates to degrees of freedom. You'll remember in several of our formulas, we averaged not by dividing by N but by $N - 1$. This, too, is related to degrees of freedom.

Degrees of freedom refers to the number of quantities that can vary if others are given. For example, if we know that A + B = C, we know that A and B are free to vary. You can put any number in the A and B slots and call the sum C. But if you change C to a number so that A + B = 100, then only one of the numbers (A or B) can vary. As soon as you plug in one number, the other is set. If A = 35, then B is not free to vary. It has to be 65. Only one was free, the other is fixed. So we say there is one degree of freedom. If we said that A + B + C = 100, then two of the numbers (for A, B, or C) can vary and the third is fixed. Two are free--two degrees of freedom. To find the degrees of freedom we subtract $N - 1$. This concept of degrees of freedom also applies to groups. The number of degrees of freedom is important, for it determines the shape of the t distribution. Mathematicians have already described these distributions for us according to the degrees of freedom. And, fortunately for us, mathematicians have also worked out the probabilities for each of these distributions. We *are* in luck. We can now find the *df* for our study and check the probability to determine whether we can or cannot reject the null hypothesis.

To obtain the *df* we use $N - 1$. The *N* of our sample was 36 so *df* = 35. To find the probability, we will consult the appropriate distribution in table 2, appendix C. Now we can find the answer to our question.

In the table, notice that the probability levels are given across the top of the table. In the first column are the degrees of freedom. If the *df* were 1, you would look at the values in the first row to determine whether you could or could not reject the null hypothesis. For example, if you chose an .05 level for rejecting the null hypothesis, you would look across the first row to the second column. The number 12.706 is the *t* critical value that you need to meet or exceed in order to reject the null hypothesis. If you chose an .01 α (rejection point), you would need a *t* value of 63.657 or better. If your study had 2 degrees of freedom, you would need a *t* value of 4.303 or better to reject the null hypothesis at the .05 level.

Let's see how this works with our study. We have 35 degrees of freedom. Look down the *df* column for the appropriate number of degrees of freedom. Unfortunately, there is no 35 in this particular table. If there is no number for the *df* of your study, move to the next *lower* value on the chart (as the more conservative estimate). The closest *df* row to 35 *df* in this table is 30. Assuming you chose an .05 α, look at the critical value of *t* given in the column labeled .05. The intersection of *df* row and *p* column shows the critical value needed to reject the null hypothesis.

The table, then, shows that you need to obtain or exceed a *t* value of 2.042 to reject the null hypothesis. For an .01 level, you would need to meet or exceed a *t* value of 2.750. These cut-off values are called the *critical value* of *t* or *t critical*. When the observed value of *t* meets or exceeds the critical value for the level selected (.05 or .01), you can reject the null hypothesis. (The critical value works for either positive or negative *t* values.)

We can reject the null hypothesis in this case because our observed *t* value of 3.0 exceeds the critical value (*t* critical) of 2.042 needed for a probability level of .05. In the research report, this information would be given as the simple statement: $t = 3.0$, $df = 35$, $p < .05$. We can reject the H_o and conclude that, indeed, our German class excelled!

The probability levels given in this table are for two-tailed, nondirectional hypotheses. If your particular study has led you to state a directional, one-tailed hypothesis, you need to "double" these values. That is, a one-tailed hypothesis puts the rejection under only one tail (rather than splitting it between the two tails). So, to find a one-tailed critical value for an .05 level, use the .10 column. To set an .01 rejection level, use the column labeled .02. Thus, for 1 *df* and a one-tailed .05 rejection area, you need a *t* critical value of 6.314 or better. For an .01 level, the one-tailed critical value of *t* would be 31.821. If your study had 16 *df* and you wished to reject a one-tailed hypothesis at the .05 level, you would need a *t* value of 1.746 or greater. If your study had 29 *df*, a *t* critical of 2.462 would be needed for rejection at the .01 level. For the more normal two-tailed

When observed value of t meets or exceeds t critical

hypothesis at the .01 level, the values needed would be 2.921 for 16 *df*, and 2.756 for 29 *df*.

Now let's review a few of the points discussed in the chapter on design. You will remember that there are many pitfalls in planning research. In this case, even if you find that the class did remarkably well on a published test, you cannot say that this "proves" the materials are effective. When research has been conducted with intact classes, and when we have not examined possible threats to internal and external validity, the results must be interpreted with care (i.e., conservatively). However, the results do allow you to reject the null hypothesis with confidence and conclude that the performance of the class is statistically better than the published mean. What caused the difference is open to interpretation.   *despite ex/in. validity threats?*

Practice 9.1

▶ 1. Use the *t*-test table in the Appendix to determine the *t* critical value needed to reject the following null hypotheses:

1.761 + 14 *df*, .05 α, one-tailed hypothesis
2.508 + 22 *df*, .01 α, one-tailed hypothesis
1.684 + 55 *df*, .05 α, one-tailed hypothesis
2.228 + 10 *df*, .05 α, two-tailed hypothesis
2.771 + 27 *df*, .01 α, two-tailed hypothesis

2. If you were to teach the course again, and if there were three other sections of German I, how might you design an evaluation that would be more convincing? (You might be able to persuade your chair to contact the program designers to see if they would allow you to keep the materials in exchange for a formal evaluation!)

Redesigned evaluation _____

_____

_____

_____

_____

_____

_____

▶ 3. Suppose there are 14 students in your class. The school requires that students take a standard reading test at the beginning of the term. The $\overline{X}$ for your class is 80 and the *s* is 5. The published mean for your class grade on this national test is 85. To paraphrase Garrison Keillor, you thought all your children were "better than average." Were they?

Box diagram:

	CLASS	POP
$\overline{X}$	80	85

The formula again is:

sd of sample

$$t_{obs} = \frac{\overline{X} - \mu}{s_{\overline{X}}} \qquad s_{\overline{X}} = \frac{s_X}{\sqrt{N}}$$

Enter your calculations below:

$$\frac{5}{\sqrt{14}} = \frac{5}{3.74} = 1.337$$

$$t_{obs} = \frac{80 - 85}{1.337} = -3.74$$

How many df are there ($N - 1$)? __13__ . Look at the t-test table in the Appendix. Find the df in the first column. Then find the intersection with the significance level you chose. What critical t value is listed? __2.160__ . (You can disregard the negative sign on t observed.) Does your observed t value exceed the critical value of t? __exceeds__

4. Think for a minute about the design of this study. If your class $\overline{X}$ were statistically different from the published $\overline{X}$, could you have attributed this sterling performance in terms of your classroom instruction? Why (not)? __Not causal__

5. Notice that the standard deviation for your group was relatively small. The class members all performed in a similar way, so you can't say that the mean was

biased by extreme scores of some few students. It looks like Garrison Keillor was wrong--the group was not better but worse. What other factors might have been involved in poor performance on the test?_____

_____

_____

6. You may have noticed an interesting phenomenon in checking the *t*-test table in the Appendix. As the sample size becomes smaller, the *t* critical value for rejecting the null hypothesis becomes higher. *The smaller the number of Ss, the larger the differences must be between the two means.* Discuss this phenomenon in your study group. Write your consensus as to why this should be so.

_____

_____

_____

_____

_____

◇◇

Case 2 Comparisons

Case 2 studies are much more common in applied linguistics research than are Case 1. We often want to compare the performance of two groups. Perhaps the scores are of an experimental group vs. a control group, Spanish vs. Korean ESL students, or field dependent vs. field independent learners.

Let's assume that you have two bilingual classrooms. In one classroom, instruction is conducted in Spanish in the morning by one teacher and in English in the afternoon by a second teacher. In the second classroom, two teachers take turns instructing children throughout the day. One uses Spanish and the other uses English. At the end of the year, the children are tested in each language. The $\overline{X}$ for the first class is 82.7; the $\overline{X}$ for the second is 78.1 (and the distribution shows that $\overline{X}$ and s.d. are appropriate measures of central tendency and variability or dispersion for these data). The question is whether the test performance of the children in the two classrooms differed significantly. By "eyeballing" the means, it appears that the first class "did better" than the second.

As you might imagine, the process by which we test the difference between these two groups requires that we look not only at the difference between the two means but that we also place that difference in a sampling distribution of such differences. This procedure will differ from that described for a Case 1 *t*-test because instead of placing a mean in a distribution of $\overline{X}$s, we want to look at a distribution of differences between $\overline{X}$s.

The basic problem is finding this sampling distribution. Once again, we will use sample statistics to estimate population parameters. Using our statistics, we will estimate the differences that we would get if we found and tested another two classes and compared their means, then found another two classes and tested them to compare their means, and so on until we felt we had tested the population. We would find the difference between each pair of classes on the test and plot these in a sampling distribution. Then we would place our difference in means in that distribution and decide whether the difference "belongs" or "is typical" of that distribution. If it is, we will not be able to reject the null hypothesis because the difference is normal (not extreme) for the distribution of differences.

Sampling Distribution of Differences Between Means

Whenever we want to compare the means of two different groups, we can visualize the procedure where we collect data on the test from two classes, another two classes, and another two until we have enough differences between means to represent the population. We compute the differences between the means for each set of two classes. Then we construct a frequency distribution of all these differences which will be called a *sampling distribution of differences between means*. The distribution--if it includes many, many differences between means-- should have the following characteristics:

1. The distribution is normally distributed.

2. It has a mean of zero.

3. It has a standard deviation called the *standard error of differences between means*.

The distribution will be bell-shaped, and we will need a "ruler" to discover the place of the difference between our two means. We will use one which measures the standard error of difference between means. This should ring a bell. This is the third time around for finding the place of our data in a distribution in exactly the same way.

To review, to find an *individual* score in a *normal distribution*, we use a *z*-score formula:

$$z = \frac{\text{difference between score and mean}}{\text{standard deviation}}$$

$$z = \frac{X - \overline{X}}{s}$$

To place a sample *mean* in a *distribution of means*, we used a *t*-test formula that said:

$$t = \frac{\text{difference between sample mean and population mean}}{\text{standard error of means}}$$

or

$$t = \frac{\overline{X} - \mu}{s_{\overline{X}}}$$

Now, in comparing the *difference between two means*, the formula is:

$$t = \frac{\text{diff. between 2 means} - \text{diff. between 2 population means}}{\text{standard error of differences between means}}$$

Now, since we believe that the difference between the two population means will be zero (because they are from the same population), we can immediately simplify this formula by deleting the second part of the numerator.

$$t = \frac{\text{difference between 2 sample means}}{\text{standard error of diff. between means}}$$

$$t = \frac{\overline{X}_e - \overline{X}_c}{s_{(\overline{X}_e - \overline{X}_c)}}$$

Let's apply this formula now to some data. Lazaraton (1985) planned to evaluate a set of authentic language materials used in a beginning-level ESL class. There were two sections of beginning ESL, one of which would form the experimental group and the other the control group. While students were placed in the class on the basis of a placement test, it was important to equate the listening skills of the two classes prior to giving the instruction. Here is a table showing the scores of the two groups:

ESLPE Listening Scores & Total Scores
Two Classes

Group	n	Mean	s	t value	df	p
LISTENING SCORE						
Control	19	11.7	4.0			
Exper.	19	10.5	4.7			
TOTAL ESL SCORE						
Control	19	66.9	7.7			
Exper.	20	63.4	8.4			

Let's fill out the chart for this example.

> *Research hypothesis?* There is no *effect* of group on listening com-
> prehension (i.e., there is no difference in the means of the exper-
> imental and control groups)
>   *Significance level?* .05
>   *1- or 2-tailed?* 2-tailed
> *Design*
>   *Dependent variable(s)?* Listening comprehension
>   *Measurement?* Scores (interval)
>   *Independent variable(s)?* Group
>   *Measurement?* Nominal (experimental vs. control)
>   *Independent or repeated-measures?* Independent
> *Other features?* Intact groups
> *Statistical procedure?* t-test

Box diagram: *for listening or total ESL scores?*

$$\overline{X}$$

EXPER	CONT

In statistics books, you may find the null hypothesis stated in the following way
for the *t*-test:

> H_o = The two samples are from the same population; the difference
> between the two sample means which represent population means
> is zero ($\mu_1 - \mu_2 = 0$). $\}$ H_o

The null hypothesis says that we expect that any difference found between the
two sample groups falls well within the normal differences found for any two
means in the population. To reject the null hypothesis, we must show that the
difference falls in the extreme left or right tail of the distribution.

Here is the formula:

$$t_{obs} = \frac{\overline{X}_e - \overline{X}_c}{s_{(\overline{X}_e - \overline{X}_c)}}$$

The denominator is the standard error of differences between means. The subscripts in the numerator just identify one mean as coming from the experimental
group and the other from the control group.

The numerator is the easy part. The difference between the two means (10.5 −
11.7) is −1.2. The question is whether that difference is significant. To find out,
we must place this difference in a sampling distribution and discover how far it
is from the central point of that distribution. We measure the distance with a
"ruler"--in this case the *standard error of differences between means.*

The denominator *is* the ruler. You remember from our discussions of Case 1
studies that we will use sample statistics (in this case, the standard deviations

from the mean of the two groups) to estimate the mean of the population. We know that in making this estimate, we need to correct the "ruler" for the size of the classes (the *n*'s of the two groups).

The formula for the "ruler" is:

$$s_{(\bar{X}_e - \bar{X}_c)} = \sqrt{\frac{s_e^2}{n_e} + \frac{s_c^2}{n_c}}$$

Since we have the *s* and the *n* for each group, we call fill in this information as follows:

$$s_{(\bar{X}_e - \bar{X}_c)} = \sqrt{\frac{4.7^2}{19} + \frac{4.0^2}{19}}$$

$$\sqrt{1.163 + 0.842}$$
$$\sqrt{2} = 1.416$$

Use your calculator to compute the value for the standard error of differences between the means. It should be:

$$s_{(\bar{X}_e - \bar{X}_c)} = 1.42$$

Now that we have the values of both the numerator and the denominator, we can find the value of *t* observed.

$$t_{obs} = \frac{\bar{X}_e - \bar{X}_c}{s_{(\bar{X}_e - \bar{X}_c)}}$$

$$t_{obs} = .845$$

At this point, we will place the observed value of *t* into the sampling distribution of differences between means for the appropriate degrees of freedom. Since there were 19 *S*s in each group for this test, each group has 18 *df*. We *add* these together to get the *df* for the study. $18 + 18 = 36$ *df*. Another way of saying the same thing is $df = n_1 + n_2 - 2$. We turn to the *t*-test table in the Appendix and look at the intersection of 36 *df* and .05. It's not there, so we choose the 30 *df* row instead (to be more conservative). The *t* critical needed for rejection of the null hypothesis is 2.042. We cannot reject the null hypothesis. This information may be presented in the simple statement: $t = .845$, $df = 36$, p = n.s. The abbreviation *n.s.* stands for a "non-significant difference." If there is sufficient space, a table such as the following may be used to give the same information.

ESLPE Listening Scores
Two Classes

Group	n	Mean	s	t value	df	p
Control	19	11.7	4.0	.845	36	n.s.
Exper.	19	10.5	4.7			

The conclusion we can draw about the differences between these two groups before the treatment began is that their listening scores did not differ; the groups are of approximately the same listening ability. (We cannot say, however, that they are *significantly similar* since we have only tested the null hypothesis of no difference.)

◇◇

Practice 9.2

▶ 1. Perform a *t*-test to test the difference between the two groups on the total ESL test scores given in the data table on page 260. Show your calculations.

_____

_____

_____

Can you reject the null hypothesis? Why (not)? _____

_____

_____

What can you conclude? _____

_____

◇◇

Assumptions Underlying t-tests

Before applying any statistical test it is important to check to make sure the assumptions of the test have been met. Because the *t*-test is meant to compare two means, it is very widely used. Unfortunately, it is also the case that it is very widely misused. The following assumptions must be met.

Assumption 1: There are only two levels (groups) of one independent variable to compare. For example, the independent variable "native language" can be defined as Indo-European and non-Indo-European. There are only *two* levels of the variable. However, if we defined "native language" by typology as subject-prominent, topic-prominent, and mixed (shows features of both), there are now three levels of the variable. Only two levels can be compared in the *t*-test procedure. You *cannot* cross-compare groups. This means you cannot compare group 1 and 2, 1 and 3, and then 2 and 3, etc. If you try to use the *t*-test for such comparisons, you make it very easy to reject the null hypothesis. (For example, if you set the significance level at .05 and then run four comparisons, you can check the level by the formula $\alpha = 1 - (1 - \alpha)^c$ where the *c* refers to the number of comparisons. So for four comparisons, the actual level would be $\alpha = 1 - (1 - .05)^4 = 1 - (.95)^4 = 1 - .82 = .18$. So the probability level has changed from .05 to .18.) In at least one of the comparisons you will not know which significant differences are spurious and which are not. Thus, interpretation becomes impossible.

Assumption 2: Each S (or observation) is assigned to one and only one group.
That is, the procedure is not appropriate for repeated-measures designs. There
is another procedure, the matched-pairs *t*-test, for such designs.

*Assumption 3: The data are truly continuous (interval or strongly continuous
ordinal scores).* This means you cannot do a *t*-test on raw frequencies. You may
be able to convert frequencies to continuous data by changing them to rates or
proportions but that conversion must be justified. In addition, you must be able
to show that the converted data approaches interval measurement. If you have
ordinal data or converted frequency data, you may question whether the scale is
continuous and/or whether the data are distributed normally across the points
of the scale (a common problem with 5-point or 7-point scales). In such cases,
the *median* rather than the *mean* may be the better estimate of central tendency
and you would be much wiser to use a nonparametric test (e.g., Median or Rank
Sums).

*Assumption 4: The mean and standard deviation are the most appropriate mea-
sures to describe the data.* If the distribution is skewed, the median is a more
appropriate measure of central tendency. Use a nonparametric procedure (Median or Rank Sums) for the comparison.

*Assumption 5: The distribution in the respective populations from which the sam-
ples were drawn is normal, and variances are equivalent.* It is, indeed, difficult to
know if the distribution in the population is or is not normal. This is a special
problem when Ss are not randomly selected but come from intact groups (i.e., our
ESL classes). For example, it would be difficult to know if population performance on a listening comprehension test of groups of ESL students is or is not
normal. If the test used by Lazaraton in the previous example (page 260) were
administered to successive groups of Ss (16 Ss in each group), we could begin to
build a sampling distribution of means. It's possible that the result would be
normal but it's also possible it might not be. For example, it's possible a bimodal
distribution would occur if, for example, groups of immigrant students clustered
around the top end of the distribution and groups of foreign students around the
bottom. You might not be at all interested in the immigrant/foreign student dichotomy but, because the data come from intact groups which show these characteristics (rather than from random samples), the data might not be normally
distributed. As for the equal variance assumption, statisticians state that, if the
n size of the two groups is equal, the *t*-test is "robust" to violations of this assumption. Magically, *t*-test procedures in some computer packages (e.g., SAS
and SPSS-X statistical packages) give information that allows you to judge
normality of distribution and equivalence of variance.

It's extremely important to observe the assumptions underlying the *t*-test procedure. Failure to do so could lead you to claims that are not warranted. Even
though the claims might have been correct if another statistical procedure were
used, the misapplication of any statistical test may cause others to lose confidence
in your work. Unfortunately, the computer will never tell you if you have violated the assumption of any test you ask it to run. You must check this yourself.

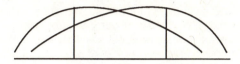

You might wonder why we spend all this time and effort. Why can't we just "eyeball" the two means and tell if they are truly different? It is possible that the means of two groups look different and yet they might not be. The diagram below helps explain why this is so.

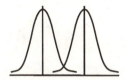

While the $\overline{X}$s appear far apart, their distributions overlap. Individual scores in one distribution could easily fit into those of the other distribution. They almost form one single distribution curve.

The next diagram shows why two means that look quite similar might, in fact, be different.

While the $\overline{X}$s appear close together, their distributions overlap only slightly. The scores in one distribution do not appear to fit into the other.

Think back to your explanation of why the critical values required for an .05 level of significance become higher as the n in the groups becomes smaller. Remember, too, that the "ruler" by which we measure the placement of the difference relative to the normal distribution also changes with group size. Can you weave this into your understanding of why a statistical test is necessary if we are to know whether differences are or are not significant? (You might want to try reworking one of the problems for a Case 2 t-test and increase or decrease the n size for each group. What happens?)

You can look at two means and say that they are *numerically* the same or different. However, there is no way to look at two means and conclude they are *statistically* the same or different without using a t-test. (If you understand how a t-test is done and have additional information on n size and s, you can, of course, make a very good guess.)

Strength of Association: eta²

When we use a t-test to compare two groups, we obtain a figure which does or does not allow us to reject our H_o. By rejecting the H_o, we can show that there is an effect of the levels of the independent variable on the dependent variable. The two levels differ in their performance on the dependent variable.

That may be all that you wish to show. If you have compared, for example, females vs. males (independent variable = sex) on a language aptitude test and found that there is a statistical difference, that may suffice. However, in the spirit of research as a process of enquiry, you might wonder just how much of the difference in the performance of the two groups is really related to male vs. female differences. You reason that there is a natural distribution of spread of scores in the data of each group which may be related to being male or female but that there are probably other factors (i.e., "error" as far as your research is concerned) that also contributed to pushing apart the means of the two groups.

When the sample statistic is significant, one rough way of determining how much of the overall variability in the data can be accounted for by the independent variable is to determine its *strength of association.* For the t-test and matched t-test this measure of strength of association is called *eta squared* (η^2). It's very simple to do. The formula uses values that can be found in your t-test calculations or your computer output.

$$\eta^2 = \frac{t^2}{t^2 + df}$$

Imagine that we had carried out the above study, comparing the performance of males and females on a language aptitude test and that we obtained a t value of 4.65. There were 20 Ss in our study, 10 females and 10 males. The df for the study are, therefore, $(10 - 1) + (10 - 1)$ or 18 df. Let's determine the strength of association between sex and performance.

$$\eta^2 = \frac{t^2}{t^2 + df}$$

$$\eta^2 = \frac{4.65^2}{4.65^2 + 18}$$

$$\eta^2 = .55$$

The η^2 of .55 in the above example is a very strong association. It tells us that 55% of the variability *in this sample* can be accounted for by sex. (45% of the variability cannot be accounted for by the independent variable. This variance is yet to be explained.)

One reason eta^2 is such a nice measure to have is that it lets you think more about findings and how you might rework the study. For example, if you obtained a significant effect (i.e., could reject the H_o on the basis of the t-test) yet found that the strength of association did not allow you to account for more than say 5 or 10% of the variability in performance, you might think about what other special features the sample showed. You might find that some of the Ss seemed to have high test anxiety and others not. If you could remove this factor, perhaps sex would turn out to be a stronger predictor of language aptitude. Or perhaps, you reason, sex is not an overriding factor in language aptitude and you want to add more independent variables to the study and try again. As you can see, if your interest is in understanding *language aptitude* rather than trying to show sex differences, the strength of association test will help start you on your way to improving the research.

Strength of association measures are sometimes reported in correlational research in our field. They are (to our knowledge) rarely included in reports in our field that give the results of the parametric and nonparametric statistical procedures discussed in this chapter. They are, however, extremely useful measures that should help you interpret your results. For example, if you ran a t-test procedure, found a statistical difference and claimed that group A did better than group B on the basis of the statistical procedure, you and your readers still do not know exactly how important that finding is. This is especially true when you have large numbers of Ss in the groups. (Remember that when you have more Ss, the degrees of freedom go up and the t critical value needed to reject the H_o gets smaller. Thus, it becomes easier to reject the H_o.) If you do a strength of association test, then you will know how important the variable is. If it turns out that you can show an association like 50% or better, you can make a big deal about your findings. If it turns out that it's, say, less than 10%, you might want to be more conservative and say that there are, of course, other factors that need to be highlighted in future research (research you have in mind to better answer your broad research question).

◇◇◇◇◇◇◇◇◇◇◇◇◇◇◇◇◇◇◇◇◇◇◇◇◇◇◇◇◇◇◇◇◇◇◇◇◇◇◇

Practice 9.3

Do a strength of association test on the outcomes of the t-test problems in this chapter. Give the results and the interpretation in the space below.

▶ 1. German example (page 254)

_____
_____
_____

▶ 2. Keillor example (page 256)

_____
_____
_____

◇◇◇◇◇◇◇◇◇◇◇◇◇◇◇◇◇◇◇◇◇◇◇◇◇◇◇◇◇◇◇◇◇◇◇◇◇◇◇

Let's review once again some of the caveats regarding the use of the t-test procedure.

1. The data that represent the dependent variable should be measured as interval scores. If used with ordinal scaled (rank-ordered) data, it is assumed the scales approach interval measurement (so that $\overline{X}$ and *s.d.* are appropriate descriptive statistics).

2. Each *S* (or observation) is assigned to one and only one group if you wish to use the regular *t*-test formula. If the observations are from the same or matched groups, use the matched *t*-test formula.

3. The scores are assumed to be normally distributed so that the $\overline{X}$ and *s.d.* are appropriate measures of central tendency and variability.

4. The scores in the populations from which each sample was drawn are assumed to be normally distributed and the variances are assumed to be equivalent.

5. Multiple comparisons cannot be done using the *t*-test procedure. (You cannot compare mean 1 with mean 2, mean 2 with mean 3, mean 1 with mean 3, and so forth.)

Even when we observe all these warnings regarding the use of the *t*-test, we may run into trouble in interpreting the results. First, the results of the *t*-test procedure tell us whether a difference exists. When we reject the null hypothesis, we feel confident in claiming that a difference exists. In many cases, however, we cannot feel confident in saying what caused the difference. That confidence can only come from a well-designed study where all the threats to internal validity have been carefully controlled.

When we do evaluation research, research that investigates effectiveness of treatments, we are advised to use random selection of *S*s and random assignment of *S*s to treatments. If we are careful in this process, we can assume that *S*s are equally representative of the population and that they are equally represented in the two groups being compared. We believe the two groups are truly the same (except for the treatment). However, we often use intact groups of *S*s--the students in our classes. If these *S*s are not randomly selected and randomly assigned to the two groups, we must be extremely conservative in interpreting *t*-test results. We cannot *generalize* from the study although we can use the test for descriptive purposes if the data are normally distributed. Even so, any difference we discover between the groups (no matter how large or small the *t* value may be) is still suspect from a design standpoint. That is, we can be confident there is a difference between the groups but we cannot be confident that there wasn't a difference to begin with (there was no pretest in the design).

To get around this problem, we can use a pretest. If we use gain scores to try to avoid the problem of preexisting differences between the two groups, we still need to be careful and take into account the nature of the groups. For example, all teachers marvel at the progress low-level students can make in a school term and despair at the slow progress made by students at the upper-intermediate level. If you have taught a beginning-level language class and an advanced class, you know that students at the beginning level make the greatest observable gains. If we use gain scores, the lower group will make the greater gain. (Smart business people are happy to promise money-back guarantees for beginners, but few will offer such guarantees for advanced Ss!) When the treatment groups are not equivalent, the *t*-test procedure should not be used (there are other procedures available and we will discuss them later).

In non-evaluative research, research where two groups are compared, the same problem obtains. We have already noticed this in the German example (page 254). The data there are from an intact class. Students were not randomly selected or randomly assigned to the class. We may use the *t*-test for descriptive purposes, but we cannot generalize the findings to other classes.

Finally, there are two related problems in interpreting results of *t*-tests in applied linguistics research which may not be so obvious in other fields. The first has to do with the assumptions of normal distribution and equal variances in the population. In the Keillor example on reading scores (page 256), the sample data came from 14 students. In running the analysis, you envision collecting scores from many different classes of 14 students. Is there reason to believe that as you continue to collect the data, compute the $\overline{X}$s and place them in the sampling distribution of means, that the distribution will be normal? That depends. Each year, the Los Angeles Unified School District publishes results of reading test scores by grade level. The distribution at each grade level is clearly bimodal! Some schools from certain school districts form a normal distribution curve near the top of the range for the means. Schools from other districts form a normal distribution curve near the bottom of the range. However, the overall curve is bimodal. Since information on the distribution of means in a population is not usually available (we estimate it from the sample statistics), we need to be both careful and realistic in deciding whether or not this particular assumption of the *t*-test has been met.

The second is more clearly an interpretation issue. We often compare the performance of a group of learners with that of a group of native speakers because we truly do not know whether they will perform in similar ways. For example, we may not know whether learners will structure narratives using the same story components used by native speakers. We may not know whether learners and native speakers use the same amount of pause time between turns at talk, or whether they take the same amount of time before responding to questions. However, we can be sure that learners and native speakers will perform differently on a language achievement test. It makes sense, then, to assume that when we compare native speakers and learners on some segment of language--say on grammaticality judgments of relative clauses--we will find highly significant differences. The differences, however, may have less to do with types of relative clauses than with general language proficiency. Large differences can be expected in such research but the differences may be due as much to language proficiency as to the variable being tested. In any case, no causal claims can be made because it is not possible to randomly assign Ss to native or nonnative groups. Common sense, then, should guide our interpretation of the *t*-test results. At the very least, we should temper our claims--pointing out this problem in interpreting the results.

t-test procedures are extremely useful and powerful statistical tests for comparing two means (assuming $\overline{X}$ is the best measure of central tendency for the data). They can be used when the means are independent (i.e., between-groups) and when they are paired (i.e., within pairs). As with all tests, care must be taken to observe the requirements for the test. Prior to applying the procedure, be sure to check each of these. And, after applying the procedure, interpret the findings with care and common sense.

Nonparametric Comparisons of Two Groups

There are times when data from two groups are to be compared, but the assumptions of the *t*-test cannot be met. Since the *t*-test compares $\overline{X}$s, it is important to make sure that the $\overline{X}$ and *s.d.* are the most appropriate measures to describe the distribution of the data in the two samples. You will remember that the larger the sample size, the more likely it is that a normal distribution will be obtained. The *t*-test is especially designed for small sample sizes, so it is safe to go below a sample size of 30. However, it is important to check the normality of the distribution. If there are "outliers" in the sample, the data are not normally distributed and the *median* rather than the *mean* is the best measure of central tendency.

Another assumption that relates to normal distribution is that the data are interval scored. Nonetheless, you will often find that the *t*-test is used for ordinal data and, worse yet, with frequency data. The rationale for using the procedure with rank-order scales is that the data are linear, that there is an underlying linearity in all continuous data which can approach interval measurement. Statisticians differ in the advice they give novice researchers in this regard. *If* the measure used is truly continuous (the distance between a 1 and a 2 is approximately the same as the distance between a 3 and a 4) *and* the data are normally distributed throughout the scale so that the $\overline{X}$ and *s* are the best measures for the data, then a parametric procedure is quite appropriate. Nonparametric tests also assume that there is some underlying continuity to scales and normality in the distribution, but these assumptions are much weaker. When you are not sure, it is best to select a nonparametric procedure.

The third assumption is that of a normal distribution in the population. The *t*-test requires that this be the case. If you have strong doubts, use nonparametric procedures (procedures which do not ask you to make estimates about the population based on knowledge of the normal distribution).

Selecting the Appropriate Nonparametric Test

To select the appropriate procedure, the first question is whether the comparison is between two independent groups or a comparison of the same *S*s at two different times. In this section, we present two nonparametric tests for comparisons between two groups: the Median test and the Rank sums test (also known as the

Wilcoxon Rank sums test, or Mann Whitney U). The comparisons for repeated-measures designs are given in chapter 10.

Median Test

The Median test is a very simple procedure for determining differences between data of two groups. If the data of the two groups have the same or similar medians, we would expect that half of the Ss (or observations) in each of the groups would fall above and below the median of the *combined* groups. That is, we expect that if we find the median for all the Ss or all the observations, there would be as many from group 1 as from group 2 above the median and as many from each group below the median.

Once we have computed the median, we can set up a contingency table for the data like this:

Sample Contingency Table

Position to Median	Gp. 1	Gp. 2	Total
Above Med.	A	B	A + B
Below Med.	C	D	C + D
Total	$A + C = n_1$	$B + D = n_2$	$N = n_1 + n_2$

If the null hypothesis is true, then half the observations in the first group should be in A and half in C; half those in the second group should be in B and half in D. If the actual frequencies are quite different from this expectation, then we can reject the null hypothesis.

The formula for the Median test is:

$$T = \frac{(A \div n_1) - (B \div n_2)}{\sqrt{\hat{p}(1 - \hat{p})(1 \div n_1 + 1 \div n_2)}}$$

$$\text{where } \hat{p} = (A + B) \div N$$

Let's see how the formula works. First of all, it uses the values of A and B--the number of Ss or observations in each group that are above the median. However, it also takes into account the total number of Ss or observations in each group. The top part of the formula, as always, is the easy part. It checks to see if, indeed, half the observations (or Ss) in each group are above the median. how?

We do expect the groups will be different and the numerator will have a value other than 0. How large does that value need to be before we can say the difference is an important one? It seems that we should just be able to divide by the square root of the number of scores above the median divided by N. That's what the classy symbol $\hat{p}$ represents. However, the denominator is adjusted to take into account the number of Ss (or observations) in each group as well.

Here is a data set that can be used for this analysis.

Foreign Ss				Immigrant Ss	
25	13	9	46	31	43
25	30	17	20	21	42
17	20	37	25	38	30
26	23	20	17	19	20
18	26	11	36	38	29
30	12	32	54	41	13
24	20	16	8	68	32
21	37	31	26	28	30

The above data are scores achieved by a group of foreign students and a group of immigrant students on a three-part test. The total scores (out of a possible 70 points) are given above. Note that there are some extreme scores (the $\overline{X}$ is not an appropriate measure of central tendency).

The first task, then, is to count the number of observations above and below the median for each group and place that information into a contingency table.

	Foreign	Immigrant	Total
Above	12	12	24
Below	20	4	24
Total	32	16	48

Now we can compute the value of $\hat{p}$.

$(A + B) \div N$ $\qquad \hat{p} = (12 + 12) \div 48 = .50$

and substitute all this information into the formula:

$$T = \frac{(12 \div 32) - (12 \div 16)}{\sqrt{(.5)(1 - .5)(1 \div 32 + 1 \div 16)}}$$

$$T = -2.45$$

Next we need to be able to place the T value in an appropriate distribution to determine whether or not we can reject the null hypothesis. Fortunately for us, the T value corresponds to the z values presented in the z table in the appendix. We already know how to read this table. However, we don't really need to refer to the table anymore because we know that we need a z score of 1.96 or better to reject the null hypothesis at the .05 level. If we set the α at .01, we need to meet or exceed a z value of 2.33.

Assume we set the α at .05. The critical value of z for .05 is ≥ 1.96. We can, therefore, reject the null hypothesis and conclude that for these data there is a relationship between groups and performance on this test. There is a significant difference between the two groups (the immigrant group outperformed the foreign student group).

You might have wondered how to classify a score which is *at* the median. In the data for this example, we managed to ignore this problem. If you have a very large data set, you can safely discard scores at the median. However, in applied linguistics studies we seldom have such large numbers of subjects or observations that this is a safe procedure. A second solution is to compare all scores above the median with those not above the median. In this case, the scores on the median are combined with those below the median. A safer solution would be to run the procedure twice, once grouping these cases with those above the median and once grouping them with those below the median. Hopefully, the results will be so similar that you will find it makes no real difference in the results. If there is a large difference, see your statistical consultant.

As you have seen, we have lost information in the process of applying the Median test to the data. The actual value of each score has played a role in determining the median. Once that is done, each score is either above or below the median. We do not care how far above or below the median each observation is from this point onward. This differs from the process used in a *t*-test where we used our "ruler" to check for distance from the mean.

Practice 9.4

1. Look back at the data examples in the section on the *t*-test procedure. Which do you feel may have violated the assumption of normal distribution (i.e., $\overline{X}$ and *s.d.* are not appropriate measures of central tendency and dispersion)?

_____
_____
_____

2. We would prefer not to lose any information that exists in our data. Yet, at the same time, we must observe the assumptions underlying any statistical procedure. If this were your data, which procedure--Median test or *t*-test--would you select? Why?

_____
_____
_____

▶ 3. Prior to instruction, *S*s wishing to enroll in an oral skills class were interviewed. The *S* received ratings on three 5-point scales: pronunciation, fluency, and grammar. On the basis of their scores, *S*s were assigned to an intermediate or an advanced oral skills class. Here are the data, the sum of the three 5-point scales for each S:

Assignment

Interm	Adv
12	15
10	10
10	15
11	15
8	15
7	12
15	10
14	12
9	12
10	14
10	9
	12

Median = 12

Do a Median test. Show your calculations in the space provided below:

	Intermed.	advi
above	2	5
below	8	3
on	1	4

Can you reject the null hypothesis? Or is there really no meaningful difference in the ratings of the two groups of Ss?

◇◇

Rank Sums Tests (Wilcoxon Rank Sums, Mann Whitney U)

The Wilcoxon Rank sums test and the Mann Whitney U are actually the same test. The test compares two groups on the basis of their ranks above and below the median. The Rank sums test is often used when ordinal rating scales rather than interval type scores are to be used. The researcher may not be confident that the scales are strongly interval or that $\bar{X}$ is the best measure of central tendency, but is certain that each S (or observation) can be ranked in respect to other Ss (or observations). In such cases, the Rank sums test, rather than the t-test, should be selected to compare the two groups.

Imagine that you have developed a set of materials to teach a unit on description (one of the course objectives for your low-intermediate ESL composition class). Your class has 21 students and you have randomly assigned 11 Ss to use the new materials and 10 Ss to use the old materials for this unit. While you realize that you cannot generalize the results (due to sampling problems), you still wish to know whether the Ss using your new materials outperform those in the control group when asked to write descriptive compositions. A panel of judges (who are unaware of the treatment) assign scores to each S's descriptive composition. The judges were guided in their scoring procedure by a checklist, but (even after being trained to use this checklist) they seemed unhappy with their ability to score each person accurately. However, they agree that their combined scores do allow you to rank-order the Ss. The best S is ranked 1, second best 2, and so on. Students with the same score are given a tie rank. The question is whether Ss in the experimental group will place closer to the top than those in the control group. The design follows.

Research hypothesis? There is no difference in the ranks assigned to the compositions of the two groups.
  Significance level? .05
  1- or 2-tailed? <mark>Always 2-tailed for this procedure</mark>   *why?*
Design
  Dependent variable(s)? (Descriptive) composition rating
  Measurement? Rank-order scale
  Independent variable(s)? Group
  Measurement? Nominal (experimental vs. control)
  Independent or repeated-measures? Independent
Other features? Subdivided intact class
Statistical procedure? Rank sums test

Box diagram:

EXPER	CONTROL

The data are arranged below. Remember that a low number equals a high rank. Ties are assigned to the same rank. However, be careful. A tie for third place gives each person a rank of 3.5, *and* the next person receives a rank of 5.

Rank	Group	Exper.	Control
1	NM	1	
2	NM	2	
3.5	NM	3.5	
3.5	NM	3.5	
5	OM		5
6	NM	6	
7	NM	7	
8	NM	8	
9	OM		9
10	NM	10	
11.5	NM	11.5	
11.5	NM	11.5	
13	OM		13
14	OM		14
15	OM		15
16	OM		16
17	OM		17
18	NM	18	
19	OM		19
20	OM		20
21	OM		21
		T1 = 82	T2 = 149

— why add?

From the rankings, it certainly looks as though the group with the new materials outperformed the control group since more new-material Ss ranked high. To find out how much confidence we can have in claiming a true difference, we will apply a special z formula for rank sums. The test, as you can see from the way the data are set up, compares the two groups but also considers the spread of the ranks within each group.

Here is the formula:

total ranks, group 1.

$$z = \frac{2T_1 - n_1(N + 1)}{\sqrt{\dfrac{(n_1)(n_2)(N + 1)}{3}}}$$

The numbers 3 and 2 in the formula are constants. That is, they do not come from the data. The formula asks how likely the total ranks for the Ss in each group might be (given the number in each group and the total N for the study). The obtained z value is then placed in the z distribution to tell us whether or not we can reject the null hypothesis.

Let's carry out the calculations by placing the values in the formula. The n for the experimental group is 11. That of the control group is 10. The total N for the study is 21. The total for the ranks given the experimental group (T_1) is 82. (The total for the ranks of the control group (T_2) is 149, but this information is not needed in the formula.)

Let's carry out the calculations for these data using the formula.

$$z = \frac{2T_1 - n_1(N + 1)}{\sqrt{\dfrac{(n_1)(n_2)(N + 1)}{3}}}$$

$$z = \frac{2(82) - 11(22)}{\sqrt{\dfrac{11 \times 10 \times 22}{3}}}$$

$$z = -2.75$$

Now we can turn to table 1 in appendix C for the distribution of z scores. You read the table in exactly the same way that you did before. However, by now, you may remember the value you need to keep in your head--the z critical for α of .05: 1.96. Knowing this, we can reject the null hypothesis.

Notice that the obtained z score is a negative value. This is because the highest ranking is 1, the lowest number, and not because the experimental group did worse than the control! (Many a researcher has come close to shock having forgotten for an instant that the highest rank is the lowest number. For this reason researchers who carry out this procedure by hand sometimes reverse the order of the numbers assigned to ranks before carrying out the procedure.) We can reject the null hypothesis and should have confidence in the conclusion that the Ss in the class who used the experimental materials outperformed those who used the old materials. However, we cannot claim that these same results might obtain for other learners in other classrooms since the design (particularly the use of intact classes) does not allow us to generalize. The procedure is used here for descriptive, rather than inferential, purposes.

Practice 9.5

▶ 1. When you carry out any statistical test by hand that works with ranks, it's important to be accurate in assigning ranks to the data. If two scores that would be ranks 2 and 3 are tied, they are each given the rank of 2.5. The *next* available rank is 4. The following table may help you in assigning ranks:

Assigning Ranks to Tied Scores

Scores	Ranks	
2	1	
6	2	
8	3	
10	4.5	average ranks 4 and 5 = 4.5 for each
10	4.5	
11	6	
12	8	average ranks 7, 8, and 9 = 8 for each
12	8	
12	8	
16	10	
22	11	CHECK: The final rank corresponds to $N = 11$ here

 CHECK: Count the total number of scores (*N*). Be sure that the highest rank equals *N* (unless there is a tie for the highest rank). If it doesn't, there is an error (most likely in the assignment of tied ranks).

Assign ranks to the following data:

Score	Rank
12	1
13	2.5
13	2.5
14	4
15	5
16	6
17	7.5
17	7.5
18	9.5
18	9.5
19	11
20	12

Check: N = __12__   Top rank = __12__

▶ 2. In an ESL reading class, *S*s were given a cloze test (where they must fill in every *n*th word in a reading passage). The students are from two different first-language groups and so you wonder whether there is a difference in the cloze scores of the two groups. Here are the data:

Gp. 2	Gp. 1
18	22
13	20
16	21
15	19
14	16
21	24
20	23
	13

Calculate the z value.

$$z = \frac{2T_1 - n_1(N + 1)}{\sqrt{\dfrac{(n_1)(n_2)(N + 1)}{3}}}$$

$$z = \underline{\hspace{2cm}}$$

Can you reject the null hypothesis? _____ What conclusion can you draw? ___

_____

3. The test gives us confidence in interpreting the descriptive statistics. If we wanted to replicate the study so that the findings could be generalized (using parametric inferential statistics), how might we redesign the study?

_____
_____
_____
_____
_____

4. Look back through the examples given for the t-test procedure. Would you recommend the use of the Rank sums test for any of the examples? If so, why?

_____
_____

5. Is the Rank sums test one that you might use for any of the research questions you have defined for your own work? If so, why? What other possible tests might you use?

_____
_____
_____
_____
_____

◇◇

Strength of Association: eta^2

There is also an η^2 formula for the Rank sums test. It can be used with any statistical test that yields a z score. Since the T in the Median test equals z, this formula is appropriate for it as well.

$$\eta^2 = \frac{z^2}{N - 1}$$

Again, all the information that you need to do a strength of association test is available in your printout or from your calculations. Assume that we had 18 Ss classified as exceptional language learners and 12 classified as poor language learners. Perhaps you asked teachers to nominate the best learners they have ever had and the learners who had the most difficulty. Ideally, this list of nominations would form a pool from which you might draw a random sample of 30 each. However, let's assume you couldn't do this but did find 18 exceptional and 12 not so exceptional learners. Your research question is whether good vs. poor learners show differences in auditory short-term memory. After testing each person, you use their scores to rank-order all the learners and then perform a Rank sums test which gives you a z statistic of $+3.8$. Good language learners did significantly better than the poor language learners on the test of auditory short-term memory. Now, you wonder how much of the variability in the short-term memory scores from all the Ss can be associated with being a "good" vs. "poor" learner.

$$\eta^2 = \frac{z^2}{N-1}$$

$$\eta^2 = \frac{3.8^2}{30-1}$$

(Notice, this time, that N [the total number of Ss] rather than df is used.) The strength of association found in this case is $\eta^2 = .498$. Thus, you can say that 49.8% of the variance in the ranks of auditory short-term memory ability may be attributed to learner classification type. Again, one independent variable has accounted for much of the variability in short-term memory (STM). Yet, there is still variance left to be explained. At this point, that variance is all "error"--that is, attributable to something other than the independent variable you have chosen to study.

This strength test is for the association *in your sample* (i.e., not in the population). It should make you begin to wonder just what the components of such classifications as "good learners" and "poor learners" might be. Certainly the outcome makes it look like a good short-term auditory memory might be one of these components. Of course, we are reasoning in a backward direction this time. But by looking at the strength of association, we should begin to form our ideas about how to improve the research, what other things we might want to enter into the equation in our future research on this question.

◇◇◇◇◇◇◇◇◇◇◇◇◇◇◇◇◇◇◇◇◇◇◇◇◇◇◇◇◇◇◇◇◇◇◇◇◇◇

Practice 9.6

Do a strength of association test on the Rank sums problems in this chapter. How strong an association is there for the levels of the variable? Report the results below.

▶ 1. Composition study (page 275)

_____

_____

_____

◇◇◇

Deciding Among Procedures

The Wilcoxon Rank sums test was used by Hensley and Hatch (1986) in a pre-liminary analysis of data on the language lab listening comprehension program in a refugee camp on Bataan, the Philippines. Scores on a set of ratings (ratings of pronunciation, syntax, confidence, communication ability, etc.) were given to individual Ss (based on their performance during an informal conversation exchange). These ratings were summed. We could not assume that the data, most of which were 5-point scales, showed interval continuity. The data at this preliminary point in the analysis were from 29 Ss in the experimental (language lab) group and 32 Ss in the control group. It was probably not safe to assume the data were normally distributed. The data were run on the computer using procedures for comparing two groups in the SAS statistical computing package. The printout reported the means of the two groups as 37.69 for the experimental group and 24.94 for the control group, and it gave us a t-test approximation of probability at .006. Then it showed us the z value as 2.8009 and the probability as .005 on the Wilcoxon Rank sums test.

Though less of the available information in the data was used by the Wilcoxon, the result of the Rank sums test was not very different from that of the t-test. Therefore, we had confidence in the difference found between the two groups in the preliminary data set.

While running the Rank sums test on SAS, it was also possible to request another analysis--the Median test. You'll remember that when we have extreme scores, the median is the more appropriate estimate of central tendency. Since we had not yet plotted the data, it seemed wise to run this analysis in case we had "outliers," Ss with extreme scores in either group.

The Median test, you'll recall, counts the number of scores above vs. below the median for each group. If the two groups were the same, there should be a similar number of people above and below the median in each group. The frequencies (number above and below the median) for each group are then compared with these expected frequencies, and a z value is obtained. In this case the z value was 1.684 and the probability was .0922. Should this lessen our confidence?

How can we decide which of these three tests--the Wilcoxon Rank sums, the t-test approximation, or the Median test--gives us the most accurate information? If we select the Median test, we cannot say the two groups differed. Both the Rank sums test and the t-test say the groups *did* differ.

Think for a moment of our earlier discussion of power. The most powerful test is the test which uses the most information and is the least likely to lead us into error in claiming a difference exists when none does or in claiming that no difference exists when, in fact, there is a difference in the groups. The Median test uses only information related to position above or below the median. The Rank sums procedure uses not only a score's relation to the median but its relative distance from the median as well. The t-test does the same, except that it uses the $\overline{X}$ and a "ruler" for distance from the $\overline{X}$.

The most powerful test, then, is the t-test, but we argued that the data did not meet the assumptions of the t-test. The second most powerful test was the Rank sums test. The confidence it gave us in our claims that the two groups differed was as great as that from the t-test approximation. Since we had a fairly substantial number of Ss at this point, the power of the two tests was approximately equal. We therefore used the Rank sums test to give us confidence in our interpretation of the findings.

To review, we have presented two nonparametric "equivalents" to the t-test.

1. The Median test has the least power since it throws away much information. It tallies the number of Ss (or observations) above and below the median for each group, compares this with the expected frequencies for each group, and calculates a T score which is evaluated like a z score. (It does *not* measure distance from the median.)

2. The Rank sums test rank-orders Ss or observations and then locates those from each group in the ranking. Both groups should be equally distributed in the ranking if there is no difference between the two groups. It uses information about the actual rank of each S or observation in drawing the comparison between groups. With large sample sizes, it approaches the power of the t-test.

3. Both tests compare the values of two groups, and check the difference between the groups for statistical significance. The parallel parametric test is the t-test.

4. There are other nonparametric tests that compare two groups. You might, for example, encounter the Kolmogorov-Smirnov test in reports. This test counts the number of Ss (or responses) at each point on a scale (for example, a 5-point scale), and uses the information on the cumulative differences between two groups in the analysis. Thus, it uses more information than the Median test. However, it requires an n of 40 in each group. For a full range of nonparametric tests equivalent to the t-test, please consult statistical computing packages (SAS, SPSS-X) or Siegel (1956).

In this chapter we have discussed methods for testing the differences between two groups. While you may never need to calculate any of these procedures by hand, it *is* important to know how they test differences and the assumptions behind the procedures. This understanding will allow you to select the most appropriate procedure for your own research. It will also help you to evaluate the research reports you read. In the next chapter we will discuss statistical procedures that allow us to make these comparisons for repeated-measures designs.

Activities

Read each of the following summaries. Decide whether the requirements of a *t*-test procedure were met. Decide whether a nonparametric test would be appropriate. Determine which statistical procedure you would use for each study. If you feel that none of the procedures we have described so far is appropriate, explain why.

1. J. D. Brown (1988. Components of engineering-English reading ability. *SYSTEM, 16*, 2, 193-200) describes the evolution of a reading test on engineering English. Among the research questions asked about the test were (a) which types of items (engineering content, linguistic content) best distinguish the ability to read engineering English, and (b) to what extent could ability to read engineering English be accounted for by general English proficiency. One of the first issues to be answered, however, was whether there was any difference between EFL students who were or were not engineers in their ability to read engineering-English texts.

Fifty-eight Chinese students of English participated in the study: 29 were engineers studying at Guangzhou English Language Center and 29 were TEFL trainees studying in the Foreign Language Department of Zhongshan University.

Here are the descriptive statistics comparing the reading test scores of TEFL and engineering *S*s:

	Engineers	TEFL
Mean	36.97	27.38
range	17-54	17-43
s.d.	8.22	6.63
SEM	3.39	3.57
n	29	29

The observed value of *t* was 4.89. The research hypothesis was two-tailed. Interpret the table and state the conclusions that can be drawn. Then answer the questions posed in the activity instructions.

2. M. A. Snow & D. Brinton (1988. Content-based language instruction: investigating the effectiveness of the adjunct model. *TESOL Quarterly, 22*, 4, 553-574) report on a variety of measures evaluating the adjunct model (where English instruction is tailored to an academic content course). One question asked was whether students enrolled in such classes were better prepared to meet the academic demands of university content classes. A special exam was given which required *S*s to both read and listen to content material (taking notes) and then

(a) answer a series of true/false and multiple-choice questions on content, and (b) write an essay which required synthesis of content information. The experimental group were 12 students enrolled in an adjunct class and the control group consisted of 15 students in a regular ESL class. Each group also took the ESLPE, an English language exam. Here are the findings in table form:

Exam		Exper.	Control	z	p
Objective test	M	25.4	26.1	0.63	n.s.
	s.d.	5.4	7.8		
Essay	M	66.5	67.2	0.42	n.s.
	s.d.	13.3	16.3		
ESLPE	M	90.8	99.4	2.11	.05
	s.d.	11.0	13.5		

The Wilcoxon Rank sums test was used to test the comparisons. Interpret the above table and state your conclusions. Then answer the questions given in the directions to this activity section. *T-test needs 2 groups only*

3. C. E. Ford (1984. The influence of speech variety on teachers' evaluation of students with comparable academic ability. *TESOL Quarterly, 18,* 1, 25-40.) presented 40 teachers with speech and writing samples of children and asked them to evaluate each child. Prior to the study, the written samples had been rated as equal. Half of the oral English samples exhibited features of Spanish phonology; the other half did not. After reading and listening to each sample, the 40 teachers assigned it a rating on a set of semantic differential scales related to potential for academic success. The results showed lower semantic differential ratings for the samples in the Spanish-accent group. The conclusion was that teachers held lower expectations for students who spoke the Spanish-accented English.

4. A. Ramirez & R. Milk (1986. Notions of grammaticality among teachers of bilingual pupils. *TESOL Quarterly, 20,* 3, 495-513.) asked teachers attending summer institutes to evaluate and rank four varieties of spoken English and spoken Spanish (standard English/Spanish, hispanicized English/Spanish with phonological and morphological deviations from standard, ungrammatical English/Spanish, and English/Spanish code switching) for classroom appropriateness, grammatical correctness, and speaker's academic potential. Evaluations of both the English and Spanish language samples appear to have been made on a standard language continuum, with code-switching the least acceptable and correct.

A table presented in the study states that "All *t*-tests for pair comparisons are significant at the .05 level with the exception of those indicated with a bracket." Four varieties of Spanish and four of English are then compared for appropriateness, for correctness, for speaker's academic potential, and for a total global reaction (the sum of the means of the other three types of ratings).

5. F. Mangubhai (1986. The literate bias of classrooms: helping the ESL learner. *TESL Canada Journal, Special Issue 1*, 43-54.) conducted a national survey in Fiji that showed sixth-grade students were unable to read the simple English prose required for successful schooling. Students in high-level achievement groups invariably came from schools with large libraries. This study evaluated a project called Book Flood where selected schools in rural areas of Fiji received 250 books. Programs where fourth- and fifth-grade students read the books silently and programs with a "shared-book" treatment (teacher introduces the book and reads all or portions of the book aloud to children as pictures, or a "blown-up" version of the text is projected and then students are encouraged to join in the reading and discuss the book together) were compared to control schools which did not participate in Book Flood. The *n* sizes for the grade 4 classes were: shared-book = 71, silent reading = 84, and control = 65. For grade 5, the *n* sizes were: shared-book = 89, silent reading = 86, and control = 87.

After eight months, all the classes were tested. The Book Flood schools were compared with the controls using *t*-tests. The measures for the fourth grade were reading comprehension tests, English structures, word recognition, and oral sentence repetition. The fifth- grade students were tested on reading comprehension, listening comprehension, English structures, and composition. *t*-tests were again used to compare the Book Flood schools with the controls. The program was continued into the next year, following the same *S*s. The gains that the Book Flood groups made in comparison to the control group continued into the second year. No significant differences were found between the shared-book group and the silent reading group.

6. D. Cross (1988. Selection, setting and streaming in language teaching. *SYSTEM, 16,* 1, 13-22) presents a series of *t*-test comparisons of "upper set" and "lower set" groups of students. (These terms relate to ability level and were made prior to the research when children first entered the program.) The two groups were compared on various measures such as reading, cloze, fluency, listening to numbers, attitudes, etc. The null hypothesis could be rejected in each case, with the upper set outperforming the lower set. By checking through the scores of individuals within each group, it was possible to locate students who had been misplaced and reassign them to a more appropriate group. In addition, Cross checked to see if students in both the "upper set" and in the "lower set" improved in language skills over time. Tables show gain or loss for each group as mean score gain or loss (from pretest to posttest). The tables also give a percent change figure for these gains or losses. No statistical procedures were used to analyze the data in these particular tables. The author concludes that both groups did show improvement.

References

Hensley, A. & Hatch, E. 1986. Innovation in language labs: an evaluation report. Report prepared for the Philippine Refugee Center, ICNC, Bataan, The Philippines.

Lazaraton, A. 1985. An analysis of listening comprehension using alternate statistical procedures. Unpublished master's thesis, TESL, UCLA.

Siegel, S. 1956. *Nonparametric Statistics for the Behavioral Sciences.* New York, NY: McGraw-Hill.

Chapter 10
Comparing Two Groups: Repeated-Measures

- *Parametric comparisons: Matched t-test*
  Strength of association: eta^2
- *Nonparametric comparisons: repeated-measures*
  Sign test
  Wilcoxon Matched-pairs signed-ranks test
  Strength of association: eta^2
- *Deciding among procedures*
- *Advantages/disadvantages of nonparametric procedures*

Parametric Comparisons: Matched t-test

In the Case 1 and Case 2 *t*-tests that we have discussed so far, the means have always come from two different groups. In Case 1 studies, the group mean ($\overline{X}$) is compared with a population mean (μ). In Case 2 studies, two group means are compared. These are all *between-groups* designs.

Repeated-measures designs, where the comparison is within one group, are quite common too. In such designs, the means are from the *same* group of Ss. For example, we may wish to compare the performance of a group of Ss prior to instruction and after the instruction. The scores are from the same Ss at two different times. It's also possible that we might want to compare the performance of a group of Ss on two different measures at one period in time. Again, the design is a repeated-measures design.

It is also possible to compare paired data of another sort. For example, you might have a pool of Ss who have all taken a general proficiency examination. From that pool you might select 30 pairs of Ss who have the same score on the examination. One S from each pair is randomly assigned to group 1 and the other to group 2. The pairs of Ss are *matched* on the basis of language proficiency. One group becomes the experimental group and the other the control group. The performance of the two groups can then be compared. (Matching is not a substitute for random assignment, but can supplement it.)

When we compare the performance of the *same* Ss, or of *matched* Ss, we must change the *t*-test formula slightly. This is because we expect that the performance of the same person (or of two Ss who have been matched) on two measures will be closer than the performance of two different people on the two measures. That is, the scores for the paired means are not independent. Therefore, the formula must be changed slightly to take this into account.

The basic difference in the formula is that our N, now, will be for number of pairs rather than number of Ss or observations. The standard error of difference between means will be computed by dividing by the number of pairs minus one (df for pairs) rather than number of observations minus 1. So, $df = n_{pairs} - 1$.

Imagine that the data collected by Lazaraton on a listening comprehension test prior to a special instruction unit and after the unit looked like this:

Scores on listening comprehension

S	Pretest	Posttest	D	D^2
1	21	33	12	144
2	17	17	0	0
3	22	30	8	64
4	13	23	10	100
5	33	36	3	9
6	20	25	5	25
7	19	21	2	4
8	14	19	5	25
9	20	19	-1	1
10	31	35	4	16
	$\Sigma X = 210$	$\Sigma Y = 258$	$\Sigma D = 48$	$\Sigma D^2 = 388$
	$\overline{X}_1 = 21$	$\overline{X}_2 = 25.8$		

The research question asks whether Ss improved following instruction--is the jump of 4.8 points in the mean a significant change? (The 4.8 is obtained by subtracting $\overline{X}_1$ from $\overline{X}_2$ or by dividing N by ΣD.) As you can see, the first step is to see what difference there is between each pair of scores. The answer to this is at the bottom of the column labeled D (difference): ΣD. To guard against negative values, each difference value is squared and placed in the column labeled D^2. The column is added, and the sum (ΣD^2) is placed at the bottom of the column. We can now plug the values into the paired t-test formula.

$$t = \frac{\overline{X}_1 - \overline{X}_2}{s_{\overline{D}}}$$

As always, the top half of the formula is the easy part. It gives us the difference between the two means. And, as always, the bottom half of the formula is a type of "ruler" that measures off the distance in terms of the standard error of differences between two means. The standard error of differences between the two means, however, is adjusted to account for the fact that the means are from the same S (or from matched pairs). To remind you that we are using matched pairs, we use the symbol $s_{\overline{D}}$.

The formula for $s_{\overline{D}}$ is as follows:

$$s_{\overline{D}} = \frac{s_D}{\sqrt{n}}$$

To find s_D use the following formula:

$$s_D = \sqrt{\frac{\Sigma D^2 - (1 \div n)(\Sigma D)^2}{n - 1}}$$

In the matched t formula, the n is the number of pairs (not the n for scores). Thus, the standard deviation of the differences is adjusted for the number of pairs.

If this is clear, let's put the values into the formula:

$$s_D = \sqrt{\frac{388 - (1 \div 10)(48)^2}{10 - 1}}$$

$$s_D = \sqrt{\frac{157.6}{9}}$$

$$s_D = 4.18$$

Now we can calculate $s_{\overline{D}}$, the standard error of differences between the two means, in order to obtain our "ruler."

$$s_{\overline{D}} = \frac{s_D}{\sqrt{n}}$$

$$s_{\overline{D}} = \frac{4.18}{\sqrt{10}}$$

$$s_{\overline{D}} = 1.323$$

Now that we have our "ruler," we can check the difference between the two means to find our observed t value. The formula for this should be familiar.

$$t_{obs} = \frac{\overline{X}_1 - \overline{X}_2}{s_{\overline{D}}}$$

$$t_{obs} = \frac{21 - 25.8}{1.323}$$

$$t_{obs} = -3.63$$

As you will have guessed, our next step is to check this observed t value against the t critical value in the t distribution table--table 2 in appendix C. We use the same t-test table as before (the changes in the formula have adjusted the observed t value to compensate for the paired nature of the data).

There is a small difference in terms of degrees of freedom. In the regular t-test, we calculated the df as $n_1 - 1 + n_2 - 1$. In the Matched t-test, we work with pairs. The df is the *number of pairs* $- 1$. Since there are 10 pairs in this study, $df = 9$. We need to check the value to see whether the difference is significant at the .05 level. The critical value for t is 2.262. We can reject the null hypothesis because our value of 3.63 exceeds 2.262. We can have confidence in concluding that treatment does have an *effect* on performance in these data. Student scores differ significantly from pretest to posttest. Again, the information may be summarized in a simple statement: $t = 2.262$, $df = 9$, $p < .05$.

On the basis of the findings, we can reject the null hypothesis of no difference between pretest and posttest. The (hypothetical) class did improve. The t-test gives us confidence that the difference is real *in these data*. That is, the test is being used for *descriptive* purposes only. Why can't we use the test for *inferential* purposes? The reason is that there are many threats to the external validity of the study. The students are not randomly selected or randomly assigned. It is an intact class. So, even though the t-test allows us to generalize, the design of the study precludes such generalization.

For descriptive purposes, the results are also open to question. We have claimed that treatment has an effect on scores. The students performed significantly better on the posttest. However, the design has so many threats to internal validity that we need to temper any claims. We cannot be sure that it was primarily the treatment that caused the change. Improvement might be due to many different things (including, of course, the instruction).

In this example, we used two scores from the same group of Ss--a repeated-measures comparison of means. Paired t-test data could also be obtained from pairs of Ss who have been carefully matched (so that we can assume that they will perform similarly, all things being equal). In this example they might be matched according to the pretest results, on the basis of a hearing test, by first language, by sex, or other relevant characteristics. The calculations are the same whether the comparison is for the same group or matched-pairs--in either case we expect the means ($\overline{X}$s) to be closer than they would be if two groups of randomly selected Ss were compared. The Matched t-test is designed to deal with this assumption. What would happen if you used a regular t-test for a repeated-measures design? Think about it for a moment. Differences that might turn out to be statistically significant on a matched-pairs test might only be a "trend" (and statistically not significant) with a regular t-test. This is because we expect *smaller* differences in the performance of the same S on two measures. The Matched t-test has been designed with this fact in mind.

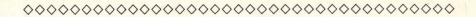

Practice 10.1

1. The data we worked with are hypothetical data. Here is the actual table used by Lazaraton to report her results:

Matched t-test on Gains after Treatment

Group	n	Mean	s.d.	t value	df	p
Pretest	38	17.3	5.1	2.81	37	.008
Posttest	38	19.4	4.9			

Give your interpretation of the table: _____ p > .01 , reject null
_____ critical t 2.750 df = 30 _____

_____

_____
_____
_____

▶ 2.   Imagine that you have been given reading test scores of two carefully matched groups of university students. These students are studying electrical engineering at the University of Guadalajara and, as part of that training, have a course in technical English. Ss have been matched for English proficiency and reading subtest scores and one member of each pair is assigned to group 1 and the other to group 2. Group 1, by a toss of a coin, becomes the experimental group and group 2 the control. The experimental group receives an intensive reading program that stresses top-down reading strategies (using publications and papers from chemical engineering). The control group receives a four-skills technical English course. At the end of the course, all students are tested again and gain scores on the reading subtest are computed for each student. As you might imagine, not all students appear for the posttest but 10 matched pairs are still there. Their gain scores must now be compared as matched groups. Here are the (fictitious) data:

Gain Scores on Reading Subtest

Gain scores

Pairs	Experim.	Control	D	D²
A	8	6	*2*	*4*
B	7	5	*2*	*0*
C	5	5	*0*	*1*
D	3	4	*-1*	*9* *18*
E	1	4	*-3*	*16* *26*
F	6	2	*4*	*9* *41*
G	8	5	*3*	*36* *84*
H	9	3	*6*	*1*
I	5	4	*1*	*4*
J	5	3	*2*	

$\Sigma X = \underline{57}$ $\Sigma X = \underline{41}$ $\Sigma D = \underline{16}$ $\Sigma D^2 = \underline{84}$

$n = 10$ $n = 10$

$\bar{X} = 5.7$ $\bar{X} = 4.1$

The means of the two groups are closer together than those in the previous example, but you cannot conclude from this that the difference in the two groups is or is not statistically significant. Other information must be taken into account.

Once again, you will find the standard error of differences between two means and then adjust it for pairs.

$$s_D = \sqrt{\frac{\Sigma D^2 - (1 \div n)(\Sigma D)^2}{n-1}}$$

Remember that n means the number of pairs, so with 10 pairs the denominator is 9.

$$s_D = \sqrt{\frac{84 - (1 \div 10)^2}{10-1}}$$

Complete the computation. $s_D = \underline{2.55}$

To find the standard error of differences between pairs of means ($s_{\bar{D}}$), divide by the number of pairs:

$$s_{\bar{D}} = \frac{s_D}{\sqrt{n}}$$

$$s_{\bar{D}} = \frac{2.55}{\sqrt{10}}$$

So, $s_{\bar{D}} = \underline{.806}$.

Now compute the t value:

$$t_{obs} = \frac{\overline{X}_1 - \overline{X}_2}{s_{\overline{D}}}$$

$$t_{obs} = \frac{57 - 41}{.806}$$

The t value = __1.99__. How many df are there? __9__. What is the critical value of t for .05? __2.26__

Can the null hypothesis be rejected? Why (not)?

_____

_____

What can you conclude? _____

_____

_____

Does the design allow you to generalize the results? Why (not)? _____

_____

_____

3. Whenever we analyze interval or ordinal scale data, we always look first at the mean (or other measure of central tendency) and the s. When we want to compare two groups, our first reaction on seeing means which are very similar is to assume that there is no significant difference between the two groups. When we see fairly large differences between two means, we assume there is a true difference between the groups. Explain why this may not turn out to be the case.

_____

_____

_____

_____

◇◇

Strength of Association: eta²

While the Matched t-test allows us to test the difference in the two means of a group, it does not tell us how "important" this difference is. We can check this for any particular data set by applying a strength of association formula--eta². The formula is exactly the same as that presented in the last chapter for the between-groups t-test.

$$\eta^2 = \frac{t^2}{t^2 + df}$$

Let's apply this to the pretest-posttest data on page 288. The observed value of t was -3.63 and there were 10 pairs of Ss (so the df is 9).

$$\eta^2 = \frac{t^2}{t^2 + 9}$$

$$\eta^2 = \frac{t^2}{t^2 + df}$$

$$\eta^2 = \frac{3.63^2}{3.63^2 + 9}$$

$$\eta^2 = .594$$

The Matched *t*-test allowed us to reject the null hypothesis and conclude that students did improve. The strength of association between the pretest and posttest is .594, showing that 59% of the variance in posttest scores can be accounted for by the pretest scores. That leaves 41% still unaccounted for ("error" as far as your research is concerned).

◇◇

Practice 10.2

▶ 1. In the Guadalajara research problem (practice 10.1.2), the observed value of *t* was 1.99. It makes no sense in this case to do an eta² since the *t* value was not statistically significant. Imagine, however, that *t*-observed had been 2.99. Compute the strength of association and interpret your finding. *3*

eta² = ___.50___. Interpretation: ___50% of variability accounted for by group___

_____

_____

◇◇

Nonparametric Comparisons: Repeated-Measures

We will turn now to other nonparametric tests that allow us to compare paired data--that from the same *S*s on two different measures or that of matched pairs. These are the nonparametric equivalents to the Matched-pairs *t*-test.

Sign Test

The goal of the Sign test is similar to that of a Matched-pairs *t*-test. That is, it is used to discover whether the same *S*s (or matched pairs of *S*s) perform in different ways over time (or on two tests).

Let's use the example we have cited before where a teacher wondered whether information from conversational analysis could be used to teach these cultural conventions in an ESL class. The study involved the conversational openings, closings, and turn-taking signals used in phone conversations. The teacher asked all students to call her during the first week of class. Each person's phone skills (the openings, preclosings, closings, and turn-taking) were scored on a 1-10 point scale. During the class a special phone conversation unit the teacher had developed was presented and practiced. At the end of the course, the teacher again had students call her and again ranked them on a 10-point scale.

Notice there is no control group. The data are not independent since the same Ss take part in the pretest and the posttest. It is also possible that the ratings given one S may influence those given the next S. (If raters were trained in using a scoring checksheet, this bias could be reduced.) Look at the data in the following table. There is evidence that suggests the data are not normally distributed. Two Ss got the maximum score on the posttest, indicating a skewed distribution.

S	Pretest	Posttest	Change
1	2	4	+
2	4	5	+
3	5	4	−
4	3	3	0
5	1	10	+
6	0	10	+
7	9	0	−
.	.	.	.
.	.	.	.
.	.	.	.

Look at the column marked "Change." This should give you a clue as to the difference between the Sign test and the Matched t-test. The Sign test asks whether or not Ss improved (the +s), regressed (the −s), or whether they showed no change (the 0s). The test does not measure degree of change but rather the presence of change.

The procedure is simple. Tally the + and − symbols under "Change." Discard Ss who do not show change (cf. S4). Let's say there were actually 29 students in the class. Twenty-one Ss improved (21 + changes) while 6 Ss did worse (6 − changes). The total number of changes would then equal 27.

The next step is to assign R to the *smaller* total of changes. In the above example, 6 Ss form one group and 21 Ss form the other. Since the group of 6 is smaller, R = 6.

Next, we turn to the Sign test table (table 3 in appendix C) to discover whether we can reject the null hypothesis. In previous tables, the first column gave us the df for the study. In this table, however, the first column (labeled N) shows that the Sign test distribution is built around the number of changes (+ or − changes) that take place in the data.

In our study the total number of changes was 27. To find the critical value α = .05 for an N of 27, locate the 27 row and check the .05 column. The R value must be *equal to or less than* that given in the chart. The R critical value for an N of
to reject the null.

27 is 7. Our *R* value is 6, so we can reject the null hypothesis. Almost all statistical tests require a value *equal to or greater than* the value listed in the table. The Sign test (and the Wilcoxon Matched-pairs test) is unusual in this regard. Remember that you need a number *smaller than* the value given in the distribution chart.

The statistical test gives us confidence in reporting that a significant number of *S*s improved in their ratings on the posttest. We would not be wise to generalize the findings, however. We have a very small *n* size and these few *S*s are from an intact class. We may not be sure about the reliability of our rating instrument. Also, *S*s might have improved anyway, regardless of the lessons presented. However, the Sign test gives us statistical evidence that supports the *description of the data.*

Practice 10.3

▶ 1. In the section on matched *t*-tests (page 288), we asked you to interpret a table reporting the comparison of *S*s' listening comprehension scores from pretest to posttest where they had received a special listening comprehension program. A *t* value of 2.81 ($df = 37$) was obtained and the probability level was better than .01. The test assessed the *degree* of change obtained by students. If Lazaraton had not been pleased with the test or thought the data were not normally distributed, she could have reported the results of a Sign test instead. This would not look at degree of change but rather the presence of change. Here are the changes:

Sign test on Gains After Treatment

+23
−13

The *N* for total changes = _____. The R_{obs} is _____. For $\alpha = .05$, $R_{crit} = 11$.

Interpret this finding _____

_____

_____

_____

2. If you believed the test was highly reliable and valid, that the scores were interval measurements, and that the data were normally distributed, in which report would you have most confidence? Why? _____

_____

If you felt the scores only crudely represented interval data, which report would you feel was most accurate? Why? _____

_____

In either case, why was Lazaraton not able to generalize her findings to claim that the materials would be equally effective for all ESL students? Even though we cannot generalize, we use statistical tests to analyze the data. Why?

_____

_____

_____

_____

_____

◇◇◇◇◇◇◇◇◇◇◇◇◇◇◇◇◇◇◇◇◇◇◇◇◇◇◇◇◇◇◇◇◇◇◇◇◇◇

This example shows us how much information can be lost when turning from a Matched *t*-test to a Sign test. Large positive changes may occur for some students and no change or small negative changes for others. The Matched *t*-test measures all these degrees of change in its analysis. The Sign test throws away all the information on amount of change, keeping only the notion of ± change. Fortunately, there is a test that is a more effective nonparametric test of matched pairs than the Sign test. We will turn to that next.

Wilcoxon Matched-Pairs Signed-Ranks Test

The Sign test uses information about the *existence* and *direction* of change in paired data. If we want to consider the *degree* of change as well as the direction of the differences, a more powerful nonparametric procedure can be used. The Wilcoxon Matched-pairs signed-ranks test does this by giving more weight to a pair which shows a large difference between the two groups than a pair which shows a small difference.

The Wilcoxon Matched-pairs test assumes that the researcher can tell which member of a pair is greater (or better) than the other. It also assumes that the differences between pairs can be rank-ordered for absolute size. That is, the researcher can make a judgment of "greater" for one of any pair's two performances and can also scale pairs as to degree of difference. This ability to give information not only about the difference within each pair but also the differences between pairs is sometimes called measuring an *ordered metric scale*. In strength this makes the test somewhere between an ordinal scale and an interval scale.

As an example, let's imagine that you wanted to explore the effectiveness of a listening comprehension program given in a language lab setting on overall communicative competence. To carry out the study you found eight pairs of students that you could match in terms of their L1, sex, scores on a language proficiency exam, and a listening comprehension test. In the interest of good design (not as a requirement of the statistical procedure), one member of each pair was randomly assigned to the experimental language lab program and the other member to a regular language lab program. After the treatment all *S*s were given a test of communicative competence which has five 5-point scales (possible total = 25). Here is our design table yet again:

Box diagram:

	EXPER	CONTROL
Diff.		

Here are the data:

Pair	Exp	Cont	d	Rank of d	T
a	25	14	11	+7	
b	24	12	12	+8	
c	22	23	−1	−1	1
d	18	12	6	+4	
e	17	10	7	+5	
f	20	10	10	+6	
g	18	22	−4	−3	3
h	16	13	3	+2	
					$T = 4$

To carry out a Wilcoxon Matched-pairs test, the first step is to compute the difference between each pair of observations. Pairs which have the same values (where the difference is 0) are dropped from the analysis and the *n* size reduced accordingly. Each pair, then, has a *d* score. The *d*s are next ranked without regard to sign, with the rank of 1 given to the smallest *d* group. A *d* of −3 is ranked the same as a +3 *d*. If there are ties for a rank, the rank is averaged as it was for the Ranks sums test.

Once ranked, each rank is assigned a sign of + or − to indicate whether it is from a positive or negative difference. If the null hypothesis is true, some of the high ranks will have +s and some will have −s, so that when we add up the positive ranks and the negative ranks for each group, they would be nearly equal. To reject the null hypothesis the sum of ranks either for the +s or for the −s must be much higher.

As with the Rank sums test, the Wilcoxon has us add up the ranks of the +s and the −s. The *smaller* of these becomes T. T is the sum of the ranks of whichever sum is smaller. Our next problem is to determine the level of significance of T. This determination depends on whether the study used only a few pairs or used more than 25 pairs. If the sample size is small, as it is in our example study, the T can be checked against table 4 in appendix C.

Our T value $= 4$, and there are 8 matched pairs. Check the table to be sure we can reject the null hypothesis. If the observed T value is *equal to or less than* the critical value given, we can reject the null hypothesis. The $N = 8$ and the table says that we can reject the null hypothesis at the .05 level because T *critical* $= 4$, which is equal to our T *observed*. In reading the table, remember that (as with the Sign test) your obtained value must be equal to or less than the value given in the chart. It's easy to misread the chart, but you will notice that the numbers get smaller, not larger, as you move from .05 to .01 on the chart. That should help to remind you that the value needs to be small enough (not large enough) to allow you to reject the null hypothesis.

You could, of course, use the Sign test on these data. Before you do so, however, think about the information you would lose if you chose a Sign test instead. Notice that the two minus *d*s are among the smallest differences found. The Sign test is not affected by the degree of difference between the pairs. It is less likely that you will be able to reject the null hypothesis if you lose this information. (If you are not sure about this, try the Sign test on the data.) The Sign test, because it is less powerful, gives you more chances of being wrong in rejecting the null hypothesis when you shouldn't and accepting it when you should not.

When the sample size (the N for number of pairs) is greater than 25, we cannot use the T table in the appendix to check the significance of the T value. When the number of pairs is greater than 25, the z formula is used:

$$z = \frac{T - \dfrac{N(N+1)}{4}}{\sqrt{\dfrac{N(N+1)(2N+1)}{24}}}$$

The numbers 4 and 24 are constants in the formula; they do not come from the data. Actually, this formula will work even with small sample sizes. Let's plug in the values from the above example and see what happens.

$$z = \frac{4 - \dfrac{(8)(9)}{4}}{\sqrt{\dfrac{(8)(9)(17)}{24}}}$$

$$z = -1.96$$

Checking this z value in the z score table in the Appendix shows that the probability of a z value this extreme is .05 for a two-tailed test. This is the same probability as we found using the T value distribution table.

Actually, the above example was part of an evaluation study of the language lab program in the Philippines (Hensley & Hatch). Twenty-nine pairs of Ss participated in the study. The z score was 2.05 (two-tailed probability = .04). The students who participated in the listening comprehension program in the language lab were rated higher than the control group on the communicative skills following the special program.

Strength of Association: eta²

eta² may be used to show the strength of association for data analyzed using the Wilcoxon Matched-pairs signed-ranks test. Since the Wilcoxon yields a z value, the eta² formula is:

$$\eta^2 = \frac{z^2}{N-1}$$

If we apply this formula to the *fictitious* data above, we find:

$$\eta^2 = \frac{z^2}{N-1}$$

$$\eta^2 = \frac{-1.96^2}{8-1}$$

$$\eta^2 = .549$$

There is a strong relation of the two variables in this particular data set (probably more than would be found in real data). The overlap of the two variables is 55%, leaving only 45% yet to be accounted for. With this association, we would be very confident of our conclusion (that the two variables are, indeed, related in an important way). We are free to consider which variables we want to research next to reduce the remaining "error."

There is no strength of association formula for the Sign test.

Practice 10.4

1. If you would like to compare all three procedures for matched pairs of data, apply the Matched-pairs t-test and the Sign test to the data on page 298. How do you account for the differences in the results of these three procedures?

_____

_____

_____

▶ 2. To give you the opportunity to practice the Wilcoxon, try the following problem. Imagine that you wish to replicate Weinstein's (1984) study which looked at the use of reduced forms by speakers in formal and informal talk. As part of the replication, you want to determine whether the rate speakers use differs under the two conditions (formal/informal). Here are fictitious data for the replication study (remember each *S* was observed twice):

	Syllables per Second Formal	Informal
S1	6.3	6.4
S2	3.6	3.4
S3	4.5	4.8
S4	5.7	5.3
S5	4.8	5.1
S6	6.6	5.8
S7	5.8	6.3
S8	5.4	6.8
S9	4.2	4.8
S10	3.1	4.4
S11	4.0	4.7
S12	5.5	6.8
S13	5.6	6.3
S14	4.7	5.8
S15	6.3	6.3

Give your calculations in the space below. Remember that when there is no change in a pair, that pair is dropped from the analysis and the number of pairs reduced accordingly.

Can you reject the null hypothesis of no difference in rate for the two conditions?

_____

▶ 3. The Wilcoxon test gives us a *z* value, so the test of association is the same as for the Median test:

$$\eta^2 = \frac{z^2}{N - 1}$$

Calculate and interpret the strength of association (eta^2) for these data:
eta^2 = _____ Interpretation:_____

Deciding Among Procedures

In chapters 9 and 10, we have discussed a variety of tests which can be used to determine whether the data from two groups differ. The tests used to compare two groups of different Ss (between-groups comparisons) contrast with those that compare the same Ss or matched Ss (paired comparisons). The statistical tests used are also determined by the nature of the data. If the data are measured on an interval or strongly continuous ordinal scale (rank-ordered) and if the data are normally distributed (i.e., the $\overline{X}$ is the best measure of central tendency), a parametric test should be used. A regular or Matched-pairs t-test is the best choice. These tests use the most information in the data and, therefore, are more powerful tests.

When the data do not meet these requirements, a nonparametric test should be selected. When the data are between-groups, then the Wilcoxon Rank sums or the Median test should be used. For repeated-measures designs, use the Wilcoxon Matched-pairs signed-ranks test. If the data have only the crudest of ordinal measurement, the Sign test can be used.

There are other choices available. For example, you may see the Walsh test and the Randomization test reported in some studies. (The Walsh test is sometimes used for 15 or fewer pairs and the Randomization test is sometimes used as an alternative to the Matched t-test where interval data is available.) If you are interested in the range of tests available, please consult the SAS and SPSS-X manuals or Siegel (1956).

The following chart may be helpful in selecting the most appropriate test for comparing groups.

Msrmt	Between-groups	Repeated or Paired

Ordinal Median	Median
	Wilcoxon Rank sums
	  (aka Mann Whitney U)
	Komogorov-Smirnov
		Sign test
		Wilcoxon Match.-pairs
		  signed-ranks
		Walsh
		Randomization

Interval Mean	t-test	Matched t-test

We will conclude this chapter by listing some of the advantanges and disadvantages inherent in selecting a nonparametric test over the parametric *t*-test procedures.

Advantages/Disadvantages of Nonparametric Procedures

Advantages

1. Probability statements of nonparametric tests are *exact* probabilities regardless of the shape of the population distribution from which the sample was drawn. The test does not depend on an assumption of normal distribution in the population.

2. If sample sizes are small, a nonparametric test is best *unless* the nature of the population distribution is known to be normal.

3. Nonparametric tests can treat data which inherently can be ranked as well as data whose seemingly numerical scores have the strength of ranks. That is, we may only be able to say that a *S* is *more X* than another *S* without knowing exactly *how much* more. Whenever a scale is "less" to "more" or "better" to "worse," the numbers on the scale can be treated using nonparametric tests.

4. Nonparametric tests (e.g., Chi-square and McNemar's tests in chapter 14) can be used with frequency data (nominal variables).

5. Nonparametric statistical tests typically are easier to calculate by hand. Most statistical packages for computers include nonparametric as well as parametric procedures.

Disadvantages

1. Nonparametric tests are "wasteful" of data. Information is lost when we change interval measurements to ordinal ranks or nominal measurements. Parametric tests use more information and thus are more powerful tests. (If you use approximately 10% more *S*s or observations with a nonparametric procedure, you can capture back some of this power.)

2. Less powerful tests are more likely to lead the researcher to err in claiming differences where none exist or in claiming no differences when they actually do exist (Type 1 and Type 2 errors, respectively). *Strictly speaking, power refers only to Type 2 errors.*

3. Tables for the probability of nonparametric tests do not appear in most statistics books so, if the analysis is done by hand, they may not be as easy to find.

4. Not all computer packages include a full range of nonparametric tests. You may have to search through several to find the procedure you want. Most packages carry a full range of parametric tests.

Activities

Read each of the following summaries. Decide which might meet the requirements of a Matched-pairs t-test procedure. Decide which might best be analyzed using a nonparametric test. Determine which statistical procedure(s) you would use for each study. If you feel that none of the procedures we have described so far is appropriate, explain why.

1. M. Benson & E. Benson (1988. Trying out a new dictionary. *TESOL Quarterly, 22*, 2, 340-345) asked whether the *BBI Combinatory Dictionary of English*--a dictionary which provides information on grammatical and lexical collocations--could be used to improve the ability of advanced learners to supply appropriate lexical collocations. Thirty-six EFL teachers (19 Hungarian and 17 Soviet teachers of English participating in a summer program in the United States) served as Ss. A collocation test was devised with 25 items such as:

Her lawyer wanted to _____(enter) a plea of not guilty.
This drug is effective _____(against) the common cold.

$$t = \frac{\bar{X}_1 - \bar{X}_2}{S_D}$$

Pretest and posttest results are given in the following table.

Group	Pretest	Posttest
Hungarian	43	92
Soviet	32	93

The authors say the data indicate remarkable improvement by the participants in each group. Decide what statistical procedure you would use to test this improvement. What statistics, aside from these figures, would you need in order to carry out the procedure(s)? need S_p

2. R. Budd (1988. Measuring proficiency in using English syntax. *SYSTEM, 16*, 2, 171-185) applied K. Hunt's sentence-combining method to encourage development of syntactic complexity in the writing of school children in the United States. The author was especially interested to see what effect this method might have when used with ESL students--in this case, Malaysian adolescents. Among several tables is the following which shows the results for various indices of syntactic proficiency for one such group of students:

Synopsis Scores for 1st-year Malaysians

Measure	Start of Year	End of Year
w/c	6.81	7.38
c/T	1.30	1.43
w/T	8.85	10.50
T/s	1.18	1.61
w/s	10.46	12.08

w/c = words per clause; c/T = clauses per T-unit; w/T = words per T-unit; T/s = T-units per sentence; w/s = words per sentence.

These indices allow the author to state that after nine months (approximately 144 hours of instruction), the scores of these students showed them jumping from 8th to 10th grade on w/c and w/T indices and from the 6-8 grade range to the 10-12 grade range on c/T and w/s indices. No procedure was used to test the differences shown in the above table. Decide what procedure(s) might be appropriate for the data. What further statistics would you need in order to be able to test the differences?

3. D. L. August (1987. The effects of peer tutoring on the second language acquisition of Mexican-American children in elementary school. *TESOL Quarterly, 21*, 4, 717-736.) August examined the effect of a special type of peer tutoring on the second language development of two groups--children acquiring English (experiment 1) and those acquiring Spanish (experiment 2). Peer tutoring, here, featured the learner as the "knower" of information. The learners were shown how to play a game or perform an enjoyable task such as baking cookies. They then selected a fluent speaker of the target language to instruct in a one-to-one interaction. The general research question was whether peer interaction would better promote acquisition than small-group instruction. Prior to the experiment, learners were matched on several criteria and then randomly assigned to either experimental or control groups. There were six experimental and six control *S*s in experiment 1 (ESL) and seven experimental and seven control *S*s in experiment 2 (SSL). Both experimental and control groups made gains over the instructional period. In the ESL experiment, peer interaction promoted greater use of the target language as measured by mean frequency of target language utterances to peers and proportion of target language to peers before, during, and following treatment. In the SSL experiment, peer interaction resulted in an almost total absence of Spanish use. The author concluded that interaction was beneficial to ESL students and discussed the difficulty of helping SSL children acquire Spanish in an environment where English is the language with more status.

4. D. Fuller & R. Wilbur (1987. The effect of visual metaphor cueing on recall of phonologically similar signs. *Sign Language Studies, 54*, 59-80.) noted that sign-naive adults recall newly learned manual signs better if they are grouped by semantic similarity (e.g., *apple, orange, banana*) than by phonological similarity (e.g., similar handshape, location, or movement of the sign). However, the authors provided visual metaphor cues to phonologically similar signs by demonstrating, for example, the *pouring* metaphor presented with an extended thumb in a pouring action (signs: *chemistry, drunk, pour, put gas in car*). The *scales of*

justice metaphor was shown where hands move simultaneously and in vertically opposite directions to give a visual illusion of balance (signs: *balance, depend, doubt, if, weigh, which*). Nevertheless, learners still recalled signs presented in semantic groups better than the signs presented in the two conditions of phonological similarity (with and without metaphor cues). The visual metaphor explanations did not significantly improve recall of phonologically similar signs.

5. Draw a chart of *your own design* which shows when each of the following tests might be used: Rank sums, Wilcoxon Matched-pairs, Sign test, *t*-test, Median test, and the Guttman test of scalability. (Try to include the notion of nominal/ordinal/interval or noncontinuous/continuous in your chart.)

References

Hensley, A. & Hatch, E. 1986. Innovation in language labs: an evaluation report. Report prepared for the Philippine Refugee Center, ICNC, Bataan, The Philippines.

Lazaraton, A. 1985. An analysis of listening comprehension using alternate statistical procedures. Unpublished master's thesis, TESL, UCLA.

Siegel, S. 1956. *Nonparametric Statistics for the Behavioral Sciences.* New York, NY: McGraw-Hill.

Weinstein, N. 1984. The effects of levels of formality and tempo on reduced forms. Unpublished master's thesis, TESL, UCLA.

Chapter 11

Comparisons Between Three or More Groups

Parametric/Nonparametric Choice

As was the case in comparing two groups, the first decision in selecting a statistical procedure to compare three or more groups is that of a powerful parametric test or of its nonparametric counterpart. Parametric tests, whether they compare means of two groups (as does the t-test) or the means of three or more groups, make the same assumption that the $\overline{X}$ is the best measure of central tendency for the data and that there is a normal distribution in the population. As we have said many times, one way to promote normal distribution is through random selection. A second method that might improve the chance of getting a normal distribution is to use a large number of subjects and randomly assign them to groups. When the basic assumption of normality cannot be met, it is always best to select a procedure that does not use these measures to estimate parameters in the population. On the other hand, when normality can be assumed, it would be a serious mistake to use a nonparametric procedure because we want to use a powerful test which uses as much information as possible in the data.

Parametric tests allow us to compare group means. These means are obtained from continuous data where the spread of scores can be appropriately captured by $\overline{X}$ and *s.d.* or variance. A second assumption of such tests, then, is that of a strong underlying continuity to the data. Ordinal scale data show such continuity when the scale approaches interval measurement. When you are not sure about the linearity of the scale itself or when the distribution of data on the scale do not appear normal (i.e., tend to cluster around one or two points), a nonparametric procedure is the better choice.

Nonparametric tests are, indeed, easier to do by hand. However, this should not be a reason for selecting a nonparametric procedure!

Parametric Tests for Comparing Three or More Groups

In chapter 10, we said that we cannot use the *t*-test procedure to make multiple comparisons. That is, the *t*-test allows us to compare two means--not cross-compare group 1 with group 2, group 1 with group 3, and group 2 with group 3. To do this, we will turn to an Analysis of Variance procedure, or ANOVA. In the *t*-test we compared two $\bar{X}$s and we also used the variability of the data in each group as well. The measurement of variability was *standard deviation*. In ANOVA, we will compare three or more $\bar{X}$s and the measure of variability used is *variance*. Hence the name *Analysis of Variance*. You should remember that variance and standard deviation differ only in that the variance equals s^2.

The ANOVA procedure is a powerful and versatile test, for it allows us to compare several means simultaneously. The type of ANOVA used will depend on the design of the research project. Imagine that you have administered a placement examination to a large groups of *S*s from five different schools. You want to know if the performance differs across the five schools. The design box for this study would look like this:

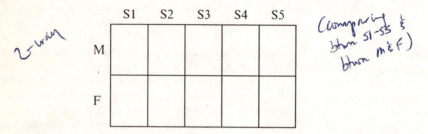

There is one dependent variable, performance on the examination. There is one independent variable with five levels. In the box diagram, the comparisons are made in only *one* direction--that of the independent variable. Therefore, the ANOVA used is called a "One-way" ANOVA. (only comparing btwn S1-S5)

It's possible that you might want to compare student scores on the test not only across five schools but by sex of the *S*s. The amended design box would be:

	S1	S2	S3	S4	S5
M					
F					

(comparing btwn S1-S5 & btwn m & F)

The comparisons are now drawn in two directions--for school and for sex--and the interaction (between sex and school) is also shown. This is a two-way design. A One-way ANOVA can no longer be used.

It's possible that as an administrator of an ESL program, you might want a breakdown of scores by L1 membership (say four major language groups). The comparison will be drawn in three ways:

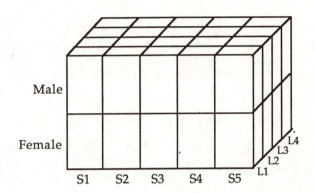

As you can see, the designs that use ANOVA may be 1-way to n-way comparisons. The more directions in which comparisons are drawn, however, the more difficult the interpretation of results becomes. This is because it is very hard to interpret higher-order interactions. (Also, as the design becomes more complex, there are more cells to fill with observations, so you need more Ss.)

It is possible that the design will be a *between-groups* comparison. In this case, the data from a S appears only once in the analysis. A S's score is never compared with a second score from the same S. In some studies, *repeated-measures* comparisons will be drawn. And in others, a *mixed* design will be used where comparisons are drawn between groups and within groups as well. The type of ANOVA to use changes according to the design.

◇◇

Practice 11.1

▶ 1. Foreign students in a literature class were asked to rate short stories covered during a course. Each story had a particular theme which might influence the "appreciation" ratings. The data, then, consist of scaled ratings of four separate themes. Research question: Are the ratings the same for each theme? Between-groups, repeated-measures, or mixed design?_____

▶ 2.   McMeans (1986) compared the CTBS (California Test of Basic Skills) scores of a group of second-grade immersion students according to their reports on when they first began reading in Spanish (preschool, kindergarten or first grade).   Research question: Do *S*s who report beginning reading in Spanish at different times have different scores on the CTBS?
Between-groups, repeated-measures, or mixed design?

▶ 3.   In chapter 6, page 182, we displayed a graph based on McGirt's study comparing composition scores of ESL and regular English classes. The graph showed the scores when the compositions were simply typed and presented to the raters.   In a second condition, the morphology and syntactic errors of all the compositions were corrected, and the compositions were scored by raters.   Research question: Are the ratings given native speaker and ESL compositions the same or different, and does this change if the morphology and syntax errors are removed from both sets of compositions?
Between-groups, repeated-measures, or mixed design?

Balanced and Unbalanced Designs

Because ANOVA is a fairly lengthy statistical procedure, it is not often carried out by hand.   If you do plan to use an ANOVA procedure and expect to do it by hand, it is important to try to get a "balanced" design.

Designs that are *balanced* (sometimes called *orthogonal*) have equal (or proportional) *n* sizes for all the groups and subgroups to be compared.   *Unbalanced* designs (*nonorthogonal*) are those where some groups have more *S*s or observations than others.   The statistics for a balanced design are *much* easier to carry out by hand than those for an unbalanced design.   For the computer this is no problem; it can easily make all the necessary adjustments in computation.   There is an additional reason for using a balanced design, and this has to do with the assumption of equal variances.   When cell sizes are not equal, the assumption of equal variance may be violated.   (If you use a computer program, it will give you information on the assumption of equal variance.)   While ANOVA is known as being a robust test (that is, we can violate the assumptions to some degree and still have confidence in the outcome), it is still sensitive to violation of both assumptions.

Let's first consider the notion of balance before we turn to the details of the ANOVA procedure.   Thirty students from each of five schools were given a language aptitude test.   If the comparison is to be drawn across the five schools, this is a balanced design because there are 30 *S*s in each of the 5 cells; the *n* is equal in each cell.   Of the 30 *S*s, 15 were females and 15 males.   The design is still balanced at this point.   There are 15 *S*s in each of 10 cells.   Five males and 5 females at each school were Spanish speakers, 5 males and 5 females were Korean speakers, and 5 males and 5 females were Vietnamese speakers.   It is still a balanced design; there are 5 *S*s in each of 30 cells.

The box diagram for the study and the *n* size in each cell are shown below. Each cell has five observations, the minimal size possible for ANOVA. (Many statisticians would argue that the cell size is too low. That argument is based on two issues. First, with such small *n* sizes, it is difficult to find an effect. Second, all you need is one person to throw everything off. For example, one Korean female at school 3 might for some reason perform in a very atypical way and distort the observations for all females. However, for simplicity of calculations and to demonstrate the notion of balance, we have used a minimal 5 *S*s per cell.)

	School 1	2	3	4	5
Spanish	5	5	5	5	5
Korean	5	5	5	5	5
Vietnamese	5	5	5	5	5

In Lazaraton's study evaluating a listening comprehension program (chapter 9, page 260), comparisons of gain scores in listening comprehension were drawn between an experimental class with 19 *S*s and a control class with 20 *S*s. This is not a balanced design because there are an unequal number of *S*s in each cell. Comparisons were also drawn for visa status (immigrant vs. foreign student) of *S*s in these intact classes. It is likely that this variable was unbalanced as well. Comparisons for male and female *S*s were also made. It is improbable that this variable was balanced. This is typical of research which involves intact classes. Designs for such studies are seldom balanced.

If your design does not have equal *n*s for cells, it is still possible to do the analysis by hand. However, we would recommend that you consider either dropping or adding *S*s (or observations) so that the cells are equal in size. If you have a substantial number of cases per cell, it is possible to drop a few cases to equate cell sizes. This must be done with care. You cannot go through the data to see which do not fit your hypotheses! The best solution is to delete cases *randomly* within cells. That is, each *S* (or observation) should have an equal chance of deletion. If you had three groups with 33, 30, and 32 cases, you could delete three from group 1 and two from group 3 simply by numbering each case and then randomly selecting numbers for deletion. The outcome should not be substantially changed if the Ss were randomly selected in the first place. For intact classes, particularly those with small *n* sizes, deletion of even one *S* or observation could dramatically change the outcome. In such cases, a better method for equating groups is to add *S*s. This can be done by adding data at the $\bar{X}$. To do this, compute the $\bar{X}$ *for the cell with missing data* (not the mean for all the data). Since this will not change the mean for the group, it will not change the results. It will also be necessary to adjust the "error" term (which we will talk about later). If at all possible, the best solution is to use a computer to run ANOVA. It can easily accomodate unbalanced data. If that is not possible, consult your advisor or statistical consultant to be sure that you have used the best method of equating the *n* for each group prior to running the statistical procedures. To calculate an unbalanced design by hand is a very involved procedure. We recommend you avoid it if at all possible.

Fixed Effects and Random Effects Designs

There is one final consideration in using ANOVA for group comparisons. Designs are classified as either *random effects* or *fixed effects* designs. A fixed effects study is one where the levels of a variable have been specified according to the research question. That is, we might wish to compare the levels of beginning, intermediate, and advanced learners: three fixed levels of the variable *language learner*. This is a "fixed effects" design. In the analysis, we can test for differences among these fixed levels. In turn, we can *only* generalize our findings to these same levels in the population. In a random effects design, the *S*s are randomly selected and the levels are also randomly set. For example, in large-scale questionnaire research, various proficiency levels or age levels might be randomly sampled from the population. In this case, the researcher hopes to be able to generalize not just to set levels in the population, but across the population at large. Usually a randomly selected stratified sample has been drawn from that population. If the data are randomly sampled, the design is a random effects design. Since we seldom carry out research using a random effects design, the procedures illustrated in this chapter and the next will be that of fixed effects designs.

One-way Balanced ANOVA

The goal of ANOVA is to explain the variance in the dependent variable in terms of variance in the independent variables. In a one-way design, there is *only* one dependent variable and *only* one independent variable with three or more levels. The comparisons of the means on the dependent variable are made across the levels. The levels, however, may be within-groups, a repeated-measures design where the same *S*s do different tasks or the same task at different times, or between-subjects, where each group is composed of different *S*s. When we compare the scores of our students before instruction, and every two weeks thereafter, the comparison is within-groups. When we compare the final exam scores of students in five sections of a course, the comparison is between groups. In the explanations that follow we will be discussing the use of One-way ANOVA with between-groups design. There are ANOVA procedures for repeated-measures designs so by understanding how ANOVA works, you will also understand how a repeated-measures ANOVA works. We will discuss ANOVA with repeated-measures in the next chapter.

Assume that you have taught one class level five different times. Each time you varied the methodology. One time you used the Natural Approach, another time Total Physical Response, then Silent Way, the Situational/Functional Approach, and Language Through Drama.

While the methodologies do overlap, you still wonder whether there are differences on final exam scores following these five approaches. Remember that there are several threats to the validity and reliability of this study. It is *not* an experimental study. The Ss were not randomly selected or randomly assigned. Whatever the findings, the results cannot be generalized to all learners at the level you teach. The ANOVA procedure is being used for descriptive rather than inferential purposes.

The design box looks like this:

		Approach Used		
	Natural	TPR	Silent	Sit/Func	Drama
Scores	$n = 15$	$n = 15$	$n = 15$	$n = 15$	$n = 15$

In displaying the data on the final exam scores, we could place the $\overline{X}$ and the s in each box. We want to be able to reject the H_o which states there is no difference in final exam scores for the five methodologies. In statistical terms, the H_o for this study is $\overline{X}_1 = \overline{X}_2 = \overline{X}_3 = \overline{X}_4 = \overline{X}_5$.

We would, of course, be surprised if each group obtained exactly the same $\overline{X}$ and s. The question is whether the means are far enough apart that we can say they are not five sample means drawn from the same population (with an unknown μ and σ^2). To answer this question we will again use sample statistics to estimate these parameters in the population.

In the example, there are 15 Ss for each of the treatments. It is unlikely that the mean for each group will be exactly the same. If there are differences among the groups, this is hopefully due to the treatment (i.e., methodology used). In addition, there is variability of the data within each group (ANOVA uses variance rather than standard deviation to examine this distribution of scores within each group) and this variability within groups will not be exactly the same for each. The variability within the group is due to individual differences among Ss rather than to the treatment. This is called *error variability*, symbolized as s^2_{within}. It is "error" not because it's wrong in any way but rather because it is not the focus of the research. The variance is due to something other than the treatment.

$$\text{Error variability} = \text{within-group variance} = s^2_{within}$$

This value for within-group variance will be our first estimate of the population variance, σ^2. We expect that the variance within each group is the result of normal distribution of scores (rather than the effect of the method). The within-group variance is an unbiased estimate of σ^2 because it does not include the effect of the treatment.

The second estimate is based on the differences across the groups. Each group will perform differently if the methods are not all equally effective. In ANOVA, this variability among the groups, called $s^2_{between}$, is attributed to two things:

1. Nonrandom, systematic variation between the groups due to the treatment effect.

2. Random, unsystematic, or chance variability between groups which is error variability.

Between-groups variance, then, is:

$$\text{Error variability} + \text{treatment effect} = \text{between-groups variance} = s^2_{between}$$

$s^2_{between}$ is our second estimate of σ^2. We said that within-group variance was not biased by treatment. Between-groups variance is biased by treatment because it contains variation due to treatment as well as variation due to error.

If the methods are truly different, we expect the scores for the five groups to be pushed far apart, so the variance across this estimate should be large. We expect the variability within the groups to be relatively stable across each group. In the best of all worlds, we would expect the *error variance*--variance due to the normal distribution of individual scores--to be the same between groups as within groups.

Since we want to be able to reject the null hypothesis, we hope the between-groups variance will be large and we want those differences to be due to treatment rather than to error. If the treatment effect is strong, the between-groups variance should be large, showing the groups pushed far apart rather than overlapping. A simple, common-sense understanding of ANOVA is the comparison of variance between groups and variance within groups. If the variance between groups (which includes the treatment effect) is not greater than the variance within groups (which does not include the treatment effect), then we know the treatments are all similar. We will not be able to reject the H_o. We must consider them all as just similar samples from the same population.

On the other hand, if the value of between-groups variance is greater than within-group variance, we are set to go. There is some difference between the five groups. Now the problem is discovering whether they are different enough that the difference is not due to chance. So (guess what), we will again place the difference in a sampling distribution to discover the probability of finding a difference as large as that we obtained. The sampling distribution for ANOVA is called the *F distribution*.

Fortunately for us, mathematicians have already constructed this distribution (see appendix C, table 5). Like the *t* distribution, it is made up of families with the same number of degrees of freedom in the sample size, but, unlike the *t* distribution, the *F* distribution also considers the degrees of freedom for number of groups. We don't have to consider the degrees of freedom for number of groups in the *t*-test because in the *t*-test there are always only two groups and the *df* for groups is always 1.

$S^2_{between}$ must be $>$ S^2_{within} to reject null Hyp. that all the groups are similar

To discover whether we can reject the null hypothesis, we once again consult the critical values given in the table for the sampling distribution.

In the *t*-test, we obtained a *t*-value. In ANOVA, we will obtain an *F value*. The *F* value is the ratio of the two sources of variance--between-groups variance over within-group variance.

$$F_{obs} = \frac{s^2_{between}}{s^2_{within}}$$

Another way of saying the same thing--

$$F_{obs} = \frac{s^2_{between}}{s^2_{within}} = \frac{error + treatment}{error}$$

If there is *no* effect for treatment we would end up with a ratio of 1, right?

$$\frac{error + treatment}{error} = \frac{error}{error} = 1$$

Thus, we need an *F* ratio > 1 to show any difference at all among groups. How much larger than 1 we need depends on the number of degrees of freedom within the groups and the degrees of freedom for the number of groups.

Let's apply this to the example to see how it works. The data from the exam scores of the five different groups follow.

Exam Scores for Five Methods

	Natural	TPR	Silent	Sit/Func	Drama
Mean	64	60	61	65	57
s^2	110	90	95	100	110
n	15	15	15	15	15
df	14	14	14	14	14

Number of groups (K) = 5
Total observations (N) = 75 (15 per group)

Arithmetically, the means of the groups differ. It appears that the situational-functional approach is best, while the natural approach is second best. Worst appears to be drama. We cannot, however, be confident that they are truly different without taking the *n* size and variance into account.

Look at the following two visuals.

need $F_{ratio} > 1$ to reject H_o.

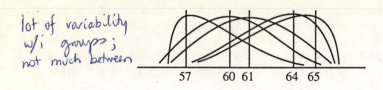

lot of variability w/i groups; not much between

57 60 61 64 65

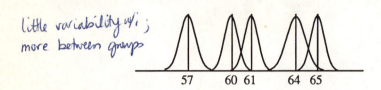

little variability w/i; more between groups

57 60 61 64 65

In the first figure, there is a lot of variability within groups, but not much between. There is a lot of overlap. These differences probably are not statistically significant. However, in the second diagram, there is little variability within groups and much more between. There is not much overlap. And since statistical significance for ANOVA is determined by the ratio of variability between to variability within, the second diagram probably shows differences which are statistically significant. In any case, we cannot know for sure without calculating the F ratio.

Remember that s^2 is used to represent population variance. This value is estimated by squaring the standard deviation. You know that we must look at the F ratio--the ratio of variance *between* over the variance *within* groups. We won't do the calculations just yet, but let's assume that we found a between-groups variance of 264. This represents the total variability present between the scores of the five groups. The within-group variance turned out to be 95. This represents the total variability of scores within each of the five groups.

We can, then, compute the F ratio:

$$F = \frac{s_B^2}{s_W^2} = \frac{264}{95} = 2.78$$

The subscripts B and W stand for *between* and *within*. The ratio is larger than 1. So, there is some effect for treatment. To discover whether the F value is large enough to give us confidence in rejecting the H_o, turn to the F distribution in table 5, appendix C. We know the probability level will depend on the number of *df* for groups. There are five groups (K). The *df* for groups is $K - 1 = 4$. There are 15 Ss in each group. To find the *df* for each group we use $n - 1$ or 14. There are five groups, so we multiply $n - 1$ by 5, 14×5; the *df* for within-group variance is 70.

$$(K-1)(n-1) = df$$

The numbers across the top of the table are the degrees of freedom for groups. The numbers down the side of the table are the degrees of freedom for Ss or

316   **The Research Manual**

number of observations. For our example, look across the top of the table for the *F* distribution to column 4 (*df* for *K*). Then go down the column to row 70 (*df* for the number of observations). Notice that there are two sets of numbers in each place. The top set are for a critical value where $p = .05$. The lower set is for a critical value where $p = .01$. We should use the .05 critical values of *F* because that's what we specified before the analyses. F_{crit} for an .05 level of confidence (for *df* of 4, 70) is 2.50. We can reject the H_o since F_{obs} is greater than F_{crit}. We can, therefore, claim that scores on the exam differ across the groups.

In this example, the data are from a relatively small number of *S*s. Remember that the smaller the number of *S*s (or observations), the larger the differences required to obtain statistically significant results.

Now that we have gone over the basic concept of ANOVA, let's actually compute an *F* ratio for a One-way ANOVA working from raw data.

The first step is to arrange the data in a sensible, organized way. This is important whether you expect to enter the data directly into the computer or plan to work from a data table and carry out the procedure by hand. If the data are organized in the following way, it will be easy for you to find all the figures you need for hand computation.

Because we don't want to make the hand calculation too cumbersome a chore, we will limit the number of groups to 5 and the number of *S*s within each of these groups to 10. We decided to use equal numbers of *S*s in each group because the computations are simpler with a balanced design. (Aren't you glad we did?)

Since the number of *S*s is relatively small, we also know that the *F* ratio will have to be relatively large before we can feel confident in rejecting the H_o.

The table for our research example follows:

Research hypothesis? There is no effect of first language on vocabulary test scores (i.e., the means of the five groups will not differ).
  Significance level? .05
  1- or 2-tailed? 2-tailed
Design
  Dependent variable(s)? Vocabulary test scores   1 d. var. ──influences──> d. var.
  Measurement? Scores (interval)
  Independent variable(s)? L1 group
  Measurement? Nominal (5 levels)
  Independent or repeated-measures? Independent groups
Other features? Fixed effects design
Statistical procedure? One-way ANOVA

As the above box shows, the H_o for the study is that there is no difference in vocabulary scores for different L1 groups. The dependent variable is vocabulary score. The independent variable is L1. This is a one-way design because there is one dependent variable and only one independent variable (with five levels).

We assume the test scores are interval data and this is a fixed-effects design. Therefore, we cannot generalize from the study to other language groups not included in the study.

Vocabulary Test Data

S	Gp1	Gp2	Gp3	Gp4	Gp5
1	16	15	14	14	10
2	14	13	13	10	8
3	10	12	15	9	10
4	13	13	17	11	9
5	12	13	11	11	12
6	20	20	11	12	5
7	20	19	12	10	8
8	23	22	10	13	8
9	19	19	13	9	7
10	18	17	12	8	9
n	10	10	10	10	10
ΣX	165	163	128	107	86
ΣX^2	2879	2771	1678	1177	772

$$N = 50 \qquad \Sigma X = 649 \quad \Sigma X^2 = 9277 \qquad (\Sigma X)^2 = 421201$$

◇◇◇

Practice 11.2

1. Let's be sure that the figures for the row totals (Σ rows) are clear. Row 1, labeled n shows ___# of observations in each group___

How many Ss are there in each group? ___10___.
What is the N for the study? ___50___.
How many df are there for the number of observations in each group? _____.
The df for Ss, then, is _____.

2. ΣX is obtained by _____

ΣX^2 is obtained by _____

(If you are not sure, guess and then use your calculator to check your answer.)
$(\Sigma X)^2$ is obtained by _____

(Again, if you are not sure, guess and do the calculations to check.)

3. Look at the raw data. Mathematically, which group appears to be best?____
Worst?_____ Do the differences appear to be large?_____.

How much variability does there appear to be in each group? _____

_____

Do you think we will be able to reject the H_o? _____

_____

◇◇

With the data in table form, we can compute the within-group and between-groups variances fairly easily and then find the F ratio.

There are several ways to compute the F ratio from raw data. We could begin by finding the grand $\overline{X}$ for all the Ss, then subtracting each individual score from the grand $\overline{X}$ and squaring all these individual differences from the $\overline{X}$ as we have before in many of our computations. While this may make the concept easier to understand (since it's exactly the same kind of thing we have done in computing standard deviation, z scores and in the t-test procedure), it's not the easiest computation to do. So let's start with an easier computation and try the other method later. This is called the *sum of squares* method.

Step 1
Square each score and add. This is the first step in determining the sum of squares total, abbreviated SST in most computer printouts. We will use that abbreviation here.

$$SST = \sum X^2 - \frac{\left(\sum X\right)^2}{N}$$

If you look at the data sheet, you will find that the scores of all the Ss have been squared and totaled. The ΣX^2 value is 9277. N is 50. $(\Sigma X)^2$ is $(649)^2$. Placing these figures in the formula and computing the value for SST:

$$SST = \sum X^2 - \frac{\left(\sum X\right)^2}{N}$$

$$SST = 9277 - \frac{421201}{50} = 852.98$$

Step 2
Find the sum of squares between groups. This is often abbreviated as SSB (for *sum of squares between*), an abbreviation we will use here.

To find SSB, we add up the scores for each group. Square each sum and then divide by the n for the group $((\Sigma X_1)^2 \div n_1)$. Add these. Then subtract the total scores squared divided by N $((\Sigma X)^2 \div N)$. You have this value since you used it in step 1. All the figures are readily available from the data table.

$$SSB = \left[\frac{\left(\sum X_1\right)^2}{n_1} + \frac{\left(\sum X_2\right)^2}{n_2} + \frac{\left(\sum X_3\right)^2}{n_3} + \cdots + \frac{\left(\sum X_k\right)^2}{n_k} \right] - \frac{\left(\sum X\right)^2}{N}$$

Here is the intermediate calculation step.

$$SSB = (2722.5 + 2656.9 + 1638.4 + 1144.9 + 739.6) - 8424.02$$

$$SSB = 478.28$$

The total sum of squares for all the data (SST) is 852.98. The sum of squares between groups (SSB) is 478.28.

Step 3

Find the sum of squares within each group. This is labeled as SSW.

Since we know that SST = SSB + SSW, we can easily find this value by subtracting SSB from SST. What's left must be the value of SSW.

$$SSW = SST - SSB$$

We can enter the figures and do the computation for SSW.

$$SSW = 852.98 - 478.28 = 374.7$$

Step 4

The next step "averages" each of these figures (SSW and SSB) to make them sensitive to their respective degrees of freedom. The result is the *variance* values. To find the variance between groups, divide SSB by $K - 1$. Let's do that now.

$$s_B^2 = MSB = \frac{SSB}{K-1}$$

$$s_B^2 = MSB = \frac{478.28}{4}$$

$$s_B^2 = MSB = 119.57$$

$s_B^2 = MSB$

You will notice that s_B^2 is also abbreviated as MSB. This stands for *mean squares between.* It is often used in computer printouts and in ANOVA tables. While s_B^2 better represents the notion of variance between groups, the MSB abbreviation appears more often in ANOVA charts in reports. Feel free to use whichever annotation you prefer.

To find the variance within groups, divide SSW by $N - K$. Since there were 50 Ss in the study, 10 in each of five groups, the df is $50 - 5$ ($N - K$) or 45. Let's place these values in the formula for MSW.

$$s_W^2 = MSW = \frac{SSW}{(N-K)}$$

$$s_W^2 = MSW = \frac{374.7}{45}$$

$$s_W^2 = MSW = 8.33$$

Step 5
Calculate the *F ratio.* You can annotate this calculation as $\frac{s_B^2}{s_W^2}$ or as $\frac{MSB}{MSW}$.

$$F = \frac{MSB}{MSW}$$

$$F = \frac{119.57}{8.33}$$

$$F = 14.35$$

The *F* ratio must be larger than 1.0 to show that there is *some* difference between the groups. This is the case here--our *F* ratio greatly exceeds 1.0.

Now we must decide whether we can reject the H_o. To do this we use our sample statistics as estimators of the population parameters. Our MSB and MSW are the two available estimates of σ^2. Remember, σ^2 represents population variance.

The MSB estimate is biased for treatment. This estimate belongs to a distribution with 4 *df* $(K - 1 = 5 - 1 = 4)$. The second estimate of σ^2 is MSW. It is not biased for treatment since it includes only error variability within the groups. MSW, in our example, belongs to a distribution with 45 *df* $(N - K = 50 - 5 = 45)$. The *F* distribution is made up of families with special distributions according to the *df* for groups and for observations. Since our study belongs in the family with 4 *df* for groups and 45 *df* for observations, we check the intersection of 4 and 45 on the *F* distribution chart in appendix C. Across the top of the chart the columns are labeled for the *df* of the numerator. In the *F* ratio, MSB is the numerator and our *df* for MSB is 4. Find that column. The *df* for the denominator runs down the side of the table and is the *df* for MSW. That's 45. There is a 44 and a 46 but no 45. So we select the line for 44 *df*. The critical value needed to reject the H_o at the .05 level of confidence is 2.58. We can safely reject the H_o at the .05 level.

Research reports published in journals often include a special table called a "source table" to display the ANOVA values. The tables are a summary of the results. You should make maximum use of this information in reading reports. One good way to do this is to first turn to the abstract of the study; identify the question(s), and the dependent and independent variables. Next turn to the tables and interpret them as best you can without further information. Then, with your own interpretation in mind, read the complete article and check your interpretation against that of the author. The following chart gives the summary information for our data.

Source of variance	SS	df	MS	F
Between Groups	478.28	4	119.57	14.35*
Within Groups	374.70	45	8.33	

$*p < .05$

Some reports include means square (MSW and MSB) but not the sum of squares within and between groups (SSW and SSB). If you think about it, this will make sense. You could recover SSW and SSB (if you know MSW and MSB and the df) simply by multiplying MSW by df_W and MSB by df_B. Some journals, in order to save space, ask authors to delete tables and just include the result of the statistical test. In this case a statement such as the following would be used: $F = 14.35 (4, 45), p < .05$.

You might wonder why the probability level is reported as $p < .05$ when it actually qualifies easily for $p < .01$. The reason is that an .05 level was selected for rejecting the H_o. Many fields (and/or journal editors) require that you state the level for rejecting the H_o and then simply report whether or not that level was met. If you exceed that, fine, but report it as $< .05$. Since computers can calculate the exact probabilities, many researchers (and journal editors) use the probability specified by the computer program. So it is quite possible that you will find research where an .05 level has been selected but where the report will give the actual probability. (In many studies, you never know what probability was selected to reject the H_o--the researcher simply reports the obtained probability from the computer analysis.) It is wise to consult your research advisor or the journal editor for their views on this before deciding how to present information on probability for your findings.

Since One-way ANOVA is more complex than the t-test, let's go through another example. Imagine that we hope to gather evidence to show that "story grammar" is not as universal as has been claimed. We prepare a reading passage which has the universal story-grammar components: orientation (setting, time, introduction of characters), the problem, a set of ordered actions addressing the problem, the solution, and a coda. We add this story with a set of 20 questions as a "research caboose" to our general English proficiency exam. If story grammar is universal then Ss from all first language groups should be able to access this discourse organization to understand and remember story components. Since five major language groups are represented in the student body that takes the exam, we can compare their performance according to L1 membership. From Ss taking the test, we randomly select Ss who scored in the 80th to 90th percentile on the rest of the examination. This assures us that we have controlled for L2 language proficiency. To simplify the computations here, we have selected five Ss from each of the five L1 groups. While these five Ss from each group have been randomly selected from the proficiency range (and we hope, therefore, that their means and variances will represent those of the population), we recommend much larger n sizes for each group in real research where inferences are to be drawn.

Scores on Story Grammar Questions

Ss	Lang.Gp.1	Lang.Gp.2	Lang.Gp.3	Lang.Gp.4	Lang.Gp.5
1	18	16	18	16	18
2	18	15	16	13	16
3	16	14	15	14	15
4	15	11	15	12	12
5	11	12	10	12	13
ΣX	78	68	74	67	74
n	5	5	5	5	5
Mean	15.6	13.6	14.8	13.4	14.8

$N = 25$ Grand mean ($\overline{X}_G = 14.44$)

If Ss from these five language backgrounds perform differently, we would be able to reject the H_o which states there is no difference in story grammar scores for different L1 groups. This would give us preliminary evidence that for these language groups the proposed universal story grammar has not been used equally to promote understanding and retention of story information. Thus, it may not be universal at all.

Now, to show that we can indeed do a One-way ANOVA by working with the grand $\overline{X}$ and computing the individual differences from that $\overline{X}$, we will present this second method of computing ANOVA. It may better illustrate how ANOVA works.

Step 1
Compute the grand mean by adding all the scores and dividing by N. The grand mean is symbolized as $\overline{X}_G$. $\overline{X}_G$ for the data is 14.44.

Step 2
Subtract each *score* from the $\overline{X}_G$ and square the difference. When we add all these squared individual differences from the $\overline{X}_G$, the result is SST.

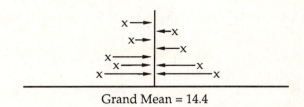

Grand Mean = 14.4

To compute SST, then, the formula says:

$$SST = \Sigma(X - \overline{X}_G)^2$$

$$SST = (18 - 14.44)^2 + (18 - 14.44)^2 + (16 - 14.44)^2 + \cdots + (13 - 14.44)^2$$
$$SST = 136.16$$

Step 3

Find SSB. To do this, subtract the $\overline{X}_G$ from the average score of each *group*, $\overline{S}_K$, squaring these differences as well. These differences will be multiplied by the n for the group and then summed. The formula, therefore, is:

$$SSB = \sum n(\overline{X} - \overline{X}_G)^2$$

For our data, then, SSB would be:

$$SSB = \sum n(\overline{X} - \overline{X}_G)^2$$
$$SSB = 5(15.6 - 14.44)^2 + 5(13.6 - 14.44)^2 +$$
$$5(14.8 - 14.44)^2 + 5(13.4 - 14.44)^2 + 5(14.8 - 14.44)^2$$
$$SSB = 16.96$$

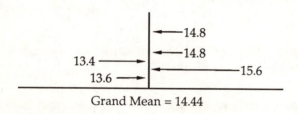

Grand Mean = 14.44

Step 4

Now that we have the sum of squares between groups, we can find SSW by subtracting.

$$SSW = SST - SSB$$
$$SSW = 136.16 - 16.96$$
$$SSW = 119.2$$

Step 5

These values for variability within and between groups must, of course, be adjusted for their respective degrees of freedom. The *df* between groups is $K - 1$. We have 5 groups, so the *df* for groups is 4. The degrees of freedom within the groups is $N - K$. The N for the study is 25 and the number of groups is 5, so the *df* for observations is 20.

$$MSB = \frac{SSB}{df_B} = \frac{16.96}{4} = 4.24$$

$$MSW = \frac{SSW}{df_W} = \frac{119.2}{20} = 5.96$$

Step 6
Compute the *F* ratio.

$$F = \frac{MSB}{MSW} = \frac{4.24}{5.96} = .711$$

Now, let us show you that the two methods of computing the *F* ratio do obtain the same results.

Step 1

$$SST = \sum X^2 - \frac{\left(\sum X\right)^2}{N}$$

$$SST = (18^2 + 18^2 + 16^2 + \cdots + 13^2) - \frac{(18 + 18 + 16 + \cdots + 13)^2}{20}$$

$$SST = 136.16$$

Step 2

$$SSB = \left[\frac{\left(\sum X_1\right)^2}{n_1} + \frac{\left(\sum X_2\right)^2}{n_2} + \frac{\left(\sum X_3\right)^2}{n_3} + \frac{\left(\sum X_4\right)^2}{n_4} + \frac{\left(\sum X_5\right)^2}{n_5}\right] - \frac{\left(\sum X\right)^2}{N}$$

$$SSB = \left[\frac{78^2}{5} + \frac{68^2}{5} + \frac{74^2}{5} + \frac{67^2}{5} + \frac{74^2}{5}\right] - \frac{361^2}{25}$$

$$SSB = 16.96$$

Step 3

$$SSW = SST - SSB$$
$$SSW = 136.16 - 16.96$$
$$SSW = 119.2$$

Again, the values for SSB and SSW must be adjusted by the number of degrees of freedom.

Step 4

$$MSB = \frac{SSB}{K-1} = \frac{16.96}{4} = 4.24$$

Step 5

$$MSW = \frac{SSW}{N-K} = \frac{119.2}{20} = 5.96$$

And the *F* ratio is:

Step 6

$$F = \frac{MSB}{MSW} = \frac{4.24}{5.96} = .711$$

The table for the results (regardless of which method is used to compute the *F* statistic) would look like this

Story Grammar Scores Across 5 L1 Groups

Source of variance	SS	df	MS	F
Between groups	16.96	4	4.24	.711
Within groups	119.20	20	5.96	
Total	136.16	24		

The *F* ratio is less than 1 so we know there is no meaningful difference among the five groups. They are all equally able to process and retain information from a reading passage which conforms to story grammar principles.

Practice 11.3

1. Can we say that these *S*s from these language groups *use* a universal story grammar to process and retain the information? Why (not)? _____
_____
_____

2. How might we design a better study to find the answer to this question? ____
_____
_____
_____
_____

▶ 3. Imagine your ESL program decided to find out "once and for all" the best method for teaching composition. Three methods were devised: method 1, 2, and 3. *S*s who were required to take the regular composition course were randomly assigned to one of the three methods. *S*s were given the same composition topics. At the end of the quarter, the final compositions were graded by five raters and averaged. The scores obtained were:

Average Final Composition Score

Method 1	Method 2	Method 3
23	12	19
20	14	18
19	19	10
21	16	18
15	12	18
19	15	20
23	18	19
24	11	16
23	15	20
20	17	21

Fill in the box diagram below for this study:

Research hypothesis? _____
    Significance level? _____
    1- or 2-tailed? _____
Design
    Dependent variable(s)? _____
    Measurement? _____
    Independent variable(s)? _____
    Measurement? _____
    Independent or repeated-measures? _____
Other features? _____
Statistical procedure? _____

Using either the sum of squares or the deviation method, do an ANOVA. Show your calculations below.

_____
_____
_____
_____

Can you reject the H_o? What do you conclude?

_____
_____
_____

4. We have given you three examples of One-way ANOVA in this chapter. In one case we were able to reject the H_o and in the other two we could not. From an examination of the $\bar{X}$ for each group in these studies, could you have easily predicted which would and which would not allow us to reject the H_o? Why (not)? _____

_____

_____

◇◇

Assumptions Underlying ANOVA

We have touched on some of the assumptions underlying ANOVA in a general way. Just to put it all together, the assumptions of One-way ANOVA are:

1. There is one dependent variable and one independent variable with three or more levels. In the story grammar example (page 322), the independent variable has five levels (five different L1 groups).

2. The data are score or ordinal scale data that are continuous. In the story grammar example, we assume the test items yield scores that are continuous, fairly equal-interval in nature, so that $\bar{X}$ and variance are the best measures of central tendency and variability for the data.

3. The data are independent (not repeated-measures). In the story grammar example, each S contributes one score to only one group. The comparison is between groups.

4. There is a normal distribution of scores in each group. That is, $\bar{X}$ and variance are the best descriptions of the data. We used the absolute minimum (five per cell) in this example. If you plot out the actual scores, the polygon is not that of a normal distribution. Even though ANOVA is said to be fairly robust in this regard, we recommend a much larger n size to guarantee that the sample distributions are not skewed.

5. ANOVA assumes that the data in the respective populations from which the samples are drawn are normally distributed. Therefore, we have an interpretation problem similar to that discussed for the t-test (chapter 9). It is legitimate to compare nonnative speakers with several different NNS groups. However, care must be taken in interpreting the results. That is, large differences can be expected, but the differences may be due to language proficiency rather than to the variable being tested. In this type of design, it is impossible to *randomly assign* Ss to either native speaker or nonnative speaker groups, and so no causal claims can be made in such research.

6. There are equal variances of scores in each group. We assume this is the case since the design is balanced. If we use a computer program for the analysis, the printout will give us this information.

7. The design is balanced (if calculations are done by hand). In the example, the dependent variable was the test score and the independent variable was first language, a variable with five levels of equal n sizes.

8. There is a minimum of 5 observations per cell. Some statisticians recommend a minimum of 10 observations per cell. It is often difficult to obtain a normal distribution with a small n size. That is, apparent differences within a cell may be due to a real difference or just to one highly variable observation which distorts the cell mean. In addition, with a small number of observations, the power to reject H_o is low, so the F must be very large to obtain statistical significance.

9. The F statistic allows us to reject or accept the null hypothesis. If there is a statistically significant difference in the groups, it does not pinpoint precisely where that difference lies. (We will deal with this next.)

(You might find it useful to review these assumptions by applying them to the test of composition methodology--page 326. Check to see if all assumptions were met in that example.)

Let's look back at the example where a statistically significant difference was found between the groups. This is the comparison of performance of five different L1 groups on a vocabulary test. We know that the groups did not perform in the same way on the test because we could reject the H_o at the .05 level. However, we still do not know exactly where the difference lies. We cannot simply check the $\bar{X}$ for each group and decide.

To discover the precise location of differences, we need to perform a post hoc comparison of the means. If no difference among the means was found in the ANOVA procedure, you can stop at that point. That is, it is not appropriate to search for differences among sets of means *unless* the F ratio is significant. When there is a significant difference among the means and we need to identify precisely where that difference lies, a post hoc comparison is possible.

Tests for Locating Differences Among Means

There are two ways to precisely locate differences among means. The first is by planning the comparison ahead of time. In this case there are preplanned comparisons and hypotheses to test. For example, in the vocabulary example (page 318) we may believe that language groups 1 and 2 will perform quite differently than Ss in language groups 3, 4, and 5. This belief would be built on previous research or on strong theoretical arguments. Perhaps previous research has shown that the first two groups share many cognate vocabulary items with English and that these two groups usually perform very well on English vocabulary tests. The preplanned comparison, then, builds on previous work and the hypothesis is directional (groups 1 and 2 will do *better* than the other three). The H_o for the comparison would be that there is no difference in vocabulary scores for Ss whose languages are either +cognate or −cognate. The H_1 for a preplanned, directional comparison allows us to use a *one-tailed* hypothesis.

The second way to locate differences is a post hoc comparison of means. In this case the researcher has a H_o of no difference among the five groups. After rejecting this H_o, it is still not clear exactly where the difference lies, so exploratory comparisons are made between all the different groups or between some groups selected on a post hoc basis. The analyses will be *two-tailed* tests.

The two methods are sometimes called *a priori* for the preplanned comparisons and *post hoc* for those carried out after the fact. There are a wealth of computer procedures that make these comparisons. Some of them are best used to compare each group with every other group. Others, such as the Scheffé, allow very powerful testing of grouped means against other grouped means.

We will not present the computations for the Scheffé, the Duncan, the Tukey, or other multiple-range tests here since they are very complex. See Kirk (1982) for a discussion of *a priori* and *post hoc* comparisons using these tests (and for the formulas for computation). Most computer software programs will generate these on request. We will, however, present a table here to show the output from one such test, the Scheffé.

Scheffé Test of Differences Across Language Groups

Group	Group 1 Mean = 4.05	Group 2 Mean = 3.30	Group 3 Mean = 2.90	Group 4 Mean = 2.75	Group 5
1		1.70**	1.75**	2.10**	2.25**
2			1.45**	1.50**	2.00**
3				1.15**	1.30**
4					.40

$**p < .01$

The chart shows which groups differ from each other. Notice the group number for the column and also for the rows. The value 1.70 compares group 1 and group 2 (it is at the intersection of these two groups on the table). The 1.75 is for group 1 and group 3. The 1.45 is for group 2 and group 3, and so forth. Each comparison is significant with the exception of the comparison between group 4 and group 5. It is also possible to group variables (e.g., groups 1 + 2 vs. groups 3 + 4 + 5) for comparison using the Scheffé test.

The combination of a One-way ANOVA and a Scheffé test allows us to discover whether there are differences among the $\overline{X}$s of different groups, and it also allows us to see, in a post hoc comparison, exactly where the differences lie.

Strength of Association: omega²

There is another very nice feature that you can add to a One-way ANOVA that, like η^2 for the *t*-test, will allow you to think about the strength of association. It will let you talk about the strength of the association in the data for balanced designs. That is, you can determine the proportion of the variability in the dependent variable that can be accounted for by the independent variable. This is called ω^2 (omega squared). The formula is very simple and you can easily do it by hand.

$$\omega^2 = \frac{SSB - (K - 1)MSW}{SST + MSW}$$

Let's try this for our vocabulary test example.

$$\omega^2 = \frac{478.28 - (4)(8.33)}{852.98 + 8.33}$$

$$\omega^2 = \frac{444.96}{861.31}$$

$$\omega^2 = .52$$

This tells us that we can account for 52% of the variability in the vocabulary score simply by knowing the L1 group. The strength of association of the independent variable is, thus, quite strong. As you will see when we turn to correlation, a relation in the .40 to .60 range is quite impressive in dealing with this type of data. However, it leaves us wondering how we might account for the remaining 48% of the variance!

(The omega^2 formula can only be used for balanced designs. If the design is not balanced, you can use the eta^2 formula which is presented in chapter 12.)

Once you have found a statistical difference in a One-way ANOVA, you can reject the H_o. A multiple-range test, such as Duncan or Scheffé, will show you precisely which means differ from each other. And, finally, once you have rejected the H_o, you can also discuss the strength of the relationship using ω^2.

◇◇◇◇◇◇◇◇◇◇◇◇◇◇◇◇◇◇◇◇◇◇◇◇◇◇◇◇◇◇◇◇◇◇◇◇

Practice 11.4

▶ 1. Calculate and interpret omega^2 for the methodology problem on page 315. You will have to derive the SS from the MS and *df*.

_____

_____

▶ 2. Calculate and interpret omega^2 for the composition problem in practice 11.3.

_____

_____

_____

◇◇◇◇◇◇◇◇◇◇◇◇◇◇◇◇◇◇◇◇◇◇◇◇◇◇◇◇◇◇◇◇◇◇◇◇

Nonparametric Tests for Comparing Three or More Groups

When the assumptions of ANOVA cannot be met, there are still nonparametric tests that can be used. The nonparametric equivalent to the one-way between-groups ANOVA is the Kruskal-Wallis test.

It is often the case that researchers in our field cannot meet the assumptions of ANOVA. It is true that ANOVA is quite robust to violations of its assumption of normal distribution. Often, though, we work with intact groups. Ss are not randomly selected, and so we cannot be sure that our estimates of population variance, σ^2, are accurate. In addition, we may not be content with the "interval" nature of the data. In such cases, a nonparametric comparison of the data seems more appropriate than does ANOVA.

Kruskal-Wallis Test

There is one caution to keep in mind regarding the Kruskal-Wallis test. If you have three levels and the n of any level is 5 or less, use an "Exact test" (see Wike, 1971) instead.

Let's begin with an example and work through the procedure. Imagine that you wished to test Schumann's (1978) acculturation hypothesis. From all the adult, immigrant, untutored learners of ESL in your community, you have found seven people who can be classified as "acrolangs" (Schumann's terminology for learners who have fossilized in syntactic development but at a fairly high level), eight "mesolangs" (roughly those who have fossilized at a medium level of syntax development), and nine "basilangs" (learners who fossilized early in development of syntax). You have revised and improved a test which measures degree of acculturation. Some of these items are on 5-point scales, some are yes/no questions, some ask the learners to give opinions. Before we turn to the calculations, please complete the following practice as a review that highlights when a nonparametric procedure such as Kruskal-Wallis should be used.

◇◇

Practice 11.5

1. Is it likely that the data are equal-interval? _____
Has random selection of Ss been used? _____.
Would the $\overline{X}$s and variances obtained for each group allow you to make an accurate prediction of population variance? _____.
Is the design orthogonal (i.e., is it a balanced design)? _____. (Fortunately, in Kruskal-Wallis unbalanced designs do not complicate computation.)

2. There is one dependent variable: _____. There is one independent variable: _____ with three levels (_____,

_____, _____). Is the comparison between-groups or repeated-measures? _____.

The data for the study began as scores on the acculturation measure. These have been changed to ranks as shown below. The lowest score has been given a rank of 1, the next a 2, and so forth. The highest score is ranked 24th.

Basilect			Mesolect			Acrolect	
Score	_Rank_		_Score_	_Rank_		_Score_	_Rank_
18	3.5		12	1		18	3.5
28	8		16	2		21	5
32	9		37	11		26	6.5
46	13.5		40	12		26	6.5
52	16.5		46	13.5		33	10.0
62	20		52	16.5		51	15
63	21.5		61	19		53	18
			63	21.5		68	23
						70	24
n1 = 7	T1 = 92		n2 = 8	T2 = 96.5		n3 = 9	T3 = 111.5
			N = 24				

The formula for Kruskal-Wallis follows. The numbers 12 and 3 are constants in the formula--that is, they do not come from the data but are part of the formula.

$$H = \frac{12}{N(N+1)} \sum_{A=1}^{a} \frac{T_A^2}{N_A} - 3(N+1)$$

In this formula, A = number of levels.

To use the formula, we will go through the following steps.

Step 1
Divide 12 by $N(N+1)$. The N for our data is 24.

$$\frac{12}{N(N+1)} = \frac{12}{24(25)} = \frac{12}{600} = .02$$

Step 2

$$\sum_{A=1}^{a}$$

is just a symbol that tells us that the next operation is to be done for however many groups (a = group) we have. The following operation says to square the sum of ranks for each group and divide by the n for the group. So the total instruction for step 2 is: square each sum and divide by the n for the group; then total these.

$$\sum_{A=1}^{a} \frac{T_A^2}{N_A} = \frac{92^2}{7} + \frac{96.5^2}{8} + \frac{111.5^2}{9} =$$

$$\frac{8464}{7} + \frac{9312.25}{8} + \frac{12432.25}{9} =$$

$$1209.14 + 1164.03 + 1381.36 = 3754.53$$

Step 3
The formula says to multiply the result of step 1 and step 2.

$$\frac{12}{N(N+1)} \sum_{A=1}^{a} \frac{T_A^2}{N_A} = .02 \times 3754.53 = 75.09$$

Step 4
Multiply $3 \times (N+1)$.

$$3(N+1) = 3(25) = 75$$

Step 5
Subtract the result of step 4 from step 3. If you look at the formula, you will see that everything up to the $3(N+1)$ was completed in step 3 and that $3(N+1)$ was computed in step 4.

$$H = \frac{12}{N(N+1)} \sum_{A=1}^{a} \frac{T_A^2}{N_A} - 3(N+1)$$

$$H = .02 \times 3754.53 - 75$$

$$H = 75.09 - 75$$

$$H = .09$$

There is still one step left--that of placing the value of H in a distribution. The distribution that we will use is that of a related statistical procedure, Chi-square, table 7 in appendix C. If you consult that table, you will see that the degrees of freedom are listed down the left side of the table. The degrees of freedom for Kruskal-Wallis are computed using the number of *levels* minus 1. In this study, the number of levels is 3, so the $df = 2$. Across the top of the table you will find the probability levels. Since we have selected an alpha of .05 to reject the null hypothesis, we consult that column. The intersection of .05 and 2 df is 5.991. We need to meet or exceed this critical value, 5.991, in order to reject the null hypothesis.

We cannot reject the H_o. Our H value is far below the critical value needed, 5.99. The conclusion the researcher could draw from these results is that Ss at differing levels did not show significantly different scores on the acculturation measure. If the observed level of H had been, say, 12.40, the researcher could have concluded that the Ss at different levels *did* get different scores on the measure.

Here is the information given for the data using SPSS-X. Notice that the printout also gives the mean ranks for each group. This is useful information that you might want to give in a report.

ACCULT   ACCULTURATION
BY LEVEL   PROFIC LEVEL

LEVEL	1	2	3
NUMBER	7	8	9
MEAN RANKS	13.14	12.06	12.39
CASES 24	χ^2 .091	SIG .956	

In a research article, the statistical findings might simply be summarized as: No difference was found among the three groups on the acculturation measure (Kruskal-Wallis χ^2 = .091, p = n.s.). You might report the mean ranks, but not interpret them. That is, the mean ranks of 13.14, 12.06, and 12.39 differ *numerically*, but they do *not* differ *statistically*. Therefore, it would be incorrect to say that these three particular groups differ in any way on the acculturation measure.

◇◇

Practice 11.6

1. How would you interpret a significance level of .956?

_____

_____

▶ 2. Now that you have a model from which to work, try to use the formula with the following data. Riggenbach and Lazaraton (1987) rated ESL students at four levels on their oral discourse skills. Five skills were tested, so the score represents a composite of five subtests. The total score, thus, is a composite of scale and score data. The students are from intact classes. The research question is whether students at different class levels (as determined by their scores on the ESL Placement Test) differ in oral communication skills. Fill in the information below regarding the study:

Research hypothesis? _Students differ in_____

Significance level? _.05_____

1- or 2-tailed? _2-tailed_____

Design

Dependent variable(s)? _____

Measurement? _____

Independent variable(s)? _____

Measurement? _____

Independent or repeated-measures? _____

Other features? _____

Statistical procedure? _____

Level 1		Level 2		Level 3		Level 4	
Mean Score	*Rank*	*Mean Score*	*Rank*	*Mean Score*	*Rank*	*Mean Score*	*Rank*
21.5	8.5	30.5	24.5	16.5	4	35.5	31.5
26.5	16	28	19.5	35.5	31.5	30	23
32.5	27.5	30.5	24.5	28	19.5	29.5	22
15.5	2	31	26	24.5	13	27	17
18	6	18.5	7	29	21	32.5	27.5
23.5	11.5	23.5	11.5	16	3	25.5	15
23	10	17	5	34.5	30		
10	1	25	14	27.5	18		
21.5	8.5			34	29		
$n1 = 9$		$n2 = 8$		$n3 = 9$		$n4 = 6$	
$T1 =$ ____		$T2 =$ ____		$T3 =$ ____		$T4 =$ ____	

Fill in the blanks for the totals above and then finish the computations using the formula below. In this procedure, it is important to carry out all calculations to four or five decimal places. (If you don't, your answer won't agree with the key!)

$$H = \frac{12}{N(N+1)} \sum_{A=1}^{a} \frac{T_A^2}{N_A} - 3(N+1)$$

Complete step 1:

$$\frac{12}{N(N+1)} = \text{_____}$$

Complete step 2:

$$\sum_{A=1}^{a} \frac{T_A^2}{N_A} = \text{_____}$$

Complete step 3.

$$H = \frac{12}{N(N+1)} \sum_{A=1}^{a} \frac{T_A^2}{N_A} = \text{_____}$$

Complete step 4.

$$3(N+1) = \text{_____}$$

Find the value of H.

$$H = \frac{12}{N(N+1)} \sum_{A=1}^{a} \frac{T_A^2}{N_A} - 3(N+1) = \text{_____}$$

How many degrees of freedom are there in this study? _____. Check the observed value of H against that shown in the Chi-square distribution table (table 7, appendix C). What is the critical value required to reject the H_o? _____. Can you reject the H_o? _____

What conclusion can you draw regarding this study?

_____

_____

◇◇

As with the t-test and One-way ANOVA, we can apply a strength of association test to the value of H in Kruskal-Wallis as well. The values needed for the formula are readily available in your printout (or hand calculations).

$$\eta^2 = \frac{H}{N-1}$$

(Pretty complicated, huh?)

◇◇

Practice 11.7

1. Imagine that in the test of the acculturation hypothesis, the value of H had turned out to be 20.09 instead of .09. This result would be significant. Using the above eta^2 formula, comment on the strength of association connected with $H = 20.09$.

_____

_____

◇◇

Nonparametric Tests for Locating Differences Among Means

The Kruskal-Wallis test, like ANOVA, allows us to determine whether there are significant differences between groups. When significant differences are found, we need other tests to determine the precise location of the differences. The Ryan procedure is used as a follow-up when overall differences are found using Kruskal-Wallis. We present the formula for the procedure here since there is only one nonparametric range test and because it may not be readily available in other references.

As with Scheffé or other multiple-range tests used with One-way ANOVA, it is *not* appropriate to use a Ryan procedure unless there is a significant difference among the groups compared in the Kruskal-Wallis.

Ryan Procedure for Ordered Data

The way the Ryan procedure works is to order the medians of the groups. Then the procedure computes a series of Rank sums tests, testing them against a tabled value of Z whose value is determined by three things: (1) the selected α for rejecting the H_o, (2) the number of groups (i.e., the number of levels of the independent variable) designated as "a," and (3) "d," which will be explained in a moment. If the value for the Ryan procedure turns out to exceed the table value for any of the differences between individual groups, the difference is significant at the .05 level.

As an example, let's assume that you decided to replicate the Riggenbach and Lazaraton study the following quarter. You revised the tasks which made up the composite score and feel that you may be able to show differences across the four levels. You run the Kruskal-Wallis and find that, indeed, a significant difference does exist across the levels. The question, now, is to locate precisely where the difference(s) lies. To do this, you apply the Ryan procedure. The procedure begins by assigning a rank-order number to the scores. The individual with the lowest score receives a 1, the next lowest a 2, and so forth. Here are the fictitious data in rank orders.

	Level 1	Level 2	Level 3	Level 4
	1	2	4	13
	3	8	17	17
	5	9	19	21
	6	12	22	23
	7	18	26	25
	10	20	29	32
	11	24	30	35
	14	28	34	38
	15	31	36	39
	16	33	37	40
Total	88	185	254	283
Median	8.5	19	27.5	28.5

Now let's work through the steps needed to locate the significant differences.

Step 1
First, in the column labeled a in table 6, appendix C, find the number of groups for your study. Then, for the selected α (the level of significance you have chosen), find the value of Z for each value of $d - 1$. The symbol d stands for the number of ordered levels spanned in the comparison. Since we have four groups we want first to compare the lowest and highest group. Level 1 has the lowest score and level 4 the highest. The span compared is four levels. So $d = 4$ and $d - 1 = 3$. The critical level of Z for 3 df in table 6 is 2.64. When we compare level 1 and level 3, the span is 3 levels, so $d - 1 = 2$ and the critical level of Z for 2 df is 2.50. Comparing the lowest level 1 with level 2 is a span of 2, so

$d - 1 = 1$, and the critical value of Z is 2.24. These critical values work for any data with the specified number of groups.

Step 2
If there are four or more groups, we can prepare a special table that will let us summarize the comparisons. To do this, compute the median for each group and arrange them in terms of increasing magnitude of the median both across the top and down the side of the table.

	Gp 1 8.5	Gp 2 19	Gp 3 27.5	Gp 4 28.5	d	d − 1	Z crit
Gp 1 (8.5)		X	X	X			
					4	3	±2.64
Gp 2 (19)			X	X			
					3	2	±2.50
Gp 3 (27.5)				X			
					2	1	±2.24
Gp 4 (28.5)							

Step 3
Compute a Rank sums test for each pair of medians indicated on the table (each X). If you have forgotten how to do this, review chapter 10. Since we are comparing two groups each time, we use only the data from the two groups being compared. We start with the two ranks that are the most different--level 1 and Level 4. First, rerank the two levels in relation to each other. The resulting ranks will be from 1 to 20 since only these two are being compared.

> Level 1 has ranks 1, 2, 3, 4, 5, 6, 7, 9, 10, 11.
> Level 4 has ranks 8, 12, 13, 14, 15, 16, 17, 18, 19, 20
> The total of ranks for level 1 is 58. This is T_i - the lowest level.
> The total of ranks for level 4 is 152.

The Rank sums test for this comparison is:

$$Z = \frac{2T_i - n_i(N + 1)}{\sqrt{\frac{n_1 n_2(N + 1)}{3}}}$$

$$Z = \frac{2(58) - 10(21)}{\sqrt{\frac{(10)(10)(21)}{3}}} = -3.55$$

The 2 and 3 in the formula are constants (i.e., they are part of the formula; they do not come from the data). The Z value is greater than 2.64 (for $\alpha = .05$, $d - 1 = 3$). Therefore, we can conclude that levels 1 and 4 differ significantly from each other. The scores for group 4 are significantly higher than those of group 1.

Now, let's compare level 1 and level 3. Levels 1 and 3 are the next most different across the range. Again, rerank the data for level 1 and level 3 in relation to each other.

> Level 1 has ranks of 1, 2, 4, 5, 6, 7, 8, 9, 10, 11.
> Level 3 has ranks of 3, 12, 13, 14, 15, 16, 17, 18, 19, 20.
> Total of ranks for level 1 = 63.
> Total of ranks for level 3 = 147.

Now we can compute the Rank sums test for this data. Make sure you understand where each number in the formula comes from.

$$Z = \frac{2(63) - 10(21)}{\sqrt{\frac{(10)(10)(21)}{3}}} = -3.17$$

The value of Z critical for $\alpha = .05$ and $d - 1 = 2$ is 2.50. We can reject the null hypothesis of no difference between the medians of these two groups. We can conclude that levels 1 and 3 are significantly different. The scores in level 3 are significantly higher than those in level 1.

◇◇◇◇◇◇◇◇◇◇◇◇◇◇◇◇◇◇◇◇◇◇◇◇◇◇◇◇◇◇◇◇◇◇◇◇◇◇

Practice 11.8

▶ 1. The Z critical for the level 1 vs. level 2 comparison is 2.24. Compute Z. Can you reject the null hypothesis of no difference between level 1 and level 2? Why (not)? What conclusion can you draw? _____

_____

_____

▶ 2. Do the comparisons between levels 2 and 3, 2 and 4, and 3 and 4 for the data above. Interpret your findings. _____

_____

_____

_____

_____

◇◇◇◇◇◇◇◇◇◇◇◇◇◇◇◇◇◇◇◇◇◇◇◇◇◇◇◇◇◇◇◇◇◇◇◇◇◇

To review, there are a variety of multiple-range tests that can be applied when a One-way ANOVA is significant that will allow us to pinpoint precisely where the differences are. The Ryan procedure can be used for this same purpose when a nonparametric Kruskal-Wallis shows significant differences in comparing the performance of groups.

Activities

1. In the H. Riggenbach & A. Lazaraton study (1987. A task-based approach to oral proficiency testing. Unpublished UCLA ESL Service Course research report, UCLA.) the researchers also included an imitation task designed by Henning (1981). In this test, the Ss were asked to repeat longer and longer utterances. A possible score of 70 could be obtained on the test. Ss from three different levels (low intermediate, high intermediate, and advanced) took the test. Here are the $\bar{X}$s and s.d.s for the three groups:

Group	Count	Mean	Std.Dev.
Gp 1	17	45.9706	13.4812
Gp 2	17	52.1176	11.6827
Gp 3	17	59.7941	13.5314
Total	51	52.6275	12.8984

From this information, what statistical procedure would you use? Why?

Here is the ANOVA printout from this study:

Source	D.F.	SS	MS	F ratio	Prob.
Between-Gps	2	1633.8922	815.4461	5.2022	.0090
Within-Gps	48	7524.0294	156.7506		
Total	50	9154.9216			

① are sig. differences across 3 groups because prob for F ratio is < .05

not on exam Scheffé Post Hoc Comparisons Table

② Look at mean scores gr 1 doing poorest

Groups	Mean	Mean
1 vs 3	59.794	45.971*
1 vs 2	59.794	52.118
2 vs 3	52.118	45.971

* p < .05

Interpret the tables. What conclusions could you legitimately draw from the analysis? If you were asked to review this study for *Language Learning*, what suggestions would you make to the authors? Explain why your options would improve the study.

2. M. Ghadessy (1988. Testing the perception of the paralinguistic features of spoken English. *IRAL, 26*, 1, 52-61.) gave a listening test to 307 Ss at the National University of Singapore. The students listened to a voice saying a statement such as "Come up and see me sometime" as they read the statement. To test their perception of the suprasegmental features overlaying the spoken utterance, Ss then selected one of four possible completions such as (a) she said gratingly, (b) she said huskily, (c) shrieked the miserable woman, (d) said Mary sternly. A

One-way ANOVA was done to see if L1 group made a difference in perception of paralinguistic features. The means of the five groups were:

Group	Mean
Chinese	11.50
Malay	11.76
Tamil	12.14
English	12.21
Other	12.50

The difference in means for the groups was not significant at the .05 level. That is, the groups did not perform differently. Imagine that you believe that Ss from all language groups are equally able to interpret the meanings of speakers' paralinguistic features. Therefore, you are not surprised at this lack of difference among the various L1 groups. To test this hypothesis, you might wish to replicate this study but with Ss from other language backgrounds. How might you design the study in such a way that it would be possible to combine your results with that of the 307 Ss in this study? If you were to replicate the study but could not obtain access to the tapes used in the experiment, what changes might you make in redesigning the study?

3. L. Goldstein (1987. Standard English: the only target for nonnative speakers of English? *TESOL Quarterly, 21,* 3, 417-436.) examined the implicit unstated assumption of much of SLA research that there is a homogeneous, standard-English-speaking target language group which nonnative speakers come in contact with. In particular, Goldstein looked at the language use and attitudes of 28 Hispanic boys who were exposed to Black English in the New York City area. Data were collected via interviews and test measures. Linguistic data came from the former; two linguistic variables were isolated: negative concord within the clause (e.g., "I don't have none") and distributive *be* (e.g., "I be here"). Negative concord was quantified as the number of times it occurred divided by the number of times it could have occurred while distributive *be* was tabulated as the number of times it occurred. These two linguistic phenomena became dependent variables. Two independent variables were examined: (1) extent of black contact-- extensive ($n = 4$), medium ($n = 6$), limited ($n = 8$), and none ($n = 10$), (2) reference group--black ($n = 5$), white ($n = 23$). One-way ANOVAs were run for the linguistic variables to see if differences among the $\overline{X}$s of the four levels of "extent of contact" groupings were significant. The following two tables are presented:

Negative Concord and Extent of Black Contact

Source	SS	df	MS	F
Between	11836.97	3	3945.66	3.32*
Within	28542.04	24	1189.25	

$p < .05$

Distributive Be and Extent of Black Contact				
Source	SS	df	MS	F
Between	14.803	3	7.321	25.54*
Within	7.162	24	.298	

$p < .01$

Based on the statistical analyses and an examination of data from individual Ss, the author concluded that extent of contact is a necessary but not sufficient condition for acquisition of these two linguistic forms. Which strength of association test should be used (ω^2 or η^2)? What is the strength of association? What statistical procedure could be used to check for the effect of the second independent variable, reference group, on these two linguistic forms? What strength of association test would you use in that case?

References

Henning, G. 1981. Oral proficiency testing: comparative validities of interview, imitation, and completion methods. *Language Learning, 33,* 3, 315-322.

Kirk, R. E. 1982. *Experimental Design: Procedures for the Behavioral Sciences.* Second edition. Belmont, CA: Brooks Cole.

McMeans, S. 1986. Metacognition and reading: a study of second graders in the Culver City Spanish immersion program. Unpublished master's thesis, UCLA.

Schumann, J. 1978. The acculturation model of second language acquisition. In R. Gringas (Ed.). *Second Language Acquisition and Foreign Language Teaching.* Arlington, VA: Center for Applied Linguistics.

Wike, E. L. 1971. *Data Analysis: A Statistical Primer for Psychologists.* Chicago, IL: Aldine-Atherton.

Chapter 12

Repeated-Measures Comparison of Three or More Groups

- *Parametric comparisons: Repeated-measures one-way ANOVA*
  Interpreting the F ratio
  eta² for repeated-measures
- *Nonparametric comparisons: Friedman test*
  Strength of association: eta²
  Nemenyi's test

In the previous chapter we compared the performance of three or more groups when the data came from *different* data sources. That is, data from different Ss appeared in each group. The comparison was *between* groups. In this chapter we will compare three or more groups when the data are taken from the *same* data source. That is, data are taken from the same Ss at different points in time or on a set of different tasks at one time. The data are not independent.

As in the previous chapter, we will begin with the parametric procedure and then move to the nonparametric equivalent.

Parametric Comparisons: Repeated-Measures One-way ANOVA

We can compare the $\overline{X}$s drawn from the same Ss on several different measures (or the same measure at several different times) using a modified ANOVA procedure. The data must meet the assumptions of ANOVA (just as in the last chapter). These assumptions include:

1. There is one dependent variable and one independent variable with three or more levels.

2. The data are from the same Ss (repeated-measures).

3. The data have been measured as ordinal scales or interval scores (continuous measurement). The distribution of data in the ordinal scales is appropriately captured by $\overline{X}$ and variance.

4. Scores in each sample are distributed such that $\overline{X}$ and variance are appropriate measures to use in the analysis.

5. The data in the population from which the samples were drawn is normally distributed with equal variances.

6. The design is balanced (if calculations are done by hand).

7. There is a minimum of five observations per cell (and more is better).

8. The *F* statistic allows us to reject or accept the null hypothesis. If there is a statistically significant difference in the samples, it does not pinpoint precisely where that difference lies. (We will deal with this later.)

The regular ANOVA procedure will have to be modified. This is because *Xbars* taken from the same *S*s will resemble each other more than those taken from different *S*s.

Let's use an example and work through the amended procedure. Irujo (1986) has written a report on the acquisition of idioms. Imagine that we, too, plan to carry out research on idioms in a second language. As part of this research, we first wish to replicate Irujo's study to see whether *S*s would perform differently with three types of idioms. The idioms Irujo selected were those identical to idioms in Spanish, similar to those in Spanish, or completely different from Spanish idioms. One of the measures used was a multiple-choice task where native speakers of Spanish selected the appropriate paraphrase of an idiom. Here are the $\overline{X}$ and *s* for each of these three subgroups of idiom type in Irujo's data:

Idiom Type	*Multiple-Choice Task*
Identical	
Mean	14.58
SD	0.79
Similar	
Mean	14.67
SD	0.65
Different	
Mean	12.25
SD	2.01

$$F (2, 22) = 15.45 \ (p < .001)$$

Note that the numerical difference among the means does not appear to be great. Remember, though, that we expect the same *S*s to perform more similarly on different tasks than would different *S*s. Also note the differences in spread of scores (*SD* is used here as the abbreviation instead of *s*) for the three idiom types. This difference in variability from the $\overline{X}$ for the three measures should seem reasonable. Less variability would be expected for identical and similar idioms: the problem arises when idioms are different. Notice the two numbers in parentheses following *F*. These indicate the number of degrees of freedom. The first number refers to the number of levels of the independent variable. For regular one-way ANOVA, this would be the number of groups; for Repeated-measures ANOVA it is the number of tasks or times data were collected. Since here each *S* had a score for three different types of idioms, there were three tasks and, therefore, 2 *df*. Don't worry now about how the second number was obtained. (If you can guess, that's fine.) The probability reported for the *F* value tells us that we can have great confidence that there is a statistical difference somewhere in the data (though we still have not located precisely which pairs of $\overline{X}$ values differ from each other). If you had read the abstract of this article and then interpreted the table, you would now be ready to read the total article, checking your predictions against the author's interpretations.

We don't have the actual data so we cannot rerun the analysis using a one-way ANOVA with repeated-measures. However, let's use some fictitious data. Let's imagine that we carried out a replication study using the second of Irujo's tasks. Twelve randomly selected *S*s (the same *n* size as in the original study) were asked to give a definition for idioms which were classified in the same way (as identical, similar, or different from those in the L1). Each student received a score for the number of correct definitions.

As always, we begin with stating the H_o.

> *There is no difference in accuracy of definitions given by Ss to three types of idioms (which vary in similarity to idioms in the L1).*

The study is a replication study (using the same materials as those in the original study and with *S*s from the same L1 group); we will select an .05 level of significance for rejecting the H_o. While the study replicates Irujo's original research in most ways, the proficiency level of the *S*s is different. Irujo's *S*s were "advanced" learners and our *S*s are randomly selected low-intermediate *S*s. This is a replication study, but one thing has been changed. Would you argue for a two-tailed test of significance rather than a one-tailed test? This is a choice the researcher needs to justify; there are no strict guidelines that bind you to one or the other. We would argue for (but not insist on) a two-tailed hypothesis on the basis that the *S*s are quite different and we would need a two-tailed .05 (.025 from each tail) to feel confident that we do not err in rejecting or accepting the null hypothesis.

We would like a large sample size and balanced design to be sure we don't violate the assumptions of normal distribution and equal variances. However, since the test is fairly robust when the design is balanced, it will certainly make our computations easier if we use a small *n* to illustrate the procedure.

Whatever our findings, we want to expand the population to which Irujo's description might apply. The characteristics of the population covered by the original study and this replication are alike in terms of L1 and *n* size. Proficiency level differs. Obviously we still will not be able to generalize the findings beyond the population from which *S*s in the two studies were drawn. That is, we cannot make claims about L1 and L2 idioms for other ESL groups. Further replications with other L1 and L2 groups would enlarge the scope of generalizability.

Here are the data:

S	Identical	Similar	Different	Total	n
1	13	10	8	31	3
2	12	10	6	28	3
3	14	11	5	30	3
4	12	9	6	27	3
5	14	8	8	30	3
6	12	8	3	23	3
7	14	11	4	29	3
8	12	10	6	28	3
9	9	9	3	21	3
10	13	10	7	30	3
11	14	8	5	27	3
12	12	10	9	31	3
Totals	151	114	70	$G = 335$	
	(12)	(12)	(12)		$(N = 36)$

The first step in carrying out the procedure is to arrange the information above in a way that will give you the information that you will need for ANOVA. After the three data columns, there is a column marked "Total"; this is the total score for each S. So, for example, S1 had scores of 13 + 10 + 8 for a total score of 31.

Second, we added all the scores in the column labeled "Identical," (13 + 12 + 14 + 12, etc.) and placed the total at the bottom of the column. Let's label this column total T_{A1}. The "subscript A" shows that this is a total for a group (remember "A" and "K" are often used to represent groups with "A" more commonly used for within-group levels), in this case the first group, "Identical Idiom." We can label the totals of the other two columns as T_{A2} and T_{A3}.

To help keep the n figures straight, we put a number 3 next to the individual total scores (the total at the far right) for each S. This is n_S. We could also place a number 12 in parentheses at the bottom of each column to show the total number of scores in this direction too. This is n_A.

This starts us with step 1 in the ANOVA process.

Step 1
Find T_{A1}, T_{A2}, T_{A3}.
We have already done this and entered the totals at the bottom of the columns. $T_{A1} = 151$, $T_{A2} = 114$, $T_{A3} = 70$. The n for number of observations in each sample is 12.

Step 2
Find $T_{S1}, T_{S2}, T_{S3} \dots T_{Sn}$.

We have already done this too. By adding the scores of the first S on the three measures, we have T_{S1}. The little subscript S shows the totals are for Ss rather than for types of idioms.

Find the n for number of scores. Each S has three scores, so the n_S is 3.

Step 3
Find G. Sum all the scores. You can do this most easily by totaling $T_{A1} + T_{A2} + T_{A3}$. $G = 335$.

At this point you could "check" if you like to be sure G is correct by adding each S's total score (in the far right column) and see if the two figures for G are identical. Fortunately, they are. If they were not, this would be the place to stop and recheck the calculations.

Find N. Count the total number of scores. This number is N. We have recorded it in parentheses next to the figure for G on the data chart. $N = 36$.

Step 4
Find $G^2 \div N$.
To do this step, we square G and divide this value by N. $G^2 = 112225$ and $G^2 \div N = 3117.36$.

Step 5
Find $\sum X^2$.
To do this, we square each raw score and sum these squared values.

$$13^2 + 10^2 + 8^2 + 12^2 + 10^2 \ldots + 9^2 = 3469$$

Step 6
Find SST.

$$SST = \sum X^2 - \frac{G^2}{N}$$

This is easy since it asks us to subtract the results of step 4 from step 5. The answer is 351.64. This number must be positive. $G^2 \div N$ must be smaller than or equal to $\sum X^2$. This is a check to make sure everything is okay so far. If the number is negative, you should stop and find your error.

Step 7
Find $[\sum_{A=1}^{a} T_A^2] \div n_A$.

To do this, we first square each of the column totals and then sum these three squared values.

$$T_{A1}^2 + T_{A2}^2 + T_{A3}^2 = 40697$$

And, now, divide this by the number of scores in each column (i.e., 12). The answer should be 3391.42.

$$\frac{40697}{12} = 3391.42$$

Step 8
Find SS_A. This is the sum of squares between the groups (SSB).

$$SS_A = [\sum_{A=1}^{a} T_A^2] \div n_A - \frac{G^2}{N}$$

To do this subtract the result of step 4 from that of step 7.

$$SS_A = 3391.42 - 3117.36 = 274.06$$

The $SS_A = 274.06$.

Step 9
Find:

$$\sum_{S=1}^{s} \frac{T_S^2}{n_s}$$

To do this, we first square each of the total scores for each individual subject and sum them.

$$31^2 + 28^2 + 30^2 + \cdots + 31^2 = 9459$$

Then we divide by the number of scores for each S which in this case is 3.

$$9459 \div 3 = 3153$$

Step 10
Find SS_S. This is the sum of squares within (SSW).

$$SS_S = \sum_{S=1}^{s} T_S^2 \div n_s - \frac{G^2}{N}$$

To find SS_S, subtract the figure found in step 4 from the figure found in step 9.

$$3153 - 3117.36 = 35.64$$

Step 11
Find $SS_{AS} = SS_{Total} - SS_A - SS_S$. This is the sum of squares for the interaction of types of idioms and subjects (SS_{BW}).

Subtract the resulting figures: step 6 minus step 8 minus step 10.

$$351.64 - 274.05 - 35.64 = 41.94$$

Now let's stop and see how these computations fit into an ANOVA table.

Here is the ANOVA table for our study.

One-way ANOVA with Repeated-Measures

Source	df	SS	MS	F
Idiom Type (A)	2	274.06	137.03	71.74
Subjects (S)	11	35.64		
Types X Subjects (A X S)	22	41.94	1.91	
Total	35	351.64		

The first column in the ANOVA table identifies the variables: idiom type, subjects, and the interaction. The interaction is read as a "types by subject interaction" with X used as the symbol for *by*.

The next column gives the degrees of freedom. The *df* for idiom type is easy. There were three types, so $3 - 1 = 2df$. There were 12 Ss, so the *df* for Ss is $12 - 1 = 11$. Next, you will find the *df* for the interaction. The *df* for interaction are $(a - 1) \times (s - 1)$. The symbol *a* is for the number of levels of the independent variable *idiom type*. There were three types, so $a - 1 = 2$. The symbol *s* is for the *subject* variable. There were 12 Ss, so $s - 1 = 11$. The total *df* for the interaction, therefore, is $2 \times 11 = 22$. (If you had problems understanding the (2, 22) figures in the Irujo study, the source of both these figures should now be clear.)

The figures that go in the SS column are the answers to the computation steps we've just completed. Step 8 gave us the sum of squares for types, SS_A. Step 10 gave us the sum of squares for subjects, SS_S. Step 11 is SS_{AS}. We have inserted each of these values into the above table. The SST value found in step 6 goes in the total row of the SS column.

The MS column was completed as follows. The *df* for type of idiom is 2, so we can divide the SS for type of idiom by 2. The answer is 137.03. The MS value for type by Ss can be obtained by dividing the SS_{AS} by 22. The answer is 1.91.

You will notice that we have not computed the MS for subjects. In ordinary ANOVA we expect Ss to differ from each other and so the MSW figure is used to determine the *F* ratio. In Repeated-measures ANOVA this is not the case. We are not interested in how Ss differ from each other, but in how *each S* differs on the repeated-measures. So, the *F* ratio is found by dividing MSB by MS_{BW}.

The final step in computing the *F* ratio is step 12.

Step 12
To find the F ratio, we divide: $MS_A \div MS_{AS}$. These figures are in the summary table. The *F* ratio is 71.74.

Now, as always, we place this value in a distribution of F ratios with the same df. Since the F ratio in this one-way Repeated-measures ANOVA is computed by dividing the MS for idiom type (A) by the MS of the interaction (AS), the two df we must consult are those for type (2) and for the interaction (22). The F distribution table is used for both between-groups and within-group designs. The repeated-measures ANOVA formula yields an F ratio which has the same distribution properties as that for between-groups designs. In the F distribution table (table 5, appendix C), find the intersection of 2 and 22 df. If the obtained F ratio is larger than the critical value given in the table, we can reject the H_o. We must choose between .05 or .01 levels of probability. Prior to the study, we selected .05 as our critical level, so $F_{crit} = 3.44$. We can reject the H_o because our F_{obs} is greater than F_{crit}.

After all this work, we would hope that there would be space in the report to include not only the $\overline{X}$ and s for each idiom type but the ANOVA table as well. However, all this information might be summarized in the statement: $F = 71.74$ (2, 22), $p < .05$.

◇◇

Practice 12.1

1. How will you interpret the findings? Do they support those reported by Irujo? Can you enlarge the descriptive scope of the original study? And the population to which the findings might generalize? Why (not)? _____

_____

_____

2. A parametric ANOVA was chosen for this study because the data were *scores*. Do you believe the data met the other requirements for using ANOVA? Why (not)? _____

_____

3. ANOVA is reputed to be quite "robust" to violations of the assumptions on which it is based, particularly that of normal distribution and equal variance. That is, if there is a violation of this assumption and you find you can reject the H_o at the .05 level, the actual probability may not be far off. It might be in the .07 or .09 range. Would it concern you if you rejected the H_o at the .05 level and then found there really were 7 or 9 chances (rather than 5) in 100 that you are wrong in rejecting the H_o? Why (not)? _____

_____

_____

4. A study of reading scores of students on five tests reported an F (4, 116) = 1.036 (p = n.s.). Explain the numbers 4, 116. How would you interpret the F ratio?

_____

_____

_____

▶ 5. Imagine you teach three classes of 15 students each. They are different sections of the same class, so Ss are assumed to be at the same level of proficiency. You want to see which reading lessons have the most beneficial effect on biweekly reading quizzes. The first week you work on scanning, then skimming, reading for the main idea, prereading skills, and finally guessing vocabulary from context. You randomly select 9 Ss from the classes. The test results are listed below. Do a one-way ANOVA with repeated-measures.

Fictitious Reading Test Scores

Week	2	4	6	8	10
S1	24	29	33	42	37
S2	25	27	36	44	43
S3	28	38	29	47	48
S4	21	26	34	30	39
S5	27	22	31	40	35
S6	26	27	45	36	46
S7	10	18	20	21	31
S8	34	36	39	50	41
S9	49	42	53	52	64

Show your calculations below. Can you reject the H_o? How would you interpret the results?

_____
_____
_____
_____
_____

◇◇

Interpreting the F Ratio

The F ratio allows us to reject or accept the null hypothesis. If the F ratio is statistically significant we know that the means that have been compared are significantly different. However, it does not allow us to locate the difference precisely. If a researcher compares group performance at five different time periods and obtains a statistically significant difference, it is possible that the difference might be between time 1 + 2 vs. 3 + 4 + 5, between time 1 + 2 + 3 vs. time 4 vs. time 5, or many other possible combinations. In order to pinpoint the location of the difference, the researcher can use a multiple-range test. Again, the Scheffé, Tukey, Newman-Keuls are commonly used for this purpose. We ask that you consult a computer manual for more details on the actual statistics for these tests. However, for reading practice, we have included a SAS printout showing a multiple-range comparison for the data in practice 12.1.5.

Scheffé Test for Comparison of Means

Minimum significant difference = 6.86.
Means with the same letter are not significantly different.

Scheffé	Grouping	Mean	N	Week
	A	42.667	9	5
B	A	40.222	9	4
B	C	35.556	9	3
D	C	29.444	9	2
D		27.111	9	1

The table shows that performance at week 5 is better than for weeks 1, 2, and 3 (but not week 4). Performance at week 4 differs from that at weeks 1 and 2 (but not weeks 3 and 5). There is no difference between weeks 3 and 2, but week 3 is higher than week 1. There is no difference between weeks 1 and 2.

The ANOVA showed that student performance varies across the testing periods and the Scheffé shows that the difference is statistically significant only between certain time periods. The differences, however, are not distinct between adjoining weeks. Rather, there is an overlap, so that performance levels at weeks 1 and 2 are not different, weeks 2 and 3 are not different, weeks 3 and 4 are not different, and 4 and 5 are not different. This makes it difficult to make a connection between the specific skill taught and test performance. Even if there were significant differences week by week, we could not claim a causal relationship between specific skill instruction and test score improvement. If we wanted to check to see if weeks 4 + 5 differ from weeks 1 + 2 + 3, we could do another Scheffé to make this comparison. If the result were significant, we might be able to show that the treatment needs three weeks before it "takes effect." Otherwise, the scores may increase simply due to more practice time (no matter what the type of practice). To provide a strong link between instruction and skill improvement, we would need to redesign the study with appropriate control groups.

In this study, we first found a significant F ratio using ANOVA. We then turned to the Scheffé to show us where the differences were located. There is, however, a strange phenomenon that sometimes occurs. The F ratio is statistically significant, but when other multiple-range tests (e.g., Duncan or Tukey) are run, some of them do and some do not locate significant differences among the levels. This occurs because some multiple-range tests are more "conservative" than others. The Scheffé is notoriously "conservative"--that is, it is more demanding than some of the other multiple-range procedures in locating statistically significant differences among means. It's unlikely that it would ever allow you to err in rejecting the null hypothesis. If you run several multiple-range tests and they do not agree, please discuss this issue with your advisor or statistical consultant so that your interpretation is well-informed.

eta² for Repeated-Measures

It is not possible to use the omega² strength of association test with Repeated-measures ANOVA. Instead, we use a special eta² formula to test the degree of association between the variables. (This special formula can also be used for between-groups comparisons with unbalanced designs.) The formula for eta² in Repeated-measures ANOVA is:

$$\eta^2 = \frac{SS_x}{SST}$$

The formula just says to take the sum of squares of the factor you are interested in and divide by the sum of squares total. For the reading study mentioned in practice 12.1.5, eta² would be:

$$\eta^2 = \frac{SS \text{ types}}{SST}$$

$$\eta^2 = \frac{1615.11}{5220}$$

$$\eta^2 = .309$$

The relationship shows that 31% of the variability in the exam has been accounted for (in these data) by the five different reading lessons. This is a healthy relationship (with real data the association would not likely be this high).

If you used omega² as the strength of association measure with these data, you would obtain a lower association; omega² gives a more conservative estimate than eta². However, with repeated-measures or unbalanced designs, remember to use the appropriate test of association--eta².

◇◇◇◇◇◇◇◇◇◇◇◇◇◇◇◇◇◇◇◇◇◇◇◇◇◇◇◇◇◇◇◇◇◇◇◇◇

Practice 12.2

▶1. For the Irujo replication on page 347, calculate eta² for idiom type.
eta ² = _____ .
Interpretation: _____

_____

_____

_____

◇◇◇◇◇◇◇◇◇◇◇◇◇◇◇◇◇◇◇◇◇◇◇◇◇◇◇◇◇◇◇◇◇◇◇◇◇

Nonparametric Comparisons: Friedman Test

If you cannot meet all the assumptions of ANOVA (whether for descriptive or inferential purposes), then you would be better served by a nonparametric test such as the Friedman. The Kruskal-Wallis test parallels one-way ANOVA where the comparisons are *between* groups. A parallel nonparametric test for a Repeated-measures ANOVA is the Friedman test.

There are some cautions to remember when using the Friedman test. With three levels, you need at least 10 observations per group. With four levels, you need at least 5 per group. Let's work through the formula, now, with an example that meets this requirement.

One of the objectives in an advanced ESL composition class was that of persuasive discourse. The ESL teacher decided to use a current topic which concerns both teachers and students--whether separate, special composition classes for ESL students should be offered for this advanced level. So, the topic for the persuasive discourse unit was whether nonnative speakers of English should take this advanced course with native speakers in a regular English class or whether it should be offered as an ESL course. The students first discussed the issue and then voted to show their opinion of taking the course in the regular English program. The vote is on a 7-point scale. Second, the students read a short article in the campus newspaper which argued that nonnative speakers would be better served taking a course especially geared to their needs. A second vote was taken at this point. Next, a foreign student graduate working at IBM came to the class and argued forcefully for taking the course with native speakers. A third vote was taken. Finally, the students listened as the teachers of the two courses went over the course syllabi for the regular English class and the ESL class. A final vote was taken. The research question is whether the votes remained constant over time (impervious to persuasion) or changed according to the arguments presented at each time period.

Research hypothesis? There is no difference in votes due to type of persuasion (e.g., vote $1 = 2 = 3 = 4$).
    Significance level? .05
    1- or 2-tailed? 2-tailed
Design
    Dependent variable(s)? Votes
    Measurement? 7-point scale
    Independent variable(s)? Persuasive argument
    Measurement? Nominal--4 levels (discussion, news article, guest speaker, syllabi)
    Independent or repeated-measures? Repeated-measures
Other features? Intact group
Statistical procedure? Friedman

The data are displayed in the table below. The first column identifies the *S*. At time 1, *S*1 gave a vote of 5 on the 7-point scale; at time 2, *S*1 gave a vote of 2; at time 3 a 4; and at time 4, a vote of 1. This *S*s lowest vote was a 1 and so it is assigned a rank of 1; the next lowest was the vote at time 2, so this is ranked 2. The next rank is for time 3 with a vote of 4, and the highest rank is for time 1 with a vote of 5. Thus, there is a rank order within each *S*'s votes. The ranks are across each *row*, not down each column.

S	Time 1 Score	Rank	Time 2 Score	Rank	Time 3 Score	Rank	Time 4 Score	Rank
1	5	4	2	2	4	3	1	1
2	6	4	4	2	5	3	2	1
3	7	4	3	2.5	3	2.5	2	1
4	7	4	4	2	5	3	3	1
5	6	3.5	5	2	6	3.5	2	1
6	4	1	5	2.5	5	2.5	6	4
7	5	3	4	1.5	6	4	4	1.5
8	7	3.5	6	2	7	3.5	3	1
9	6	3.5	5	2	6	3.5	3	1

$$T1 = 30.5 \qquad T2 = 18.5 \qquad T3 = 28.5 \qquad T4 = 12.5$$

The Friedman formula doesn't start with "Friedman equals." Rather it starts with "Chi-square of ranks" (χ^2_R), perhaps because the distribution table to be used is the Chi-square table. We will present the Friedman formula as a series of steps. The numbers 12 and 3 are, again, constants in the formula.

$$\chi^2_R = \frac{12}{(a)(s)(a + 1)} \sum_{A=1}^{a} T_A^2 - 3(s)(a + 1)$$

Step 1

Sum the ranks for each time. Time 1 = 30.5, time 2 = 18.5, time 3 = 28.5, and time 4 = 12.5.

Step 2

Square each sum of ranks and total these.

$$\sum_{A=1}^{a} T_A^2 = 30.5^2 + 18.5^2 + 28.5^2 + 12.5^2$$

$$= 930.25 + 342.25 + 812.25 + 156.25$$

$$\doteq 2241$$

Step 3

Divide 12 by the number of levels (a), times number of observations per level (s), times levels plus 1 ($a + 1$).

$$\frac{12}{(a)(s)(a + 1)} = \frac{12}{4 \times 9 \times 5} = \frac{12}{180} = .066$$

Step 4
Multiply the results of steps 2 and 3.

$$\frac{12}{(a)(s)(a + 1)} \sum_{A=1}^{a} T_A^2 = .066 \times 2241 = 147.9$$

Step 5
Compute 3 times s, the number of observations per level, times $a + 1$, the number of levels plus 1.

$$3(s)(a + 1) = 3(9)(5) = 135$$

Step 6
Subtract the result of step 5 from that of step 4.

$$\chi_R^2 = 147.9 - 135 = 12.91$$

Now that we have the value of χ^2, we can check the critical value needed for the appropriate degrees of freedom in the Chi-square distribution table (table 7 in appendix C). This time, the df is the number of *levels* minus 1. In this study the number of levels was 4, so the degrees of freedom for the study is $4 - 1 = 3$. Since we have selected an α of .05, and our df is 3, we look at the intersection of column 2 and row 3 to find the critical value.

χ^2 critical for 3 df is 7.81. We can reject the H_o and conclude that Ss' ratings did change over time as the persuasive discourse changed. We can show that the scaled votes vary from time to time and we can show, numerically, how they differed. However, we cannot say which kinds of persuasive discourse were *most effective* in influencing votes on the basis of the statistical procedure. The procedure tells us that we can feel confident about saying that the scores do, indeed, differ, and we show that confidence by displaying a simple statement: Friedman $\chi^2 = 12.91$, 3 df, $p < .05$.

Strength of Association: *eta²*

When the outcome of the Friedman allows us to reject the null hypothesis, we can then turn to a test of association to discover how strong a relationship exists. The strength of association formula for the Friedman is eta²:

$$\eta^2 = \frac{\chi_R^2}{N^* - 1}$$

In the above formula, χ_R^2 is the statistic you calculated for the Friedman. The N^* is the number of Ss times the number of observations on each S. The calculations are simple. Let's apply it to the example above:

$$\eta^2 = \frac{\chi_R^2}{N^* - 1}$$

$$\eta^2 = \frac{12.91}{(9 \times 4) - 1}$$

$$\eta^2 = .37$$

While the Friedman test told us that votes did change over time as the persuasive discourse changed, eta² tells us that the strength of association between persuasive arguments and voting behavior for these data was really quite strong (we should be pleased). We've made an excellent start in understanding the relationship between persuasion and voting behavior on this issue. However, persuasion alone doesn't cover all the variability in the data. "Error" (normal variability in performance *and* that due to other variables yet to be researched) is still large. That should suggest redesigning the study to include other variables to see if we *can* enlarge our view as to what influences attitudes (expressed as votes) on the issue of separating or integrating native speakers and nonnative speakers in composition courses.

Practice 12.3

1. Following this exercise, the teacher asked the students to write an explanatory essay on why different types of evidence were/weren't effective as persuasion. How might this become a new research project? What is a candidate research question? _____

_____

_____

_____

▶ 2. For the problem below, please compute the value of χ_R^2. We will give you the answer based on a computer run of the same data. Carry out the calculations and see whether the computer gives you exactly the same values.

People often say that immediate feedback is valuable for correcting errors. We wondered if perhaps such feedback might simply make people more anxious (and thus lead to more error). To test this, we gave three different computer assignments, each of which had two parts. For the first assignment, we sat beside students and each time they were about to make an error, we stopped the Ss and explained what was wrong. In the second assignment, we sat beside students and helped to correct errors after they occurred. In the third assignment, we let the students get error messages from the computer after they ran the program. Each of these assignments had a second part where the Ss did a similar problem on their own. There were 10 possible errors in each exercise. A perfect score would be 0 and a score of 10 would show that every possible error occurred. These scores became the data for the study.

Research hypothesis? _____

Research hypothesis? _____

    Significance level? _____

    1- or 2-tailed? _____

Design

    Dependent variable(s)? _____

    Measurement? _____

    Independent variable(s)? _____

    Measurement? _____

      Independent or repeated-measures? _____

Other features? _____

Statistical procedure? _____

The data are from 18 Ss.

S	T1	T2	T3
1	2	6	4
2	4	6	2
3	3	9	6
4	1	2	3
5	3	1	2
6	6	9	3
7	9	8	7
8	1	3	2
9	3	1	2
10	4	2	3
11	2	3	1
12	2	3	1
13	3	2	1
14	2	3	1
15	5	5	2
16	3	2	1
17	6	4	2
18	2	3	1
Totals	____	____	____

Place your calculations in the space provided below. (*Warning*: Remember that this time, the best score is the low score. The worst possible score is a 10. If there were someone with a score of 10, they would receive the rank of 1.)

Here is the computer output (using the SPSS-X program).

Friedman Test
TS   TEACHER STOPS
TC   TEACHER CORRECTS
DC   DELAYED CORRECTION

	TS	TC	DC
MEAN RANKS	1.80	1.64	2.56

CASES = 18 χ^2 = 8.583   D.F. = 2 p = .014

Did your calculation agree with the computer printout? If not, where do they differ?

_____

Interpret these findings. _____

_____

_____

▶ 3.   Calculate eta^2 and add this information to your interpretation of the findings. _____

_____

_____

◇◇◇◇◇◇◇◇◇◇◇◇◇◇◇◇◇◇◇◇◇◇◇◇◇◇◇◇◇◇◇◇◇◇◇◇

Nemenyi's Test

We have noted that there are a variety of tests (e.g., Scheffé, Tukey) that allow us to make post hoc comparisons of means following ANOVA. The Nemenyi's test allows us to accomplish the same type of post hoc comparisons following

Friedman. If the results of the Friedman allow us to reject the H_o, we may want to use Nemenyi's test to show us precisely where the differences are. We can outline the Nemenyi procedure in six steps.

Step 1
First, be sure the overall Friedman χ_R^2 statistic was significant. Determine the critical value of χ_R^2 for your selected α level. For the example on page 356 regarding change of votes in response to type of persuasion, the $\chi_R^2 = 12.91$ and the critical value is 7.81.

Step 2
Find $a(a + 1) \div 6n$
The symbol a is the number of measures in the study and n is the number of Ss. In the vote example, there were four times at which votes were taken, so $a = 4$ and $a + 1 = 5$. There were 9 Ss, so $n = 9$.

$$\frac{4(4 + 1)}{6(9)} = \frac{20}{54} = .370$$

Step 3
Multiply the result of step 1 by that of step 2. Find the square root of that value.

$$\sqrt{(\chi_R^2\alpha)\frac{a(a + 1)}{6n}}$$

$$\sqrt{(7.81)(.370)}$$

$$\sqrt{2.887}$$

$$1.70$$

This is the critical value for the data for Nemenyi.

Step 4
Compute the *mean* sum of ranks for each group. That is, divide the sum of ranks by n, the number of Ss in each measure.

$$\overline{X}_{T1} = 30.5 \div 9 = 3.39$$
$$\overline{X}_{T2} = 18.5 \div 9 = 2.05$$
$$\overline{X}_{T3} = 28.5 \div 9 = 3.17$$
$$\overline{X}_{T4} = 12.5 \div 9 = 1.39$$

Step 5
Make a table with the mean sum ranks arranged in ascending order across the top and down the sides.

	Mean T4 1.39	Mean T2 2.05	Mean T3 3.17	Mean T1 3.39
Mean T4	1.39			
Mean T2	2.05			
Mean T3	3.17			
Mean T1	3.39			

To fill in the table, list the differences in mean sum of ranks in the table that you have set up. For the above example, the differences would be:

$$3.39 - 3.17 = .12$$
$$3.39 - 2.05 = 1.34$$
$$3.17 - 2.05 = 1.12$$
$$3.39 - 1.39 = 2.00$$
$$2.05 - 1.39 = .66$$
$$3.17 - 1.39 = 1.78$$

		Mean T4 1.39	Mean T2 2.05	Mean T3 3.17	Mean T1 3.39
Mean T4	1.39	—	.66	1.78*	2.00*
Mean T2	2.05		—	1.12	1.34
Mean T3	3.17			—	.12
Mean T1	3.39				—

$$* = > 1.70$$

Step 6
Any difference between sum of ranks that exceeds the critical value (step 4) is a significant difference. 1.70 is the critical value.

$$T4 - T3 = 1.78 = > 1.70$$
$$T4 - T1 = 2.00 = > 1.70$$

Step 7
Conclude that Ss voted significantly higher after the guest speaker than after the syllabi presentation; they also voted significantly higher after the class discussion than after the syllabi presentation. Thus, the Friedman test told us that we could reject the H_o and conclude that there was a difference in how different types of persuasion affected voting outcomes. The Nemenyi test has allowed us to pinpoint more precisely where these differences occurred.

◇◇◇◇◇◇◇◇◇◇◇◇◇◇◇◇◇◇◇◇◇◇◇◇◇◇◇◇◇◇◇◇◇◇◇◇

Practice 12.4

▶ 1. For the Friedman problem in practice 12.3, perform a Nemenyi analysis. Interpret your findings.

◇◇

To summarize, there are several nonparametric tests that can be used to compare the performance of different groups or of the same group at different times. Two tests have been presented here. The Kruskal-Wallis parallels a between-groups one-way ANOVA; the Friedman can be used as the parallel of a one-way Repeated-measures ANOVA. These tests are especially valuable given the following conditions.

1. You need a test that does not depend on the shape of the population distribution.

2. You need a test that allows you to work with small sample sizes while not knowing exactly the nature of the population distribution.

3. You need a test that has samples made up of observations from several *different* populations. For example, you might say that Japanese, Egyptian, and Venezuelan Ss are all from one population--L2 learners of English. If you add native speakers of English to the comparison, it would be difficult to say they are from the same population. No parametric test can handle such data without requiring us to make unrealistic assumptions.

4. You need a test that can treat data which are in ranks as well as data whose seemingly interval scores have only the strength of ranks.

The tests presented here have the same major disadvantage as reported for tests that parallel the *t*-test. That is, they are wasteful of data. Information is lost, and the tests are not as powerful as the parametric alternatives.

Activities

1. R. W. Gibbs & R. A. G. Mueller (1988. Conversational sequences and preferences for indirect speech acts. *Discourse Processes, 11,* 1, 101-116.) had 40 Ss read different conversational sequences involving indirect requests. They examined two situations: "service encounters," where the addressee's main job is to fill requests (such as a store clerk), and "detour situations," in which the addressee's activities or plans are interrupted by the speaker. The authors asked Ss to show their preference for sequence and expected the Ss would show sequence preferences similar to those suggested by Levinson (1983). These are arranged below so that the most preferred sequence (according to Levinson) is at the top and the least preferred at the bottom.

Example Stimuli--Service Encounter

(A) prerequest   Do you have D-size batteries?
    response to prerequest   Yes, here you go.

(B) prerequest   Do you have D-size batteries?
    offer   Would you like some?
    acceptance of offer   Yes, I'd like two.
(C) prerequest   Do you have D-size batteries?
    go ahead   Yes.
    request   I'll take two.
    compliance   Here you go.

Each *S* read hypothetical situations of both service encounters and detour situations with stimuli like those above. For each situation, they selected the most appropriate sequence (A, B, or C). The stimuli for each situation differed but the sequence choices (A, B, or C) were the same.

Results showed the following mean rankings (from a Friedman test):

Service encounter:	B	1.65	$\chi_R = 24.69, \ p < .001$
	C	1.84	
	A	2.50	
Detour situation:	B	1.74	$\chi_R = 36.26, \ p < .001$
	C	1.90	
	A	2.36	

Explain the above table. (The general conclusion drawn was that conversational organization has a strong influence on people's language behavior in making indirect requests.)

The activities below are a review of tests that compare two or three (or more) groups. Look at each of the following examples and decide which statistical test you would use. Since there is no one correct answer for each item, it is important that you justify your choice.

2. H. Kinjo (1987. Oral refusals of invitations and requests in English and Japanese. *Journal of Asian Culture, 11,* 83-106.) wanted to know how native speakers and second language learners do "refusals." After you read her thesis, you decided to work out a methodology to look at refusals of requests for a favor. You waited until the very end of the term when everyone was very busy and then asked 10 randomly selected native speakers of English (5 male and 5 female) and 10 nonnative speakers (again 5 men and 5 women) for help in entering all your data on the computer. You told them you only have about 500 scores and you would like them to read these off to you while you enter them. With your trusty hidden microphone, you tape-recorded their responses. Hopefully, these all turned out to be refusals. (And of course you got permission from all 20 *S*s to use the data for the research project.) You asked two experts in intercultural communication to rank the acceptability of each refusal on a 7-point scale. Each point was carefully defined and discussed with the raters. You wonder whether these ratings will be different for native and nonnative speakers (i.e., you were not going to compare male and female respondents). What statistical procedure would you use and why?

3. After running the above analysis, you found there was no difference in ratings that could be attributed to first language of the Ss. You wondered whether your experts' ratings of appropriateness was influenced by their acceptance of differences and that this led them to judge everyone about the same. So, you decided to ask the judges to listen to the refusals once again and judge whether the refusal was "direct" or "indirect." Fortunately, the judges always agreed in their judgments so you had confidence in them. You want to know whether language background makes any difference in whether refusals were judged as direct or as indirect (you might also wonder whether the sex of the refuser might also make a difference in the (in)directness of the response, but we haven't learned how to do this yet!) What statistical procedure would you use and why?

4. In the language lab evaluation study mentioned earlier in this text, you may have noticed that all the Ss were Vietnamese refugees. Later, the teachers decided to include Khmer and Lao students in the evaluation. Since some of the tests require basic literacy skills (and only Vietnamese of these three languages uses a Roman script), they decided to look to see if the groups were equally literate in English. A reading test developed at the camp was used to measure reading skill. It is difficult to get a feel for how "interval" the data might be. Not being confident about the test, we advised a nonparametric test. Which test would you suggest and why?

5. Differences in literacy were found among the groups in the above example. A set of lab materials were then designed that would integrate listening comprehension and literacy training. Once the materials were ready, the lab staff taught this as a new ten-week course. At the end of the course, the Lao and Khmer students were tested on the same reading test. The question was whether there would be improvement in scores for these two groups of special Ss. Which statistical procedure would you suggest and why?

6. All entering EFL/ESL students at your university have taken a general proficiency test. All items related to verb morphology in the test are the data for a study of how Ss from different L1 backgrounds perform on English tense and aspect. The verb morphology of some of these L1 groups is rather similar to that of English; for other L1 groups the morphology is not similar at all. You are undecided as to whether to group them in this way first and do the analysis or whether to do a more straightforward comparison across the languages first and then compare those that are or are not similar to English later. A number of statistical procedures might be used. Which would you select and why?

7. Another research question for the data in example 6 might be whether the verb morphemes form a scale or not. If so, you might form a "natural-order" hypothesis. If this is the research question, what statistical test would you use and why?

In your study group, compare your responses to each of these items. Try to reach a consensus regarding which choices would be best considering the information given in each justification.

References

Irujo, S. 1986. Don't put your leg in your mouth: transfer in the acquisition of idioms in a second language, *TESOL Quarterly, 20*, 2, 287-304.

Levinson, S. 1983. *Pragmatics.* Cambridge: Cambridge University Press.

Chapter 13
Comparisons of Means in
Factorial Designs

- *Factorial designs*
- *Calculating ANOVA for a 2 X 2 design*
  Interpreting Factorial ANOVA
  Strength of relationship: omega^2
- *Assumptions underlying Factorial ANOVA*
- *Selecting Factorial ANOVA programs*

Factorial Designs

In chapter 11, we discussed ways in which we might test the differences in the performance of three or more groups. In that discussion the groups represented levels of *one* independent variable. The research question was always whether performance on the dependent variable differed across the groups represented in the levels of only one independent variable.

Factorial designs are those where more than one independent variable is involved in the design. For example, you might investigate whether *S*s taught using one method outperform those taught by other methods. The *dependent* variable might be performance on a language achievement test. The first *independent* variable is *method*, and there might be several methods compared. In the same study, you might have tried to balance the number of female and male *S*s, but you do wonder whether females and males might perform differently on the achievement test. *Sex*, a moderating variable, is the second *independent* variable.

Here is the box design represented in the study. Two methods are being compared and two levels for sex make this a 2 X 2 factorial design.

	Sex	
Method	Male	Female
Teacher Centered		
Cooperative Learning		

The analysis, then, compares four different groups:

Group 1--Males in teacher-centered class
Group 2--Females in teacher-centered class
Group 3--Males in cooperative-learning class
Group 4--Females in cooperative-learning class

You want to check performance of all Ss in the teacher-centered classroom with all Ss in the cooperative-learning classroom (groups 1 + 2 vs. groups 3 + 4). You also want to be sure that females and males perform in similar ways, and so you will compare all males vs. all females on the test outcome (groups 1 + 3 vs. groups 2 + 4). However, it is also possible that one methodology may "work better" for males or for females in the sense that one or the other may benefit more from one method (group 1 vs. 2 vs. 3 vs. 4).

In this study, we hope that one method "works better" for all Ss and that this shows up in the "main effect" of method. If we are advocates of cooperative learning, then we hope that the Ss in the cooperative-learning group will outperform those in the teacher-centered group. We hope that men and women perform in the same way and that there is no interaction where, say, males in the cooperative-learning group do better than females and that females do better than males in the teacher-centered class. If there were such an interaction, it would weaken the argument in favor of cooperative-learning techniques. (And, as a practical matter, it is unlikely that we could apply such results by setting up separate classes for males and females.)

In One-way ANOVA, we saw that there was only one independent variable. When we compared SSB and SSW and computed the F ratio, we attributed the difference between SSB and SSW to the levels of that one independent variable. In our example, we expect that there will be variability in the performance of Ss on the achievement test. We want to know what effect the methodology factor had on that variability. We also want to know what effect the sex factor had on variability in the data. And, further, we want to know the effect of the combination of method and sex on variability in test performance.

1. Effect of method (factor A): teacher-centered vs. cooperative-learning

2. Effect of sex (factor B): male vs. female

3. Interaction effect (factor A X B)

The advantage of using a Factorial ANOVA is that we can look not only at the effect of each independent variable but also the interaction effects in the combination of different independent variables.

Imagine that all the Ss participating in this study were selected at random from a population of learners. In addition, they have been randomly assigned to a French I class taught using teacher-centered procedures or to a French I class using cooperative-learning techniques. The curriculum objectives for the classes are the same. The same teacher teaches the two classes, so the design is not confounded in a technical sense. However, it would be important that the teacher not know which is the experimental treatment group and not feel that one technique is any better than the other (an unrealistic hope, of course). Since none of the *S*s had previously studied French, no pretest was given.

At the end of the semester, an achievement test consisting of 25 items was given and we assume that the scores reflect equal-interval measurement. Fortunately, the test turned out to be highly reliable even though relatively short. Further, since random selection and random assignment were used, we believe that the *S*s form samples which are representative of the population of college students enrolling in our French I classes.

Let's fill in the chart for this study:

Research hypothesis? There is no effect on achievement for sex or method, and there is no effect for the interaction.
  Significance level? .05
  1- or 2-tailed? 2-tailed
Design
  Dependent variable(s)? Achievement
  Measurement? Scores (interval)
  Independent variable(s)? Sex, Method
  Measurement? Nominal (two levels for each independent variable)
  Independent or repeated-measures? Independent
Other features? Random selection and assignment
Statistical procedure? Factorial ANOVA

In One-way ANOVA, we were able to look for "treatment" effect by comparing the two components of variance:

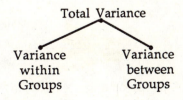

Total Variance

Variance within Groups   Variance between Groups

In Factorial ANOVA, the variance for this study will be divided in the following way:

Factorial ANOVA

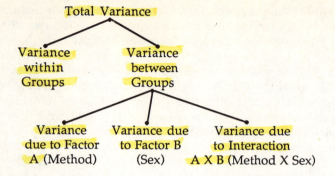

Total Variance

Variance within Groups

Variance between Groups

Variance due to Factor A (Method)

Variance due to Factor B (Sex)

Variance due to Interaction A X B (Method X Sex)

The within-group variance is ordinary "error" variability--it results from the normal distribution of individual scores within each of the groups. However, the between-groups variance contains within it the effect of factor A, factor B, or factor A X B. As in One-way ANOVA, we want to compute the values of variance for each component and then put each in an F ratio to see which, if any, exceed the normal within-group variance.

$$F_{FactorA} = \frac{s_A^2}{s_W^2}$$

(effect of method--factor A)

$$F_{FactorB} = \frac{s_B^2}{s_W^2}$$

(effect of sex--factor B)

$$F_{AB} = \frac{s_{AB}^2}{s_W^2}$$

(effect of interaction of sex X method--A X B)

Before we go on to the calculations used in computing these F ratios (don't worry, they are very similar to those used for One-way ANOVA), stop and chart the partialing of the total variance in each of the following studies.

◇◇◇◇◇◇◇◇◇◇◇◇◇◇◇◇◇◇◇◇◇◇◇◇◇◇◇◇◇◇◇◇◇◇◇◇

Practice 13.1

Use the "tree diagram" given in the previous discussion as a guide. Chart the partialing of total variance into that for each independent variable.

▶ 1. Abraham (1985) studied the differential effects of two methods for teaching participial formation on 28 field-dependent and 28 field-independent students. Two CAI-ESL lessons were used, one using a traditional deductive-rule approach and the other using examples in context. Field-independent learners got higher posttest scores (dependent variable) with instruction from the deductive lesson; the example lesson was more beneficial for field-dependent students.

▶ 2. Pritchard (1987) collected 10 essays each from 383 junior and senior high school students whose teachers either had or had not been trained in the National Writing Project Model. A 6-point rating scale (with detailed operational definitions for each point on the scale) was used to rate the compositions. Among many other findings in this study, the author notes that differences were found between students from classes taught by NWP-trained teachers vs. nontrained teachers, but an interaction showed that this difference was really valid only at the junior high level.

3. Do you think that the authors were pleased that the interactions turned out to be significant? Why (not)? _____
_____
_____

This should give you a forewarning about interpretation of the results of Factorial ANOVA. That is, when an interaction turns out to be significant, the findings must be interpreted in light of the interaction (rather than in terms of the individual independent variables).

Calculating ANOVA for a 2 X 2 Design

Researchers seldom, if ever, carry out Factorial ANOVA calculations by hand. However, it is something that everyone should try once (and perhaps only once) in order to understand how ANOVA works.

There are six steps in the computations:

1. Compute sum of squares total (SST).

2. Compute sum of squares between (SSB).

3. Compute sum of squares within (SSW).

4. Compute sum of squares for factor A (SS_A).

5. Compute sum of squares for factor B (SS_B).

6. Compute sum of squares for the interaction of factors A and B (SS_{AB}).

We will use the example of *method* (teacher-centered vs. cooperative-learning instruction) and *sex* as independent variables with an achievement test as the dependent variable. There are three null hypotheses to be tested:

1. There is no difference in achievement test scores according to method.

2. There is no difference in achievement test scores according to sex.

3. There is no interaction effect between sex and method on achievement.

In order to simplify the calculations, we have limited the number of Ss to five in each group. Again, in a real study, we recommend a larger *n* size for each group. Five is an absolute minimum. Thirty per group give us a much better population estimate. The data given in the following table are fictitious.

	Female		Male	
	X	X^2	X	X^2
	9	81	14	196
	10	100	12	144
Tchr	8	64	9	81
Ctrd	7	49	9	81
	10	100	14	196
	$\Sigma X = 44$ $\Sigma X^2 = 394$		$\Sigma X = 58$ $\Sigma X^2 = 698$	
	Mean $= 8.8$		Mean $= 11.6$	

Method (factor A)	16	256	11	121
	15	225	10	100
Coop	20	400	9	81
Lrng	14	196	7	49
	12	144	9	81
	$\Sigma X = 77$ $\Sigma X^2 = 1221$		$\Sigma X = 46$ $\Sigma X^2 = 432$	
	Mean $= 15.4$		Mean $= 9.2$	

Mean for Females $= 12.1$ Mean for Males $= 10.4$
Mean Coop Lrng $= 12.3$ Mean for Tchr Ctr $= 10.2$
Grand Mean $= 11.25$

The $\overline{X}$s for the cells do appear to be quite different. There is a large difference, for example, between a $\overline{X}$ of 8.8 and a $\overline{X}$ of 15.4. However, remember that the smaller the sample size, the larger the difference among $\overline{X}$s must be in order to achieve statistical significance. The raw $\overline{X}$s also look as though there may be an interaction in that females in the cooperative-learning group have the higher $\overline{X}$ while the higher male $\overline{X}$ is for the teacher-centered group. To know whether this is the case, we must carry out the statistical procedure.

Step 1
Compute the sum of square total (SST).

$$SST = \sum X^2 - \frac{\left(\sum X\right)^2}{N}$$

The value of $\sum X^2$ should be familiar to you by now. Square each individual score and then sum these.

$$\sum X^2 = 9^2 + 10^2 + 8^2 + \cdots + 7^2 + 9^2$$

$$\sum X^2 = 2745$$

To find $(\sum X)^2$, first sum the individual scores and square that value.

$$\left(\sum X\right)^2 = (9 + 10 + 8 + \cdots + 7 + 9)^2$$

$$\left(\sum X\right)^2 = 225^2$$

$$\left(\sum X\right)^2 = 50625$$

There are five Ss in each of the cells of the design. The N, therefore, is 20. Now that we have all the values needed for SST, we can complete the following computations.

$$SST = \sum X^2 - \frac{\left(\sum X\right)^2}{N}$$

$$SST = 2745 - \frac{50625}{20}$$

$$SST = 213.75$$

Step 2
Find the sum of squares between (SSB).

The sum of squares between (SSB) contains the treatment effects (just as it did for One-way ANOVA). It also includes the effect of sex and of the interaction between method and sex on the test. Once we find the value of SSB, then, it will be further partialed out so that we can see the effect of each of these individually.

Since we are working from raw data, the formula we will use for SSB is:

$$SSB = \left[\frac{\left(\sum X_1\right)^2}{n_1} + \frac{\left(\sum X_2\right)^2}{n_2} + \frac{\left(\sum X_3\right)^2}{n_3} + \frac{\left(\sum X_4\right)^2}{n_4}\right] - \frac{\left(\sum X\right)^2}{N}$$

$$SSB = \left[\frac{44^2}{5} + \frac{58^2}{5} + \frac{77^2}{5} + \frac{46^2}{5}\right] - \frac{225^2}{20}$$

$$SSB = 137.75$$

Step 3
Compute the sum of squares within (SSW).

This step is easy since we already have SST and SSB. All we need to do is subtract the between-groups variance from the total variance.

$$SSW = SST - SSB$$

$$SSW = 213.75 - 137.75$$

(We hope these are the same values that you got.)

$$SSW = 76.0$$

Remember that SSW is the variance associated with normal variability ("error" variability) in performance. That is, it is not influenced by either method or sex or the interaction.

Step 4
Compute the sum of squares for factor A--*method* (SS_A).

SSB includes all the variance due to the effects of the independent variables (i.e., *method* and *sex* and the interaction). We need to divide up the variance in SSB to show us that for factor A, *method*. To do this, we will add up the total score for each level of *method* (that for cooperative-learning and that for teacher-centered instruction). Then we will divide each of these by the *n* for the level.

At the end of the upper left quadrant of the data table, you will find the ΣX for the total scores for women in the teacher-centered group. It is 44. In the upper right quadrant is ΣX for the total scores for men. So ΣX for everyone in the teacher-centered group is 102.

There are 10 Ss in the cooperative-learning group. Now, let's find ΣX for the cooperative-learning instruction. That for females is 77 and for males is 46, so the total ΣX for this treatment is 123.

Now we can put this information into the formula for the sum of squares for factor A (*method*).

$$SS_A = \left[\frac{\left(\sum scores A_1\right)^2}{n_{A1}} + \frac{\left(\sum scores A_2\right)^2}{n_{A2}} \right] - \frac{\left(\sum X\right)^2}{N}$$

$$SS_A = \left[\frac{102^2}{10} + \frac{123^2}{10} \right] - \frac{225^2}{20}$$

$$SS_A = 22.05$$

Now that we have the portion of SSB that belongs to method, we can find the part for sex.

Step 5
Compute the sum of squares for factor B--*sex* (SS_B).

Now we need to partial out the part of the SSB variance for the effect of sex. The information we need, once again, is in the data chart. We add the scores for females in the upper left quadrant (where $\Sigma X = 44$) with that of females in the lower left quadrant (where $\Sigma X = 77$). The total ΣX for females is 121. The total for males is 104. There are 10 females and 10 males in the total study. (A balanced design--hooray for small mercies!)

$$SS_B = \left[\frac{\left(\sum scores\, B_1\right)^2}{n_{B1}} + \frac{\left(\sum scores\, B_2\right)^2}{n_{B2}} \right] - \frac{\left(\sum X\right)^2}{N}$$

$$SS_B = \left[\frac{121^2}{10} + \frac{104^2}{10} \right] - \frac{225^2}{20}$$

$$SS_B = 14.45$$

Now that we have the sum of squares for each of the main effects in the study, we need to compute the sum of squares for the interaction of the two.

Step 6
Compute the sum of squares for the interaction (SS_{AB}).

This will be easy since we already have the SS for factor A (*method*) and factor B (*sex*). SSB contains the effect of both of these main factors and that of the interaction. So, all we need to do is subtract.

$$SS_{AB} = SSB - (SS_A + SS_B)$$

$$SS_{AB} = 137.75 - (22.05 + 14.45)$$

$$SS_{AB} = 101.25$$

We hope that you are checking these calculations as we go along. Do the given values of SSB and SS_A and SS_B agree with the values you computed? If not, check with your study group to see where you went wrong.

Now that we have worked through each of the six steps and have found the sum of squares for each, we need to divide them by their respective degrees of freedom.

The total *df* for the study $= N - 1$. There were 20 *S*s in the study, so the total *df* $= 19$. The *df* for SSW is $N - K$. There were 20 *S*s and 4 groups so $N - K = 16$ *df*. For factor A, there were 2 levels, so $a - 1 = 1$ *df* for method. For factor B, there were also 2 levels, so $a - 1 = 1$ *df* for sex. The *df* for the interaction is found by multiplying the *df* for factor A by the *df* of factor B. $1 \times 1 = 1$ *df*.

You can check these degrees of freedom for accuracy by adding them to see if they are the same as the total *df* for the study. $16 + 1 + 1 + 1 = 19$, which the total *df*, $N - 1$.

Now we can divide each sum of squares by its respective degrees of freedom to obtain the variance that can be attributed to each. These variance values are (as before in the other ANOVAs we have computed) called the mean squares (MS). Let's fill in the ANOVA table for the values we have obtained so far.

Source	df	SS	MS	F ratio
Between Groups				
Method	1	22.05	22.05	4.64 *
Sex	1	14.45	14.45	3.04
A X B Method x Sex	1	101.25	101.25	21.32 *
Within Groups	16	76.00	4.75	
Total	19	213.75		

Now we are ready to compute the F ratios for each factor and for the interaction.

$$F - \text{ratio } A(Method) = \frac{S_A^2}{S_W^2} = \frac{MS_A}{MSW} = \frac{22.05}{4.75} = 4.64$$

$$F - \text{ratio } B(Sex) = \frac{S_B^2}{S_W^2} = \frac{MS_B}{MSW} = \frac{14.45}{4.75} = 3.04$$

$$F - \text{ratio } A \times B = \frac{MS_{AB}}{MSW} = \frac{101.25}{4.75} = 21.32$$

You can place each of these F ratios in the appropriate row in the column labeled F ratio above.

The final step in our calculations, of course, is to discover whether the obtained F ratios are sufficiently larger than 1 to allow us to reject the H_o. We can find the critical value of F for 1,16 df for *each* of the three effects (*method, sex,* A X B) in the F distribution table, table 5 of appendix C. The intersection of 1 and 16 df shows that a critical value of 4.49 is needed to reject the H_o for an α of .05. Our ratio for *method* is larger than the required critical value of F. We can place an asterisk next to the method F ratio to show this. The F ratio for *sex* is not larger than the critical value, so we cannot reject the H_o for sex. Unfortunately, the F ratio for the interaction of method X sex *is* also larger than the critical value of F. This leads us to the issue of interpretation.

Interpreting the Interaction and Main Effects in Factorial ANOVA

In the above example, the interaction of method and sex is significant. This means that the effect of method was moderated by that of sex. To see how this works, let's chart the $\overline{X}$s of our groups. The $\overline{X}$ for women in the teacher-centered approach was 8.8 and for the cooperative-learning approach, 15.4. The $\overline{X}$ for men in the teacher-centered approach was 11.6 and in the cooperative-learning method, 9.2 These are charted on the following figure.

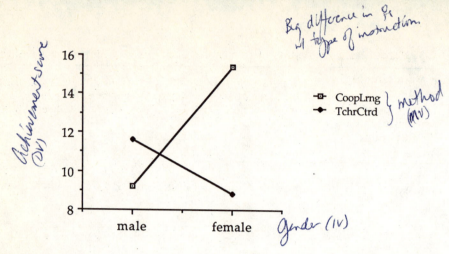

Achievement score (DV)

CoopLrng
TchrCtrd *} method (MV)*

male   female   *Gender (IV)*

To draw this figure we located the $\bar{X}$ for cooperative learning for males and for females and drew a line connecting these two points. This line is labeled *cooperative learning*. Then we located the $\bar{X}$ for males and females for the teacher-centered method and drew a line to connect these two $\bar{X}$'s. It is labeled teacher centered.

This graph shows that while women did much better if they were in the cooperative-learning group, men showed somewhat better performance in the teacher-centered group. Since there is such a strong interaction, we would naturally be suspicious of any claim that said the two methods differed and that one was better than the other overall. Rather, we must interpret the findings in light of the interaction. *The interaction overrides the main effect.*

It is true that we almost always hope that our main effects (such as *method* in this case) turn out to be significant. Then we can say there is a clear difference which relates to the independent variable. When we add moderator variables (such as *sex* in this case), we are checking to make sure nothing else may play an important role. We may hope that this particular variable will not turn out to be significant. However, if it is significant in the study, a chart of the means will help us interpret the findings.

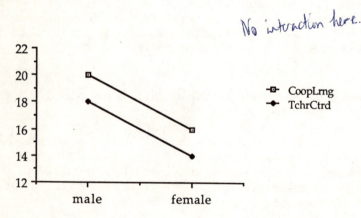

CoopLrng
TchrCtrd

male   female

In this case, our interpretation would be that the H_o of no difference between the two methods could be rejected. The methods differ significantly with Ss performing better in the cooperative-learning group. The H_o of no difference for sex could also be rejected. Males did better than females regardless of method. The figure shows no interaction. Therefore, the main effects can be interpreted independently.

More important, we hope that the interaction of the main variables will *not* be significant. We want a clear-cut difference in *method* without any "interference" from the interaction with other variables. When an interaction is significant, we must focus our interpretation on it and not make claims about the significance of the main variables.

Our interpretation of the ANOVA table in this example, then, is that any difference found in the two methods must be attributed to the fact that women did better on the achievement exam if they were in the cooperative-learning group. To apply this information would be difficult. It's unlikely that we could or would want to segregate women into a cooperative-learning class because they seemed to do much better with this methodology. However, it is also true that the difference between the two methods was not so pronounced for men, so perhaps we could argue that they might not be harmed and women would be helped if they all enrolled in classes that used cooperative learning. Obviously, the best solution would be to vary techniques to take advantage of both methods in teaching French I at our university. It would also be important to check to see if there were any important differences in the Ss (despite random assignment) in the teacher-centered and cooperative-learning classes. There might be other factors which challenge the validity of subject selection in the study.

When we plot an interaction using the $\overline{X}$s of each subgroup, it is not always the case that the figure for the interaction will form a crossover pattern. It is possible that a figure such as the following might be found.

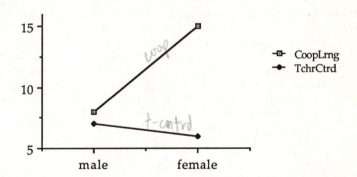

Even though there is no crossover, the effect of method is still clearly due to better performance of females in the cooperative-learning approach. The difference in methods for males appears trivial.

It is always helpful to chart the $\bar{X}$s in order to understand exactly how best to interpret a Factorial ANOVA. Again, it is important to remember that inter-action effects must qualify any statements we make about the effect of the main variables by themselves. The interaction effect washes out the main effect. That is why the interpretation of the results of ANOVA must be carefully done. The interpretation *must* focus on the interaction effect when it is significant. When the interaction effects are not significant, stronger statements can be made about the effect of the independent variables on the dependent variable.

We have said that researchers almost always hope that no significant interaction effects are found. However, there are cases--such as in cross-cultural research-- where researchers do expect to find significant interaction effects. For example, if you had test data where Ss from several different L1 groups judged the ap-propriateness of information-request forms, you might include sex as another major variable. In this case, you might not expect males and females to differ in their judgment scores, but you would probably expect to find that judgments vary not just by L1 membership (the other main effect being tested) but in interaction with sex. This would show, for example, that male or female Ss within certain L1 groups judge the appropriateness of requests differently than male or female Ss in another L1 group. Again, the interpretation would be in terms of this interaction rather than in terms of simple L1 membership.

As always, it is helpful in reading a research report to begin with the abstract and then turn to the tables and interpret the findings. With complex designs that use ANOVA this is an especially important step in evaluating research. Read and interpret the tables and then turn to the full article, checking your own under-standing of the results against that of the author. ANOVA is an excellent sta-tistical test precisely because it allows us to look at interaction effects and to interpret the main effects in light of the interactions. If you train yourself to do this as you read the research reports of others, it will become much easier to offer an interpretation of your own research findings.

We have said that it is possible to design a Factorial ANOVA with many differ-ent factors. From our discussion of interaction effects, we hope you can see why it is often so difficult to interpret complex designs. The more independent vari-ables are added into a Factorial design, the more difficult it becomes to interpret the multiple interactions that may result. Rather than combining many inde-pendent variables in one study, we might design a series of studies where we vary the independent variables. As you will see in future chapters, another solution is to use correlation-based statistical procedures to get at the importance of large numbers of independent variables.

Strength of Relationship: omega^2

As part of interpretation, we can get a rough measure of strength of relationship by using the omega^2 procedure. There were two main effect variables and one interaction in our example, so there are three possible omega^2 computations:

$$\omega_A^2 = \frac{SS_A - (df_A)MSW}{SST + MSW}$$

$$\omega_B^2 = \frac{SS_B - (df_B)(MSW)}{SST + MSW}$$

$$\omega_{AB}^2 = \frac{SS_{AB} - (df_{AB})(MSW)}{SST + MSW}$$

However, for the methodology problem we just completed, remember that the effects for *method* (A) and the interaction (AB) were significant. *Sex* (B) was not. Therefore, we have no reason to do an omega^2 for *sex*.

$$\omega_A^2 = \frac{22.05 - (1)4.75}{213.75 + 4.75}$$

$$\omega_A^2 = \frac{17.3}{218.5} = .08$$

$$\omega_{AB}^2 = \frac{101.25 - (1)4.75}{213.75 + 4.75}$$

$$\omega_{AB}^2 = \frac{96.5}{218.5} = .44$$

So, we can see that although the effect for method was significant in the ANOVA, the strength of that relationship is not great, only 8%. The interaction of *sex X method* accounts for much more of the variance, 44%. Obviously, the interaction is much more important than method alone.

Using omega^2 helps us to understand why it is so important to interpret ANOVA with reference to any significant interactions. It also lets us know how much variance is left unaccounted for. The 48% does cover almost half of the variance, but it still leaves 51.4%--the result of "error"--random variation that is not accounted for in the design. This suggests we might try to discover what factors other than sex (perhaps learning styles) might interact with these particular teaching methodologies.

(Remember that omega^2 is used for balanced designs. If the design is unbalanced, use the eta^2 formula presented in chapter 12 ($\eta^2 = SS_X \div SST$) as an estimate of the strength of the relationship.)

Assumptions Underlying Factorial ANOVA

The assumptions underlying a regular between-groups Factorial ANOVA are those of all ANOVA procedures.

1. The data are score or rank-order data that are truly continuous.

2. The data are independent. If the design includes repeated-measures or within-group comparisons, there are special ANOVA procedures available in SAS, SPSS-X, and BMDP that can be used instead.

3. The distributions of scores in the samples are normal enough that $\overline{X}$ and variance are appropriate measures of central tendency and variability.

4. The data form a normal distribution and equal variances in the respective populations.

5. The design is balanced (otherwise use general linear modeling procedures--GLM in computer statistics packages).

6. There are at least five observations per cell.

7. The F statistic allows the researcher only to accept or reject the H_o (other statistical procedures can be used to locate differences among levels of those variables where the F statistic is statistically significant).

For a thorough discussion of Factorial ANOVA and the assumptions underlying the procedures, see Kirk (1982) or Winer (1971).

Practice 13.2

▶1. Chapter 11, practice 11.3, presented a problem about determining the best method for teaching composition. In that study, three methods were devised for teaching composition. Ss were randomly assigned to one of the three methods. All Ss had the same topics for their compositions. At the end of the semester, the final compositions were graded by five raters and the scores were averaged. Imagine the ESL director wanted to see if the same results hold for the remedial ESL composition class as well. The methods and topics were as they were in the regular classes. The final composition results from three classes to which the remedial Ss were assigned were:

Method 1	Method 2	Method 3
12	19	13
14	20	15
10	10	9
13	19	15
11	12	10
12	14	13
15	18	14
10	21	12
12	19	13
14	16	14

For the regular ESL composition classes:

Method 1	Method 2	Method 3
$\sum X = 207$	$\sum X = 149$	$\sum X = 179$
$\bar{X} = 20.7$	$\bar{X} = 14.9$	$\bar{X} = 17.9$
$\sum X^2 = 4351$	$\sum X^2 = 2285$	$\sum X^2 = 3291$
$n = 10$	$n = 10$	$n = 10$

Make *class* be factor A, and *method* be factor B.

a. Do a 3 X 2 Factorial ANOVA for these data. Note that for some of the steps you will have more factors in the equation. SSB will have 6 expressions in the brackets instead of 4. Likewise, SSB in step 5 will have 3 expressions in brackets instead of 2. The *df* for factor B (*method*) will be 2 instead of 1, right?

Step 1: SST = _____
Step 2: SSB = _____
Step 3: SSW = _____
Step 4: SS_A = _____
Step 5: SS_B = _____
Step 6: SS_{AB} = _____
F ratio for A = _____
F ratio for B = _____
F ratio for A X B = _____

b. Which null hypotheses can be rejected?

c. Calculate omega^2 for significant F ratios.

$$\omega_A^2 = \frac{SS_A - (df_A)(MSW)}{SST + MSW}$$

$$\omega_A^2 = \underline{\quad\quad}$$

$$\omega_B^2 = \frac{SS_B - (df_B)(MSW)}{SST + MSW}$$

$$\omega_B^2 = \underline{\quad\quad}$$

$$\omega_{AB}^2 = \frac{SS_{AB} - (df_{AB})MS_w}{SST + MSW}$$

$$\omega_{AB}^2 = \underline{\quad\quad}$$

d. Draw a graph of the interaction and interpret it. You can make either *method* or *class* the *X*-axis.

e. What conclusions can you draw?

_____
_____
_____
_____
_____

◇◇◇

Selecting Factorial ANOVA Programs

The kind of Factorial ANOVA you use to test differences among $\overline{X}$s of groups will depend on a number of considerations. These include:

1. Is the design for fixed effects or random?

2. Is the design a between-groups design?

3. Is the design a repeated-measures design?

4. Is it a mixed design where some variables are between-groups and others are within-group comparisons?

5. Is it a balanced or unbalanced design?

The exact type of ANOVA procedure you use must be specified in research reports. Obviously, we do not expect the researcher to carry out complex mixed designs by hand. There are, however, a wide range of possibilities open to you using SAS, SPSS-X, or BMDP programs. In SAS, we recommend that you use GLM (General Linear Modeling) for both one-way and factorial designs. In SAS, ANOVA only handles balanced designs while GLM does the same work for both balanced and unbalanced designs. Since SAS won't give you an error message if you run an unbalanced design on ANOVA, it's better to play safe and use GLM.

GLM carries out a variety of ANOVA procedures. In research reports, you may see abbreviations that look much like ANOVA. One GLM subcommand, MANOVA, may be used. This stands for "multivariate analysis of variance" and is used when the research design includes more than one *dependent* variable. For example, the research might include two measures from different tests.

Another abbreviation you may see in the literature is ANCOVA. This stands for "analysis of covariance." This procedure allows you to control for some variable factor--perhaps a pretest score or a language aptitude score--so that the measurement of the dependent variable is adjusted taking into account this initial difference among Ss.

We haven't presented formulas for calculating ANOVA in these complex designs, but they can be found in Kirk (1982). Readable explanations of these complex designs are given in the SPSS-X manual (1986). In addition, a nonparametric Factorial ANOVA procedure is covered in Meddis (1984). In order to help you when you must decide among these procedures, you need to be able to identify variables and know which are repeated-measures (within-group) and which are between-groups comparisons. The activities section at the end of this chapter gives you additional opportunity to practice this decision-making process.

In part III, we have presented statistical tests that compare the performance of groups. The statistical procedures which allow us to make the comparisons are selected according to the number of groups (two, or more than two), the independence of the data (between-groups or repeated-measures designs), and the type of measurement used (continuous data that is normally distributed so that the $\overline{X}$ and *s.d.* are the best measures of central tendency and dispersion, or continuous data where the median and rank order are more appropriate). As a guide to selection of an appropriate statistical test, turn to the flow chart on page 543. You will find the procedures presented in part III grouped immediately below the entry for Guttman (Implicational scaling). The flow chart is a quick guide. The assumptions for each test must also be consulted. To do this, check the assumptions and solutions for the procedure in the appropriate section of the review beginning on page 548. The flow chart and the information contained in the review of assumptions of tests are not meant to supplant the information given in each chapter. Once a procedure is selected, it will always be a good idea to go back and review the chapter in which it is presented. That is, these charts are supplements or quick guides, rather than the final word on options and assumptions.

You will notice that each procedure in part III has compared performance of two or more groups on some dependent variable. The basic question answered has been whether there is variation in performance that can be traced to differences in the groups identified by the independent variable(s). In part IV, we will look at *relationships* among variables rather than the effect of independent variables on a dependent variable. Instead of comparing group means (or medians), the statistical tests, for the most part, will examine how well the data for one variable relate or correlate with the data for other variable(s).

Activities

Read the brief descriptions of the following studies, all of which used some type of Factorial ANOVA in data analysis. First, draw a design box for each study. Then determine the type of ANOVA (number of dependent and independent variables; between-groups or repeated-measures, etc.). From such a brief description it is difficult to tell whether the basic assumptions of ANOVA have been met. However, try to decide whether you think this is the case. Consider yourself as the researcher and comment on changes you might want to make to simplify (or further complicate) the research. In cases where you are not certain whether the basic assumptions of ANOVA have been met, suggest alternative procedures if you can.

1. E. Henly & A. Sheldon (1986. Duration and context effects on the perception of English /r/ and /l/: a comparison of Cantonese and Japanese speakers. *Language Learning, 36,* 4, 505-521.) used a procedure where five native speakers of Cantonese were given identification tests consisting of words containing English /r/ and /l/ in four positions: initial, medial, consonant cluster, and final. Results showed that accuracy of perception depended on location of the sound (perception was best in initial and medial position), not the duration of the sound. This finding did not support the Duration Hypothesis, which was based on Japanese speakers finding final position easiest to perceive. In discussing their findings, the authors hypothesized that these differences might be due to the status of these phonemic contrasts (or lack thereof) in Cantonese and Japanese.

2. J. Vaid (1987. Visual field asymmetries for rhyme and syntactic category judgments in monolinguals and fluent early and late bilinguals. *Brain and Language, 30,* 263-277.) conducted another study to support the notion that most language tasks require preferential use of the left hemisphere of the brain. In this study, Ss heard a word and then had to identify a different visually projected word as a ±rhyme. When the projected word was flashed in the right visual field (and thus processed in the left hemisphere), both monolingual and bilingual Ss responded more quickly than when the word was presented to the left visual field. Second, Ss heard a word and then a sentence containing that word. This was followed by a different word flashed in the right or left visual field. Ss had to decide whether the word was the same part of speech as in the heard stimuli. Again, material flashed to the right visual field was responded to more rapidly by monolinguals and bilinguals. In both tasks, late bilinguals responded more slowly than early bilinguals.

3. J. Reid (1987. The learning style preferences of ESL students. *TESOL Quarterly, 21,* 1, 87-111.) conducted a survey of 1,388 students to discover their perceptual learning style preferences. Subjects from nine language backgrounds indicated their attitudes about statements which reflected six learning styles: visual, auditory, kinesthetic, tactile, group learning, and individual learning. Results show that ESL learners strongly preferred kinesthetic and tactile learning styles, with a negative preference for group learning. Japanese speakers were most frequently different in their preferences.

4. R. Scarcella (1984. How writers orient their readers in expository essays: a comparative study of native and non-native English writers. *TESOL Quarterly, 18,* 4, 671-688.) analyzed 110 essays (30 native English and 80 ESL) for orientation, the preparatory material before the statement of the theme. Nonnative speakers wrote significantly longer orientations than native speakers, but the longer orientations tended to contain more "known," and thus unnecessary information. Japanese speakers wrote significantly shorter orientations than the other three first language groups studied, but they wrote lengthy orientations following the theme.

5. R. J. Vann, D. E. Meyer, & F. O. Lorenz (1984. Error gravity: a study of faculty opinion of ESL errors. *TESOL Quarterly, 18,* 3, 427-440.) asked 164 faculty members to rate the relative seriousness of 12 common ESL written errors. Their judgments generated a hierarchy of errors, with word order errors being the least acceptable and spelling errors being the most acceptable. The age and academic field of respondents appeared to be important factors in responses.

6. W. K. Tsang (1987. Text modifications in ESL reading comprehension. *RELC Journal, 18,* 2, 31-44.) undertook a study to examine the effects of text version (native speaker, input modified, interactional structure modified) and form level (forms 3-7, roughly equivalent to grades 9-13) on reading comprehension. Four hundred and one Cantonese speakers were randomly placed in one of three groups representing the three kinds of text versions. *S*s then read the text version assigned to their group; all *S*s answered the same multiple-choice comprehension questions after reading the passage.

A two-way ANOVA showed significant effects for the two main effects and the interaction. Post hoc comparisons show that the modified texts were more effective in fostering comprehension than the unmodified native speaker versions, while the modified input was more effective than the interactionally modified version. Input modified texts were better for *S*s in form 3 while input and interactionally modified ones were best for form 4 *S*s.

The following table for strength of effect is also presented:

	omega^2 Analysis	
Source	ω^2	% of variance
Text version	0.055	5.5
Form level	0.287	28.7
Interaction (text X form)	0.049	4.9
Error	0.609	60.9
Total	1.000	100%

In light of the ω^2 figures, which is the most important effect? What does this mean? How much variability has yet to be explained?

7. E. Shohamy (1987. Does the testing method make a difference? The case of reading comprehension. *Language Testing, 1,* 2, 147-170.) studied the effects of various methods of testing reading comprehension. Six hundred fifty-five *S*s were randomly assigned to one of eight groups representing various combinations of

three independent variables: (1) question type--multiple-choice or open-ended; (2) questions in L1 (Hebrew) or L2 (English); and (3) version of the text (2 topics). All *S*s read a text in English (the L2) and answered questions based on the text. Results of a Factorial ANOVA showed significant effects for the independent variables. The addition of a fourth variable, proficiency level, showed that effects were more pronounced in the lower-level *S*s.

References

Abraham, R. 1985. Field independence-dependence and the teaching of grammar. *TESOL Quarterly, 19,* 4, 689-702.

Kirk, R. E. 1982. *Experimental Design: Procedures for the Behavioral Sciences.* Second Edition. Belmont, CA: Brooks Cole.

Meddis, R. 1984. *Statistics Using Ranks.* New York, NY: Basil Blackwell Inc.

Pritchard, R. J. 1987. Effects on student writing of teachers trained in the National Writing Project Model. *Written Communication, 4,* 1, 51-67.

SPSS Inc.. 1986. *SPSS-X Users Guide.* Second edition. Chicago, IL: SPSS Inc.

Winer, B. J. 1971. *Statistical Principles in Experimental Design.* New York, NY: McGraw-Hill.

Part IV. Describing Relationships

Chapter 14

Relationships in Nominal Data

- •*Chi-square procedure*
    Computing χ^2 for one-way designs
    Chi-square for two-way designs
- •*Yates' correction factor*
- •*Assumptions underlying Chi-square*
- •*Interpreting χ^2*
- •*Strength of association*
    Phi
    Cramer's V
- •*McNemar's test for related samples*

Chi-square Procedure

Nominal data are facts that can be sorted into categories such as L1 background (sorted into Mandarin, Farsi, Korean, etc.), sex (sorted as male, female), or ESL course level (sorted as beginning, intermediate, advanced). The category may be represented by a number, but the number is arbitrary (1 may equal Mandarin, 2 Farsi, and so forth). Nominal variables are discrete--one either is or is not a native speaker of Mandarin. Nominal variables are not meant to handle the subtleties of degree. Rather, they are measured as frequencies.

In part I of this manual we talked about how we can display frequency data in terms of proportions, percents, rates, or ratios and how these might be shown in various types of figures. The frequencies might be the number of beginning, intermediate, and advanced students who used special listening comprehension materials in a language lab. (We want to know if there is a relation between lab use and student level.) They might represent the frequencies of special hedges (such as *perhaps, appears, seems*) in science vs. economics textbooks. (We want to know if there is a relation between type of hedge and text genre.) The frequencies could show a comparison between the number of people who answered "yes" or "no" on a questionnaire (where we want to know if response type and sex are related).

When we look at frequencies in a display table (e.g., the number of men vs. women who voted "yes" or "no"), they "look" similar or different. We turn to a statistical test, though, to tell us how different frequencies have to be before we can make claims about the relation of the variables with some degree of certainty.

For frequency data, an appropriate statistical procedure to test the relationship is the Chi-square (χ^2) test. Notice that it tests the *relationship* between the variables (how well they go together) rather than how one variable *affects* another. The Chi-square procedure does not allow us to make cause → effect claims.

Assume you were about to design materials to teach relative clauses and you wanted to know whether the "noun accessibility hierarchy" is correct. Actually, you don't care about the more esoteric types shown in the hierarchy but only relative clauses that follow subjects (e.g., The team *that wins the series* will advance to the finals), objects (e.g., I always like the team *that wins the game*), or the object of a preposition (e.g., The series tickets are in the envelope *that's on the table*) since these are the three types that must be sequenced for teaching purposes.

As a first step, you decide to use the Brown corpus as a data base since it is available for computer analysis. You randomly sample 10,000 sentences from the total corpus. Then, to find the relative clauses in these sentences, you use relative pronouns (*that, who, which,* etc.) as prompts. You sort through the examples that the computer lists to get rid of examples where the prompt word is not a relative pronoun (for example, where *who* is a question word rather than a relative pronoun). Then you categorize the relative clauses by position. The table showing the frequencies might look like this:

	SUBJ NP	OBJ NP	PrepPH NP
REL CL	442	334	94

From these frequencies, it is obvious that there are more relative clauses following subjects and objects than following prepositions. Numerically, the frequencies in these cells differ. Despite our confidence that this is so, we will perform a test to be certain of this relationship between position and frequency.

> *Research hypothesis?* There is no relation between position and number of relative clauses.
> *Significance level?* .05
> *1- or 2-tailed?* Always 2-tailed for this procedure
> *Design*
> *Dependent variable(s)?* Relative clauses
> *Measurement?* Frequency tally
> *Independent variable(s)?* Position
> *Measurement?* Nominal--3 levels (following a subject, object, or prepositional phrase)
> *Independent or repeated-measures?* Independent (Chi-square requires that the data from each subject or piece of text appear in one and only one cell. The comparisons here are *between* cells.)
> *Other features?* Data source: randomly selected sentences from a large data base thought to be representative of written text.
> *Statistical procedure?* Chi-square test

Box diagram: 1 X 3 design (1 level of dependent; 3 of independent)

REL.CL.

SUBJ	OBJ	PrepPH

Computing χ^2 for One-way Designs

Goodness of fit

step (1)

The first step in the Chi-square procedure is to prepare a frequency chart such as the one below. As before, in a one-way design, the dependent variable is the row and the independent variable is shown in the columns. The design is one-way--that is, we are investigating the relationship of the levels of *one* independent variable and the dependent variable. There is only *one* row of cells in the design.

indep. variables?

	SUBJ	OBJ	PrepPH
REL.CL.	442	334	94

dependent

The second step is to decide what the frequencies would have been if there were *no* relationship between position and number of relative clauses. If the number of relative clauses were the same, we would expect that each position would have the same frequency (1/3 for subject, 1/3 for object, and 1/3 for prepositional phrases). There are a total of 870 relative clauses, so there should be approximately 290 in each position if the H_o is correct. *(2)*

	Obs. f	Exp. f
SUBJ	442	290
OBJ	334	290
PrepPH	94	290

Looking at the actual distribution of relative clauses, the frequencies seem quite different from this "expected" distribution. But, is the difference great enough that we can feel confident in making claims that a difference exists?

The third step is to find how far the number of relative clauses in each cell departs from this expected value. That is, we subtract the "expected frequencies" (E) from the "observed frequencies" (O). These values have been filled in on the following table: *(3)*

	Obs. f	Exp. f	O − E
SUBJ	442	290	+152
OBJ	334	290	+44
PrepPH	94	290	−196

You can probably guess what we do next. We square these differences from the expected values, and these values become the column of differences squared.

	Obs. f	Exp. f	O − E	(O − E)²
SUBJ	442	290	+152	23104
OBJ	334	290	+44	1936
PrepPH	94	290	−196	38416

In the formulas we've worked with so far, the next step would be to sum these values and find the average. Chi-square is different in this regard. It weights the difference in each cell according to the expected frequency for that cell. This means it gives more weight to those categories where the mismatch is greatest. To do this, we divide this squared difference by the expected value.

	Obs.f	Exp.f	O−E	(O − E)²	(O−E)²÷E
SUBJ	442	290	+152	23104	79.67
OBJ	334	290	+44	1936	6.68
PrepPH	94	290	−196	38416	132.47

As you can see, we are comparing a table of frequency values with a table of expected frequencies (where everything is equal as it would be if there were no relationship between the two variables). We compare these frequencies to discover how far each cell in the frequency table differs from its respective cell in the table of expected values. The difference for each cell is then squared. Next, we divide the difference value for each cell by the expected value for the cell and sum these. We can see that the weighted differences in the $(O - E)^2 \div E$ column are greatest for the prepositional phrase. There are many fewer than we would expect. The next strongest weight is given to subject. There are more than expected if the distribution of relative clauses was not affected by the type of noun phrase. Then, we add the values in the final column (79.67 + 6.68 + 132.47 = 218.82). 218.82 is the observed value of χ^2.

The formula that captures the steps we have gone through is:

$$\chi^2 = \sum \frac{(Observed - Expected)^2}{E}$$

What does this χ^2 value tell us about confidence in our finding? To explain this, we must turn again to the notion of distribution and probability.

In our example, we know that if there were no relationship between position and frequency of relative clauses, each position would show an equal number of relative clauses. Each position should have the same opportunity (the same probability) to exhibit relative clauses as every other position.

This expected distribution is, then, something like our normal distribution. We believe that the frequencies in each cell will be equally distributed if the levels of the independent variable are the same. The distribution may not be exactly that of the expected distribution since there is always "error." However, if the null hypothesis is correct, whatever variation there is will have nothing to do with the position of the noun phrase.

The question is how much variation from this expected distribution is normal, and how different should the cell frequencies be in order for us to conclude that position *is* related to frequency of relative clauses? The χ^2 value tells us the magnitude of the variation in cell frequencies from the expected distribution. And, fortunately for us, mathematicians have figured out the probabilities for the distribution of χ^2 values for all the possible number of levels of dependent and independent variables. They are presented in the χ^2 table in appendix C (table 7).

Our χ^2 value is 218.82. Turn to appendix C and find table 7, labeled "χ^2 Distribution." In the first column of the table you will see the numbers for the degrees of freedom. The most probable value for χ^2 with 2 *df* in this table is 4.605. The probability of getting this value is .10--one chance in ten--*if* the levels (positions in this case) are the same. The next column for 2 *df* shows a value of 5.99 and the probability of getting this value, a value close to the expected value is .05--one chance in twenty. As you continue across the table, you see that the χ^2 values are getting larger--the difference from the expected value is getting larger too. The probability, the chances of getting the value, *if* the levels are the same, begins to drop. The higher the χ^2 value, the lower the probability that the levels are the same (that is, the easier it will be to reject the null hypothesis).

When we get to the very last column, we see that with a χ^2 value of 13.816, the chances are indeed slim that the levels (positions) are the same. The probability level has sunk to .001.

This means that there is only 1 chance in 1,000 that you could get a value as high as 13.816 *if* the number of relative clauses were the same in each position. It's very unlikely that you would get a result this far from the expected values if the levels were the same. Another way of saying this is that there is 1 chance in 1,000 that you would be wrong if you said that the number of relative clauses (in these data) differs in the three positions. Or, there are 999 chances in 1,000 that you would be wrong if you said that there was no difference in the number of relative clauses in the three positions. Our χ^2 value is 218.82, and that's so high that the probability isn't even on the page! Perhaps 1 chance in 1,000,000. We can feel great confidence in rejecting the null hypothesis. The number of relative clauses is definitely related to position in this text data base.

If you use this example as a guide, there is one thing to keep in mind: the sticky issue of independence. To assure independence, we randomly selected sentences from a very large data base. Assume, instead, that we had analyzed the relative clauses in one short story--a typical repeated-measures design where the same person produced all the relative clauses. The data would not be independent across cells and a Chi-square analysis should not be done. To avoid this, you might decide to analyze the relative clauses in science texts, a subcategory of the Brown corpus. Each passage is produced by a different writer. Again, there is a problem of independence, this time within the cells. It is possible that one passage by one author would contribute a very large number of relative clauses and this might radically influence the measure of relationship. In this case, the data within cells would *not* be independent of author. One author, because of personal writing style, might unfairly influence the outcome. (To avoid this problem in our example, we randomly selected sentences from the total data base and hoped to obtain no more than one sentence per author.)

The example we have used is unusual in that it is a one-way design. In fact, we very rarely have one-way Chi-square designs in applied linguistics research. Following the practice, we will consider more complex designs.

◇◇

Practice 14.1

1. If there were just two relative clause positions in the example (using random sampling techniques), how many of each would we expect to have if the total number of relative clauses in the example (using a random sample) was 870? ___435___ If there were five types? __175__

If we have no special information that tells us otherwise, our best estimate of the number of relative clauses for each can be calculated by ___avg___

2. Turn to the probability chart for χ^2 values. If the χ^2 value for our example were larger than 9.21 but less than 13.816, the probability level would be .01. This means that you would have 1 chance in 100 of being wrong if you rejected the null hypothesis. How many chances of being right would you have? ___99___.

If your χ^2 value were 6.1, how many chances would you have of being wrong if you rejected the null hypothesis? __5 in 100__.

3. Imagine that you wanted to compare the frequency of other types of relative clauses as a test of the the NP (noun phrase) accessibility hierarchy. Keenan and Comrie (1979) claimed that there is a hierarchy in terms of which noun phrases can be most easily relativized. The hierarchy is based on the types of relative clauses that appear across languages. Those most accessible should be those that appear in most languages. The less accessible the NP, the fewer the number of languages that should allow relative clauses for the NP. (Predictions are similar to those tested with a Guttman scalogram, right? That is, if a language allows relative clauses with indirect objects, it should also allow them with direct objects and subjects.) We should, then, be able to use the hierarchy to determine which types of relative clauses should be most difficult for second language learners. It is also possible that those highest in the hierarchy would also be those most frequently found in texts and those lowest in the hierarchy would have the lowest frequency. The hierarchy predicts the following order: subject NP, direct object NP, indirect object NP, oblique object NP (i.e., object of preposition), genitive NP (i.e., possessive), and object NP of a comparison. The degrees of freedom for positions of relative clauses is now ___5___. Suppose that the χ^2 value for the study, using a random sample of 10,000 sentences, was 10.276. The null hypothesis is that there is no difference in the frequency of relative clauses across these six types. That is, position is not related to the frequency of relative clauses.

What is the probability that you would be wrong if you rejected the null hypothesis? _10 in 100_ Would you reject the null hypothesis? Why (not)? _No._
To high a level for error

For practice, you might want to recalculate the values for the expected cell frequencies with six types, add fictitious data counts, and recompute the value of χ^2 for relative clauses.

Chi-square for Two-way Designs

In our examples so far, we have used Chi-square to check to see if frequencies on one variable (the dependent variable) change with levels of another independent variable. Let's turn now to an example which compares the relation of frequencies for two variables, both of which have several levels. Since levels of two variables are compared, this will be a *two-way design*.

Imagine your school district has entered a national campaign to encourage reading in the elementary schools. The school district wants to use this opportunity to study the relation of type of reward to increased reading. Students can select a material reward (stickers, chips, etc.), peer recognition (honor list with stars, videolog star of the week in reading), or special privileges (computer use, videorecording, etc.). Since there are children from several different ethnic groups, the school also wonders if this might have any relation with choice of reward. The children report the number of books they read each month and select whatever reward they wish.

> *Research hypothesis?* There is no relation between ethnicity and choice of reward.
>   *Significance level?* .05
>   *1- or 2-tailed?* Always 2-tailed for this procedure
> *Design*
>   *Dependent variable(s)?* Reward choice
>   *Measurement?* Frequency tally
>   *Independent variable(s)?* Ethnicity
>   *Measurement?* Nominal--3 levels (Vietnamese, Mexican-American, Chinese)
>   *Independent or repeated-measures?* Independent
> *Other features?* Intact class
> *Statistical procedure?* Chi-square

Box diagram:

	Vietnamese	Mex-Am	Chinese
Material			
Recognition			
Privilege			

Here are fictitious data on three groups of fourth grade children:

Reward Type	Vietnamese	Mex-Am	Chinese
Material	2	21	27
Recognition	8	17	7
Privilege	26	11	6

The above table gives us our observed values for each cell. To discover the expected values, we can't just divide the total frequencies this time by the number of cells. The expected values depend on the number of children in each group and the number of children in each group selecting each reward type.

First, we total the frequencies across the rows and enter this as a row total:

Reward	Vietnamese	Mex-Am	Chinese	Total
Material	2	21	27	$n1 = 50$
Recognition	8	17	7	$n2 = 32$
Privilege	26	11	6	$n3 = 43$
Total	$n1 = 36$	$n2 = 49$	$n3 = 40$	$N = 125$

At the bottom of each column are the number of Vietnamese responses (n_1), and so forth. If we sum the *row* frequencies, we can enter this under N in the bottom right-hand corner of the table. If we add the *column* frequencies, we should get the same value for N. These column totals and row totals are called the marginals.

To find the expected value for each cell, multiply the row total by the column total and divide this by N:

$$E_{ij} = \frac{n_i \times n_j}{N}$$

where E = expected frequency, i = row, and j = column.

Let's do this for the first cell in the upper left corner (f for Vietnamese selecting a material reward). The row total for material is 50. This equals n_i. The column total for Vietnamese is 36. This equals n_j. Multiplying n_i and n_j gives us 1,800. When we divide this by N (the total frequency for all groups on all rewards), the answer is 14.4. We place this number in the boxes drawn for the expected values below. $\frac{1800}{N} = 14.4$

	Vietnamese	Mex-Am	Chinese	
Material	14.40			50
Recognition				32
Privilege				43
	36	49	40	125

Let's go to the next cell, the number of Mexican-American children selecting a material reward. The row total is again 50, but the column total this time is 49. We multiply these and divide by N and insert the number in the corresponding cell below. Then we repeat the operation for the next cell, the number of Chinese students selecting a material reward.

When we move to the next row, the row total has now changed. The row total for recognition is 32. When we multiply this by the first column total and divide by N, we have the expected frequency for the number of Vietnamese children selecting a recognition reward (9.22). We continue on until all the cells are filled for the expected frequency table.

	Vietnamese	Mex-Am	Chinese
Material	14.40	19.60	16.00
Recognition	9.22	12.54	10.24
Privilege	12.38	16.86	13.76

Now we can find the differences between the observed frequencies and the expected frequencies in each cell. These are shown in the $O - E$ column in the table below. The next step is to square each of these values and enter the results in the column labeled $(O - E)^2$. Then we divide each $(O - E)^2$ value by the expected value for that cell and enter the answers in the last column of the table. Finally, we can total the values in this last column to obtain the value of χ^2.

Row	Col	Obs	E	*residual* $O-E$	$(O-E)^2$	$(O-E)^2/E$
1	1	2	14.40	−12.40	153.76	10.68
1	2	21	19.60	1.40	1.96	.10
1	3	27	16.00	11.00	121.00	7.56
2	1	8	9.22	−1.22	1.49	.16
2	2	17	12.54	4.46	19.89	1.59
2	3	7	10.24	−3.24	10.50	1.03
3	1	26	12.38	13.62	185.50	14.98
3	2	11	16.86	−5.86	34.34	2.04
3	3	6	13.76	−7.76	60.22	4.38
						$\chi^2 = 42.52$

Consulting the $(O - E)^2 \div E$ column, we see that the largest weightings are for cell 1-1 and cell 3-1. These relate to the Vietnamese group. Cell 1-1 shows they chose fewer material rewards than expected and (cell 1-3) more privilege rewards.

cell 1-1 = row 1, cell 1

3-1

Cells 1-3 and 3-3 relate to the Chinese group which chose more material rewards and fewer privilege rewards than expected.

The next step is to find out whether we can or cannot reject the null hypothesis. That is, are these weightings strong enough that we can say that the three groups do differ in their choice of rewards? You'll remember that the χ^2 value has to be placed in the appropriate Chi-square distribution. To do that, we need to know the degrees of freedom. We can't just subtract $K - 1$ for groups. We also have to subtract $K - 1$ for type of reward. In the study there are three groups of Ss. So the degrees of freedom for groups is $3 - 1 = 2$ (that's the hard part!). There are three types of reward. So the degrees of freedom for type of reward is $3 - 1 = 2$. To find the total degrees of freedom, we multiply these together. Perhaps an easier way to remember how to do this is take the number of rows minus 1 and the number of columns minus 1 and multiply them to find the degrees of freedom; i.e., $(3 - 1)(3 - 1) = 4$. The Chi-square distribution in which we will locate our χ^2 value is that which mathematicians have determined for 4 df.

Now we turn to table 7 in the Appendix and find the row marked for 4 df and look across the table until we find the location of the χ^2 value needed for the .05 level. The probability level listed is 9.49. Since we selected the .05 level, we can feel confident in rejecting the null hypothesis because our χ^2 of 42.52 is larger than 9.49.

If this were a real study, we could conclude that:

1. The two variables are related (ethnic membership is related to choice of rewards offered as an incentive to encourage free reading) for our sample Ss.

2. If the Ss were randomly selected and if all threats to internal and external validity had been met in the study, we would claim that our results could be generalized to other Ss of the same ethnic groups. Since this is not the case here, we will use the statistical procedure to be confident that our description of the results for our Ss is correct.

3. Even though the choice of reward was related to ethnic group membership, we cannot say that ethnicity caused the choice of reward. Nor do we know just how much weight to give ethnicity in terms of choice of reward. Other variables (e.g., sex, socioeconomic status, intrinsic vs. extrinsic motivation) might be as important or even more important in relation to choice of reward.

4. We are surprised (if we are) that the results turned out this way and we would like to replicate the study, taking greater care to be sure we have a representative sample, that we have better operational definitions for reward types, and so forth.

In practical terms, given that we cannot generalize, we might want to continue to give everybody whatever reward they want to select. Still, we should be willing to share the results with others, giving, of course, fair warning regarding lack of generalizability.

Practice 14.2

▶ 1. Ss in a study were categorized as being either analytic problem solvers, holistic problem solvers, or some mix of these two types. To see whether problem solving style related to the acquisition of discourse skills, these Ss were given a number of communication tasks. A composite score for each S was obtained and S were then given a "grade" based on their composite score. The data classify the Ss as follows.

Problem Solving Type

Grade	Holistic	Analytic	Mixed
< 25 (D)	11	9	10
25 - 49 (C)	12	11	11
50 - 74 (B)	35	34	30
> 75 (A)	32	37	28

Is performance on communication tasks related to problem solving styles? State the H_o, do a Chi-square analysis, and state your conclusions.

Ho Type of problem solver is not related to discourse skill (measured by grade).

Can you generalize the findings? Why (not)? *No. Don't know enough about who Ss were, etc.*

2. The following table is one of many presented by Shibata (1988) in her report of language use in three ethnic Japanese language schools. The table is based on 30 minutes of coded interactions per classroom. Three classrooms were observed in school 1, 3 classrooms in school 2, and 4 classrooms in school 3, for a total of 10 classrooms.

Student Utterances by Language and School

	School 1		School 2		School 3	
English	91	17%	69	14%	339	45.5%
Japanese	442	82%	406	85%	403	54.1%
Mixing	4	1%	4	1%	3	.4%
Total	537	100%	479	100%	745	100%

The basic question is whether the amount of Japanese and English usage differs in the three schools. We cannot use a Chi-square analysis of these data because we do not know whether certain children in the classes may have contributed more (or fewer) mixed, Japanese, or English utterances. If we counted the number of children who used Japanese, the number who used English, and the number who used both Japanese and English, we could do a Chi-square analysis. Explain why this is so. How much information would be lost if we did this?

_____

_____

_____

_____

_____

_____

◇◇

Yates' Correction Factor

In our examples, we have taken care that the degrees of freedom should always be greater than 1. Yet, it is possible we might want to compare frequencies where the independent variable has only two levels (where $K - 1 = 1$ df) or when we have a 2 X 2 design (where $K - 1 = 1$ and $K - 1 = 1$ so that $1 \times 1 = 1$ df). In the first case, the design is one-way and in the second case the design is two-way, but in each the degrees of freedom $= 1$. With 1 df, the comparison between the Chi-square distribution and the observed χ^2 value is not as close as mathematicians would like. So, there are special correction procedures to take care of the discrepancy. This is called the *Yates' correction factor*. Most computer routines build in this correction since it compensates for cell sizes less than 5 and doesn't negatively affect the outcome.

For one-way designs the correction factor is simple. If the observed value (O) is greater than the expected value (E), subtract .5 from O and enter this as the "corrected O." If the observed value (O) is less than the expected value (E), add .5 to O and enter this as the "corrected O" value. Then continue computing the χ^2 using the corrected values of O.

Actually, researchers seldom run a one-way Chi-square with only two cells (and a df of 1). The reason is that one can easily look at the raw frequencies and tell whether one cell has more than 50% of the frequencies. There is no real reason to run a Chi-square test and a correction procedure to determine if this is the case.

If you have a 2 X 2 design (2 levels of one variable and 2 levels of the other), you also have 1 df. A correction is required. The method by which we calculate this correction, however, is slightly different than for a one-way design. Instead of just adding or subtracting .5 from observed values, we have an amended Chi-square formula. Here it is in all its glory:

$$\chi^2 = \frac{N(|ad - bc| - N \div 2)^2}{(a + b)(c + d)(a + c)(b + d)}$$

To understand all the as, bs, and cs, look at this diagram of a 2 X 2 table:

	Var X		
Var Y	a	b	$a+b$
	c	d	$c+d$
	$a+c$	$b+d$	

The letters a, b, c, and d represent the frequencies that fall into the four cells in the design. The two-letter symbols in the margins simply represent the sums of the cells in each row and column.

To see how this works, consider the following example. To encourage language minority students to continue their studies at the university, special tutorials were offered to students identified early as being "at risk." At the end of their freshman year, some "at risk" students were placed on probation and others not. The research question is whether students who took advantage of tutorial help were more likely to succeed (i.e., not be placed on probation). Here are the frequencies.

	+Tutorial	−Tutorial
+Probation	34	73
−Probation	432	377

Let's plug these frequencies into our formula:

$$\chi^2 = \frac{916(|34 \times 377 - 432 \times 73| - 916 \div 2)^2}{107 \times 809 \times 466 \times 450}$$

$$\chi^2 = \frac{916(18718 - 458)^2}{18,152,261,000}$$

$$\chi^2 = \frac{305,419,680,000}{18,152,261,000}$$

$$\chi^2 = 16.825$$

The critical value of χ^2 for 1 df is 3.84. The value we obtained is higher, so we can reject the H_o at the .05 probability level. We can conclude that for these students there is a relation between tutorials and probation--fewer students who participated in tutorials were placed on probation.

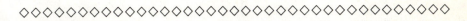

Practice 14.3

▶ 1. To better understand student dropout rates, a questionnaire was administered to a (stratified) random sample of 50 Ss who had dropped out of school and 50 who continued in the sophomore year. Each questionnaire item was subjected to Chi-square analysis. Here are the frequencies for a question regarding work hours.

	Wk < 4 hrs	Wk > 4 hrs.
Drop	19	33
Continue	31	17

In the space below write out the formula and do the calculations.

The value of χ^2 is _____. What is the critical value needed to reject the null hypothesis? _____. Can you reject the null hypothesis? _____ What can you conclude? _____
_____

In this case, do you think you can generalize the findings? Why (not)? If so, to what population can you generalize? _____
_____
_____
_____
_____

◇◇

Assumptions Underlying Chi-square

As always, there are some cautions to remember before using the Chi-square procedure. The following assumptions must be met:

1. The data must consist of frequencies.

The Chi-square procedure is appropriate when the data are counts of numbers of items or people in particular classifications or cross-classifications. Do not attempt to perform a Chi-square analysis using proportions. Change the proportions to raw frequencies and then perform the analysis if this is appropriate. Or, find a different procedure that is appropriate for proportions.

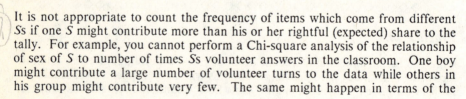

It is not appropriate to count the frequency of items which come from different Ss if one S might contribute more than his or her rightful (expected) share to the tally. For example, you cannot perform a Chi-square analysis of the relationship of sex of S to number of times Ss volunteer answers in the classroom. One boy might contribute a large number of volunteer turns to the data while others in his group might contribute very few. The same might happen in terms of the number of turns taken by the girls. Instead, count the number of *S*s who take turns and the number of *S*s who do not and perform the Chi-square analysis on these data.

	M	F
+ Turns		
− Turns		

Or, count the number of turns each *S* takes in, say, an hour class period and use these to set levels for the dependent variable.

No. Turns	M	F
< 5		
5-9		
10-14		
> 15		

In the above contingency table, the data that go in each cell are *frequency* data. Don't be confused by the rank scales on the side of the table. These are *levels* of the dependent variable set on an ordinal scale, but the data consist of frequency counts.

As you can see, we are trying to meet the same criticism mentioned earlier for text analysis studies. The data in such studies are traditionally sampled across a genre. It is possible that some individual samples may contribute more heavily than others to the frequency counts and thus give the researcher a spurious relationship where none exists. While tradition appears to approve of this use of the Chi-square procedure for such data, it seems inadvisable to us. Your research advisor or consultant may also feel that a Chi-square analysis is inappropriate for such data. (In other words, don't just accept tradition. Check with your advisors before attempting the analysis in such cases. You don't want to put your research at risk by making the wrong choice.)

2. The categories should form a logical classification.

It is simple to see that two levels for sex--male and female--form a logical classification. Oral and written modes also form a logical classification. L1 membership (Chinese, Japanese, Korean, Farsi, etc.) forms another logical classification. However, in some studies it might be more logical to group subject-prominent languages in one group, topic-prominent languages in another, and those which use both into a "both S-P and T-P" group. The logic of the classification is related to the research question.

When the research question relates to grammar categories such as clause types, the logic of the classification may not be so easily determined. How many different clause types form the possible "set" of clauses (as in our relative clause example)? Why are some types included in studies and others not? Again, the overall logic of the classification must relate to the study and be justified by the researcher.

3. *Whenever the frequency of an event is counted, the frequency of nonoccurrence must also be counted.*

where? if totals on edges

This is a fairly simple matter to remember. For example, if we want to discover the relationship between the number of Ss who pass an ESL course and L1 membership, we must count the number who pass *and* the number who do not pass. If we want to look at the relationship of sex and the number of Ss who take turns in class, we need to count the number of boys and the number of girls who take turns *and* the number who do not. In the case where there are several levels of a variable, this may not be so obvious. The frequencies in one level contrast with all those in the other levels. In L1 membership, the number of Chinese Ss contrasts with Ss who are not Chinese (Japanese, Korean, Farsi, etc.). The number who are Japanese contrasts with those who are not Japanese (Chinese, Korean, Farsi, etc.). As you can see, this reinforces assumption 2. If the category levels are not logical and complete in terms of the research questions, it will become impossible to meet assumption 3.

4. *The data must be independent.*

There are two ways in which this assumption might be violated. First, there might not be independence between the cells in the design. Second, there might not be independence of data within each cell. Let's look first at the problem of maintaining independence between the cells in the design.

Each S or observation can be entered in *only* one cell. That is, the Ss in our study of reward type were tallied under only one type of reward. The same S couldn't be entered under *material* and also under *recognition*. If a student wavers back and forth in reward choice, we would have to add another level to reward type--perhaps *material + recognition*--and place that person in this category. If you have sent out a questionnaire and you have questions for which you want to compare the number of people who answer "yes" and "no," you can't enter a person in both categories. You can add the response category "undecided" and place the person there. If you are looking at semantic functions of *if clauses*, you can enter each *if clause* under one and only one function.

In addition, you can't count frequencies on a variable at one time, count them again later and compare the frequencies using Chi-square. That is, a regular Chi-square analysis is not appropriate for repeated-measures designs. Thus, you couldn't count the number of ESL students who used the language lab during their introductory course and the number of ESL students (the same students) who used it one year later and compare these with a Chi-square analysis.

The data must also be independent within each cell. As an example, assume we wanted to look at changing forms in pidgin languages. To do this, we collected data from children, adolescents, adults, and elderly adults. We singled out some area where we expect change may be found--perhaps the emerging use of one certain modal. We expect to find the highest frequency in the data of children with a decrease as we cross the age groups. We go through the data counting the presence and absence of the modal (where native speakers would use the modal). The table is divided into eight cells (four age group levels and two presence/absence levels for the modal). Again, each piece of data goes into one and only one cell of the box design. However, it is possible that certain Ss contributed more than their fair share to the data within each cell. There is not independence of data within the cell. This lack of independence threatens the validity of the study.

As a second example, assume we ran a concordance program on the Brown corpus searching for instances of "resemble" in hopes of validating the finding that in sentences such as "X resembles Y" (which should be symmetric with "Y resembles X"), the Y is always the standard of comparison. Thus "Y resembles X" is not a synonymous form. The data base might be limited to the "science" and "science fiction" sections of the Brown corpus. This gives us four cells (where Y is or isn't the standard of comparison in science or science fiction text). Again, the frequencies fall within one and only one box of the design, but there is a problem in that certain authors within the science or science fiction base might be fond of the word "resemble" while others might never use such constructions. The counts within the cell are not really independent. The data are not representative of the category (science or science fiction text) but only of certain contributors in each category. The validity of the study is at risk if the data are analyzed using a Chi-square analysis.

The data must be independent. If the data are not independent across the cells, you might be able to use McNemar's test (which we will illustrate in a moment) or CATMOD (categorical modeling), a special procedure available on computer programs which will be discussed in chapter 16. If the data are not independent within the cells, you might want to use solutions such as those shown on page 407. Another option, if you convert such data to rates (mean number of instances per 1,000 words, number of instances per 100 clauses, etc.), might be to use nonparametric procedures presented in chapters 9 through 12 of this manual.

5. *The sample size must be large enough* to obtain an expected cell frequency of five.

In cases where you have small sample sizes, some of the expected cell frequencies may dip below five. If this happens and your design has only 1 df, the best thing to do is to use *Fisher's Exact test.* This is available in SAS, or you can read about it in Hays (1973), Siegel (1956), or Kendall and Stuart (1977). If your study has more than 1 df, and some of the cells have an expected cell frequency less than 5, it is possible that some of the cells could be collapsed without damaging your study. For example, if you used a separate cell for every grade from kindergarten through 12, you would have 12 cells. You might be able to group these into K-3, 4-6, 7-9, 10-12. This would, in all likelihood, give you a large enough expected cell frequency to allow you to apply the Chi-square test.

When you do a Chi-square procedure by hand, you will have to remember to check the expected cell size frequencies yourself. If you run Chi-square on any computer program, you should automatically receive a warning message when the cell sizes drop below an allowable level.

Interestingly, not all statisticians agree on the minimum size allowed for Chi-square. Some writers suggest that if the *df* is only 1, a minimum expected frequency of 10 (not 5) be used, and 5 is the minimum for designs with more than 1 *df*. This seems rather conservative, but do not be surprised if your advisor or statistical consultant suggests an expected cell size of 10 for a study with 1 *df*. Others specify 5 as the minimum for 1 *df* and 2 as the minimum for larger *df*. On some computer printouts you will find a warning only when 20% of the cells have dropped below an expected cell frequency of 5. Again, be sure to discuss this issue with your research advisor or statistical consultant prior to interpreting your results.

6. *When the number of df equals 1, apply the Yates' correction factor.*

We have already discussed how to compute the correction in the previous section. Most computer packages automatically make this correction in carrying out the procedure.

Given these assumptions, you should now be able to draw design boxes for Chi-square contingency tables and decide on the appropriateness of the procedure for data. Before doing this, though, complete the following practice.

◇◇◇◇◇◇◇◇◇◇◇◇◇◇◇◇◇◇◇◇◇◇◇◇◇◇◇◇◇◇◇◇◇◇◇◇◇◇

Practice 14.4

1. Consider an example where a foreign language department surveyed student interest in taking conversation classes in foreign languages. A Chi-square analysis was used to relate interest of *S*s (low, moderate, high) to the information they gave on each questionnaire item. What advice would you give the department regarding one question which relates interest in such classes to whether or not *S*s have friends who speak the language. The following contingency table data box show the choices. Cell 1, for example, would show the number of *S*s who have low interest in conversation classes and who have friends who speak the foreign language.

Ss' Interest	+ Friends spk lang.	− Friends spk lang.	Have no real friends
Low			
Moderate			
High			

Advice _____

_____

_____

▶ 2. Draw a Chi-square contingency table (design box) to match each of the following (fictitious) study descriptions. Feel free to set up your own levels of the dependent and independent variable. There is no one "right" design. Compare your contingency tables with those given in the answer key.

Example A
This study tests the relationship of geographic area to the importance attached to bilingual education. In a national survey, respondents were asked how they would vote on the issue of mandatory bilingual education in elementary schools.

Example B
A study related the choice of university major to the first language membership of foreign students.

Example C
An interlanguage study related the "age of arrival" (i.e., how old each S was on arriving in a country where the second language is spoken) to stages of negation (taken from Schumann's [1979] stages of *no* + verb, unanalyzed *don't*, aux + neg, analyzed *do* + neg).

Example D
The study relates the cognitive styles sometimes called "field-independent" vs. "field-dependent" to self-correction of errors in revision of compositions.

▶ 3. Review each of the assumptions that must be met in order to use a Chi-square procedure. Then, decide whether Chi-square is an appropriate test for the data described in each of the following examples. Give the rationale for your answer. If the procedure is not appropriate, show how the study might be amended so a Chi-square procedure could be done.

Example A
Students in community adult school programs were asked about their reactions to group-work activities scheduled in ESL classes. Students voted for, against, or undecided regarding continuance of these activities. The students came from three major L1 groups: Spanish, Far East languages, and Middle East languages. The question is whether students from these three backgrounds have different views of the value of group work in language classes.

_____
_____
_____
_____
_____

Example B
The school district keeps records of testing related to language disorders. Among many tables are those that show the number of bilingual children for whom stuttering is a problem only in L1, only in L2, and in both L1 and L2. The tables also show the number of boys and girls in each category, since sex is expected to relate to stuttering.

_____
_____
_____
_____
_____

Example C
In chapter 5 (page 137) we presented a table showing the frequencies for seven clause types in oral and written samples of fourth-grade children. The null hypothesis is that there is no relationship between language mode (written vs. oral) and frequency of clause types (seven types of clauses) in the data.

_____
_____
_____
_____
_____
_____

Example D
You taught your ESL students using two different methods--a teacher-centered approach and a cooperative-learning approach. You counted the number of clauses the students produced in each lesson. You hoped to show more student participation in the cooperative-learning session than in the teacher-centered session.

_____
_____
_____
_____
_____
_____

4. Look back through your own research questions and find those for which the Chi-square test might be appropriate. Check with your study partners to be sure you can meet the assumptions. If you are not sure, note your uncertainty below and discuss with members of your study group.

_____
_____
_____
_____
_____

List the number of cells in each of the studies for which you think the Chi-square is an appropriate procedure. Will correction factors be required? _____
_____
_____
_____

◇◇

Interpreting χ^2

As we have seen in a few of our earlier examples, there may be several variables (independent and moderating variables) which we would like to relate to the dependent variable. This means that the table for the observed frequencies will have several cells.

In the example of relation of position and frequency of relative clauses we had three cells (three different NP positions). There were 442 relative clauses in subject position, 334 following direct objects, and 94 with prepositional phrases. In our research article, we would report the results of our statistical test as: $\chi^2 = 218.82$, $df = 2$, $p < .05$. When the χ^2 value allowed us to reject the null hypothesis, we could say that the frequency of relative clauses differed in these three positions. From the frequencies, it is obvious there were fewer relative clauses after prepositional phrases than following subjects or objects. It is this cell which shows the greatest difference from the expected cell frequency. In addition, the $(O - E)^2 \div E$ column shows that subject and object NPs have *more* relative clauses than expected and that prepositional phrase NPs have *fewer* relative clauses than expected.

This is a legitimate interpretation of the χ^2 value for this study. The problem is that the full table is seldom included in research articles, so it is difficult for the reader to know whether or not the interpretation is correct. The writer should explain the basis for the interpretation when the table is not included.

The table makes it possible for us to interpret the data quite easily, but this isn't always the case. Sometimes we want to compare the relation of several independent variables or several levels of one independent variable to the dependent variable. This was the case in our (fictitious) example of ethnic background and reward preference. There were nine cells in the design. We found we could reject the null hypothesis (that is, there was a difference in preference of reward type according to ethnic background), but we could not say exactly where the difference occurred by looking at the χ^2 value. Again, the research article might simply report the results of the statistical test as: $\chi^2 = 42.52$, $df = 4$, $p < .05$. That tells us that the frequencies in the cells differ from those expected (given the total number of responses and the degrees of freedom). It doesn't say *where* the difference is. It might be in any of the nine cells or in some combination of them.

The best thing to do (when you need to locate precisely which cells compared with which other cells resulted in a high χ^2 value) is to carry out a *Ryan's procedure* (see Linton & Gallo, 1975). This procedure compares the frequencies in all the cells against each other in ways that allow you to see exactly where the differences are the greatest (most significant).

However, at this point what is most important is that you use the probability level to give you confidence in accepting or rejecting the null hypothesis. Further interpretation of the actual cell frequencies can be done by looking at the $(Q - E)^2 \div E$ values for each cell (those that are largest are those which depart most from the expected cell frequency). You can interpret your computer printouts for χ^2 in exactly this way.

Once you have located the cells where the $(O - E)^2 \div E$ are the largest, be sure to note whether the value is *higher* or *lower* than the expected value as you give your interpretation. In the reward type study on page 401, cell 1 (row 1, column

1) and cell 7 (row 3, column 1) made the largest contribution to the χ^2 value. Compared with the other two groups, the Vietnamese students selected fewer materials rewards and more privilege rewards than expected. If you wish, you can request (from your consultant or from the computer) a Ryan's procedure analysis to accomplish the same thing.

The Chi-square test gives us a useful way of dealing with frequency data in a systematic way. It allows us to talk about frequencies not just in terms of percent, proportion, or ratio, but in terms of whether or not the frequencies reflect a relationship between variables.

Strength of Association

Chi-square allows us to test the null hypothesis of *no* relationship between variables. When we reject the null hypothesis, we can conclude that a relationship exists. A Ryan's procedure can show precisely where the relation differs from that "expected." However, the test does not show how strong the relationship between the variables in the *present* research might be.

When the χ^2 value is significant, we can estimate how strong the association between variables is for a particular data set by using association measures. For research with 1 *df*, you may use *Phi* (Φ). For research with more than 1 *df*, use Cramer's V.

Phi (Φ)

When the χ^2 is significant (the H_o can be rejected), it is possible to determine the association between the variables for your particular data set. The formula is very simple since the information needed is already available on your data sheet or your computer printout. (In fact, your computer package may automatically generate these strength of association figures.)

$$\Phi = \sqrt{\frac{\chi^2}{N}}$$

(χ^2 equals the χ^2 value itself, not the value squared.) Let's apply the formula to our Chi-square analysis of the relation between dropout rates and work hours (page 405).

$$\Phi = \sqrt{\frac{\chi^2}{N}}$$

$$\Phi = \sqrt{\frac{6.77}{100}}$$

(?) *see p. 405*

$$\Phi = .26$$

The two variables (in *these* data) share a 26% overlap. That's a fairly strong relationship, but it should lead us to wonder what other variables might account for the remaining 74%.

Cramer's V

Phi isn't an accurate strength of association measure with tables where the *df* is greater than 1. Cramer's V should be used for these tables. You need to calculate Phi first, and then use the following formula:

$$Cramer's\ V = \sqrt{\frac{\Phi^2}{(\min r - 1, c - 1)}}$$

Use the instructions above to calculate Phi. The (min *r* − 1, *c* − 1) means 1 from *either* the number of rows or the number of columns in the design, *whichever is smaller*.

In the problem regarding the relation between ethnicity and reward type (page 399), there are three rows and three columns. Since they are the same, the denominator for the problem is 2, and Φ is .58, so Cramer's V is:

$$Cramer's\ V = \sqrt{\frac{\Phi^2}{(\min r - 1, c - 1)}}$$

$$Cramer's\ V = \sqrt{\frac{.58^2}{2}}$$

$$Cramer's\ V = .41$$

Again, the relationship was significant so a relation exists between the variables. Cramer's V shows us that not only does a relationship exists but that it is a strong one.

Practice 14.5

▶1. Calculate Phi (Φ) for the tutorial example on page 405. The χ^2 value is 16.825. _____

_____

_____

▶ 2. Imagine that the χ^2 value for the problem solving example in practice 14.2 was 13.01 instead of .901. Then calculate Cramer's V. _____

_____

_____

With the Chi-square procedure, as with the procedures presented in part II, we have used a statistical test to test our hypotheses. It is extremely important to know which statistical test to select in testing hypotheses. The Chi-square test is appropriate when the data are nominal and the measurement is in terms of frequencies. The data must be independent.

McNemar's Test for Related Samples

Here is an example where the data are *not* independent. A student you tutor has great trouble with verb tense. You ask her to underline every verb in a composition you have just returned to her. Then you ask her to correct any errors that she sees. This makes it possible for you to do a frequency count of the number of verbs which were incorrect in the original and which are now correct, the number incorrect which are still incorrect, the number correct which are still correct, and the number correct which are now incorrect. The comparison is between the original version (time 1) and the revised version (time 2) and so the comparison is "within" Ss, a repeated-measures design.

The table might look like this:

		Revision	
		Correct	Incorrect
Original	Correct	4	4
	Incorrect	14	3

Look at the number in the lower left of the table. It shows that 14 items were incorrect in the original and are now correct. Three items were incorrect and still are incorrect. The top row shows four items were correct and are still correct, and four were correct and are now incorrect. The McNemar's analysis checks these changes and uses an adjusted χ^2 formula to give us a χ^2 value of 2.36 and a two-tailed probability of .02. The largest change is in the cell which shows change from incorrect to correct, so we can interpret the McNemar's analysis as giving us confidence that this procedure of self-guided correction was effective for the student. While the example given here is from an individual S, the data could have been drawn from a class of Ss at two points in time. That is, the procedure can be applied to an individual case study or to a group. (The data here are observations rather than Ss.)

In case you should want to do a McNemar's procedure by hand, it's a very simple task. Since the test is for matched pairs of Ss or observations as well as two responses from the same Ss, let's try it with a new example. Suppose that you wondered whether maintenance of the L1 (native language) could be linked to being a first child in a bilingual immigrant family. Each firstborn child in the study was matched with a non-firstborn child of the same age and same sex, enrolled in the same high school. Successful L1 maintenance was determined by an oral interview conducted by a native speaker of each language. The data were five ratings yielding a possible total of 25 points. A cut-off point of 18 was established (and justified) for ±maintenance.

The first step is to place the observations into a contingency table, just as we did for the Chi-square test:

		Controls		Total
		+Maint.	−Maint.	
1st Child	+Maint.	A	B	A + B
	−Maint.	C	D	C + D
	Total	A+C	B+D	N Pairs

Here are the fictitious data. To read the table, the A cell shows the number of pairs where the first child and the control both successfully maintained the language. The B cell shows the number of pairs where the first child was successful but the paired control was not. C shows the number of pairs where the first child was not successful but the paired control was. D shows the number of pairs where both members of the pair failed to maintain the L1.

		Controls		Total
		+Maint.	−Maint.	
1st Child	+Maint.	26	15	41
	−Maint.	7	37	44
	Total	33	52	85

The formula is simple.

$$z = \frac{B - C}{\sqrt{B + C}}$$

We can place the data from the table into the formula to compute the z value.

$$z = \frac{15 - 7}{\sqrt{15 + 7}}$$

$$z = 1.70$$

Using table 1 in appendix C, we see that the critical value of z for .05 (two-tailed hypothesis) is 1.96. (Remember from our earlier discussion of the z score table in chapter 8 that 1.96 is the critical value that allows us to reject the null hypothesis at the .05 level of significance.) We cannot reject the null hypothesis because our z value is less than the critical value of 1.96. Our conclusion, if the data were real, must be that L1 maintenance for these Ss is not strongly related to being the first child in a bilingual immigrant family. The two groups do not differ significantly. However, since the probability is .089 ($z = 1.70$, area beyond $z = .0446$, times 2 tails $= .089$), we could say there is a "trend" in this direction in the data which warrants further investigation. We might want to revise the research so that we could see if language maintenance is related to other factors as well.

There is one important caution to keep in mind when doing the McNemar's test by hand. The number of changes must be ≥ 10. That is, B + C must be 10 or more. Most computer programs automatically correct for this and uses a Chi-square distribution (with a Yates' correction factor) instead of the z distribution to calculate probability. The z distribution is much easier to do by hand. Just remember, though, that the number of changes (whether positive or negative) must exceed 10 before you can estimate the probability in this way.

Practice 14.6

▶ 1. Your school district is considering establishing an immersion program. Beginning in kindergarten, one class at one elementary school would be taught completely in the "heritage language" of the community (Swedish in this case). Elementary school teachers in the district attend a weekend seminar on the issue, listening to the arguments of community leaders, immersion experts, parents, and administrators, and then discuss the issue themselves in small group workshops. Teachers cast a straw vote at the beginning of the seminar and again at the close of the seminar.

		Before	
		Yes	No
After	Yes	15	28
	No	10	21

In the space below, compute the value of z using a McNemar's procedure.

$$z = \frac{B - C}{\sqrt{B + C}}$$

$$z =$$

Can you reject the H_o? What can you conclude? _____

_____

_____

2. Seminars often have an immediate effect on opinions but, later, opinions may again change. To improve the study, what suggestions might you make? Would you still be able to use a McNemar's procedure to analyze the data? Why (not)?

_____

_____

_____

_____

◇◇

To summarize this chapter:

1. Frequency data on separate Ss or observations = Chi-square analysis.

2. Frequency data on samples from the same or matched Ss = McNemar's test (or CATMOD in SAS).

When computing χ^2 by hand, it is important to remember that two adjustments must be made in certain circumstances. First, when the number of degrees of freedom equals 1, an adjustment is needed--use the Yates' correction factor. Second, if expected values for cells drop below five, either collapse some of the cells (if this makes sense in the study) or use the Fisher's Exact test. In summary:

1. $df \geq 2$, apply Chi-square.

2. $df = 1$, apply the Yates' correction factor.

3. Expected cell frequency ≥ 5, apply Chi-square.

4. Expected cell frequency < 5, collapse cells or use Fisher's Exact test if the df is only 1.

In interpreting the results, discuss the findings in terms of the cells where the observed values differ most from expected cell frequencies--the $(O - E)^2 \div E$ values. Ryan's procedure may be used to locate more precisely the difference among the cells.

In the following chapter, we will consider tests that allow us to discover relationships between variables when the data are measured using rank-order scales or interval scores.

Activities

Read each of the following abstracts. Decide whether Chi-square might be an appropriate statistical test for the data (or some part of the data). Give a rationale for your decision. Draw the design box(es). Note any special corrections that might need to be made if the data were analyzed by hand.

1. J. Holmes (1986. Functions of *you know* in women's and men's speech. *Language in Society, 15*, 1, 1-21.) set out to investigate the assumption that *you know*, often regarded as a lexical hedge, is more characteristic of women's speech than men's. A 50,000-word spoken corpus, roughly 40% formal speech and 60% informal speech, was examined for instances of *you know*. Half of the corpus was men's speech, the other half women's. The analysis indicated that there were no differences in the number of *you know*s produced by men and women, but there were sex differences in the functions of *you know*. Women used *you know* more frequently than men as a token of certainty, while men tended to use *you know* as a mark of uncertainty.

2. K. L. Porreca (1984. Sexism in current ESL textbooks. *TESOL Quarterly, 19*, 4, 705-724.) did a content analysis of the 15 most widely used ESL textbooks. Results show that men were mentioned twice as often as women in text and pictures; that men were mentioned first in exercises, sentences, etc., three times as often as women; and that there were six male workers appearing for every working female. Masculine generic constructions were used extensively; the adjectives used to describe women focused on emotions, appearance, and marriage while renown, education, and intelligence characterized men.

3. U. Connor (1984. Recall of text: differences between first and second language readers. *TESOL Quarterly, 18*, 2, 239-256.) asked 10 native English speakers and 21 ESL learners to read a passage from the *Washington Post* and then to write immediate recalls of its content. L1 subjects recalled more propositions than ESL students, but there was no significant difference between these groups in recall of "high-level" ideas from the text.

4. S. Blum-Kulka & E. Levenston (1987. Lexical-grammatical pragmatic indicators. *Studies in Second Language Acquisition, Special Issue 9*, 2, 155-170.) used Chi-square tests to compare the request strategies of native speakers and nonnative speakers of Hebrew. Here is one table from the study that compares the request as to whether it is hearer oriented (e.g., "Could you lend me your notes"), speaker oriented (e.g., "Could I borrow your notes"), a combination of hearer and speaker oriented, or impersonal. Each analysis has a 4 X 2 contingency table (although the data are presented on one line in the table). The numbers in the parentheses are the raw data for the study. They show the number of Ss whose request fell into each category. The percentage figures are given directly above these data. (If you add percentages for each NS cell, you will see that they total 100%, as do those for NNS.) The χ^2 value given refers to the contingency table for that particular situation. Select one situation and, using the raw score data, recompute the χ^2 value for that situation. Interpret the value in terms of the larger $(O - E)^2 \div E$.

	Hearer oriented		Speaker oriented		Hear/Spkr oriented		Impersonal	
	N %	NN %	N %	NN %	N %	NN %	N %	NN %
Situation 1 $\chi^2 = 7.669$ 3 df, p <.05	82.7 (234)	70.8 (165)	4.9 (8)	8.2 (19)	4.3 (7)	9.0 (21)	8.0 (13)	12.0 (28)
Situation 5 $\chi^2 = 5.908$ 2 df, p <.05	50.6 (86)	42.6 (101)	19.4 (33)	30.0 (71)			30.0 (51)	27.4 (65)
Situation 7 $\chi^2 = 14.662$ 2 df, p <.03	21.2 (35)	29.2 (62)	23.6 (39)	28.6 (61)			55.2 (91)	42.8 (89)
Situation 11 $\chi^2 = $ n.s.	81.7 (134)	82.3 (149)	10.4 (17)	5.0 (9)			7.3 (12)	12.7 (23)
Situation 15 $\chi^2 = 12.535$ 4 df, p <.01	71.3 (107)	63.6 (84)	25.3 (38)	22.6 (30)	.7 (1)	.8 (1)	2.0 (3)	12.9 (17)

Situation 1 = Student asks roommate to clean up the kitchen, which roommate left in a mess.
Situation 5 = A student asks another student to lend lecture notes.
Situation 7 = A student asks people living on the same street for a ride home.
Situation 11 = A policeman asks a driver to move her car.
Situation 15 = A university teacher asks a student to give his lecture a week earlier than scheduled.

5. D. Tannen (1982. Ethnic style in male-female conversation. In J. J. Gumperz [Ed.]. *Language and Social Identity*. New York, NY: Cambridge University Press, 217-231.) discusses misunderstandings in male-female conversations where one party is being more or less "direct" while the other is being rather "indirect." The "indirect" party gives out hints which are missed while acting on hints which were never intended; the "direct" party misses hints and is unaware that the partner is acting in response to perceived hints. Such misunderstandings are common among members of the same culture group, but mix-ups may be even more characteristic of cross-cultural communication. To show this, Tannen did a mini-experiment where she asked Americans, Greeks, and Greek-Americans to interpret transcripts of real conversations such as the following:

Wife: John's having a party. Wanna go?
Husband: OK.
Wife: I'll call and tell him we're coming.

Then Tannen directed the *S*s: "Based on this conversation only, put a check next to the statement which you think explains what the husband really meant when he answered 'OK.'"

1. ___My wife wants to go to this party, and since she asked, I'll go to make her happy.
2. ___My wife is asking if I want to go to a party. I feel like going, so I'll say yes.

Later, the same couple had this conversation:

Wife: Are you sure you want to go to the party?
Husband: OK, let's not go. I'm tired anyway.

The *S*s then put a check next to the statement which explains what the wife really meant by "Are you sure you want to go to the party?"

3.___It sounds like my wife doesn't really want to go, since she's asking me about it again. I'll say I'm tired, so we don't have to go, and she won't feel bad about preventing me from going.
4___Now that I think about it again, I don't really feel like going to a party because I'm tired.

The table for choice 1 shows the following frequencies:

American		Greek		Greek-American	
Female	Male	Female	Male	Female	Male
5	3	8	5	9	4

The focus of Tannen's paper is not on this mini-study but rather on the interpretive analysis of conversations. However, for our purposes, let's consider how we might expand the mini-study. Unfortunately we do not have the tapes of the actual conversations (and suprasegmentals would be very important in this study). Nevertheless, reproduce the questionnaire and administer it to four Americans (two male and two female) and four *S*s from other ethnic groups (two male and two female). In your study group, combine the data to form your own contingency tables for the responses to items 1-4. If the data warrant it (i.e., your expected cell frequencies are large enough), do a Chi-square analysis and interpret your findings.

6. In chapter 10 (page 306) we asked you to draw a chart showing options for statistical procedures. Add the procedures given in this chapter to your chart along with those of chapters 11 through 13.

References

Hays, W. 1973. *Statistics for the Social Sciences*. Second Edition. New York, NY: Holt, Rinehart and Winston.

Keenan, E. L. and Comrie, B. 1979. Data on the noun phrase accessibility hierarchy. *Language, 55,* 333-351.

Kendall, H. G. & Stuart, A. 1977. *The Advanced Theory of Statistics.* Fourth Edition. New York, NY: Macmillan.

Linton, M. & Gallo, P. S. 1975. *The Practical Statistician: A Simplified Handbook of Statistics.* Monterey, CA.: Brooks/Cole.

Schumann, J. 1979. The acquisition of English negation by speakers of Spanish: a review of the literature. In R. Andersen (Ed.). *The Acquisition and Use of Spanish and English as First and Second Languages.* Washington, DC: TESOL, 3-32.

Shibata, B. 1988. Ethnic Japanese language schools in the Los Angeles area: a descriptive study. Unpublished master's thesis, TESL, UCLA.

Siegel, S. 1956. *Nonparametric Statistics for the Behavioral Sciences.* New York, NY: McGraw-Hill.

Chapter 15

Correlation

Measuring Relationships

In previous chapters, we have tested differences in the means of two or more groups with the aim of establishing the *effect* of the independent variable(s) on a dependent variable. In our research, however, we often hope to establish a relationship between the scaled or scored data of one variable with those of another. For example, if we wonder whether a good short-term memory is related to success in language learning, we might want to know the relationship of Ss' scores on a short-term memory test and their scores on a language proficiency test. Do students who score well on one exam also score well on the other, and do students whose scores are low on one also do poorly on the other? We need a way to measure this relationship directly (rather than as an exploratory strength of association estimate following a *t*-test or ANOVA procedure).

In selecting any statistical procedure to measure relationships, we begin by asking several basic questions.

1. How many variables are being compared? What are they?

2. Is the comparison between groups or repeated-measures of the same or matched groups?

3. How have the data been measured: frequencies, rank-order scales, or interval scores?

For the above example, there are two variables being compared: short-term memory and language proficiency. The comparison involves repeated observations of the same Ss (repeated-measures), and the data have been measured as scores (interval measurement).

As a second example, imagine that you and a friend team-taught two composition classes. At the end of the course you both read all the final exam compositions, rating them using a department guidesheet which gives 25 possible points (five 5-point scales). You wonder how strong an agreement there is between your ratings. That is, when you give high marks to a student, does your team teacher also give high marks? When one of you gives a student a low mark, does the other also give a low mark? Again, you want to describe the strength of the relationship between these two sets of ratings.

Here there are still two variables: your ratings and those of your partner. Fortunately, correlations can be carried out where data are from the *same Ss* on different measures or when ratings of performance are obtained from *different Ss.* This time, though, the data are measured using an ordinal 5-point scale (and the distribution may or may not be continuous) rather than an interval score. Most correlations are for linear (i.e., interval) data, but special correlation formulas are available that allow us to compare rank-ordered and even dichotomous (nominal) data.

You may also see correlation used when the data are really open-ended frequency data. For example, a frequency count of some particular linguistic feature might be correlated with the frequency tally of a second feature. The number of questions a teacher asks might be correlated with the number of questions students produce (again, open-ended frequency tallies). In such correlations, the researcher assumes the open-ended counts, since they are *incremental* in nature, are the same as equal-interval scores. Clearly, they are not if the observations are open-ended in length. That is, if you count instances of code-switching of students and want to relate that to, say, vocabulary use of students, neither variable may be continuous. There is not an equal opportunity for all Ss to accumulate some optimal number of code-switches. If the vocabulary measure is the number of words each S produces, again Ss have unequal opportunities to produce words. Some researchers solve this problem by converting frequency tallies to rates, ratios, or percentage values. For example, each S might have a $\overline{X}$ number of switches per 100 words, per turn, or whatever and the vocabulary measure might be turned into a type-token ratio. This conversion (as we mentioned in chapter 5) must be justified to the satisfaction of the field. Then, the researcher should check the data for normality of distribution to be confident that they spread evenly throughout the range. (As you can tell, we are less happy with converting data from frequency to ordinal to interval measurement than the reverse! There are too many studies in our field where frequencies are converted to percentages [e.g., $f = 2 = .50$], averaged for a group [$\overline{X}$ percent], and then entered into statistical calculations as if they were interval measures.)

This doesn't mean that we cannot use correlations to discover relations where one variable may be a category (i.e., nominal) and the other an interval or ordinal scaled variable. There are *special* correlation formulas for such data. There is also a special correlation for two category variables. The Pearson correlation, however, is restricted to variables where measurement is truly continuous.

Pearson Correlation

The Pearson correlation allows us to establish the strength of relationships of continuous variables. One of the easiest ways to visualize the relationship between two variables is to plot the values of one variable against the values of the other. Let's use fictitious data on short-term memory and language proficiency as an example. Assume that data have been collected from a group of students on each of the two variables. If we have only a few students, it will be easy for us to plot the data. The plot is called a *scatterplot* or *scattergram*.

To show the relationship, the first step is to draw a horizontal line and a vertical line at the left of the horizontal line. It is conventional to label the vertical axis with the name of the dependent variable and the horizontal axis with the independent (though these designations are arbitrary). Short-term memory will be the independent variable in this example and proficiency the dependent variable. This classification is fairly arbitrary, for we are *not* looking for the *effect* of an independent variable on a dependent variable (as in *t*-tests or ANOVA). Rather, we are searching for the *degree of relationship* between the two.

Here are the scores for the first five *S*s.

S	STM Score	Prof. Score
1	25	100
2	27	130
3	28	200
4	30	160
5	35	180

The first *S*'s proficiency score is 100 and we located that score on the horizontal axis. The student's short-term memory score is 25 and we located that on the vertical axis. Imagine a line straight out from each of these points; we placed a symbol where the two lines would meet.

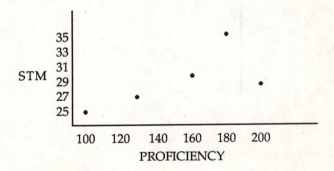

Each S's place is now marked on the scatterplot. It appears that as the scores on one test increased, the scores on the other test also increased. $S5$, however, looks a bit different from the others. If we look at the first four Ss, we would expect that $S5$ would have scored higher on STM so that the dot would line up more closely with those of the other Ss.

Imagine that there was a *perfect* relation between the two variables. Such things do not happen in reality (not even if we measure exactly the same thing twice), but let's imagine anyway. Assume that you and your team teacher actually gave each student exactly the same rating on their final compositions. The assignment of the variables to the x and y axes is really arbitrary. But, again, we want to know the strength of agreement between the two sets of values just as we did in the previous example. Here is the scatterplot:

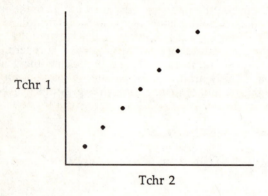

If we draw a line through the symbols, the line is perfectly straight. There is a perfect positive relationship between the two sets of scores. As the ratings assigned by one teacher rise, the ratings by the other rise--so the relationship is positive.

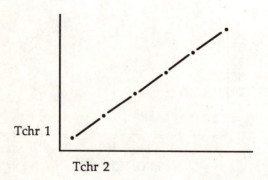

Now, imagine that you and your team teacher never agree on anything. In fact, the higher you rate a composition, the lower she rates it. (Again, this wouldn't happen in reality--especially since you are using a guidesheet in scoring the compositions!) The resulting scatterplot would look like this:

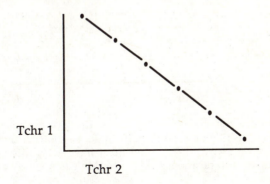

Tchr 1

Tchr 2

The relationship is now a perfect *negative* correlation. That is, increase in your ratings is perfectly matched by an equivalent decrease in your team teacher's ratings.

Perfect correlations, whether positive or negative, are really impossible (except when data are correlated with themselves!). That is, if you try to draw a line through all the points (symbols) placed on a scatterplot, the result will not be a straight line. The data do not usually line up in this way. However, it is possible to see the general direction that a straight line would take if the two variables are related.

Look at the following diagrams. Notice that the line does not touch all the points but that it does reflect the general direction of the relationship. If you draw a straight line to show the direction of the relationship, you can see whether the correlation is positive or negative.

It is also possible that no relationship will be apparent from the scatterplot. Imagine that you and your team teacher were asked to judge composition of students from another school. Here is the scatterplot for your ratings:

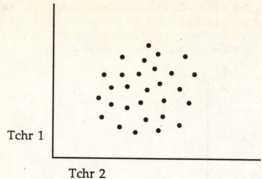

Tchr 1

Tchr 2

It is impossible to draw a straight line in this scatterplot to show the direction of the relationship because there is no pattern to go by--that is, there is no real relationship between the two ratings. You must have very different standards of excellence for judging compositions. This shouldn't happen if raters are trained beforehand.

Before we look at the statistical procedure that pinpoints the strength of the relationship in correlation, look at the three scatterplots below. In the first example, the points most tightly clustered around the straight line. In the second, they are moderately scattered out from the straight line, and in the third figure, the scatter is greatest and no line is possible.

The actual strength of the correlation is reflected in these scatterplots. The tighter the points cluster around the straight line, the stronger the relationship between the two variables. (Remember that in a *perfect* correlation, the points were right on the line.).

Of course, when you draw a scatterplot (or ask the computer to draw the scatterplot for your data), the straight line doesn't appear. You have to imagine it. However, there is a technical term for the imaginary straight line around which all the points cluster. It is called the *regression line*, and the angle of the regression line is called the *slope*. The amount of variation of the points from the regression line and the tightness of the clustering of the points to the line determine the *magnitude*, the strength of the correlation coefficient.

◇◇◇◇◇◇◇◇◇◇◇◇◇◇◇◇◇◇◇◇◇◇◇◇◇◇◇◇◇◇◇◇◇◇◇◇◇◇◇

Practice 15.1

1. As a review, what does each point on the scatterplot represent?_____
_____

If the straight line rises, the correlation is said to be _____. If it falls, the correlation is _____. If it is impossible to visualize a straight line in the data display, the relation is so weak that no correlation can be seen.

2. Review your own research questions. For which might you want to establish a relationship via correlation?
_____
_____
_____

Draw a sample scatterplot for the correlation that you hope to obtain. If you expect the correlation to be strong, how will the points be placed relative to a straight line?
_____

If you expect a correlation to exist but expect that it will not be extremely strong, how will the points appear relative to a straight line? _____
_____

◇◇◇◇◇◇◇◇◇◇◇◇◇◇◇◇◇◇◇◇◇◇◇◇◇◇◇◇◇◇◇◇◇◇◇◇◇◇◇

Computing the Correlation Coefficient

Now that the concept of correlation has been presented, we will turn to the ways of measuring the strength of the correlation in more precise terms. If you remember the discussion of z scores in chapter 7, you may already have an inkling as to how we might compare scores when they are from different data sources.

Suppose that we wanted to discover the relationship between scores on two tests. Let's take the example where the university wonders whether they can use information obtained from SAT verbal scores (information available with a student's application for admission) instead of an ESL language test to determine whether or not students should be required to take ESL classes. If the scores on the verbal portion of the SAT are very strongly related to those on the ESL language test, then perhaps this would be possible. The first problem, of course, is that a score of 80 on one test does not equal a score of 80 on the other. The means for the two tests are not the same, nor is the standard deviation the same since the tests have different properties. However, we can equate the values of the two variables (verbal SAT and ESL test) by converting them to z scores. (You will remember that the z score is a way to standardize scores across tests and is computed as $z = \dfrac{X - \overline{X}}{s}$.)

Suppose that you asked the computer to convert each student's score on the verbal SAT and on the ESL test to a z score. The scores are now equivalent. (That is, a z score of 1.1 on one variable will equal a score of 1.1 on the other.) If a student has a positive z score on one variable, we expect the same student will have a positive z score on the second variable. If this is the case for all students, the correlation will be positive. If students who have positive z scores on one variable have negative z scores on the second variable, the correlation will be negative. The closer each student's z score is on the two ratings (whether positive or negative), the greater the strength of the relationship between the two tests.

Here are the z scores of nine students on the two measures:

S	SAT Verbal	ESL Test	Product
1	+1.5	+1.5	2.25
2	+1.2	+1.2	1.44
3	+.8	+.8	.64
4	+.4	+.4	.16
5	.0	.0	.00
6	−.4	−.4	.16
7	−.8	−.8	.64
8	−1.2	−1.2	1.44
9	−1.5	−1.5	2.25

In the above table, S5 scored at the mean for each test since her z score is 0 on each. The Ss with positive z scores on one measure also have positive z scores on the second. Those with negative z scores on the first measure also have negative z scores on the second. If you look at the z scores, you can see that each student's score on one test *exactly* matches that on the other. This is another one of those impossible perfect correlations. But how, other than comparing the z scores, do we know this is a perfect correlation?

You will notice that there is a column labeled "product" in the above table. This was obtained by multiplying each S's z scores. If we add the cross products in this column, the answer is 8.98. Actually, the answer would be 9.0 if we had not rounded off the number. If we take the average (divide the total by 9, since there are 9 Ss in this table), the answer is 1. This is the value of the correlation coefficient for these data, the value of an absolutely perfect correlation.

Here is the z score formula for the Pearson correlation. (Notice that this formula uses $N - 1$ in the denominator while the previous example used N. $N - 1$ is an adjustment for sample data.)

$$r_{xy} = \frac{\sum(z_x z_y)}{N-1}$$

It is possible that you might someday have z score data and need to use this version of the formula. However, it is more likely that you will start with raw scores. ✓

The correlation coefficient, symbolized by the letter r, can be calculated in several ways. Whatever method is chosen, the value r will always be somewhere between -1 and 0 or 0 and $+1$. The closer the r is to ± 1, the stronger the relationship between the variables.

Computing Correlation from Raw Scores

When we assign a value (a rating or a score) to a variable, we usually enter this value as raw data on a scoring sheet (or directly into the computer). We don't want to go to the trouble of converting each of these values into z scores. The conventional formula for the correlation coefficient takes care of this conversion for us. Let's work through an example using raw score data.

Imagine that you have undertaken a study that requires you to have valid pronunciation ratings for bilingual children in their first language. To do this, your study group advisors suggest that you ask two native speakers to listen to the taped data and judge each child on a 15-point scale (from three 5-point scales for segmental phonology, general prosodic features, and absence of L2 features--nativeness).

Here are the fictitious data:

S	Judge 1	Judge 2
1	12	8
2	10	12
3	11	5
4	9	8
5	8	4
6	7	13
7	7	7
8	5	3
9	4	8
10	3	5

Because the formula looks complicated, let's go through the computations in five separate steps.

1. List the scores for each S in parallel columns on a data sheet. (Arbitrarily designate one score as X and one as Y as we did for the scatterplots.)

2. Square each score and enter these values in the columns labeled X^2 and Y^2.

3. Multiply the scores ($X \times Y$) and enter this value in the XY column.

4. Add the values in each column.

5. Insert the values in the formula.

The information from steps 1 through 4 are entered in the following chart.

S	X	Y	X²	Y²	XY
1	12	8	144	64	96
2	10	12	100	144	120
3	11	5	121	25	55
4	9	8	81	64	72
5	8	4	64	16	32
6	7	13	49	169	91
7	7	7	49	49	49
8	5	3	25	9	15
9	4	8	16	64	32
10	3	5	9	25	15
Totals	76	73	658	629	577

The formula for the correlation coefficient, sometimes called the *Pearson Product-moment correlation*, follows. r is the symbol for the Pearson correlation coefficient. The subscripts x and y stand for the two variables being compared (the somewhat arbitrarily specified dependent and independent variables).

raw score formula

$$r_{xy} = \frac{N(\sum XY) - (\sum X)(\sum Y)}{\sqrt{[N\sum X^2 - (\sum X)^2][N\sum Y^2 - (\sum Y)^2]}}$$

Since all the symbols may be a bit overwhelming, we have filled in the values from the data table. Check to make sure that you can match the symbols and the values. Then use your calculator to check the computations shown below.

$$r_{xy} = \frac{N(\sum XY) - (\sum X)(\sum Y)}{\sqrt{[N\sum X^2 - (\sum X)^2][N\sum Y^2 - (\sum Y)^2]}}$$

$$r_{xy} = \frac{(10)(577) - (76)(73)}{\sqrt{[(10)(658) - (76)^2][(10)(629) - (73)^2]}}$$

$$r_{xy} = \frac{222}{\sqrt{804 \times 961}}$$

$$r_{xy} = .25$$

The final value of r shows a positive correlation. You remember that the value of r will always be between 0 and 1. If it isn't, you will need to recheck your calculations.

We also said that the closer the r value is to 1, the stronger the relationship between the variables. This does not look like a very strong relationship. We'll discuss just how you can interpret the strength of the correlation in a moment.

Practice 15.2

1. What suggestions could you give the raters that might might help them reach a closer agreement on the ratings?

_____

_____

_____

▶ 2. Calculate the correlation between these z scores from two tests, one a writing error detection test (where Ss locate grammar errors in paragraphs) and the other a multiple-choice grammar test.

S	WED	Gram
1	−.40	0.00
2	0.00	−.36
3	−.80	−.73
4	.80	0.00
5	1.20	1.09
6	−1.60	−1.45
7	.80	1.45

$$r_{xy} = \underline{\hspace{2cm}}$$

▶ 3. The data in the following table are fictitious but are given to show ratings of 10 students over five conversations on factors related to Grice's (1975) maxims of cooperative conversation. According to Grice, a cooperative conversationalist does not violate constraints on quality and quantity in his or her contributions to conversational exchanges. Responses must be topic-relevant, truthful, of appropriate quantity and appropriate quality. In the following table are scores for 10 students for five factors that reflect these constraints. For each conversation, the S was rated on a 6-point scale for topic maintenance (Grice's maxim of "Be relevant"), for appropriate level of informativeness of content (Grice's maxim of "Be truthful"), for clarity (Grice's maxim to "Be clear"), and two scales for appropriate quantity--appropriate turn-taking and appropriate turn length (Grice's maxim of quantity: "Say enough but not too much"). A perfect score for each factor, then, would be 30 points (6-point scale and 5 conversations) and a perfect total test score would be 150. Do a correlation of any two variables. Use either the z score or the raw score method, whichever you like best. (If you want to check to make sure you really do get the same value for r with each formula, you can do it both ways!)

S	Relev.	Inform.	Clarity	T-take	T-length
1	14	23	19	15	10
2	12	24	20	18	18
3	13	15	18	22	21
4	12	18	20	21	25
5	24	14	16	20	25
6	25	24	20	23	25
7	18	8	10	15	20
8	28	2	2	19	26
9	14	17	15	22	19
10	16	12	7	14	22

Variables correlated: _____

$r =$ _____

4. Which formula do you think helps you the most to understand exactly what r represents? Why? _____
_____
_____
_____
_____

◇◇

Assumptions Underlying Pearson Correlation

There are four basic assumptions that must be met before applying the Pearson correlation as a measure of how well any two variables "go together."

1. The data are measured as scores or ordinal scales that are truly continuous.

Interval and ordinal data are appropriate data for correlation. (Remember that statisticians call these measures *continuous*?) However, it is important that the ordinal measurement be truly continuous (i.e., approach equal-interval measurement and a normal distribution).

2. The scores on the two variables, X and Y, are independent

We know that the rating on one variable should not influence the rating on the second. One very obvious violation of this assumption may pass unnoticed when the Pearson correlation it used to test the relationship that exists among many pairs of variables in the same study. For example, you might want to know how well scores students obtain on subtests of a test battery "go together." For instance, is the relation between vocabulary and reading strong--does a high, positive correlation exist between these two subtests? What about the correlation between grammar and reading? Between a section which tests cultural appropriateness of speech acts such as warnings, compliments, threats, or condolences and a grammar subtest? Or cultural appropriateness and reading scores? Students' subscores on all these tests *can* legitimately be correlated with each other. It is also possible to correlate subscores with the total score for the battery. There is, however, one very important thing to remember. The total test score contains all the values of the subtest scores. The test scores on X and Y are *not* independent. To solve this problem, *subtract the subtest score from the total test score before running the correlation* or use other corrections available in computer packages. When reading journal articles or reports where part-to-whole correlations such as these are given, it is difficult--if not impossible--to be certain that the assumption of independence of the variables has been met. Each researcher must remember to meet the assumption, and it would be helpful if such comparisons were reported as *corrected* part-to-whole correlations.

3. The data should be normally distributed through their range.

The range of possible scores in each variable should not be restricted. For example, with a 5-point scale, the scores should not all fall between 3 and 4 or the correlation will be spurious. It is also important that extreme scores at the far edges of the range for each variable not distort the findings. Check for outliers and consider the influence of these scores in interpreting the strength of correlation.

4. The relationship between X and Y must be linear.   —*But not know until test?*

By linearity we mean that we expect that it is possible to draw an imaginary *straight* line through the points on the scatterplot (and measure how tightly the points cluster around that straight line).

Sometimes the line that would connect the points is not straight, not linear but curvilinear. The classic example of this is the relationship between anxiety and test scores. We all need a little anxiety to sharpen our responses. As anxiety increases our performance increases and so test scores should rise. However, a *lot* of anxiety can have a very debilitating effect on our performance. As anxiety increases at the upper ends of the anxiety scale, scores on tests should fall.

Here is the scatterplot for this relationship:

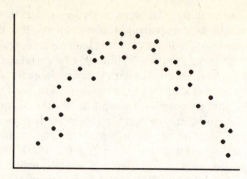

The correlation starts out strongly positive and ends up strongly negative, and the actual *r* value would, of course, be distorted.

It's also possible to have a curvilinear relationship in the other direction. For example, in teaching an introductory course in linguistics, the notion of comparing sound inventories and phonological rules across languages is extremely difficult for many students. In the early stages, the more students work on the homework assignments, the more confused they become. The relation between time devoted to study and success on phonology quizzes may be negatively correlated. At some point, these same students magically "get" the concept, and from that point on, the time devoted to study is positively correlated to success on quiz scores.

The Pearson correlation is not appropriate when the relationship is curvilinear. The problem is that the researcher may not always be aware that a relationship might turn out to be curvilinear. The best way to avoid this possible problem is to ask the computer to produce a scatterplot for each correlation. If the scatterplot shows a curvilinear relationship, either make an appointment with a statistical consultant or read Kirk (1982) for appropriate statistical procedures for measuring the strength of curvilinear relationships or transforming the data.

Practice 15.3

1. Look back at the example in practice 14.2. Do you believe that five 6-point scales for a possible total of 30 points for each variable really meets the requirements of the Pearson correlation? Why (not)?

_____

_____

_____

2. Look at the following examples and determine whether a Pearson correlation would be an appropriate measure for determining the strength of the relation of the variables.

Example A: You wonder whether first language is related to the accuracy of grammatical judgments ESL students make on such sentences as *She asked me to write the report, She made me to write the report, She advised me to be careful, She recommended me to be careful.*

Variable *X*: _____ L1 _____
Variable *Y*: _____ gr judg score _____
Rationale for (not) using Pearson correlation: _____
_____ cos nominal variable not truly continuous _____

Example B: You believe that the amount of time students spend outside class using a language is as important as time devoted to language instruction in class. You ask every student to keep a diary of the amount of interaction time spent outside of class where the new language is used. You want to know how this relates to the scores they receive on your final examination.

Variable *X*: _____ L2 prac outside class _____
Variable *Y*: _____ Final exam Score _____
Rationale for (not) using the Pearson correlation: _____ Pearson. Continuous _____
_____ Interv data _____
_____ linear relationship _____

3. If you have data already available on your computer, you might want to run a correlation of a subtest with a total test score first without heeding the warning about part-to-whole correlations. Then rerun the correlation, subtracting the values for the subtest from the total test score. How much difference does this make in the correlation?) _____

4. Draw the curvilinear relationship between the variables in the introductory linguistics course example (page 438) below:

5. A teacher asked *S*s to rate their course for "course satisfaction" using a 5-point scale (5 showing high satisfaction). She wondered whether course satisfaction and grades were related. She converted the grades to 1 = F, 2 = D, 3 = C, 4 = B, 5 = A and then ran a correlation for the two variables. Which assumptions seem to be met and which do not? Would you advise using a Pearson correlation for the analysis? Why (not)?

_____

Interpreting the Correlation Coefficient

Once you have obtained the *r* value for the correlation, you still must interpret what it means, and caution is warranted. Remember that the magnitude of *r* indicates how well two sets of scores go together. The closer the value is to 1, the stronger the relationship between the two variables.

Researchers use different cutoff points in deciding when a relationship is high enough or strong enough to support their hypotheses. The most sensible way of interpreting a correlation coefficient is to convert it into overlap between the two measures. To compute the overlap, square the value of *r*. This allows us to see how much of the variance (the variability of scores around the mean) in one measure can be accounted for by the other. To the degree that the two measures correlate, they share variance. The following figures represent this overlap.

If there is no correlation between the two measures, the *r* is 0 and the overlap of variance between the two measures is also 0.

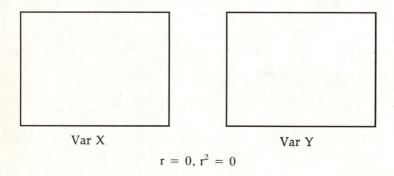

$$r = 0, r^2 = 0$$

If the correlation of two measures is .60, the variance overlap between the two measures is $.6^2$ or .36.

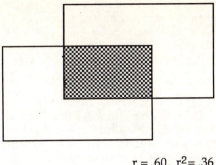

$$r = .60, \; r^2 = .36$$

If the correlation is .85, the shared variance is r^2 or .72.

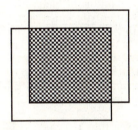

$$r = .85, \; r^2 = .72$$

The overlap tells us that the two measures are providing similar information. Or, the magnitude of r^2 indicates the amount of variance in X which is accounted for by Y or vice versa. If there were a perfect correlation between two variables, the overlap would be complete--the boxes would match perfectly. To the extent that the correlation deviates from the perfect overlap of 1, we lose space shared by the two measures. The strength of the relationship becomes weaker.

If we computed a correlation between a test of grammar and a test of general language proficiency, and the correlation turned out to be .71, we could say that the two tests overlap to the extent of r^2 (or .504). This is a fairly strong correlation; the overlap is 50.4%. However, if you hoped to show that the two tests measured basically the same thing, the correlation isn't very strong. You would want an r in the high .80s or .90s. You would want a very high overlap of the two measures.

If you wanted to have confidence in the ratings that two raters assign to students' oral reports, you would also expect that the r would be in the high .80s or .90s. That is, you want the ratings to overlap as much as possible.

On the other hand, if you ran a correlation between a test of cultural appropriateness of various speech act expressions and general language proficiency, the r would probably be lower than .80 because language proficiency might have several components, only one of which is "cultural appropriateness." Since you would not expect that the two tests measure the same thing, a correlation of .30 to .50 (an overlap of 9% to 25%) might be expected, and therefore be an acceptable correlation.

A correlation in the .30s or lower may appear weak, but in educational research such a correlation might be very important. For example, if you could show a correlation between early success in learning to read and later success in second language acquisition, this might be important if you wanted to locate prospective students for a FLES (foreign language in elementary school) program. While no causal claim could be made, in the absence of any information on other variables more strongly related to FLES achievement, you would do well to select early readers for the program.

Beginning researchers often make the mistake of asking the computer to judge the "significance" of a Pearson correlation. Remember that judging "significance" in this case only determines whether you can reject the null hypothesis of *no* relationship between the variables (i.e., whether you can reject the "no overlap" figure shown on page 440). A fairly weak correlation will allow you to do this. The critical values needed to reject the null hypothesis of no correlation are given in table 8, appendix C. Imagine that you have data from your class of 37 Ss on the TOEFL and your final exam score. Let's see how strong a correlation you would need in order to reject the null hypothesis.

Turning to table 8, you will see that the degrees of freedom for Pearson correlation is the total $N - 2$. If there are 37 students in your class, the df is 35. In the row for 35 df, you will find the critical value ($\alpha = .05$) is .3246. If the correlation is equal or higher than .3246, you can reject the null hypothesis of no relationship.

However, this procedure won't tell you how to judge the importance of the discovered relationship. Look back at the scatterplots at the beginning of this chapter. The figure for teacher 1 and teacher 2 on page 430 shows little relation between the ratings. Yet, the H_o could be rejected if the correlation were statistically significant at the .05 level: that is, there is *some* relationship--not much, but some. By looking at this scatterplot, you should be able to see that a "significant correlation" doesn't mean very much. The important thing to do is look at the *strength* of the relationship. To do that, it is best to talk about the relationship in terms of the overlap between the two measures (r^2). The overlap should be high (with an r in the .80 to 1 range) if the two measures are claiming to test the same thing. The correlation can be much lower (with an r in the .35 to .80s range) and still be very important.

To make this superclear, let's use a silly example. Assume you wondered whether people who are good at languages also make lots of money. You get the scores of all the people who took the ETS tests of French, German, Russian, and Spanish at the last administration, look up their phone numbers, and call them all up to ask how much money they earn. And they told you! You have 1,000 Ss in this study. You run the correlation and obtain an r of $+.063$. Heart pounding and fingers atremble, you consult the distribution table for the Pearson correlation. Hooray, it's significant at the .05 level! You can reject the H_o and say that there is a relationship.

However, when you present these results at the next meeting of the MLA Association, some smart heckler asks you how you could be so stupid. Of course there's a relationship with that many Ss, yet the strength of association is $.063^2$ or $.00397$. Only 4/1000 of the variability in income earned is accounted for by foreign language proficiency. You sink to the floor and hope the rug will cover you. Checking the probability of Pearson r tells you if there is a nonchance relationship, but it is the strength of relationship that is the important part. *often overlooked in rls. reports.*

Pearson correlation is often used to correlate several pairs of variables at once. For example, having given a proficiency test, you might want to know whether students who do well on one section of the test do well on another section of the test. If there are several sections, the correlations can all be done at once and the results displayed in a table. It doesn't make sense to use a table if only two variables are correlated.

Correlation tables, or matrices, usually look like triangles. That's because the computer prints out the correlations among all the variables so each correlation is printed twice. To make the table easier to read, only half of it is reproduced.

For example, here are the Pearson correlation figures for a sitting of UCLA's ESL placement exam. The figures show the correlations among the various subtests (dictation, cloze, listening comprehension, grammar, and reading).

	DICT	CLOZE	LISTEN	GRAM	READ
DICT	1.000	.919	.874	.925	.838
CLOZE		1.000	.826	.883	.880
LISTEN			1.000	.854	.774
GRAM				1.000	.796
READ					1.000

The 1.000 figures on the diagonal are, of course, the correlation of one variable with itself, so the 1.000 below the column marked DICT is of dictation with dictation. The next column, marked CLOZE, shows first the correlation of cloze with dictation (.919) and then cloze with cloze (1.000). The next variable, LISTEN, shows the correlation of listening comprehension with dictation (.874), then with cloze (.826), and then with itself (1.000). Then grammar is correlated with dictation (.925), with cloze (.883), with listening (.854), and itself. Finally, reading is correlated with dictation, cloze, listening, grammar, and itself. Now, if we tried to fill in the other half of the triangle, we would repeat all this information. For example, in the first column, we would add the correlation for dictation and cloze. That value would be .919 and is already available as the first figure in the cloze column. Then we would add the correlation for dictation and listening and that is already available as the first value under the LISTEN column. If you get a computer printout that gives all these values, use the row of 1.000 values (the

correlation of a variable with itself) as the place at which to divide the table to avoid redundant information. Please remember that the correlations are based on the data. Unless the observations were randomly selected and the study meets all threats to internal and external validity, you cannot generalize. The correlation is for *these* data, not some others. The correlation is also influenced by the quality of the test as applied to these Ss--that is, test reliability. We assume that the subtests are all equally reliable tests. If they are not, interpretation problems arise.

Correction for Attenuation

When correlating a group of variables, we assume that the method of measuring each of the variables is reliable. But, if each measurement is not of comparable reliability, the correlation itself may be distorted. For example, if we ran correlations in a "fishing expedition" where we wanted to see the relation of many different variables to a test of language proficiency, we might expect that all the data entered would not be equally reliable. It is possible that the proficiency test is highly reliable, the test of short-term memory not so reliable, the test of anxiety could have medium reliability, and several of our "home-grown" tests of listening comprehension, speech act recognition, and so forth might also vary in terms of reliability. With so much difference in reliability of measurement, the correlations obtained between the proficiency test and each of these other measures cannot be compared.

We have not yet discussed ways of determining measurement reliability (see chapter 18) but, if we know the reliability of our tests, we can easily hold reliability constant and correct the correlation.

The formula for this correction is:

$$r_{CA} = \frac{r_{xy}}{\sqrt{r_{ttx}r_{tty}}}$$

In this formula, r_{CA} is the corrected correlation. r_{xy} is the value of the uncorrected correlation. r_{ttx} is the reliability coefficient for the first variable and r_{tty} is the reliability of the second.

Let's imagine that we ran a correlation between our home-grown test of speech act appropriacy, the short-term memory test, and the proficiency examination. The uncorrected correlation values were: speech act and proficiency = .65, short-term memory and proficiency = .60. However, when we look at the reliability of the speech act test we find that it is .60 while the reliability of the short-term memory test is .90. The reliability of the proficiency test is .95. Let's see how this affects the correlation.

$$r_{CA} = \frac{r_{xy}}{\sqrt{r_{ttx}r_{tty}}}$$

$$r_{CA} = \frac{.65}{\sqrt{.95 \times .60}}$$

$$r_{CA} = .86$$

$$r_{CA} = \frac{r_{xy}}{\sqrt{r_{ttx}r_{tty}}}$$

$$r_{CA} = \frac{.60}{\sqrt{.95 \times .90}}$$

$$r_{CA} = .65$$

Without the correction for attenuation, the two measures (speech act appropriacy and short-term memory) appear to relate about equally to language proficiency. Once the correction has been done, this picture changes in such a way that the relation between speech acts and proficiency is actually much stronger (for these fictitious data) than the relation between short-term memory and proficiency.

Practice 15.4

▶ 1. At the end of the semester, ESL university students in a composition class were given three tests: a composition test, a multiple-choice grammar test, and a written error detection test (where the S must spot errors in short written passages). The correlation of composition and multiple-choice is .70; that of composition and written error detection is .75. The reliability of these three tests is composition test .80, written error detection .90, and multiple-choice grammar test .95. The question is which of the two tests (the discrete point grammar test or the more global error detection test) relates better to the composition test. Correct the correlations (between each of these tests with the composition test) for attenuation. What can you conclude?

_____

_____

_____

A final word of warning regarding the interpretation of correlation. ==Correlations measure overlap, how well two variables "go together." This is _not_ the same thing as effect or causation.== Correlations are never to be interpreted in the light of one variable affecting a second variable or causing it to change. That is, in the example that tries to establish a relationship between hours spent using the language outside class and success on a language achievement test, there can be no claim that this extra outside class practice _causes_ an increase in test scores. ==(ANOVA and the _t_-test procedure investigate effect.)== If you use those procedures for descriptive purposes and have met the threats to internal validity, you can talk about the effect of the independent on the dependent variable for the data.

And it is possible to generalize if you have met all the threats to external validity as well. Remember that we use eta^2 and omega^2 to determine strength of *relationship* in the sample and thus decide how much importance to attribute to the effect.)

Nevertheless, it isn't uncommon to find causal claims being made in the literature. We are all familiar with junk mail circulars where language schools promise to have us "speaking like a diplomat" in a new language within weeks of enrolling in the course. If they are smart, such programs test our speaking ability prior to *any* exposure to the language. Depending on how the school legally defines "speaking like a diplomat," they can easily show a positive correlation between time spent in the program and gains toward speaking like a diplomat. Readers of such ads interpret the relationship as causal. Obviously, that's a mistake.

Factors Affecting Correlation

Let's review the factors that can influence the value of *r*. First, if you have a restricted range of scores on either of the variables, this will reduce the value of *r*. For example, if you wanted to correlate age with success on an exam, and the age range of your *S*s was from 18 to 20, you have a very restricted range for one of the variables. If a full range of scores is used, the correlation coefficient will be more "interpretable."

A second factor that might influence the value of *r* is the existence of scores which do not "belong"--that is, extreme "outliers" in the data. If you can justify removing an outlier and doing a case study on that particular *S*, then it is best to do so because that one extreme case can change the value of *r*. Again, you can't just throw out data when they do not fit. You must explain why certain responses are exceptional in order to justify their removal.

A third factor which can influence the value of *r* is the presence of extremely high and extremely low scores on a variable with little in the middle. That is, if the data are not normally distributed throughout the range, this will throw the correlation coefficient off. The data need to be normally distributed in the sample. You might, however, reconstitute the data as nominal (high vs. low) and do a different type of correlation (point biserial or phi).

A fourth factor that can affect the value of the correlation is the reliability of the data. Statistical tests assume that data is reliable. In the case of correlation, it is important that the reliability of measurement actually be checked. If the measurement of each variable is not of comparable reliability, the correlation must be corrected using the correction for attenuation formula.

After all these warnings, the most important thing is to use common sense. It is possible to have a very high correlation coefficient--high but meaningless--or a very low correlation that still can be important. For example, you might correlate the scores *S*s receive on their driver's license exam with their scores on a Spanish achievement test. It's possible you might obtain a fairly high correlation, but obviously it wouldn't mean much. Or you might get a low correlation between, say, musical ability and scores on an achievement test in Chinese. However, with other components of language aptitude, this might be an important and useful correlation that can enter into predicting success in the acquisition of Chinese (particularly if you want to look later at the acquisition of tone).

Next to using common sense in interpreting correlations, the most important thing to remember is not to make causal claims. A correlation does *not* show that success on one variable *causes* success on the related variable. Instead, it shows us how strongly related the two variables are.

◇◇◇◇◇◇◇◇◇◇◇◇◇◇◇◇◇◇◇◇◇◇◇◇◇◇◇◇◇◇◇◇◇◇◇◇◇◇◇

Practice 15.5

1. Interpret the meaning of the correlations presented for the ESL placement exam (page 443) table.

2. Imagine you wished to replicate Guiora et al.'s (1972) study of the relationship between relaxation and pronunciation in a second language. The notion is that the more relaxed and less inhibited the *S* becomes, the better the pronunciation. To induce relaxation in the *S*s, you gave them measured amounts of alcohol, tape-recording their pronunciation after each additional drink. Why can't you expect to measure the relationship of relaxation and pronunciation accuracy using a Pearson correlation? *Not true interval? Restricted range on drinks. Reliability of measurement*

3. Imagine that you developed a set of special materials on appropriate complaint procedures. This is one of the objectives of a course in communication skills. At the end of the course, *S*s are given a course final which tests all the communication skills taught in the course. As further validation of your materials, you ran a correlation between *S*s' scores on the items for complaints and the total final exam score. You present the correlation to your supervisor, who says "This correlation can't be interpreted--it violates one of the basic assumptions required for Pearson correlation!" Gee whiz--what's wrong with it? _____

4. After all the data from your ESL placement exam is in, you run a series of Pearson correlations. Surprisingly, you find that the Pearson correlation between the total test score and L1 is significant at the .001 level. Duhhh. What went wrong here? _____

◇◇◇◇◇◇◇◇◇◇◇◇◇◇◇◇◇◇◇◇◇◇◇◇◇◇◇◇◇◇◇◇◇◇◇◇◇◇◇

Correlations with Noncontinuous Variables

While the Pearson correlation is the most common correlation in applied linguistics research, there are times when the Pearson formula cannot be used to measure the strength of the relationship between two variables.

When the assumptions which underlie the Pearson Product-moment correlation are violated, relationships can sometimes still be measured using other formulas. We will present three of them here--point biserial correlation (which is used when one variable has continuous measurement and the other is a true dichotomous and nominal variable), Spearman's correlation (which is used when the data of two variables have the continuity of the strength of ordered ranks), and Kendall's Coefficient of concordance (a procedure which searches for relationships among three or more noncontinuous variables).

Point Biserial Correlation

As you have noted, the Pearson correlation is used when the data for each variable are continuous. Point biserial correlation can be computed when one variable is a dichotomous nominal variable and the other is interval. Point biserial correlations are frequently used in test analysis. For example, answers to a *single* test item are either right or wrong. This is a dichotomy where 1 might = wrong and 2 might = right. Thus, it is possible to run a correlation of the performance on a single test item with the total test score (minus that one item, of course). If there are several subtests within the test for, say, reading, grammar, vocabulary, listening comprehension, and so forth, it would be possible to correlate the single test item with each subtest score. The single test item should correlate most with the subtest in which it appears. In addition, those Ss who do well on the subtest should pass the item and those who fail the item should have lower subtest scores. If not, then it is probably a poor item to use to test that particular skill. That is, the point biserial correlation will tell you how well single items are related to, or "fit" with, other items which purport to test the same thing.

The formula for point biserial correlation is

$$r_{pbi} = \frac{\overline{X}_p - \overline{X}_q}{s_x}\sqrt{pq}$$

In the r represents correlation and the subscript *pbi* is for "point biserial." The subscript letters p and k in the remainder of the formula are the two parts of the dichotomy being compared (*e.g.*, yes/no, pass/fail, and so forth). The $\overline{X}_p$ is the mean total test score for Ss who answered the item correctly. $\overline{X}_q$ is the mean total test score for Ss who answered the item incorrectly. s_x is the standard deviation of all the scores on the test. p is the proportion of Ss who got the item right, and q is the proportion of Ss who got it wrong.

If you gave the language test to 200 students, the point biserial correlation between this test item and the total test would be .33 if:

1. The mean for Ss answering the item right was 72.3.

2. The mean for Ss who answered the item wrong was 62.5.

3. The proportion of Ss answering the item right (p) was .42.

4. The proportion of Ss answering it wrong (q) was .58.

5. The standard deviation (s) was 14.4.

Let's put the values in the formula, and see how this works:

$$r_{pbi} = \frac{\overline{X}_p - \overline{X}_q}{s_X}\sqrt{pq}$$

$$r_{pbi} = \frac{72.3 - 62.5}{14.4}\sqrt{.42 \times .58}$$

$$r_{pbi} = .33$$

Test developers typically look for items which are *negatively* correlated with the subtest they should represent. These are "bad" items and should be removed if possible. Correlations in the .20 to .40 range are typical of "good" test items because they show test items where Ss with high test scores pass the item and those with low scores fail the item.

One very interesting example is that presented by Hudson and Lynch (1984) where point biserial correlations are given for test items with subtest scores. Two different sets of correlations are given. The first is for Ss who have had instruction on the objectives tested by the items and the second is a comparable class just prior to instruction. Here are the correlations for five listening test items.

Listening Item Point Biserial Correlations

Item	+Instruct.	−Instruct.
1	.23	.29
2	.14	.15
3	.06	.31
4	−.60	.19
5	.09	.02

We expect Ss who have been instructed to show a small range in scores and lower point biserial correlations. The point biserial correlation values will be higher for the uninstructed group because Ss in the uninstructed group have greater variance. The reason this example is especially interesting here is that the correlations help to show which items most discriminate between high and low scorers on the test. For example, some of the items show a high correlation for uninstructed (for example, item 3 is .31--the item is good for this group, they don't all already know it) and a lower correlation for the instructed group (.06). The item is weaker for this group; there is little variation in their responses, they "know" it (which can be taken to reflect successful instruction since there was ample variation for the uninstructed group). Thus, <mark>point biserial correlation can be useful in examining criterion-referenced tests and criterion-based instruction.</mark>

Point biserial correlations are occasionally used for purposes other than test evaluation in applied linguistics. We've already noted that a Pearson correlation is spurious when the data are not well distributed in the range. In cases where one variable is continuous but the second consists of scores at the top and bottom of the distribution with few scores in the center, the second variable could be changed to a "high/low" dichotomous variable. A point biserial correlation would then be appropriate. Interpretation of the strength of the correlation would, of course, depend on the purpose of the correlation. For more information, see Guilford and Fruchter (1978).

Practice 15.6

1. Can you think of an example from questionnaire research in which the way respondents answered one question might be correlated with responses on parts of the questionnaire or on the total? (If so, you've thought of a new application for point biserial correlation!)

_____

_____

_____

▶ 2. Calculate the point biserial correlation for the following data. The mean for Ss who answered a test item correctly was $\overline{X} = 80$. The mean for Ss who answered the item incorrectly was $\overline{X} = 70$. The proportion of Ss who answered the item right was .60. The proportion of Ss who answered it incorrectly was .40. The s was 15. Is this a "good" item for the test? Why (not)?

$$r_{pbi} = \frac{\overline{X}_p - \overline{X}_q}{s_X}\sqrt{pq}$$

$$r_{pbi} = \underline{\quad.33\quad}$$

Yes 33mm   .20 – .40

_____

_____

Spearman Rank-Order Correlation (Rho)

Most statisticians argue that the Pearson correlation should not be used unless the data are normally distributed (for example, when we have a large sample size and the data are spread throughout the range). When the distribution is not normal, they argue for Spearman's correlation. This might lead you to believe that the Spearman correlation would be used much more frequently than the Pearson. However, this is not the case.

The Spearman correlation is appropriate for both rank-order data and interval data with the strength of ranks. When the computer computes the value of ρ, it automatically changes the interval data to rank-order data (and thus loses some precision of information in the data). When you do the calculation by hand and have determined that interval data are not normally distributed but have the strength of ranks, you will arrange the scores in an order and assign them ranks. Rho (ρ) tells us how the *rankings* of data from two variables are related.

In our field, Spearman *rho* has often been used to look at the order of morpheme acquisition by second language learners. If you collect test data (perhaps using Fathman's [1975] SLOPE test or the Bilingual Syntax Measure [1973]) on a group of second language learners, you can score each person's use of, say, the morphemes that have often been used in such studies. This would allow you to rank-order the morphemes for your group and then compare the obtained order with that shown in the literature for other second language learners. The ranking of the morphemes in your data would be compared with the ranking in previous studies.

Another possibility would be to establish a scale (using the Guttman Implicational scaling procedure) for the grammar points taught in, say, a series for teaching beginning German. (This might or might not agree with the sequence in the materials.) The data that let you establish the scale might come from test items for each grammar point obtained from all the students in first-year German classes. These data are *cross-sectional*. To check whether this scale also reflects an *acquisition* order, you might then have a project where you tape-record at regular intervals a learner who is not receiving instruction in German but who is living in a German-speaking environment. You might set up a matrix of the grammar points and check to see at what point each grammar item appears with some set degree of accuracy in the tape-recorded data. Again, this would allow you to determine a rank-order of the grammar points. The order for the acquisition data could then be correlated with the scale from the cross-sectional accuracy data.

It is also possible that you might make a case study of two learners and chart the accuracy of their use of a set of forms at one time. Each grammar point would be rank-ordered for each S and the two orders related using a Spearman ρ.

As always, it will be much easier to compute the value of ρ if the data are first displayed on a data sheet. Let's imagine that you have the classroom data on the German test and that it has turned out to be scalable using a Guttman analysis.

In a case study of one learner, you have charted a "percent correct in obligatory instances" for each item over time. This has allowed you to rank-order the data.

The first step is to use the Guttman analysis order and, then, place the case study order next to it.

Gr. Point	Guttman	Case Data
9	1	3
10	2	1
8	3	2
4	4	8
3	5	7
1	6	4
2	7	6
6	8	5
7	9	10
5	10	9

The numbers in the first column are the grammar points (actually the I.D. number represents the order in which these items are sequenced in the book, but that is not a concern in this particular study.) The number in the second column orders these points according to how accurately Ss in the German class used them on a test. It is rank-ordered. The third column gives the order for the same grammar points in the acquisition data. So, for example, the grammar point presented first in the series was sixth on the Guttman scale in terms of difficulty and was acquired fourth overall by the case study learner. The grammar point presented ninth in the series was the easiest for the students in the class and was the third item acquired by the case study learner.

Once the two orders are displayed, the next step is to compute the differences in the rank-orders. We have placed this in a new column, labeled d for difference, and squared that value. (We squared the obtained values to get rid of negative numbers.)

Gr.Point	Guttman	Case Data	d	d^2
9	1	3	−2	4
10	2	1	1	1
8	3	2	−1	1
4	4	8	−4	16
3	5	7	−2	4
1	6	4	2	4
2	7	6	1	1
6	8	5	3	9
7	9	10	−1	1
5	10	9	1	1

The sum of the squared differences ($\sum d^2$) for the above data is 42. With the information displayed in a table, it is an easy matter to place the values in the formula for rho (ρ). The number 6 in the formula is a constant. It does not come from the data. All the other values, of course, do.

$$\rho = 1 - \frac{6(\sum d^2)}{N(N^2 - 1)}$$

The N for the study is 10 because the number of grammar points ranked is 10. (Notice that it is *not* 20--the number of items ranked in the class data plus the number in the case data.) Let's place these values in the formula and compute ρ (rho).

$$\rho = 1 - \frac{6(\sum d^2)}{N(N^2 - 1)}$$

$$\rho = 1 - \frac{6 \times 42}{10(10^2 - 1)}$$

$$\rho = .746$$

To interpret the obtained value of rho, once again we talk about the magnitude of rho and the direction of the relationship. The value, as with r, will always be somewhere between -1 and 0, or between 0 and $+1$. You can have a negative or a positive correlation (just as with r). The closer the obtained value of ρ is to ± 1.0, the stronger the relationship between the two orders.

Unfortunately, we cannot talk about the strength of rho in terms of ρ^2. That is, we *cannot* square the value we obtain and talk about the overlap between the two orders. This is because we have already squared differences in computing the value of rho.

Instead, we can check for the significance of ρ using the correlation table, table 9 of appendix C. While probability levels obtained for Spearman are more often used than they are with Pearson, again it makes more sense to talk about the strength of the correlation (how close to ± 1 it is rather than the fact that we feel confident in rejecting the H_o of no relationship between the two ranks). The probability level does, however, let us say that the two orders are or are not related. For this problem, the critical value of rho (with an N of 10) is .648 for a probability cutoff point of .05. We can, therefore, say the variables are related. The strength of the correlation, however, tells how well correlated they are. For the example above, we would conclude that, despite the obvious difference in actual ranks between the accuracy and acquisition data, they are quite closely related. Certainly we would feel that some reordering of presentation in teaching would be worth trying on an experimental basis.

While the Spearman Rank-order correlation is used in many studies in our field, there are some problems with it. Researchers sometimes opt for another rank-order correlation, *Kendall's tau.* Kendall's tau is better able to handle the problem of tied ranks. When there are a number of ties in the ranks, Spearman is not a good procedure to use. Computer packages adjust Spearman correlations for ties, but hand computations are rather cumbersome so we haven't presented or discussed the formula here. If you have many ties, use a Kendall tau procedure instead. (See Daniel [1978] for the formula to compute a Kendall's tau.)

Practice 15.7

▶ 1. Compute Spearman's rho for the following data. Students in a teacher training program were required to take 12 different classes to obtain their credentials. After graduation, students from two succeeding years were asked to judge the "helpfulness" of each class as preparation for their teaching tasks. The data rank the classes as follows:

Class	Gp1 rank	Gp2 rank
1	1	3
2	2	9
3	3	5
4	4	1
5	5	2
6	6	10
7	7	4
8	8	8
9	9	12
10	10	6
11	11	7
12	12	11

How well do the two groups of graduates agree in their ratings of the usefulness of the classes?

_____

_____

Kendall's Coefficient of Concordance

In the Spearman correlation we are concerned with how well data on two variables correlate. However, we cannot use the Spearman to look for a relationship among more than two variables. Kendall's W allows us to do this, the only stipulation being that the data are at least ordinal. That is, the data must have the strength of ranks.

The following fictitious data set shows us the ranking by six "good language learners" of 10 factors which are assumed to relate to success in second language learning. As gifted language learners, they were asked to give a rating of 0 to 10 for each factor. The factors were then converted to ranks so that for each learner the 10 factors are now rank-ordered. The 10 factors are: intrinsic motivation, extrinsic motivation, personal need achievement, field independence, integrative motivation, short-term memory, tolerance for ambiguity, risk-taking, extroversion, and convergent thought processes.

To set up a table for the Kendall Concordance, remember that the people who are doing the ranking go down the side of the table, and the items (or, in some cases, people) being rank-ordered go across the top of the table. The procedure will compare the ranks given by each S (the data shown in each row) across all Ss. Your actual raw data may first consist of ratings or scores but they must be converted to ranks.

S	A	B	C	D	E	F	G	H	I	J	
S1	4	6	1	2	8	10	9	3	5	7	55
S2	5	2	8	6	1	3	7	4	9	10	55
S3	7	1	9	5	2	4	6	3	8	10	55
S4	6	5	2	10	8	3	4	1	7	9	55
S5	5	7	2	1	9	8	10	4	6	3	55
S6	1	4	9	7	5	3	2	8	10	6	55
Tot	28	25	31	31	33	31	38	23	45	45	330

A = intrinsic motivation, B = extrinsic motivation, C = personal need achievement, D = field independence, E = integrative motivation, F = short-term memory, G = tolerance for ambiguity, H = risk-taking, I = extroversion, J = convergent thought processes.

The H_o would be that there is no relationship among the factors. If this is correct, then we would expect that the distribution of the ranks would be random. Since we have 10 factors, we would expect that each would receive a total of $330 \div 10 = 33$ if there were no relationship. The totals at the bottom of the table vary from 28 to 45.

The formula for Kendall's W is algebraically derived, so like most nonparametric procedures, it's not easy to see what's going on. The formula is based on a procedure where the difference of the total ranks for each factor from 33 is found and squared and then totaled (sounds like an ANOVA sum of squares method, right?). The amount that these totals differ from 33 gives us a measure of association among the 10 factors.

$$(28 - 33)^2 + (25 - 33)^2 + (31 - 33)^2 + \cdots + (45 - 33)^2 = 514$$

Second, we need a measure of agreement in the ranks assigned to each factor. If there were a perfect association, the best factor (the one ranked highest by everyone) would be ranked 1 by all learners and thus have a total of 6. The second best should be ranked 2 by all learners for a total of 12. The third best should have $3 \times 6 = 18$ points and the worst S should have $10 \times 6 = 60$ points. Look at the total points for each factor. They are not close at all to this "perfect" ranking.

If there were a perfect correlation, then we could subtract the expected total rank for each factor (33) from the perfect rank scores of each factor, square these and total the squared differences:

$$(6 - 33)^2 + (12 - 33)^2 + (18 - 33)^2 + \cdots + (60 - 33)^2 = 2970$$

The ratio of these two measures will always be somewhere between 0 and 1. If it isn't, recheck your calculations. The correlation in our case is quite low:

$$\frac{514}{2970} = 0.173$$

The formula for Kendall's W, however, is not so transparent since mathematicians have done what is called "appropriate algebraic manipulation" to make it more precise. The formula is (gasp!):

$$W = \frac{12\sum_{j=1}^{n} R_j^2 - 3m^2 n(n + 1)^2}{m^2 n(n^2 - 1)}$$

Don't worry about the formula. It will be clear in a minute. The easiest parts are the 12 and 3 because they are constants in the formula. That is, they are part of the formula - they don't come from the data.

Step 1

Find the value of $\sum_{j=1}^{n} R_j^2$

To do this, we simply square the total for each factor (the "total" row at the bottom of the data table) and sum these: $(28^2 + 25^2 + \cdots + 45^2) = 11404$.

Step 2
Multiply the result of step 1 by 12 (the constant in the formula). The answer for this data is 136848.

Step 3
Subtract $3m^2 n(n + 1)^2$

So, we multiply 3 by m^2. m is the number of learners doing the rankings. We have 6 learners. n is the number of factors (or objects or Ss) being ranked, and that's 10. So $3 \times 6^2 \times 10(10 + 1)^2 = 130680$.

Step 4
Find the value of $m^2 n(n^2 - 1)$. The result is 35640.

Step 5
Enter the values from steps 1 through 3 in the formula and complete the calculation.

$$W = \frac{136848 - 130680}{35640} = \frac{6168}{35640} = .173$$

As you can see, the actual Kendall's Concordance figure matches that given in our explanation even though "algebraic manipulation" has been used to correct the basic formula.

To interpret the coefficient, we must convert the value of W into a χ^2 statistic by using the following formula:

$$\chi^2 = m(n - 1)(W)$$

Since m in this example is 6, n is 10, and the obtained value for W was .173, the χ^2 value is:

$$\chi^2 = 6 \times 9 \times .173 = 9.34$$

Checking this value of χ^2 in the Chi-square table (table 7 of appendix C), we see that we need to know the df to read the table. Our df is $n - 1$ or $10 - 1 = 9$. The χ^2 critical value needed for 9 df is 16.92. So we cannot reject the H_o. We have to conclude that there is no significant relationship (agreement or disagreement) in how these learners view the importance of these factors.

Practice 15.8

▶ 1. At the conclusion of instruction, your language department asks students to rank-order the usefulness of various classroom activities. You want to know whether there is general consensus among the students as to what is useful and what is not. There are 10 activities: (a) composition, (b) composition revisions, (c) listening comprehension activities, (d) vocabulary exercises, (e) grammar exercises, (f) examinations, (g) problem solving activities, (h) diary writing, (i) watching target language soap opera, (j) activities based on soap opera. Here are the fictitious data:

S	a	b	c	d	e	f	g	h	i	j
1	9	10	6	1	7	8	2	4	3	5
2	10	9	7	2	6	8	3	5	4	1
3	9	8	6	1	5	10	4	3	2	7
4	4	9	6	8	10	3	7	2	5	1
5	10	9	6	1	7	8	3	5	2	4
6	9	10	6	1	7	8	3	5	2	4
7	6	7	1	4	9	2	10	5	8	3
8	10	9	7	2	5	8	3	6	4	1
9	9	10	6	1	8	7	3	5	1	4
10	8	6	2	5	10	9	7	4	3	1
11	9	8	6	1	5	10	4	3	2	7
12	9	10	6	1	7	8	4	5	3	2
13	1	6	7	10	9	8	2	4	3	5
14	9	10	6	1	8	7	3	5	2	4
15	6	3	10	8	1	2	5	4	7	9
Tot	118	124	88	47	104	106	63	64	52	59

The H_o is that there is no agreement among the Ss as to the relative merit of the different activities used in class.

Compute W.

$$W = \frac{12 \sum_{j=1}^{n} R_j^2 - 3m^2 n(n+1)^2}{m^2 n(n^2 - 1)}$$

$$W = \underline{\hspace{2cm}}$$

▶ 2. The coefficient of concordance is higher this time than in our previous example. To interpret the values, though, we must check the critical values for an .05 level (or less, depending on the level you select for rejecting the H_o). So, once again, convert the value to a χ^2 statistic:

$$\chi^2 = \underline{\hspace{2cm}}$$

Check the χ^2_{crit} for $n - 1 = 9$ df in the Chi-square table in the Appendix to see if we can reject the H_o. Can we reject the H_o? Why (not)? What can you conclude?

_____

_____

_____

◇◇◇

As always, the calculations are tedious when we must do the work by hand. The problem is compounded when we have ties. When two or more observations are equal, we assign each the mean of the rank positions for which it is tied. The problem is that the formula must then be adjusted to take care of the ties. To do this we change the denominator of the formula to:

$$m^2 n(n^2 - 1) - m \sum (t^3 - t)$$

t stands for the number of observations in any set of rankings that is tied for a given rank.

phi: Correlation of Two Dichotomous Variables

It's true that when we work with nominal variables, our first thought is to turn to a Chi-square analysis. However, in language testing the phi correlation is another possibility. It looks at association in two dichotomous variables. That is, each variable is a dichotomy measured as yes/no, present/absent, correct/incorrect, pass/fail, etc.

In language testing, the relation of two test items might be assessed according to how many people failed both items, passed both items, or got item A correct and item B wrong or item A wrong and item B correct. It's possible to use the procedure, however, in other areas of language research as well. For example, we could test the relationship between early (kindergarten to grade 3) vs. late (grade 4 to grade 6) instruction in FLES (foreign language in elementary schools) and subsequent study of foreign languages--yes/no--in high school. Or, we might correlate Korean surname--yes/no--of Americans applying for a university's study abroad program to Korea or other countries--again, yes/no in respect to requesting Korea. The table for each of these would look something like this:

	no	yes
no	A	B
yes	C	D

The formula for phi is:

$$r_{phi} = \frac{BC - AD}{\sqrt{(A + B)(C + D)(A + C)(B + D)}}$$

Let's add data to our table and calculate an example phi coefficient. As an example, you know that most people who apply to applied linguistics doctoral programs send applications to several schools. Imagine that university A (our very own) wants to know whether the result of its selection process correlates with that of university B (our cross-state rival institution). Here are the figures:

	Reject	Accept
Reject	6	16
Accept	8	6

$$r_{phi} = \frac{BC - AD}{\sqrt{(A + B)(C + D)(A + C)(B + D)}}$$

$$r_{phi} = \frac{128 - 36}{\sqrt{(22)(14)(14)(22)}}$$

$$r_{phi} = .299$$

The value of the phi coefficient is converted to a χ^2 value by placing it in the equation:

$$\chi^2 = N\Phi^2$$

For our data, this would be:

$$\chi^2 = 36(.299^2)$$

$$\chi^2 = 3.21$$

We can then use our regular Chi-square table in appendix C to find the critical value needed to reject the null hypothesis of no relationship between the two schools' acceptance/rejection results. The χ^2_{crit} needed is 3.84. The correlation is, indeed, weak.

There is a second formula that some researchers find easier to use. It is:

$$r_{phi} = \frac{p_{ik} - p_i p_k}{\sqrt{p_i q_i p_k q_k}}$$

The subscripts i and k refer to the two parts of the dichotomy being tested (e.g., yes vs. no, pass vs. fail, and so forth). In our example, i would be acceptance at university A and k would be acceptance at university B. In the formula p_{ik} = the proportion of Ss getting both "correct," p_i = the proportion getting i correct, p_k = proportion getting k correct, q_i = proportion getting i wrong, and q_k = proportion getting k wrong. Again, once the value of Φ is found, it is placed in the χ^2 formula, and the result is checked against the critical value in the Chi-square table to determine whether the null hypothesis of no relationship can be rejected.

As you can see, a phi correlation is very similar to the Chi-square test. In Chi-square, we first test to see whether a relationship exists--that is, can we reject the null hypothesis? Then, as a follow-up to see just how strong the relationship is in the data, we can use phi. Here, we begin by asking whether the two variables are related. The value of Φ tells us how related the variables are. We can then ask whether this correlation will allow us to reject the null hypothesis by inserting the value into a χ^2 formula.

The phi correlation has been subject to some criticism when applied to language tests (where correlations are carried out between test items each of which are correct or incorrect). Many test experts have turned to tetrachoric correlation as a correlation less sensitive to possible distortion caused by the relative difficulty

of each test item. To learn more about this correlation and the use of interitem correlation in factor analysis, please consult Davidson (1988).

◇◇

Practice 15.9

▶ 1. The number of American children who were early entrants (K-2nd grade) into a Spanish immersion program was 82; the number of late entrants (3rd-5th grade) was 112. The number of Ss who elected to continue Spanish in high school from the early group was 68; from the late group, 71. Is there a significant Φ coefficient for the correlation?

$\Phi =$ _____ $\chi^2 =$ _____ $\chi^2_{crit} =$ _____

Conclusion _____

_____

◇◇

We have discussed five kinds of correlations in this chapter: Pearson, point biserial, Spearman's rho, Kendall's W, and phi (Φ). There are many other kinds of correlations, some of which will allow you to work with curvilinear data (that obtained for scores on such variables as anxiety). For these, we suggest you consult your local statistician or textbook references such as Hays (1973) or Daniel (1978). Perhaps the best reference to consult for all correlations is Guilford and Fruchter (1978).

Activities

1. Check your research journal to find examples of studies where you would wish to run a correlation. What are the variables? Do you expect to find a positive or a negative correlation? Which type of correlation will you use? What strength of correlation do you hope to obtain? Why?

2. R. Guarino & K. Perkins (1986. Awareness of form class as a factor in ESL reading comprehension. *Language Learning, 36,* 1, 77-82.) gave 35 ESL learners a standard reading comprehension test and a test meant to assess knowledge of form class, or a word's morphemes/structural units. Results indicated a significant relationship between the two tests. Although the authors concluded that awareness of form class relates to success in reading, they cautioned that reading also involves metalinguistic skills. If this were your study, approximately what strength would you want the correlation to obtain in order to claim the two variables are related? Justify your choice.

3. Look back at the correlation table for the ESL placement subtests (page 443). Given that the correlations are so very high among the subtests, do you think that

the point biserial correlation figures for test items within each subtest will always show stronger correlation with the subtest they represent than with other subtests? Why (not)?

4. T. Pica, R. Young & C. Doughty (1987. The impact of interaction on comprehension. *TESOL Quarterly, 21*, 4, 737-758.) used point biserial correlation in an interesting way. They compared NNSs' comprehension of directives under two conditions--premodified simplified input and negotiated input. Before answering this question, to be sure the premodified simplified commands were good items to use, they ran a point biserial correlation on each directive. Of the 15 commands, 13 had a r_{pbi} of .30 or above. In your own words, explain how the researchers (or their computer program) performed the point biserial correlation.

5. E. Geva (1986. Reading comprehension in a second language: the role of conjunctions. *TESL Canada Journal, Special Issue 1,* 85-110.) designed several tasks to investigate the importance of intrasentential, intersentential, and discourse level comprehension of conjunctions on reading comprehension. Sixty university ESL students performed a "fill in the blank" task which tested comprehension at the intrasentential level (e.g., "We could not see the man, although _____" with four options given for the blank), a sentence continuation task (e.g., "It was cold outside, although it was sunny" with two choices for continuation, "So it was a good day for skiing" or "So Johnny's mother made him wear a sweater"). Two methods were used to test intersentential comprehension: a cloze passage to test comprehension at the discourse level, and comprehension tests based on academic text passages. Oral proficiency ratings were also available for each student.

Consider the following correlation matrix to decide whether oral proficiency is related to the tasks which test conjunction comprehension. How would you interpret the correlations between oral proficiency and the comprehension of conjunctions at intrasentential, intersentential, and discourse levels? How would you interpret the correlation of cloze scores (the discourse level measure) and ATC?

Intercorrelations Between Oral Proficiency Ratings, Predictor
Variables and Total Score on the Dependent Measure

	Oral Prof.	FBT	SCT	Cloze	ATC (total)
Oral Prof.	1.00				
FBT	.37	1.00			
SCT	.24	.43	1.00		
Cloze	.69	.26	.30	1.00	
ATC (total)	.43	.27	.40	.49	1.00

FBT = fill in the blank task, SCT = sentence continuation task, ATC = academic text comprehension

6. R. Altman (1985. Subtle distinctions: *should* versus *had better*. Research Note, *Studies in Second Language Acquisition*, *8*, 1, 80-89.) developed and administered

several measures of modal usage to 12 nonnative and 12 native speakers of English. The results showed that understanding of expressions of modals of obligation is different for these native and nonnative groups. Examine the following table which reports the value of *W* (Kendall Concordance analysis) within *each* group on one of these measures, that of modal strength.

Average Ranking of Seven Modal Test Items
(from strongest to weakest)

Native speakers*		Nonnative speakers**
must	1	must
have to	2	have to
'd better	3	should
should	4	BE supposed to
BE supposed to	5	could
can	6	can
could	7	'd better

*$W = .90, p < .001$ **$W = .615, p < .005$

Interpret the meaning of the *W* statistic for each group. Then look at the order shown for each group. For which modals are the ranks most similar, and for which are they dissimilar? If you are interested in modals of obligation, you will want to consult the other measures Altman devised (not analyzed using this procedure) which were administered to larger groups of *S*s.

7. V. Nell (1988. The psychology of reading for pleasure: needs and gratifications. *Reading Research Quarterly, 23,* 1, 6-50.) explored (among many other things) readers' ranking of books for preference and literary merit. Three groups of *S*s (129 college students, 44 librarians, and 14 English lecturers, or "professional critics") read short extracts for 30 books which spanned the continuum from highest literary quality to total trash. *S*s ranked the extracts for preference (what they would read for pleasure) and merit (what is good literature).

Kendall's Concordance for preference rankings and for merit rankings showed that within the three groups of *S*s, rankings were significantly similar. Spearman rho coefficients showed that preference rankings were the same for students and librarians; for merit rankings, all three groups ranked the extracts in significantly similar sequences. The author concludes that all groups share a common set of literary value judgments.

In addition, negative Spearman rho coefficients indicated that merit and preference ratings are inversely related. For all groups, the higher merit an extract was given, the less desirable it was for pleasure reading.

If this were your study, what coefficient values (i.e., what range of values) would you want to obtain in order to make these claims for the findings? Justify your decision.

8. K. Bardovi-Harlig (1987. Markedness and salience in second language acquisition. *Language Learning, 37,* 3, 385-407.) examined the acquisition of preposition "pied piping" by 95 ESL learners representing 8 proficiency levels. An elicitation task was used to look at preposition use for dative Wh-questions and relative clauses. Results indicated that *S*s show an order of No Preposition > Preposition Stranding > Pied Piping. Examples given for No Preposition are "Who did Mary give a book?" and "The man Mary baked a cake was Joe"; for Preposition Stranding, "Who did Phillip throw the football to?" "The guard was watching the player who Phillip threw the football to"; and for Pied Piping: "For whom did George design the house?" "The teacher helped the student for whom the lesson was difficult."

A Kendall tau correlation for two structures (Wh-questions and relative clauses) showed the order of No Prep > Prep Stranding > Pied Piping to be correct: tau $= -.25, p < .01$. The Kendall tau for another order, which would be predicted by markedness theory (namely No Prep > Pied piping [unmarked form]) > Prep Stranding [marked form]), had a tau $= .05$, n.s.. The author explains this apparent counterexample to markedness theory by suggesting that salience also plays an important role.

If you are interested in markedness theory, read the article. Consider other explanations you might be able to give for the findings. Also consider what advantages the Kendall tau procedure has to either the Spearman Rank-order correlation or a Pearson correlation. If you were to replicate this study, how would you decide which correlational or other parametric and nonparametric procedure to use for the data?

References

Burt, M., Dulay, H., and Hernandez, E. 1973. *Bilingual Syntax Measure.* New York, NY: Harcourt Brace Jovanovich.

Daniel, W. W. 1978. *Applied Nonparametric Statistics.* Boston, MA: Houghton Mifflin Co.

Davidson, F. 1988. An exploratory modeling survey of the trait structures of some existing language test datasets. Unpublished doctoral dissertation, Applied Linguistics, UCLA.

Fathman, A. 1975. The relationship between age and second language production ability. *Language Learning 25,* 2, 245-254.

Grice, H. P. 1975. Logic and conversation. In P. Cole and J. P. Morgan (Eds.). *Syntax and Semantics: Speech Acts.* Vol. 3. New York, NY: Academic Press.

Guilford, J. P. & Fruchter, B. 1978. *Fundamental Statistics in Psychology and Education.* Sixth Ed. New York: McGraw-Hill.

Guiora, A., Beit-Hallahmi, B., Brannon, R., and Dull, C. 1972. The effects of experimentally induced changes in ego status on pronunciation ability in a second language: an exploratory study. *Comprehensive Psychiatry, 13,* 421-428.

Hays, W. L. 1973. *Statistics for the Social Sciences.* Second Edition. New York: Holt Rinehart & Winston.

Hudson, T. and Lynch, B. 1984. A criterion-referenced measurement approach to ESL achievement testing. *Language Testing, 1,* 2, 171-201.

Kirk, R. E. 1982. *Experimental Design: Procedures for the Behavioral Sciences.* Second Edition. Belmont, CA: Brooks Cole.

Chapter 16

Regression

- *Linear regression*
- *Multiple regression*
  Restrictions related to multiple regression
  Interpreting multiple regression
  Relation between ANOVA and regression

When we calculate the mean ($\overline{X}$), we think of it as the central point of the distribution. If we gave a test, calculated the $\overline{X}$, and then found that one of our Ss missed the test, our very best guess as to that S's score (assuming we know nothing about the S's ability) would be the $\overline{X}$. However, if we *do* know something about the student, we may be able to make a better guess. If the S has shown outstanding abilities in the classroom, we would likely guess a score higher than the $\overline{X}$. If the S was not doing well in class, we'd guess some score lower than the $\overline{X}$.

When we have no other information, the best guess we can make about anyone's performance on a test is the $\overline{X}$. If we knew, on the basis of a strength of association η^2 (eta squared) that some of the variance in performance on this test was due to sex or on the basis of ω^2 (omega squared) that some was due to L1 membership, then by knowing the student's L1 and sex, we could improve our guess. If we knew, on the basis of a Pearson r^2 that there was a strong overlap of scores on this test and scores on the SAT, then by knowing the student's score on the SAT, we could improve our guess. If we knew that SAT scores, sex, and L1 membership (and perhaps length of residence or age of arrival or a host of other variables) were possibly related to performance on this test measure, then by having all this information on the student, we could be quite accurate in predicting the student's score. We would not need to guess the $\overline{X}$; we could be much more accurate in our predictions.

Regression, then, is a way of predicting performance on the dependent variable via one or more independent variables. In simple regression, we predict scores on one variable on the basis of scores on a second. In multiple regression, we expand the possible sources of prediction and test to see which of many variables and which combination of variables allow us to make the best prediction.

You can see that simple regression is useful when we need to predict scores on a test on the basis of another test. For example, we might have TOEFL scores on students and use those scores to predict the Ss' scores on our ESL placement test. If accurate predictions are possible, then we can spare students the joy of taking another test and ourselves the correcting of more exams.

Multiple regression is more frequently used when we want to know how much "weight" to give to a variety of possible independent variables that relate to performance on the dependent variable. For example, if we have an achievement test for Spanish and previous research has shown that success on this test is related to a number of things (e.g., one study shows that age at which Spanish instruction was begun relates to achievement; another study shows that amount of interaction with native speakers is related to achievement; another that reading scores relate to achievement; and so forth), we can determine which of all these variables best predicts achievement and/or which combination of these variables most accurately predicts achievement, and which do not add much information to the prediction.

Linear Regression

Regression and correlation are related procedures. The correlation coefficient, which we discussed in the last chapter, is central to simple linear regression. While we cannot make *causal* claims on the basis of correlation, we can use correlation to *predict* one variable from another.

Let's assume we have the following scores for Ss on two tests, a reading test score and a cloze test score.

S	Reading	Cloze
1	10	5
2	20	10
3	30	15
4	40	20
5	50	25

The data form a perfect relationship ($r = 1, r^2 = 1$). For each increase of 10 points in reading, there is a corresponding increase of 5 points on the cloze test. With such a perfect relationship, you can predict with complete accuracy where any S will score on one test on the basis of the score on the other.

If the correlation were ever perfect, all we would need to do to predict one score on a variable from the score on the second is to locate the person's score on one axis of the scatterplot and then look up to where the line drawn from that score hit the correlation line, and then check across.

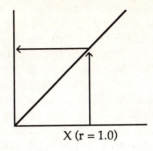

X (r = 1.0)

The chance of ever finding a perfect correlation is, of course, next to never. In addition, few people want to go to the trouble of drawing a scatterplot and then plotting out all the scores to see where the scores intersect in order to find the score of Y given the score on X.

Since correlations are not perfect, the scores will not all fall right on our imaginary straight line. For example, here is a scatterplot that shows the (fictitious) correlation of scores on the MLAT (Modern Language Aptitude Test) and an achievement test on learning a computer language. The research question asked was whether there is a relationship between language learning aptitude and the learning of an artificial machine language.

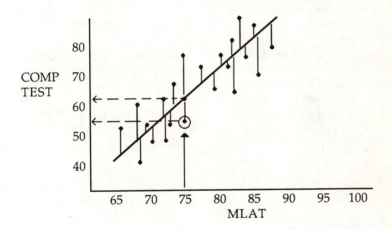

If we drew in the best-fitting straight line for our correlation, it might look something like that drawn on the scatterplot. Look at the circled dot on the scatterplot. This is the intersection of one S's score on the MLAT (75 points) and the score on the computer-language achievement test. If we drew a straight line up to the best-fitting straight line, we would expect the score on the computer-language achievement test to be around 61. However, it is not. The actual score was 56. We make a 5-point error in our estimate for this particular S.

The closer the correlation is to ± 1, the smaller the error will be in predicting performance on one variable to that of the second. The smaller the correlation (the closer it is to 0), the greater the error in predicting performance on a second variable from that on the first. Think back to the various scatterplots we showed in the previous chapter. When the value of r was close to ± 1, the points clustered close together along the best-fitting straight line. Thus, there would be little error in predicting scores in such a distribution. In analyzing your own data, you might first ask the computer to give you a scatterplot in order to see the correlation and also to allow you to identify cases (if there are such) where Ss do not seem to fit the correlation "picture." The printout will also allow you to *see* the amount of error (sometimes that means more to us than seeing a numerical value for error); the error, however, will be labeled "residual" in most computer programs.

Four pieces of information are needed to allow us to predict scores using regression. These are (1) the mean for scores on one variable ($\overline{X}$), (2) the mean for scores on the second variable ($\overline{Y}$), (3) the S's score on X, and (4) the slope of the best-fitting straight line of the joint distribution. With this information, we can predict the S's score on Y from X on a mathematical basis. By "regressing" Y on X, predicting Y from X will be possible.

We already know how to compute $\overline{X}$, so that part is no problem. However, we have not yet discussed how to determine slope (which is usually abbreviated as b). If we try to connect all the dots in scatterplot, we obviously will not have a straight line (more likely a picture of George Washington?). We need to find the best-fitting *straight* line. Look at the following scatterplot. You can see that lines drawn to the straight line show the amount of error. Suppose that we square each of these errors and then find the mean of the sum of these squared errors. This best-fitting straight line is called the *regression line* and is technically defined as the line that results in the smallest mean of the sum of the squared errors. We can think of the regression line as being that which comes closest to all the dots but, more precisely, it is the one that results in a mean of the squared errors that is less than any other line we might produce.

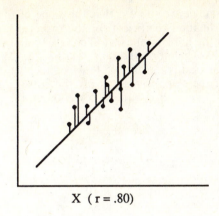

X (r = .80)

Before we give you the raw score formula for _b (slope of the regression line)_, let's make a link between the concept of slope and that of correlation. Imagine that we had the scores on the computer test and on the MLAT. Because the scores come from different measures, we convert each of these scores to a z score. This makes them comparable. Then we could plot the intersection of each S's z score on the MLAT and on the computer test. These would form the dots on the scatterplot. The best-fitting straight line would have a slope to it. As the z scores on the MLAT increase they form a "run," the horizontal line of a triangle. At the same time, the z scores on the computer test increase to form a "rise," the vertical line of the triangle. The slope (_b_) of the regression line is shown as we connect these two lines to form the third side of the triangle.

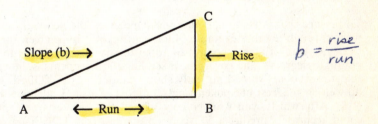

In the above diagram, an increase of six units on the run (MLAT) would equal two units of increase on the rise (computer test). The slope is the rise divided by the run. The result is a fraction. That fraction is the correlation coefficient. _The_ Pearson _correlation coefficient is the same as the slope of the best-fitting line in a z-score scatterplot._ If, in our example, we knew that the standard deviation on the MLAT is 10, a z score of 1 is 10 points above the mean. A z score of 2 is 20 points above the mean. Imagine, too, that the standard deviation on the computer test was 8 points. A +2 z score would be 16 points above the mean. A −1 z score would be 8 points below the mean. For a z-score scatterplot, we know that the slope of the best-fitting straight line is related to the correlation coefficient. In the little triangle we showed that the slope of the regression line was $2 \div 6$, and so the correlation coefficient for the two is .33. We now know that each shift in units on the horizontal axis (X) equals 10 and each shift on the vertical axis (Y) equals 8. Therefore, the slope will be .26. That is, 2 z units when the s is 8 = 16, and 6 z units for an s of 10 = 60, and $16 \div 60 = .26$. All we have to do to obtain the slope is to multiply the correlation coefficient by the standard deviation of Y over the standard deviation of X.

$$b = r_{xy}\frac{s_Y}{s_X}$$

Pearson correlation coefficient

$$b = .33\frac{8}{10}$$

$$b = .26$$

It is very easy to find the slope if you have the correlation coefficient and the standard deviation for X and Y. However, sometimes we do not already have the correlation coefficient, and do not have the time to compute and plot out the z scores for each S on the two measures. Still, you can as easily compute b using raw score data. The formula for slope follows.

$$b = \frac{N(\sum XY) - (\sum X)(\sum Y)}{N\sum X^2 - (\sum X)^2}$$

Whenever you need to do regression but do not yet have the correlation, you can use this "long" formula and work from the raw data.

To be sure that you can compute the slope given the necessary information, let's work through another example. Imagine that you have given the TOEFL exam to a group of students hoping to come to the United States to complete their graduate degrees. The government sending these students is, however, concerned that the students should not only show abilities on the TOEFL but should also do well on the Test of Spoken English (TSE). So the students also are given this test. Afterwards, you wonder how related the two tests are and whether you could accurately predict a S's score on one test (the TOEFL) given the score on the other (TSE).

The $\overline{X}$ on the TOEFL for your group was 540 and the standard deviation was 40. The $\overline{X}$ on the TSE was 30 and the standard deviation was 4. The correlation computation showed that $r = .80$. We can, then, determine the slope.

$$b = r_{xy}\frac{s_Y}{s_X}$$

$$b = .80 \times \frac{40}{4} = 8.0$$

The scatterplot might look like this. Notice that we have marked the means on each test as $\overline{X}$ and $\overline{Y}$. The point where these two means intersect has been labeled with a zero (0). Notice that the scatterplot is set out in z score intervals and the $\overline{X}$ for each, therefore, is a z score of 0. The regression line passes through this intersection.

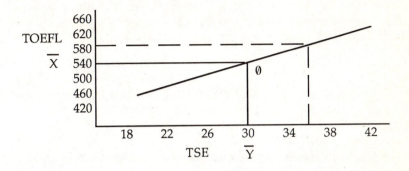

Assume that after the last administration of the TOEFL in this country, a new candidate for study abroad appeared. It would be possible to give her an interview for the TSE. Once you obtained her score of 36 on the TSE, you could convert it to a z score and place it in the scatterplot diagram, look across and discover what the corresponding z score might be on the TOEFL.

The problem is that nobody (that we know) ever actually converts all the scores to z scores and draws a scatterplot that would allow one to do this. Instead, we need a mathematical way of computing this result.

We know that the slope is 8 ($b \doteq 8$). So for every 4-point shift in the X line, there will be a 32-point shift in the Y line (4 x 8 = 32). For a 2-point shift in X, there will be a 2 x 8 = 16-point shift in Y. Looking back at the diagram, we see that if we begin at the intersection 0 and move to the right on the X axis (above the TSE mean), there will a consequent increase on the Y axis (above the TOEFL mean). The amount of increase depends on the slope. We can calculate this increase without reference to the scatterplot by using the slope. For example, with a TSE score of 36, the shift from the mean of 30 is 6 points. Multiplying that by the slope, we get 8 x 6 = 48. So our prediction of the TOEFL score is the mean of Y, 540, plus 48, or 588.

Let's convert all these words into a formula for predicting an individual S's score on the Y variable given his or her performance on the X variable. The formula follows.

$$\hat{Y} \text{ (predicted Y)} = \overline{Y} + b(X - \overline{X})$$

$$\hat{Y} = 540 + (8)(36 - 30)$$

$$\hat{Y} = 588$$

The formula for this prediction is sometimes called the *regression equation* or the *prediction formula*. Another regression equation that is more useful with computer output is:

$$\hat{Y} = a + bx$$

In this formula, a is the y-intercept, information which is routinely generated by the computer. b is the slope, and x is the score we use to predict y. Obviously, this formula is much easier if you are using a computer package that gives you this information.

Practice 16.1

1. Look at the following scatterplots. In which would the error (residual) be greatest and in which smallest?

smallest   greatest

▶2. In the TSE and TOEFL example, assume that once you made an exception and interviewed the first person, another candidate appeared and demanded like treatment. Without information from the TSE, what is the best estimate for the TOEFL score of this candidate? _____ This time the S's TSE score was below the mean for that test, a score of 25. The student's predicted score on the TOEFL exam would be below the $\overline{X}$. Calculate the predicted value. How different is this prediction from that obtained without the TSE information?

$$\hat{Y} = \overline{Y} + b(X - \overline{X})$$

$$\hat{Y} = \underline{\qquad}$$

Difference in predictions: _____

We will do one more example of simple regression, working directly with raw data this time. Imagine that you have scores on an error detection test for a group of Ss. This is a test where students are given sentences containing grammar errors. The S must correctly identify the location of the error. Say there are 15 such items so the S has a possible score of 0 to 15 on the test. In addition, you have scores derived from scale ratings given by teachers to their written compositions. After the tests and compositions have been scored, you hope to be able to use the error detection test (since it is so easy to score) to predict the next S's score on composition.

X	Y	X^2	Y^2	XY
1	5	1	25	5
2	6	4	36	12
3	8	9	64	24
4	9	16	81	36
5	8	25	64	40
6	10	36	100	60
7	13	49	169	91
8	12	64	144	96
9	13	81	169	117
10	11	100	121	110
11	13	121	169	143
12	14	144	196	168
13	14	169	196	182
14	13	196	169	182
15	13	225	169	195
Σ	120 162	1240	1872	1461

120

$\overline{X}_x = 8.00; \overline{X}_y = 10.8 ; s_x = 4.47; s_y = 2.96$

Let's do a correlation and then use the correlation and information on the slope to predict composition scores given error detection scores.

The first step is to calculate the correlation between the two measures:

$$r_{xy} = \frac{N(\sum XY) - (\sum X)(\sum Y)}{\sqrt{[N\sum X^2 - (\sum X)^2][N\sum Y^2 - (\sum Y)^2]}}$$

$$r_{xy} = \frac{(15)(1461) - (120)(162)}{\sqrt{[15(1240) - (120)^2][15(1872) - (162)^2]}}$$

$$r_{xy} = .89$$

The second step is to determine the slope.

$$b = r_{xy}\frac{s_y}{s_x}$$

$$b = .89 \times \frac{2.96}{4.47}$$

$$b = .59$$

Since we had such a high value for r, we should feel confident in predicting the composition scores from the written error detection test. The overlap between the two measures is .79. The next student who missed the composition section of the test scored 10 on the error detection test. Let's calculate her predicted composition score.

$$\hat{Y} = \overline{Y} + b(X - \overline{X})$$

$$\hat{Y} = 10.8 + .59(10 - 8)$$

$$\hat{Y} = 11.98$$

Just to be sure all our calculations are correct, let's use the raw score formula for slope, and see if the results match.

$$b = \frac{N(\sum XY) - (\sum X)(\sum Y)}{N\sum X^2 - (\sum X)^2}$$

$$b = \frac{(15)(1461) - (120)(162)}{(15)(1240) - (120)^2}$$

$$b = \frac{2475}{4200} = .59$$

Hooray, they match!

In our discussion so far, we have used correlation to help us improve our guess when we want to predict a person's score on the basis of his or her score on another test. When we do this, we know that the prediction will not be exact. There is "error" in the prediction. This is because the correlation between the two tests is not perfect. If we continuously make errors in our predictions (the residuals are large), the question we need to ask is how much do we gain by using simple regression for this purpose. We know that our best guess, if we have no other information, is the $\overline{X}$. The amount we can improve on that guess is determined by the strength of the correlation between the two measures. If the correlation is relatively weak, we gain a little but not much in prediction. If the correlation is strong, then our guessing improves a great deal. If you visualize the scatterplot of a weak and a strong correlation, you can see why this is the case. In a strong correlation, the scores all cluster around the regression line. When the scores are close to the line, there is only a small amount of error involved in the prediction. When the scores are spread out away from the line, then the amount of error increases. The weaker the correlation, the more error we make in our predictions.

Let's think about this issue in another way. Imagine that we have found a correlation of .50 between the type/token ratios in Ss' writing (a rough measure of vocabulary flexibility) and their reading vocabulary scores. The mean for the reading vocabulary test was 35 and the s was 8. If you plot the type/token ratios with vocabulary scores on a scatterplot, you can see the difference between using the $\overline{X}$ as the best estimate vs. using the regression formula.

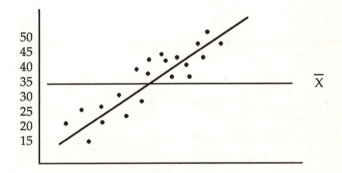

Remember that there will be some overlap in the variance of the two scores. When we square the value of r, we find the degree of shared variance. Of the original 100% of the variance, with an $r = .50$, we have accurately accounted for 25% of the variance using this straight line as the basis for prediction. We have reduced the error variance now to 75%. So we have substantially increased the accuracy of our prediction by using linear regression rather than the $\overline{X}$, but there is still much error in the prediction.

When we square r, we have the proportion of variance in one variable accounted for by the other. When we remove that proportion of variance from 1.00 (the total variance), we remove that overlap and what is left is the error associated with predicting from the regression line. We can change this into a formula which will give us the *standard error of estimate*, which is usually symbolized as s_{yx} or SEE in computer printouts. Visualize the dispersion of the data around the regression line in analogy to spread of scores in a normal distribution. The straight line represents all the *predicted Y* values. The "data" around the line are the *actual Y* values. The standard deviation is a figure that tells us about variability of individual scores away from the mean. In regression, SEE does the same job regarding the dispersion of scores away from the straight line. In the case of standard deviation, the larger the standard deviation, the greater the dispersion of scores away from the mean; the larger the SEE, the greater the dispersion from the straight line. In a normal distribution, if the standard deviation is very small, we would not make much error in predicting new scores using the mean. In regression, if all the data are tightly clustered on the line, little error is made in predicting scores on one variable from scores on a second variable.

SEE is an important figure for it tells us how much error is likely to occur in prediction. That is, the SEE gives us a more exact idea of how far off our prediction may be. Once you have predicted a score, you should look at the SEE to see if it is large. The larger the SEE, the greater the amount of error in prediction. If it is very large, then you may do just as well using the mean. (There is no set "too high" value. You might judge this value in the same way that you do standard deviation. There is no set "too high" value for standard deviation, but we know, in both cases, that the value gives us a way of judging how far off we might be. For SEE, it tells us how great the error may be in prediction. In standard deviation, it also gives us a rough estimate of how far off we might be if we thought that all scores were similar to the mean.)

To compute SEE, we need to know the error variance. The error variance is the sum of squares of actual scores minus predicted scores divided by $N - 2$.

$$Error\ Variance = \frac{\sum(Y - \hat{Y})^2}{N - 2}$$

The square root of this variance is referred to as the SEE:

$$SEE = \sqrt{\frac{\sum(Y - \hat{Y})^2}{N - 2}}$$

Another formula for SEE that uses values often more easy to find is the following:

$$SEE = s_y\sqrt{1 - r_{yx}^2}$$

For the error detection problem, $s_y = 2.96$ and $r_{yx} = .89$. So, we can easily compute the SEE for those data.

$$SEE = 2.96\sqrt{1 - .89^2}$$

$$SEE = 2.96 \times .458$$

$$SEE = 1.35$$

If our data are normally distributed, this means that 68% of actual Y scores would fall within $\pm s_{yx}$, or ± 1.35 of the predicted Y score.

One way to interpret the SEE is to make a *confidence interval* around the regression line. If we had a set of predicted Y scores and actual Y scores and calculated the difference between each predicted vs. actual, we would be left with a set of *errors* in the estimate which are distributed around the regression line. We can then use our knowledge of z scores and the normal distribution to determine how much confidence we can place in our predictions of Y, based on these "errors." You remember that 68% of a normal distribution is $\pm 1\ s$; 95% within $\pm 1.96\ s$, and $\pm 2.58\ s$ covers 99% of the distribution. Since SEE is the "standard deviation" for regression, we can use these figures to determine our confidence.

For a $\hat{Y}$ of 11.98 on the error detection test, we can be 95% sure the actual score is between 9.33 ($11.98 - 2.65 = 9.33$) and 14.63 ($11.98 + 2.65 = 14.63$). Similarly, we'd be 99% sure the actual score would be between 8.50 ($11.98 - 3.48$) and 15.46 ($11.98 + 3.48$). This shows us that our predicted scores are somewhat close to actual scores.

SEE is important because it gives an indication of how large the error is in estimating scores for one test on the basis of scores from another. We also know that if the correlation between the scores for the two tests is low to begin with, the error will be high. That is, we don't increase the accuracy much above that which we would have by simply using the *mean* as the best estimate. When this happens, there is no point in using one test to predict scores on a second measure. The two tests are simply too different to allow for successful prediction.

◇◇

Practice 16.2

▶ 1. For the TOEFL/TSE problem on page 472, calculate the standard error of estimate (SEE). $s_y = 40$ and $r_{xy} = .80$. How do you interpret this value? _____

_____

_____

◇◇

Simple linear regression, then, provides us a way of predicting a S's performance on one measure based on his or her performance on another measure. It is an especially useful procedure for student placement. (Some researchers use this method to supply scores for missing data. When balanced designs are required and data are missing, we may not want to delete a S for whom we have most measures but who is missing one score. Rather than use the mean as a neutral figure for the missing data, some researchers use regression to give a better estimate of the predicted score. Again, we are not recommending this procedure but simply saying this is one use of regression. Most computer programs allow for the entry of missing data as missing and rework the computation around that information.)

Simple regression has rather limited uses in our field. Multiple regression, on the other hand, is very widely used, and it works on the same principles of prediction.

Multiple Regression

In simple regression we use the score on one variable to predict a second. Our ability to do this successfully depends on how closely the two measures are related. In our field, we usually use multiple regression when we want to discover how well we can predict scores on a dependent variable from those of two or more independent variables. With this method we can determine which of all the independent variables best predicts performance on the dependent variable. Or, it will allow us to see what combination of variables we need in order to predict performance on the dependent variable.

For example, we might want to know what combination of subtests best predict scores on a total placement test. If we know that some subtests give little additional information, we might be able to drop some of these, making the test less time-consuming for everyone. Another example might be attempting to see what particular qualities or combination of qualities lead to successful language learning as measured by an overall achievement test. Perhaps we want to look at all the "cognitive" values associated with successful learning--field independence, tolerance of ambiguity, intrinsic motivation, and so forth. Multiple regression would allow us to see which of these--or which combination of these--best predicts performance on a test of "successful learning."

Restrictions Related to Multiple Regression

Some words of caution are in order before undertaking analyses using multiple regression. First, as a general rule, multiple regression requires that variables be interval or truly continuous and that the relationship be linear in nature. That is, the same general rules apply as for a Pearson correlation. This is not an absolute law, however. There are ways in which category variables (such as *method* or *sex* or *semester level*) can be entered into regression through the use of special procedures. (If you wish to do this, please consult with your adviser or statistical consultant on how this is to be accomplished.)

Second, since the procedure builds on correlation, it is doubly important that the correlation values be accurate. We know that the reliability of measurement of the individual variables may not be equivalent. The reliability of each measure must be reported and reliability held constant in measuring correlation (using correction for attenuation).

Third, if the variables entered in the regression formula are highly intercorrelated (i.e., the correlation among some of the independent variables is in the high .80s or .90s), there will be a problem in using multiple regression. This is referred to as *multicolinearity*. (Another big word for your collection!) Consult with an expert if this is the case. You may want to omit some of the variables or collapse them to take care of this problem.

Fourth, remember that the more variables we put into the regression equation, the larger the N size for the study must be. As a rough rule of thumb, we want to have 30 Ss for each independent variable. So a study where multiple regression includes, say six variables, would need an N of approximately 180 Ss. Some researchers argue that multiple regression should have a minimum of 200 Ss. In any case, this is not a small n-size procedure.

Fifth, if the procedure is being used for inferential purposes rather than as a descriptive tool, the sample must be drawn at random, normal distribution and equal variances must be found, and the regression relationship must be linear (not curvilinear).

Interpreting Multiple Regression

The principles underlying multiple regression are the same as those of simple regression. Since the mathematical formulation of the procedure is beyond the scope of this book, we will only discuss the practical aspects of the procedure and interpretation of tables here. We refer you to Kerlinger and Pedhazur (1973) for more information on this procedure.

In multiple regression, more than one independent variable is used to improve prediction of performance on the dependent variable. As an example, let's turn to Call's research on listening comprehension (1985). The study assesses the contribution of five types of auditory input to predicting scores on a standard listening comprehension test (*Michigan Test of Aural Comprehension*). The first type tested memory where a discourse context was supplied. Ss heard a brief story which was interrupted. At the interruption, a "probe word" (the first content word in the last-heard sentence) was given and Ss were to repeat what they had heard after that word. A second test removed discourse context as a memory aid. Ss repeated individual sentences. The third task removed the element of syntax as a memory aid. Ss were required to repeat strings of content words arranged in random order. Next, the lexical aid to memory was removed and Ss repeated strings of random digits (from four to eight digits in length). This was a test of symbolic memory. Finally, the tone memory section of the *Seashore Test* was used. It was predicted that the first three subtests would explain the greatest amount of variance in listening comprehension scores.

The motivation behind this study was the description of "comprehensible input" as being comprised of material that is familiar to the student (the i of "$i + 1$") and a certain amount of unfamiliar material whose meaning can be induced from the context (the "$+1$" of "$i + 1$"). According to Krashen, Terrell, Ehrman, and Herzog (1984), when students are presented with such input, they make use of "key vocabulary items (nouns, verbs, adjectives, and sometimes adverbs)" that are familiar to them in order to understand the global meaning carried by the input.

Context (linguistic and nonlinguistic) clarifies the meanings of familiar words. Comprehensible input is therefore defined in terms of context and content word vocabulary; the contribution of syntax is not given much weight. The subtests of Call's study were meant to show which kinds of memory best predict success in listening comprehension. Since the tasks vary context, syntax, and other memory components, the results could serve as *indirect* evidence in support or nonsupport of the Krashen et al. hypothesis.

The correlations show that each of the tests is related to the listening comprehension test.

Correlations of Tests with Listening Comprehension

	Discourse	Syntax	Words	Digits	Tone	List.Comp.
Discourse	1.00	.78	.56	.42	.25	.57
Syntax		1.00	.66	.50	.38	.65
Words			1.00	.46	.06	.39
Digits				1.00	.22	.34
Tone					1.00	.42

However, it also shows that each of the memory tests correlates to some extent with every other test. This is to be expected since all are components of auditory memory. However, we do not need to worry about colinearity--e.g., that any of these correlations among the independent variables make it impossible to interpret the multiple regression--because the correlations are all below .80.

For simplicity's sake, let's just look at the first three memory subtests--discourse context, syntax, and words. Imagine that we wanted to run a multiple regression to find out how well these three predict scores on the listening comprehension test. Each correlates with the test. But each also correlates with the other two subtests. In the following diagram you can see the overlap for each with listening comprehension. The central shaded area shows that much of that overlap is shared by all three subtests. The lightly shaded areas show the *unique* contribution--the unique overlap of each variable with listening comprehension.

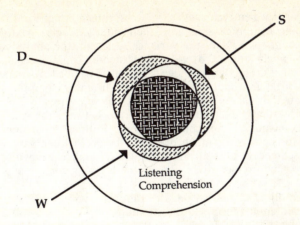

D

S

W

Listening
Comprehension

Now, you can see that an important decision must be made. If we enter *discourse context* into the regression first, it will take the central shaded area of overlap with it, and the two areas of overlap from *syntax* and *words*, leaving *syntax* and *words* with much diminished importance. If we enter *syntax* next, it takes its unique contribution and the area of overlap with *words*. *Words* is entered third and now consists only of the unique area which does not overlap with *syntax* or *discourse*. Whichever variable is entered into the regression equation first will always have a much higher contribution than those entered after it.

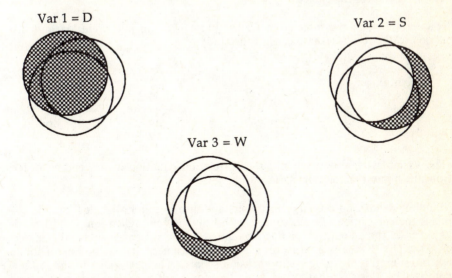

Var 1 = D

Var 2 = S

Var 3 = W

Interpreting the results in such a way that the other variables, those entered after it, have little importance is obviously unwarranted. Look at the correlation table. If we enter *syntax* first, we can account for $.65^2$ or 42% of the variance. If we enter *discourse* first, we can account for $.57^2$ or 32% of the variance in listening comprehension. If we entered *syntax* first and, thus account for 42% of the variance in listening comprehension, and then enter *discourse* next, *discourse* no longer will account for 32% of the variance. Instead, the analysis will check to determine how much "unique" overlap with listening comprehension is left separated from all other correlations. Indeed, very little will be left, and so this second variable adds little information in predicting listening comprehension scores. Does this mean that the second variable is not important? No, it does not. Rather, we know that there is a strong overlap between the role of context in sentence syntax memory and discourse memory. Both are important and *together* they allow us to account for much of the variation in listening comprehension. However, the sentence syntax memory task, since it correlates with the discourse task, gives us a good predictor of scores on the listening comprehension test.

In running a multiple regression on the computer, you can leave the choice of which variable to enter first up to the computer. If you do, it will automatically select the variable with the strongest correlation with the dependent variable first. Then, it will add in the independent variable that will add most in terms of unique explained variance next, and so forth. Sometimes this doesn't make sense and you will want to tell the computer the order in which to enter the variables. (For example, in predicting placement test scores, you might want to enter certain variables first not because they have the strongest correlation but because they are those which are usually most accessible. If these variables serve as good predictors, then those which are less often available could be omitted in future work. In such cases, you are not testing theoretical issues but rather practical issues). When you (rather than the computer) determine the order of entry, justification must be given for the choice.

Now let's look at the table from Call's study. For an interpretation and discussion of the results, please consult the study.

Subtest	Simple r	R^2	Change in R^2
Syntax	.65	.42	.42
Discourse	.57	.43	.01
Tone	.42	.47	.04
Words	.39	.47	.00
Digits	.34	.47	.00

(The variables were entered into the correlation equation in descending order, from the highest simple correlation to the lowest.)

You should have no difficulty in understanding the column labeled "simple r"-- this is the correlation of each subtest with listening comprehension. The R^2 column shows the amount of overlap accounted for by sentence syntax (this is $.65^2$ or .42). That is, the two measures share 42% variance. It is a good predictor to use in estimating listening comprehension scores. The next value in the R^2 column is .43. This says that the first and second variable *together* (i.e., syntax plus discourse memory tasks) have a 43% overlap with listening comprehension. Notice that this is only a 1% gain in prediction. When the third variable, *tone memory*, is added to the equation, the three variables now account for 47% of the variance in listening comprehension. Another 4% has been added in terms of prediction of scores. Notice that adding the last two variables brings about no change. They add nothing *unique* to prediction. It's not that they are not important, but that their contribution has already been made by the previously entered variables.

Interestingly, Call presents a second table, showing what happens if the variables are entered in ascending order from the lowest to the highest simple correlations.

Subtest	Simple r	R^2	Change in R^2
Digits	.34	.11	.11
Words	.39	.18	.07
Tone	.42	.32	.14
Discourse	.57	.42	.10
Syntax	.65	.47	.05

The results do not differ in terms of the R^2 column. That is, the five subtests still account for .47 of the variance. With this order of entry, however, all five subtests are needed to account for information shown by three subtests in the previous table.

In the first table, you can see that, using three of the independent variables, we have accounted for 47% of the variation in scores on the dependent variable, *listening comprehension*. This leaves 53% of the variance still unaccounted for. The digit and word variables did not increase the amount of variance accounted for in *listening comprehension*. Other variables must be found before we can increase R^2.

Interestingly, analysis of variance and multiple regression are probably the two most used statistical procedures in applied linguistics research. This is because we so often want to investigate the relationship of many different independent variables with the dependent variable. Our designs are often amazingly complex.

As we have noted before, ANOVA and multiple regression can be used for either descriptive or inferential purposes. When they are used for inferential purposes, certain assumptions absolutely must be met. We have specified these in this chapter for multiple regression. However, even for descriptive purposes there are warnings that must be observed. In reviewing studies using multiple regression (as with those using Factorial ANOVA), it has been difficult to find research reports where all the assumptions have been met. *N* size is often a problem; the assumptions of Pearson have not been met. One point many of us forget is the necessity of correction for the effect of different test reliabilities ("correction for attenuation"). Researchers have a habit of saying "everyone violates assumptions of statistical tests, and so it's a matter of where you decide to draw the line-- which will you decide are okay to overlook and which will you decide are too important to ignore." While that indeed may be the case, it is our contention that when we use a statistical procedure for either descriptive or inferential purposes, we state whether we have violated any of the assumptions that underlie the computation and then justify our use of the procedure. When we simply ignore assumptions, readers either do not know we have done so, wonder why we have done so, or wonder what difference it might have made in our results. If the purpose of using a statistical procedure is to give us (and our readers) confidence in our findings, then appropriate choice of procedures and appropriate interpretation of results of the procedure are of importance.

Relation Between ANOVA and Regression

There is a strong resemblance between ANOVA and Regression. In ANOVA, we try to account for the variance in a dependent variable on the basis of two major components: the variance between groups (which includes the treatment effect and error) and the variance within groups (error only). We use sums of squares and the formula SST = SSB + SSW to show how the variance can be partialed out to these two major components.

In regression analysis, we can conceive of the sum of squares for the predicted value of Y as the sum of squares regression (the predicted variation) and the leftover variation as sum of squares residual (which is the variance left unaccounted for). So, in regression, $SST = SS_{reg} + SS_{res}$.

In ANOVA, we formed an observed F ratio using the formula

$$F = \frac{SSB \div df_{Betw}}{SSW \div df_{Within}} = \frac{MSB}{MSW}$$

In regression, we also can form an observed F statistic using the formula

$$F = \frac{SS_{reg} \div df_{reg}}{SS_{res} \div df_{res}}$$

The $df_{reg} = K$ (number of groups) and $df_{res} = N - K - 1$.

Thus, both procedures are dealing with variance in the dependent variable. Both try to account for as much variance as possible as an "effect of" (ANOVA) or as "accounted for by" (regression) various independent variables. Understanding the similarity between these procedures may help you in deciding which (if, indeed, either) might be the best route to take in your own research projects.

Activities

Each of the following studies employed multiple regression in analyzing data. For the article that most interests you, assume you were asked to critique the article prior to its publication. Note whether the procedure is used for descriptive or for inferential purposes. Evaluate the appropriateness of the procedure for the study and critique the interpretation given the results of the procedure. As an evaluator, what suggestions would you make to the author(s)?

1. M. E. Call (1985. Auditory short-term memory, listening comprehension, and the input hypothesis. *TESOL Quarterly, 19,* 4, 765-781.) tested 41 ESL students

to assess the role of five short-term memory components (sentences in context, isolated sentences, random words, random digits, and random tones) of listening comprehension. Memory for syntax, specifically sentences in isolation or sentences in context, proved to be the best predictor of successful listening comprehension.

2. C. Chapelle & C. Roberts (1986. Ambiguity tolerance and field independence as predictors of proficiency in English as a second language. *Language Learning, 36,* 1, 27-45.) administered a variety of tests and attitude measures to 48 ESL learners from two language groups at three times during the semester. Field independence was measured by the Group Embedded Figures Test, and ambiguity tolerance was tested by the MAT-50, a Likert-scale measure. Proficiency was assessed by the TOEFL, grammar, dictation, cloze, and oral tests. Results showed that field independence and ambiguity tolerance explained a significant amount of variance in posttest proficiency measures. The authors concluded that good language learners may be, among other things, field independent and tolerant of ambiguity.

3. B. S. K. Morris & L. J. Gerstman (1986. Age contrasts in the learning of language-relevant materials: some challenges to critical period hypotheses. *Language Learning, 36,* 3, 311-352.) studied 182 children in three public school grades (4th, 7-8th, and 11th) who were given a lesson in Hawaiian (a language none of the Ss had any contact with) and were then immediately given a test to measure semantic and syntactic content retention. Another test was given one week later. (Results from an ANOVA showed grade 4 students had the poorest retention, and grade 7-8 students did better than the 11th-graders on some tasks.) Among the demographic variables studied (sex, reading level, attitudes, socioeconomic status), reading level proved to be the best predictor of immediate retention. The best predictor of retention after one week was the immediate retention test score. The authors concluded that the capacity to learn a language cannot be solely related to age.

4. C. Chapelle & J. Jamieson (1986. Computer-assisted language learning as a predictor of success in acquiring ESL. *TESOL Quarterly, 20,* 1, 27-46.) reported on 20 Arabic and 28 Spanish speakers who used lessons from several series of CALL lessons outside ESL classes during the course of a semester. Data gathered on the Ss included time spent using CALL materials, attitudes towards CALL lessons, field independence, tolerance of ambiguity, motivation intensity, English class anxiety, TOEFL scores, and scores on an oral test of communicative competence. The study showed that motivational intensity and field independence accounted for a significant amount of the variance in time spent using CALL and attitude towards CALL. One would expect motivated students to have positive attitudes towards, and spend time on, many academic activities, including CALL. But field independence accounted for variance in time and attitude even after motivation had been entered into the regression.

5. M. Zeidner (1987. A comparison of ethnic, sex, and age bias in the predictive validity of English language aptitude tests. *Language Testing, 4,* 1, 55-71.) presents a series of simple regression analyses aimed at discovering possible bias in an English language aptitude test which is part of a college entrance exam in

Israel. "Bias" in this study was operationally defined as error in the predictive validity of the English test for three population subgroups. First year GPA was predicted by the English test for three subgroups of 824 Ss: males and females, Western and Oriental students, and Ss in four age groups: 18-21, 22-25, 26-29, and 30+. The analyses show that first-year GPAs are overpredicted for males and Orientals while they are underpredicted for females and Western students. Test scores predicted GPA scores less well for the oldest age group (30+) than for the other age categories. However, since all errors in prediction were modest, the author concludes that the results do not support contentions by some that universities should use different criteria for selecting members of subgroups in the population of applicants.

References

Call, M. 1985. Auditory short-term memory, listening comprehension, and the input hypothesis. *TESOL Quarterly, 19,* 4, 765-781.

Kerlinger, F. & Pedhazur, J. 1973. *Multiple Regression in Behavioral Research.* New York, NY: Holt, Rinehart and Winston, Inc..

Krashen, S., Terrell, T., Ehrman, M., & Herzog, M. 1984. A theoretical basis for teaching the receptive skills. *Foreign Language Annals, 17,* 4, 261-275.

Chapter 17

Other Statistical Tests Used in Applied Linguistics

- *Principal component analysis and factor analysis*
  Interpreting components or factors
- *Multidimensional scaling*
- *Path analysis*
- *Loglinear and categorical modeling*
  Categorical modeling and causal analysis
  Categorical modeling with repeated-measures

As you read through the research literature in applied linguistics, you may find statistical procedures which have not been presented in this book. We have tried to include those that are most used in the field. This means that some procedures not often used or those that are alternatives to procedures already presented will not be discussed here.

There are, however, other very useful procedures that ought to be included in any book for researchers or consumers of research in applied linguistics. These are important because they hold promise of helping us better understand language learning in all its complexity.

In the first section of this manual, we asked that you narrow the scope of your research so that it would be feasible. Often this means looking at the relation between just two variables. When we do this, we inevitably think of a third variable that may play a role or may influence the relation between the original two variables. That is, our expertise in the field of language learning tells us that in the "real world" the picture is much more complex--that we must add more pieces to the puzzle if we want to capture the essence of language learning. As we add more variables, the research becomes increasingly complex--sometimes so complex that we need to reduce large numbers of variables in some meaningful way. Our picture of the "real world" may also suggest that those variables discovered to be important in language learning should be arranged in a particular way. And so, models are proposed (for some reason, these untested models are sometimes called theories) for the learning process. The statistical procedures included in this chapter are important because they give us a way of discovering factors that underlie language proficiency (and, hopefully, language learning) and ways of testing the relationships among them.

By and large, these procedures require relatively large numbers of Ss or observations, require some mathematical training to understand, and can only realistically be carried out using computer programs. While most of our research involves small *n* sizes, there are times when the data are sufficient for appropriate use of these procedures. Our goal will be to give you a brief introduction to each without much attention to the statistical details. These introductions are heuristic in nature. Since they cover complex statistical procedures, they will, of necessity, be misleading if taken at face value. We therefore strongly urge that you read the listed references and talk with a statistical consultant before selecting any of the procedures presented in this chapter (and that you ask for assistance in selecting the best computer programs).

The first group of procedures--principal component and factor analysis, multidimensional scaling, and path analysis--all relate to correlation or to variance/covariance. With the exception of interitem correlations of language tests, the data are continuous (interval) in nature. The second group--loglinear procedures--relate to such distributions as those typically presented in Chi-square analyses. The data for this second group consist of frequencies of nominal (categorical) variables.

Principal Component Analysis and Factor Analysis

Principal component analysis and factor analysis are techniques used to determine whether it is possible to reduce a large number of variables to one or more values that will still let us reproduce the information found in the original variables. These new values are called *components* or *factors*. They do not exist on the surface of the observed data but they can be captured by these analytic techniques.

The task undertaken in each analysis is that of extracting what is common among various tests and thereby reducing the number of tests (or variables). For example, you might administer several general achievement tests to large numbers of *S*s. The tests purport to be general achievement measures, but you wonder whether they aren't, perhaps, testing several different things. If you run a correlation of the test results, you might find that some correlate highly with each other while others may not be highly correlated. Certainly if there are subtests, you would expect that the tests which measure reading must be measuring something different than those which measure, say, spelling abilities or, perhaps, functional communication skills. If a large number of tests are available, we would like to know (statistically) whether there are components that are shared in common by the tests and whether we can capture them in a meaningful way. And we would like to know just how many different components actually exist that underlie all the tests (or variables).

Consider another example where you have data from many different tests for a group of *S*s. Say that you surveyed the literature and decided that there are many independent variables that might influence language achievement (as measured by a proficiency test). You had planned, perhaps, to do a multiple regression to find out which of these many variables can best predict language achievement. Imagine you have scores on field dependence/independence, tolerance of ambiguity, introversion/extroversion, short-term memory, extrinsic/intrinsic motivation, integrative/instrumental motivation, years of language study, a cultural attitude measure, an acculturation measure, a role values measure, a cultural contact measure, a metalinguistic awareness test, a self-concept test, the Peabody Picture Vocabulary Test, a self-report on degree of bilingualism, an impulsivity test, and so forth. Each of these might or might not be an important predictor of language achievement. There are two potential problems to be faced at once. First, we know that the correlation of these tests is sensitive to the relative reliability of each test. So, prior to running the procedure, you will want to check test reliability and, where appropriate, correct the correlation values (correction for attenuation). A second potential problem is sometimes called *multicolinearity*. If many of the measures are highly intercorrelated (multicolinear), it may be impossible to carry out your plan. Because there are so many variables to look at, you might begin to wonder if some of these measures might be collapsed into just a few factors, perhaps those that measure acculturation, those that seem to be personal need-achievement tests, and those which are related to memory. Aside from logic, there is no way to collapse variables into a smaller number of variables in a meaningful way unless we use an analysis that searches for these factors. The analysis will use statistical procedures (the researcher later supplies logic) to discover these shared, underlying factors.

Principal Component Analysis (PCA)

Principal component analysis is used to discover components that underlie performance on a group of variables. It is best utilized as a precursor to factor analysis. Why this is so will be explained as we discuss these two procedures.

Depending on the software program used, PCA starts with either a correlation matrix of all the tests or with a covariance matrix of the tests. The procedure searches through the data of all the tests to find a first principal component. It will produce a value for this first component. This first component will explain as much of the total variability in the original data as possible. The value produced is called an *eigenvalue*, a weight of sorts, for the first component.

The procedure then searches through all the tests for a second component that is *not* correlated with the first component. This component, again, should account for as much of the total remaining variance in the data as possible. And, again, this will be isolated and presented as a value for the second principal component.

The procedure will then search for a third component that is uncorrelated with the first two components and present a coefficient for this component. The process of extracting components from the matrix (whether it is a correlation or a covariance matrix) will continue until as many components as there are tests (or variables) have been extracted.

Once the components are extracted, the researcher looks to see how much of the variance has been accounted for by the first component, the second component, and so forth. To do this the researcher compares the relative magnitude of each eigenvalue to each successive eigenvalue. If one or two or three components account for most of the information in all the tests, then we can talk about the tests as measuring these few components (rather than the many original variables).

If the new components capture most of the information in the original data, then we have succeeded in reducing a large number of variables to a few, hopefully meaningful, components. These components indicate the possible number of factors to extract in a subsequent factor analysis.

Factor Analysis

Following upon PCA, the goal of factor analysis is to discover factors that underlie a series of items or tests that measure many variables. It does this by decomposing the score variances to isolate common variance (common because it appears in more than one test) and looking for factors there. This is one of the basic differences between factor analysis and PCA. Factor analysis looks only at common variance, while PCA looks at all variance present in the data.

Like PCA, factor analysis (there are several different types) usually begins with a correlation matrix, the correlations of all the tests. In extracting factors, the procedure examines the variance in the tests in terms of three components:

1. Common variance--the variance that is shared because there is some underlying factor or factors that appear in more than one test.

2. Specific variance--the variance that is specific to a test, not shared with others.

3. Error variance--ordinary sampling error.

The common variance may divide into several factors or only one. In the example on page 490, we had many variables (field dependence, and so forth) that might relate to language achievement. The goal is to reduce all these to a small number of factors. These factors will be found in the common variance shared by the tests. In addition, the procedure will identify unique variance. This is specific variance which is not shared across tests plus ordinary error variance. The total variance, then, will be: align = center.

$$V_{tot} = V_{common} + V_{spec} + V_{err}$$

Total variance equals common variance + specific variance + error variance. The specific and error variance together are called *unique variance*.

Common variance will be made up of a combination of one or more common underlying factors shared by all the tests. Therefore,

$$V_{total} = V_A + V_B + V_n + V_{specific} + V_{error}$$

If the researcher has already used PCA, the range of possible factors would already be known. Factor analysis can be used to confirm that information. If PCA and factor analysis are doing the same thing, how do they differ? Principle component analysis starts with a correlation matrix. Think for a minute what such a matrix looks like. Across the diagonal are a series of 1.00s. This is the correlation of each variable with itself, right? These are the diagonals used in principal component analysis. What happens in factor analysis is that these values are replaced by the communalities, values for the common variance shared by the tests (or variables). Specific and error variance are removed. Communalities take the place of the 1.00s in the principal diagonal.

The effect of this replacement (communalities for 1.00s in the diagonal) is that the matrix algebra of the factor analysis will only work with common variance. That's important--factor analysis seeks the parsimony of the best set of common factors. It does not also try to explain specific and error variance (as does PCA). This feature is central to the difference between PCA and factor analysis and is the primary motivation to use factor analysis in place of, or following, principal component analysis. *oblique = correlated*
orthogonal = NOT correlated

In factor analysis, the matrix is next rotated to achieve "maximum parsimony." The type of rotation used is "oblique" if the factors are presupposed to be correlated and it is "orthogonal" if the factors are thought to be uncorrelated. (In language research, it is rather difficult to think of factors that would not be correlated, so the type of rotation is more frequently oblique.) It is the result of this final step, the rotated factor analysis, which is presented in research reports. Printouts and journal tables usually list the number of factors found and additional information on common variance and specific variance. The common variances represent the correlation coefficient of each test score with the underlying factor(s). The portion of the total variance contributed to each factor is referred to as *factor loading*. Let's look at one such table and work through an interpretation here.

Suppose that we had three tests--a general proficiency test for French, a test of spoken French, and a French reading test. Imagine that since there are three tests, you requested at least three factors. Depending on the computer program you use, at least some of the following information will be supplied.

Test	F1	F2	F3	Spec	Err	Comm	Tot
Profic.	.16	.36	.25	.09	.14	.77	1.00
Spkn. Fr.	.49	.16	.00	.25	.10	.65	1.00
Rdg.	.36	.00	.16	.36	.12	.52	1.00

Look at the top row. The general proficiency test shows factor loadings for each of the three factors (.16, .36, .25). These three factors make up the common variance of .77 for the achievement test. The unique variance is .23 (.09 specific + .14 error). That accounts for the total variance of the test. Now if you look just at the "specific variance" column, you will see that each test shows some specific variance. Of the three, the reading test is the one which seems to have the most specific variance (variance not linked to the three factors). The achievement test has the least amount of specific variance. It has the highest common (shared) variance of the three tests.

A loading of .30 or above is considered to be a substantial link of a factor and test. Let's look, then, at the loadings for factor 1. The test of spoken French and the reading test contribute most heavily to this factor; the general proficiency test loading is much less. Immediately we start to wonder what common ground there is between speaking and reading which is less common in general achievement. No answer springs ready-made to mind. Turning to factor 2, we see that the reading test contributes nothing to factor 2, and the speaking test adds little to the factor. Only the achievement test seems to contribute much to this factor. Again, what is there that an achievement test might measure which would not also appear in speaking and reading tests or, conversely, what isn't in speaking and reading but is present in achievement tests? Factor 3 shows very little. The speaking test contributes nothing to the factor and the loadings from the other two tests are slight. If we look at the factors themselves, it should be clear that factor 3 has low factor loadings from the three tests; it could be safely dropped from the analysis. Eigenvalues, supplied in the printout, should confirm this. Actually, a one-factor solution seems likely. We are, however, still left with the problem of identifying at least factor 1 and, depending on information from the eigenvalues in this analysis, perhaps, factor 2.

Interpreting Components or Factors

As you might guess, the hard part is that after detecting underlying factors from factor analysis, we need to find an appropriate label for each. In the example on page 490, perhaps cultural contact, acculturation, integrative motivation, and cultural role values all load on one factor which can conveniently be labeled something like *cultural factor*.

It's possible, however, that introversion/extroversion, the Peabody vocabulary test, and short-term memory would load on one factor. Imagine nothing else loads on this factor. What label could we attach to such a factor? Or, perhaps, self-concept is included in a factor that has high loadings for short-term memory, field dependence/independence, and metalinguistic awareness (and low loadings from all the other test instruments). Again, we would be better able to find a cover term for this factor if the contribution of self-concept were not there. We always hope that we will be able to interpret the factors in a reasonable way. Since it is often difficult to name the underlying traits accurately, researchers often leave the categories as "factor A" and "factor B" and allow the consumer of the research determine the meaning of the factor.

Let's turn to another example, and see what real loadings sometimes look like and the difficulty in interpretation researchers face. Jafarpur (1987) demonstrated, in a variety of ways, the reliability and validity of the short context technique (SCT) for testing reading. The technique tests reading using passages of one, two, or three sentences in length with one or two questions on overall meaning of each passage. The study includes the correlations of the test with various subtests of the Michigan Test of English Proficiency (Upshur, Corrigan, Dobson, Spaan, and

Strowe, 1975) and the ALIGU test (Harris, 1965) as showing concurrent validity. Finally, he produces a table showing a factor analysis of the SCT (short context technique test), the grammar, vocabulary, and reading subtests of the Michigan battery, and a cloze test for sample group 1 (91 Ss in the M.S./Education program at Shiraz University).

Varimax Rotated Factor Matrix--Group 1

Test	A	B	C	h^2
MTELP--Gr	.43	.41	.65	.78
MTELP--V	.13	.63	.21	.46
MTELP--Rd	.69	.14	.37	.63
SCT	.63	.58	.29	.81
Cloze 1	.40	.30	.56	.57
V	2.82	.29	.14	
%	87.00	8.90	4.20	

h^2 is the common factor variance. If you look at the bottom of the table, you will see that the first factor accounts for 87% of the total variance in the tests, the second for 8.9% and the third for 4.2%. Obviously the first factor is the major component underlying the tests. You can tell this by comparing the successive eigenvalues in the row labeled V (2.82 − .29 − .14). In this case, the researcher might opt for a one-factor solution and talk about the unidimensionality of these tests. However, let's look at each factor in turn to see what information they can give us. If you look at the numbers under factor A, you will see that the grammar subtest contributes a loading of .43 to the factor, vocabulary contributes .13, the reading test of the Michigan battery is .69, the SCT is .63, and Cloze 1 is .40. By convention a loading of .30 or above is considered to signal that the test does load on the factor. So the two reading tests, the cloze, and the grammar test group together on this factor while the loading from vocabulary is low. Since the SCT is a reading test and loads on factor A along with the Michigan reading and grammar tests, and a cloze test (which might also measure, in part, whatever reading tests measure), calling this a *reading factor* seems to make some sense. Cloze is something of a predict-as-you-read process. Still, it doesn't really make sense that vocabulary should not contribute as much to the factor as grammar (since reading research has shown vocabulary, particularly, and grammar, less so, are related to reading proficiency). If we look at the SCT row, we see that the test also contributes to factor B. This second factor links vocabulary, the SCT reading test and the Michigan grammar test. This would not appear strange if the Michigan reading test were also included. Then perhaps a more vocabulary + reading connection could be made. As it is, the factor is difficult to interpret. Perhaps grammar and vocabulary are more important with short passages such as those used in SCT than they are for the longer passages in the Michigan reading test. SCT, in part, measures something that grammar and vocabulary also measure.

SCT does not contribute to the third factor. Grammar and the cloze test do. The factor, however, accounts for very little of the variance in the data (.14) and could, possibly, be due to normal sampling error. From the eigenvalues, it appears that the tests are unidimensional--that is, the common variance need not be broken down into three factors; one will do.

The above discussion should not detract from the findings of this study. In fact, if a unidimensional solution is accepted, SCT fits well--it shares much of its variance with these other tests. The study includes a variety of procedures and displays that give confidence regarding the use of SCT as an alternative approach for testing reading.

The discussion above results from a procedure that we have urged you to adopt in reviewing research articles. As always, when you read a research article, begin with the abstract, then turn to the tables. Try to interpret the factors by looking at the factor loadings. Once you are satisfied with your own labels for the factors, read the study, comparing your perceptions with those of the author. Test your ability to identify and label factors in the following practice.

Practice 17.1

1. Svanes (1987) administered a questionnaire to 167 foreign students enrolled in special Norwegian classes in order to study their motivation for studying Norwegian. A factor analysis of questionnaire responses was used to reduce the 20 items. The table lists three factors obtained from the factor analysis with varimax rotation.

Factor Loadings for 20 Motivation Variables

Motivation Variable	Factor 1	Factor 2	Factor 3
Reasons for Coming to Norway			
Seeing Norway, scenery	.73	−.140	−.13
Getting to know Norwegians	.80	−.070	−.06
Getting a degree	−.06	.800	−.21
Finding out how people live	.81	−.200	.04
Study in Norway	.07	.740	−.27
Get training in field	.12	.470	−.04
Chance to live in another country	.70	−.190	.03
Find how students live	.58	.160	.04
Joining family members	.03	−.260	.26
Have new experiences	.67	.020	−.14
Meet different kinds of people	.70	.090	−.05
Fleeing from my country	−.28	.060	.45

Reasons for Studying Norwegian

To be able to study at the university	.04	.068	.16
Interest in Norwegian culture	.62	−.051	.33
Interest in Norwegian language	.38	.004	.26
To get a job in Norway	−.07	−.140	.67
To begin to think and behave as Norwegians	.28	.150	.38
To get a good job in home country	−.05	.570	.09
To establish better relations with Norwegians	.46	.010	.44
To get an education in order to serve my country	−.17	.790	.17

First circle all loadings greater than .30. Within each factor, compare the descriptions of variables above .30 with those below .30. Then decide on a label for each. Svanes labeled the first two factors as integrative and instrumental motivation, respectively. Do you agree with this classification? Why (not)?

_____

_____

_____

_____

Can you think of a label for the third factor? _____

Look at each of the three factors. Since the heaviest loadings are on the first factor, on what grounds would you argue for retaining a second or third factor? What additional information would you need?

_____

_____

_____

_____

(Authors usually do include the h^2 and eigenvalues in tables. Sometimes such details are deleted to make tables simpler for the general reader, resulting in tables that are difficult for researchers to interpret accurately. All authors face this dilemma--how to give all important information and not, at the same time, overload the reader with detail.)

◇◇◇◇◇◇◇◇◇◇◇◇◇◇◇◇◇◇◇◇◇◇◇◇◇◇◇◇◇◇◇◇◇◇◇◇

Principal component analysis, followed by factor analysis, are techniques that allow us to reduce a large number of tests (or test items) to a smaller number of variables (called factors or components) that will retain as much of the original information in the data as possible. The techniques are quite common in studies that include information from many different tests--or many items of a single test. Since the techniques begin with correlation or covariance matrices, the techniques are only appropriate when the assumptions that underlie these procedures have been met. In some cases these include the notion of normal distribution. To obtain a normal distribution, a rule of thumb is that 30 observations per variable are needed. For this reason, factor and principal component analysis are really only appropriate for large-scale studies (determined by the number of variables but usually over 200 *S*s). The problem in our field, of course, is that we are seldom able to obtain so much data. For example, to use an *n* of 30 per variable or test in the Svanes example, would require $30 \times 20 = 600$ *S*s. Until some sort of research consortium is formed in applied linguistics, it is unlikely that any single researcher would have access to such numbers. When these procedures are used with smaller sample sizes, the interpretation of the findings must be conservative, and the reader should be warned that the procedure has only been carried out as an exploratory measure and that the results of the exploration need to be replicated.

For an overview of principal component analysis and factor analysis, see Kerlinger (1986) and Kim and Mueller (1978).

Multidimensional Scaling

Multidimensional scaling is a data reduction/clustering procedure similar to factor analysis. In addition to interval data, it can take rank-order (ordinal scale) data as its input, data such as respondents' ratings of the difference/distance between stimuli. For example, *S*s might be asked to respond to a set of questions that measure their attitudes towards particular aspects of an ESL program. Their responses would be on a scale of, say, 7 points. It is possible to view the correlations of the items as "similarities," where high correlations represent greater similarity, and the lower correlations show "dissimilarity." The procedure will convert these similarities and dissimilarities to distances in space. Tests (used loosely here to mean tests or items or *S*s or other observations) that show strong similarity will cluster together and those that are dissimilar will cluster together in space at an appropriate distance from the first cluster. This gives us one dimension in space. Then the procedure goes back to the same items or tests and repeats the process for a second dimension and plots it in space. A third dimension will give a three-dimensional grouping in space.

To do all this, multidimensional scaling internally converts scales, scores, or correlations to difference/distance values. It models the distances as follows: it plots all the data points so that the plotted distance between each pair of points most closely approximates the observed distance, a value derived from the correlations.

The researcher determines the number of dimensions to extract by allowing the program to run multidimensional scaling solutions with increasing numbers of dimensions and then checking to see which best fits the original data. The computer program gives a "stress" value. The lower the stress value, the better the match to the data. In recent work, researchers have been able to use special plots (something like the scree plots generated for factor analysis) to judge accurately the true number of dimensions in the data. Aside from the area of test analysis, however, this new plotting possibility has not yet been used. Researchers, instead, have used the MDS solutions, the stress values, and common sense to determine the number of dimensions.

One of the especially appealing features of MDS is that it can analyze noninterval ratings, e.g., sorts. For example, Kellerman (1978), in a study of lexical transfer, asked Ss to sort cards on which were written sentences containing the word *break* (actually *breken*). As Ss sort cards into piles, they are, in effect, determining the semantic similarities of meanings by the number of piles they use in sorting. The MDS procedure can use ratings or correlations as input and is much more sophisticated in plotting the dimensions since, figuratively, the cards are being resorted in an iterative fashion to find the best number of dimensions. When MDS was employed for this experiment, the procedure showed a reasonable two-dimensional solution. The two major dimensions appeared to relate to core/noncore (since relabeled as unmarked/marked) and an imageable/nonimageable (or concrete/abstract) dimension.

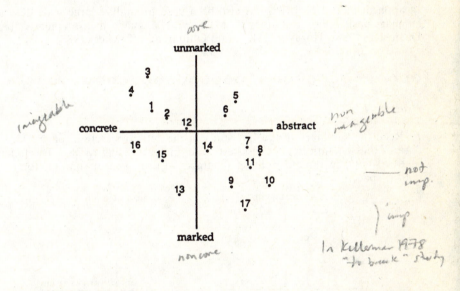

The numbers set in space show *break* in sentences with particular collocations (1 = waves, 2 = light rays, 3 = leg, 4 = cup, 5 = man, 6 = heart, 7 = word, 8 = oath, 9 = ceasefire, 10 = strike, 11 = law, 12 = ice, 13 = game, 14 = record, 15 = voice, 16 = fall, 17 = resistance). Since the horizontal axis is concrete/abstract, those numbers toward the left side of the line are the most concrete and those toward the right, the most abstract. Those numbers close to the top of the vertical line are most unmarked and those to the bottom are more marked meanings. This makes sense since 3, *break a leg* is concrete and imageable compared with 11, *breaking the law*, and 4, *break a cup* is more corelike or unmarked in meaning than 13, *using a game to break up an afternoon*. Interestingly, this experiment also showed that the marked/unmarked dimension was important in determining students' willingness to translate *breken* as *break* while the abstract/concrete dimension had little effect.

As we have said, one particular advantage of multidimensional scaling is that it can take a variety of statistics as input. For example, while factor analysis is not appropriate with Spearman rank coefficients, MDS is appropriate because it can effectively analyze Spearman coefficients. This advantage of MDS over factor analysis is particularly relevant in our field when the data are not clearly interval in nature, and the researcher therefore elects to use the Spearman coefficient.

Usually, interpretable MDS solutions do not exceed four dimensions. Since the analysis is spatial, comments about a five-dimensional hyperspace would be an interpretation nightmare. When interpretable, MDS produces not loadings, but coordinates in Cartesian space (as shown in the above plots). The researcher examines these resulting plots for neighboring or aligning groups of variables. Neighboring clusters or aligning groups are then interpreted in the same manner as factors in factor analysis; the researcher draws conclusions based on those clusterings, and labels the dimensions.

In applied linguistics, MDS has also been used to analyze large-scale data from language tests. For examples of MDS with language measurement data, see Davidson (1988), Hozayin (1987), and Oltman and Stricker (1988).

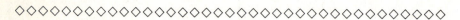

Practice 17.2

1. Read the summary of the Ijaz study in the activities section (page 523). The data of the semantic relatedness test were analyzed using MDS. The following figures show the three-dimension (contact, vertical, space) solution for the semantic space of *on*.

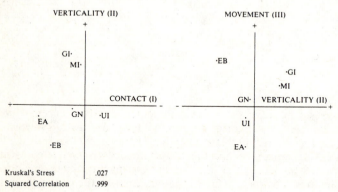

*The dimensions are indicated between brackets.

The first dimension, *contact* was the most "salient"; the second most "salient" was *vertical*; the third was *motion*. The letters placed on the dimensions refer to the five groups of *S*s: EA (*n* = 87) and EB (*n* = 33) are native speakers of English--the B group have parents with a different native language. GI are German immigrants to Canada (*n* = 45); GN are German high school teachers of English; UI are 50 Urdu speakers who immigrated to Canada; and MI are foreign students or immigrants from other language groups. Look at the placement of each group on each dimension. Do the similarities/differences in placements of the groups make sense to you? Which puzzle you? Compare your figure reading skills with those of others in your study group. Give your consensus on figure interpretation below:

_____

_____
_____
_____
_____
_____

2. In order to arrive at names for the dimensions, the author used three criteria: (1) the nature of the most salient semantic dimension of each word as became apparent in a pilot study; (2) the nature of pairs which were rated significantly differently by the L2 and native speaker groups; and (3) the nature of group-specific erroneous lexical uses on the second test involving the different words. We know that naming factors and dimensions is not an easy task. This is one of the few studies that gives criteria for labeling. Have one member of your study group read the article and explain study details to you. Do you feel the criteria are sensible guidelines for labeling? Why (not)?

_____

_____
_____
_____

◇◇

The MDS procedure is used to determine the number of dimensions that exist in the data. As is the case in factor analysis, a decision must be made by the researcher as to which solution (in MDS, how many dimensions) to accept. Recently, computer programs have been used to generate visual plots that allow us to judge accurately the true number of dimensions. However, all MDS programs generate a "stress coefficient" value which can be helpful. This value reveals how far the solution differs from the data on which it is based. The lower the stress coefficient, the closer the match. Needless to say, the determination of an acceptable stress range is arguable, and this means that both substantive and statistical support must be given to the solution (number of dimensions) accepted.

Finally, Davidson (1988) notes that MDS consistently underestimates the number of factors from a factor analysis extraction. This is because geometrically the factor analysis model includes a point of origin, whereas MDS is more of an arbitrary free-space plotting technique. This is not necessarily a weakness; i.e., factor extraction is not necessarily better because it provides more detail--more dimensions. There comes a point in all dimensional modeling where the researcher confronts over-large factor models, models which are uninterpretable under current theory. Davidson concludes that competing model extraction methodologies, like MDS and factor analysis, merely provide alternatives to each other--neither, nor either's metaphor of the world, is inherently correct. Mental abilities, such as language proficiency, may be better served by a factor analytic metaphor, by a MDS analogue, or by some as yet unused or unforeseen statistical clustering technique.

For overviews of MDS, see Coxon (1982) and Kruskal and Wish (1978).

Path Analysis

The intent of the preceding techniques has been to discover components or factors that underlie a group of tests or to discover how they group together to form clusters. In a very real sense, then, they are exploratory procedures (although they may also be used to confirm the existence of factors). Path analysis is concerned with a very different goal. In this case, the researcher has identified some particular goal and the variables that relate to that goal. The analysis is meant to test whether, in fact, the variables not only predict performance on the final goal but explain that performance. That is, path analysis allows us to test causal claims.

You will remember from the discussion of regression that it is possible to accurately *predict* performance on one variable from performance on another variable if the two variables are highly correlated. One of the caveats of correlation, however, is that no causal claims can be made about this relationship. That is, if you find that TOEFL scores are highly correlated with scores on your homegrown proficiency examination, you can say they are related. If you use regression, you will be able to predict performance on one measure given performance on the other. Though you can predict performance with confidence, you cannot say that performance on your proficiency exam *causes* the predicted performance on the TOEFL.

Path analysis is used to study the direct and indirect effects of a set of variables the researcher believes *cause* differences on a final goal, performance on the dependent variable. Because it looks for causal links among the variables, it is thought of as a theory-testing procedure rather than a discovery technique to generate theory. The researcher already has in mind which variables are important (perhaps on the basis of previous experiments set up to see how much variation in final outcome can be produced by varying certain independent variables) and hopes that the procedure will confirm these beliefs or that the procedure will allow for some of the variables to be dropped, "trimmed" from the theory.

There are a number of general assumptions in path analysis.

1. *The variables are linear, additive, and causal.* This means that the data cannot be curvilinear. Additivity means that the variables cannot be interactive (i.e., they should be independent of each other). And finally, logic should argue that there is a causal direction to the relationship.

2. *The data are normally distributed and the variances are equal.* You know that one method of obtaining a normal distribution with equal variances is to increase the sample size. This is not a small-sample technique.

3. *The residuals are not correlated with variables preceding them in the model nor among themselves.* This implies that all relevant variables are included in the system.

4. *There is a one-way causal flow in the system.* That is, the final goal (dependent variable) cannot be seen as causal for the preceding independent variables. If your model is recursive, consult a statistician for help.

5. *The data are interval, continuous data.* That is, the procedure is not appropriate for nominal, categorical variables.

On the basis of previous research or theoretical reasoning, a researcher sets up a path diagram such as the following.

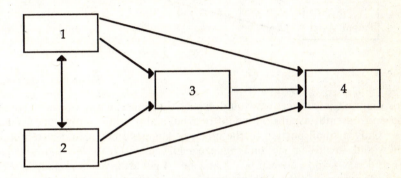

The connections shown in the figure imply that independent variables 1 and 2 may be related to each other. Each may also be related to variable 3. Variable 3 may be linked with the dependent variable 4. Variables 1 and 2 may also be linked with the dependent variable without the intermediary variable 3. The analysis will test the model to see if some of these "paths" can be eliminated.

Perhaps this example will be clearer if we fill in the diagram. Imagine that we wish to explain language learning success. This is the dependent variable, and we have operationally defined language learning success in terms of performance on a respected language achievement test. The data are interval in nature. We have decided to test the "theory" that national language policy, parental aspirations, and the learner's own need achievement determine achievement. A score for national policy has been arrived at by converting a group of five 7-point scales to a final "score" which we believe is interval in nature. This is box 1, the first independent variable. The data on parental aspirations also consists of a final score derived from a series of questionnaire scales. These data fill box 2, the second independent variable. *Ss'* need achievement has been measured using a need-achievement test, again score data which is placed in box 3, the third independent variable. We have placed need achievement in this position because we hypothesize that it is a mediating variable, mediating the effect of the first two variables. (We don't believe that the *Ss'* need achievement influences either national language policy or parental aspirations, but these variables may influence need achievement.)

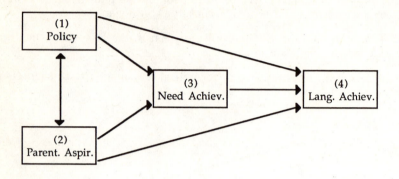

If this diagram is correct, we would expect that most of the effect of language policy and parental aspiration would be mediated by the *S*'s own need achievement. Only a small portion of the effect of language policy and parental aspiration would directly impact on language achievement. If so, the "paths" between box 1 and box 4 and between box 2 and box 4 could be deleted, and the theory revised. Perhaps even the path between box 1 and box 3 will be deleted, showing that the effect of national language policy is mediated through parental aspirations which, in turn, may influence *Ss*' need achievement and final language achievement.

The "test" of this path diagram is accomplished by a procedure similar to regression. Regression would regress the single dependent variable (language achievement) on all the independent variables to see how many are really needed to account for most of the variance. Path analysis regresses each variable on all preceding variables. Thus, it traces direct and indirect effects (paths). The effect may be correlated so that the following pathway is shown:

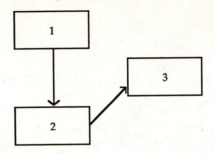

The regression path may show that some or all of the effect of one variable is mediated by another:

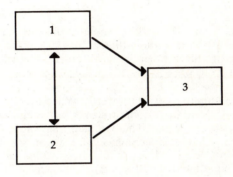

Or it may show that the effect of each variable on the following variable is independent.

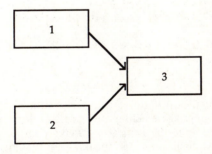

While we talk about path analysis as theory testing, it is really most useful in that it allows us to do theory trimming. For example, we might argue that the important variables that cause differences in performance in second language achievement are proficiency in the L1, age, school quality, self-concept, level of aspiration, and acculturation. Assume that we have operationally defined each of these factors in a reasonable way and that we have ordered them (on the basis of previous research or our own intuitions) as follows:

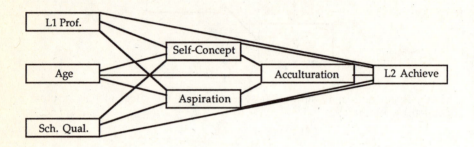

We hope that the analysis will show that some of the connecting lines are strong links and that others are weak enough that we can delete them. The fewer paths left after this trimming, the simpler (and, by most conventions, the better) the theory will be.

The question for which there is no set answer is: When are the paths weak enough that they can be safely trimmed? Some researchers argue that paths can be cut if the path coefficient is below .05. The path can then safely be eliminated. It is often argued, though, that the decision should be on meaningful substantive grounds as well. The decision level should be justified by the individual researcher (and included in the research report). The decision is often made on how close a fit is obtained, that is, whether it is possible to reproduce the correlation matrix R in a reasonable fashion once paths are deleted. Again, this information should be included in the report.

For more information on path analysis, please consult Kerlinger and Pedhazur (1973) and Duncan (1966).

Practice 17.3

1. Bernstein (1985) noted that unidirectional claims have often been made about skills development in language teaching or learning. For example, audiolingual methodologists claimed that the skill areas were separate and that instruction should be sequenced from listening → speaking → reading → writing. Noting that Krashen (1984) also advocates a reading → writing sequence and that comprehension-based instruction argues for listening → speaking, it seemed ap-

propriate to test out these claims. Assuming that each skill area is, indeed, a separate skill and that these differ in some way from global language competence, Bernstein set up a number of path diagrams (listening model, vocabulary model, reading model, grammar-translation model, and the audiolingual model.) One model, the listening model, is shown below. This model says that aural comprehension precedes oral production, that development of oral skills precedes development of reading skills, and that there is a transfer of learning from listening competence to the other skills. (Note that Bernstein didn't test oral production or writing skills in this model, so they don't appear.)

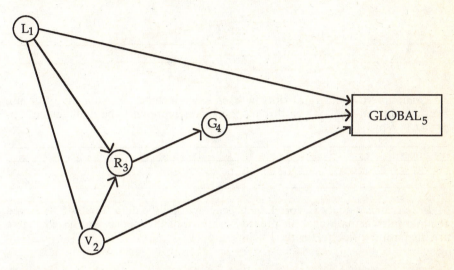

▶ 2. Draw a model that incorporates all four of the following premises of the audiolingual approach. Compare your model with Bernstein's model which is given in the answer key.

    a. There should be strict sequencing of skills: listening → speaking → reading → writing.
    b. Primary emphasis is on oral repetition rather than aural comprehension.
    c. Language is learned through repetition and manipulation of structural patterns.
    d. Vocabulary is limited, and relatively little emphasis is given to reading and writing.

3. Compare your diagram with those of other members in your study group. How do they differ? Which do you think best represents the audiolingual approach? Why?

_____

_____

_____

_____

4. In Bernstein's analysis, correlations generated by the data from 446 Ss served as input into the path analysis procedure. Each of the models was tested. Here are the path coefficients for the listening model.

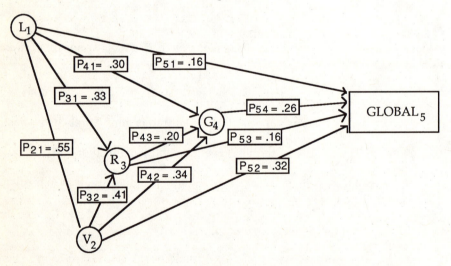

For the model to be successful, we would like to be able to trim all paths except those shown in the first diagram. Can we do so? Why (not)?_____

_____

In some of the models, path coefficients do drop into the .16 range; however, the results did not support any of these "theories" about skill sequence. In discussing the findings, Bernstein notes that "language proficiency" is a composite of these skills. ("Global," however, was not measured as a composite but by cloze procedure.) Multicolinearity, therefore, is a problem since there is a strong relation among the skill areas and between skill areas and total language proficiency. Bernstein also reports that measurement experts, having performed principal component analysis and factor analysis, have not discovered separate dimensions for skill areas. Given that information, he suggests neither individual skill data nor general language competence data reflect separate components. Therefore, he argues, path analysis should not be used with such data.

Do you agree with his final conclusion regarding the use of path analysis for such data? Why (not)?_____

_____

_____

_____

◇◇◇

Loglinear and Categorical Modeling

The procedures discussed so far in this chapter are based primarily on correlation or regression of continuous (interval) data that are normally distributed. When our data are nominal categories, we know we cannot use these procedures.

We have already shown that Chi-square (χ^2) is a good procedure when working with frequency data, where we count, for example, the number of monolinguals and bilinguals who are or are not required to take remedial English classes in college. *Student type* is a nominal category with two levels, and *remedial class* could also be a nominal variable with two levels (no remedial classes vs. one or more remedial classes). We might also believe that *sex of student* affects assignment to such classes and so we add this as a second dichotomous nominal variable. Perhaps we believe that *socioeconomic status* (SES) might mediate the effect of these other independent variables, and so we might add a three-level SES variable to the study. The problem with Chi-square is that we cannot add more independent variables to the table and interpret the results. Nor can Chi-square analysis tell us about the interaction of variables. It cannot tell us which of these independent variables best predicts the actual distribution. Nor can Chi-square be used to test causal claims.

Categorical modeling procedures can do all these things for nominal data. The basic loglinear procedure is analogous to regression for continuous data. It allows us to consider how many of the independent variables and interactions affect the dependent variable.

You will remember that the Chi-square procedure is concerned with proportions. If we are concerned with the distribution of students who do or do not have to take remedial English classes and who are or are not bilingual, the expected cell frequencies are calculated using proportions (*column × row totals ÷ N*). Loglinear, on the other hand, looks at how a nominal variable such as ±*bilingual* affects the *odds* that a student will or will not need to take a remedial course. In loglinear, these odds are found by dividing the frequency of being in one category by the frequency of not being in the category. So, in our example, the odds would be that an individual selected at random would or would not be required to take remedial courses. If we had access to national survey data and found that 1006 *S*s had no requirement for remedial work and 419 did, the odds ratio would be 1006/419 or 2.40. The odds are approximately two and a half to one against assignment to remedial classes. This odds ratio is called *marginal odds*.

We do, however, want to test whether the marginal odds are affected by the independent variables. So, we calculate the *conditional odds* to discover whether the chances of being required to take remedial classes change if the *S* is monolingual or bilingual.

Let's assume the following fictitious distribution:

Assignment to Remedial Classes and Bilingualism

	Monolingual	Bilingual	Total
−Remed.	694	312	1006
+Remed.	221	198	419
Total	915	510	1425

The table shows that the odds of being excused from remedial classes are 1.57 (312 ÷ 198) among bilinguals and 3.14 (694 ÷ 221) among monolinguals. An *odds ratio* is then found by dividing these (3.14 ÷ 1.57). The odds of being required to take remedial classes are two times greater among bilinguals than monolinguals. Not a very happy finding even for fictitious data!

So far, a regular Chi-square analysis could handle the data quite well. 2 X 2 contingency tables present no problem for Chi-square (aside from the necessary correction factor). However, it is quite possible that the findings might really be due to socioeconomic status (SES) of the *S*s. When SES is added to the equation, we may find that the odds are really more a reflection of SES than of bilingualism. We could then propose a "model" that says it is the interaction between SES and bilingualism that influences the odds of needing remedial instruction and test it against a "model" that links bilingualism and the need for remedial instruction. Chi-square could not help us here. Instead, we use loglinear procedures to compare these two models and test for interactions in each.

Model is used to stand for a statement of expectations regarding the categorical variables and their relationships to each other. In the above data, we might propose a model where ±*bilingualism* (variable A) is related to ±*remedial course requirement* (variable B). Using loglinear notation, this is model {AB}. Or, we might propose a model where *SES* (variable C) mediates the odds effect of ±*bilingualism* on the odds of ±*remedial course requirement* {ABC}. Alternatively, we could propose a model where *bilingualism* and *remedial courses* are separately related, that these two are jointly related to *sex* (variable D), a three-way interaction, and that *bilingualism, SES*, and *sex* are also mutually related. The model would be {AB} {ABD} {BCD}. The loglinear programs can test the competing models. There are several iterative algorithms that can be used to generate estimates of the expected cell frequencies for each model. These expected cell frequencies (called maximum likelihood estimates) are calculated using natural logarithms. (In the old days we would have had to look all of these up in logarithm tables and then do the calculations. Groan. But it's no problem for the computer.)

Once the program has produced the expected frequencies for the model, these are entered into the program to produce what are called effect estimates (symbolized by tau τ, or lambda λ, or even χ^2) for the variables and their interactions.

Perhaps an example will help to make this complex process less opaque. De Haan (1987) used a very large text data base to replicate the finding that complexity of noun phrases depends on the function of the noun phrase. Previous research had been partly successful in showing that simple noun phrases tend to appear in subject function while structurally more complex noun phrases do not. Since Chi-square analysis cannot look at interactions, the research had been unable to determine whether this finding holds across different text types (i.e., whether there is an interaction between NP function and text type).

Using loglinear analysis, de Haan examined 25,210 NPs in either fiction or non-fiction text (using the Nijmegen corpus). The NPs were classified as BASIC head nouns (such as *he, Harry, water* or *books*), SIMPLE determiner + head nouns (e.g., *this article* or *my car*), EXTENDED head nouns where the head is preceded by anything but a single determiner (e.g., *my old car* or *expensive books*), or COMPLEX with at least one postmodifier irrespective of the structure of the rest of the NP (e.g., *books for sale* or *that very tall man who just walked in*). This gives us four levels of NP complexity: basic, simple, extended, and complex. Three functions were selected: subject, object, prepositional complement. And, two text types were chosen from the corpus: fiction and nonfiction. The design, therefore, is 4 X 3 X 2--a design that Chi-square cannot handle.

The particular loglinear procedure used by de Haan produced lambda effects for each main variable, for all the two-way interactions, and all the three-way interactions. This is the so-called *saturated model*, a model which includes all the variables and interactions. The table gives the reader what are sometimes called parameter effects. It lists the effect for each main effect variable, then for each two-way interaction (and there are many of these because of the number of levels within each of the variables), and finally for all the possible three-way interactions.

A small portion of the lambda table for the de Haan data is shown here:

effect	lambda	effect	lambda
BasicN	0.792*	BasicXFict	−0.232*
Simple	−0.091*	SimpleXNFict	−0.037
Extend	−0.499*	ExtendXNFict	−0.007
Complex	−0.203*	ComplexXNFict	0.275*
.	.	.	.
.	.	.	.
.	.	.	.

n a sense, the parameter table (lambda table in this example) is something like ı combined ANOVA and multiple-range test report. It shows which of all the variables and interactions are significant in the study. De Haan chose to interpret the significant parameters in this table. Using the table in a way analogous to ANOVA would mean beginning with interpretation of the three-way interactions (if they are interpretable), then the two-way interactions, and finally interpreting the main effects in light of the interactions.

Using the saturated model (where all the variables and interactions are included), there are many interpretations to be made. There is a problem, however, when statistics are calculated for such a large number of lambdas. With multiple comparisons, the possibility of finding some estimates significant when there really is no effect increases with the number of estimates. In the article, of course, the author interpreted those which are most central to the question of interest (i.e., does the number of NPs vary by function in the different text types). As with ANOVA, the best way to illustrate interactions is with a figure. The following figures show the interaction between text type, function, and NP complexity.

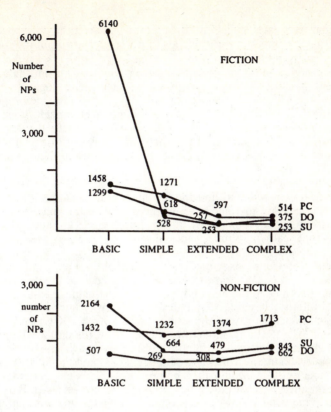

From this picture, it appears that subject NPs are usually basic nouns, but this is more true for fiction than for nonfiction. Nonfiction does not so clearly obey the "basic N in subject function" prediction.

We have said that the loglinear process tests models. Actually, researchers usually posit several models and evaluate them to see which best fits the data. In the example above, the researcher did not test alternative models but interpreted the saturated model where all the main effects and interactions are left in. In essence, this uses loglinear as an alternative to ANOVA for nominal, categorical variables. It doesn't, then, show the major strength of loglinear modeling, which is to test and compare models.

When models are tested against each other, the use of loglinear is analogous to multiple regression. When models are tested against each other, the one with the fewest variables and/or fewest interactions that successfully predict the observed odds is the winner. Think of this in terms of multiple regression. There, the "winning" variable is that which explains most of the variance. We can then look to see how much more can be explained if we add the next variable, and so forth.

Here, loglinear tests each model and then allows us to test the difference between them to see which can best cover the odds that were derived from the frequencies.

In testing the models (note, now, that we have moved away from the parameters and are testing models), some computer packages with loglinear programs produce a χ^2 statistic while others print out a likelihood ratio (abbreviated L^2). The larger the L^2 or χ^2 (relative to the df), the more the model *differs* from the observed data. Since we want to find a model which *does* fit the data, we look for the *lowest* L^2 or χ^2 value relative to the df. This is contrary to the usual interpretation of χ^2, and is similar to χ^2 fit statistics found in factor analysis programs.

It is possible, since we want to find the one model that includes all the variables and interactions needed to come close to the original data, that we will select a model that is "too good." That is, we may potentially select a model that includes relationships that really only reflect normal sampling error.

Consider our previous example for $\pm$bilingual, $\pm$remedial class, and SES--variables A, B, C. We want to find the best model for the data. If we start with the saturated model, the one that includes everything, we will have a perfect fit. Our first alternative model eliminates the three-way interaction. The model is {AB BC}--a model with two interactions (A X B and B X C) and three main variables (A, B, C). Say this model has a close fit to the data. The χ^2 (2 df) is .01, $p = .9931$. It is very close to the full saturated model (which would include a three-way interaction and where p would equal 1.00 and the $df = 0$). A second alternative model {BC A} could then be proposed. This has one interaction (B X C); the main effects are still there but A no longer interacts with B or C. (That is, SES and $\pm$remedial classes interact but $\pm$bilingual does not interact with $\pm$remedial classes. Say this model also fits the data: χ^2 (3 df) is 4.43, $p = .2187$. The saturated model and the first alternative model gave us a super fit to the data. The fit for the first alternative may still be "too good." Many researchers prefer a p between .10 and .30 to assure a good fit and a parsimonious solution. With a p of .22, the second alternative model looks like the better model--a close fit but not so close that it may include "error" relationships.

If this model fits the data and is more parsimonious than the others, common sense would say to accept the model. But there is another check that can be made. If we subtract the first alternative model from the second, we can check to see if they differ significantly in how well they predict the data. Unfortunately, they do. χ^2 (3 df) minus χ^2 (2 df) = 4.42, $p = .0356$. This indicates that the two models are different and that the A X B interaction is significant. So, although the last model is more parsimonious, the researcher is left having to decide on substantive grounds whether the interaction can or cannot be dropped.

The procedure may seem confusing, so we will give another illustration. Unfortunately, we have found no applied linguistics studies that have used loglinear to test models, so we must give you another fictitious example. The values that are used to illustrate the procedure are based on a study by Ries and Smith (1963); the actual loglinear analysis is from the *SAS User's Guide: Statistics* (1985, 225-228).

Imagine that you wanted to know students' preference for two different language teaching methods. Method A is project-based (where students work both individually and in groups to carry out a project such as researching and drawing up a plan for improving student counseling) and method B is teacher-centered instruction (where students work primarily on an individual basis to meet course objectives). You believe that these preferences may vary depending on age level (three age groups 18-20, 20-30, 30 and over). You also think that preference may be influenced by whether Ss have had previous experience with the method. Finally, you decide to include sex as a third variable that might relate to preference.

The design includes one dichotomous dependent variable: method choice: A or B. There are three independent variables: Age has 3 levels, Previous Experience (with the preferred method) has 2 (yes = 1, no = 2), and Sex has 2 (female = 1, male = 2). Assume that through the magic of the research committee and the Adult Education Special Interest Group of TESOL, you were able to obtain the following data.

Population and Response Profiles

Sample	AgeGp	PrExp	Sex	N	MethA	MethB	ProbA	ProbB
1	3	2	2	72	30	42	.417	.583
2	3	2	1	110	42	68	.382	.618
3	3	1	2	67	43	24	.642	.358
4	3	1	1	89	52	37	.584	.416
5	2	2	2	57	23	33	.412	.589
6	2	2	1	116	50	66	.431	.569
7	2	1	2	70	47	23	.671	.329
8	2	1	1	102	55	47	.671	.329
9	1	2	2	56	27	29	.482	.518
10	1	2	2	116	53	63	.457	.543
11	1	1	2	48	29	19	.604	.396
12	1	1	1	106	49	57	.462	.538

Look at the top line of the table. There were 72 students in age group 3 who had no previous experience with the method they chose, and who were male. Of these 72 students, 30 chose method A and 42 chose method B. The probability of selecting method A for this group of students was .417, and .583 for method B. The second line shows the choices of the 110 students who belonged to age group 3, who had no previous experience with the method they selected, and who were female. Since there were three age groups, two experience levels, and two levels for sex, there were $3 \times 2 \times 2 = 12$ samples.

The saturated model, the one which includes all the variables and all the interactions gives us a χ^2 value for each variable and interaction (called *parameters*). The χ^2 statistics here are *not* "goodness of fit" statistics. They are read as ordinary χ^2 statistics. Those with high χ^2 values and low probabilities are the parameters that should be retained in formulating alternative models. (You will notice there is an extra parameter for age because this is a three-level [trichotomy] category rather than a dichotomy.)

Analysis of Individual Parameters

Effect	Parameter	Estimate	Std.Err.	χ^2	p
Intercept	1	.031	.067	0.21	.651
Age	2	−.004	.094	.00	.960
	3	.028	.095	.09	.769
Prev Exp	4	−.314	.067	21.80	.001
AgeXPrev Exp	5	−.121	.094	1.67	.196
	6	−.064	.095	1.67	.196
Sex	7	.128	.067	3.63	.057
AgeXSex	8	−.031	.094	.11	.741
	9	−.009	.095	.01	.919
Prev ExpXSex	10	−.101	.067	2.25	.134
AgeXPrExpXSex	11	.077	.093	.66	.415
	12	−.059	.094	.39	.531

This is the saturated model with all variables left in. The SAS printout has given us χ^2 values to interpret, and a quick glance at them shows that previous experience is significant, sex approaches significance in predicting preference, and previous experience and sex interact to some degree in shaping preferences though the interaction is not statistically significant.

The residuals left for the saturated model are nil, since everything is included; the model matches the observed data perfectly. Let's see what happens when we try to get rid of the interactions. Can the main effect variables give us a good estimate of the actual odds in the original data?

Here are the results for the main effects model:

Analysis of Individual Parameters

Effect	Parameter	Estimate	Std.Err.	χ^2	p
Intercept	1	.020	.067	.20	.652
Age	2	−.009	.091	.01	.913
	3	.039	.090	.190	.664
Prev Exp	4	−.28	.064	19.28	.001
Sex	5	.128	.067	3.63	.057

From the table it appears that only previous experience with method is significant. Let's look, though, at how well this model fits the original data. If you compare the χ^2 values in the two tables, you will see that the shifts are small. The computer also gives a value for a "residual." This is a measure of how well the data fit the model. The residual "goodness of fit" statistic for this model is 8.18, 7 df, and the probability is .317. (In a perfect fit, the probability would be .00.) We have already noted that researchers usually look for probabilities somewhere between .10 and .30 to assure that all important variables and interactions are left in but that nothing extraneous is included when it shouldn't be. We don't want too good a fit. A probability of .317 seems to be fairly acceptable. If you compare the two tables, you can see that this difference in probability is perhaps connected to the interaction between previous experience with the method selected and sex. We might, then, propose and test another model, adding this particular interaction to the main effects. We could compare it with the main effects model and make a final decision on the best fitting model for the data. The final decision would be tempered by substantive argument as well as by the *p* levels.

Categorical Models and Causal Analysis

Loglinear has several variations that fit different uses. For example, it is possible to do "path analysis" on nominal data using loglinear techniques. The resulting figures are very similar to those used in path analysis. For example, assume we thought we could predict attitudes towards bilingual education by some combination of respondent's age, education, and the geographical area of residence. It is impossible to run a regular path analysis because not all of the variables are really continuous in nature. Loglinear, as with regular path analysis, will allow us to determine whether the model can be "trimmed" so that all of the paths do not need to be maintained. The following diagram is based on fictitious data.

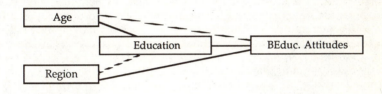

Depending on our cutoff point for trimming paths, we might trim the one between region and education and the one between age and attitudes. The result would show that while the effect of age on attitudes was mediated by education, the effect for region was not.

Categorical Modeling with Repeated-Measures

In loglinear procedures, models are tested to see which best fit the observed data. One of the loglinear procedures which is called "loglinear" makes no distinction between independent and dependent variables (although, as in our examples, they can be interpreted in this way). Another related loglinear procedure called CATMOD (for categorical modeling) does distinguish dependent and independent variables. These two procedures are basically the same. SAS calls them both categorical modeling; other books call them both loglinear. The time when it is really important to make a distinction is when the data appear in a repeated-measures design.

Both loglinear and CATMOD programs can be used for time series studies. They both can be used for between-Ss designs (where, say, questionnaires are collected from different Ss over time). For example, either method could be used to look at the attitudes towards bilingual education at five-year time periods. If *region* was an important variable, the country might be divided into, say, five major areas (Northeast, Midwest, South, Northwest, Southwest). Attitudes might be placed in five levels (highly positive, positive, neutral, negative, highly negative). The frequencies at the two time levels could then be subjected to either loglinear or CATMOD to find the best fit for the data.

CATMOD is, however, special because it can be used to analyze time series studies for nominal variables where the data are from the same Ss. You will remember that one of the assumptions of the Chi-square analysis is that the data are independent. Chi-square cannot be used for repeated-measures designs. CATMOD is a procedure which can handle data such as those given in the following examples. This is a fairly complex design. Since, again, we were unable to find examples of repeated-measures categorical modeling in applied linguistics literature, we have adapted an example from Koch et al. (1977) using the data which appears in the SAS manual (*SAS User's Guide: Statistics*, 1985, 234-236).

Imagine that you worked in a private language school which dealt with students who had intercultural communication problems. Some portion of the students have suprasegmentals that are judged as either highly annoying or moderately annoying because they do not match those of native speakers. The school offers a special program which these students may elect to take. Alternatively, they can take a regular communication class which treats many different areas of communication. The school wants to know whether there is any difference in outcomes for these two groups of Ss (moderately annoying vs. highly annoying) given these two treatments. Data were gathered from both groups. At three times (weeks 1, 2, and 4), the students were videotaped as they carried out a conversation with a native speaker. Three raters reviewed a one-minute segment from each conversation, judging the learner's speech as either "acceptable" or "irritating." In cases of disagreement, a second one-minute segment was reviewed. In all cases, judges were able to agree following two ratings. The population profiles are as follows:

Population Profiles

Sample	Group	Class	N
1	moderate	commun	80
2	moderate	supraseg	70
3	high	commun	100
4	high	supraseg	90

There are three repeated ratings. It is possible to obtain one of 8 different response patterns. If these are abbreviated A = acceptable and I = irritating, the response patterns for the three weeks could be III, IIA, IAI, IAA, AII, AIA, AAA. These are 8 different possible response patterns which are numbered 1 through 8 respectively.

The individual ratings over the three periods are entered into the computer along with information on each person's original referral status (moderately vs. highly annoying) and the class selected (communication class vs. suprasegmental class). SAS then gives this information back in the form of response frequencies.

Pattern Response Frequencies

Samp.	1	2	3	4	5	6	7	8
1	16	13	9	3	14	4	15	6
2	31	0	6	0	22	2	9	0
3	2	2	8	9	9	15	27	28
4	7	2	5	2	31	5	32	6

To read this table, first identify the sample group. Sample group 1 includes those people who are prediagnosed as having suprasegmentals that are moderately irritating and who took the regular communication class. There are 80 such people. These 80 people each received a rating at three separate times. Those who did not improve (i.e., were rated as I, irritating, at each of the three time periods) are in response group 1. Sixteen of the 80 S are in that response group. Thirteen received IIA ratings, 9 received IAI ratings, and so forth.

CATMOD works out the odds ratios and runs the analysis for the saturated model. Then, on request, it reruns the analysis for the main effects (original diagnosis and class selected without the interactions).

The parameter output (which is read as a regular χ^2, not as goodness of fit) is shown below. It shows which parameters to keep if we want to try a subsequent model.

Analysis of Individual Parameters

Param	Estimate	Std.Err.	χ^2	p
mod-comm	−.072	.135	.28	.5960
mod-supra	−1.353	.135	100.48	.0001
high-comm	.494	.096	26.35	.0001
high-supra	1.455	.130	125.09	.0001

This table shows precisely where significant results (improvement) were obtained. Students who entered the program with suprasegmentals that were highly annoying improved in either treatment. That is, they improved if they were in the communication class ($\chi^2 = 26.35$, $p < .0001$) and they improved if they were in the suprasegmental class ($\chi^2 = 125.09$, $p < .0001$). Those Ss who entered the program with moderately annoying suprasegmentals improved significantly in the suprasegmental class ($\chi^2 = 100.48$, $p < .0001$), but not in the regular communication class.

This should suggest that while CATMOD gives χ^2 values and while it uses statistical procedures akin to loglinear, the final printout and interpretation is not dissimilar to analysis of variance followed by a multiple-range test. Of course, data such as those described above could not be analyzed via analysis of variance since the data do not meet the requirements of such tests.

The question still remains as to whether this "main effects" model fits the original data. To find out, we check the residual "goodness of fit" statistic in the printout. Yes, it does. The residual "goodness of fit" statistic shows a low χ^2 value and a high probability (χ^2, 8 $df = 4.20$, $p = .8387$) . That's a very good fit to the original observed data.

The goodness of fit statistic argues for acceptance of this model as a more parsimonious solution. However, the fit may still be "too good" given the .8387 probability for fit. We would want to see what changes we could make to have the model even more concise. However, looking back at the parameter table, we see that the only parameter left to eliminate would be the first parameter (moderate-communication class). It makes no sense to delete this from the model.

The example we have just presented is very complex since it contains so many different response patterns. However, it is not atypical of the types of designs and tasks used in applied linguistics. We wanted to show you the possibilities for analysis using categorical modeling for complex designs. Let's turn to something simpler as a practice exercise.

Practice 17.4

1. Immigrant and foreign students either do or do not take advantage of a university counseling program. Their status ($\pm$probation) is recorded at three time periods. The research asks whether counseling has any effect on probationary status.

Dependent variable?_____

Independent variables?_____

Explain why this is both a between-subjects and a repeated-measures design. __

_____

Assume you had 80 Ss in the +counseled immigrant group and 100 in the −counseled immigrant group. There are 180 +counseled foreign students and 70 −counseled. The "response" pattern for status over the three time periods could be + + +, + + −, + − +, − + +, − + −, etc. Pretend you are a computer, and give a response profile for your own fictitious data set.

Sample	Group	1	2	3	4	5
1	+Cons Immig					
2	+Cons FS					
3	−Cons Immig					
4	−Cons FS					

Assume that the saturated model showed that the +counseled group does improve probationary status over time. It appears this is somewhat more true of immigrant than foreign students. The printout for the reduced model with only main effects (no interaction) shows a residual χ^2 of 5.09 and a probability of .532.

Would you accept the reduced model, try another model, or go with the saturated model? Why? _____

_____
_____
_____

The results of the procedures used in this chapter are not always easy to interpret. Each procedure performs a variety of statistical manipulations which are so complex that they cannot readily be carried out by hand. Because they are so complex, it is often difficult to get a handle on the logic behind the procedures. In addition, the researcher is asked, in the end, to make crucial decisions regarding, for example, the number of factors to accept and the naming of the factors in principal component analysis and factor analysis, and multidimensional scaling. In categorical modeling, the researcher must decide which model best predicts the observed distribution of frequencies in a way that doesn't over- or underpredict the number of variables or interactions to include. Path analysis and the use of causal modeling in loglinear procedures also require that the researcher make reasoned decisions, first, in theory formation and, second, in deciding on cutoff points that will allow paths to be "trimmed" in theory testing. These decisions should be influenced not just by statistical arguments but by the substantive issues inherent in the research question. All of this assumes a sophistication beyond that which one can normally expect to attain without sustained practice in use of the techniques. It is, therefore, especially important that you read as many source manuals as possible on each procedure and work with a seasoned statistical consultant when applying these procedures.

This is not meant to discourage you from use of the procedures. As our field moves into more sophisticated studies with complex designs and large numbers of observations or *S*s, these procedures open up many new avenues for data analysis, exploratory work towards theory, and theory testing particularly with large-sample-size studies. The use of all these procedures in applied linguistics research will surely grow over the next few years.

Activities

1. J. Oller (1983. Evidence for a general language proficiency factor: an expectancy grammar. In Oller, J. [Ed.]. *Issues in Language Testing Research*. New York, NY: Newbury House, 3-11) performed a PCA analysis on the UCLA ESL Proficiency Exam which consisted, then, of five parts: vocabulary, grammar, reading, dictation, and cloze. Four different data sets were analyzed in the study. The part illustrated below is for one set consisting of 119 *S*s. The first component accounted for 76.1% of the total variance. Each test contributed most of its variance to this first component.

Subtests	1st Component
Vocabulary	.85
Grammar	.88
Reading	.83
Dictation	.89
Cloze Test	.91

Oller (following Nunnally [1967]) notes that if the principal components analysis exhausts the reliable variance in the contributing variables, then the simple correlations of pairs of tests should equal the loading of one variable on the first component multiplied by that of the second variable. So, for example, the correlation of vocabulary and grammar should be close to .85 × .88. Checking the correlation matrix, we find the actual correlation is .67. Estimating the correlation for each pair of variables from their loading on the principal component shows how well the first component, alone, predicts the original correlation matrix. The "residuals" table below shows what would be left if the first component were removed.

Residuals from Correlations Minus Multiples of Factor Loadings

	Vocab	Grammar	Rdg	Dict	Cloze
Vocab	—	−.07	−.06	−.07	−.07
Grammar		—	−.11	.01	−.04
Rdg			—	−.09	−.03
Dictation				—	.00
Cloze					—

Since the residuals are small, it appears that the component does indeed cover most of the variance.

This particular article has been the center of much controversy since it used an unrotated principal component analysis. Because this is a critical issue, Oller included the original paper and Farhady's criticism (1983) in this volume. Review the statistical and substantive arguments in the original paper and the criticism of the procedure in Farhady. Do these arguments lead you accept the sequence of procedures proposed by Davidson (1988) for PCA and FA: "PCA → scree plot of PCA evaluations → FA extraction to a range of possible n factors (e.g. 1 to 4 or 5) and rotate each extraction both orthogonally and obliquely → check the substance of each n factor extraction (i.e. does it make sense, or put another way, can the criterion of interpretability help decide on an n factor?) → commit to one n factor, interpret it further, and report it"? Why (not)?

2. T. Robb, S. Ross, & I. Shortreed (1986. Salience of feedback on error and its effect on EFL writing quality. *TESOL Quarterly, 20*, 1, 83-95.) did a factor analysis as a preliminary procedure to an analysis of feedback methodology on EFL writing. The authors analyzed and graded 676 narrative compositions (written by 134 Japanese college students at five equal time intervals). A factor analysis was performed on each of these five sets individually. The factor analyses essentially showed the same results. Three factors were found: those grouped by "error-free" criteria (accuracy factor), by amount of information pre-

sented, such as the number of words or clauses (fluency factor), and by "additional" clauses (complexity factor).

Before reading the article, review the table on pages 94-95 of the article. Look at each measure that contributes to factor 1. Do you agree that "accuracy" is a good name for this factor?

Repeat this process for factors 2 and 3. Now look at the communality column. Which measure has the lowest communality? Which has the highest? On which measure does communality seem to vary across the five time groups? Remember that total variance of a test consists of common variance and unique variance (specific variance + error variance). How do you interpret the differences in communality across measures and the occasional differences within a measure across time periods? Fortunately for the reader, the authors present only loadings above .30 in this table (this makes it much easier to read). Would you like to know the value of those below .30? Why (not)? Look at those tests which load on more than one factor. Do the measures which contribute to more than one factor do so across each test administration? If this is not the case, how would you explain these discrepancies? Now read the article and check your interpretation of the table against that given by the authors in the results section.

3. D. Biber (1986. Spoken and written textual dimensions in English: resolving the contradictory findings. *Language, 2*, 384-414.) used factor analysis to reduce some 41 linguistic features in 545 text samples consisting of approximately 2000 words each. The analysis yielded three underlying factors which he labeled Interactive vs. Edited text, Abstract vs. Situated Content, and Reported vs. Immediate Style. In this article, the author then goes on to show how specific findings from earlier studies fit with this three-factor model. If this were your study, what other possible procedures might you want to use? What rationale can you give for each choice?

4. I. H. Ijaz (1986. Linguistic and cognitive determinants of lexical acquisition in a second language. *Language Learning, 36*, 4, 401-451.) investigated the meanings of six spatial prepositions in two categories, ON (*on, upon, onto, on top of*) and OVER (*over, above*). Two hundred sixty-nine *S*s, both native speakers and ESL learners, were given two tests to ascertain the meaning of these prepositions. The semantic relatedness test had subjects draw an X, in relation to a line, which showed the relationship in question; the other test was a cloze-sentence completion. Results drawn from an MDS analysis showed that ESL learners differed significantly from native speakers in the semantic boundaries they ascribed to these spatial prepositions. The author concluded that the meanings that words have for ESL learners are influenced by contextual constraints, cognitive factors, and L1 transfer.

This study has a great deal of information packed into a small space. Authors with dissertation research are often faced with this problem: should all the findings be shared at once (as they are here) or might the dissertation be reasonably presented in two or three articles? If this were your dissertation, which route would you choose? Why?

5. R. Hozayin (1987. The graphic representation of language competence: mapping EFL proficiency using a multidimensional scaling technique. *Language Testing Research: Selected Papers from the 1986 Colloquium*. Defense Language Institute, Monterey, California.) notes that one of the ways of answering the question "What is the test actually testing?" is to ask, "How many significant identifiably separate factors is the test testing?" The data here consisted of responses to 36 items on a cloze, an elision test (where extraneous words are to be crossed out), and a multiple-choice vocabulary test, tests taken by adult Egyptian EFL students. The paper presents the argument that factor analysis is not really appropriate when searching for unidimensionality within tests where the items are usually ± dichotomies (i.e., right or wrong) rather than linear measures. Therefore, an MDS analysis was performed and 2-dimension, 3-dimension, 4-dimension and 5-dimension solutions given. The displays, to the extent that they are interpretable, show the cloze test items as neighboring clusters. Particular cloze items cluster more closely to each other than to other cloze items in the diagrams. By and large, the elision items are closer to each other than to the cloze items (though the clustering among them is not so tight).

The author also raises the issue of whether stress levels might be higher (and acceptably so) when MDS is used to analyze items within a test. If your interest is in test development or language testing in general, review this excellent article. If your group shares research reports, prepare a summary of the arguments presented in the paper, explain how Rasch statistics are integrated into the interpretation of the results. Finally, think about the practical explanation given for the cloze vs. elision clusters and report your conclusions.

6. R. Kirsner (1989. Does sign-oriented linguistics have a future? In Y. Tobin [Ed.]. *From Sign to Text: A Semiotic View of Communication*. Amsterdam: John Benjamins, 161-178.) posited a "retrieval distance" or "referential distance" hypothesis to explain the position of Dutch deictic terms in the sentence. The path coefficients are given in the diagram below.

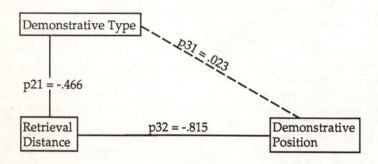

The coefficient indicates, in each case, the relative effect of the second variable on the first. Thus, the diagonal path from Demonstrative Type to Demonstrative Position with a coefficient of .023 shows that the direct influence of Demonstrative Type on Demonstrative Position is negligible. Since .023 is below the .05 cutoff point, the path can be deleted. In contrast, the influence of Retrieval Distance on Demonstrative Position is very high, $p = -.815$. And the influence of Demonstrative Type on Retrieval Distance is also meaningful ($p = -.466$). Kirsner, therefore, concluded that there is no direct effect of Demonstrative Type on Demonstrative Position. The effect is mediated through the intermediate variable of Retrieval Distance. This allowed him to refute an opposing hypothesis (the "attraction hypothesis") and make a causal claim that Retrieval Distance determines Demonstrative Position.

If this were your study, which of the two types of path analysis would you select? Why?

7. W. Tunmer, M. Herriman, & A. Nesdale (1988. Metalinguistic abilities and beginning reading. *Reading Research Quarterly, 23,* 2, 134-158.) present the results of a two-year longitudinal study which examined the metalinguistic abilities of beginning readers. One hundred eighteen Ss were given a variety of tests at the beginning of first grade, at the end of first grade, and at the end of second grade. The pre-first-grade measures were (a) three tests of metalinguistic ability (phonological, syntactic, and pragmatic awareness), (b) three prereading tests (letter identification, concepts about print, and ready to read word), (c) the Peabody Picture Vocabulary Test (verbal intelligence), and (d) a test of concrete operational thought.

The post-first-grade measures consisted of the three tests of metalinguistic awareness, the three of prereading skills, and three reading achievement tests (real word decoding, pseudoword decoding, and reading comprehension). The three reading achievement tests served as the post-second-grade measures.

The authors present a number of analyses, including three path analyses. The figure reproduced below is the causal path diagram for reading comprehension at the end of the second grade.

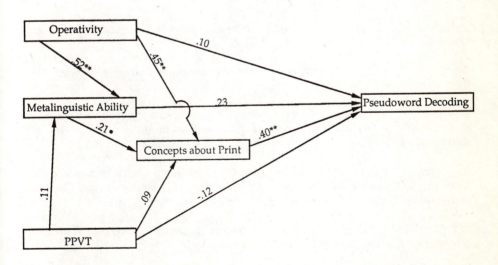

Decide which of the paths you believe could be trimmed. (Remember that trim decisions are based on both statistical and substantive arguments.) When you have trimmed these paths, write a causal statement about the relation of the remaining variables to reading comprehension for the Ss at this grade level. Before you compare your statement with that of the authors, decide which type of path analysis was used (one based on regression or one based on loglinear analysis). Then turn to the article to compare interpretations.

8. C. M. Ely (1986. An analysis of discomfort, risktaking, sociability, and motivation in the L2 classroom. *Language Learning, 36,* 1, 1-25.) proposed a model of language learning which included class participation and ultimately language proficiency. Seventy-five Ss in six Spanish language classes responded to a variety of attitude measures reflecting discomfort, risk-taking, and sociability in the language class, as well as feelings toward the class, importance of the grade, and strength of motivation. Ss were also observed for classroom participation. These factors became independent variables. The dependent variable, language proficiency, was measured by a story retelling task (scored for correctness and fluency) and a final written exam. Results showed that risk-taking positively predicted participation. Discomfort negatively predicted risk-taking and sociability. Finally, participation positively predicted oral correctness. The model is presented with a path diagram and a series of tables give regression results.

If you are interested in classroom research, this study presents a useful model. Are these the variables that you would want to include in a model of classroom learning? Why (not)? What factors would you include and how would you arrange them in the model? Look at the variables you have chosen. If this were your research, which path analysis would you use (regression-based or loglinear)? Why? What other statistical tests might you use for the data? Justify your choice.

References

Bernstein, L. 1985. The role of listening comprehension in linguistic performance. Unpublished master's thesis, TESL, UCLA.

Coxon, A. P. 1982. *The User's Guide to Multidimensional Scaling.* Exeter, NH: Sage Publications.

Davidson, F. 1988. An exploratory modeling survey of the trait structures of some existing language test datasets. Unpublished doctoral dissertation, Applied Linguistics, UCLA.

De Haan, P. 1987. Exploring the linguistic database: noun phrase complexity and language variation. In W. Meijs (Ed.). *Corpus Linguistics and Beyond.* Amsterdam: Rodopi.

Duncan, O. D. 1966. Path analysis: Sociological examples. *American Journal of Sociology, 72,* 1-16.

Farhady, H. 1983. On the plausibility of the unitary language proficiency factor. In J. Oller (Ed.). *Issues in Language Testing Research*. New York, NY: Newbury House, 11-29.

Harris, D.P. 1965. *A vocabulary and reading test for students of English as a second language*. Form A, revised edition. Washington, DC: American Language Institute, Georgetown University.

Hozayin, R. 1987. The graphic representation of language competence: mapping EFL proficiency using a multidimensional scaling technique. *Language Testing Research: Selected Papers from the 1986 Colloquium*. Monterey, CA: Defense Language Institute.

Jafarpur, A. 1987. The short context technique. *Language Testing, 4*, 2, 195-220.

Kerlinger, F.N. 1986. *Foundations of Behavioral Research*. Third edition. New York, NY: Holt, Rinehart, and Winston, Inc.

Kellerman, E. 1978. Giving learners a break: native language intuitions as a source of predictions about transferability. *Working Papers on Bilingualism, 15*, 59-92.

Kerlinger, F. & Pedhazur, J. 1973. *Multiple Regression in Behavioral Research*. New York, NY: Holt, Rinehart and Winston, Inc..

Kim, J. & Mueller, C. W. 1978. *Introduction to Factor Analysis: What It Is and How to Do It*. Beverly Hills, CA: Sage Publications.

Koch, G. G., Landis, J. R., Freeman, J. L., Freeman, D. H., and Lehnen, R. G. 1977. A general methodology for the analysis of experiments with repeated measurement of categorical data. *Biometrics, 33*, 133-158.

Krashen, S. 1984. *Writing: Research, Theory and Applications*. New York, NY: Pergamon Press.

Kruskal, J. & Wish, M. 1978. *Multidimensional Scaling*. Beverly Hills, CA: Sage Publications.

Nunnally, J. C. 1967. *Psychometric Theory*. NY: McGraw-Hill.

Oltman, P. K. & Stricker, L. J. 1988. How native language and level of English proficiency affect the structure of the Test of English as a Foreign Language (TOEFL). Paper presented at the 10th Annual Language Testing Research Colloquium. Urbana, Illinois, March.

Ries, S. and Smith, J. 1963. *Chemical Engineering Progress, 59*, 39-43.

SAS Institute, Inc. 1985. *SAS User's Guide: Statistics, Version 5 Edition*. Cary, NC: SAS Institute, Inc..

Svanes, B. 1987. Motivation and cultural distance in second language acquisition. *Language Learning, 37,* 3, 341-359.

Upshur, J., Corrigan, A., Dobson, B., Spaan, M. and Strowe, L. 1975. *Michigan Test of English Language Proficiency.* Form O. Ann Arbor, MI: University of Michigan Press.

Chapter 18
Assumptions of Statistical Tests

- *Reliability of measurement*
- *Estimating reliability*
  Test-retest method
  Parallel test method
  Interrater reliability
  Internal consistency (split-half, K-R 20, K-R 21)
- *Validity of measurement*
- *Validity of research*
- *Guide to selecting the appropriate statistical procedure*
- *Assumptions of specific statistical tests*

Reliability of Measurement

Before *any* statistical procedure is applied to test hypotheses, we *assume* that the researcher has checked to be certain that the measurement of variables is both valid and reliable. (In some cases, of course, the research question may be whether a particular test *is* a reliable and valid test.) The reliability of measures used in research projects should *always* be reported. Reliability of the data is an assumption behind all statistical procedures, but to satisfy the researcher and the reader we must report just how reliable the data are. Even when a test has been shown to be a reliable and valid measure in previous research, you will want to check to see how reliable it is in *your* research. That is, just because a test has been shown to be reliable for one group of Ss does not mean it will (or won't) be for your Ss.

We have not included a thorough discussion of test reliability and validity in this manual since these topics are treated in books on testing and measurement (rather than in research design and statistics). We suggest that you consult such excellent sources as Henning (1987), Bachman (1990), or Popham (1981) for a full discussion of this issue. These authors give careful consideration for all types of validity--face validity, construct validity, content validity and both predictive and concurrent criterion-related validity. Bachman also deals with the grey area between reliability and validity. However, in case you are not able to find other resources for estimating reliability, we will present the classical formulas for reliability in this chapter.

A perfectly reliable measurement is completely accurate, free of "error." We already know that some error will occur; measurement is never perfect. Our goal is to minimize error in measurement so that the results are true, accurate measures of performance. *Reliability* is usually defined as the extent to which a test produces consistent, accurate results when administered under similar conditions. Whatever type of data you collect, you trust that they are reliable. If you took a test on Monday and scored 100 points, you would be surprised if you took the test the following day and scored 20. The results would not be consistent or reliable. You would have little confidence in the accuracy of the scores obtained. You might wonder if the proctors used the wrong correction key. If you asked a child to copy a set of words on five different days and the results were radically different each day, the results would not be consistent or reliable. Without reliable results, there is no point in subjecting the data to any statistical analysis. Rather, the data would be described in terms of inconsistent or variable performance.

There are many factors that contribute to unreliable data--measurement error, fatigue of *S*s, problems with the data collection environment, *S*s' lack of familiarity with a particular type of test, and so forth. All of these things cause error in measurement. Think back again to chapter 1 where we gave you the following diagrams related to design.

LITTLE threat to validity:

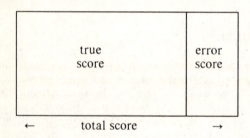

EXTENSIVE threat to validity:

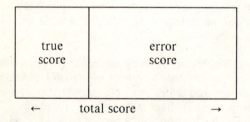

These figures are helpful in thinking about measurement reliability as well as validity of design. Obviously, we want our measurement to be accurate, with as little "error" as possible. We know that in any distribution, scores spread out from the point of central tendency. That variability of performance is partly true variance (individuals place where their true scores fall) and partly error variance (the scores aren't perfect reflections of true ability and so fall in slightly different places). A logical definition of reliability is the proportion of variance that is true variance.

If you think about it for a moment, you will probably be able to predict that we will use correlational methods to estimate reliability. If we score 100 points today, we expect to stay in the same relative place in the distribution tomorrow. We may not score exactly 100 the next day, but if we scored 20, we would be surprised. We expect a high correlation. If there is high error variance--scores do not yield accurate placement in the distribution--our relative placement will not be the same from moment to moment. The correlation and the reliability will be low.

From your work on correlation, you know that if the data are not normally spread throughout the distribution, the correlation will be meaningless. In terms of reliability, when the test is too easy or too difficult, the scores will clump together at one or the other end of the scale. The resulting correlation will be uninterpretable and the reliability low. Similarly, if Ss have a wide range of ability so that their scores spread out across the range, the correlation and reliability will be interpretable. However, if everyone has the same ability (e.g., if Ss just took an intensive program of instruction and the test is referenced to the content of instruction), the range will be so small that the correlation and reliability of measurement will be low. This does not mean that the data are unreliable, only that ordinary correlational methods are not the best methods for establishing the reliability of the data.

In addition, it is difficult to obtain reliable data from some Ss.. Data of preschool and kindergarten children are particularly variable. Data are often collected at several different sessions and carefully checked for reliability of performance. Data from beginner-level second language learners may also be inconsistent. While researchers should report the reliability of measurement for all studies, it is especially important that reliability of performance be studied in fields such as ours.

Estimating Reliability

In classical theory, there are several ways to estimate reliability: (1) for consistency over time--correlation between test-retest scores; (2) for equivalence in form--correlation of parallel or comparable tests; (3) for equivalence in judgment--interrater reliability checks; and (4) for consistency *within* a test.

Test-Retest Method

Test-retest correlation shows us stability over time. Ss may improve from time 1 to time 2, but they still will be rank-ordered in the same way. The Ss at the top in the first test will still be at the top in the second, and so forth. (To minimize the impact of learning/forgetting and maturation, Henning [1987] suggests that the time lapse should be less than two weeks.) If you give a test twice to the same Ss (or collect data from the same Ss or texts twice), you can run a Pearson correlation on the results and report this as the reliability coefficient. An r in the high .80s or .90s would show that the data are reliable (i.e., consistent and trustworthy).

Possible sources of error variance (and lower reliability) inherent in this method include setting, time span, history, and the Ss' physical and psychological state. If the room is hot, ventilation poor, lighting dim, the results may change. The time span may be too long. If Ss have been given feedback on the results of the first test, this history factor could change the distribution of scores at time 2. It may be difficult to obtain the same enthusiasm for the procedure the second time; some Ss may become bored. These factors should not discourage you from using this method. Rather, they are potential effects that you should try to minimize.

◇◇◇◇◇◇◇◇◇◇◇◇◇◇◇◇◇◇◇◇◇◇◇◇◇◇◇◇◇◇◇◇◇◇◇◇◇◇

Practice 18.1

1. Plann (1979) investigated the acquisition of Spanish gender (agreement of adjectives and articles with nouns) by Anglo elementary school children in an immersion program. She devised a puzzle game where children had to request puzzle pieces (e.g., *los conejos blancos* (masculine plural), *la mariposa amarilla* (feminine singular), or other familiar animal and color names) in order to complete their puzzle. Separate scores were tallied for agreement by number and gender (masculine and feminine) of each adjective and article. However, a total score could be assigned to each child by computing the total scores on these items. If you wanted to estimate the reliability of the data, what problems would you need to address using the test-retest method? _____

_____

_____

2. Give two suggestions that might help encourage retest enthusiasm of adult Ss for a reading test. _____

_____

_____

_____

◇◇◇◇◇◇◇◇◇◇◇◇◇◇◇◇◇◇◇◇◇◇◇◇◇◇◇◇◇◇◇◇◇◇◇◇◇◇

Parallel Test Method

Parallel tests are sometimes administered to the same Ss at the same time. If Ss' scores on these two measures of the same thing correlate in the high .80s or .90s, we can assume that the data are reliable and trustworthy. (Equating tests is another field of research in itself.)

There are possible sources of error inherent in this method as well. The two tests may not be exactly the same. The content in "parallel" tests may differ, the procedure may differ, or the two tests may require slightly different skills. In addition, Ss may become fatigued when the two tests are given at the same sitting. If the tests are "speeded," pressure plus fatigue may result in low test reliability. Again, the researcher (who is fortunate in having located two parallel tests) must consider these issues in planning test administration.

◇◇◇◇◇◇◇◇◇◇◇◇◇◇◇◇◇◇◇◇◇◇◇◇◇◇◇◇◇◇◇◇◇◇◇◇

Practice 18.2

1. Following a reading improvement course, you want a reliable measure of reading comprehension. You administer the ESLPE reading comprehension subtest (passages show general academic content and questions are multiple choice) and the TOEFL reading subtest. If you use the parallel test method to estimate reliability, what difficulties would you need to address?_____

_____

_____

◇◇◇◇◇◇◇◇◇◇◇◇◇◇◇◇◇◇◇◇◇◇◇◇◇◇◇◇◇◇◇◇◇◇◇◇

Interrater Reliability

In research reports you will frequently find figures given for interrater reliability where several judges have been asked to rate compositions or, perhaps, the speaking performance of language learners. To have confidence in the ratings, we need information on interrater reliability. Since the S's final score is the combination or average of the ratings, reliability depends on the number of raters. (The more raters, the more we trust the ratings and so the more raters, the higher the reliability.)

To compute interrater reliability for more than two raters, we first correlate all the ratings (producing a Pearson correlation matrix) and then derive an average of all the correlation coefficients. You'll remember in the chapter on correlation, we used Spearman correlation for rank-ordered data. Here we have used the Pearson. In order to correct the distortion inherent in using the Pearson for ordinal data, we apply a Fisher Z transformation. (If the original correlations are very similar or are very close to .50, there is very little distortion. In such cases, it is not necessary to correct for attenuation.) We won't give you the formula for this since we can supply a conversion table (see appendix C, table 10). Once you have obtained the correlations, check the table and convert the values before placing them in the formula below.

$$r_{tt} = \frac{n \, r_{AB}}{1 + (n-1) \, r_{AB}}$$

In this formula, r_{tt} stands for the reliability of all the judges' ratings. n is the number of raters, and r_{AB} is the correlation between the two raters (if there are only two) or the average correlation if there are more than two judges.

Let's see how this works. Riggenbach (1989) asked 12 ESL teachers to rate the fluency of 6 NNS (taped during conversations with native-speaker friends). Let's assume that we had collected similar data on 16 ESL students and asked 6 ESL teachers to rate them for fluency. Here is the Pearson correlation matrix:

Pearson Correlation for Raters

	R1	R2	R3	R4	R5	R6
R1	1.00	.69	.87	.52	.75	.74
R2		1.00	.80	.62	.57	.77
R3			1.00	.79	.81	.83
R4				1.00	.67	.61
R5					1.00	.67
R6						1.00

The correlations must now be corrected using the Fisher Z transformation table.

Z Transformation for Data

	R1	R2	R3	R4	R5	R6
R1		.85	1.33	.58	.97	.95
R2			1.10	.72	.65	1.02
R3				1.07	1.13	1.19
R4					.81	.71
R5						.81
R6						

The average for these correlations would be:

$$\overline{X} = \frac{13.89}{15}$$

$$\overline{X} = .926$$

We can now use these corrected values to obtain the overall reliability.

$$r_{tt} = \frac{n\, r_{AB}}{1 + (n - 1)\, r_{AB}}$$

$$r_{tt} = \frac{6(.926)}{1 + (5 \times .926)}$$

$$r_{tt} = .987$$

Having used the Z transformation as a correction, we now must change this value back to that of a Pearson correlation. We turn once again to the chart and find that .987 equals a Pearson correlation between .75 and .76. The interrater reliability is marginal. However, if these ratings of fluency were given without setting any predetermined definitions of *fluency* (hoping there would be a strong shared notion of *fluency* that would result in better agreement), such a correlation is not unusual. With a predetermined definition of fluency and with a training session for the raters, a much higher correlation would result.

534   **The Research Manual**

Since it is likely that you may need to calculate interrater reliability for ratings, let's practice this procedure.

Practice 18.3

▶ 1. Riggenbach also had teachers rate the fluency of the learners on their monologue performance. Here are fictitious ratings for fluency. Calculate the interrater reliability.

	1	2	3	4	5	6
1		.47	.57	.44	.68	.68
2			.40	.55	.67	.69
3				.56	.48	.78
4					.53	.62
5						.65

The Pearson interrater reliability with Z transformation was _____. We can, therefore, conclude _____

_____

2. If your data consist of ratings obtained from judges, compute the interrater reliability and report the results below.

_____

_____

_____

Internal Consistency

Internal consistency methods are used when it is not convenient to collect data twice or to use parallel tests. There are three classic methods for calculating reliability from the internal consistency of a test: split-half method, Kuder-Richardson 20, and Kuder-Richardson 21.

For the *split-half method*, the test data are divided into two similar parts. The scores of the Ss on the two halves are treated as though they came from two separate tests. If the test items are homogeneous, you might put the even-numbered items in one test and the odd-numbered in the second. If the test is not homogeneous, be sure to first match items that test the same thing, and then randomly assign one of each pair to one test and the other to the second test. The correlation between the two halves gives us the reliability for 1/2 of the test. When we have the Pearson r for the half-test, the *Spearman-Brown Prophecy formula* determines the reliability of the full test:

$$r_{tt} = \frac{2r_{AB}}{1 + r_{AB}}$$

r_{tt} is the reliability of the total test. r_{AB} is the correlation of the half tests, which we multiply by 2. This value is then corrected by dividing by 1 plus the correlation of the two half-tests.

Imagine that you gave the Peabody Picture Vocabulary Test to two groups of bilingual children (Spanish/English and Korean/English). The research question is whether the scores of the two groups differ. However, prior to answering this, it is important to establish reliability of measurement. To do this, the responses of all the children to half of the test items are assigned to one "test" and their responses to the other half to a second "test." Imagine that the obtained correlation between the two halves was .87. This is the reliability of the half-test. The Spearman-Brown Prophecy formula gives us the reliability of the total test:

$$r_{tt} = \frac{2r_{AB}}{1 + r_{AB}}$$

$$r_{tt} = \frac{2 \times .87}{1 + .87}$$

$$r_{tt} = \frac{1.74}{1.87}$$

$$t = .93$$

The correlation shows us that the test data are reliable. We can feel comfortable about continuing on with our investigation of the research question.

However, let's assume that the correlation shows us that the data are not accurate (i.e., not consistent). What can we do? Remember that reliability is derived in part by the number of items or, in interrater reliability, the number of judges. If we add similar items, or additional judges, the reliability should increase. The question is how much more data are needed. (Notice that the total test in the example above has more items and that the reliability estimate improves from the half-test to the total test.) We can use the Spearman-Brown prophecy formula to determine this. Henning (1987) offers the following Spearman formula to allow the researcher to relate test length, or number of raters, to reliability.

$$r_{ttn} = \frac{nr_{tt}}{1 + (n - 1)r_{tt}}$$

Here, r_{ttn} is the reliability of the test when adjusted to n times its original length. r_{tt} is the observed reliability at the present length. n is the number of times that the length is augmented. For example, if you had used 6 raters and wanted to increase reliability by adding 2 more raters, the n would be 1.33. If you had 40 test items and wanted to add 10 to increase reliability, the n would be 1.25.

To determine the optimal number of items, or raters, to reach the level of reliability you have selected as a goal, use the following formula:

$$n = \frac{r_{ttd}(1 - r_{tt})}{r_{tt}(1 - r_{ttd})}$$

n is the number of times that the test must be increased with similar items or raters. r_{ttd} is the desired level of reliability. r_{tt} is the present level of reliability or correlation between two raters or sets of items.

As an example, assume the Riggenbach data for interrater reliability was not high enough to justify confidence. Imagine that there were three raters and the interrater reliability were .70. The desired reliability is .80.

$$n = \frac{.80(1 - .70)}{.70(1 - .80)}$$

$$n = 1.71$$

This tells us that we must increase the number of raters 1.71 times. We must add two raters in order to obtain data with a .80 reliability estimate. Of course, we could also improve reliability by giving the raters additional training in the rating procedure.

◇◇◇◇◇◇◇◇◇◇◇◇◇◇◇◇◇◇◇◇◇◇◇◇◇◇◇◇◇◇◇◇◇◇◇◇◇

Practice 18.4

1. Check the reliability for the monologue data. Set a slightly higher reliability level as your goal. How many raters would you need to add?

_____

_____

2. Assume that the split-half reliability in the Plann study (page 532) was .75. What level of reliability would you hope to achieve for such data? What measures could you take to increase the reliability?_____

_____

_____

◇◇◇◇◇◇◇◇◇◇◇◇◇◇◇◇◇◇◇◇◇◇◇◇◇◇◇◇◇◇◇◇◇◇◇◇◇

A second way to estimate reliability via internal consistency is to use the _Kuder-Richardson 20_ formula. You can think of K-R 20 as giving an average item reliability that has been adjusted for the number of items on the test. (Note: K-R 20 is equivalent to Cronbach's α coefficient in the case of 0-1, right vs. wrong data. Cronbach's α can also be applied to ordinal scale data whereas K-R 20 cannot. For a real example, you might look at the article by Yopp (1988) which presents Cronbach's alpha values for 10 tests of phonemic awareness.) Since we don't want to have to run correlations on every pair of items in a test, we can shortcut the process by estimating reliability using the following formula:

The formula for K-R 20 is:

$$\text{K-R } 20 = \frac{n}{n-1}\left[\frac{s_t^2 - \sum s_i^2}{s_t^2}\right]$$

Here *K-R 20* is the reliability of the test, n is the number of items, s_t^2 is the variance of the test scores, and $\sum s_i^2$ is the sum of the variance of all items.

Imagine that you gave a 9-item test (*n* in the formula) to a group of *S*s. The variance of the test scores was 8.00 (the s_t^2 in the formula), and the sum of the variances of all the items was 1.72 (the sum of s_i^2 in the formula). So, the K-R 20 for the test would be:

$$\text{K-R } 20 = \frac{9}{8}\left[\frac{8.00 - 1.72}{8.00}\right]$$

$$\text{K-R } 20 = .883$$

The *K-R 21* formula is also frequently reported in applied linguistics literature. For example, Ilyin, Spurling, and Seymour (1987) used K-R 21 figures to report the reliability of six ESL tests. The Kuder-Richardson 21 formula is even simpler to compute. In this formula, n is the number of items in the test, $\bar{X}$ is the mean of the test scores, and s^2 is the variance of the scores in the sample.

Imagine that you gave a 100-item grammar test to your students. The test developers have reported high reliability for this test in its brochures. The $\bar{X}$ for your group was 65, and the *s* was 10. With this information, it is easy to compute the reliability of the test when applied to your *S*s.

$$\text{K-R } 21 = \frac{n}{n-1}\left[1 - \frac{\bar{X} - (\bar{X}^2 \div n)}{s_t^2}\right]$$

$$\text{K-R } 21 = \frac{100}{99}\left[1 - \frac{65 - (65^2 \div 100)}{10^2}\right]$$

$$\text{K-R } 21 = 1.01\left[1 - \frac{65 - 42.25}{1000}\right]$$

$$\text{K-R } 21 = .987$$

These fictitious data are highly reliable (perhaps because they are so fictitious!). Henning (1987) notes that K-R 21 is less accurate than K-R 20 as it slightly *underestimates* the actual reliability. Both K-R formulas are especially prone to distorting reliability when the number of items is small. In this example, the number of items (100) is large, so the distortion, if any, should be small.

The different ways of estimating reliability are obviously not exactly the same. If the items on the test do measure the same ability or abilities throughout the test, then it makes sense to use one of the internal consistency measures (even though these are less valued measures of reliability than test-retest or parallel test methods).

In our discussion of methods of estimating reliability we have mentioned a number of characteristics of the test itself which may influence reliability. Let's summarize them here.

1. The longer the test, the more reliable it will be (assuming it's not so long that fatigue sets in!).

2. If the task items are too easy or too difficult, reliability will be low (scores will all group together at high or low points). Consult your advisor for alternate ways of estimating reliability.

3. Items which discriminate well among Ss will contribute to test reliability.

4. If Ss have a wide range of ability, test reliability will increase.

5. The more homogeneous the items, the higher the reliability.

6. Reliability estimates are better on "power" tests than on "speeded" tests (don't use a split-half method comparing the first half with the last half if speed is a factor!).

Test length is probably the most important test characteristic in terms of increasing reliability. The more data you have, for example, on your Ss' performance on present perfect, the surer you can be that the performance is reliable. Of course, an increase in number of items will result in improved reliability only up to a point (which you can determine using the Spearman formula). From then on, the reliability will not change as more items are added. It also makes no sense to add items if it means that Ss become bored or exhausted. Trying to increase reliability by constructing many items may not work. When testing young children, or when it is likely that Ss will become frustrated by a task, it is always a good idea to schedule plenty of "rest periods" to be sure that you get consistent, high-level performance.

One final note on reliability of data--the reliability formulas given here were devised for data where there is variance. They obviously should not be used with criterion-referenced tests (since these tests are devised to get high scores from all Ss and, thus, little variance in performance). If the data you have collected come from a criterion-referenced test, consult Thorndike (1971). Hudson and Lynch (1984) provide an excellent discussion of ways to estimate reliability and validity of such tests. The article contains a good example of application of these techniques to a sample data set.

Validity of Measurement

Researchers know that if a test measure is not reliable it cannot be a valid measure. However, validity is almost always couched in terms of valid *for* something else. An instrument is valid for the purpose of testing reading, a test is valid for some certain group of advanced learners, or it is a valid test for children.

Nevertheless, there are different types of validity, three of which are most central to applied linguistics research. The first of these is *content validity*. Content validity represents our judgment regarding how representative and comprehensive a test is. Our data-gathering procedures are usually selective. That is, we can't look at all of written language in doing a text analysis. We select a representative sample--say comparative structures--in a written language data base. In a grammar test, we can't test every grammar point--there isn't time. We select a representative sample for test purposes. If we study speaker overlap in natural conversations, we can't look at every overlap in all conversations of learners. We have to select a representative sample of the data for analysis. Not only should the data we select for analysis be representative of the phenomenon we wish to research, but they must be comprehensive. Thus, in the grammar example, the items selected for test purposes must not only be representative but cover as wide a range of grammar points as possible. A grammar test that only tests verb morphology is not a valid grammar test in terms of the comprehensiveness of its content. If the data selected for overlaps relate only to greetings and leave-takings, the measurement is not comprehensive and lacks content validity (if the test purports to measure overlaps in conversation in general). In the same vein, if a text analysis of comparatives only selects samples related to *more* and *most* and neglects the *-er, -est* forms, the data are not comprehensive and so the measures lack content validity.

Content validity, then, has to do with how well a test or observation instrument tests what it purports to test. The key elements in the judgment are representativeness and comprehensiveness. There is no statistical measurement of content validity. Rather, panels of experts may be asked to rate the representativeness and comprehensiveness of each part of a test. They may be asked to draw up specifications so that test items can be written that will be representative and comprehensive in nature.

Face validity relates to content validity. However, face validity has more to do with how easy it will be to convince our *S*s, our peers, and other researchers that a particular test actually measures what we say it measures. For example, it may be difficult to convince some teachers or administrators of the face validity of a cloze passage test as a measure of reading comprehension. Somehow, since it is not in the traditional form of "read this passage and answer these questions based on the passage," it does not have the same acceptance, the same face validity as an ordinary reading test.

Predictive validity refers to the use of tests as valid *for* the predictive purposes. If a student does well on a general language proficiency test, we expect that we can predict how well the student will do in a variety of nontest situations. Conversely, we expect that if a student does poorly on a language proficiency test, this can be used to predict nonsuccess in other areas. For example, you may have noticed that students applying to foreign universities are asked to give information on their abilities in the language of instruction at the university. People who write reference letters are often asked about the language proficiency of students wishing to study in foreign universities. The assumption is that language proficiency can predict at least to some degree success in academic life in general. Researchers have been interested in how well ESL placement exams (e.g., TOEFL or ESLPE) can predict grades (GPA) of entering foreign students. If the ESL tests have good predictive validity, we would expect that they might be very good predictors at the lower proficiency levels. Henning (1987) suggests that as students become more and more proficient, the relationship between test scores and GPA should weaken. That is, hypotheses on the predictive validity of the ESL test in terms of general academic performance could be made and tested.

A third type of validity has been mentioned several times in this manual: construct validity. We have demonstrated that there are many constructs in our field for which we have no direct measures--constructs such as motivation, need achievement, attitude, role identification, acculturation, communicative competence, and so forth. We can, however, say that someone who is highly motivated in language learning will exhibit traits a, b, and c for which we may have direct measures. The motivated S will not exhibit traits x, y, and z for which we have direct measures. Once we have formed our hypotheses regarding the construct, we can then test these predictions in our research. If our predictions hold, we can say that we have a valid construct which was defined by theory and tested in our research.

Another kind of construct validation is more closely tied to second language acquisition research. In a series of theoretical papers, SLA researchers have suggested that there are a number of components that make up "communicative competence." If there are direct measures for the components, then we should be able to test the construct indirectly. In addition, if it can be shown that a person who is competent exhibits traits a, b, and c and not x, y, and z, then we can begin to establish the reality of the construct itself. You might think of this as analogous to establishing the validity of a construct such as listening comprehension. If the items on a listening subtest correlate (point biserial correlation) with the listening subtest score better than, say, with a vocabulary subtest score, then we have helped to establish the construct validity of listening comprehension. In the same way, construct validity can be established for many constructs for which we have no direct measures. Since there are so many such constructs related to language learning, construct validation is important to our field.

As was the case with reliability, there are many threats to measurement validity. Henning lists five major threats to validity. In most cases, it takes only a few minutes of planning to avoid these problems.

1. *Invalid application of tests.* For example, you might select a Spanish reading test to assess the L1 reading skills of a group of Spanish-English bilingual children in the American Southwest. Later, someone points out that the Spanish test was written in Spain with cultural content related to that country. Most of the children come from Mexico and Central America--the test has been misapplied. There are many possibilities for misapplication of tests: tests written for native speakers given to immigrant students, tests written for adults administered to children, vocabulary tests given as tests of reading, and so forth. The tests are not valid for these particular purposes or groups.

2. *Inappropriate content.* Students may not know the vocabulary used in test items meant to test other skills. For example, students may be given a reading test where the passages are about physical sciences even though the student has never been exposed to such content. The content is not valid for the purpose of testing reading.

3. *Lack of cooperation from the examinees.* When the people who contribute the data have no stake in the data, it's likely the data will not be valid. If the participants view the exercise as a great waste of time, and you hope to use the results to decide who should or should not be selected for a special language program, the data will not be valid for your purposes.

4. *Inappropriate norming population.* It's possible that you will see a test referenced as both valid and reliable. For example, UCLA uses a placement examination which is believed to be valid and for which we have obtained consistently high reliability. The Ss who take this test are from many different countries but primarily from Asian countries. These Ss may be newly arrived students or students who have lived in the United States for several years prior to admission to the university. Imagine, then, taking the test normed on this group (diverse in some respects) and using it as a valid placement test at the University of Copenhagen. We have no way of knowing whether the test would be valid for placement purposes in a different area of the world where all the Ss are from one language background.

5. *Invalid constructs.* We have talked about this problem many times in this chapter and elsewhere. We need to be careful in our operational definitions of constructs such as motivation, success, fluency, intelligibility, and so forth. We must be able to show that our measures are valid as tests of these constructs.

Validity of Research

Whether planning our own research or reading research reports of the field, we should think about the project from at least two perspectives. First, what can this particular piece of research contribute to our understanding of language acquisition theory or language teaching practice? The potential for advancing theory or practice is our main guideline in evaluating research. That potential, however, can be reached only if the research is carried out in a way that allows us to feel confident in the results.

The issue of confidence has been central, lurking behind all the discussions and problem solving activities in this manual. We want to carry out our research in such a way that we all will feel confident in claims made on the basis of the results. This depends on the answer to at least three questions:

1. Is the design valid?

   a. Internal validity of design: What threats are left unsolved?

b. External validity of design: What threats are left unsolved (especially stratified sampling, random selection, and random assignment)?

2. Is the measurement valid?

   a. Do operational definitions match the construct?

   b. Are the measures representative and inclusive?

3. Is the measurement reliable?

   a. Is the measurement internally consistent (split-half, K-R 20, K-R 21)?

   b. Is the measurement consistent over time (correlation)?

   c. Is there consistency in form (correlation)?

   d. Is there consistency in judgment (interrater reliability)?

Our ability to describe and, beyond description, to generalize depends in large part on the answers to these questions.

We have already said that computers can never judge data--they know not whence the data came. The same can be said about any statistical test. Once we move over to selection of a statistical test to test our hypotheses, we *assume* that the answers regarding the source of the data have been satisfactorily answered. All statistical tests share the assumption that the data are both valid and reliable. There are, however, specific assumptions related to each procedure. We have talked about these as we discussed each procedure in turn. In order to help you select the appropriate procedure and to check the assumptions of each test, we present a flow chart and a list of assumptions in the following sections.

Guide to Selecting the Appropriate Procedure

Once you have determined reliability of your data, you still must select the appropriate procedure for analyzing the data. The assumptions listed for each procedure may help you determine the appropriate statistical procedure. At several points throughout the manual we have given you pointers or asked that you draw your own chart to help guide you in the selection process.

The following flow chart includes the statistical procedures covered in the manual. With care, the chart may be used as a guide in the selection process. Once a statistical procedure has been selected, check the assumptions for that procedure in the following lists.

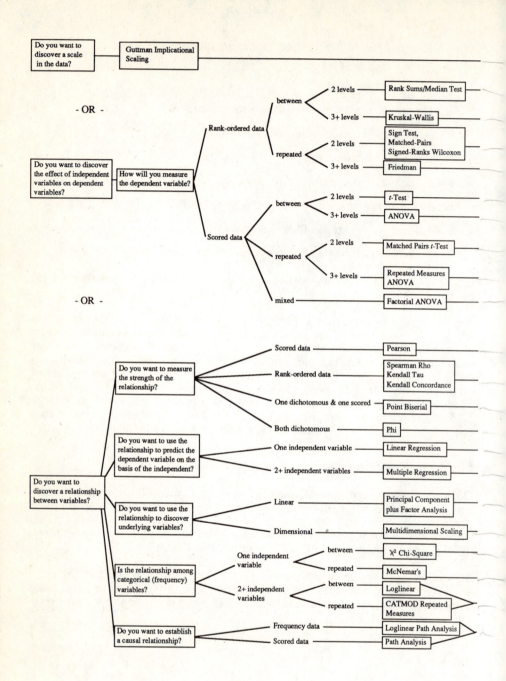

Check that the coefficient of scalability is over .60 — Interpret scale in light of reasonableness of the cutoff point, number of instances required, missing values, and context used to elicit forms.

Compare the groups
Check z value — If the z score is significant, then one group has more Ss in higher ranks than the other . Use eta² for strength of association.

Compare the groups
Check H value — If H is significant, the groups differ; use Ryan's procedure to locate which groups differ. Use eta² for strength of association.

Compare the groups
Check R or z value — If the Sign test R or Wilcoxon z is significant, there is a change from time 1 to time 2. Use eta² for strength of association for Wilcoxon.

Compare the groups
Check X^2 — If X^2 is significant, there is a change over several time points (or msrs.) To locate the difference more precisely report the results of the Nemenyi's procedure. Use eta² for strength of association.

Compare the two means
Check t value — If the t value is significant, the two groups differ. Use eta² to show strength of association.

Compare 3+ means
Check F ratio — If the F ratio is significant, the groups differ. To locate the difference more precisely, interpret the multiple-range test (Scheffé, Tukey, or Newman-Keuls). Use omega² or eta² for strength of association.

Compare the two means
Check t value — If the t value is significant, there is a difference in the means for the two times or measures. Use eta² for strength of association.

Compare 3+ means
Check F ratio — If the F ratio is significant, the same (or matched) Ss perform differently on repeated measures. Use a multiple-range test to locate precise differences. Use eta² for strength of association.

Compare the means
Check F ratios — Step 1. If the interaction is significant, chart the means to show the interaction and interpret it. Interpret main effects in light of the interaction.
Step 2. If the interaction is not significant, interpret the difference in the main effects. Use a multiple-range test to locate precise differences. Use eta² to show the strength of association.

Check the strength of each correlation — r^2 shows the amount of overlap between each pair of variables. Be sure to correct for attenuation if measures are not of equal reliability.

Check the probability of the correlation — If the correlation is significant, it shows that the H_o of no relation can be rejected. Interpret the value "sensibly" in terms of strength of relationship.

Check the value of the correlation — Explain the correlation in a "sensible" way.

Check X^2 for significance — Explain the correlation in a "sensible" way.

Report predicted scores
Check the SEE — The stronger the correlation and the smaller the SEE, the better the prediction will be.

Check each added variable — Identify the first independent variable, then the overlap of the second with the first to see how much each contributes (as well as their joint contribution) to explain variance in the dependent variable. Explain how much additional information is given by each succeeding independent variable.

Check each factor loading — If possible, once the number of factors has been determined, label each factor by consulting variables with high loadings vs. variables with low loadings on each. Else, label them as factor A, B, C, etc.

Check solutions and stress — Once a solution (about number of dimensions) has been identified or selected, label each dimension by consulting items in the cluster and those distant from cluster. Else, label them as dimension A, B, C, etc.

Check X^2 value & $(O-E)^2/E$ values — If X^2 is significant, the distribution differs from the expected distribution. Show which cells differ most from expected cell frequency or do a Ryan's procedure to locate the difference more precisely. Use Phi or Cramers V for strength of association.

Check z value — If z is significant, conclude there is a change in proportion of Ss from time 1 to time 2.

Check parameter estimates to reduce model, compare models — The parameter estimates show which interactions and main effects are significant. To "pare" the model, compare various models with the saturated model. Decisions should be based on statistical and substantive arguments.

Check the paths to see which can be trimmed from the model — Use the analysis to trim "paths" from the model. Interpret the findings on both statistical and substantive grounds.

Chapter 18. Assumptions of Statistical Tests 545

Assumptions of Specific Statistical Tests

All statistical tests have certain assumptions underlying their formulation. When the assumptions are violated, it is difficult for the researcher or the reader of the research to know how much confidence to place in the findings. If one assumption is ignored and the statistical test applied, the probability is distorted. If more than one assumption is violated, or some combination of assumptions is violated, the resulting probability level is meaningless.

The kinds of assumptions differ depending on the kinds of claims researchers hope to make. When the researcher uses a statistical test for inferential purposes--i.e., when the researcher wishes to generalize--then the basic assumptions of the test must be met, and, in addition, good design must be employed.

For example, in using a statistical study for inferential purposes, we make the following assumptions:

1. The population is well described and a *representative* sample is drawn from the population.

2. A (stratified) *random* sample is drawn from the population.

3. *S*s (or observations) are *randomly assigned* to treatment groups.

4. Threats to *internal* validity of the study have been met.

5. Threats to *external* validity of the study have been met.

In our field, we seldom are able to meet all of these requirements. Therefore, when parametric statistical procedures are used, they are used primarily for descriptive purposes. They give us confidence that what we say about the sample is correct (rather than confidence that what we say about the sample can be generalized to the population at large). In using parametric procedures for descriptive purposes, we also do *not* make causal claims. Even for inferential purposes, we cannot say that we have "proved" anything, but rather, that we have found evidence in support of (or contrary to) our hypotheses.

Nevertheless, whether we use statistical procedures for inferential purposes or descriptive purposes, we must meet the assumptions that underlie the statistical test. In some cases, this relates to normal distribution; in other cases, it may be the number of observations or *S*s required; and in other instances, it may have to do with whether the observations are from different *S*s or from the same *S*s at different times.

Once you have selected a statistical procedure, you should always check the assumptions that underlie the test. In general, many tests can suffer from a small *n* size because a single outlier or a few outliers will influence the results. That is why *n* size appears again and again in the suggestions below. If you cannot meet the assumptions of a statistical test, then it is better not to apply the test. If you go ahead and run the procedure and report the results, the results must be qualified so that readers can make up their own minds whether they feel the circumstances warrant the exceptional use of the test.

Since we want to use as much information in the data as possible, our first choice is for a parametric procedure. When we cannot meet the assumptions of these procedures, however, we can turn to alternative nonparametric procedures. The following lists reflect this bias. Please consult the appropriate chapter for a full discussion of the assumptions underlying each test.

t-test: Comparing Two Means

1. The data are scores (or ordinal scale data appropriate for parametric procedures).

2. The data are independent (between-groups design).

3. The data in the two samples are normally distributed so that $\overline{X}$ is an appropriate measure of central tendency.

4. The distribution of the data in the respective populations is normally distributed with equal variances.

5. Only two means are compared (no cross-comparisons allowed).

6. The t statistic shows if an effect exists, not its strength.

Solutions when assumptions cannot be met.

1. For assumption 1 (and 3 and 4), use a Rank sums test or a Median test instead. (If you have 40 or more Ss, you can also use the Komogorov-Smirnov test.)

2. If the data are from the same Ss or highly correlated samples (i.e., matched groups), use a matched t-test. If the design is repeated-measures and you can't meet the normal distribution and equal variance assumptions, use a Wilcoxon Matched-pairs signed-ranks test or (last resort!) a Sign test.

3. If the data are not normally distributed (the $\overline{X}$ is not a good measure of central tendency), use a Rank sums or Median test for a between-groups comparison or a Wilcoxon Matched-pairs signed-ranks for a repeated-measures comparison.

4. If you run the t-test on the computer, you can check for equal variances in the printout. If calculated by hand and the design is balanced, you can assume they are equal. If the variances are not equal, use the nonparametric tests listed above and compare the results. Or, add data to make a balanced design.

5. To compare more than two groups, use a test which allows for such comparisons (e.g., ANOVA, GLM, or Friedman).

6. Report eta² for strength of association.

ANOVA: Comparing More Than Two Means

1. The data are scores (or ordinal scale data appropriate for parametric procedures).

2. The data are independent (between-groups designs).

3. The data in the samples are normally distributed so that $\overline{X}$ is an appropriate measure of central tendency.

4. The data in the respective populations are normally distributed with equal variances.

5. The design is balanced (unless specific ANOVA procedure adjusts for unbalanced nonorthogonal designs).

6. There are a minimum of 5 Ss or observations per cell.

7. The F statistic allows us only to (not) reject the null hypothesis (i.e., it shows the groups differ but not where the difference lies).

8. The F statistic shows if an effect exists, not its strength.

Solutions when assumptions cannot be met.

1. If data are not interval, use a Kruskal-Wallis or Friedman test.

2. If the data are not independent, use a Repeated-measures ANOVA or GLM. If it is a mixed design, use Factorial ANOVA or consult a statistician to determine which member of the ANOVA family is appropriate for the data.

3. If data are not normally distributed, use a nonparametric test (Kruskal-Wallis or Friedman).

4. Apply a nonparametric procedure (Kruskal-Wallis or Friedman) if the distribution in the population cannot be assumed to be normal.

5. If the design is not balanced, use SAS procedure GLM, and consult the Type III results.

6. Collect additional data to meet minimum cell size.

7. When the F statistic is statistically significant, use a multiple-range test (e.g., Scheffé, Tukey, Newman-Keuls) to determine which groups differ from each other.

8. Report omega² as the strength of association.

Chi-square: Relating Categorical Variables

1. The data are frequencies.

2. The data are independent. This means, first, that each observation or S appears in only one cell. The comparisons are between-Ss or between-texts; i.e., no repeated-measures. Second, the data within each cell are independent. Each S or observation contributes just one piece of information.

3. Correction factors are applied to tables with 1 df.

4. Expected cell frequencies are $\geq$ 10 for tables with 1 df. Expected cell frequencies are $\geq$ 5 for all other tables.

5. In the report of results, the observed χ^2 value allows us only to (not) reject the null hypothesis (not to locate precisely where the difference is).

6. The results show a relationship among the variables but not the strength of the relationship.

Solutions when assumptions cannot be met.

1. If the data are continuous, use the appropriate correlation (Pearson or Spearman) to show relationship. Or, if the data are categorical and can be appropriately converted to raw frequencies, do so.

2. For nonindependent data between cells (i.e., repeated-measures), use McNemar's test or CATMOD. For nonindependence of the data within cells (i.e., individual Ss or texts contribute different frequencies to one cell), convert the data as shown on page 407 of this manual or convert the data to rates (X per 100 or whatever) and apply an appropriate nonparametric procedure.

3. For 1 df, use Yates' Correction factor.

4. For small cell sizes, collapse cells or use a Fisher's Exact test (see Siegel, 1956).

5. To locate differences when the χ^2 is significant overall, interpret the larger $(O - E)^2 \div E$ values, or do a Ryan's procedure to locate differences among cells.

6. Use phi (Φ) or Cramer's V for strength of association.

Pearson Correlation: Relating Interval Variables

1. The two data sets are measured with scores or ordinal scales that are truly continuous.

2. The two data sets have equivalent reliability.

3. The data are independent (i.e., no uncorrected part-to-whole correlations).

4. The data on both measures are normally distributed. To obtain a normal distribution, n size should ≥ 30 or 35 for each.

   a. The range of scores on both variables is "large enough"; i.e., scores are not grouped tightly together with little range.

   b. There are no extreme scores at each end of the range with little in the middle of the distribution.

5. The relationship is linear, not curvilinear.

6. Checking the probability of any correlation coefficient simply allows us to reject the null hypothesis of *no* relationship. The probability does not reflect the strength of the relationship.

7. Pearson correlations used for interrater reliability with more than two raters will likely be distorted.

Solutions when assumptions cannot be met.

1. When data are not score data or when not normally distributed:

   a. Use point biserial correlation when one variable is a dichotomous (as in pass/fail) nominal variable and the other is score data.

   b. Use Spearman or Kendall tau correlations for rank-order data. Be sure to check number of ties when using Spearman if you do the procedure by hand (computer programs correct for ties).

   c. Use phi for two categorical variables or eta where one is a category and the other score.

   d. Use Kendall's Concordance when checking agreement in rank orders across many cases (rather than just two).

2. If the tests being correlated are not equivalent in terms of reliability, correct for attenuation.

3. Remove the contribution of the part from the whole before correlating part and whole.

4. When data are not normally distributed, use Spearman or gather additional representative data.

5. Consult a statistical consultant when the scatterplot shows a curvilinear relationship. There are special methods for curvilinear data.

6. Interpret the strength of correlation with r^2 (rather than the probability level). Remember that correlations of tests are to some extent dependent on the reliability of each test. This is not reflected in a correlation matrix which has not been corrected for attenuation.

7. Use a Fisher Z transformation to correct distortion in interrater reliability (when there are more than two raters).

Regression: Predicting Y from X

1. Since regression is related to Pearson correlations, the assumptions of the Pearson must be met.

2. The correlations must be accurate (corrected for attenuation).

3. Check that there is no multicolinearity.

4. A minimum of 30 to 35 Ss or observations per independent variable is required. As a general rule, regression should not be done with n sizes below 200.

Solutions when assumptions cannot be met.

1. If data are ordinal and a Spearman correlation was performed, talk with a statistical consultant to determine whether the data are appropriate for regression.

2. Correct for different test reliabilities (correction for attenuation).

3. Collapse or omit variables which overlap above .80. Or consult a statistician for assistance.

4. Don't perform regression with small n sizes. Collect additional data instead.

PCA, Factor Analysis, and Multidimensional Scaling

1. Since these procedures build on Pearson correlations or, in the case of MDS, on Spearman, the data must meet the assumptions associated with these correlations.

    a. For principal component and factor analysis, check all the assumptions of Pearson's correlation.

    b. For multidimensional scaling, check either the assumptions of Pearson or Spearman, depending on which is used as input to the MDS procedure.

2. Normal distribution is best assured by having approximately 35 Ss or observations per variable. These are not small n-size procedures.

3. Cutoff points and interpretation of factors or dimensions (or clusters) must be guided by substantive arguments as well as statistical evidence.

Solutions when assumptions cannot be met.

1. If data are nominal, use a categorical (loglinear) modeling procedure.

2. If the *n* is too small, add more data. If this is impossible, interpret the study as exploratory in nature and warn readers that even this exploration must be considered tentative.

3. When interpretation is difficult, discuss the issues with your advisor, statistical consultant, or a member of the testing or research special interest groups of TESOL.

Path Analysis

1. Path analysis has the same assumptions as regression. Review each of these carefully.

2. The variables are linear, additive, and causal (i.e., no curvilinear relations, variables are independent, and logic or previous research/theory argues that there is a causal direction to the relationship).

3. All relevant variables are included in the system.

4. There is a one-way causal flow in the path diagram that is being tested.

5. And, as with regression, the data are normally distributed and the variances are equal. Again this is not a small sample technique. To approximate normal distribution with equal variances, be sure the sample size is as large as possible.

6. Before causal claims can be made (beyond the sample), be certain that the data are randomly selected and are representative of the population, and that all threats to internal and external validity have been met.

Solutions if the assumptions cannot be met.

1. If the data are frequency distributions rather than interval data, use a loglinear path analysis.

2. If the data are recursive, consult a statistician for help.

3. If the sample size is insufficient and the analysis is performed as an exploratory test, do not make causal claims. Caution the reader that this is a pilot study and attempt to collect additional data.

4. If there are design faults that threaten external validity, caution the reader that causal links apply only to the data sample.

Categorical Modeling

1. The data are for nominal, categorical variables (with two or more levels).

2. The data are representative and randomly selected.

3. The particular procedure matches the design.

   a. Between-groups designs: loglinear or CATMOD

   b. Path analysis: loglinear

   c. Repeated-measures designs: CATMOD

4. When using loglinear to test effects, interpret interaction before main effects (as with ANOVA). When using the procedures to test competing models, interpret the differences in models based on both substantive and statistical arguments.

Solutions when the assumptions cannot be met.

1. If data are interval, use PCA, factor analysis, or multidimensional scaling.

2. When interpretation is difficult, consult your advisor, statistical consultant, or a member of the testing or research special interest groups of TESOL.

References

Bachman, L. 1990. *Fundamental Considerations in Language Testing.* Oxford: Oxford University Press.

Henning, G. 1987. *A Guide to Language Testing.* New York, NY: Newbury House.

Hudson, T. & Lynch, B. 1984. A criterion-referenced measurement approach to ESL achievement testing. *Language Testing, 1,* 2, 171-201.

Ilyin, D., Spurling, S., and Seymour, S. 1987. Do learner variables affect cloze correlations? *SYSTEM, 15,* 2, 149-160.

Plann S. 1979. Morphological problems in the acquisition of Spanish in an immersion classroom. In R. Andersen (Ed.)., *The Acquisition of Spanish and English as First and Second Languages.* Washington, DC: TESOL, 119-132.

Popham, W. J. 1981. *Modern Educational Measurement.* Englewood Cliffs, NJ: Prentice-Hall.

Riggenbach, H. 1989. Towards an understanding of fluency: descriptive "profiles" of 6 nonnative speakers in dialogue and monologue speech. Unpublished Ph.D. dissertation, Applied Linguistics, UCLA.

Siegel, S. 1956. *Nonparametric Statistics for the Behavioral Sciences.* New York, NY: McGraw-Hill.

Thorndike, R. L. 1971. *Educational Measurement.* Washington, DC: American Council on Education.

Yopp, H. 1988. The validity and reliability of phonemic awareness tests. *Reading Research Quarterly, 23,* 2, 159-177.

Conclusion

Applied linguistics, at our university, is part of the division of humanities. Humanities, by its nature, includes all the fields that help to define what it means to be human. For most people, music, art, and dance are important, but it is language and language use that is central to that definition. Whether the language is that of child or of poet, it helps to define what we are.

Within humanities there are many fields, and each looks at language in a different way. Linguists see their research agenda, in part, as describing languages in a way that will reveal something of the language faculty of humankind. The sociologist looks at how society uses language to carry out oral and written communication and how that communication is shaped by social groups. Language use is also a concern of anthropologists who document how groups and individuals within groups use language to carry out their roles and organize their worlds. Developmental and cognitive psychologists have as one of their central concerns the connections between language and cognitive and social development. For many psychologists, the gift of literacy is as puzzling as language acquisition itself. The cognitive processes underlying reading and composing come to define humanness and creativity in parallel to that of the spoken language. The psychologist, too, is intrigued by the way we "turn words"--for example, the use of everyday metaphor--to form and transform our realities.

For a very large portion of the world, bilingualism and even multilingualism is the expected state of affairs. If language--and the arts--together with cognitive and social knowledge are defining qualities of humans, then these qualities expand in all directions as new languages, new social knowledge, and new ways of organizing cognitive concepts are added.

Our research agenda in applied linguistics overlaps with linguistics in that we too are interested in descriptions of language that brighten our understanding of language acquisition. We share the interest of sociologists and anthropologists in understanding the organization of talk and written communication in social groups. Those of us working on child bilingualism and second language acquisition share the same interests as those of developmental and cognitive psychologists. We want to understand not only the patterns of early second language development but also the creative use of language by bilingual and multilingual writers. Here our interests merge with those of literature.

Since the interests of all these fields overlap, what is it that makes ours different? Certainly the major difference must be our interest in teaching languages. As we learn about language acquisition outside the classroom, we wonder about language acquisition within the classroom. How do they differ? What can we do to promote the process? As we learn about language use within social groups (whether these groups are in academic disciplines, in immigrant neighborhoods, in the factory or workplace), we wonder how we can transform the classroom to teach communicative competence and appropriate register variation. When we compare the rhetorical organization of genres across languages, we think about the comparison in terms of better ways to teach composition and reading in our classes. We can begin to understand the learning preferences of our students if, with the anthropologist and sociologist, we investigate how language is used to organize the world of the classroom. However we define applied linguistics, one part of our research agenda must be the question of how best to help learners acquire the social-cultural knowledge of a new ethnic group and the language that puts that knowledge to use.

We have said that questions are "interesting" in our field to the extent that they inform theory (e.g., theory of acquisition, theory of reading, theory of language use) or practice (e.g., language teaching, language planning and policy, materials development, language testing, and so forth).

The problem is that it would be foolish to think that we can address theory without practice or practice without theory. One affects the other. We have, indeed, urged you to simplify your research efforts. If we think of the complexity of such questions as, What is it that makes us human? you can understand why many scholars want to look at language as separate from social knowledge, separate from other types of cognitive knowledge, separate from language use, separate from language instruction, and separate from the issues of bilingualism or multilingualism. You can understand why many educators want to look at bilingualism or multilingualism as only a cognitive issue or only a social issue. It's easy to understand why we, as teachers, want to see the question in terms of better teaching materials, new ways of organizing tasks, and ways of finding activities that focus on "just" language or "just" cognitive problems or "just" social organization. We all know this can't be done, but we struggle to do it because the task is so overwhelming otherwise.

On the other hand, life, for most people, is an attempt to answer the most complex question of all, what it means to be human. It is human nature to be curious about ourselves. So, since we are constantly asking these questions anyway, we are fortunate to be applied linguists. We get paid for looking for our own answers! The search for answers on the personal level, however, is usually quite different from that at the professional level. One difference is that as professionals we accept a framework for the search. There are, of course, many different frameworks to choose from within our field. Whichever we select, it is the framework which gives us confidence in sharing the answers we find.

We have said that research is the organized, systematic search for answers to the questions we ask. Because it is systematic, we have greater confidence in our findings. When we have thought about all the possible threats to internal and external validity and adjusted our search to deal with as many of these as possible, we have greater confidence in our findings. Statistical procedures are useful tools to increase that confidence. If we use them appropriately, we can feel confident that our descriptions and results are correct. We know when we can and cannot generalize our answers beyond the people, the place, and the time frame in which we searched for answers.

In our personal lives we each probably have a Grandmother Borgese--that mythical someone who continually says "That I knew already," "I don't believe it," and "Who cares anyway?" as we struggle with questions which are important to us. By organizing our search, we will be better equipped to answer back.

A year after visiting the school where we hoped to involve teachers in research, we received a group of papers from some of the students at the school. Not only did these teachers have questions, but they had stimulated the curiosity of their students as well. For some of these students, problem solving became a solitary research effort:

> *I thought about it last night in my dream I desided what to do. I ask 10 4th grades in Mrs. A class and I wright it down. I ask 10 people at my house and I wright it down. I ask 9 teashers and 1 lady in the offis (= the principal). I writ it and I count it and I can tell the answer. I will draw a piechart for the answer.*

For others it was a group effort:

> *We worked hard for our book rerort (= book report). Their was too many circles. What we are going to do. First we are going to Jose is going to count the red words. Then we are going to Cindy write the red words. Nix we are going to we study red words in spelling. Then we are going to Carlos read the words. Then we are going to see the words. We put stickers for good. Then we are going to count the words and see. Then we are going to write the book rerort for you.*

Systematicity in answering questions is alive and well in the world! At times, we may feel that the questions (how to get rid of "red words") are trivial in view of our larger questions. But each fits a place in our lives, in our theories, and in our understanding at a particular time.

At this particular time, we expect that you are better prepared to evaluate the evidence presented in applied linguistics research. We also believe that you are better able to undertake research yourself. We hope that you now keep a research journal, and that you have refined your broad research interests into feasible questions. You should be able to design a project with minimal threats to internal--and possibly even external--validity, a design that allows you to search for answers in appropriate ways. Finally, we trust that you can gather reliable data, analyze them appropriately and interpret the findings wisely. If you can do all these things, you have more than met the objectives of this course. At the next TESOL, AILA, AAAL, or SLRF conference, you should feel confident in saying, "I have an interesting question, I know one way to answer it, and I am willing to share that answer with you." The researcher who can say this need never again worry about Grandmother Borgese.

Appendices

Appendix A

Pretest

This pretest is a diagnostic to help you discover which sections of the Manual material you should review. The first section asks you to identify statistical procedures appropriate to a given research question. The second section is a "vocabulary test" meant to check your familiarity with basic terms used in data-based research.

Name the statistical procedure(s) needed to analyze the data described in each of the following items.

1. You borrowed data from 30 SLA researchers who had done longitudinal research on 1 *S* each. You want to know if there is any order in which these ESL learners acquire Wh-questions (*what, where, who, when, how, why*, etc.). (Chapter 7)

_____

2. As a second part of the study, you want to check to see whether the order you found (in item 1 above) compares to data in a cross-sectional study. You add a caboose (a short extra subtest) of Wh-questions to the placement exam at your school. (Chapter 15)

_____

3. Compositions of 50 entering ESL freshmen with SAT verbal scores between 250 and 300 were read and *S*s were referred either to Freshman ESL or regular English writing programs. Using strict scoring guidelines, three teachers rate each composition for a possible total of 25 points. You need to report the reliability of scoring. (Chapter 18)

_____

4. At the end of a quarter, the *S*s in item 3 above (30 were in ESL; 20 in writing programs) again wrote a final composition (assume topics were equivalent). These were scored the same way. You want to know if both/either program(s) produced results (and/or if one worked better). (Chapters 9 and 10)

_____

5. Assume that the difference between treatments in item 4 wasn't significant because there was so much variability within each group. Still, it appeared some *S*s did improve more than others irrespective of treatment. Therefore, you decided to forget about treatment altogether and instead determine whether L1 membership would account for this.

You group the ESL *S*s into five major L1 types. (Chapter 11)

6. You decide major might also be important so you divide them into science/humanities/undecided and add that to L1 (in item 5). (Chapter 13)

7. Grades (A to D) were given to all *S*s in advanced ESL classes. You wondered if attendance at tutorials would be reflected by higher grades for those who participated. You obtain a list of *S*s who attended the tutorials so that you have information in the form of "never--occasionally--regularly--very often" for each *S*. (Chapter 14)

8. You have data from 30 child ESL learners who mix/switch languages while speaking with a bilingual researcher. You have classified the switching as lexical/phrase level/sentence level switches. For each *S*, you convert the frequencies to proportions: % lexical, % phrase level, and % sentence level switches. You believe children primarily use lexical switches. (Chapter 12)

9. You believe the relationship between need achievement and foreign language proficiency should be obvious to all. It isn't, though, so you collect data to try to demonstrate this. You also collect data from each *S* using the Eysenck scale of personality factors. There are 32 personality traits that you hope to reduce to two factors--introvert/extrovert and stable/unstable. You also have data for each *S* on need achievement, and field independence. You want to know how these variables relate to language proficiency and which (or what combination) best predicts the "good language learner." The data are from 450 ESL *S*s entering your university. (Chapter 16/17)

10. In preparing a "culture course" for a program in China, you ask Americans in the United States and Chinese *S*s in China to complete a values survey. In one part of the survey *S*s rank-order the importance of 20 values statements. You want to know whether there is agreement within each group on the importance of shared values and whether the importance rating for each value is similar for the two groups. (Chapter 15)

Following are a list of statistical concepts. Place a check mark beside those you do not know.

Chapter 1
        Null hypothesis
        Alternative hypothesis
        Internal validity
        External validity
        Interaction
        Operational definition

Random sampling

Appendix B

Answer Key to Exercises

Chapter 1

1.5.1

H_o : There is no relation between language proficiency and spelling scores.

Interpretation: The spelling scores will not vary in relation to the language proficiency of the Ss.

Alternative hypothesis: There is a relation between language proficiency and spelling scores.

Interpretation: The spelling scores will vary in relation to the language proficiency of the Ss.

Directional, positive hypothesis: There is a positive relation between language proficiency and spelling scores.

Directional, negative hypothesis: There is a negative relation between language proficiency and spelling scores.

Interpretation: Positive--Students at the higher levels of language proficiency will obtain higher spelling scores; students at lower proficiency levels will obtain lower spelling scores. Negative--Students with lower levels of language proficiency will score higher on the spelling test while those with higher levels of language proficiency will score lower.

1.6.1

H_o for sex: There is no *effect* of sex on spelling scores. (If this hypothesis were rejected, males and females would show different spelling scores.)

H_o for sex and L1: There is no interaction of sex and first language membership on spelling scores. (If this hypothesis were rejected, there might be a pattern where for females the scores wouldn't change across the L1 groups while for men they would. That is, sex and L1 would interact--an interaction one would not hope to get.)

H_o for sex and language proficiency: There is no interaction of sex and language proficiency on spelling scores. (If this hypothesis were rejected, there might be a pattern where for females the scores wouldn't change across the proficiency levels while for men they would. This is another interaction one would not hope to get.)

H_o for sex, L1, and language proficiency: There is no interaction of sex, language background, and language proficiency on spelling scores. The researcher hopes this interaction will not be significant. If the null hypothesis is rejected, it might mean, for example, that females of certain first language groups who are at certain proficiency levels perform differently than others.

Chapter 2

Meas· type variable
who hit part of a.

2.5.2
Nominal variable, level, ordinal, interval

2.6.1
a. Variables: 1. Amount of information translated in information units. Measurement: frequency; or interval scores if points are set ahead of time for each piece of information so that a *S* would receive a total score based on number of correct points supplied. 2. Condition: ±pause (2 levels). Measurement: nominal.
b. Variables: 1. Technical vocabulary problems. Measurement: interval data (converted from frequencies to percentages which may be interval in nature). Change: yes, the data would be measured as frequencies. 2. Text field (3 levels). Measurement: 3-level nominal category.
c. Variables: 1. Ratings. Measurement: ratings are measured as ordinal scales. 2. Status (2 levels--MA/Ph.D.). Measurement: nominal (1 or 2).
d. Variables: 1. Cloze test score. Measurement: interval scores. 2. Type of cohesive tie (4 levels). Measurement: nominal variable with 4 categories. 3. L1 membership. Measurement: nominal with 7 categories.
e. Variables: 1. Number of misunderstandings. Measurement: frequencies. 2. Status (2 levels--NS and NNS) (The description is not very clear. It's possible that the study may have looked at dyads so that instead of student status you might have dyad type--NS/NS, NNS/NNS, NS/NNS as the status variable.) Measurement: nominal.
f. Variables: as above plus problem type (2 levels--easy/difficult), nominal with two category levels.

2.9.1
a. Dependent: frequency of 5 types of uncertainty expressions. Independent: status (teacher/student). Control: all *S*s are university persons. Possible other intervening variables not measured: sex of teacher/student, age of teacher/student, field of study/expertise of teacher/student. (This assumes that each of the six types of uncertainty expressions is a separate dependent variable. If comparisons are to be made among these six types, then the dependent variable would be frequency of uncertainty expressions and another independent variable would be type of uncertainty expression with 6 levels.)
b. Dependent: number of information units recalled *or* information score (if points assigned and a total score computed). Independent: condition (±pause). Control: passage. Possible intervening variables: length of pause, proficiency of translators in each language, age, etc.
c. Dependent: % technical words in problem list. Independent: text field. Control: all university persons; all Chinese L1. Other possible intervening variables that were not measured: English proficiency level of *S*s, years studying major.
d. Dependent: ratings. Independent: student status. Control: all university persons; all in same major area of study. Other possible intervening variables that were not measured: sex, age, professional background of *S*s.
e. Dependent: score on cloze passage. Independent: cohesive tie type. Independent (or moderator): L1 membership. Other intervening variables: ESL proficiency level, sex, age, years of study, etc.

f. Dependent: number of misunderstandings. Independent: status (NS or NNS). Intervening: proficiency level of Ss, matched sex or cross-sex dyads, years in the United States for NNSs, etc.

Chapter 3

3.1.1

a. Between-groups. The comparison will be drawn between the responses of faculty who have had such students and faculty who have not. These are two different groups of faculty.

b. Between-groups *and* repeated-measures. Between-groups since there are comparisons to be drawn across four different groups of students. Repeated-measures since the ratings given by each S to the first episode will be compared with the same S's ratings of the second, and so forth across the five episodes.

c. Between-groups. The comparison of position of the purpose clauses will be between oral and written corpora. The data come from two different sources.

d. Repeated-measures. Each S's scores on pronunciation, conversation, and oral presentation measures are compared with his or her own scores at two-week intervals. Also repeated-measures: A course report with average scores at each point would be reported.

e. Repeated-measures *and* between-groups. Each S's score in the formal context is compared with the same S's score in the informal context. Then, the scores of the nonnative speakers are compared with those of the native speakers--scores of two different groups are compared.

3.2.1a.

Faculty

	+ ESL Ss	No ESL Ss
Yes		
No		

Credit

3.2.1b.

L1 Background

	NS	Canad.	Ind.	Vietn.
1				
2				
3				
4				
5				

Episode Ratings

L1 Background

	NS	Canad.	Ind.	Vietn.
Total Rating				

3.2.1c.   Purpose Clauses

	Oral	Written
Precede		
Follow		

3.2.1d.

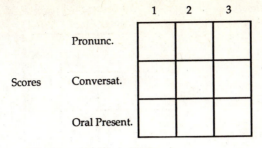

3.2.1e.

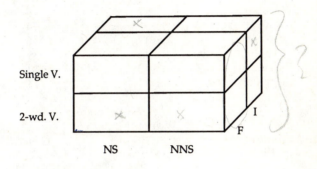

Chapter 5

5.2.1

Connector	f	cum F
to	89	490
and	72	401
prep	52	329
because	50	277
when	50	227
that	42	177
if	28	135
but	15	107
where	13	92
okay	12	79
or	12	67
like	11	55
how	11	44
what	10	33

Connector	f	cum F
who	9	23
well	5	14
after	4	9
so	3	5
as	1	2
why	1	1

5.3.1

Genre	f	cum F
account	476	1153
event cast	348	677
operation	121	329
label quest	112	208
recount	22	96
student quest	18	74
exposition	17	56
hypothesis	16	39
argument	12	23
meaning quest	11	11

5.4.1

	Written Mode	
Clause	%	Cum %
S.Finite	54.8%	100%
Complex	32.2%	45.2%
S.Nonfin	7.0%	13.0%
Coord.	3.4%	6.0%
Frag	1.5%	2.6%
Comp/Coord	0.8%	1.1%
NMSub	0.3%	0.3%

5.7.1

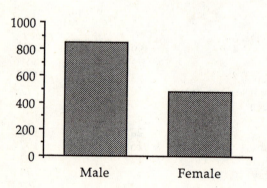

5.7.2

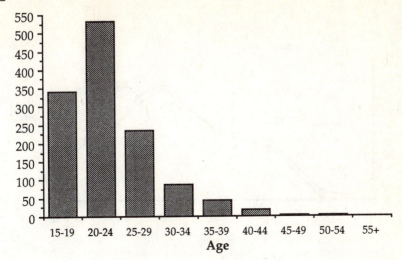

5.8.1

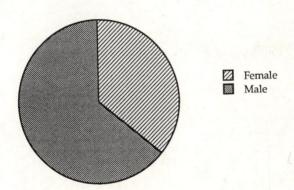

Female
Male

5.9.1

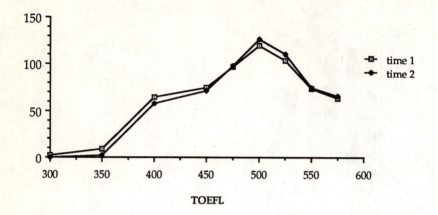

Chapter 6

6.1.3 Mode = 160, Median = 160, Mean = 179.3

6.2.1

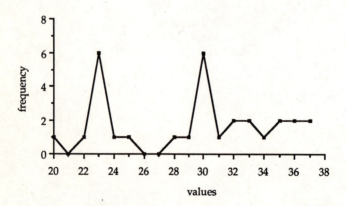

6.4.1

Mid-term Exam

Scores	$(X - \overline{X})$	x^2
16	0.6	.36
13	−2.4	5.76
13	−2.4	5.76
19	3.6	12.96
18	2.6	6.76
15	−0.4	.16
20	4.6	21.16
11	−4.4	19.36
14	−1.4	1.96
15	−0.4	.16

6.4.3

$$\frac{\sum x^2}{N - 1} = \frac{74.4}{9} = 8.27$$

6.5.2

$$s = \sqrt{8.27}$$

$$s = 2.87$$

$$\text{raw score formula } s = \sqrt{\frac{2446 - (23716 \div 10)}{9}}$$

$$s = \sqrt{8.27}$$

$$s = 2.87$$

Chapter 7

7.1.1
a. Sec 1: 54 = 62nd percentile, Sec 2: 62 = 90th percentile, Sec 3: 42 = 10th percentile.
b. 520
c. .02 × 759,768 = 15,195
d. .41 × 759,768 = 311,505
   .59 × 759,768 = 448,263

7.2.1
Score of 20 = 20th percentile

7.2.2
Score of 20 = within the 1st quartile
Score of 20 = at the 2nd decile

7.4.1

Raw Score	z
38	0
39	.17
30	−1.33
50	2.00
25	−2.17

Raw Score	T
38	50
39	51.7
30	36.7
50	70
25	28.3

7.6.1

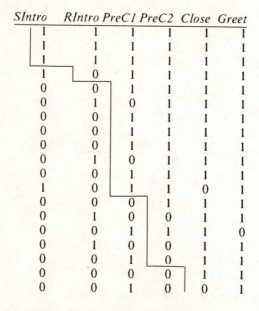

SIntro	RIntro	PreC1	PreC2	Close	Greet
1	1	1	1	1	1
1	1	1	1	1	1
1	1	1	1	1	1
1	0	1	1	1	1
0	0	1	1	1	1
0	1	0	1	1	1
0	0	1	1	1	1
0	0	1	1	1	1
0	0	1	1	1	1
0	1	0	1	1	1
0	0	1	1	1	1
1	0	1	1	0	1
0	0	0	1	1	1
0	1	0	0	1	1
0	0	1	1	1	0
0	1	0	0	1	1
0	0	1	0	1	1
0	0	0	0	1	1
0	0	1	0	0	1

Tot	14 5	12 7	6 13	5 14	2 17	1 18

2 correct = 2, 3 correct = 5, 4 correct = 8, 5 correct = 1, 6 correct = 3.

7.6.2

Errors are listed in the 'total' column above. Total errors = 18. *S*s got item right when we would predict they would get it wrong.

7.7.1

a.

$$C_{rep} = 1 - \frac{18}{(19)(6)}$$

$$C_{rep} = 1 - \frac{18}{114}$$

$$C_{rep} = 1 - .16 = .84$$

b.

$$MM_{rep} = \frac{88}{114} = .77$$

c.

$$improve = .84 - .77 = .07$$

d.

$$C_{scal} = \frac{.07}{1 - .77} = .30$$

Chapter 8

8.1.1
a. 50%, 16%, 16% (rounded from 15.87)
b. 2% (rounded from 2.28)

8.2.1
.13, .02 (rounded)

8.2.2
.10, .21, .001 (rounded)

8.2.3
.80, .98, .93 (rounded)

8.2.4
0, 1.88, 1.96

8.5.3
a.
Measurement: frequencies; Type of comparison: repeated-measures; Representativeness of sample: no information on how 25 Ss were selected; Normal distribution: questionable, so check distribution; Wish to generalize: can't; Independence of measures: no, repeated-measures; Choice: nonparametric. Rationale: data are frequencies (not interval data), normal distribution is also questionable.
b.
Measurement: ordinal; Type of comparison: between-groups; Representativeness of sample: intact class is not randomly selected and it is unknown if the Ss in the class were randomly assigned to the two treatments. Normal distribution: very questionable with small n size so check. Wish to generalize: can't. Independence

of measures: ratings may not be entirely independent, but groups are independent, we hope. Choice: nonparametric. Rationale: data are rank-ordered rather than interval measures. Normal distribution is questionable.

c.
Measurement: scores. Type of comparison: between-groups. Representativeness of sample: samples include all members of the population. Normal distribution expected: yes, given the n size. Wish to generalize: perhaps to similar new classes at same site with same materials, etc. Independence of measures: yes, if scores for each area are independently given. Choice: either parametric or nonparametric. Rationale for parametric choice: a normal distribution will obtain from the large n size; while the scores are derived from scale ratings, the ratings show a good distribution and are highly reliable; we believe the data are continuous. Since the mean and s are appropriate measures of central tendency and dispersion and we don't want to lose any of the information in the data, we want to select a parametric test. Rationale for nonparametric choice: the ratings are not equal-interval and the data are not normally distributed. Therefore, the mean and s are not appropriate measures. The data have continuity to the extent of ranks. Therefore, we will select a nonparametric test.

d.
Measurement: rank-order scales. Type of comparison: repeated-measures. Representativeness of sample: intact class so not representative. Normal distribution: questionable given small n size in a single class. Wish to generalize: can't. Independence of measures: no, since repeated-measures design. Choice: nonparametric. Rationale: rank-order scale data, small n size and nonrepresentative sample.

e.
Measurement: scores. Type of comparison: between matched pairs. Representativeness of sample: questionable since pairs had to be matched. Normal distribution: questionable so check. Wish to generalize: perhaps to the current population since pairs were chosen to represent the range of scores, but risky to generalize. Independence of measures: yes. Choice: both parametric and nonparametric procedures were run. They gave the same results and the nonparametric procedures were used in the final report.

Chapter 9

9.1.1
14 df = 1.76
22 df = 2.51
55 df = 1.67
10 df = 2.23
27 df = 2.77

9.1.3

$$t_{obs} = \frac{80 - 85}{5 \div \sqrt{14}}$$

$$t_{obs} = -3.73$$

$$t_{crit} = 2.16, df = 13, \text{ reject } H_o$$

9.2.1

$$s_{(\bar{x}_e - \bar{x}_c)} = \sqrt{\frac{8.4^2}{20} + \frac{7.7^2}{19}}$$

$$(\bar{x}_e - \bar{x}_c) = 2.58$$

$$t_{obs} = \frac{63.4 - 66.9}{2.58}$$

$$t_{obs} = -1.36$$

$$t_{crit} = 2.03, df = \cancel{37} \; 36, \text{ cannot reject } H_o$$

Conclusion: there is no difference in the total test scores for the two groups.

9.3.1 (German vocabulary example)

$$\eta^2 = \frac{3.0^2}{3.0^2 + 35}$$

$$\eta^2 = .20$$

In these data, 20% of the variability in vocabulary test scores can be accounted for by group.

9.3.2 (Keillor problem)

$$\eta^2 = \frac{3.73^2}{3.73^2 + 13}$$

$$\eta^2 = .52$$

In this sample, 20% of the variability in vocabulary test scores can be accounted for by group.

9.4.3

Median = 12. Low Group: above 2, not above 9 (n = 11). High Group: above 5, not above 7 (n = 12). Total above = 7, Total not above = 16. N = 23.

$$\hat{p} = (2 + 5) \div 23 = .304$$

$$T = \frac{(2 \div 11) - (5 \div 12)}{\sqrt{.304(1 - .304)(1 \div 11 + 1 \div 12)}}$$

$$T = 1.22$$

$z_{crit}, \alpha = .05 = 1.96$. We cannot reject H_o; there is no meaningful difference in the ratings of the two groups of Ss.

9.5.1

Score	Rank
12	1
13	2.5
13	2.5
14	4
15	5
16	6
17	7.5
17	7.5
18	9.5
18	9.5
19	11
20	12

$N = 12$ Top Rank $= 12$

9.5.2

Gp 2	Rank	Gp 1	Rank
18	9.0	22	3.0
13	14.5	20	6.5
16	10.5	21	4.5
15	12.0	19	8.0
14	13.0	16	10.5
21	4.5	24	1.0
20	6.5	23	2.0
		13	14.5

$T_2 = 70$ $T_1 = 50$
$n_2 = 7$ $n_1 = 8$

$$z = \frac{2(50) - 8(15 + 1)}{\sqrt{\dfrac{8 \times 7 \times (15 + 1)}{3}}}$$

$$z = 1.62$$

We cannot reject H_o. There is no significant difference in cloze test scores for the two language groups.

9.6.1 (composition example)

$$\eta^2 = \frac{2.7^2}{20} = .38$$

In this sample, 38% of the variability in composition ratings can be accounted for by language group.

9.6.2 (listening lab example)

$$\eta^2 = \frac{2.80^2}{60}$$

$$\eta^2 = .13$$

In this sample, 13% of the variability in ratings can be accounted for by group.

Chapter 10

10.1.2

$$s_D = \sqrt{\frac{84 - (1 \div 10)256}{10 - 1}}$$

$$s_D = 2.55$$

$$s_{\overline{D}} = \frac{2.55}{\sqrt{10}}$$

$$s_{\overline{D}} = .806$$

$$t = \frac{5.7 - 4.1}{.806}$$

$$t = 1.99$$

$$t_{crit} = 2.26, df = 9$$

No, we cannot reject H_o because t_{crit} is greater than t_{obs}. We have to conclude that the Ss who used the special materials did not make significantly greater gains than those who used the traditional materials. The results cannot be generalized because Ss were not randomly selected.

10.2.1 (Guadalajara problem)

$$\eta^2 = \frac{2.99^2}{2.99^2 + 9} = .50$$

In this sample, 50% of the variability in reading test scores can be accounted for by group.

10.3.1 $N = 36$ $R_{crit} = 11.$ $R_{obs} = 13.$
Interpretation: We cannot reject H_o; Ss did not make significant gains in listening scores.

10.4.2
T = 17, n = 14

$$z = \frac{17 - \dfrac{14(14 + 1)}{4}}{\sqrt{\dfrac{14(14 + 1)(2 \times 14 + 1)}{24}}}$$

$$z = 2.23$$

$z_{crit} = 1.96, \alpha = .05$. Reject H_o.

10.4.3 (reduced forms practice)

$$\eta^2 = \frac{2.23^2}{13} = .38$$

In this sample, 38% of the variability in rate can be accounted for by condition.

Chapter 11

11.1.1
Repeated-measures

11.1.2
Between-groups

11.1.3
Mixed

11.3.3

$$SST = 386.17$$
$$SSB = 168.27$$
$$SSW = 217.9$$
$$MSB = 84.13$$
$$MSW = 8.07$$
$$F = 10.42$$
$$df_B = 2$$
$$df_W = 27$$
$$F_{crit} = 3.35$$

Reject the null hypothesis and conclude there is a significant difference in final composition scores for subjects taught under three different methods.

11.4.1 (methodology example)

$$\omega^2 = \frac{1056 - 4(95)}{7706 + 95}$$

$$\omega^2 = .09$$

In this sample, 9% of the variability in exam scores can be accounted for by method.

11.4.2 (composition problem)

$$\omega^2 = \frac{168.27 - 2(8.07)}{386.17 + 8.07}$$

$$\omega^2 \doteq .39$$

In this sample, 39% of the variability in composition scores can be accounted for by method.

11.6.2
Step 1: .011, Step 2: 9354.22, Step 3: 102.9, Step 4: 99, H $= 3.90$.

$df = 3$, $H_{crit} = 7.81$. Cannot reject H_o; conclude that students at different levels do not get different oral communication scores.

11.8.1
Level 1 vs. Level 2

$$z = \frac{2(77) - 10(21)}{\sqrt{\dfrac{10 \times 10 \times 21}{3}}}$$

$$z = -2.12$$

$d - 1 = 1$, $z_{crit} = 2.24$. Cannot reject H_o; no statistical difference between level 1 and level 2.

11.8.2
Level 2 vs. Level 3: $Z = 1.44$, $d - 1 = 1$, $Z_{crit} = 2.24$, no statistical difference.

Level 2 vs. Level 4: $Z = 1.96$, $d - 1 = 2$, $Z_{crit} = 2.50$, no statistical difference.

Level 3 vs. Level 4: $Z = 1.13$, $d - 1 = 1$, $Z_{crit} = 2.24$, no statistical difference.

12.1.5

One-way ANOVA with Repeated-Measures

Source	df	SS	MS	F
Types (A)	4	1615.11	403.78	20.35
Subjects (S)	8	2970.00		
Types X Ss (A X S)	32	634.89	19.84	
Total	44	5220.00		

F_{crit} for (4,32 df), $\alpha = .05 = 2.67$. Reject H_o and conclude that type of lesson had a significant effect on reading test scores.

12.2.1

$$\eta^2 = \frac{274.05}{351.64} = .78$$

In this sample, 78% of the variability in definition scores can be accounted for by idiom type.

12.3.2

$$32.5^2 + 29.5^2 + 46^2 = 1056.25 + 870.25 + 2116 = 4042.5$$

$$\frac{12}{3 \times 18 \times 4} = \frac{12}{216} = .05555$$

$$4042.5 \times .055 = 224.58$$

$$3(18)(4) = 216$$

$$224.58 - 216 = 8.58$$

Interpretation: error scores vary according to the feedback method.

12.3.3 (computer practice)

$$\eta^2 = \frac{8.58}{53} = .16$$

In this sample, 16% of the variability in error scores can be accounted for by feedback type.

12.4.1
1.

$$\chi_R^2 = 8.58$$

2.

$$\chi^2_{Rcrit} = 5.99$$

3.

$$\frac{a(a+1)}{6n} = \frac{3(3+1)}{6 \times 18} = \frac{12}{108} = .111$$

4.

$$\sqrt{5.99 \times .111} = .82$$

5.

$$\overline{X}_{T1} = 1.80$$

$$\overline{X}_{T2} = 1.64$$

$$\overline{X}_{T3} = 2.56$$

6.

		T2 1.64	T1 1.80	T3 2.56
T2	1.64	---	.16	0.92*
T1	1.80		---	0.76
T3	2.56			---

difference is between T2 and T3 (.94 > .82)

Chapter 13

13.1.1

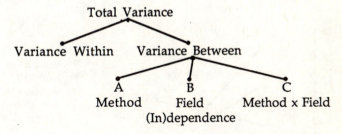

13.1.2.

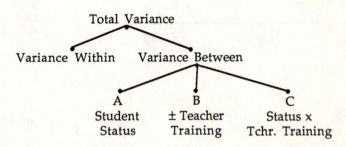

13.2.1

a.

SST = 915.4
SSB = 514.2
SSW = 401.2
SSA = 224.27
SSB = 13.3
SSAB = 276.63
$df_A = 1$
$df_B = 2$
$df_{AB} = 2$
$F_A = 30.19$
$F_B = .90$
$F_{AB} = 18.62$

b.
Reject H_o for A (class) and AB (interaction).

c.

$$\omega_A^2 = \frac{224.27 - 7.43}{915.4 + 7.43} = .235$$

$$\omega_{AB}^2 = \frac{276.63 - (2)7.43}{915.4 + 7.43} = .28$$

d.

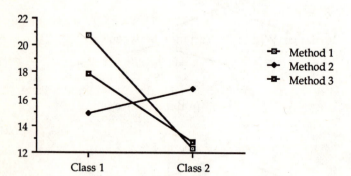

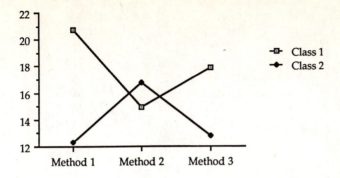

e. There was a significant interaction between *method* and *class*. Ss in *class 1* got higher composition scores than Ss in *class 2* EXCEPT in *method 2* where *class 2* Ss performed better.

Chapter 14

14.2.1
H_o : There is no relationship between problem solving type and grade on tasks.

Row	Col	Obs	E	O−E	$(O-E)^2$	$(O-E)^2 \div E$
1	1	11	10.38	.62	.384	.037
1	2	9	10.50	−1.50	2.25	.214
1	3	10	9.12	.88	.774	.085
2	1	12	11.77	.23	.053	.004
2	2	11	11.90	−.90	.810	.068
2	3	11	10.33	.67	.449	.043
3	1	35	34.27	.73	.533	.016
3	2	34	34.65	−.65	.422	.012
3	3	30	30.08	−.08	.006	.001
4	1	32	33.58	−1.58	2.50	.074
4	2	37	33.95	3.05	9.30	.274
4	3	28	29.47	−1.47	2.16	.073

$$\chi^2 = .901$$

The critical value of χ^2 for 6 df, $p = .05$, is 12.59. Therefore, the H_o cannot be rejected. Conclude that there is no relation between problem solving type and grade on tasks. Findings cannot be generalized beyond this sample of Ss.

14.3.1

$$\chi^2 = \frac{100[|19 \times 17 - 31 \times 33| - 100 \div 2]^2}{52 \times 48 \times 50 \times 50}$$

$$\chi^2 = \frac{100[|323 - 1023| - 50]^2}{6240000}$$

$$\chi^2 = 6.77$$

$\chi^2_{crit} = 3.84$, for 1 df and $\alpha = .05$. Reject the H_o and conclude that there is a relationship between dropout rates and work hours. You can generalize to Ss in similar schools with similar characteristics and similar work habits.

14.4.2

a.

Vote	S-W	S-E	N-E	N-W	Cent
pro					
against					
undecided					

US Geographic Areas

b.

Major	Korean	Farsi	Span	Japanese
Humanities				
SocSci				
BioSci				
PhysSci				
Engr				

c.

	Age of Arrival			
Neg stage	< 10	10-19	20-29	> 30
no + V				
unan. do				
aux neg				
analz do				

d.

Corrections/1000wrds	F.Indep.	F.Dep.
< 5		
5-10		
> 10		

14.4.3

a. Yes, a Chi-square test is appropriate for the data. It is a 3 X 3 contingency table (3 language groups and 3 types of votes). Given that students of the entire community adult school system were surveyed, it seems likely that the expected cell frequency size would be adequate. The data are independent.

b. Yes, a Chi-square test is appropriate. It is a 3 X 2 contingency table and since the records include a total school district, it seems likely that the sample size is large enough to get the needed expected cell frequencies. The data are independent.

c. No, a Chi-square test is inappropriate for these data. The two samples come from the same children, so the data are not independent either within or between the cells. Collect oral language from one group and written from the other. Then, since the clauses don't form a logical set, decide which clauses you believe will differ across written and oral modes. Present a separate table for each clause. Since individual children might contribute more than others to the frequency counts in each cell, change the design so the data show how many Ss used low, middle, high numbers of each clause type in the two modes.

d. No, a Chi-square test is inappropriate for these data. The two samples were obtained from the same teacher, so the data are not independent (either within or between the cells). Obtain data from two different classes. Then count the number of clauses (a rough measure of participation) each S produced in a

50-minute class period. Use this to establish levels (low, middle, high or < 5, 5-10, etc.) and count the number of Ss who fall into these levels in each treatment.

14.5.1

$$\Phi = \sqrt{\frac{16.825^2}{916}}$$

$$\Phi = .14$$

14.5.2

$$\Phi = \sqrt{\frac{13.01^2}{260}}$$

$$\Phi = .22$$

$$Cramer's\ V = \sqrt{\frac{.224^2}{2}}$$

$$Cramer's\ V = .16$$

14.6.1

$$z = \frac{28 - 10}{\sqrt{38}} = \frac{18}{\sqrt{38}} = 2.92$$

Reject null hypothesis and conclude that vote on issue is related to the seminar presentation.

Chapter 15

15.2.2

$r = .89$ (z score formula)

15.2.3
Pearson correlation coefficients: Relevance and Informativeness = $-.46$, Relevance and Clarity = $-.49$, Relevance and Turn-taking = $.15$, Relevance and Turn-length = $.57$, Informativeness and Clarity = $.90$, Informativeness and Turn-taking = $.23$, Informativeness and Turn-Length = $-.44$, Clarity and Turn-taking = $.42$, Clarity and Turn-Length = $-.30$, Turn-taking and Turn-length = $.48$.

15.4.1
Written Error Detection

$$\frac{.75}{\sqrt{.8 \times .9}} = .88$$

Grammar

$$\frac{.70}{\sqrt{.8 \times .95}} = .80$$

The overlap of each of two types of grammar tests is high (77% for the global error detection test and 64% for the discrete point grammar test). If the intent behind the research question is to eliminate one or more tests, the decision would need to be made on the basis of practical substantive issues (e.g., difficulty of test construction, time needed for administration and correction, comprehensiveness of measures) in addition to statistical evidence.

15.6.2

$$r_{pbi} = \frac{80 - 70}{15}\sqrt{.6 \times .4}$$

$$r_{pbi} = .33$$

Yes, it is a good item since it falls in the .20 to .40 range.

15.7.1

$$\rho = .50$$

$Rho_{crit} = .591$; conclude that the two groups do not agree.

15.8.1

$$W = \frac{906660 - 816750}{222750}$$

$$W = .404$$

15.8.2

$$\chi^2 = 15(9)(.404)$$

$$\chi^2 = 54.54$$

$\chi^2_{crit} = 16.90$, 9 df; reject the H_o and conclude that there is a consensus regarding useful activities.

15.9.1

$$\Phi = \frac{(112 \times 68) - (82 \times 71)}{\sqrt{(82 + 112)(68 + 71)(82 + 68)(112 + 71)}} = .066$$

$$\chi^2 = 333(.066^2) = 1.45$$

$$\chi^2_{crit} = 3.84$$

There is no relation between time of entrance to program and continuation of Spanish in high school.

Chapter 16

16.1.2

$$\hat{Y} = 540 + 8(25 - 30)$$

$$\hat{Y} = 500$$

Difference in prediction = 40 points.

16.2.1

$$s_{xy} = 40\sqrt{1 - .8^2}$$

$$s_{xy} = 24.00$$

Interpret by making confidence intervals around predicted values.

Chapter 17

17.3.2

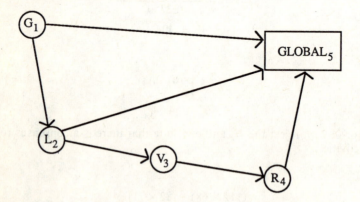

18.3.1

	1	2	3	4	5	6
1		.51	.65	.47	.83	.83
2			.42	.62	.81	.85
3				.63	.52	1.045
4					.59	.725
5						.775

Total = 10.275

$$\text{Average} = \frac{10.275}{15} = .685$$

$$r_{tt} = \frac{6(.685)}{1 + 5(.685)} = \frac{4.11}{4.425} = .93$$

Reconversion to Pearson correlation

$$r_{tt} = .73$$

Conclude the interrater reliability is marginal.

Appendix C
Statistical Tables

Table 1: Normal Distribution

Table of z Scores

(A) z	(B) area between mean and z	(C) area beyond z	(A) z	(B) area between mean and z	(C) area beyond z	(A) z	(B) area between mean and z	(C) area beyond z
0.00	.0000	.5000	0.55	.2088	.2912	1.10	.3643	.1357
0.01	.0040	.4960	0.56	.2123	.2877	1.11	.3665	.1335
0.02	.0080	.4920	0.57	.2157	.2843	1.12	.3686	.1314
0.03	.0120	.4880	0.58	.2190	.2810	1.13	.3708	.1292
0.04	.0160	.4840	0.59	.2224	.2776	1.14	.3729	.1271
0.05	.0199	.4801	0.60	.2257	.2743	1.15	.3749	.1251
0.06	.0239	.4761	0.61	.2291	.2709	1.16	.3770	.1230
0.07	.0279	.4721	0.62	.2324	.2676	1.17	.3790	.1210
0.08	.0319	.4681	0.63	.2357	.2643	1.18	.3810	.1190
0.09	.0359	.4641	0.64	.2389	.2611	1.19	.3830	.1170
0.10	.0398	.4602	0.65	.2422	.2578	1.20	.3849	.1151
0.11	.0438	.4562	0.66	.2454	.2546	1.21	.3869	.1131
0.12	.0478	.4522	0.67	.2486	.2514	1.22	.3888	.1112
0.13	.0517	.4483	0.68	.2517	.2483	1.23	.3907	.1093
0.14	.0557	.4443	0.69	.2549	.2451	1.24	.3925	.1075
0.15	.0596	.4404	0.70	.2580	.2420	1.25	.3944	.1056
0.16	.0636	.4364	0.71	.2611	.2389	1.26	.3962	.1038
0.17	.0675	.4325	0.72	.2642	.2358	1.27	.3980	.1020
0.18	.0714	.4286	0.73	.2673	.2327	1.28	.3997	.1003
0.19	.0753	.4247	0.74	.2704	.2296	1.29	.4015	.0985
0.20	.0793	.4207	0.75	.2734	.2266	1.30	.4032	.0968
0.21	.0832	.4168	0.76	.2764	.2236	1.31	.4049	.0951
0.22	.0871	.4129	0.77	.2794	.2206	1.32	.4066	.0934
0.23	.0910	.4090	0.78	.2823	.2177	1.33	.4082	.0918
0.24	.0948	.4052	0.79	.2852	.2148	1.34	.4099	.0901
0.25	.0987	.4013	0.80	.2881	.2119	1.35	.4115	.0885
0.26	.1026	.3974	0.81	.2910	.2090	1.36	.4131	.0869
0.27	.1064	.3936	0.82	.2939	.2061	1.37	.4147	.0853
0.28	.1103	.3897	0.83	.2967	.2033	1.38	.4162	.0838
0.29	.1141	.3859	0.84	.2995	.2005	1.39	.4177	.0823
0.30	.1179	.3821	0.85	.3023	.1977	1.40	.4192	.0808
0.31	.1217	.3783	0.86	.3051	.1949	1.41	.4207	.0793
0.32	.1255	.3745	0.87	.3078	.1922	1.42	.4222	.0778
0.33	.1293	.3707	0.88	.3106	.1894	1.43	.4236	.0764
0.34	.1331	.3669	0.89	.3133	.1867	1.44	.4251	.0749
0.35	.1368	.3632	0.90	.3159	.1841	1.45	.4265	.0735
0.36	.1406	.3594	0.91	.3186	.1814	1.46	.4279	.0721
0.37	.1443	.3557	0.92	.3212	.1788	1.47	.4292	.0708
0.38	.1480	.3520	0.93	.3238	.1762	1.48	.4306	.0694
0.39	.1517	.3483	0.94	.3264	.1736	1.49	.4319	.0681
0.40	.1554	.3446	0.95	.3289	.1711	1.50	.4332	.0668
0.41	.1591	.3409	0.96	.3315	.1685	1.51	.4345	.0655
0.42	.1628	.3372	0.97	.3340	.1660	1.52	.4357	.0643
0.43	.1664	.3336	0.98	.3365	.1635	1.53	.4370	.0630
0.44	.1700	.3300	0.99	.3389	.1611	1.54	.4382	.0618
0.45	.1736	.3264	1.00	.3413	.1587	1.55	.4394	.0606
0.46	.1772	.3228	1.01	.3438	.1562	1.56	.4406	.0594
0.47	.1808	.3192	1.02	.3461	.1539	1.57	.4418	.0582
0.48	.1844	.3156	1.03	.3485	.1515	1.58	.4429	.0571
0.49	.1879	.3121	1.04	.3508	.1492	1.59	.4441	.0559
0.50	.1915	.3085	1.05	.3531	.1469	1.60	.4452	.0548
0.51	.1950	.3050	1.06	.3554	.1446	1.61	.4463	.0537
0.52	.1985	.3015	1.07	.3577	.1423	1.62	.4474	.0526
0.53	.2019	.2981	1.08	.3599	.1401	1.63	.4484	.0516
0.54	.2054	.2946	1.09	.3621	.1379	1.64	.4495	.0505

(continued)

(A) z	(B) area between mean and z	(C) area beyond z	(A) z	(B) area between mean and z	(C) area beyond z	(A) z	(B) area between mean and z	(C) area beyond z
1.65	.4505	.0495	2.22	.4868	.0132	2.79	.4974	.0026
1.66	.4515	.0485	2.23	.4871	.0129	2.80	.4974	.0026
1.67	.4525	.0475	2.24	.4875	.0125	2.81	.4975	.0025
1.68	.4535	.0465	2.25	.4878	.0122	2.82	.4976	.0024
1.69	.4545	.0455	2.26	.4881	.0119	2.83	.4977	.0023
1.70	.4554	.0446	2.27	.4884	.0116	2.84	.4977	.0023
1.71	.4564	.0436	2.28	.4887	.0113	2.85	.4978	.0022
1.72	.4573	.0427	2.29	.4890	.0110	2.86	.4979	.0021
1.73	.4582	.0418	2.30	.4893	.0107	2.87	.4979	.0021
1.74	.4591	.0409	2.31	.4896	.0104	2.88	.4980	.0020
1.75	.4599	.0401	2.32	.4898	.0102	2.89	.4981	.0019
1.76	.4608	.0392	→2.33	.4901	.0099	2.90	.4981	.0019
1.77	.4616	.0384	2.34	.4904	.0096	2.91	.4982	.0018
1.78	.4625	.0375	2.35	.4906	.0094	2.92	.4982	.0018
1.79	.4633	.0367	2.36	.4909	.0091	2.93	.4983	.0017
1.80	.4641	.0359	2.37	.4911	.0089	2.94	.4984	.0016
1.81	.4649	.0351	2.38	.4913	.0087	2.95	.4984	.0016
1.82	.4656	.0344	2.39	.4916	.0084	2.96	.4985	.0015
1.83	.4664	.0336	2.40	.4918	.0082	2.97	.4985	.0015
1.84	.4671	.0329	2.41	.4920	.0080	2.98	.4986	.0014
1.85	.4678	.0322	2.42	.4922	.0078	2.99	.4986	.0014
1.86	.4686	.0314	2.43	.4925	.0075	3.00	.4987	.0013
1.87	.4693	.0307	2.44	.4927	.0073	3.01	.4987	.0013
1.88	.4699	.0301	2.45	.4929	.0071	3.02	.4987	.0013
1.89	.4706	.0294	2.46	.4931	.0069	3.03	.4988	.0012
1.90	.4713	.0287	2.47	.4932	.0068	3.04	.4988	.0012
1.91	.4719	.0281	2.48	.4934	.0066	3.05	.4989	.0011
1.92	.4726	.0274	2.49	.4936	.0064	3.06	.4989	.0011
1.93	.4732	.0268	2.50	.4938	.0062	3.07	.4989	.0011
1.94	.4738	.0262	2.51	.4940	.0060	3.08	.4990	.0010
1.95	.4744	.0256	2.52	.4941	.0059	3.09	.4990	.0010
→1.96	.4750	.0250	2.53	.4943	.0057	3.10	.4990	.0010
1.97	.4756	.0244	2.54	.4945	.0055	3.11	.4991	.0009
1.98	.4761	.0239	2.55	.4946	.0054	3.12	.4991	.0009
1.99	.4767	.0233	2.56	.4948	.0052	3.13	.4991	.0009
2.00	.4772	.0228	2.57	.4949	.0051	3.14	.4992	.0008
2.01	.4778	.0222	2.58	.4951	.0049	3.15	.4992	.0008
2.02	.4783	.0217	2.59	.4952	.0048	3.16	.4992	.0008
2.03	.4788	.0212	2.60	.4953	.0047	3.17	.4992	.0008
2.04	.4793	.0207	2.61	.4955	.0045	3.18	.4993	.0007
2.05	.4798	.0202	2.62	.4956	.0044	3.19	.4993	.0007
2.06	.4803	.0197	2.63	.4957	.0043	3.20	.4993	.0007
2.07	.4808	.0192	2.64	.4959	.0041	3.21	.4993	.0007
2.08	.4812	.0188	2.65	.4960	.0040	3.22	.4994	.0006
2.09	.4817	.0183	2.66	.4961	.0039	3.23	.4994	.0006
2.10	.4821	.0179	2.67	.4962	.0038	3.24	.4994	.0006
2.11	.4826	.0174	2.68	.4963	.0037	3.25	.4994	.0006
2.12	.4830	.0170	2.69	.4964	.0036	3.30	.4995	.0005
2.13	.4834	.0166	2.70	.4965	.0035	3.35	.4996	.0004
2.14	.4838	.0162	2.71	.4966	.0034	3.40	.4997	.0003
2.15	.4842	.0158	2.72	.4967	.0033	3.45	.4997	.0003
2.16	.4846	.0154	2.73	.4968	.0032	3.50	.4998	.0002
2.17	.4850	.0150	2.74	.4969	.0031	3.60	.4998	.0002
2.18	.4854	.0146	2.75	.4970	.0030	3.70	.4999	.0001
2.19	.4857	.0143	2.76	.4971	.0029	3.80	.4999	.0001
2.20	.4861	.0139	2.77	.4972	.0028	3.90	.49995	.00005
2.21	.4864	.0136	2.78	.4973	.0027	4.00	.49997	.00003

Find your obtained z score value in column (A). The probability of this particular z score value appears in column (C). Column C gives the probability of obtaining a z score this high *or* this low in the distribution. To find the proportion of the curve *below* the z score, add .50 to the figure in column (B). The critical z values to remember in hypothesis testing are: *z = 1.96 for p = .05 and z = 2.57 for p = .01* for two-tailed tests. The table is read in precisely the same way whether the obtained value of z is positive or negative.

Table 2: t-test

Critical Values for *t*

possibility → *p*	.10	.05	.02	.01	.001
df 1	6.314	12.706	31.821	63.657	636.619
2	2.920	4.303	6.965	9.925	31.598
3	2.353	3.182	4.541	5.841	12.941
4	2.132	2.776	3.747	4.604	8.610
5	2.015	2.571	3.365	4.032	6.859
6	1.943	2.447	3.143	3.707	5.959
7	1.895	2.365	2.998	3.499	5.405
8	1.860	2.306	2.896	3.355	5.041
9	1.833	2.262	2.821	3.250	4.781
10	1.812	2.228	2.764	3.169	4.587
11	1.796	2.201	2.718	3.106	4.437
12	1.782	2.179	2.681	3.055	4.318
13	1.771	2.160	2.650	3.012	4.221
14	1.761	2.145	2.624	2.977	4.140
15	1.753	2.131	2.602	2.947	4.073
16	1.746	2.120	2.583	2.921	4.015
17	1.740	2.110	2.567	2.898	3.965
18	1.734	2.101	2.552	2.878	3.922
19	1.729	2.093	2.539	2.861	3.883
20	1.725	2.086	2.528	2.845	3.850
21	1.721	2.080	2.518	2.831	3.819
22	1.717	2.074	2.508	2.819	3.792
23	1.714	2.069	2.500	2.807	3.767
24	1.711	2.064	2.492	2.797	3.745
25	1.708	2.060	2.485	2.787	3.725
26	1.706	2.056	2.479	2.779	3.707
27	1.703	2.052	2.473	2.771	3.690
28	1.701	2.048	2.467	2.763	3.674
29	1.699	2.045	2.462	2.756	3.659
30	1.697	2.042	2.457	2.750	3.646
40	1.684	2.021	2.423	2.704	3.551
60	1.671	2.000	2.390	2.660	3.460
120	1.658	1.980	2.358	2.617	3.373

possibility of error (handwritten annotation)

an incomplete table (handwritten annotation)

Find the row for your df in the first column. Find the column with the appropriate p level. The intersection of this row and column shows the value needed to reject the H_o. The observed level of t must be *equal to or greater than* this critical value. The critical values are the same for both positive and negative t values. Notice that not all df are given after 30. If the df you need is not in the table, use the row *before* as a conservative estimate of the critical value needed to reject the null hypothesis. Thus, if the df is 32, use the critical value for 30 df as a rough estimate.

Table 3: Sign Test

Critical Values of R for the Sign Test

p	.05	.01
N 1		
2		
3		
4		
5		
6	0	
7	0	
8	0	0
9	1	0
10	1	0
11	1	0
12	2	1
13	2	1
14	2	1
15	3	2
16	3	2
17	4	2
18	4	3
19	4	3
20	5	3
21	5	4
22	5	4
23	6	4
24	6	5
25	7	5
26	7	6
27	7	6
28	8	6
29	8	7
30	9	7
35	11	9
40	13	11
45	15	13
50	17	15

Find the appropriate row for the number of pairs in the first column. Find the column for the selected level of probability. Check the intersection to find the number of changes required to reject the H_o. The observed number of changes must be *less than* the critical number of changes.

Table 4: Wilcoxon Matched-Pairs Signed-Ranks Test

Critical Values of T for Wilcoxon Matched-Pairs Signed-Ranks

p	.05	.025	.01
N 6	0	--	--
7	2	0	--
8	4	2	0
9	6	3	2
10	8	5	3
11	11	7	5
12	14	10	7
13	17	13	10
14	21	16	13
15	25	20	16
16	30	24	20
17	35	28	23
18	40	33	28
19	46	38	32
20	52	43	38
21	59	49	43
22	66	56	49
23	73	62	55
24	81	69	61
25	89	77	68

Find the appropriate row and the column for the selected level of probability. Check the intersection for the sum of ranks required to reject the H_o. The observed sum of ranks must be *equal to or less than* the critical sum of ranks given in the intersection.

larger #s ———→ *smaller #s*

$$T_{obs} \leq T_{crit}, \text{ reject } H_o$$

Table 5: F distribution (ANOVA)

(handwritten: (K-1) between groups continues →)

Critical Values of *F*

(handwritten: df for groups)

(handwritten left margin: df for observations N-K; df for observations N-K)

df	1	2	3	4	5	6	7	8	9	10	
1	161	200	216	225	230	234	237	239	241	242	*p < .05*
	4052	4999	5403	5625	5764	5859	5928	5981	6022	6056	*p < .01*
2	18.51	19.00	19.16	19.25	19.30	19.33	19.36	19.37	19.38	19.39	
	98.49	99.01	99.17	99.25	99.30	99.33	99.34	99.36	99.38	99.40	
3	10.13	9.55	9.28	9.12	9.01	8.94	8.88	8.84	8.81	8.78	
	34.12	30.81	29.46	28.71	28.24	27.91	27.67	27.49	27.34	27.23	
4	7.71	6.94	6.59	6.39	6.26	6.16	6.09	6.04	6.00	5.96	
	21.20	18.00	16.69	15.98	15.52	15.21	14.98	14.80	14.66	14.54	
5	6.61	5.79	5.41	5.19	5.05	4.95	4.88	4.82	4.78	4.74	
	16.26	13.27	12.06	11.39	10.97	10.67	10.45	10.27	10.15	10.05	
6	5.99	5.14	4.76	4.53	4.39	4.28	4.21	4.15	4.10	4.06	
	13.74	10.92	9.78	9.15	8.75	8.47	8.26	8.10	7.98	7.87	
7	5.59	4.74	4.35	4.12	3.97	3.87	3.79	3.73	3.68	3.63	
	12.25	9.55	8.45	7.85	7.46	7.19	7.00	6.84	6.71	6.62	
8	5.32	4.46	4.07	3.84	3.69	3.58	3.50	3.44	3.39	3.34	
	11.26	8.65	7.59	7.01	6.63	6.37	6.19	6.03	5.91	5.82	
9	5.12	4.26	3.86	3.63	3.48	3.37	3.29	3.23	3.18	3.13	
	10.56	8.02	6.99	6.42	6.06	5.80	5.62	5.47	5.35	5.26	
10	4.96	4.10	3.71	3.48	3.33	3.22	3.14	3.07	3.02	2.97	
	10.04	7.56	6.55	5.99	5.64	5.39	5.21	5.06	4.95	4.85	
11	4.84	3.98	3.59	3.36	3.20	3.09	3.01	2.95	2.90	2.86	
	9.65	7.20	6.22	5.67	5.32	5.07	4.88	4.74	4.63	4.54	
12	4.75	3.88	3.49	3.26	3.11	3.00	2.92	2.85	2.80	2.76	
	9.33	6.93	5.95	5.41	5.06	4.82	4.65	4.50	4.39	4.30	
13	4.67	3.80	3.41	3.18	3.02	2.92	2.84	2.77	2.72	2.67	
	9.07	6.70	5.74	5.20	4.86	4.62	4.44	4.30	4.19	4.10	
14	4.60	3.74	3.34	3.11	2.96	2.85	2.77	2.70	2.65	2.60	
	8.86	6.51	5.56	5.03	4.69	4.46	4.28	4.14	4.03	3.94	
15	4.54	3.68	3.29	3.06	2.90	2.79	2.70	2.64	2.59	2.55	
	8.68	6.36	5.42	4.89	4.56	4.32	4.14	4.00	3.89	3.80	

Critical Values of F

df	1	2	3	4	5	6	7	8	9	10
16	4.49	3.63	3.24	3.01	2.85	2.74	2.66	2.59	2.54	2.49
	8.53	6.23	5.29	4.77	4.44	4.20	4.03	3.89	3.78	3.69
17	4.45	3.59	3.20	2.96	2.81	2.70	2.62	2.55	2.50	2.45
	8.40	6.11	5.18	4.67	4.34	4.10	3.93	3.79	3.68	3.59
18	4.41	3.55	3.16	2.93	2.77	2.66	2.58	2.51	2.46	2.41
	8.28	6.01	5.09	4.58	4.25	4.01	3.85	3.71	3.60	3.51
19	4.38	3.52	3.13	2.90	2.74	2.63	2.55	2.48	2.43	2.38
	8.18	5.93	5.01	4.50	4.17	3.94	3.77	3.63	3.52	3.43
20	4.35	3.49	3.10	2.87	2.71	2.60	2.52	2.45	2.40	2.35
	8.10	5.85	4.94	4.43	4.10	3.87	3.71	3.56	3.45	3.37
21	4.32	3.47	3.07	2.84	2.68	2.57	2.49	2.42	2.37	2.32
	8.02	5.78	4.87	4.37	4.04	3.81	3.65	3.51	3.40	3.31
22	4.30	3.44	3.05	2.82	2.66	2.55	2.47	2.40	2.35	2.30
	7.94	5.72	4.82	4.31	3.99	3.76	3.59	3.45	3.35	3.26
23	4.28	3.42	3.03	2.80	2.64	2.53	2.45	2.38	2.32	2.28
	7.88	5.66	4.76	4.26	3.94	3.71	3.54	3.41	3.30	3.21
24	4.26	3.40	3.01	2.78	2.62	2.51	2.43	2.36	2.30	2.26
	7.82	5.61	4.72	4.22	3.90	3.67	3.50	3.36	3.25	3.17
25	4.24	3.38	2.99	2.76	2.60	2.49	2.41	2.34	2.28	2.24
	7.77	5.57	4.68	4.18	3.86	3.63	3.46	3.32	3.21	3.13
26	4.22	3.37	2.89	2.74	2.59	2.47	2.39	2.32	2.27	2.22
	7.72	5.53	4.64	4.14	3.82	3.59	3.42	3.29	3.17	3.09
27	4.21	3.35	2.96	2.73	2.57	2.46	2.37	2.30	2.25	2.20
	7.68	5.49	4.60	4.11	3.79	3.56	3.39	3.26	3.14	3.06
28	4.20	3.34	2.95	2.71	2.56	2.44	2.36	2.29	2.24	2.19
	7.64	5.45	4.57	4.07	3.76	3.53	3.36	3.23	3.11	3.03
29	4.18	3.33	2.93	2.70	2.54	2.43	2.35	2.28	2.22	2.18
	7.60	5.52	4.54	4.04	3.73	3.50	3.32	3.20	3.08	3.00
30	4.17	3.32	2.92	2.69	2.53	2.42	2.34	2.27	2.21	2.16
	7.56	5.39	4.51	4.02	3.70	3.47	3.30	3.17	3.06	2.98
32	4.15	3.30	2.90	2.67	2.51	2.40	2.32	2.25	2.19	2.14
	7.50	5.34	4.46	3.97	3.66	3.42	3.25	3.12	3.01	2.94

Critical Values of F

df	1	2	3	4	5	6	7	8	9	10
34	4.13	3.28	2.88	2.65	2.49	2.38	2.30	2.23	2.17	2.12
	7.44	5.29	4.42	3.93	3.61	3.38	3.21	3.08	2.97	2.89
36	4.11	3.26	2.86	2.63	2.48	2.36	2.28	2.21	2.15	2.10
	7.39	5.25	4.38	3.89	3.58	3.35	3.18	3.04	2.94	2.86
38	4.10	3.25	2.85	2.62	2.46	2.35	2.26	2.19	2.14	2.09
	7.35	5.21	4.34	3.86	3.54	3.32	3.15	3.02	2.91	2.82
40	4.08	3.23	2.84	2.61	2.45	2.34	2.25	2.18	2.12	2.07
	7.31	5.18	4.31	3.83	3.51	3.29	3.12	2.99	2.88	2.80
42	4.07	3.22	2.83	2.59	2.44	2.32	2.24	2.17	2.11	2.06
	7.27	5.15	4.29	3.80	3.49	3.26	3.10	2.96	2.86	2.77
44	4.06	3.21	2.82	2.58	2.43	2.31	2.23	2.16	2.10	2.05
	7.24	5.12	4.26	3.78	3.46	3.24	3.07	2.94	2.84	2.75
46	4.05	3.20	2.81	2.57	2.42	2.30	2.22	2.14	2.09	2.04
	7.21	5.10	4.24	3.76	3.44	3.22	3.05	2.92	2.82	2.73
48	4.04	3.19	2.80	2.56	2.41	2.30	2.21	2.14	2.08	2.03
	7.19	5.08	4.22	3.74	3.42	3.20	3.04	2.90	2.80	2.71
50	4.03	3.18	2.79	2.56	2.40	2.29	2.20	2.13	2.07	2.02
	7.17	5.06	4.20	3.72	3.41	3.18	3.02	2.88	2.78	2.70
55	4.02	3.17	2.78	2.54	2.38	2.27	2.18	2.11	2.05	2.00
	7.12	5.01	4.16	3.68	3.37	3.15	2.98	2.85	2.75	2.66
60	4.00	3.15	2.76	2.52	2.37	2.25	2.17	2.10	2.04	1.99
	7.08	4.98	4.13	3.65	3.34	3.12	2.95	2.82	2.72	2.63
65	3.99	3.14	2.75	2.51	2.36	2.24	2.15	2.08	2.02	1.98
	7.04	4.95	4.10	3.62	3.31	3.09	2.93	2.79	2.70	2.61
70	3.98	3.13	2.74	2.50	2.35	2.32	2.14	2.07	2.01	1.97
	7.01	4.92	4.08	3.60	3.29	3.07	2.91	2.77	2.67	2.59
80	3.96	3.11	2.72	2.48	2.33	2.21	2.12	2.05	1.99	1.95
	4.06	4.88	4.04	3.56	3.25	3.04	2.87	2.74	2.64	2.55
100	3.94	3.09	2.70	2.46	2.30	2.19	2.10	2.03	1.97	1.92
	6.90	4.82	3.98	3.51	3.20	2.99	2.82	2.69	2.59	2.51

Down the side of the table, find the *df* for the degrees of freedom *within* $(N - K)$. Then find the *df* across the top of the table for *df between* $(K - 1)$. In the intersection of the row and the column, you will find the F_{crit} needed to reject the H_o. The upper value is for $p = .05$, the lower value is for $p = .01$. If the observed value of *F* is *equal to or larger than* the value shown in the table, you can reject the H_o.

Table 6: Ryan's Procedure for Kruskal-Wallis

	7	6	5	$d-1$ 4	3	2	1
a							
8	3.13	3.09	3.03	2.96	2.86	2.74	2.50
7		3.04	2.99	2.92	2.83	2.69	2.45
6			2.94	2.87	2.77	2.63	2.40
5				2.81	2.72	2.58	2.33
4					2.64	2.50	2.24
3						2.40	2.13

In the above table, a is the number of groups, d is the number of levels spanned by the comparison. For example, if you have four groups, you will look along the row labeled 4. Then, if you want to compare group 1 with group 4, that spans four levels (which is d). $d-1=3$, so you look down the column labeled 3 for the intersection (2.64). This is the critical Z value.

$\chi^2_{obs} \geq \chi^2_{crit}$ to reject H_0.

Table 7: Chi-square Distribution

Table of Critical Values for Chi-square (χ^2)

p	.10	.05	.025	.01	.001
df 1	2.706	3.841	5.024	6.635	10.828
2	4.605	5.991	7.378	9.210	13.816
3	6.251	7.815	9.348	11.345	16.266
4	7.779	9.488	11.143	13.277	18.467
5	9.236	11.070	12.832	15.086	20.515
6	10.645	12.592	14.449	16.812	22.458
7	12.017	14.067	16.013	18.475	24.322
8	13.362	15.507	17.535	20.090	26.125
9	14.684	16.919	19.023	21.666	27.877
10	15.987	18.307	20.483	23.209	29.588
11	17.275	19.675	21.920	24.725	31.264
12	18.549	21.026	23.337	26.217	32.909
13	19.812	22.362	24.736	27.688	34.528
14	21.064	23.685	26.119	29.141	36.123
15	22.307	24.996	27.488	30.578	37.697
16	23.542	26.296	28.845	31.100	39.252
17	24.769	27.587	30.191	33.409	40.790
18	25.989	28.869	31.526	24.805	42.312
19	27.204	30.144	32.852	36.191	43.820
20	28.412	31.410	34.170	37.566	45.315
25	34.382	37.653	40.647	44.314	50.620
30	40.256	43.773	46.979	50.892	59.703
40	51.805	55.759	59.342	63.691	73.402
50	63.167	67.505	71.420	76.154	86.661
60	74.397	79.082	83.298	88.379	99.607
70	85.527	90.531	95.023	100.425	112.317
80	96.578	101.879	106.629	112.329	124.839
90	107.565	113.145	118.136	124.116	137.208
100	118.498	124.342	129.561	135.807	149.449

Look for the appropriate degrees of freedom down the side of the table. Then locate the column for the probability level you selected to test the H_0. Check the intersection of this row and column for the critical value. To reject the H_0, the observed χ^2 value must be *equal to or greater than* the critical value shown in the table.

Table 8: Pearson Product-Moment Correlation

Critical Values for Pearson Product-Moment Correlation

$df = N-2$	p .05	.01	.001
1	.9969	.9999	1.000
2	.9500	.9900	.9990
3	.8783	.9587	.9912
4	.8114	.9172	.9741
5	.7545	.8745	.9507
6	.7067	.8343	.9249
7	.6664	.7977	.8982
8	.6319	.7646	.8721
9	.6021	.7348	.8471
10	.5760	.7079	.8233
11	.5529	.6835	.8010
12	.5324	.6614	.7800
13	.5139	.6411	.7603
14	.4973	.6226	.7420
15	.4821	.6055	.7246
16	.4683	.5897	7084
17	.4555	.5751	.6932
18	.4438	.5614	.6787
19	.4329	.5487	.6652
20	.4227	.5368	.6524
25	.3809	.4869	.5974
30	.3494	.4487	.5541
35	.3246	.4182	.5189
→40	.3044	.3932	.4896
45	.2875	.3721	.4648
50	.2732	.3541	.4433
60	.2500	.3248	.4078
70	.2319	.3017	.3799
80	.2172	.2830	.3568
90	.2050	.2673	.3375
100	.1946	.2540	.3211

First find the degrees of freedom for your study (number of pairs minus 2). Then find the column for the level of significance you have selected. The observed value of _r_ must be _greater than or equal to_ the value in the intersection of this column and line. The critical values are the same for positive and negative correlations.

$r_{obs} \geq r_{crit}$, reject H_0

Table 9: Spearman Rho Correlation

Critical Values of Spearman rho Rank-Order Correlation

	p	.05	.01
N	5	1.000	---
	6	.886	1.000
	7	.786	.929
	8	.738	.881
	9	.683	.833
	10	.648	.794
	12	.591	.777
	14	.544	.714
	16	.506	.665
	18	.475	.625
	20	.450	.591
	22	.428	.562
	24	.409	.537
	26	.392	.515
	28	.377	.496
	30	.364	.478

N = Number of pairs
Columns labeled .05 and .01 = the probability level

To reject H_o, the attained value of rho must be *greater than or equal to* the tabled value.

$\rho_{obs} \geq \rho_{crit}$, reject H_o

Table 10: Fisher Z--Transformation of Correlations

r	Z	r	Z	r	Z
.00	.000	.34	.354	.67	.811
.01	.010	.35	.365	.68	.829
.02	.020	.36	.377	.69	.848
.03	.030	.37	.388	.70	.867
.04	.040	.38	.400	.71	.887
.05	.050	.39	.412	.72	.908
.06	.060	.40	.424	.73	.929
.07	.070	.41	.436	.74	.950
.08	.080	.42	.448	.75	.973
.09	.090	.43	.460	.76	.996
.10	.100	.44	.472	.77	1.020
.11	.110	.45	.485	.78	1.045
.12	.121	.46	.497	.79	1.071
.13	.131	.47	.510	.80	1.099
.14	.141	.48	.523	.81	1.127
.15	.151	.49	.536	.82	1.157
.16	.161	.50	.549	.83	1.188
.17	.172	.51	.563	.84	1.221
.18	.182	.52	.576	.85	1.256
.19	.192	.53	.590	.86	1.293
.20	.203	.54	.604	.87	1.333
.21	.213	.55	.618	.88	1.376
.22	.224	.56	.633	.89	1.422
.23	.234	.57	.648	.90	1.472
.24	.245	.58	.662	.91	1.528
.25	.255	.59	.678	.92	1.589
.26	.266	.60	.693	.93	1.658
.27	.277	.61	.709	.94	1.738
.28	.288	.62	.725	.95	1.832
.29	.299	.63	.741	.96	1.946
.30	.310	.64	.758	.97	2.092
.31	.321	.65	.775	.98	2.298
.32	.332	.66	.793	.99	2.647
.33	.343			1.00	11.859

Find the value of the uncorrected correlation in the columns labeled *r*. Correct the correlation to the *Z* value given in the column to the right of the *r* value.

Appendix D
List of Formulas

Chapter 5

Descriptive statistics

Cumulative frequency = successive addition of frequency

$$\text{Proportion} = \frac{\# \text{ of } X}{\text{total}}$$

$$\text{Percentage} = 100 \times \text{proportion}$$

Cumulative percent = successive additions of percent

Rate = relative frequency per unit

$$\text{Ratio} = \frac{\# \text{ of } X}{\# \text{ of } Y}$$

Chapter 6

Central tendency

Mode = most frequently obtained score

Median = center of distribution

$$\text{Mean} = \overline{X} = \frac{\sum X}{N}$$

Formulas for variability

$$\text{Range} = X_{highest} - X_{lowest}$$

$$\text{Variance} = \frac{\sum (X - \overline{X})^2}{N - 1}$$

$$\text{Variance} = \frac{\sum x^2}{N - 1}$$ } differs from EPS 625

$$\text{Standard deviation} = s = \sqrt{\frac{\sum (X - \overline{X})^2}{N - 1}}$$

$$s = \sqrt{\frac{\sum x^2}{N - 1}}$$

$$s = \sqrt{\frac{\sum X^2 - [(\sum X)^2/N]}{N - 1}}$$

Chapter 7

Percentile

$$\text{Percentile} = (100)\frac{\text{F below the score} + 1/2 \text{ F same score}}{N}$$

z score

$$z = \frac{X - \overline{X}}{s}$$

T score

$$T \text{ score} = (10)(z) + 50$$

Guttman formulas

$$\text{Coefficient of reproducibility} = C_{rep} = 1 - \frac{\text{number of errors}}{(\# \text{ Ss})(\# \text{ items})}$$

$$\text{Minimum marginal reproducibility} = MM_{rep} = \frac{\text{maximum marginals}}{(\# \text{ Ss})(\# \text{ items})}$$

$$\% \text{ improvement in reproducibility} = C_{rep} - MM_{rep}$$

$$\text{Coefficient of scalability} = \frac{\% \text{ improvement in reproducibility}}{1 - MM_{rep}}$$

Chapter 9

Standard error of means

$$\sigma_{\overline{X}} = \frac{\sigma_X}{\sqrt{N}}$$

$$s_{\overline{x}} = \frac{s_X}{\sqrt{N}}$$

Case 1 t formula

$$t_{obs} = \frac{\overline{X} - \mu}{s_{\overline{X}}}$$

Case 2 t formula

$$t_{obs} = \frac{\overline{X}_e - \overline{X}_c}{s_{(\overline{X}_e - \overline{X}_c)}}$$

Standard error of differences between $\overline{X}'s$

$$s_{(\overline{X}_e - \overline{X}_c)} = \sqrt{\frac{s_e^2}{n_e} + \frac{s_c^2}{n_c}}$$

Median test

$$T = \frac{(A \div n_1) - (B \div n_2)}{\sqrt{\hat{p}(1 - \hat{p})(1 \div n_1 + 1 \div n_2)}}$$

where $\hat{p} = (A + B) \div N$

Rank sums test

$$z = \frac{2T_1 - n_1(N + 1)}{\sqrt{\frac{(n_1)(n_2)(N + 1)}{3}}}$$

eta^2 for t-test

$$\eta^2 = \frac{t^2}{t^2 + df}$$

eta^2 for Rank sums

$$\eta^2 = \frac{z^2}{N - 1}$$

Chapter 10

Matched (paired) t

$$t_{matched} = \frac{\overline{X}_1 - \overline{X}_2}{s_{\overline{D}}}$$

Standard error of difference between $\overline{X}s$

$$s_{\overline{D}} = \frac{s_D}{\sqrt{n}}$$

Standard error of differences

$$s_D = \sqrt{\frac{\sum D^2 - (1 \div n)(\sum D)^2}{n-1}}$$

Wilcoxon Matched-pairs

$$z = \frac{T - \dfrac{N(N+1)}{4}}{\sqrt{\dfrac{N(N+1)(2N+1)}{24}}}$$

Chapter 11

ANOVA *F*-ratio

$$F_{obs} = \frac{S^2_{between}}{S^2_{within}} = \frac{MSB}{MSW}$$

Sum of squares total

$$SST = \sum X^2 - \frac{(\sum X)^2}{N} = \sum (X - \overline{X}_G)^2$$

Sum of squares between

$$SSB = \left[\frac{(\sum X_1)^2}{n_1} + \frac{(\sum X_2)^2}{n_2} + \cdots + \frac{(\sum X_k)^2}{n_k} \right] - \frac{(\sum X)^2}{N}$$

$$SSB = \sum n[\overline{X} - \overline{X}_G]^2$$

Sum of squares within

$$SSW = SST - SSB$$

Mean squares between

$$MSB = \frac{SSB}{df_B} = \frac{SSB}{K-1}$$

Mean squares within

$$MSW = \frac{SSW}{df_W} = \frac{SSW}{N-K}$$

eta² for unbalanced or repeated-measures designs

$$\eta^2 = \frac{SS_x}{SST}$$

omega² for balanced designs, between-groups

$$\omega^2 = \frac{SSB - (K-1)MSW}{SST + MSW}$$

Kruskal-Wallis test

$$H = \frac{12}{N(N+1)} \sum_{A=1}^{a} \frac{T_A^2}{N_A} - 3(N+1)$$

eta² for Kruskal-Wallis

$$\eta^2 = \frac{H}{N-1}$$

Ryan's Procedure for Kruskal-Wallis

$$z = \frac{2T_i - n_i(N+1)}{\sqrt{\dfrac{n_1 n_2(N+1)}{3}}}$$

Chapter 12

Repeated-measures ANOVA formulas

$$G = T_{A1} + T_{A2} + T_{A3} + \cdots + T_{AN}$$

$$SST = \sum X^2 - \frac{G^2}{N}$$

$$SS_A = \left[\sum_{A=1}^{a} T_A^2 \right] \div n_A - \frac{G^2}{N}$$

$$SS_S = \sum_{S=1}^{s} T_S^2 \div n_s - \frac{G^2}{N}$$

$$SS_{AS} = SST - SS_A - SS_S$$

$$F = \frac{MS_A}{MS_{AS}}$$

Friedman

$$\chi_R^2 = \frac{12}{(a)(s)(a+1)} \sum_{A=1}^{a} T_A^2 - 3(s)(a+1)$$

Chapter 13

Factorial Anova formulas

$$F_{FactorA} = \frac{s_A^2}{s_W^2} = \frac{MS_A}{MSW}$$

$$F_{FactorB} = \frac{s_B^2}{s_W^2} = \frac{MS_B}{MSW}$$

$$F_{AB} = \frac{s_{AB}^2}{s_W^2} = \frac{MS_{AB}}{MSW}$$

$$SST = \sum X^2 - \frac{\left(\sum X\right)^2}{N}$$

$$SSB = \left[\frac{\left(\sum X_1\right)^2}{n_1} + \frac{\left(\sum X_2\right)^2}{n_2} + \frac{\left(\sum X_3\right)^2}{n_3} + \frac{\left(\sum X_4\right)^2}{n_4} \right] - \frac{\left(\sum X\right)^2}{N}$$

$$SS_A = \left[\frac{\left(\sum scores A_1\right)^2}{n_{A1}} + \frac{\left(\sum scores A_2\right)^2}{n_{A2}} \right] - \frac{\left(\sum X\right)^2}{N}$$

$$SS_B = \left[\frac{\left(\sum scores B_1\right)^2}{n_{B1}} + \frac{\left(\sum scores B_2\right)^2}{n_{B2}} \right] - \frac{\left(\sum X\right)^2}{N}$$

$$SS_{AB} = SSB - (SS_A + SS_B)$$

omega^2

$$\omega_A^2 = \frac{SS_A - (df_A)MSW}{SST + MSW}$$

$$\omega_B^2 = \frac{SS_B - (df_B)(MSW)}{SST + MSW}$$

$$\omega_{AB}^2 = \frac{SS_{AB} - (df_{AB})(MSW)}{SST + MSW}$$

Chapter 14

Chi-square

$$\chi^2 = \sum \frac{(\text{observed} - \text{expected})^2}{\text{expected}}$$

Chi-square expected cell

$$E_{ij} = \frac{n_i \times n_j}{N}$$

Yates' χ^2

$$\chi^2 = \frac{N(|ad - bc| - N \div 2)^2}{(a + b)(c + d)(a + c)(b + d)}$$

Phi

$$\Phi = \sqrt{\frac{\chi^2}{N}}$$

Cramer's V

$$Cramer's V = \sqrt{\frac{\Phi^2}{(\min \ r - 1, c - 1)}}$$

McNemar's test

$$z = \frac{B - C}{\sqrt{B + C}}$$

Chapter 15

Pearson correlation

$$r_{xy} = \frac{\sum (z_x z_y)}{N - 1}$$

$$r_{xy} = \frac{N(\sum XY) - (\sum X)(\sum Y)}{\sqrt{[N \sum X^2 - (\sum X)^2][N \sum Y^2 - (\sum Y)^2]}}$$

Correction for attenuation

$$r_{CA} = \frac{r_{xy}}{\sqrt{r_{ttx} r_{tty}}}$$

Point biserial correlation

$$r_{pbi} = \frac{\overline{X}_p - \overline{X}_q}{s_x} \sqrt{pq}$$

Spearman (rho) correlation

$$\rho = 1 - \frac{6(\sum d^2)}{N(N^2 - 1)}$$

Kendall's concordance

$$W = \frac{12 \sum_{j=1}^{n} R_j^2 - 3m^2 n(n + 1)^2}{m^2 n(n^2 - 1)}$$

$$\chi^2 = m(n - 1)(W)$$

Correction for ties

$$W = \frac{12 \sum_{j=1}^{n} R_j^2 - 3m^2 n(n + 1)^2}{m^2 n(n^2 - 1) - m \sum (t^3 - t)}$$

Phi correlation

$$r_{phi} = \frac{BC - AD}{\sqrt{(A + B)(C + D)(A + C)(B + D)}}$$

$$\chi^2 = N \, Phi^2$$

$$r_{phi} = \frac{P_{ik} - P_i P_k}{\sqrt{P_i q_i P_k q_k}}$$

Chapter 16

Regression formulas

$$b = \frac{N(\sum XY) - (\sum X)(\sum Y)}{N \sum X^2 - (\sum X)^2}$$

$$b = r_{xy}\frac{s_Y}{s_X}$$

$$\hat{Y} \text{ (predicted Y)} = \overline{Y} + b(X - \overline{X})$$

$$\hat{Y} = a + bx$$

$$\text{Error variance} = \frac{\sum(Y - \hat{Y})^2}{N - 2}$$

$$SEE = \sqrt{\frac{\sum(Y - \hat{Y})^2}{N - 2}}$$

$$SEE = s_y\sqrt{1 - r_{yx}^2}$$

Chapter 18

Reliability formulas

Interrater reliability for more than two raters:

$$r_{tt} = \frac{nr_{AB}}{1 + (n - 1)r_{AB}}$$

Internal consistency:

$$r_{tt} = \frac{2r_{AB}}{1 + r_{AB}}$$

$$\text{K-R 20} = \frac{n}{n - 1}\left[\frac{s_t^2 - \sum s_i^2}{s_t^2}\right]$$

$$\text{K-R 21} = \frac{n}{n - 1}\left[1 - \frac{\overline{X} - (\overline{X}^2 \div n)}{s_t^2}\right]$$

Appendix E
Selected Journals in Applied Linguistics

√ = at NAU, best for this class

The following list of journals is not meant to be exhaustive. Rather, it gives an indication of some of the journals you might wish to consult for research ideas or for articles that address research questions that interest you.

Journal	Publisher
Applied Psycholinguistics	Oxford Univ. Press
Applied Linguistics	Cambridge Univ. Press
Brain and Language	Academic Press
CALICO Journal	Brigham Young Univ.
Cognition	Elsevier Publishers
Cognition & Instruction	Lawrence Erlbaum
College English	NCTE
College Composition & Communication	NCTE
Discourse Processes	Ablex Publishers
English for Special Purposes Journal	Pergamom Press
English Language Teaching Journal	Oxford Univ. Press
English Today	Cambridge Univ. Press
English World-wide	John Benjamins
Foreign Language Annals	ACTFL
IAL (Issues in Applied Linguistics)	UCLA
IRAL	J. Groos Publishers
Journal of Communication	Oxford Univ. Press
Journal of Cross-Cultural Psychology	Sage Press
Journal of Language & Social Psychology	Multilingual Matters
Journal of Multilingual and Multicultural Development	Multilingual Matters
Journal of Pragmatics	North-Holland
Journal of Psycho-linguistic Research	Plenum Press
Language	Linguistic Society of America
Language and Cognitive Processes	Lawrence Erlbaum
Language & Communication	Pergamon Press

Language & Speech	Kingston Press
Language in Society	Cambridge Univ. Press
Language Learning	Concordia University
Language Problems & Language Planning	U. Texas Press
Language Testing	Edward Arnold
Linguistics	Mouton de Gruyter
Linguistic Analysis	American Elsevier
Linguistics and Education	Ablex Publishers
Mind and Language	Basil Blackwell
Modern Language Journal	NFMLTA
NABE Journal	NABE
Reading in a Foreign Language	Internat'l Educ. Centre
Reading Research Quarterly *quantitative*	Internat'l Reading Assoc.
RELC Journal	SEAMEO
Research in the Teaching of English *college level*	NCTE
Second Language Research	Edward Arnold
Sign Language Studies	Linstok Press
Studies in Language	John Benjamins
Studies in Second Language Acquisition	Cambridge Univ. Press
SYSTEM	Pergamon Press
Teaching English in the Two Year College	NCTE
Teaching English to Deaf and Second Language Students	Gallaudet University
TESL Canada Journal	TESL Canada
TESL Reporter	BYU Hawaii
TESOL Quarterly	TESOL
Word	Internat'l Linguistic Assoc.
World Englishes	Pergamon Press
Written Communication	Sage Press

Author Index

Statistical Content Index

Measurement
  continuous, 62
  interval, 58–59, 159–186
  nominal, 55–56
  noncontinuous, 62
  ordinal, 56–58, 159–186
Median, 161, 167, 181. *See also* Central
  tendency
  definition of, 161
  formula for, 161, 607
Median test, 271–273, 281, 547. *See also*
  Nonparametric tests
  formula for, 271, 609
Minimum marginal reproducibility. *See* Guttman
  procedure
Mixed designs (split-plot designs), 79–81
Mode, 160–161. *See also* Central tendency
  definition of, 160
  formula for, 160
Moderator variable, 65, 607. *See also* Variable
MSB (mean squares between), 320, 610. *See
  also* ANOVA
MSW (mean squares within), 320, 610. *See also*
  ANOVA
MU (μ) (population mean), 251
Multicolinearity, 481, 491
  definition of, 481
Multidimensional scaling (MDS), 498–500,
  551–552, 553
Multiple-range comparisons. *See* Post hoc
  comparisons
Multiple-range tests, 330, 548
  Duncan test, 331, 354
  Neuman-Keuls test, 353
  Scheffé test, 330–331, 353, 354
  Tukey test, 330, 353, 354
Multiple regression, 467–468, 480–488. *See
  also* Regression

Negative correlation, 429, 449
Nemenyi's test, 361–363
  formula for, 362–363
Neuman-Keuls test, 353. *See also* Multiple-
  range tests
Nominal measurement, 55–56, 203
Noncontinuous measurement, 62
Nonorthogonal designs, 310
Nonparametric tests, 237–239, 270–277, 303–
  304, 307. *See also* Parametric tests

Normal distribution, 164–167, 177–178, 192–
  196, 199, 498
  definition of, 164
Null hypothesis, 24–25, 74, 81–82, 224, 229,
  230, 232. *See also* Hypothesis

Omega^2 strength of association, 548
  Factorial ANOVA, 382–383
  formula for, 331, 611, 612
  One-way ANOVA, 330–331
One-tailed hypothesis. *See* Hypothesis
Operational definition, 15, 37
Ordered metric scale, 297
Ordinal measurement, 56–58, 159, 178–186
Orthogonal designs, 310
Outlier, 181

Paired *t*-test. *See* Matched *t*-test
Parameter, 252, 515–516
Parametric tests, 237–239, 307–308. *See also*
  Nonparametric tests
Path analysis, 502–506, 517, 521, 552, 553
PCA (Principal component analysis), 490–492,
  493, 551, 552, 553
Pearson correlation, 427–431, 534, 549–550
  correlation coefficient, 431, 433, 440–444,
    471
  correction for attenuation, 444–445, 480
  formula for, 434, 613
  interpreting, 440–444
  scatterplot, 427–430, 437
Percent
  definition of, 136
  formula for, 607
Percentile, 187–191
  definition of, 189–190
  formula for, 190, 608
Phi (Φ) correlation, 415–416, 459–461, 549,
  550
  formula for, 415, 459, 614
Pie chart, 150
Point biserial correlation, 448–450, 550
  formula for, 448, 614
Polygon, 151–153, 160, 164
Population, 42, 229, 234
Positive correlation, 428
Post hoc comparisons (multiple-range
  comparisons), 100–101, 330, 361
Power, 239
Pretest-posttest design, 40, 87